AF505465

RODIN
IN THE UNITED STATES

Edited by
Antoinette Le Normand-Romain

With essays by
Christina Buley-Uribe
Patrick R. Crowley
C. D. Dickerson III
Antoinette Le Normand-Romain
Laure de Margerie
Véronique Mattiussi
Elyse Nelson
and Jennifer A. Thompson

and chronology by
Nora M. Rosengarten

Clark Art Institute, Williamstown,
Massachusetts

Distributed by Yale University Press,
New Haven and London

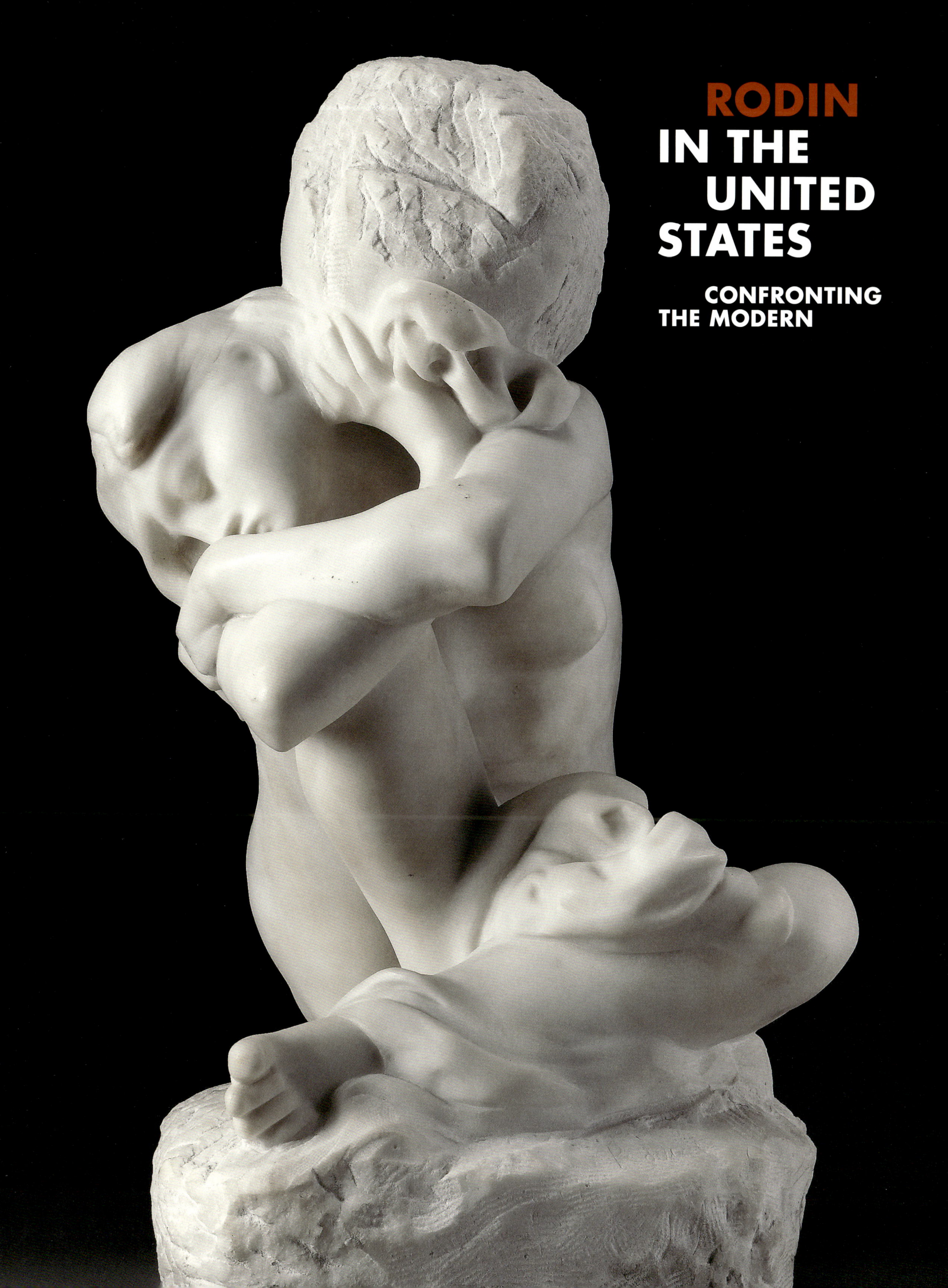

RODIN
IN THE
UNITED
STATES
CONFRONTING
THE MODERN

CONTENTS

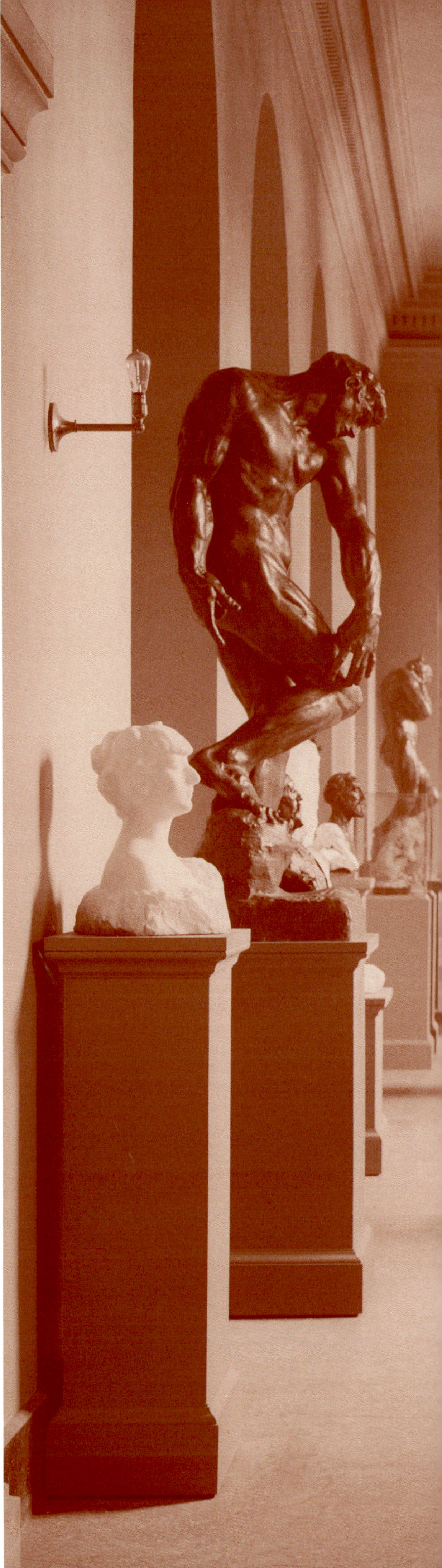

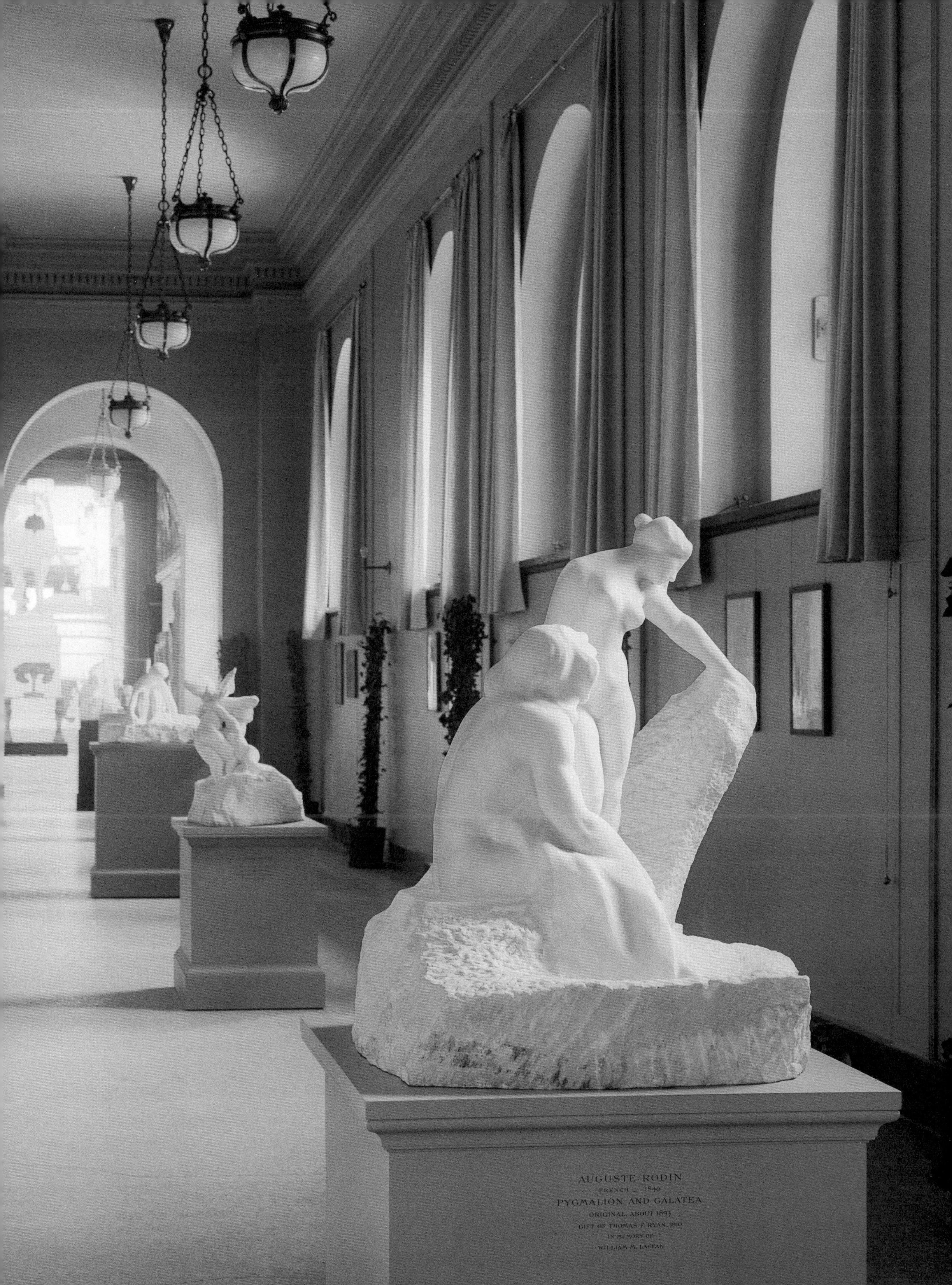

AUGUSTE·RODIN
FRENCH — 1840
PYGMALION AND GALATEA
ORIGINAL, ABOUT 1893
GIFT OF THOMAS F. RYAN, 1910
IN MEMORY OF
WILLIAM M. LAFFAN

DIRECTOR'S FOREWORD

Today, the centrality of Auguste Rodin to the development of modern sculpture seems unquestioned. This was achieved not only through his pathbreaking choice of subjects and the attention he paid to the sensuous qualities of his materials, but by a network of ardent collectors dedicated to ensuring his work's visibility. During his life, Rodin amassed a devoted following, providing him a steady stream of commissions, sales, and support. After his death, Rodin's legacy was extended through a web of individuals and institutions intent on maintaining the artist's prominence. In 1893, the American public first encountered Rodin's work at the World's Columbian Exposition in Chicago. The path from this point to the cultural ubiquity the sculptor's work enjoys today was a long one, beset by critics who perceived his art as unfinished or inappropriate and by eventual institutional neglect, as much of his work languished unseen in museum vaults for the greater first half of the twentieth century. Nonetheless, through all these twists and turns, Americans have been instrumental in creating, establishing, and maintaining Rodin's global significance.

Rodin in the United States: Confronting the Modern tells the story of the American collectors, curators, and art historians who have helped form our current understanding of the artist. The exhibition emphasizes the role of women whose contributions to Rodin's fame have been underappreciated—including the philanthropist Katherine Seney Simpson and the influential dancer Loïe Fuller, both of whom shared their appreciation of the artist by ensuring his representation in American collections. It also recognizes the contributions Rodin scholars have made through developing fresh interpretations of the artist's endlessly complex body of work.

The exhibition examines the role of these figures through an arrangement of some of Rodin's most expressive works. With sculptures in plaster, terracotta, marble, and bronze alongside the artist's sensitive and experimental drawings, *Rodin in the United States* displays the incredible breadth of Rodin's creative output. Drawn from both public and private collections, the exhibition opens at the Sterling and Francine Clark Art Institute in Williamstown before traveling to the High Museum of Art in Atlanta. Visitors are invited to appreciate Rodin's work as it was seen at different historical moments, through the eyes of those whose devotion and erudition brought the artist fame. This catalogue complements the exhibition, investigating the key players who enabled the artist's eventual status as a modern icon.

We are deeply grateful to curator Antoinette Le Normand-Romain, whose unparalleled understanding of Rodin is evident throughout the exhibition and this catalogue. It has been a distinct pleasure for me to collaborate on this project with a longtime friend. We would also like to extend our appreciation to Christina Buley-Uribe, whose contributions to this exhibition—particularly on the subject of the artist's drawings—were equally invaluable. Le Normand-Romain and Buley-Uribe have revealed a new lens through which to view the work, life, and legacy of one of modern art's most influential representatives. This new and exciting vision could not have been realized without the leadership support of Denise Littlefield Sobel and Diane and Andreas Halvorsen, as well as the generous funding provided by the Acquavella Family Foundation, Jeannene Booher, Robert D. Kraus, the Robert Lehman Foundation, Carol and Richard Seltzer, and the Malcolm Hewitt Wiener Foundation, with additional contributions from Hubert and Mireille Goldschmidt and Gregory Annenberg Weingarten, GRoW @ Annenberg. The exhibition is also supported by an indemnity from the Federal Council on the Arts and the Humanities. Lastly, we would like to thank the collectors and museums who have generously lent to the exhibition, allowing us to stage an exhibition of many of Rodin's most beloved and engaging works.

Olivier Meslay
Hardymon Director

ACKNOWLEDGMENTS

Organizing this exhibition has been a great joy. I would like to express my profound gratitude to the Clark Art Institute, particularly to Olivier Meslay, Hardymon Director, and the helpful team of Esther Bell, Robert and Martha Berman Lipp Chief Curator; Kathleen M. Morris, Sylvia and Leonard Marx Director of Collections and Exhibitions; and Alexis Goodin, curatorial research associate, whose unwavering commitment was essential. Thank you, also, to Julie Blake, assistant exhibitions project manager, and Angela Liporace, associate registrar for exhibitions. Anne Leonard, Manton Curator of Prints, Drawings, and Photographs, offered helpful advice. Nora Rosengarten and Sophie Kerwin, curatorial assistants, and Byron Otis and Delaney Keenan, graduate interns, provided much-appreciated logistical assistance. Anne Roecklein, the Clark's managing editor, oversaw the realization of this catalogue along with the skillful publications team, including image specialist David Murphy, translators Damion Searls and Eriksen Translations, editor Kristin Swan, and designer Roy Brooks, with production by Verona Libri. I also wish to acknowledge the exhibition design of Jarrod Beck and his team, who planned an engaging and innovative layout for the Clark venue of the exhibition.

This project developed over a long period of time. I began my research while I was the sculpture curator at the Musée Rodin in Paris (1994–2006). For years, the museum had been carrying out a survey of Auguste Rodin's collectors, which became my point of departure. I likewise owe a debt to Ruth Butler, who shared with me research she compiled in writing her monumental biography *Rodin, the Shape of Genius* (1993). After these years in Paris, I had the opportunity to make significant progress as an Edmond J. Safra Visiting Professor at the Center for Advanced Study in the Visual Arts at the National Gallery of Art in Washington, DC (2016–17). I would like to thank Elizabeth Cropper, Therese O'Malley, and Peter Lukehart for their warm welcome in Washington, along with Wendy Slatkin, my research assistant there, for all her help.

Sculpture is only one aspect of Rodin's oeuvre that appealed to American collectors. This exhibition has profoundly benefited from Christina Buley-Uribe's vast knowledge of Rodin's drawings. Together, Christina and I wish to thank the many colleagues in the United States and Europe, particularly the catalogue contributors, who have helped with research and have assisted in securing loans, giving generously of their time. Without their support and friendship during the challenges of the pandemic, this project could not have been completed.

I would especially like to thank Denise Allen, Stéphane Aquin, Colin B. Bailey, Andaleeb Banta, Daphne Barbour, Christopher Bedford, Emily Beeny, François Blanchetière, Sarah Ganz Blythe, Jonathan Bober, Emerson Bowyer, Maud Brezinski, André Bromberg, Julian Brooks, Elizabeth Tufts Brown, Helen Burnham, Marietta Cambareri, Thomas P. Campbell, Danielle Carrabino, Martin Chapman, Christophe Chérix, Melissa Chiu, Jay A. Clarke, Emily Conforto, Simon Crameri, Eric Crosby, Patrick Crowley, Emily Cushman, Tom Davies, Anne-Lise Desmas, C. D. Dickerson, Ashley Dunn, Kaywin Feldman, Ryan Fisher, Jonathan Freund, Lily Goldberg, Hubert and Mireille Goldschmidt, Steve Grafe, William M. Griswold, Gloria Groom, Evelyn C. Hankins, June Hargrove, Tessa Helfet, Daniel Hoffman, Rena Hoisington, Max Hollein, Maureen Holtz, Jan Howard, Frederick Ilchman, Anne E. Jarvis, Laurence Kanter, Shelley Langdale, Claude Laroque, Martina Larsson, Sarah E. Lawrence, Stuart Lochhead, Patricia Loiko, Glenn Lowry, Tony Maniaty, Louis Marchesano, John Marciari, Laure de Margerie, Akemi May, Julie Mellby, Elizabeth Mitchell, Valérie Montalbetti, Janet Moore, Clarissa Morales, Margaux Morel, Lisa Morra, Asma Naeem, Elyse Nelson, Jill Newhouse, Jessica Nicoll, Maureen O'Brien, Nadine Orenstein, Anne Pasternak, Emily Peters, Timothy Potts, Sarah Purdy, Richard Rand, Allan Rappaport, Anne Reeve, Anne Rivière, William Robinson, James Rondeau, Quentin Rose, Timothy Rub, Kevin Salatino, Nicholas Sands, Colleen Schafroth, Hugh Justin Seto and Amy T. Seto, Oliver Shell, Lisa Small, Judith Sobol, Stephanie Stebich, Shelley Sturman, Julia Sylvester, Matthew Teitelbaum, Ann Tempkin, Jennifer Thompson, Jennifer Tonkovich, Bénédicte Van Campen, and Stephanie Wiles. Many thanks also to the Musée Rodin in Paris, particularly to Sandra Boujot, Sonia Christon, Hughes Herpin, Franck Joubin, Jérôme Manoukian, Hélène Marraud, and Véronique Mattiussi.

I am deeply grateful to the lenders to this exhibition, both public institutions and private collectors, who graciously allowed their Rodin sculptures and drawings to travel to Williamstown and Atlanta. I would especially like to thank Iris Cantor, who has always shown great kindness to me and was willing, for several months, to part with the marble that, in a way, marks the beginning of this story. I also wish to acknowledge the many conservators who prepared the works in the exhibition for travel. Their efforts help preserve Rodin's remarkable sculptures and drawings for generations to come.

It has been a sincere pleasure to work with colleagues at the High Museum of Art in Atlanta who made a second venue for this exhibition possible. I would particularly like to thank Randall Suffolk, Nancy and Holcombe T. Green Jr. Director; Claudia Einecke, Bunzl Family Curator of European Art; Amy Simon, director of collections and exhibitions; Danielle Kiser, manger of exhibitions; Frances Francis, senior registrar; and Tomasina Ray, associate registrar, exhibitions.

Without the generous support of many people, this project would not have been realized. My deepest thanks again to all who have assisted with the exhibition and the catalogue. And thank you, dear readers, for your engagement.

Antoinette Le Normand-Romain

NOTES TO THE READER

ARTISTS AND OTHER PRACTITIONERS

All works in the exhibition are by Auguste Rodin (French, 1840–1917) except for one (cat. 62). Throughout the catalogue, names, nationalities, and life dates for other artists are given in image captions or, if there is no corresponding illustration, in running text.

Rodin had numerous skilled assistants in his workshop (as many as thirty to fifty), including molders, carvers, and founders (see "Media and Process" below). Working closely with these assistants was essential to Rodin's success, and the names of these specialized practitioners are given in the entries when known.

TITLES

Titles given by the artist are preferred when they exist. When the artist's title is not available, we have deferred to previously published descriptive titles except in cases where new information has emerged through our research. French titles of works are given in English translation following US spelling rules. Rodin made a great number of studies for some sculptures (for example, *Hanako* or *Dance Movements*). These different studies have been given letters (type A, B, C, D, etc.) to help to identify them.

DATES

FOR SCULPTURE

We indicate when Rodin first modeled or assembled a composition, as well as when the specific example in the exhibition was cast in bronze, carved in marble, or created in another material. If modeling and object date are the same, only one date is given. In the case of plasters, lack of documentation often means the precise date of a cast cannot be given. An original model date is provided, and the cast is assumed to have been made before it was acquired by a collector.

FOR WORKS ON PAPER

Specific dates or date ranges indicate when Rodin created the work. In some cases, inscriptions were added later (by Rodin or by owners of the sheets) and therefore have a later date.

MEDIA AND PROCESS

All the sculptural materials (clay, plaster, marble, and bronze) and techniques that Rodin used throughout his career are represented in this exhibition. Rodin used traditional techniques and created new processes to achieve unexpected, sometimes controversial sculptures. Very few extant drawings are related to sculptural compositions.

Rodin began by modeling clay or wax or by working directly in plaster to create a three-dimensional work. Assistants then used the clay model to produce a mold, which would be cast in plaster. Rodin could produce multiples in this inexpensive medium and even cut the plaster apart, recombining hands, legs, torsos, and heads to alter a composition, to form a completely new work, or to hold in reserve for use in future compositions. (The new works, based on existing material, are called "assemblages.")

Rodin exhibited plaster casts in his studio, but he also presented them in formal exhibitions, as this was less expensive (and quicker) than reproducing works in marble or bronze. When a subject appealed to a buyer, a more permanent marble was carved or a bronze version cast. The copies in marble are not identical; the composition remains the same, but specific details are changed, depending on the carver and also on the shape of the marble block used. Rodin also scaled up works to achieve distinct effects. Reductions of the most famous works were available to a larger public.

Rodin never carved marble himself but hired *praticiens* (workers who executed commissions for others) to carve for him. Some of them, mostly Italians, specialized in carving other artists' compositions using the *mise au point* system, but others were young sculptors, including Antoine Bourdelle, who needed to earn their living and were happy to gain experience and contacts by being close to Rodin. He oversaw every aspect of the transition from clay model or plaster cast to stone.

To create multiples of his sculptures in bronze, Rodin also collaborated with several founders in Paris, the most famous of whom was Alexis Rudier, who began to work for him in 1902. Liquid bronze would be poured into molds derived from Rodin's plaster casts, creating faithful copies of the originals. Rodin was attentive to this process, including the patination (surface finish) to ensure that the final sculpture met his standards.

DIMENSIONS

Dimensions are listed in inches followed by centimeters in the order of height × width × depth. Unless otherwise noted, dimensions refer to the primary object. Dimensions for works on paper include the sheet if the support is original.

SIGNATURES AND INSCRIPTIONS

FOR SCULPTURE

All inscriptions (signature, dedications, and founders' marks) are reproduced as they appear on the objects. If the name of the founder is missing but we know it through documentation, it is indicated in parentheses.

FOR WORKS ON PAPER

Signatures: Rodin seldom signed his drawings, but he would sign them for exhibitions or when the drawings were destined to be sold. Some drawings appear with a "Rodin" stamp resembling a signature (see "Collector's Marks").

Dedications: Dedications are relatively rare among the approximately 9,000 drawings created by the artist. This exhibition includes several dedicated drawings, some inscribed on the spot, others added later.

Other Inscriptions: All inscriptions are by Rodin unless otherwise noted. Rodin would often add several inscriptions on one drawing, hence drawings with multiple titles and possible orientations.

PROVENANCE

The provenance sections of the Exhibition Checklist (p. 241) provide the most complete information currently available about each work's sequence of ownership. The word "possibly" indicates cases where documentation is unconfirmed. Distinct owners are separated by semicolons. Galleries and dealers are set off in brackets, while auction houses are listed without brackets. The words "by descent" indicate ownership of a work passing from one family member to another. Dates of ownership and the life dates of each collector are also provided, when known.

COLLECTOR'S MARKS

In certain catalogue and checklist entries, the term "Lugt" references Frits Lugt's book on collector's marks. This source, Frits Lugt, *Les marques de collections de dessins et d'estampes* (1921), is accessible online, with updates released in 1956 and 2010: http://www.marquesdecollections.fr.

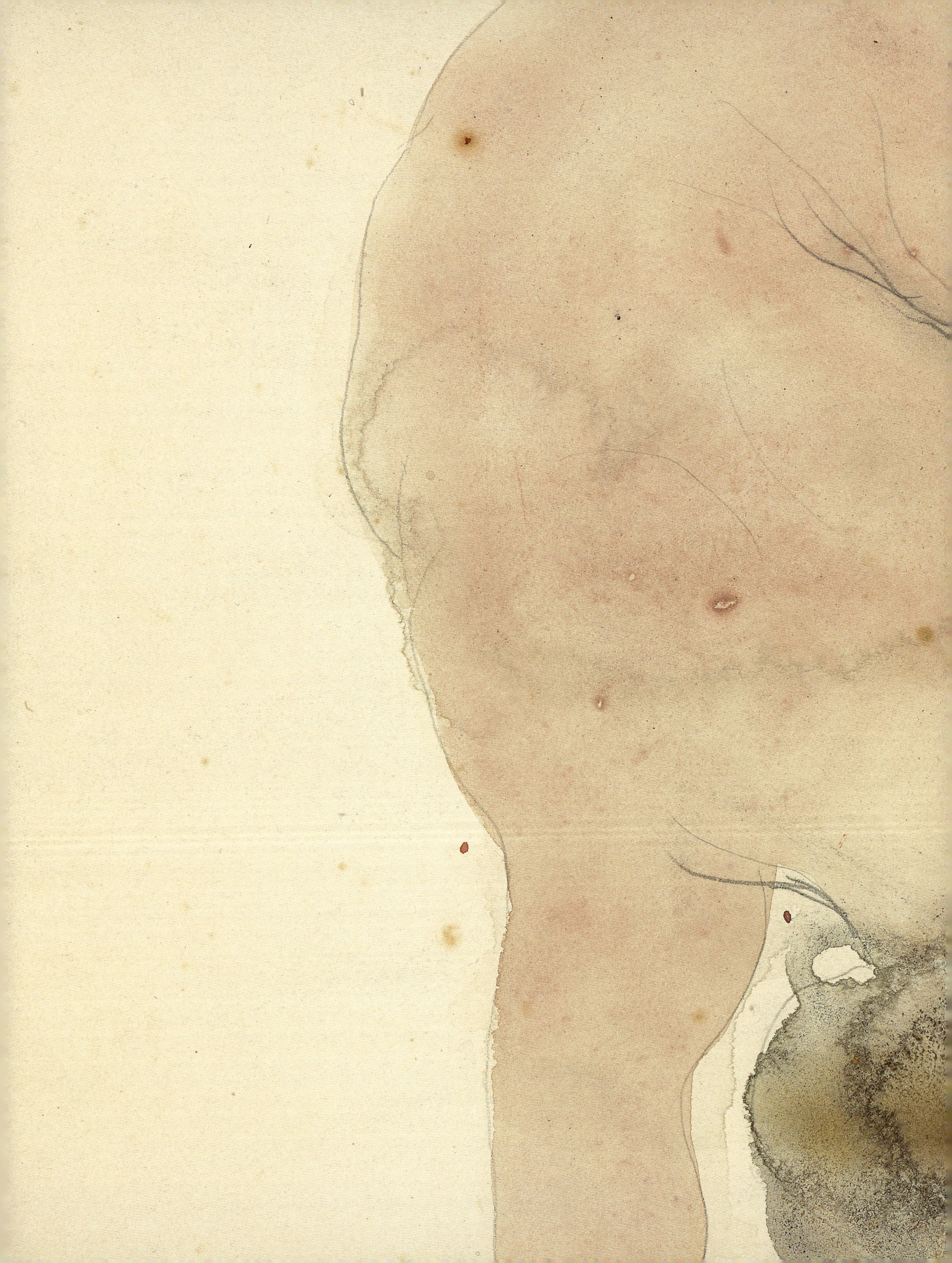

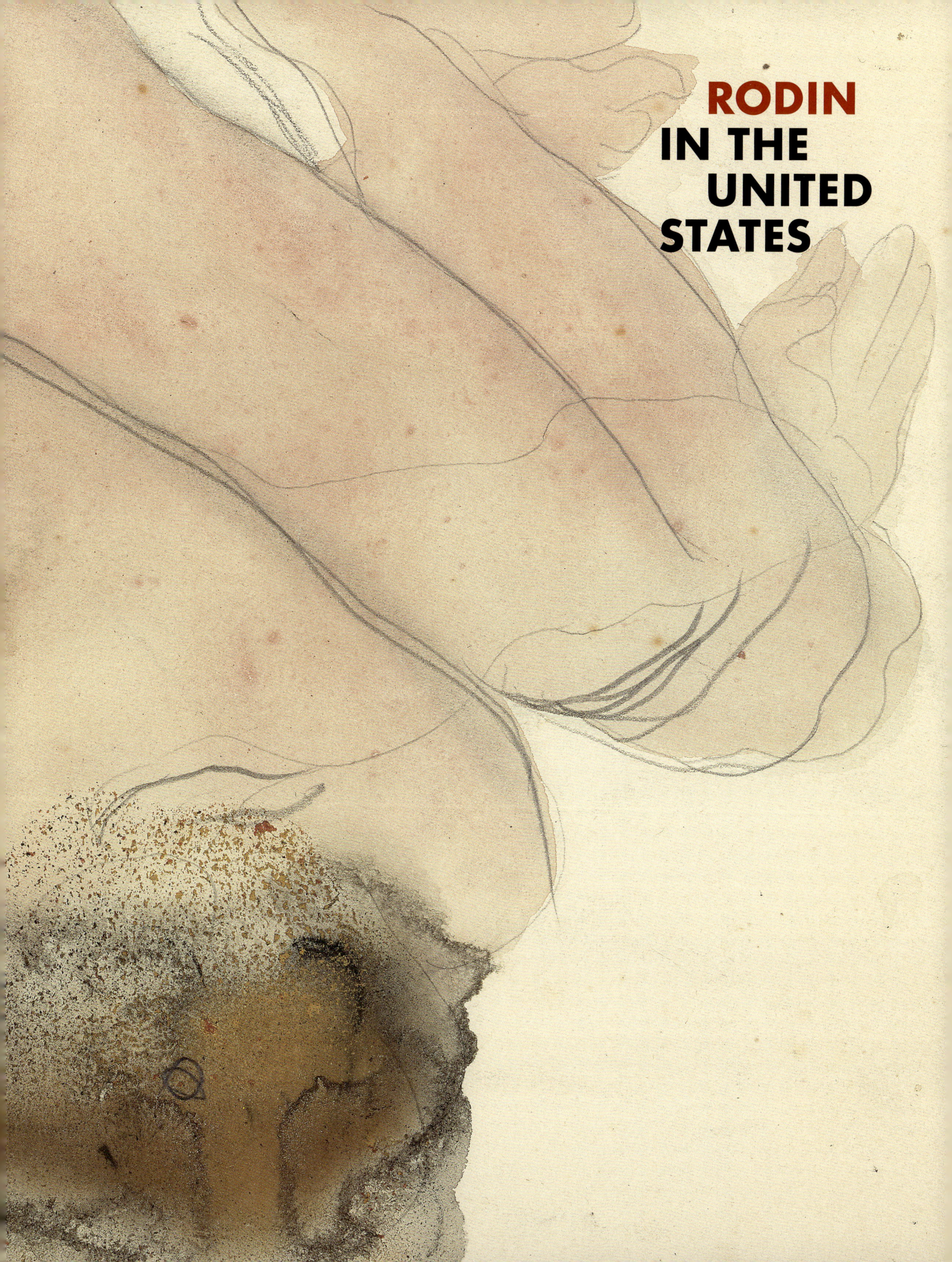
RODIN
IN THE
UNITED
STATES

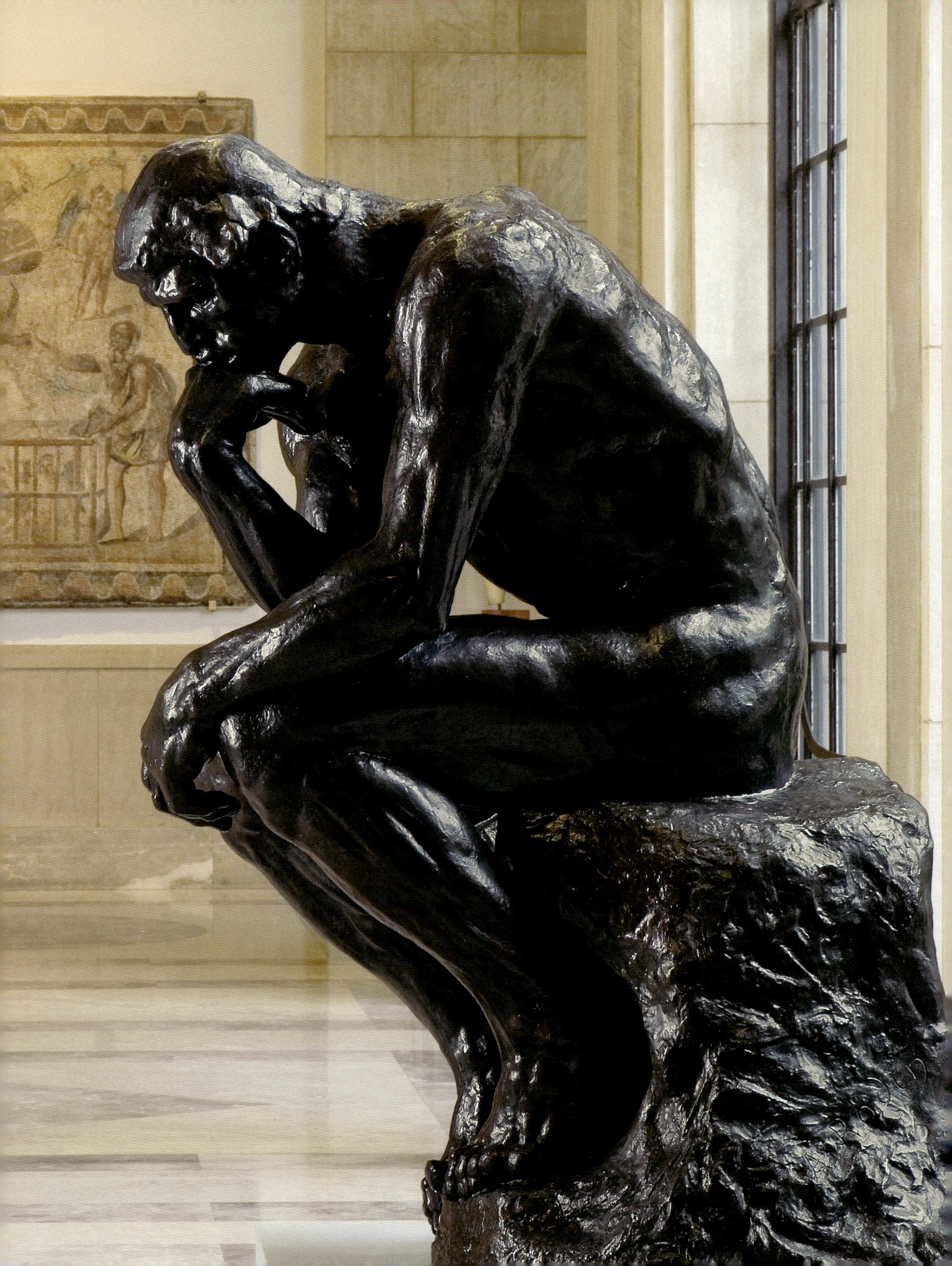

AT THE HEART OF SCULPTURE

ANTOINETTE LE NORMAND-ROMAIN

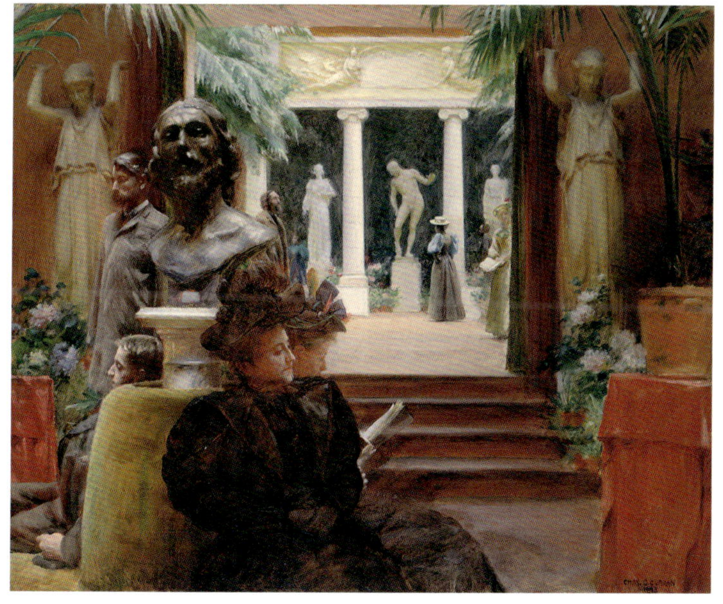

FIG. 1.1

Charles Curran (American, 1861–1942), *At the Sculpture Exhibition*, 1895. Oil on canvas, 18 × 22 in. (45.7 × 55.9 cm). Yale University Art Gallery, New Haven, Connecticut. Stephen Carlton Clark, B.A. 1903, Fund, 1973.103.

When Samuel P. Avery gave a copy of Auguste Rodin's *Bust of St. John the Baptist* (cat. 3) to the Metropolitan Museum of Art, New York, in April 1893, it was the first work by the artist to enter a museum in the United States. Two years later, another version—just a few days after it featured in an American Art Association sale[1]—appeared at the Second Annual Exhibition of the National Sculpture Society, which opened on May 7, 1895, in the American Fine Arts Society Building in New York. Charles Curran made that bust the central element in a small painting (fig. 1.1), displaying it next to plaster sculptures inspired by ancient art and surrounded by flowers. Beginning on May 1, 1893, several other works by Rodin were on view at the World's Columbian Exposition in Chicago. Rodin was represented in the south court of the Fine Arts Building (fig. 1.2), with a large figure from the *Monument to the Burghers of Calais* (cf. cat. 15), as well as in an exhibition of works by so-called foreign masters in US collections.[2] Deemed too suggestive for the world's fair general public, those three small marbles were soon moved into a separate area where they could be accessed only by request.

The last decade of the nineteenth century marked a turning point in the artist's life, one that was further accentuated by the end of his relationship with his former student and assistant Camille Claudel. He had met her in 1882 and soon developed passionate feelings for her; she eventually became his

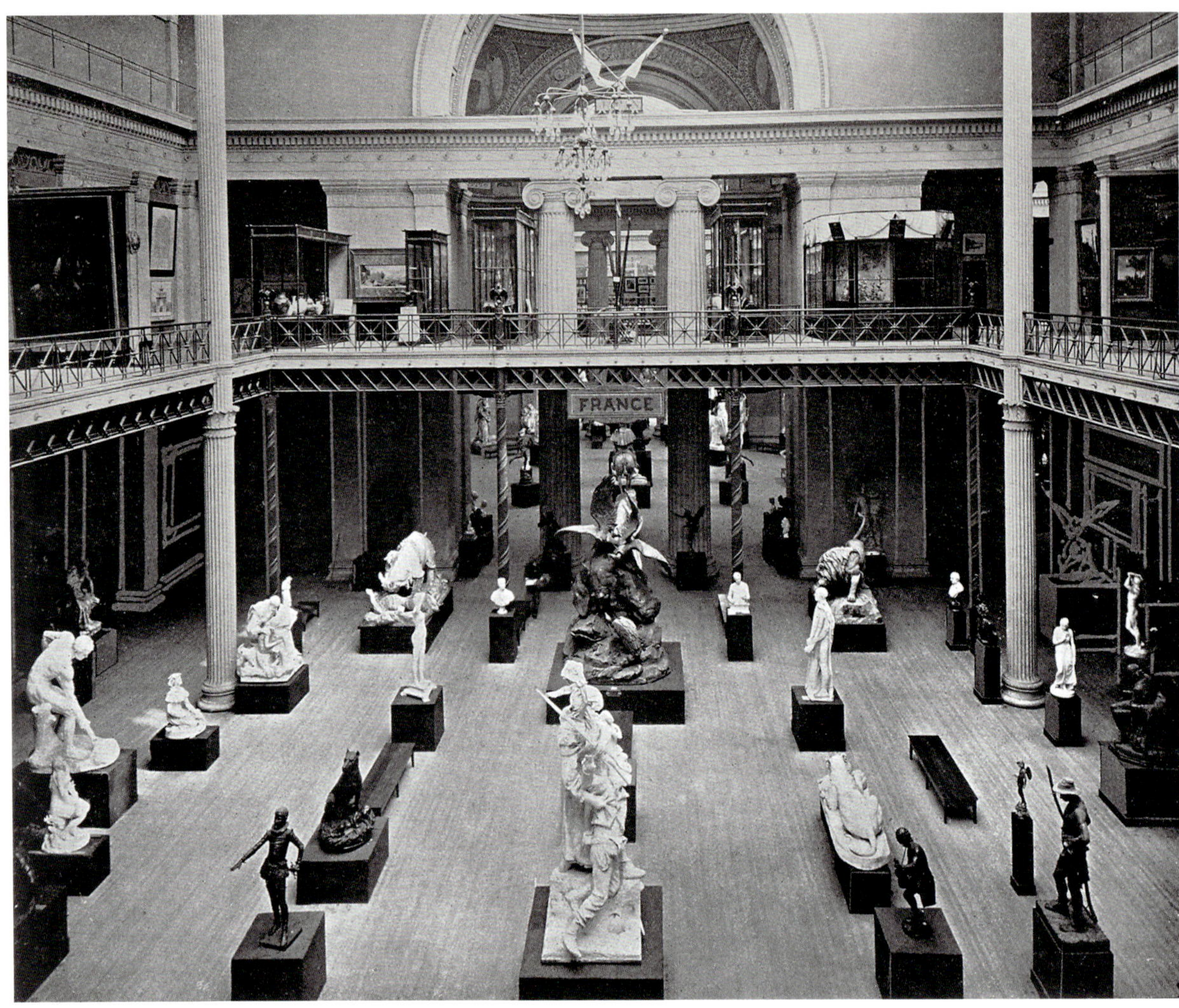

South court of the Fine Arts Building,
World's Columbian Exposition, Chicago,
1893, originally published in J. W. Buel,
*A Magic City: A Massive Portfolio of
Original Photographic Views of the Great
World's Fair and Its Treasures of Art,
Including a Vivid Representation of the
Famous Midway Plaisance*, 1894.

companion. For some time, they shared the same studio. A journalist in 1898
reported that Rodin "said the happiness of being always understood and seeing
his expectations always surpassed had been one of the great joys of his artistic
life."[3] But Claudel realized that as long as she stayed with Rodin, she would
be seen only as his student or assistant, so she decided to end their relationship
about ten years later. Rodin suffered terribly from their separation. In 1891, he
received the commission for a monument to novelist Honoré de Balzac (cf. cat. 85)
and quickly worked on several possible models, but he found it difficult to make
progress on the project, a sign of the depression that had taken hold of him.
In fact, in 1894, as several accounts attest, he returned the advance payment he
had received, feeling unable to complete the project. On July 6, 1895, Edmond
de Goncourt ran into Rodin on a train and noted in his journal that he found the
artist "greatly changed, and very melancholy on account of his worn-out state
and of the weariness he feels in working just now."[4]

This period marked, in a way, the end of the first part of his career. The
exhibition *Claude Monet–A. Rodin* held at Galerie Georges Petit in Paris from
June 21 to August 1889 can be considered the pinnacle of this phase. Rodin
declined to show at the Paris Exposition Universelle of 1889, where he might
have presented *The Gates of Hell*, a major commission he had received from the
French government in 1880; instead, he gave preference to the sphere of private
collectors by choosing to show his work at a gallery, presenting only small- or
medium-sized pieces, except for the *Burghers of Calais*, which he assembled as
a group for the first time.

Nearly fifteen years earlier, in 1875, Rodin had his first work accepted by the Salon, the official annual exhibition, where he showed the marble bust *M. B.* (Musée Rodin, Paris). Carved that year, it was none other than a new version in a more traditional style of the damaged *Mask of the Man with the Broken Nose* (cf. cat. 64), which had been rejected by the committee of the same Salon ten years earlier. In 1877, he presented *The Age of Bronze* (cf. cat. 87), which looked so lifelike that Rodin was accused of casting it directly from the human body. After spending seven years in Belgium, Rodin had just returned to Paris, and he was counting on this sculpture to establish his reputation, hoping that it would be acquired by the government, which would be a starting point for any career. "I'm very annoyed," he wrote to Rose Beuret, his companion at the time, who had remained in Brussels. "Just imagine—so close to my goal! Everyone found my figure beautiful, but they insist on saying it was cast from life! . . . I'm at my wits' end, I'm tired, I don't have enough money, I have to find a studio."[5]

Indeed, he would again have to work as a studio assistant—rather than as an independent artist under his own name—until 1880 when, with the help of a group of sculptors who were convinced of his talent for modeling, he finally managed to clear himself of the slanderous accusation of making casts from life. The Fine Arts Administration then acquired the model for *The Age of Bronze*, from which a first cast was immediately made (Musée d'Orsay, Paris), and commissioned a monumental door from him that was intended for a planned museum of decorative arts. In 1880 and 1881, he exhibited two more large figures, *St. John the Baptist* (fig. 1.3) and *Adam*, which echo the masterpieces of the Italian Renaissance. In subsequent Salon exhibitions, he presented only busts, which demonstrated his capacity for deep anatomical and psychological analysis.

Rodin was able to adapt to the great transformations then taking place in the French artistic system.[6] The reform of the Salon, from which the government withdrew in 1881, eliminated the path to prestige associated with exhibiting at an official event. New criteria for appreciation took shape with the emergence of a clientele attracted by luxurious galleries where growing numbers of dealers promoted selected artworks. The development of these galleries was supported by an unprecedented boom in the publication of journals after the Freedom of the Press Act of July 29, 1881, eliminated any type of censorship. French journalists thus enjoyed a new sense of power, and Rodin soon understood the advantage he could draw from this.

In this favorable environment, he presented his new works, including elements modeled in connection with the *Gates of Hell* that he exhibited in 1886 and 1887 at Galerie Georges Petit (cf. cat. 4), which opened in 1882. Because Rodin conceived these elements as independent works of art, the versions in marble or bronze were able to follow their own individual paths.

Artists, especially the Naturalist painters Alphonse Legros, Jules Bastien-Lepage, and Alfred Roll, made up an initial group of admirers. Rodin negotiated trades with them: a bust for a portrait by Legros; a marble to Bastien-Lepage (who died in 1884), which would soon be his first sculpture—or at least one of his very first—to enter an American collection (cat. 2); and two bronzes,[7] which ended up in the United States after the painter's death, in exchange for a painting from Roll, *Peasant Woman with Cows* (c. 1885, Musée Rodin, Paris). Writers and journalists who were drawn to Rodin's symbolism would soon join these early admirers: Léon Gauchez, editor of the journal *L'Art* and an art dealer; Edmond Bazire who, after Rodin was accused of having cast the *Age of Bronze* from life, suggested that he produce a portrait of a famous man such as Victor Hugo or Victor-Henri Rochefort, whom no one would suspect of participating in

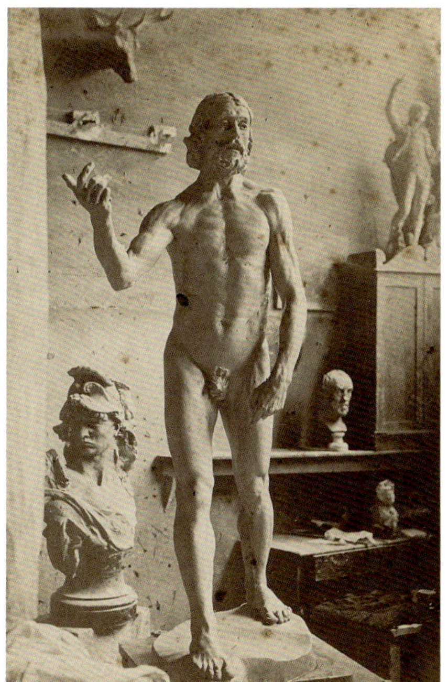

FIG. 1.3

Plaster model for *St. John the Baptist* in Rodin's studio, c. 1880. Photo by Charles Michelez. Archives du musée Rodin, Paris. PH. 662.

such a process; Gustave Geffroy, who met Rodin in 1884 and became one of the artist's staunchest defenders in his articles in *La Justice*; along with Octave Mirbeau, Félicien Champsaur, Edmond de Goncourt, Alphonse Daudet, and Roger Marx, among others. Collectors also appeared in France (Johanny Peytel, Antony Roux, and Maurice Fenaille, a pioneer in the French oil industry and an important patron and connoisseur), in Great Britain (Alexander Constantine Ionides), and in Belgium (Camille Lemonnier).

A NEW WAY OF SEEING AND UNDERSTANDING

The 1880s were a time of great activity and passion, marked by the influence of Michelangelo and a period of strenuous labor devoted almost exclusively to the prestigious commissions for the *Burghers of Calais* and the *Gates of Hell* (the original 8,000-franc budget for which was increased to 18,000 in 1881 and 25,000 in 1884, but whose completion was delayed year after year, with the project finally being canceled in February 1904). Rodin was working "with a kind of concentrated fury"[8] and modeled hundreds of small figures as studies for the two commissions, some of which soon became stand-alone works. With little imagination for titles, he settled for vague designations such as three *Tired Women* (*Andromeda*, *Caryatid*, and *Crouching Woman*), shown at Galerie Petit in 1886.[9] Some were completed immediately — the small *Eve* in bronze (1884) and in marble (1886), *Fallen Caryatid* in marble (1882–83, cat. 2), and various groups of children, including *Idyll of Ixelles* in marble (1884, Musée d'Ixelles, Brussels) or bronze (1885, Musée Rodin, Paris) — while others remained on the shelves of the studio, creating a stockpile that he would continue to draw on throughout his career.

The *Age of Bronze* and, especially, *Adam* and *St. John the Baptist*, the large figures produced around 1880, resonate with the influence of Michelangelo's Florentine-period sculptures of *Bacchus* (1496–97, Bargello National Museum, Florence) and *David* (1501–4, Galleria dell'Accademia, Florence), fully occupying their space with heads firmly turned to the side, pivoting torsos, and striding legs. Thereafter, however, Rodin's point of reference was the Italian master's *Last Judgment* fresco (1536–41) in the Sistine Chapel, with its tormented compositions. Upon receiving the commission from the Fine Arts Administration for a large decorative door, Rodin decided to represent the *Inferno* from Dante Alighieri's fourteenth-century epic poem *The Divine Comedy*. He populated the two doors and tympanum with dozens of the damned in the throes of horrendous suffering, creating a series of figures whose intense vitality was enough to justify their existence. They demonstrate what Geffroy termed "a new way of seeing and understanding."[10] Did they benefit from the "secret" that he had learned from Michelangelo in Florence, as he wrote to Beuret in 1876? Had Rodin succeeded in endowing them with "that nameless something that only he [Michelangelo] knew how to give"?[11] As Geffroy put it:

> For him [Rodin], not only can poses not be reduced to a few types, but in fact they appear infinite, engendering one another through decompositions and recompositions of movements, multiplying in transitory appearances each time the body moves. . . . The realities of life, the forms and positions provided by nature, are reproduced with rigorous accuracy and with skill that is determined to show that it can endow matter with the physical and intellectual manifestations of humanity, the movements by which it expresses its anger, sadness, desires, and passions, its need for excitement and dreams.[12]

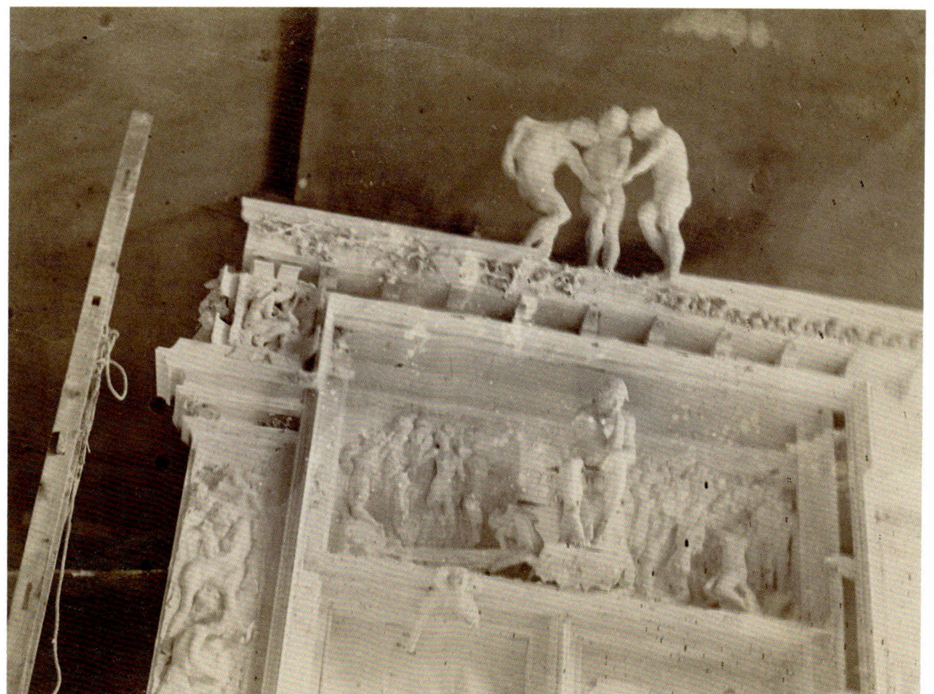

Like many of his contemporaries, Rodin invoked nature. "For an artist
worthy of the name," he told art critic Paul Gsell, "everything is beautiful in
Nature because his eyes boldly accept every external truth, read in Nature
without effort, as from an open book."[13] He attempted to depict the structure
of bodies, to make the presence of muscles and bones felt under the skin. Yet he
stood apart from the Naturalist movement because he employed anatomical
precision to express the passions. Inspired by his models—among them César
Pignatelli, who himself devised the pose of *St. John the Baptist* preaching; Adèle
Abbruzzesi, who was unafraid to adopt the most complex or audacious positions,
such as those of *Crouching Woman* or the *Caryatid*; and Marie Caira, whom
he did not hesitate to depict in all the decrepitude of old age—the Rodin of
the 1880s let the body, and the body alone, suggest the passions and torments
described by Dante. Thus, *The Kiss* (cf. cat. 68)—representing the lovers Paolo
and Francesca embracing in the moment Francesca's husband catches them—
was replaced in the *Gates* by a vision of the same couple tormented by the
violent winds of Hell, and the *Young Mother in the Grotto* by the *Fallen Caryatid*,
a dramatic allegory for human destiny (fig. 1.4). In so doing, he stripped the
figure of any specific historical or geographical context in order to give it a
universal resonance, as Geffroy observed:

> *The Gates of Hell* is the assemblage, in turbulent action, of instincts, desti-
> nies, desires, despair, of everything that cries out and moans in humanity.
> The Ghibelline poem has kept no local color and has lost all its Florentine
> meaning. It has been stripped, so to speak, and only its synthetic meaning
> has been expressed, like a collection of unchanging aspects of humanity
> from every era and every country.[14]

This approach was new. It was common for sculpture to express a message
using the traditional language of allegory, conveyed through clothing and
various accessories or attributes. Rodin, however, made bodies themselves speak.

He adopted this approach beginning in 1884 for the *Burghers of Calais*. The city had been seeking a single, heroic figure to memorialize the group of men who, after a siege that had lasted for over a year, risked their lives to bring the keys to the city to the victorious king of England. According to Gustave Coquiot, Rodin, pursuing the commission with enthusiasm,

> did research, borrowed the *Chroniques de Froissart*, and read the chapter titled "How King Philippe of France Could Not Free the City of Calais, and How King Edward of England Took It!" . . . Reading Froissart's complete narrative, Rodin was very moved and decided he could not depict *one* burgher of Calais, but six — all these heroes together. It was impossible to separate them. *Six* for the agreed-upon price.[15]

Even before the commission was definite, he renounced the traditional pyramidal model that exalted an individual, and his first maquette emphasized the notion of a collective sacrifice by positioning the six figures on the same plane. Having chosen to depict them at the moment they left Calais to surrender to the English, which meant almost certain death, Rodin was criticized for emphasizing despair over heroism, but he did not let this affect him. Any changes he made to the figures over the following four years only made them even stronger and more expressive. The German poet Rainer Maria Rilke wrote that Rodin "saw how the men started on their way, he felt how through each one of them pulsated once more his entire past life."[16]

In early 1886, the Calais banks failed, and the revenue for underwriting the monument vanished. Unsure of the project's future, but freed of any constraints, Rodin again began working on the *Gates of Hell*, which he hoped to complete for the Paris Exposition Universelle in 1889. Yet he did not abandon the *Burghers*, showing the first three figures in May 1887 at Galerie Petit and casting the last one on December 17, 1888. At this time, he had the opportunity to show his work with that of his friend Claude Monet at Galerie Petit. Needing a monumental piece to put in the center of the space, he ceased work on the *Gates* in order to focus on the assemblage of the six *Burghers*.

Adopting a different arrangement than what he had proposed in 1885, he grouped the figures around Eustache de Saint Pierre, the oldest burgher (fig. 1.5). From the side, they appear drawn by an impulse that pulls them forward. The oblique rhythm of the legs pulling away reluctantly from their native land emphasizes how painful it was for some of them to make this decision to surrender. In the artist's own words:

> They still ask themselves if they will have the strength to accomplish this supreme sacrifice. . . . Their souls push them forward and their feet refuse to walk. They drag along painfully, because of both the weakness caused by famine and the horror of their ordeal. And certainly, if I have succeeded in showing how the body, even exhausted by the cruelest forms of suffering, still holds on to life, how much influence it still has over the soul enamored of valor, I can only congratulate myself for being equal to the noble theme I had to treat.[17]

It was a new conception of a public monument, and the humanity of the group was the focus of attention when it was inaugurated in Calais in 1895. Rodin had allowed viewers to enter into the feelings of these six human beings, making the emotions of the historical figures immediate and palpable.

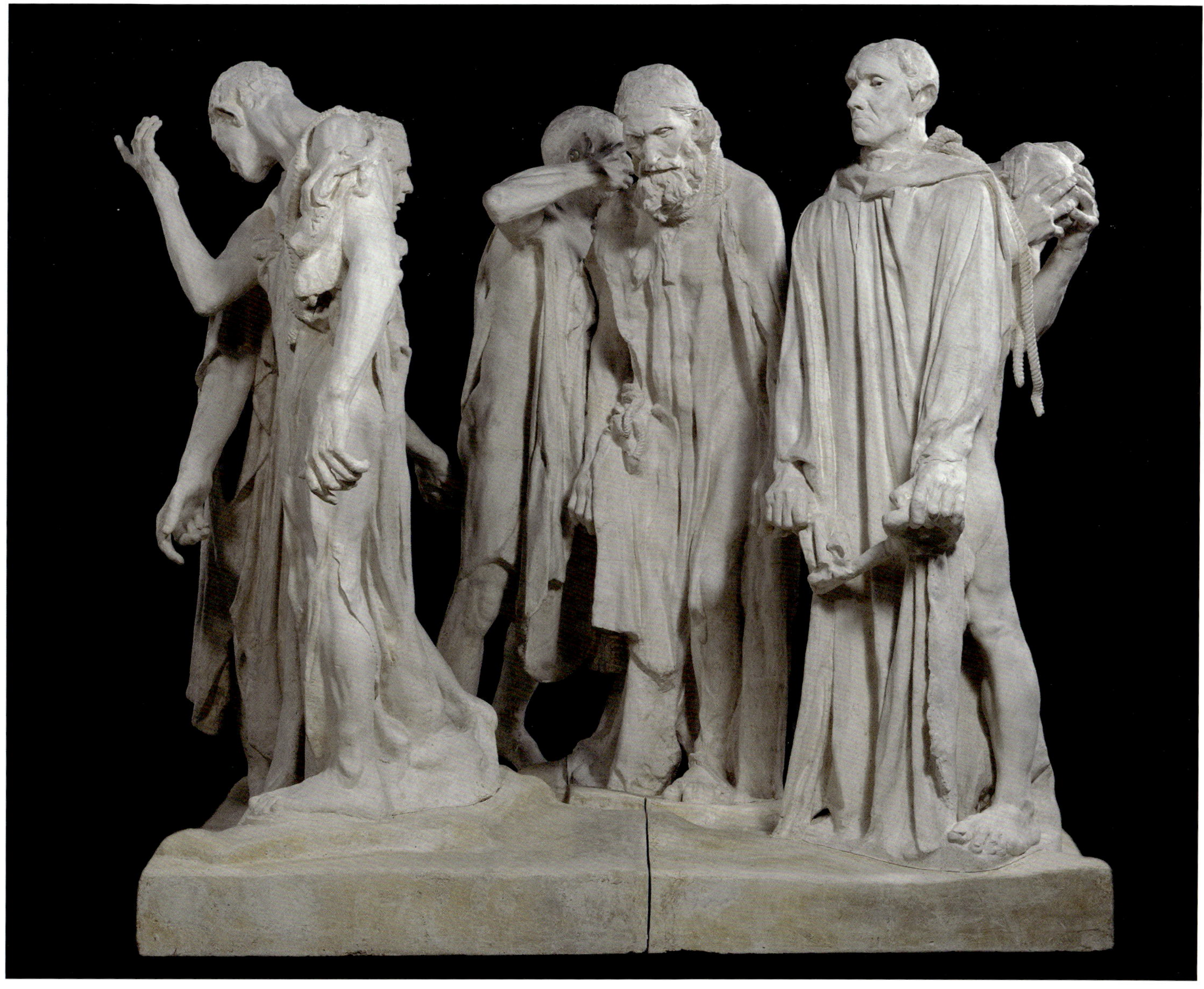

NEW VENUES, NEW AUDIENCES

Auguste Rodin (French, 1840–1917), *Monument to the Burghers of Calais*, 1889. Plaster, 88 %⁄₁₆ × 94 ½ × 78 ¾ in. (225 × 240 × 200 cm). Musée Rodin, Paris. S. 153.

In 1889, along with the large plasters for the *Burghers of Calais*, Rodin presented works that surprised viewers with the innovation and expressiveness of their poses, such as *Danaid*, *I Am Beautiful*, *Eternal Spring*, and *Fugit Amor* (cf. cat. 6). Their small dimensions were also ideal for a private clientele, and indeed many copies of each exist. In the last decade of the century, while remaining faithful to Galerie Petit, Rodin regularly participated in exhibitions at the Société Nationale des Beaux-Arts (SNBA), which was founded in 1890 and, unlike the Salon, was never controlled by the state. Welcoming new approaches to art and decoration, it was aimed at a different audience—in particular, those collectors who were interested in modernity. Rodin exhibited marbles and bronzes there, completed works that could be purchased immediately. These works were generally given Symbolist titles from poems that he liked or titles suggested by his friends, which contributed to their allure. Thus, the figure originally titled simply *Old Woman* became *She Who Was the Helmet-Maker's Once-Beautiful Wife*, echoing François Villon's poem "Les Regrets de la Belle Heaulmière" (c. 1461).

Between 1896 and 1897, the public first saw some of Rodin's most important marble sculptures: *Eternal Idol* (fig. 1.6), *Illusion, Sister of Icarus* (1894–96,

Musée Rodin, Paris), *Man and His Thought* (1896–1900, Nationalgalerie, Berlin), and *Youth Triumphant* (1896, MAK, Vienna) in 1896; and the column *Dream of Life* (fig. 1.7), *Eternal Spring* (private collection), and *Phantom Kissing a Young Girl* (1892–94, formerly Walker Art Center, Minneapolis) in 1897, some of them repeated in multiple versions. Like most of his contemporaries, Rodin ranked marble as the noblest material for sculpture, yet, also like them, he would not touch it. Instead, he modeled his works in plaster or clay and called on artisans who specialized in carving marble, which required considerable physical exertion, to translate his designs into stone. In 1874, he had asked Léon Fourquet, one of his friends from the École Impériale Spéciale de Dessin et de Mathématiques (Petite École), to execute the bust *Man with the Broken Nose* (Musée Rodin, Paris), which was intended for the Salon of 1875. He then relied on a series of outstanding sculptors who subsequently went on to successful careers. After 1900, the situation became paradoxical: as the demand for marbles was constantly increasing, Rodin himself was less busy and could thus devote significant time to drawing, which played a considerable role in the last part of his career.[18] Yet it must be understood that, as the American sculptor Lorado Taft astutely commented after visiting the artist's studio in 1900, "these artisans are literally his hands";[19] the marble works were indeed his own. He signed them and ascribed so much importance to them that he had additional examples produced of those he deemed most significant (such as *Fugit Amor*) so that his future museum would reflect his work as completely as possible.

Almost always, the marble sculptures were based on figures from the *Gates of Hell*—such as the Boston *Fallen Caryatid*. Chance sometimes brought together some of the figures, as if guiding the artist's inspiration toward new groups, as in works such as *Orpheus and Eurydice* (1893, Metropolitan Museum of Art, New York), *The Hand of God* (cat. 22), *Christ and Mary Magdalene* (cat. 101). The hundreds of figures modeled for the *Gates of Hell*, whether or not incorporated into it, constituted a veritable reservoir of forms and ideas. Rodin discovered that the simple juxtaposition of two bodies, or two parts of the body, offered a source of energy that could produce unexpected and often surprising compositions, without having to go through all the stages of modeling. Arthur Symons, a British writer and poet, understood this better than anyone:

> Often a single figure takes form under his hands, and he cannot understand what the figure means: its lines seem to will something, and to ask for the completion of their purpose. He puts it aside, and one day, happening to see it as it lies among other formless suggestions of form, [he finds that] it groups itself with another fragment, itself hitherto unexplained; suddenly there is a composition, the idea has penetrated the clay, life has given birth to the soul.[20]

His only concern was to move as quickly as intuition flashed into his mind. Carving, cutting, and attaching elements without paying any attention to anatomical realism, he did not hesitate to give the marble artisans assemblages that were sometimes very rudimentary. The details would become precise as the carving took shape and established the final dimensions. This approach privileged the nature of the block of marble, and Rodin expressed a preference for irregular or reused blocks—such as the triangular block employed for the bust of Katherine (Kate) Seney Simpson (cat. 12)—which stimulated his imagination. This method was somewhat risky, but it offered the advantage of maintaining a margin of freedom almost until the end. From the early 1890s onward, inspired by his love for Camille Claudel and encouraged by his friends Monet, Mirbeau, and Geffroy, he radically stood out from other contemporary sculptors

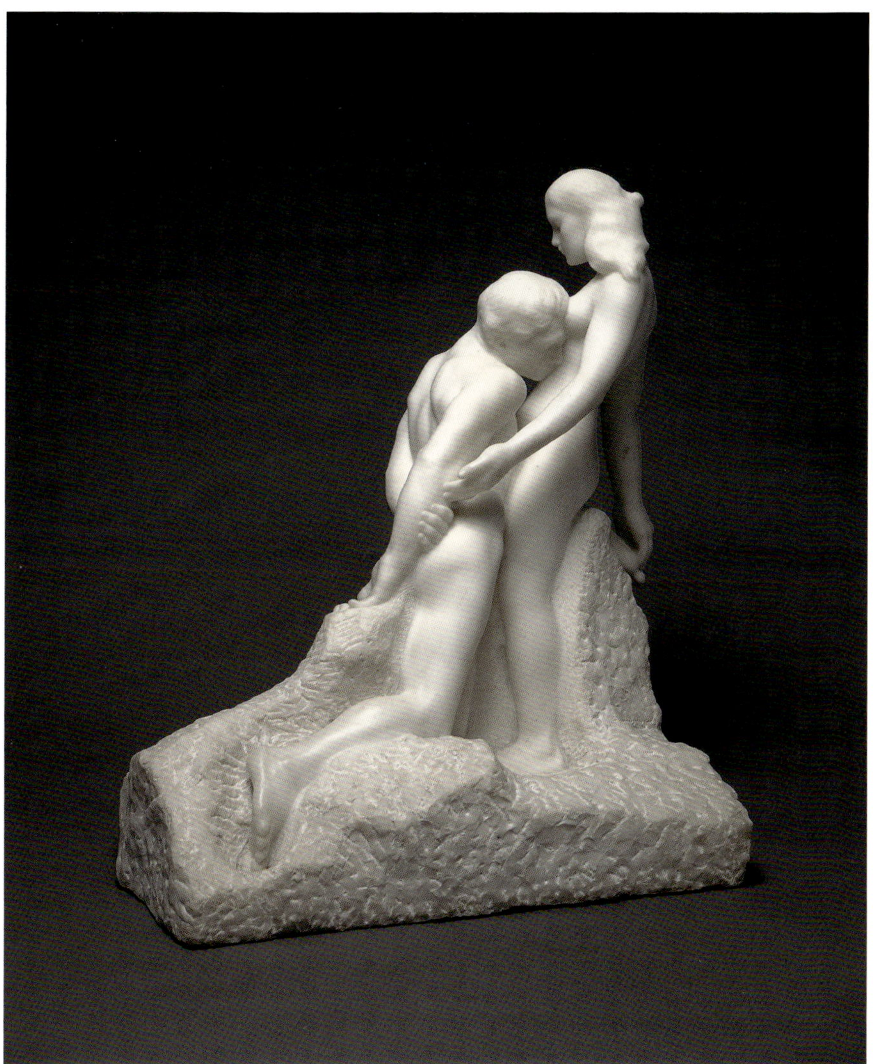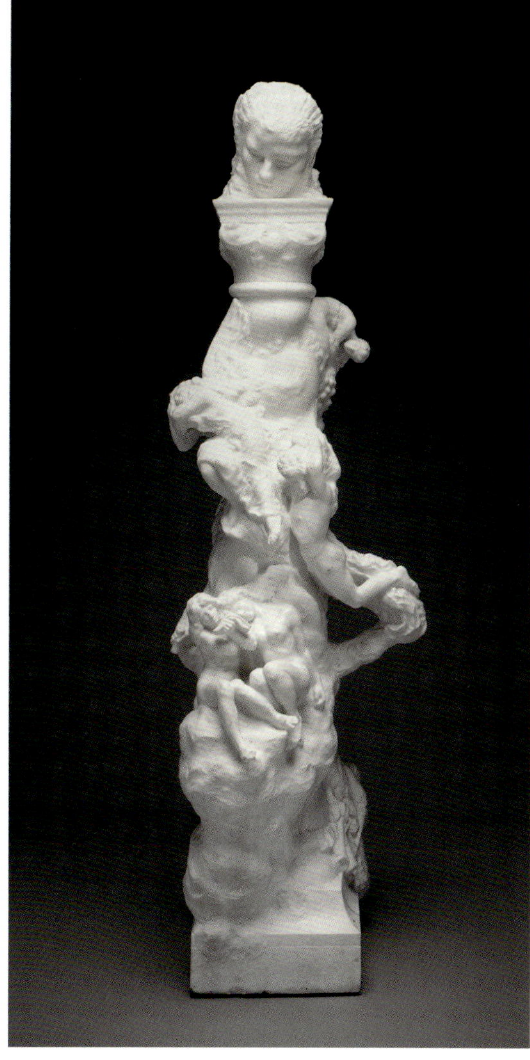

Auguste Rodin, *Eternal Idol*, original model 1891, carved by Jean Escoula, 1893. Marble, 28 ½ × 25 × 15 ¾ in. (72.4 × 63.5 × 40 cm). Harvard Art Museums / Fogg Museum, Cambridge, Massachusetts. Bequest of Grenville L. Winthrop, 1943.1034.

Auguste Rodin, *Dream of Life* or *Fenaille Column*, original model 1894, carved by A. Morlon 1894–97. Marble, 72 × 21 ¾ × 23 in. (182.9 × 55.3 × 58.4 cm). Dallas Museum of Art. The Wendy and Emery Reves Collection, 1985.R.64.

as he experimented with bold and innovative creative processes, which he did not hesitate to share with the public. The compositions' expression in marble granted them the status of completely finished works.

By the beginning of twentieth century, American collectors would seek out this more modern Rodin—even if, in 1893, the Renaissance allusions of the *Bust of St. John the Baptist* at the Metropolitan Museum of Art or the single figure from the *Burghers of Calais* shown in the world's fair Fine Arts Building in Chicago had more universal appeal. Initially, the freer and more passionate figures from the *Gates* found homes only with more audacious US collectors who were not concerned about moral criteria. As American historian and presidential scion Henry Adams explained to revered Washington hostess Elizabeth Cameron in 1895, he was torn between his admiration for the artist and his loyalty to a conservative worldview that made it impossible to have one of Rodin's works in his home.[21] But the situation soon changed. Prior to the Met's major acquisition campaign in 1910–11, collectors like Samuel Isham, Alexander Harrison, John G. Johnson, Henry Lee Higginson, Charles T. Yerkes, Kate Seney Simpson and John Woodruff Simpson, Agnes Ernst Meyer and Eugene Meyer, Isaac D. Fletcher, and others acquired the works that are today the pride of American museums, emphasizing marbles over bronzes, even if they were more difficult to obtain.

NEW CREATIVE MODES

During the last years of the nineteenth century, Rodin showed his work in Geneva with Pierre Puvis de Chavannes and Eugène Carrière in 1896, and then alone, for the first time, in Belgium and the Netherlands in 1899. The following year in Paris, alongside the Exposition Universelle, he had a solo exhibition in an independent pavilion built for this purpose at Place de l'Alma.[22] After that date, his international exhibitions multiplied. In addition to the Parisian Salons (the SNBA Salon to which Rodin remained faithful, and then the Salon d'Automne), his works were shown in Vienna, Dresden, and Venice in 1901; in Prague in 1902; in Düsseldorf, Dresden, Weimar, Leipzig, and St. Louis, Missouri, in 1904; in Rome in 1911 and 1913; in London in 1914; and in San Francisco in 1915, just to mention his most important exhibitions.

This was the time when the great Rodin collections were assembled: the Jacobsen collection in Copenhagen, the Thyssen collection in Germany, and the Simpson collection in the United States. The exhibition at the Pavillon de l'Alma allowed Rodin to attract a much broader and more international clientele. He acknowledged this himself:

> As a spiritual result, my exhibition is very beautiful, and in terms of money I will cover my costs. I sold work for 200,000 francs, and I am hoping for a bit more. Plus a few commissions, as well.
>
> Almost all the museums bought from me: Philadelphia, *The Thinker*; Copenhagen, for 80,000 francs, [works] for a separate room in the museum; Hamburg, Dresden, Budapest, etc. There were few Americans, few English, but many Germans at my exhibition.[23]

The Pavillon de l'Alma exhibition, which remained open from June 1 to the end of 1900, was somewhat unusual, with Rodin's work arranged as if in his studio (fig. 1.8). Critic Georges Morot observed:

> What makes this pavilion of Rodin's so charming is the overall impression of sketches, drawings, and projects. This isn't an official exhibition hall where everything is complete and ready for a column in a park or a plinth in a public square. It's the studio of a great artist and a powerful genius where nothing seems completely finished, where we look for the Master busy "pushing ahead," changing, or finishing a figure.[24]

Beginning in the mid-1890s, helped perhaps by the distance he gained following the rupture with Claudel, Rodin's vision of sculpture continued to evolve. Alongside assemblages that extended his creative output from the two previous decades, *The Earth*, *Tragic Muse*, *Meditation*, and *Iris, Messenger of the Gods* (cf. cat. 84) masterfully affirmed the new direction that he was now taking through the use of partial figures and enlargements, approaches that art historian Leo Steinberg saw as transforming the artistic process in a famous text from 1972.[25] The most spectacular example may be *Iris*, a version of which Edward Perry Warren donated to the Museum of Fine Arts, Boston. He had previously lent the museum the famous third-to-second-century BCE *Head of a Goddess ("The Chios Head")*, a fragmentary ancient marble, which Rodin wrote about and wanted very much to acquire.[26] In both cases, the absence of certain elements had the consequence of focusing attention on what was essential: the torso and the leap of the messenger of the gods and the sweet face of the young Greek woman, which is heightened by the violence of its damage.

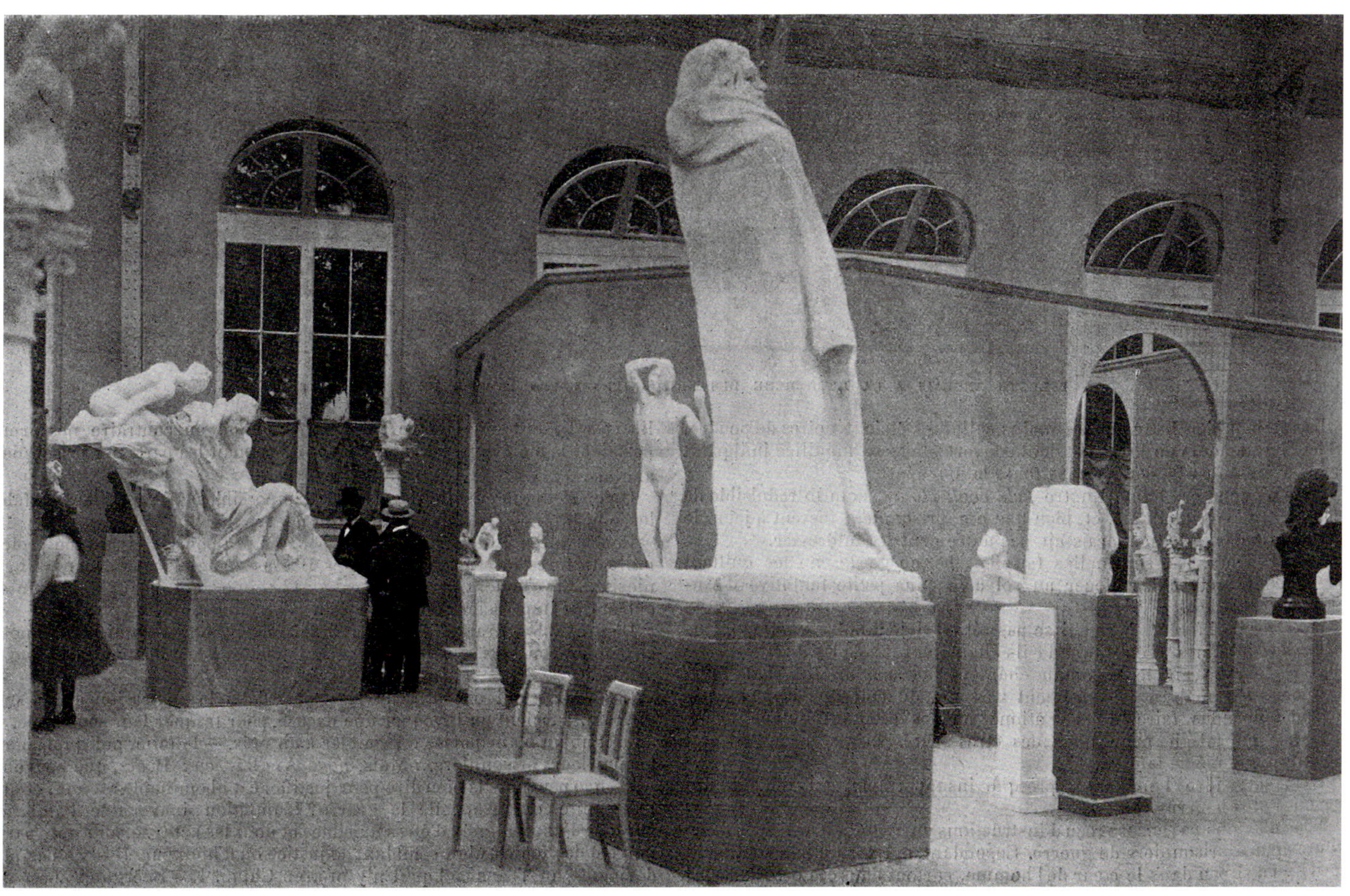

Interior View of the Pavillon de l'Alma, with *Monument to Victor Hugo*, *The Age of Bronze*, and *Balzac*, from *La Vie illustrée*, December 21, 1900.

The highly anticipated *Gates of Hell* was on view in the Pavillon de l'Alma, of course, but stripped of all its figures, which Rodin had decided at the last minute not to reinstall. The statue of Balzac, commissioned by the Société des Gens de Lettres almost a decade earlier, was aligned with the exhibition entrance as if to affirm that this was an essential step in the quest for a synthetic form. Over the course of the many studies Rodin had made for the statue, he had removed anything that could distract the viewer from the face, which he made so powerful that it was almost a caricature. Thus, for example, the hands are hidden under the cloak that Balzac was in the habit of wearing when he wrote at night, initially a monk's robe, which had lost its hood and belt in Rodin's final version. The society had rejected the work in 1898 because, they claimed, they could not "recognize" the writer, as Charles Chincholle reported in *Le Figaro*.[27] "What does it mean not to 'recognize'?" Rodin exclaimed in response. "For me, modern sculpture cannot be photography. The artist must work not only with his hands, but above all with his brain."[28] He reiterated in *Le Matin* a decade later that his *Balzac* "[would make] its way. . . . This sculpture, which people laughed at and made sure to ridicule because they couldn't destroy it, is the result of my entire life, the very pivotal point of my aesthetic."[29]

In his intense search for expressiveness, he also discovered that partial figures—that is, figures that were damaged or voluntarily stripped of nonessential details—could have even greater power. Beginning in 1895–1900, he expressed the same passion for life in partial figures that he did in the countless nudes of the *Gates of Hell*. Using plaster, which became a favorite medium, he thus showed that, at almost sixty years of age, he could change his approach based on his receptiveness to new discoveries, being humble enough to take what would have appeared insignificant to others and make it his own.

Even if the general public was unable to understand this new approach to his craft, it was still successful. His commissions continued to increase, and Rodin was able to respond to them because he was surrounded by many assistants, to the point that sculpture became essentially a mental practice for him. It was no longer a question of modeling but simply a process of composing new groups based on earlier figures. Rodin took into account the observations and suggestions of those around him and was also inspired by small events from daily life, such as accidents, a chance connection between two forms, or taking a walk and discovering eggshells or dry branches that he would immediately incorporate into his work (fig. 1.9). Moreover, he oversaw and guided the execution of his works by highlighting the nature of the selected material. For instance, he left the seams from the molds on the plasters, which were then reproduced when they were cast in bronze. With marble, he played on the contrast between highly finished areas (flesh) and others that were simply chipped away, and he did not eliminate the traces of the process, such as base points, pencil marks, holes produced by the needle during carving, or other tool marks.

While Rodin revealed the workings of his craft by preserving the seams and other traces of modeling or casting, he also respected the influence of chance, shifting the source of creativity from the hand that models to the eye that perceives. In this way, happenstance, which had played a role since the beginning of his career, became an important resource for his work.[30] Around 1885–86, he rediscovered the study of a torso that had been modeled a few years earlier in connection with the large *St. John the Baptist* (1880). Relegated to a corner of the studio and forgotten, the clay original had cracked while it dried, giving it the appearance of an archaeological fragment. A great admirer of ancient art, Rodin felt the emotion this work produced: "When [the artist] is very skillful at imitating nature," he declared in a long meditation published in 1904, "you will tell him, 'Look at the work of the ancients.' And antiquity will be for him a new source of energy."[31] Just as he recognized the expressive beauty of the damaged *Mask of the Man with the Broken Nose*, he carefully preserved the damaged torso, having it cast in bronze and exhibiting it at Galerie Petit in 1889 (as "*Torso*," no. 28; fig. 1.10).

Enlargement, too, played a role in the process of creation. After he was accused in 1877 of having made the *Age of Bronze* by means of casts from life, Rodin decided to model his figures larger than life (as in the *Burghers of Calais*, *St. John the Baptist*, and others), directly in their final size. But over the following decade, once his modeling talent had been firmly established, he made studies for *Balzac* and the elements of the *Monument to Victor Hugo* in more convenient dimensions (approximately half life-size), with the understanding that the figures would be enlarged during their production.[32] As Rodin explained to his secretary René Chéruy[33] the moldings that were to frame the *Gates of Hell* were supposed to create a connection to its surroundings. Rodin was deeply aware of the relationship between form and its context, and he also realized that the dimensions of an artwork completely changed this relationship, giving the new sculpture the quality of a unique creation. Thus, after having first practiced enlargement for the needs of his craft, he

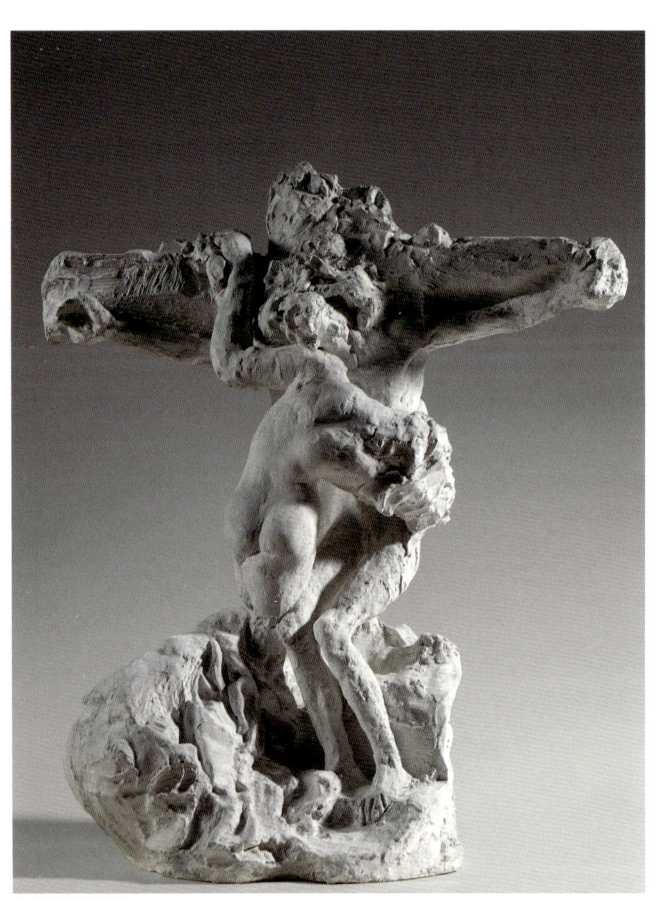

FIG. 1.9

Auguste Rodin, *Christ and Mary Magdalene*, c. 1894. Model: plaster, wood, and fabric, 33 ¼ × 29 ⅛ × 17 ⅜ in. (84.5 × 74 × 44.2 cm). Musée Rodin, Paris. S. 001097.

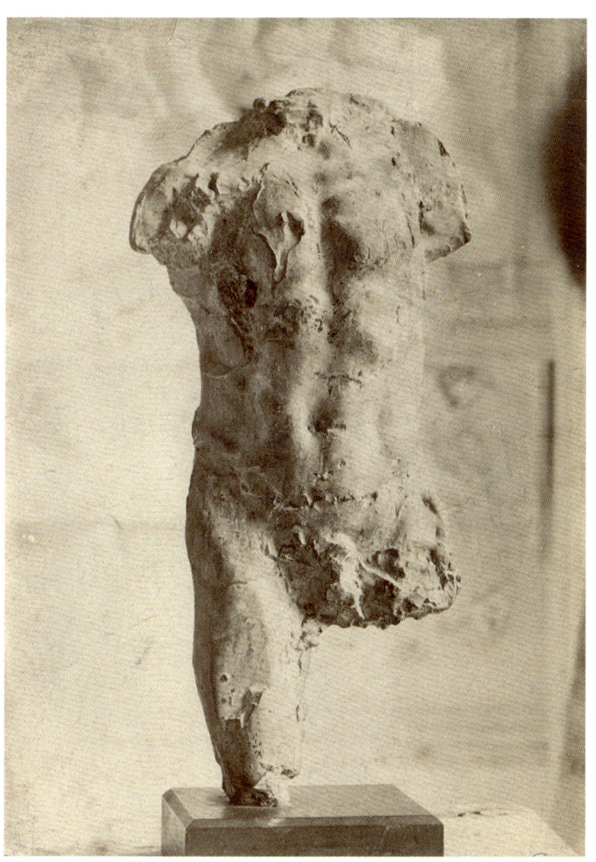

Auguste Rodin, *Torso*, study for *St. John the Baptist*, c. 1879. Photo by Ernest Freuler. Archives du musée Rodin, Paris, PH. 2656.

systematically performed this same operation on the figures he especially cared about, allowing them to attain their maximum expressive strength—as with *The Prodigal Son* (cf. cat. 42) and *The Thinker* (cf. cat. 69). In its large version, the latter, in particular, acquired the fame it enjoys today.

After 1900, Rodin's art developed in what seemed to be two opposing directions: on the one hand, the search for expression that he had pursued ever since his early enthusiastic work on the *Gates of Hell*, and, on the other, a process of simplification that invoked ancient art. However, even the works derived from the *Gates of Hell* or those created by assemblage using figures from the 1880s, such as the *Prodigal Son* or the *Hand of God*, left room for a kind of experimental approach. André Gide called such works *pathétiques*, or profoundly poignant, in 1905, in contrast with the "silence" of the work of Bach, Phidias, Raphael, and Maillol.[34] The *Hand of God* in Pittsburgh (cat. 52) and the *Prodigal Son* in San Francisco both emerge from roughly cut bases that make them less weighty, but also underscore the fact that the work is perceived at a particular moment during an evolution that is not yet complete. Time thus becomes an essential element of sculpture. Rodin also suggested the duration of action in the *Prodigal Son* or *The Walking Man* (cf. cat. 86) by representing the torso, the head, and the limbs over a series of instants: "In this way, when viewers move their eyes from one end of my statues to the other, they see their gestures unfold."[35] And, crucially, the time of creation extends over two phases: not just when the sculpture is first produced, but also later when any superfluous material is removed, exposing the form's intrinsic beauty.

Eve (cf. cat. 48) is an essential object for understanding Rodin's vision of sculpture, revealing the development of his approach between 1881–82 and 1899—that is, between when Rodin modeled the work and set it aside, because the sittings were interrupted, and when it was cast in bronze with no modifications whatsoever. The concept of "finishing," as defined by the traditional approach to sculpture, was no longer of the least interest to Rodin. At the center of his practice was form searching for itself, and, for him, sculpture was never finished. The artist explained:

> "Finishing". . . means connecting to life, which begins and never finishes, which is in constant development. Understood differently, the same word could only have a negative meaning, the meaning of death; and this is indeed what mediocre sculptors or those from the Institut unconsciously mean by it: they finish, i.e., they give their artworks the characteristics of death.[36]

In Rodin's work, by contrast, each plaster or marble sculpture is the materialization, at a given moment, of a stage in a long history that often runs throughout the artist's entire career. From the sketch to the completed version—of which there is rarely just one (four marbles exist for the *Hand of God*, two for *Christ and Mary Magdalene*, etc.)—along with enlargements (not to mention bronze casts), the same work appears and reappears in various forms over time, for it is part of an ongoing process of transformation and evolution that is life itself. This process does not end even with the artist's death.

In theory, artists may control the interpretation of their works during their own lifetimes, yet works can acquire metaphorical significance, even meanings unintended by the artist, at much later times. In front of the High Museum of

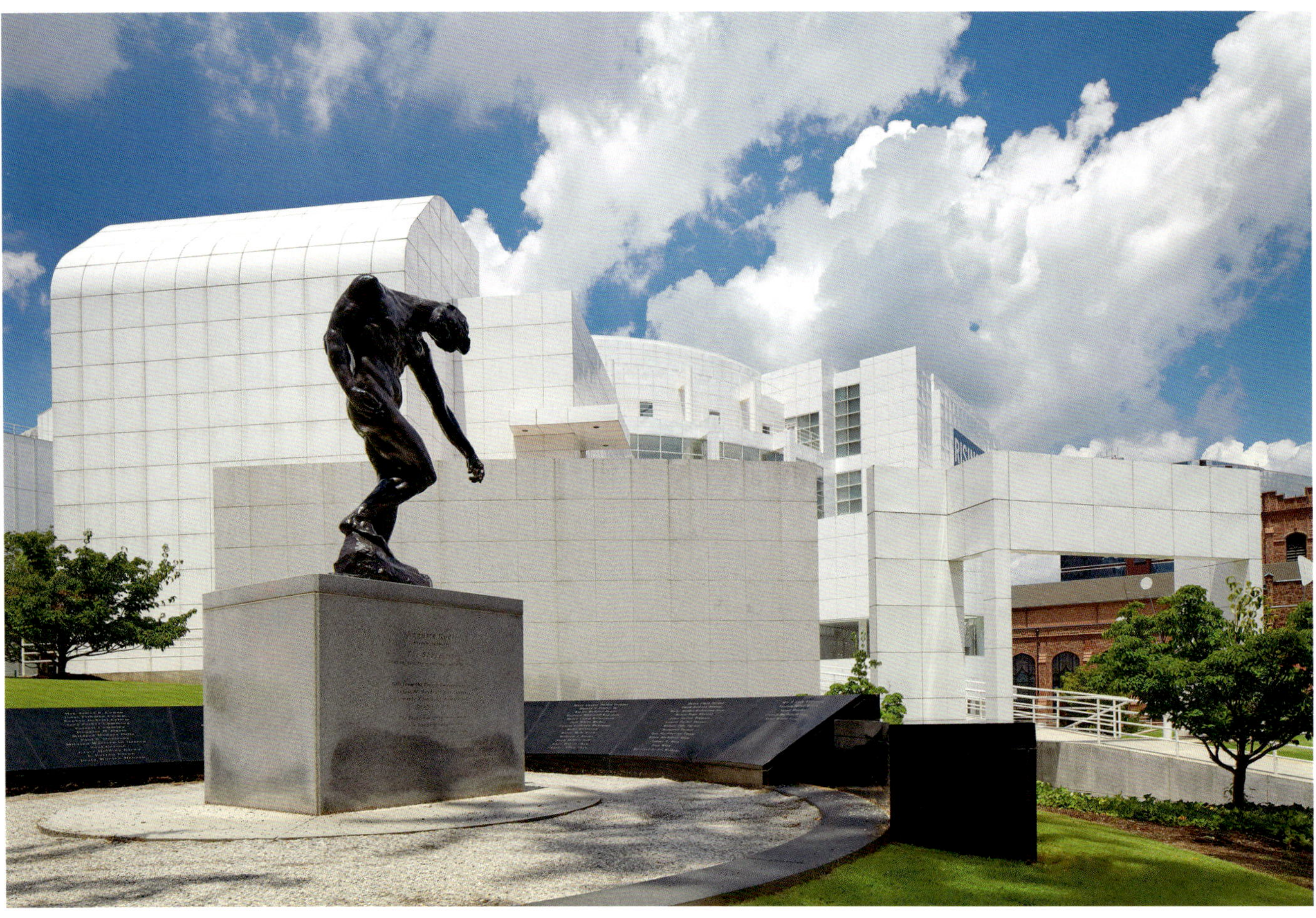

Auguste Rodin, *The Shade*, 1904, cast 1968. Bronze, 75 ½ × 44 ⅛ × 19 ¾ in. (191.8 × 112.1 × 50.2 cm). Woodruff Arts Center, Atlanta.

Art in Atlanta stands a monumental bronze version of *The Shade* (fig. 1.11) donated by France to the Woodruff Arts Center in memory of the victims of a Paris plane crash that killed 106 members of the city's arts leadership on June 3, 1962. The choice of this mournful figure, which had already been used for several tombs (such as that of collector Ernest Thiel in Stockholm and that of founder Eugène Rudier in Le Vésinet, near Paris), might seem self-evident for such a memorial, but tragedy may also be inscribed in the very flesh of a sculpture. *The Thinker* in Cleveland was blown up with dynamite on March 24, 1970, in protest against the Vietnam War (see fig. 9.19), and fragments of another *Shade* and one figure from the *Burghers of Calais* were found in the ruins of the World Trade Center in New York after the attacks of September 11, 2001. None of these objects was restored; they were simply preserved in their damaged state, as the symbolic value they acquired overtook their original status as works of art.

For the final sculptures he exhibited at the SNBA, Rodin used descriptive titles such as *Walking Man* (1907) or *Large Head of Iris* (1911). The art of sculpture, to which he had devoted his life, had become the main — if not the only — subject of his work. He realized that nothing highlighted this more powerfully than to leave his sculpture "alone and naked, so to speak," as Judith Cladel wrote in 1908. She continued:

> This is the ultimate art; a certificate that the sculptor gives himself, the sum of his efforts and his research concentrated in artistic forms. From then on, what does the completion of the details or an attractive arrangement matter to him? . . . Like a historian, Rodin calls them "essays," and these are indeed pages from the history of his art.[37]

With notable exceptions like Kate and John Simpson, who acquired a small *Walking Man* in 1904 (cat. 14), or Alma de Bretteville Spreckels, thanks to whom the *Female Figure, Half-Length* (cat. 43) sent to San Francisco remained there (perhaps due to the cost of sending it back to Paris rather than by choice), Americans largely did not understand Rodin's vital contribution to art history until the second half of the twentieth century. The influence of discerning figures such as Alfred Barr, Curt Valentin, Albert Elsen, John Steinberg, and B. Gerald Cantor would be needed in order for collectors and the general public to recognize Rodin's importance, making him the best-represented French sculptor in American collections today.

NOTES

1. American Art Association sale, New York, April 25–30, 1895.

2. *Loan Collection: Foreign Masterpieces Owned in the United States*, exh. cat. (Chicago: W. B. Conkey, 1893), http://archive.org/details/catalogueofunite00worl /page/8/mode/2up.

3. Mathias Morhardt, "Mademoiselle Camille Claudel," *Mercure de France*, March 1898, 719.

4. Julius West, ed., *The Journal of the De Goncourts: Pages from a Great Diary, Being Extracts from the Journal des Goncourt* (London: Thomas Nelson and Sons, [191-?]); electronic reproduction (Los Angeles: Internet Archive, 2012), 457.

5. Auguste Rodin to Rose Beuret, after April 13, 1877, in Auguste Rodin, *Correspondance*, vol. 1, *1860–1899* (Paris: Éditions du musée Rodin, 1985), no. 20.

6. See Harrison C. White and Cynthia A. White, *Canvases and Careers: Institutional Change in the French Painting World* (New York: John Wiley and Sons, 1965); Patricia Mainardi, *The End of the Salon: Art and the State in the Early Third Republic* (Cambridge: Cambridge University Press, 1993).

7. The two bronzes were *The Kiss* (cat. 68) and *Eternal Spring* (1884, cast 1888), Harvard Art Museums / Fogg Museum, Cambridge, Massachusetts, Bequest of Grenville L. Winthrop.

8. Judith Cladel, *Rodin*, trans. James Whitall (New York: Harcourt, Brace, 1937), 75.

9. *Vème Exposition internationale de peinture et de sculpture*, Galerie Georges Petit, Paris, 1886; cf. Alain Beausire, *Quand Rodin exposait* (Paris: Musée Rodin, 1988), 94.

10. Gustave Geffroy, "Rodin," *La Justice*, July 11, 1886.

11. Rodin to Beuret, [March 1876], in Rodin, *Correspondance*, vol. 1, no. 13.

12. Gustave Geffroy, "Auguste Rodin," in *Claude Monet–A. Rodin*, exh. cat. (Paris: Galerie Georges Petit, 1889), 61–62, 63.

13. Auguste Rodin, *Art: Conversations with Paul Gsell*, trans. Jacques de Caso and Patricia B. Sanders (Berkeley: University of California Press, 1984), 20; originally published as Auguste Rodin, *L'Art: Entretiens réunis par Paul Gsell* (Paris: Bernard Grasset, 1911), 51, 52.

14. Geffroy, "Auguste Rodin," 57.

15. Gustave Coquiot, *Le vrai Rodin* (Paris: Éditions Jules Tallandier, 1913), 133–34.

16. Rainer Maria Rilke, *Auguste Rodin* [1903], trans. Jessie Lemont and Hans Trausil (New York: Sunwise Turn, 1919), 68.

17. Auguste Rodin, quoted by Paul Gsell, "Chez Rodin," *L'art et les artistes*, 1914, 67.

18. For more on this subject, see Christina Buley-Uribe's essay in this volume, "The Role of Drawing in the Art of Rodin," pp. 45–59.

19. Lorado Taft, "Rodin in His Studio: Visit to the Great Sculptor," *Chicago Record*, June 16, 1900.

20. Arthur Symons, "Rodin," *Fortnightly Review* 71 (January–June 1902), 964; see also Ruth Butler, ed., *Rodin in Perspective* (New York: Prentice-Hall, 1980), 118.

21. Henry Adams to Elizabeth Cameron, September 25, 1895, in *The Letters of Henry Adams*, vol. 4, *1892–1899*, ed. J. C. Levenson, Ernest Samuels, Charles Vandersee, and Viola Hopkins Winner (Cambridge, MA: Belknap Press of Harvard University Press, 1989), 332.

22. On that exhibition, see *Rodin en 1900: L'exposition de l'Alma*, exh. cat. (Paris: Musée du Luxembourg, 2001).

23. Auguste Rodin to Edmond Bigand-Kaire, between December 11, 1900, and March 8, 1901, Archives du musée Rodin, Paris; see Rodin, *Correspondance*, vol. 2, *1900–1907* (Paris: Éditions du musée Rodin, 1986), no. 32.

24. Georges Morot, "Le pavillon Rodin: Étreintes et masques," *La Presse*, June 11, 1900.

25. Leo Steinberg, "Rodin," *Other Criteria: Confrontations with Twentieth-Century Art* [1972] (Chicago: University of Chicago Press, 2007), 322–403.

26. Auguste Rodin, "La tête Warren," *Le Musée: Revue d'art antique*, no. 6 (November–December 1904): 298–301.

27. Charles Chincholle, "La Vente de la statue de Balzac," *Le Figaro*, May 12, 1898.

28. Auguste Rodin, quoted in Chincholle, "La Vente de la statue de Balzac."

29. Auguste Rodin, quoted in Gaston Leroux, "A Paris: Le vernissage," *Le Matin*, July 13, 1908.

30. See *Rodin: L'accident, l'aléatoire*, exh. cat. (Geneva: Musée d'Art et d'Histoire, 2014).

31. Rodin, "La Leçon de l'antique," *Le Musée: Revue d'art antique*, no. 1 (January–February 1904): 17.

32. In the world of sculpture, enlargement was typically done using a pantograph, a machine invented by Achille Collas in 1838. Using a sliding arm equipped with triangles, the sculptor could mechanically enlarge or reduce the volume of an object.

33. René Chéruy, "Rodin's *Gates of Hell* Comes to America," *New York Herald Tribune*, January 20, 1929.

34. André Gide, "Promenade au Salon d'automne," *Gazette des Beaux-Arts*, December 1, 1905, 478.

35. Auguste Rodin, quoted in Gsell, "Chez Rodin," 63.

36. Auguste Rodin, quoted in Charles Morice, *Rodin* [transcript of lecture at the Maison d'Art in Brussels, May 2, 1899] (Paris: H. Floury, 1900), 17.

37. Judith Cladel, *Auguste Rodin, l'œuvre et l'homme* (Brussels: Librairie Nationale d'Art et d'Histoire / G. Van Oest, 1908), 97.

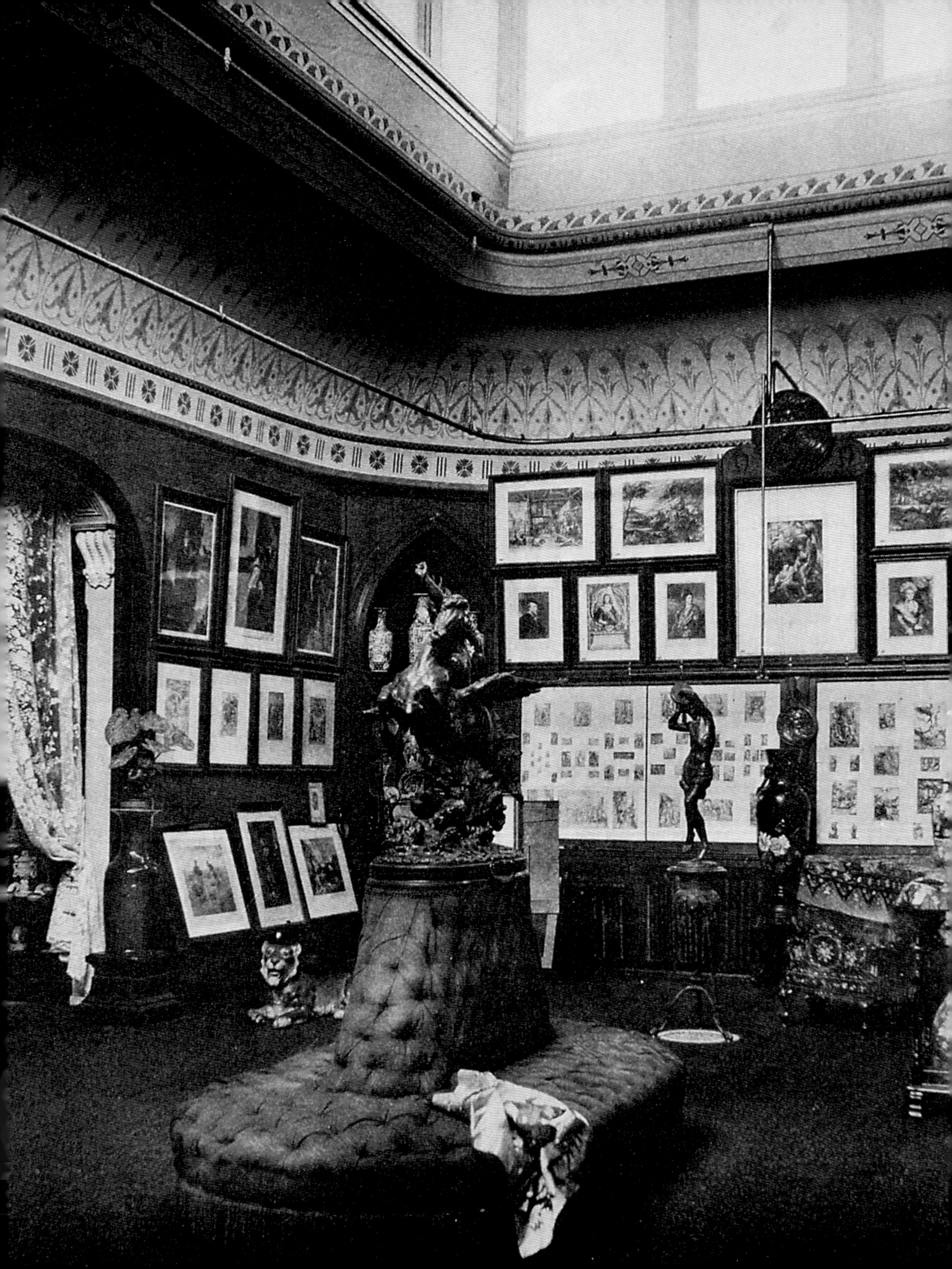

AN ESTABLISHED TASTE

COLLECTING FRENCH SCULPTURE IN AMERICA

LAURE DE MARGERIE

When the New York art dealer and collector Samuel P. Avery bought two bronzes by Auguste Rodin in 1888, he was among the first Americans to acquire the artist's work. But interest in French sculpture had already been firmly established in the United States for more than a century, with the beginnings of its appreciation inextricably linked to the founding of the new nation.[1] In the 1770s and 1780s, French sculptors were sought to erect what is considered the earliest American public monument, and then to portray the founding fathers of the country. First, the Continental Congress, which governed the thirteen colonies from 1775 to 1781 and adopted the Declaration of Independence on July 4, 1776, appointed Jean-Jacques Caffieri to create the *Monument to General Montgomery* (New York, St. Paul's Chapel) in 1777. Richard Montgomery had been killed during the Battle of Quebec on December 31, 1775. In 1784, the General Assembly of Virginia commissioned a full-length statue of future president George Washington (Richmond, Capitol) from Jean-Antoine Houdon, a portrayal that quickly became emblematic. From then on, sculpture would be closely tied to historical and political relations between the two countries.

After this initial period, primarily centered on portraiture, collectors in the 1860s were the first to take an interest in other artistic genres. Several circles of amateurs formed, from Gilded Age collectors of curios to those whose holdings were the forerunners of US museums, with relatively fluid borders between them. What differentiated these individuals were social affiliations and the scope and age of their respective fortunes, as well as their artistic education and the status they granted to sculpture: Was it décor or an object to be collected in its own right? And which French sculpture did they prefer? The taste for Rodin thus emerged within a tradition in which French sculpture was viewed, appreciated, bought, and shown—but Rodin's work was a very different kind of French sculpture.

Starting in the 1850s and especially in the 1860s, a group of American art lovers, including Samuel Avery, turned their attention to France, traveling there regularly and sometimes moving there permanently. For example, there was George A. Lucas, a broker or middleman (the term at the time was "agent") between French artists and American collectors, who supplied Avery's two Rodin bronzes. Lucas and Avery were agents, dealers, and collectors as well. The doyen of the group, William W. Corcoran, had retired from a successful career as a banker; William T. Walters, from Baltimore (like Lucas), was still active in the whiskey business. Some of them had turned to France out of a combination of artistic curiosity and political motivation: they were from the North, and thus theoretically on the Union side of the American Civil War, but their financial interests were anchored in the South, and their sympathies were with the Confederates. They therefore chose to distance themselves from the bloody theater of the fratricidal war.

This group was the first to collect French sculpture for reasons unlinked to iconography and history. Even as Houdon's portrayals of the heroes of the American Revolution (Washington, Thomas Jefferson, Benjamin Franklin, and the Marquis de Lafayette, to name a few) garnered continued appreciation, a new genre now won over these Americans in Paris: animal sculpture. Works by Antoine-Louis Barye, but also by lesser-known artists such as Christophe Fratin and Auguste Cain, were bought with remarkable consistency over several decades. The determination of William Walters, and later of his son Henry, to reconstitute the whole of Barye's vast *surtout de table*, or centerpiece, commissioned by the Duke of Orléans was comparable to that of American collectors of Rodin who tried to assemble representative sets of the sculptor's work. Their systematic planning also served their desire to share their possessions with their fellow citizens by creating museums to house them. At the openings of the Corcoran Gallery of Art in Washington, DC, in 1874, and of the Barye Room in William Walters's home in Baltimore in 1885, dozens of Barye's bronzes were on display. The presentation of the Barye Room at the Walters Art Museum in the 1930s (fig. 2.1) gives an idea of this abundance.

These true connoisseurs chose works discerningly from the artistic production of the time. The technical quality of the casting and chasing in bronze, along with the value of the materials, was important to them; this interest in craftsmanship was shared by many early Americans interested not only in sculpture but also in furniture and decorative art. Henry Walters, for instance, seemed especially drawn to works in ivory. His collection included a large number of examples from every era, including by Augustin-Jean Moreau-Vauthier, who combined expertise in carving ivory with a taste for semiprecious stones (fig. 2.2).

Several members of this group of Americans were interested in Rodin's works. In January and March 1888, George Lucas had bought the two bronzes that he immediately resold to Avery: a model of the *Monument to the Painter Jules Bastien-Lepage* (1886, Wadsworth Atheneum, Hartford, Connecticut) and the *Bust of St. John the Baptist* (cat. 3)—the first work by Rodin to enter an American public collection, when Avery gave it to the Metropolitan Museum of Art in New York (the Met) in 1893. William Walters may not have bought Rodin works himself, but his son Henry did; Henry had spent part of his childhood in Paris with his father and was close to Lucas, who bequeathed his collection to him. There is no doubt that Rodin was one of the artists Henry Walters had known since he was young.

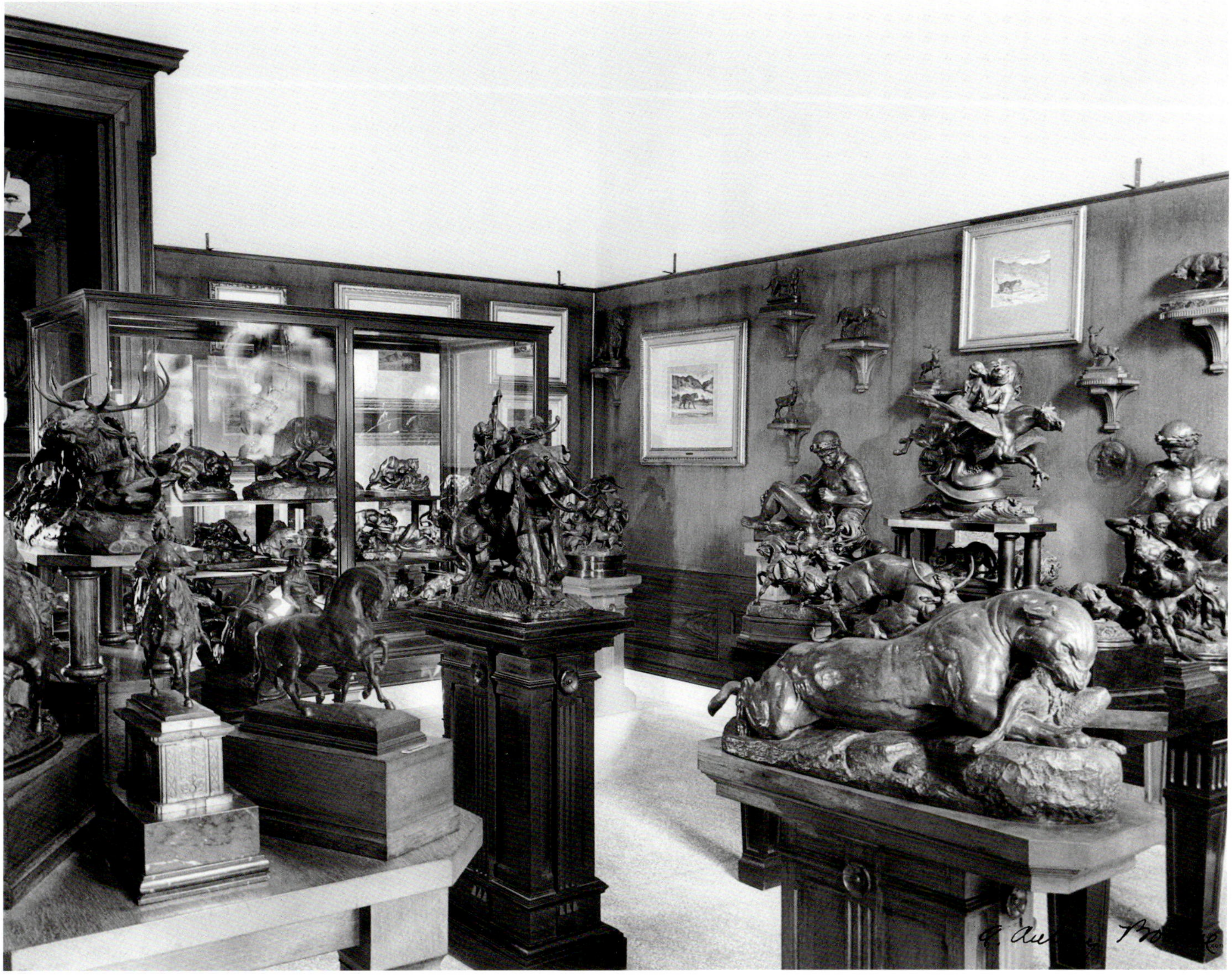

The Barye Room at the Walters Art Museum, Baltimore, in the *Sunday Sun*, Baltimore, January 25, 1931. Photo by A. Aubrey Bodine.

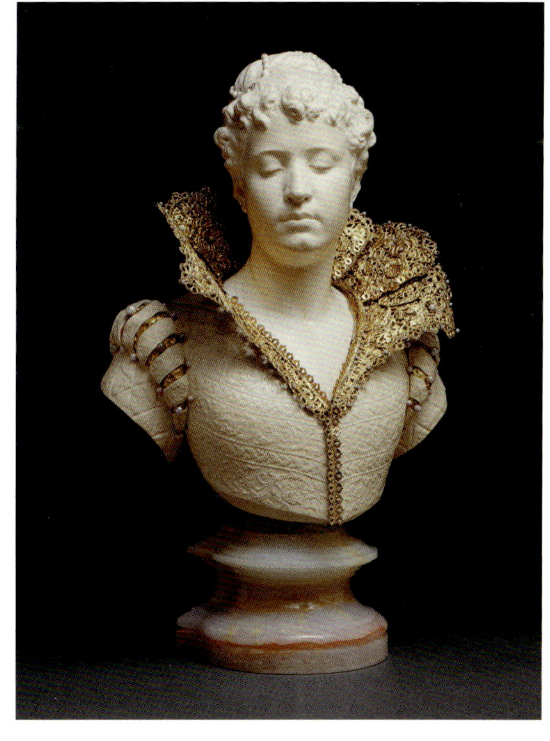

Augustin-Jean Moreau-Vauthier (French, 1831–1893), *Florentine Head* (or *Marie de Medici*?), c. 1882. Ivory, gilt silver, pearls, and onyx, height: 18 in. (45.7 cm). Walters Art Museum, Baltimore. Acquired by Henry Walters, 1898, 71.446.

THE "BRIC-A-BRAC" OF THE GILDED AGE

Very different from this group of enlightened enthusiasts were the collectors from the worlds of industry, commerce, or banking who built the great houses of the Gilded Age. Between 1880 and 1900, these townhouses multiplied in Philadelphia, Boston, and New York, and the need to decorate them generated a market of its own. Their architecture was eclectic, some of them in the French Beaux-Arts style taught in Paris, where many American architects were educated. Their interiors were singularly homogeneous in their excess—of carved wood, fabrics, worked leather, draperies, upholstered furniture, carpets, light fixtures, plants, and an abundance of works of art—an accumulation of Far Eastern, Orientalist, and European objects they referred to as "bric-a-brac."

French sculptures featured prominently in these settings (fig. 2.3), often edition bronzes or replicas of works exhibited at the Salon, the official annual exhibition that set the rhythm of the Parisian art world. French bronze founders had gained a reputation in the United States thanks to the world's fairs held on American soil—in 1876 in Philadelphia, 1893 in Chicago, 1904 in Saint Louis—in which they participated in large numbers. The founders sometimes had agreements with US firms that offered the pieces for sale in their stores. For example, bronzes by the Parisian foundry Barbedienne could be bought at Tiffany & Co. in New York, which added its own mark to the artist's signature

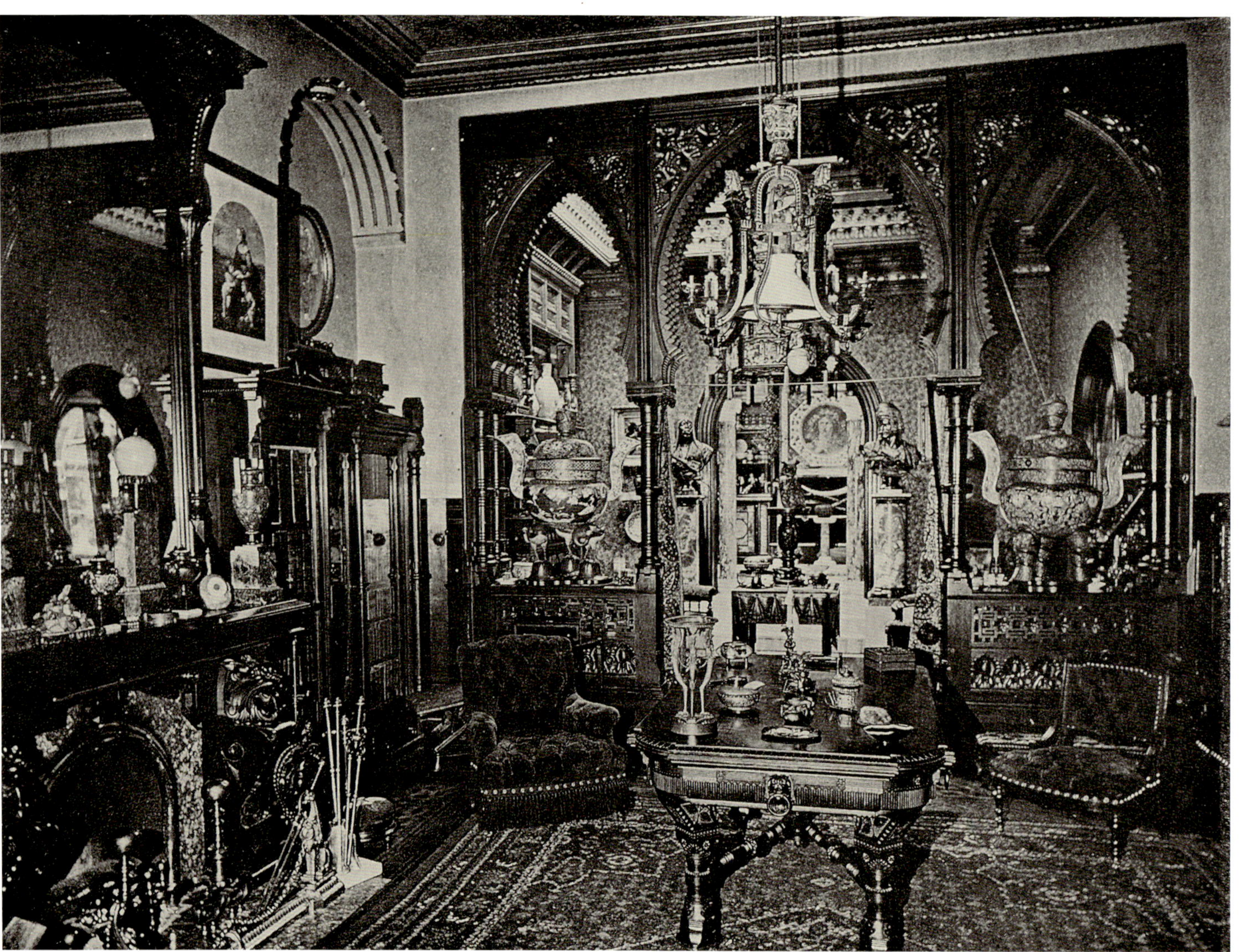

FIG. 2.3

Library, Henry C. Gibson house, Philadelphia, in *Artistic Houses* (New York: D. Appleton, 1883–84). In the rear of the room are two bronze busts by Emile Guillemin (French, 1841–1907): *Janissary of Sultan Mahmoud II*, 1880 (left), and *Zeibeck, Turkish Irregular Soldier from Near Smyrna (Asia Minor Type)*, 1879.

and the foundry's mark.[2] The nascent American bronze-casting industry benefited from the expertise of French workers who had emigrated and sometimes
even been poached from Parisian foundries. French sculptures filled Gilded Age
interiors in all the styles found at the Salon between 1870 and 1900, except for
late Neoclassicism, which Americans preferred to acquire from England or Italy.

Another factor making contemporary sculpture desirable was the reassuring
fact that the authenticity of these objects could more easily be verified than
that of works of the past. Exhibited at the Salon, created by living artists, and
sometimes accompanied by certificates, photographed, and reproduced and
discussed in journals, these sculptures were far less subject to dubious attribu-
tions. Their buyers did not yet have the educated eye that traveling abroad and
visiting museums would eventually give them. Museums in the United States
were still new, their collections still being formed. In the realm of sculpture,
plaster casts of Classical or modern works played an important didactic role: such
copies were often sold by major European museums in Paris, Berlin, Munich,
Florence, and London, among others, and they occupied the ground-floor rooms
of newly built museums, where original sculptures would later replace them.
The discipline of art history was also slowly becoming established, with art
publications proliferating. Until collectors were sufficiently educated in the field
of art, they had to trust dealers, indispensable interlocutors who sometimes
worked in close collaboration with decorators.

The superlative example of a Gilded Age home was the one built by William
Henry Vanderbilt on Fifth Avenue in New York. Occupying a whole block, it
comprised two houses (one of which was divided into two units), built for the
families of Vanderbilt and his two daughters. The extent of Vanderbilt's fortune
(he was the richest man in the world at his death in 1885) put this house in a
class of its own. It became legendary in the eyes of New Yorkers, from its construction, completed in 1883, until its demolition in 1947. The interior decoration had been entrusted to Herter Brothers, a firm founded by two German
emigrants, Gustave and Christian Herter, competitors of the Frenchman Jules
Allard. Numerous French sculptures were displayed in the various rooms.
A table in the entrance hall (fig. 2.4) displayed a pair of reduced-size, vividly
Baroque bronzes, *Marly's Horses* by Guillaume Coustou, flanking — in an
abrupt clash of styles, scales, periods, and atmospheres — the mysterious bust
Semiramis, Queen of Assyria, with half-closed eyes, by Emile Hébert. At the
base of the staircase was Tony-Noël's *Neo-Renaissance Torchère* (date and location
unknown), whose belt, diadem, and sandal ties were encrusted with crystals
reflecting the candlelight in the evening. The door to the Japanese salon was
flanked by *Japanese Torchères* (fig. 2.5) by Émile Guillemin, while two ivories by
Moreau-Vauthier were displayed under glass in the salon, thereby signaling their
great value. The leading art critic of the time, Edward Strahan, left no doubt
about the decorative role of these two objects: "Both are completely adapted
for parlor admiration; they are thoroughly elegant, refined and artistic, without
deep mythological meanings to disturb the equipoise of the evening caller."[3] It
comes as no surprise to find there these ivories, so appreciated by the Walterses,
Lucas, and Avery: the latter was Vanderbilt's agent in Paris, and it is more than
likely that he arranged the acquisition of the two statuettes.

Such grouping of works could not be called a collection per se; sculptures
were, first and foremost, meant to complement the décor. A few other collections,
however, had been assembled more purposefully, consisting primarily of paintings but sometimes including rare sculptures. Some Gilded Age homes had their
own exhibition halls where, as in the annual Salons and museums of old, canvases crowded the walls at various heights under overhead lighting. The furniture included benches or ottomans and library tables. The sculptures were

Table in the atrium of William Henry Vanderbilt's house in New York, in Edward Strahan [Earl Shinn], *Mr. Vanderbilt's House and Collection* (Boston: George Barrie, 1883–84), with reduced-size versions of *Marly's Horses*, 1743–45, after Guillaume Coustou (French, 1677–1746) flanking the bust *Semiramis, Queen of Assyria*, 1874, by Emile Hébert (French, 1828–1893).

The Japanese salon in William H. Vanderbilt's house in New York, in Edward Strahan [Earl Shinn], *Mr. Vanderbilt's House and Collection* (Boston: George Barrie, 1883–84). *Japanese Torchères*, 1881, by Émile Guillemin (French, 1841–1907), flank the doorway; visible in the salon, in a tabletop vitrine, is *Fortune*, 1881, by Augustin-Jean Moreau-Vauthier (French, 1831–1893).

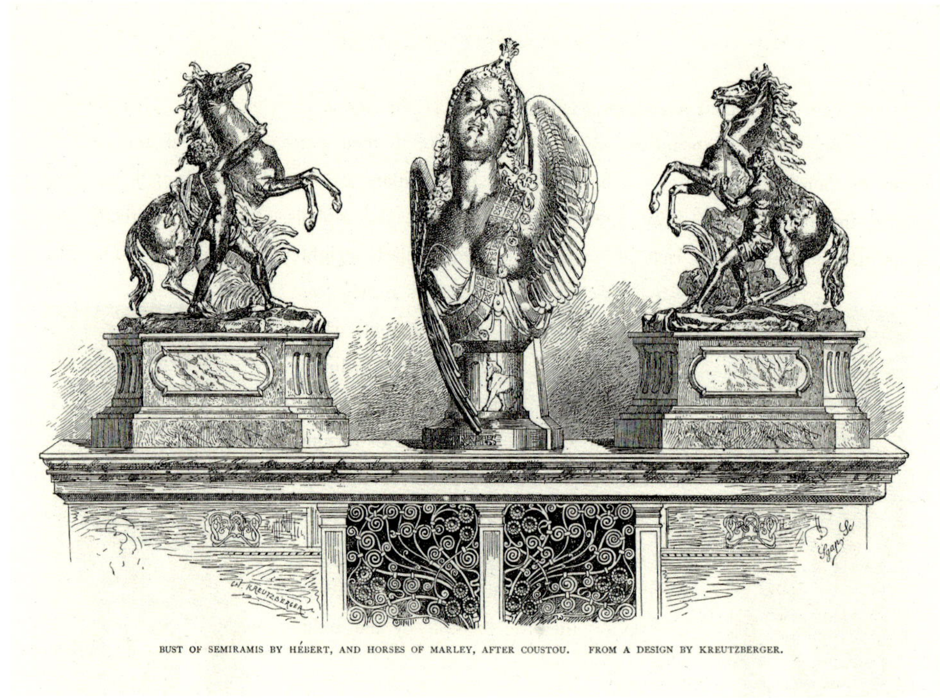

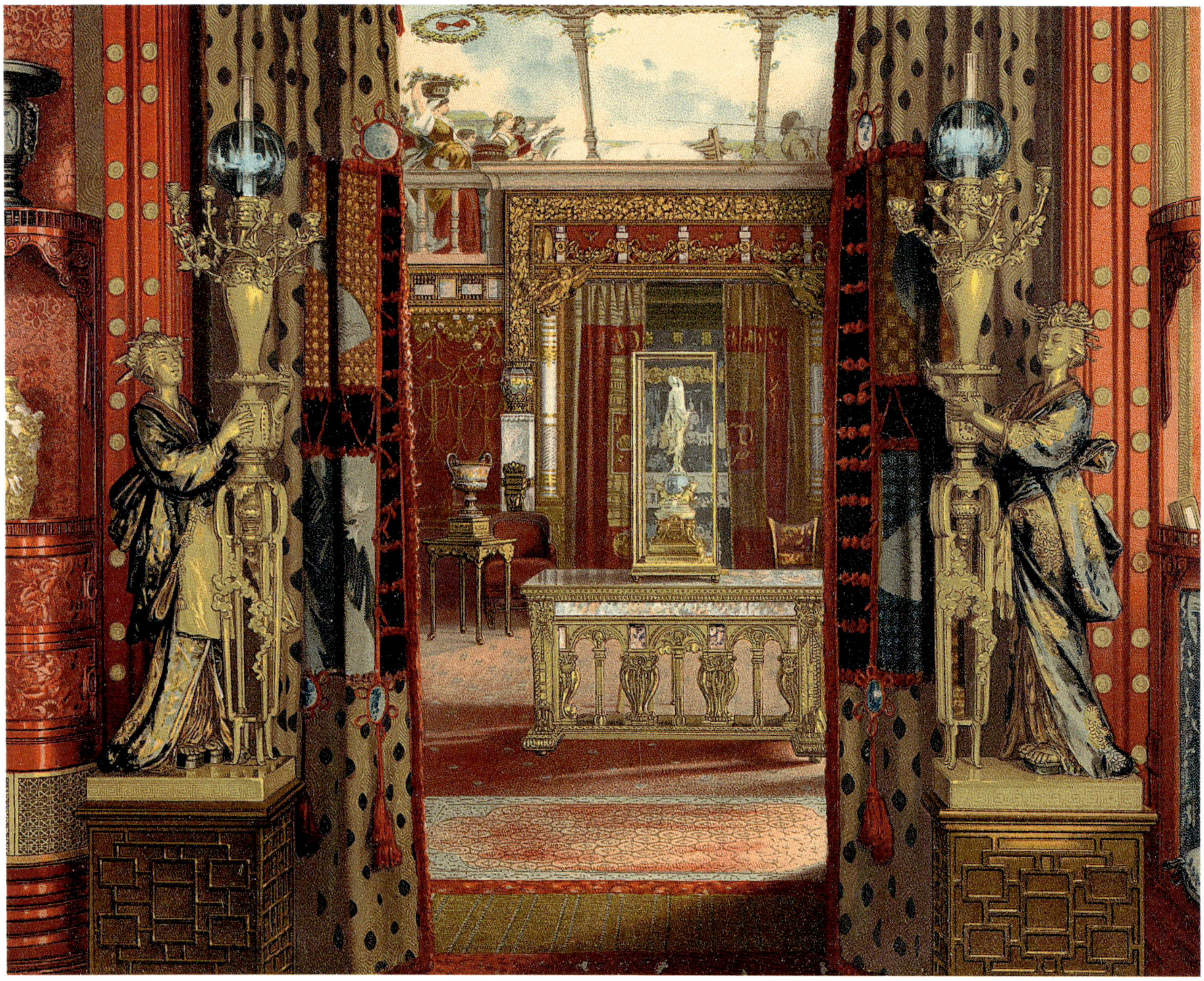

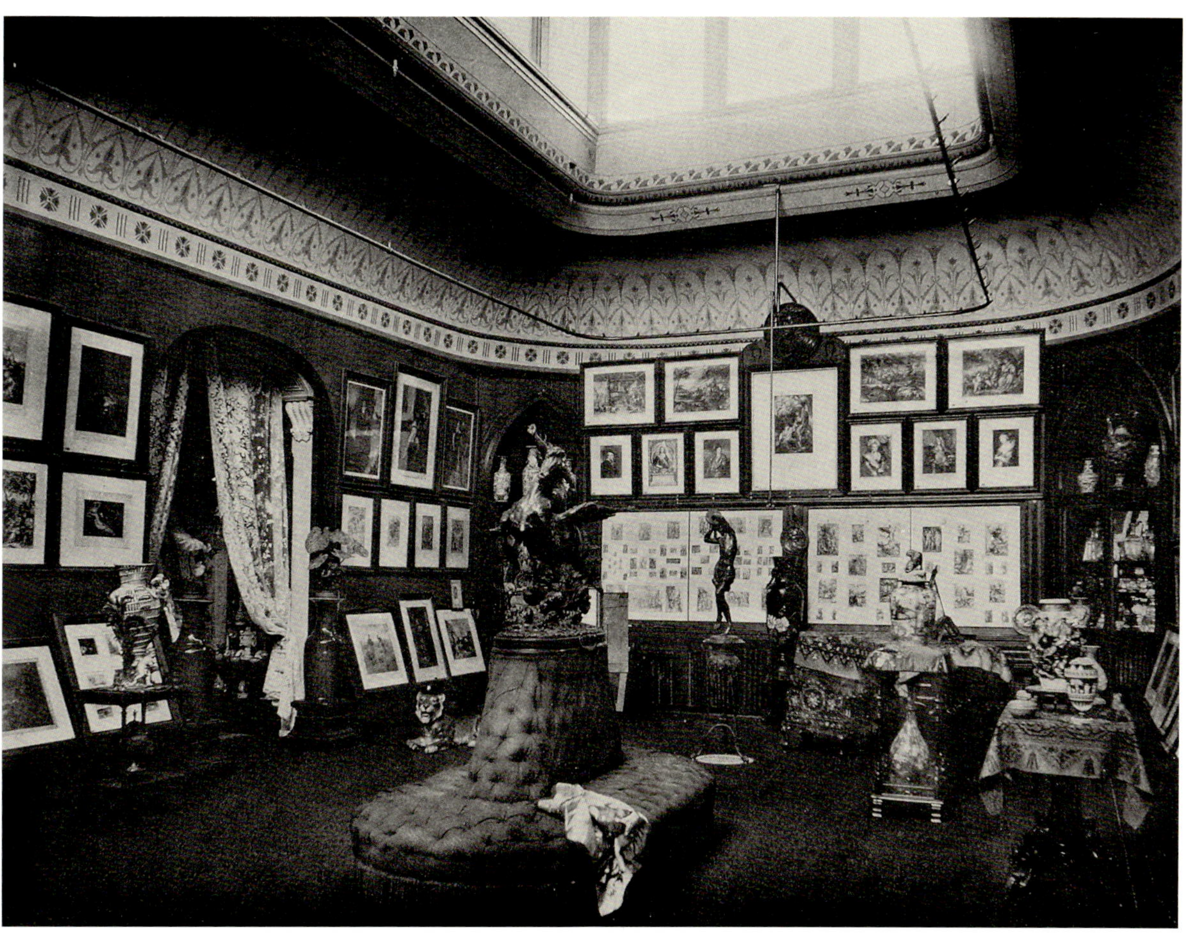

FIG. 2.6

Print gallery, James L. Claghorn house, Philadelphia, in *Artistic Houses* (New York: D. Appleton, 1883–84). In the center is *Bellerophon Vanquishing the Chimera*, 1874, by Emile Hébert.

arranged along the walls or on the tables. At the print collector James L. Claghorn's house in Philadelphia, *Bellerophon Vanquishing the Chimera* (fig. 2.6) by Emile Hébert replaced to advantage the plant that would typically spring from the top of the banquette's backrest.

Strangely enough, none of the sculptures that appear among the 203 photographs of Gilded Age interiors published in the 1883–84 volumes *Artistic Houses* have been found in an American public collection thus far.[4] Yet it is unlikely that these works crossed the Atlantic again, so they are probably still in the United States, living their life as objects, passing from hand to hand. One of them will eventually turn up in a public sale.

Members of this Gilded Age generation, active in the 1880s and 1890s, were a bit older than Rodin's first admirers, but, more importantly, they lived in distinct worlds. For those amassing bric-a-brac, sculpture was above all bronze, illustration, and decoration, while for the first collectors to appreciate Rodin, it was essentially marble, expression, and form.

COLLECTORS, THE FORERUNNERS TO MUSEUMS

The genuine collectors who emerged in the years 1890 to 1920, including William A. Clark, James J. Hill, John Pierpont Morgan, and Charles T. Yerkes, among others—were from a slightly later generation and another social class. They still belonged to the world of finance, industry, or commerce, or occasionally worked in the law, the press, or entertainment, but the scale of their possessions and their social stature had risen. Some were among the era's "robber barons," their wealth multiplied through ruthless business practices. They had also had time to acquire a certain artistic discernment, thanks to numerous trips to Europe and frequent visits to American museums, of which they were sometimes trustees. Their desire for a more direct relationship with the past and with history, their taste for patrician residences, and their determination to provide the nation with art collections comparable to those available abroad drove them to assemble consequential collections, often focused on the art of the past. Their wars in the business world sometimes translated into fiercely competitive art buying.

To build their collections, they depended on dealers who became powerful consiglieres during this period. Most of these dealers did business on both sides of the Atlantic, between Paris, London, and New York. Taking advantage of the particular economic circumstances of the time, they made themselves the perfect intermediaries between a European landed aristocracy in desperate need of money and an American social class with money to spare and a desire to solidify their status. One approach was for European men to marry rich American heiresses, as hundreds did; the other was to sell, sell, sell. The dealers' power was measured by what they had to sell and by the provenance of their objects, which they sometimes embellished. The main dealers in sculpture were M. Knoedler and Company (active in New York from 1857 to 2011), Duveen Brothers (a member of the family opened a shop in New York in 1877, and the stock was bought by Norton Simon in 1964), Wildenstein (the New York branch, still active, opened in 1903), and Jacques Seligmann (active in New York from 1904 to 1978).

Leaving behind the art of the present that had appealed to their Gilded Age predecessors, these new collectors favored art from the past. In sculpture, eighteenth-century works were the most coveted—not only the usual busts by Caffieri and Houdon, but also works by their predecessors, contemporaries, and successors. Most seemed to prefer terracotta, specifically finished objects in that medium, rather than sketches. The best-represented artist was Clodion (Claude Michel), in whose figurines all combinations were possible: a bacchante alone or accompanied by a cupid or a satyr, child or adult, sometimes even supported by two satyrs in a stumbling bacchanal. The lighthearted antiquity that animated these figures, the frivolity of feeling and action radiating from their faces and bodies, allied with a perfect mastery of material, made these terracottas particularly attractive. Department-store owner Benjamin Altman was one of the Americans who had an actual exhibition hall in his home, and his collection featured two groups by Clodion (fig. 2.7), which he would bequeath to the Met in 1913, as well as a rare marble statue, Houdon's *Bather* (figs. 2.8, 2.9). This feminine figure imbued with grace and sensitivity—an element from a fountain in a princely Parisian garden—is unusual in the work of a sculptor known primarily for his bust portraits.

Collector J. P. Morgan, whose appetite for purchases was almost insatiable, also had several terracottas by Clodion, which dealers and collectors would fight over after his death in 1913. This is how Clodion's group *Zephyrus and Flora* (fig. 2.10) ended up in the Frick Collection in New York, while *Young Woman Holding a Child before Her* (c. 1785–90) is in the Huntington Library, Art Museum, and Botanical Gardens in San Marino, California. Other collectors at the time acquired works of similar size but in less fragile materials, small groups in marble or in

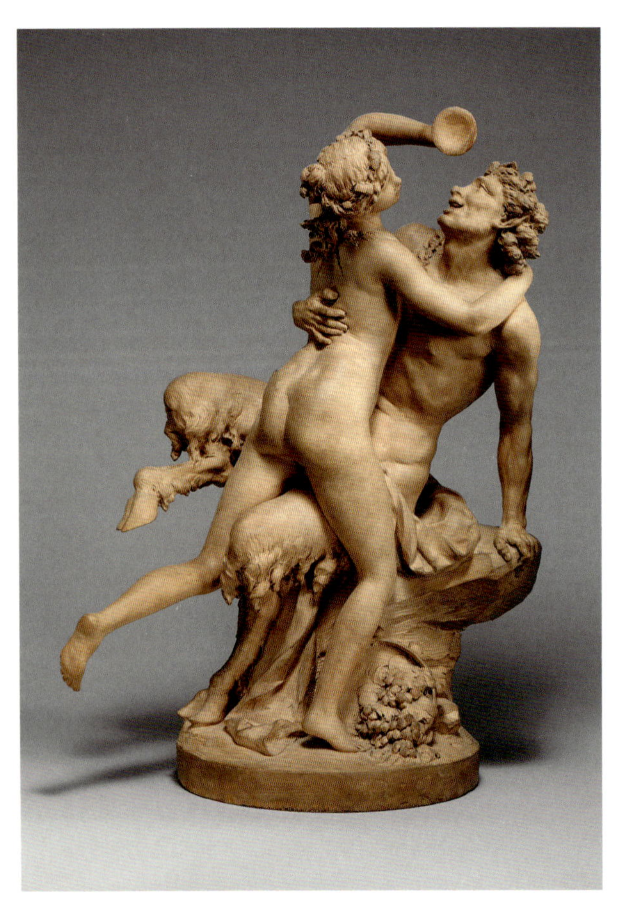

FIG. 2.8 (right)

An exhibition room in Benjamin Altman's house on Fifth Avenue, New York, after 1913, with *Bather* (from a fountain group), 1782, by Jean-Antoine Houdon (French, 1741–1828), at rear center.

FIG. 2.9 (below left)

Jean-Antoine Houdon, *Bather* (from a fountain group), 1782. Marble, 47 × 43 × 28 in. (119.4 × 109.2 × 71.1 cm). Metropolitan Museum of Art, New York. Bequest of Benjamin Altman, 1913, 14.40.673.

FIG. 2.10 (below right)

Claude Michel, known as Clodion, *Zephyrus and Flora*, 1799. Terracotta, 23 × 10 ¼ × 11 ½ in. (58.4 × 26 × 29.2 cm). Frick Collection, New York. Henry Clay Frick Bequest, 1915.2.76.

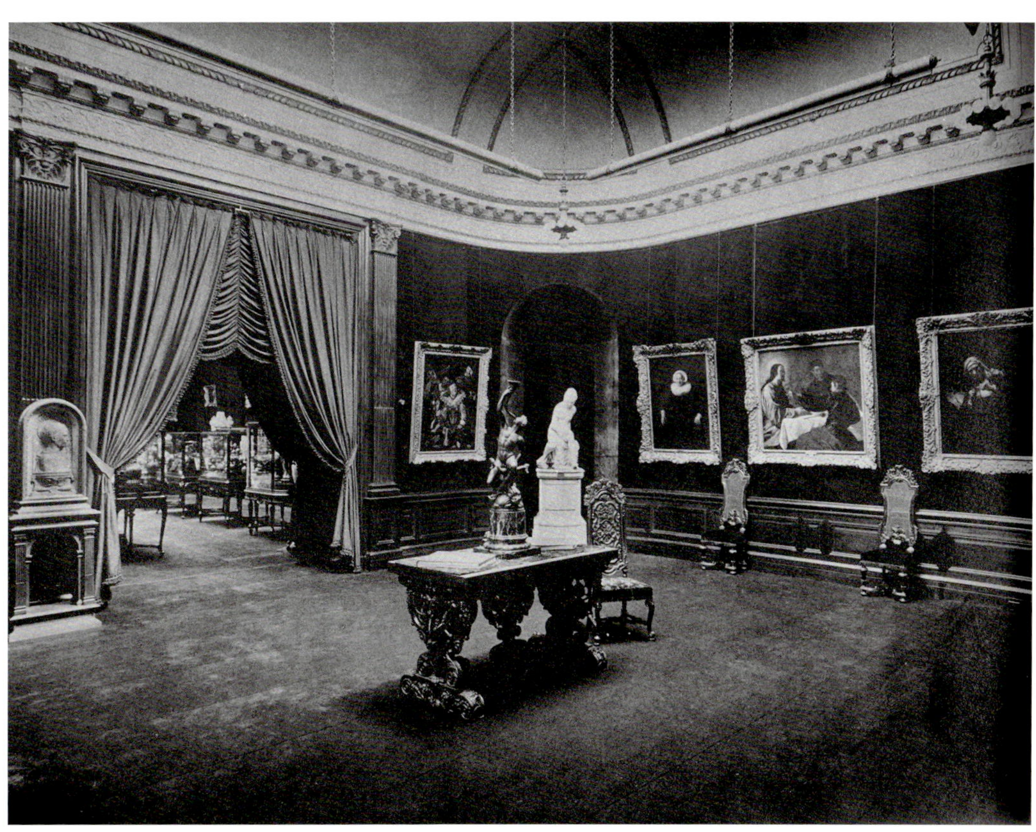

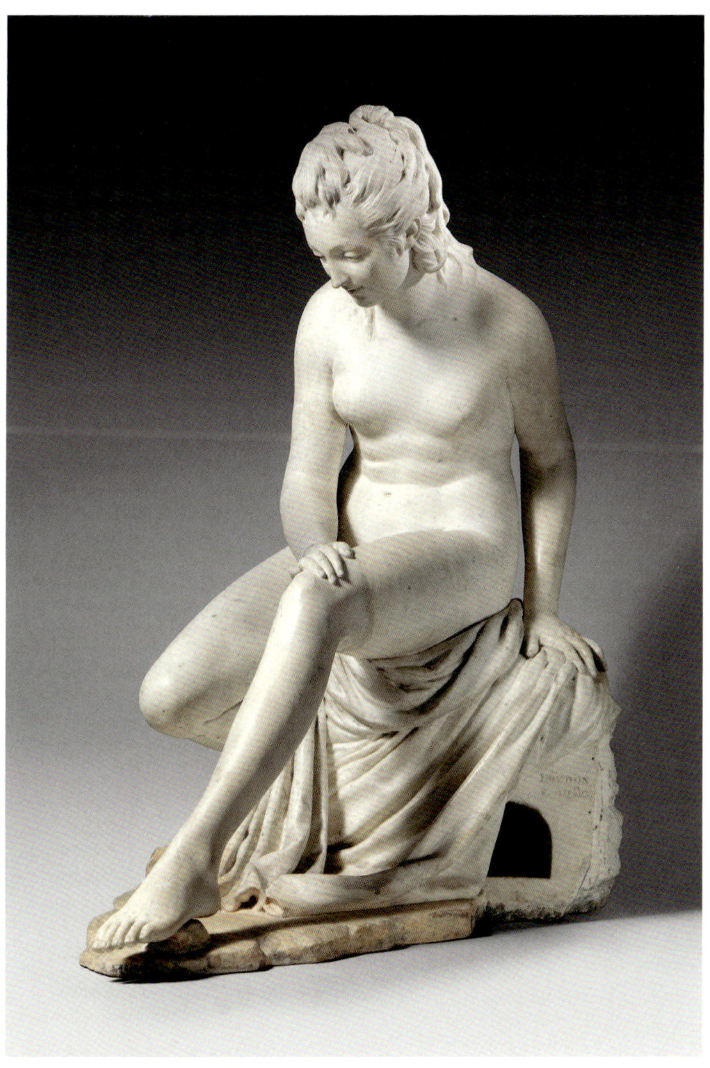

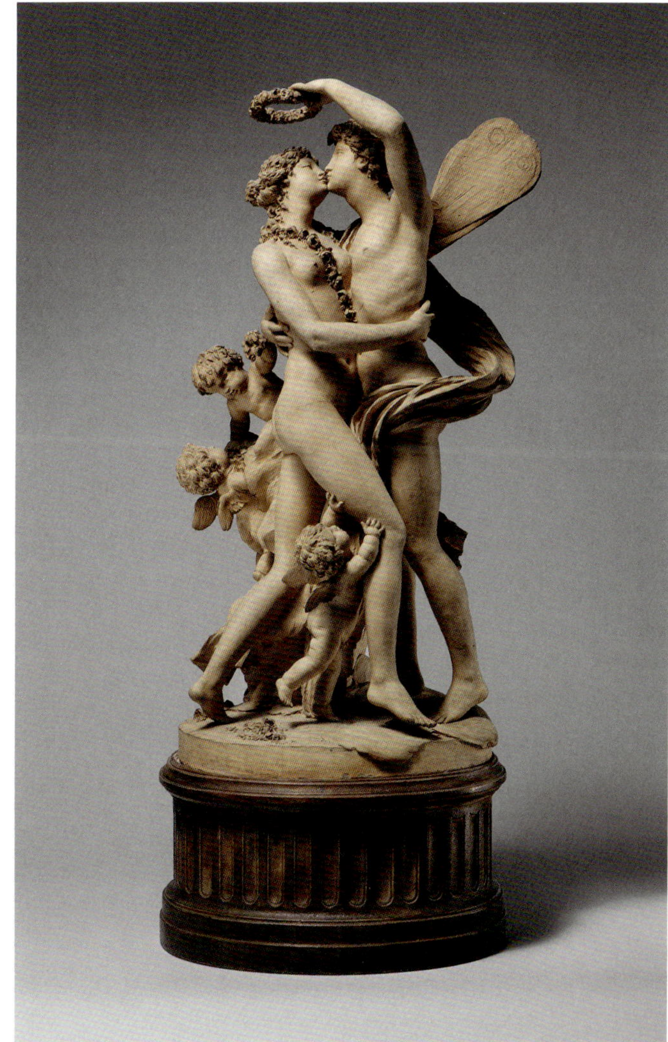

FIG. 2.11 (right)
Mathieu Jacquet (French, c. 1545–1611),
Henri IV, c. 1605. Bronze, height: 12 7/16 in.
(31.6 cm). Walters Art Museum, Baltimore.
Acquired by Henry Walters, 1910, 27.352.

FIG. 2.12 (below left)
Mathieu Jacquet, *Henri IV as Jupiter*,
c. 1605–9. Bronze, height: 18 5/16 in.
(46.5 cm). Walters Art Museum, Baltimore.
Acquired by Henry Walters, 1910, 54.667.

FIG. 2.13 (below right)
Mathieu Jacquet, *Marie de Medici as Juno*,
c. 1605–9. Bronze, height: 19 1/8 in.
(48.5 cm). Walters Art Museum, Baltimore.
Acquired by Henry Walters, 1910, 54.668.

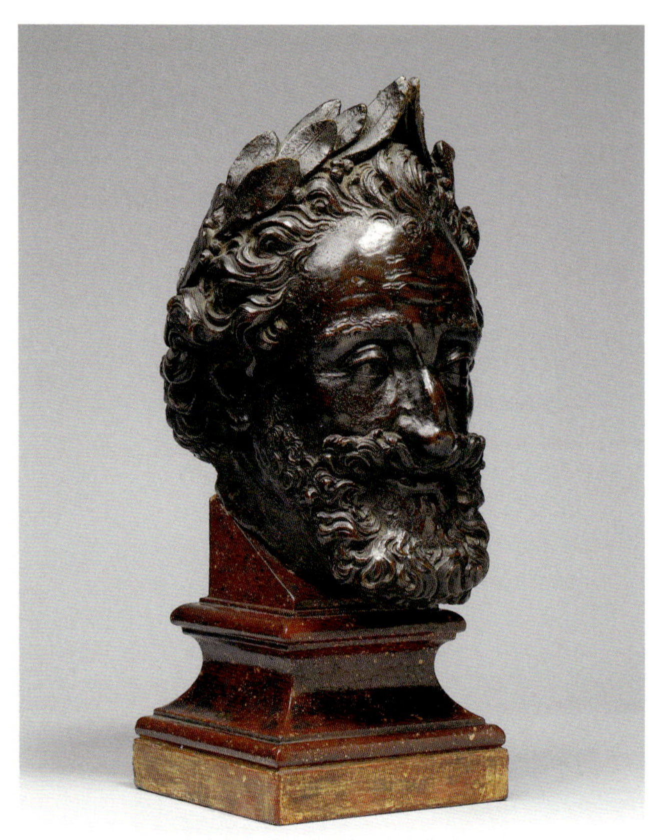

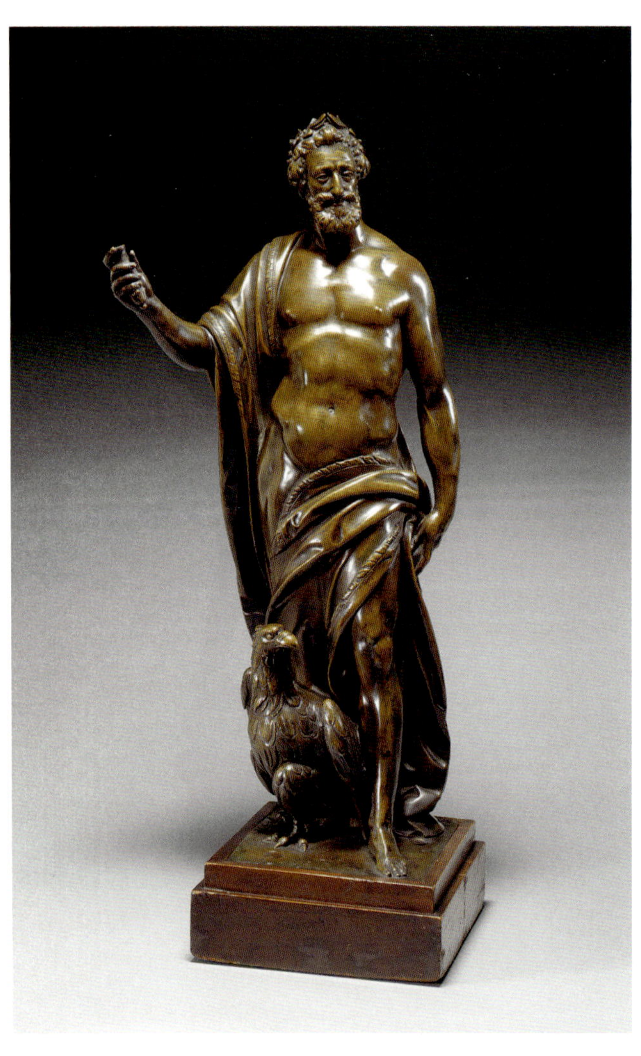

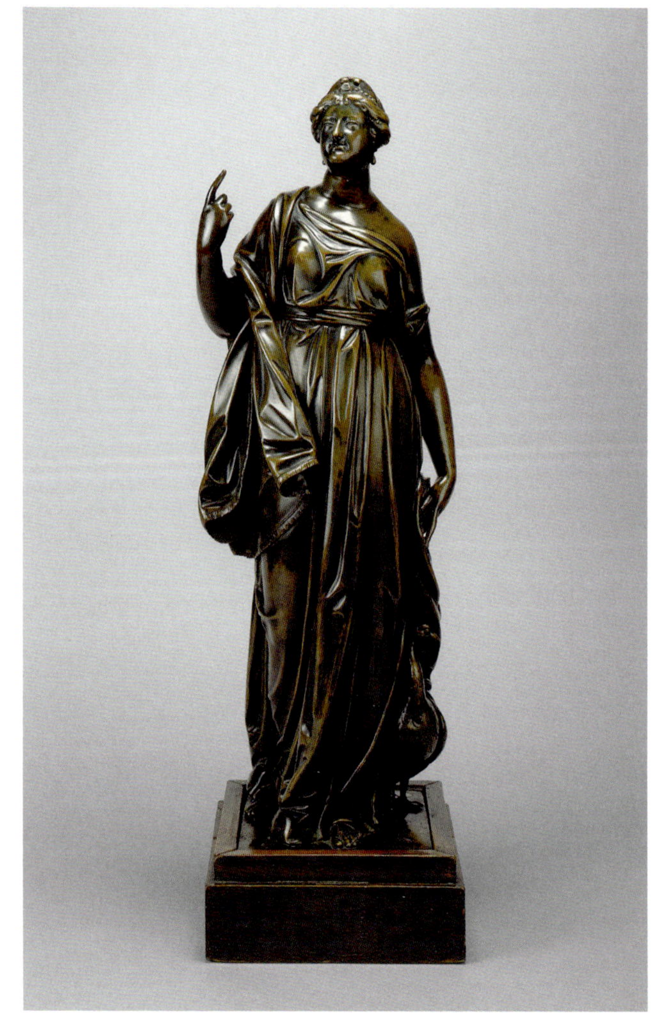

Sèvres biscuit porcelain, to place on pedestal tables in boudoirs paneled with real, or replica, Louis XVI woodwork.

The seventeenth century was represented in US collections mainly by bronzes. In the years preceding World War I, Henry Walters, heir to his father's collection, continued enriching it with sculptures by Barye while also extending it back into the seventeenth and eighteenth centuries. Walters worked mainly with the dealer Jacques Seligmann in Paris, from whom he bought a fine grouping by Mathieu Jacquet, a *Head of Henry IV*, as well as two statuettes of *Henry IV as Jupiter* and *Marie de Medici as Juno* (figs. 2.11–13). These works from the very early seventeenth century are imbued with a mannerist elegance that can also be found in slightly earlier statuettes by Barthélemy Prieur. The reign of Louis XIV had seen the development in France of a taste for small bronzes in the Italian manner. In 1652, upon his return from Italy, Michel Anguier found major success with his first series of statuettes (six gods and goddesses),[5] two of which Benjamin Altman would ultimately acquire for his collection and bequeath to the Met in 1913: *Amphitrite* and her pendant, *Neptune* (both 18th- or 19th-century casts from c. 1652 models). Reduced-size versions of Louis XIV's equestrian monuments were also much sought after for the royal grandeur they conveyed, even though the monuments themselves had been destroyed during the French Revolution. Thirty years before Altman's bequest, Henry G. Marquand, one of the founders and first patrons of the Met, had donated to the museum a reduced-size version of the *Equestrian Monument in Place Louis-le-Grand (Vendôme) in Paris* (19th-century cast of 1699 statue) by François Girardon.

Among the collectors of the 1880s through 1910s, one, whose holdings included some premier sculptures, broke free from social norms. Charles Tyson Yerkes was first and foremost a financier who did not hesitate to use blackmail and corruption to achieve his goals, which even led to him spending a few months in prison. He generally preferred the company of women much younger than him, including his two wives and the mistress for whom he had a house built a few steps away from the one he had built for his wife and himself on Fifth Avenue. Failing to find acceptance among high-society circles in Chicago, he had moved to New York with his collections. He had two wings built for exhibition rooms, one adjacent to the mansion's Fifth Avenue façade and the other at the rear, where he showed his paintings and sculptures.

In a photograph taken by 1904 (fig. 2.14), we can see, through the opening of the door on the left, *Pygmalion and Galatea* (now in Hearst Castle), the important marble group by Jean-Léon Gérôme that Yerkes had loaned to the 1893 World's Columbian Exposition in Chicago.[6] In the center of the gallery is a life-size copy, cast in Paris at Gruet Jeune, of the *Bacchante and Infant Faun* (Museum of Fine Arts, Boston) by Frederick William MacMonnies, an American sculptor living between his country and France. Behind it is another statue of a standing nude woman, but very different in style: Houdon's *Diana the Huntress* (Huntington Library, Art Museum, and Botanical Gardens), a bronze commissioned by Jean Girardot de Marigny, Benjamin Franklin's Swiss banker in Paris. On the right in the photograph is a large marble *Bacchante* (National Gallery of Art, Washington, DC), attributed at the time to Etienne-Maurice Falconet (1716–1791). Nineteenth-century French sculpture alongside nineteenth-century American (created and cast in France) and eighteenth-century French works: eclecticism was the order of the day, as further confirmed by two groups not visible in the photograph—two very important marbles by Rodin, *Cupid and Psyche* (before 1893, Metropolitan Museum of Art, New York) and *Orpheus and Eurydice* (fig. 2.15). Bought by Yerkes from the sculptor himself, they are among Rodin's finest marbles in the United States. In a letter of July 23, 1894, Rodin recommended that *Orpheus and Eurydice* "should be placed against the

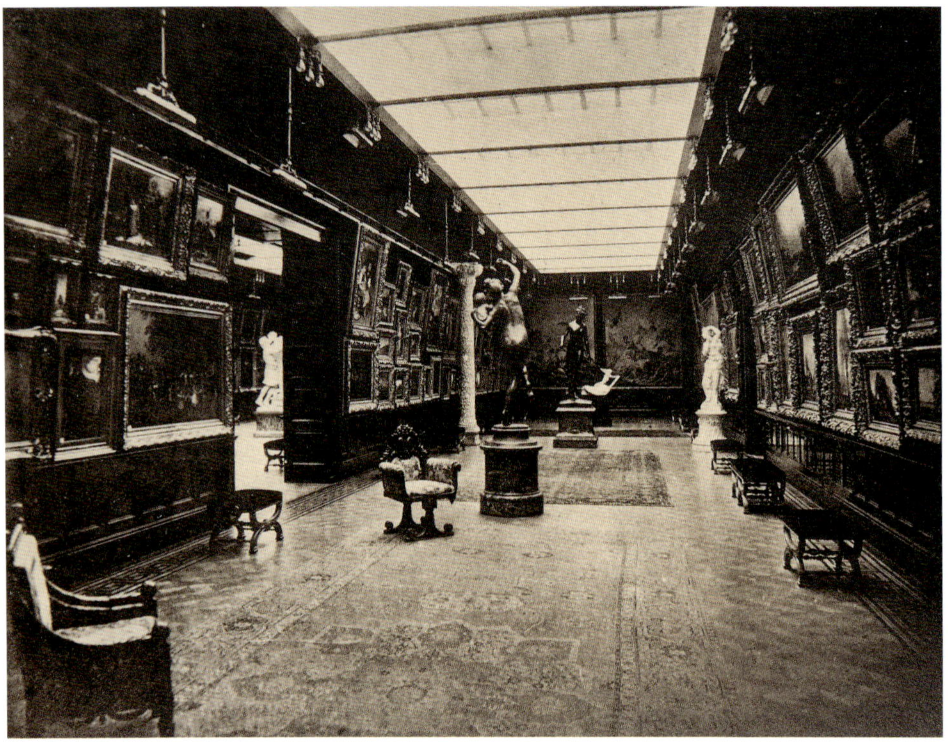

One of the exhibition rooms in Charles T. Yerkes's house at 864 Fifth Avenue, New York, in Josiah Granville Leach, *Chronicle of the Yerkes Family* (Philadelphia: J. B. Lippincott, 1904), with (left, through doorway) *Pygmalion and Galatea*, 1892, by Jean-Léon Gérôme (French, 1824–1904); (center) *Bacchante and Infant Faun*, 1893, by Frederick William MacMonnies (American, 1863–1937); (rear) *Diana the Huntress* (1782), by Jean-Antoine Houdon; and (right), *Bacchante*, 19th century, by an unknown French artist.

light, [so] that the rocky background, representing the Gate of Hell, may be engulfed in shadows."[7]

In April 1910, a few years after Yerkes's death, the American Art Association auction house broke up the collection and sold, over the course of several days, the entire contents of Yerkes's home, from the furniture to the paintings, the dishware to the tiger skins, the plants to the ostrich eggs, as well as the house itself.[8] The sculptures' buyers were among the greatest collectors of the period. Gérôme's group was bought by newspaper magnate William Randolph Hearst and is now in Hearst Castle, in California. MacMonnies's *Bacchante and Infant Faun* was immediately loaned by its buyer, pharmaceutical company owner and philanthropist George Robert White, to the Museum of Fine Arts, Boston, before ultimately being donated. Houdon's *Diana the Huntress* was bought by a dealer, Joseph Duveen, for Eduardo Guinlé, from a wealthy Brazilian family, who died two years later; Duveen then sold it to Henry Huntington. And the marble *Bacchante* was bought by the collector Samuel Untermyer, then by the Samuel H. Kress Foundation; the statue is now in the National Gallery of Art in Washington, DC. After having been attributed to Falconet, then to Clodion, it is now considered an anonymous French work from the nineteenth century.

The two Rodin marbles were purchased by Thomas Kirby, the auctioneer for the American Art Association, who was acting as an agent for an anonymous buyer. This buyer was one of Rodin's main American collectors, Thomas Fortune Ryan, who donated the marbles to the Met that same year. Fifteen years later, Ryan, who lived in the house next door to Yerkes's home and exhibition rooms, bought those buildings and had them razed to expand his garden. Barely a trace was left to evoke Yerkes, his eventful life, or his collections.

While the Yerkes collection lacked the handful of small works and terracotta sculptures that would have made it perfectly representative of the era's taste for French sculpture, its Rodin works constitute a common denominator linking several collections of different sensibilities—those of Henry Walters, Thomas Fortune Ryan, Montana Senator William A. Clark, and businessman Isaac Dudley Fletcher. Like Yerkes, Walters had two works by Rodin. First, he acquired the marble *Death of Adonis* (original model before 1881, carved 1901, Walters Art Museum, Baltimore), which had previously been purchased directly from the sculptor by a prominent Chicago collector, Mary Mitchell Blair. Then Walters acquired the large bronze of *The Thinker* (1903, University of Louisville, Kentucky) sent to the United States for the St. Louis World's Fair in 1904 but never exhibited there. Shown at the Walters Art Museum from 1904 to 1947, it was eventually sold because the Baltimore Museum of Art had acquired another bronze of *The Thinker* in 1930, and two in the same city seemed redundant.

Ryan was among the Americans passionate about history of the Middle Ages and the Renaissance and devoted to bringing those eras into the lived

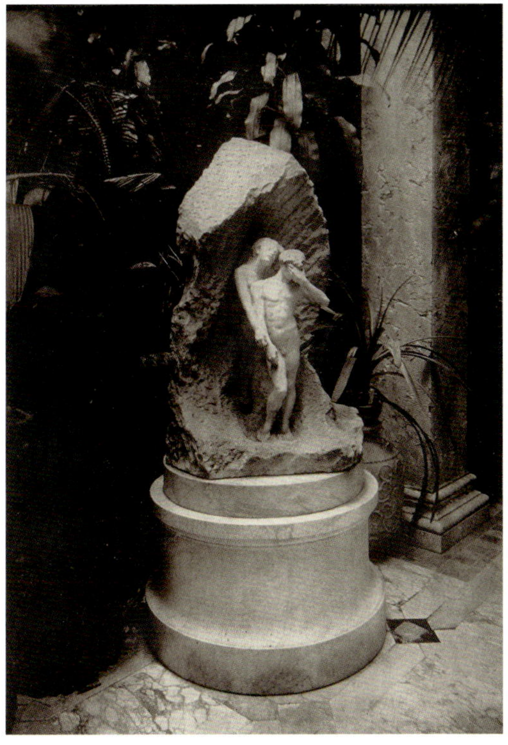

Auguste Rodin (French, 1840–1917), *Orpheus and Eurydice*, 1893, in the sales catalogue for the estate of Charles T. Yerkes, April 12, 1910, which took place in his house at 864 Fifth Avenue, New York. Today, the marble is in the Metropolitan Museum of Art, New York.

environment through *cassoni* and other furniture, Limoges enamels, Italian majolica, and Italian Renaissance sculptures. The sale of Ryan's collection in 1933,[9] after his death, included French sculptures from the sixteenth (school of Michel Colombe), eighteenth (Antoine Coysevox, Clodion, Edme Bouchardon,[10] Houdon), and nineteenth centuries, with thirty works by Barye and five by Rodin up for auction. During his lifetime, Ryan had personally purchased a total of nine Rodins, including the two Charles Yerkes marbles, and had financed the acquisition of twelve more by the Met, which the museum selected directly from the artist in 1910.[11]

William Clark, in turn, acquired French works from the eighteenth (Jacques Bousseau, Falconet, René Frémin, Alexandre Charles Renaud) and nineteenth (Emmanuel Fremiet) centuries, as well as Rodin's *Little Eve* (original model 1881, reduced 1883, carved 1890–91, National Gallery of Art, Washington, DC) commissioned by jeweler Henri Vever. Fletcher bought sculptures from the thirteenth and fourteenth centuries, two monumental bronze groups of *Boar and Deer Hunts* in seventeenth-century style,[12] a Clodion, and two Rodins, including *Eternal Spring* (original model 1884?, carved 1906–7), which he donated to the Met.

Whether they were devoted collectors who invested energy, determination, and financial resources to gathering representative sets of Rodin works, or they simply had "a Rodin" the same way they had "a Barye," many Americans shared a taste for his art. While we have a tendency to isolate artists we consider geniuses, as if their works monopolize so much attention that they could not coexist with other, necessarily less-important works, these numerous American admirers and collectors of Rodin's sculptures around the turn of the last century offer us another perspective. Meanwhile, a new history of sculpture was already being written in the wake of the 1913 Armory Show, and with it came the overture to a decidedly different world, that of modernity. It seemed that new world had to move away from Rodin in order to fully embrace modern sculpture. Yet only a few decades later, historians would understand that Rodin was opening the twentieth century rather than closing the nineteenth.

NOTES

1. This text developed out of research undertaken for the forthcoming book *French Sculpture: An American Passion* (*La sculpture française: Une passion américaine*) by Laure de Margerie, with a contribution by Antoinette Le Normand-Romain (Paris: Institut national d'histoire de l'art, 2022). The book itself relies on the "Répertoire de sculpture française (1500–1960) dans les collections publiques américaines" (Census of French Sculpture [1500–1960] in American Public Collections), accessible at http://frenchsculpture.org.
2. Florence Rionnet, *Les bronzes Barbedienne: L'œuvre d'une dynastie de fondeurs* (Paris: Arthena, 2016), 103.
3. Edward Strahan [Earl Shinn], *Mr. Vanderbilt's House and Collection*, 4 vols. (Boston: George Barrie, 1883–84), 1: 53.
4. [George William Sheldon], *Artistic Houses: Being a Series of Interior Views of a Number of the Most Beautiful and Celebrated Homes in the United States with a Description of the Art Treasures Contained*

Therein (New York: D. Appleton, 1883–84).
5. Ian Wardropper, "Michel Anguier" and following entries, in *Cast in Bronze: French Sculpture from Renaissance to Revolution*, exh. cat., ed. Geneviève Bresc-Bautier and Guilhem Scherf, with James David Draper for the English-language edition (Paris: Musée du Louvre Éditions / Somogy Art Publishers, 2009), 204–21.
6. The photograph was published in Josiah Granville Leach, *Chronicle of the Yerkes Family, with Notes on the Leech and Rutter Families* (Philadelphia: J. B. Lippincott, 1904), 194. I would like to thank Tom Miller, author of the blog daytoninmanhattan .blogspot.com, for this information.
7. Auguste Rodin, quote in American Art Association, *Catalogue of the Statuary, Bronzes, the Costly Furniture and Embellishments Contained in the Mansion of the Late Charles T. Yerkes*, sold on the premises, 864 Fifth Avenue, New York, April 8–13, 1910, no. 251.

8. American Art Association, *Catalogue of the Statuary*.
9. *Gothic and Renaissance Art: Collection of the Late Thomas Fortune Ryan*, sold by the order of the Guaranty Trust Company of New York, executor, New York, American Art Association, Anderson Galleries, November 23–25, 1933.
10. Later considered anonymous nineteenth-century French works and deaccessioned by the Metropolitan Museum of Art, New York, in 2013.
11. For more on Ryan's relationship with the Met, see the essay by Elyse Nelson in this volume, "Making the 'Little Rodin Gallery': The Rodin Collection at the Met," pp. 117–25.
12. Both bronzes by an unidentified artist, in the style of French sculptor Jacques Houzeau, dating to 1875–1900, Huntington Library, Art Museum, and Botanical Gardens, San Marino, California.

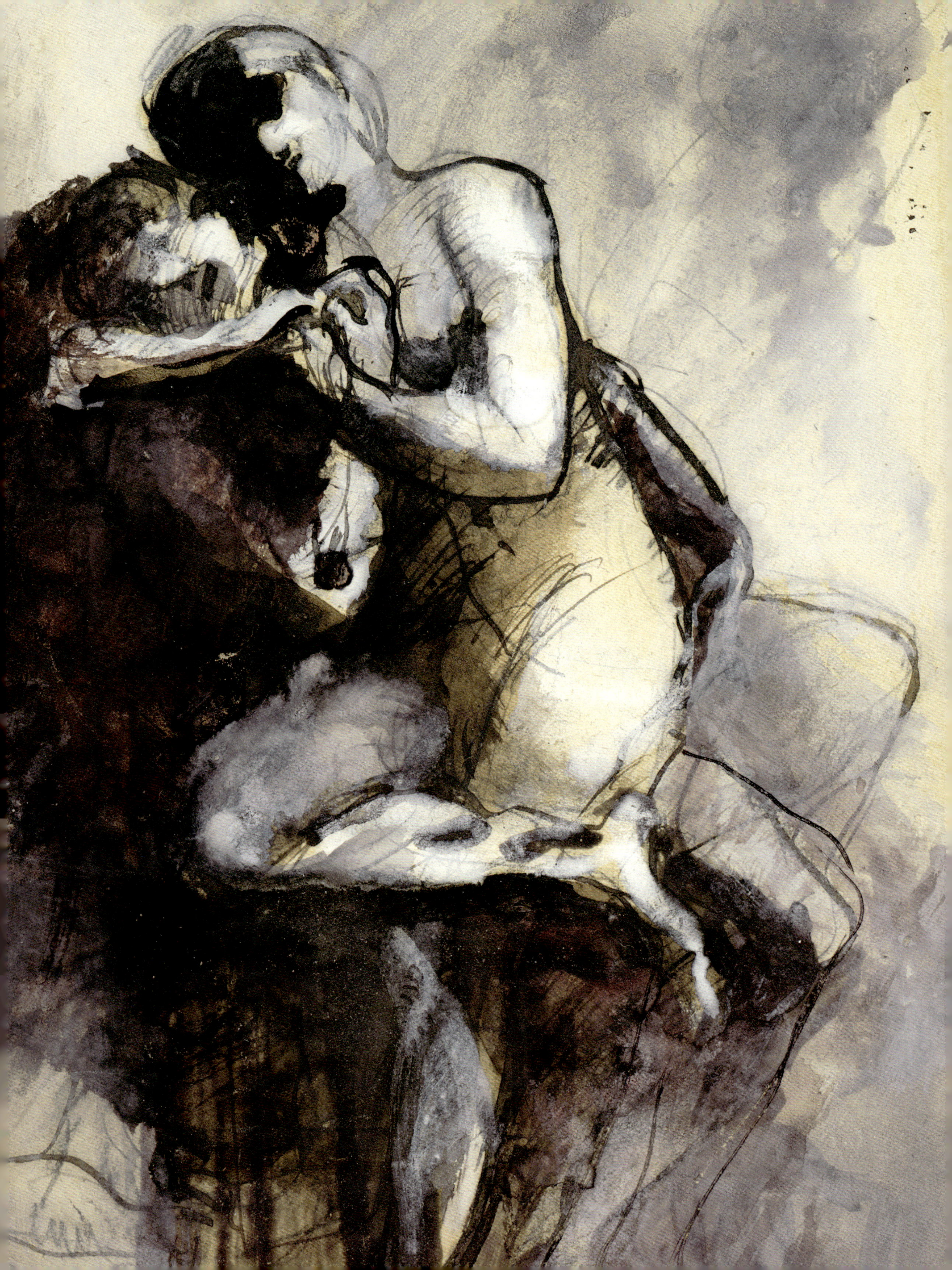

THE ROLE OF DRAWING IN THE ART OF RODIN

CHRISTINA BULEY-URIBE

My drawings are the result of my sculpture.
— Auguste Rodin

Drawing was the foundation of Rodin's development, and it deepened his approach to form: the body as a silent subject where surfaces, planes, and contours interact. Unique among his contemporaries—for whom drawing was a minor medium, a draft of more-or-less settled ideas—Rodin did not make preparatory drawings for sculptures. Instead, paper was the medium where his figures could unfold vivaciously, with an effervescence that sculpture did not allow. In studies, drawings from the imagination, copies after sculptures, sketches of models, and "instantaneous" drawings—whether loaded with matter or light and fluid—the aesthetic concerns were the same for Rodin the sculptor and Rodin the painter.

He did all he could during his life to explain these two facets to his work, but the foundational part played by drawing is generally overlooked, and Rodin's graphic output hardly weighs at all against the overwhelming impact of his sculptures. Critics and historians tend to strictly separate the two practices. Curator and art historian Catherine Lampert puts it well:

> Among those who write about Rodin, there is a difference of opinion, really one of interpretation, about whether the drawings and the sculpture are interdependent. One will look in vain for preparatory or finished drawings. If one asks the question of whether sculptures evolve through drawing, the answer is probably "no." If one asks oneself whether Rodin's grand, imaginative project, his life's work could have been achieved without the freedom and intimacy of drawing, the answer is the same.[1]

By highlighting the relationship between his sculpture and drawing, taking examples from American collections, this essay aims to reveal the balance and profound unity of Rodin's work and underlines the importance he gave to the theory of art and his own place in a theoretical continuum—an aspect of his thinking little explored until now.

THE MATERIAL RECORD

How many drawings did Rodin make? About nine thousand survive—roughly the same number as his sculptures.[2] The category of "graphic works" or "works on paper" encompasses numerous techniques: graphite, charcoal, red chalk (*sanguine*), stumped (smudged) graphite, pen and ink, brush, wash, watercolor, gouache; we could also include drypoint engraving, which is a form of drawing, and a single lithographic attempt. This heterogeneity reflects the evolution of Rodin's styles across his career, which—in the case of drawing—can be divided into several periods: youth (starting in 1854); the Belgian period, including his trip to Italy (1871–77); the "black period" for *The Gates of Hell* (the 1880s); the "transitional" female nudes, which could also be labeled the "rose" period (the 1890s); and, finally, the late nudes (after 1896).[3] More than two-thirds of the drawings date from between 1890 and his death in 1917: they are the work of a mature artist, created between the ages of fifty and seventy-seven. This output is primarily held at the Musée Rodin in Paris but also in collections around the world.

The first objective attempt to quantify the number of drawings was in 1916, when Rodin donated his works and collections to the French State to create a monographic museum. At the time, the drawings were scattered among several studios, mainly in Meudon, and some hung on the walls of the Hôtel Biron in Paris, which Rodin had occupied since 1908. He attempted to classify them with the help of close collaborators, including the sculptor Malvina Hoffman, to assess as accurately as possible the number of works covered by the donation. An initial list made by his biographer and friend Judith Cladel showed how extraordinarily abundant the drawings were: the gift to the Musée Rodin initially numbered 5,350 works. Over time the figure grew, with drawings found slipped into books or furniture and others acquired later, reaching more than 7,500 sheets today.

Several generations of curators were involved in documenting the drawings—a seemingly simple task but in reality extremely complex, considering how methodically the first catalogers went about classifying, numbering, stamping, and understanding Rodin's graphic work. What made the process more difficult was that Rodin's notebooks had been "stripped," and the albums he put together were dismembered. As well, starting in 1916, some of the drawings disappeared.[4] A further problem, still ongoing, is the matter of forgeries, which have to be identified and excluded from Rodin's corpus.

AMERICAN COLLECTIONS

Beyond the Musée Rodin, collections of Rodin's drawings were assembled quite early in Europe, North America, and Asia—at first sporadically, then with the active and ambitious goal of creating new museums or even compiling complete collections of works by an artist now of universal renown.

The United States is home to extensive Rodin collections, which this exhibition explores. There are over 150 drawings in twenty-three US cities,[5] not

FIG. 3.1

Auguste Rodin (French, 1840–1917), *Standing Nude* or *Washing Up* (*La Toilette*), 1898–1900. Graphite, stomp, and watercolor on wove paper, 12 13/16 × 9 13/16 in. (32.5 × 25 cm). Museum of Fine Arts, Boston. Denman Waldo Ross Collection, 07.858. Photograph © Museum of Fine Arts, Boston

FIG. 3.2

Auguste Rodin, *The Golden Age*, 1878. Black chalk heightened with white on faded blue paper, 18 7/16 × 12 in. (46.8 × 30.4 cm). Metropolitan Museum of Art, New York. Rogers Fund, 1963, 63.92.3.

including the fakes that mar certain collections and which American museum curators are eager to identify.[6] Regarding authenticity, the subject of pioneering studies by Dorothy Seiberling, Rodolfo Paras-Perez, and Kirk Varnedoe,[7] American collectors have been victims of counterfeiters just as the French were. Some of the drawings owned by Grenville L. Winthrop and donated to Harvard's Fogg Museum are forgeries—at least those purchased from the Leonard Clayton Gallery, with a certificate of authenticity signed by the forger himself, Ernest Durig.[8] So, too, are all the drawings donated by Alma de Bretteville Spreckels to the Legion of Honor in San Francisco.[9]

The Museum of Fine Arts, Boston, was the first institution outside France to acquire drawings by Rodin, in 1907 (fig. 3.1), and the United States remains the only country to which Rodin dedicated one symbolically (cat. 1).[10] As visitors can observe in this exhibition, the obvious quality of the drawings in American collections also deserves emphasis. Consisting of rare, private work, including sketches made at the Museum of Natural History where Antoine-Louis Barye taught, the album from Rodin's youth known as the "Mastbaum Album" (1863–64), in the Rodin Museum in Philadelphia, is unequaled. Rodin attempted to get the album back for himself at the end of his life but did not succeed.[11] American museums are the only institutions to own two of the three known drawings of projects in marble inspired by Albert-Ernest Carrier-Belleuse: *The Golden Age* at the Metropolitan Museum of Art (the Met), New York (fig. 3.2), and *Spring* at the Art Institute of Chicago, acquired in 1963 and 1984, respectively. A rare *St. John the Baptist* now at the Fogg, drawn in pen and ink from a photograph, is the counterpart of the version in the Musée d'Orsay in Paris. Stanford University

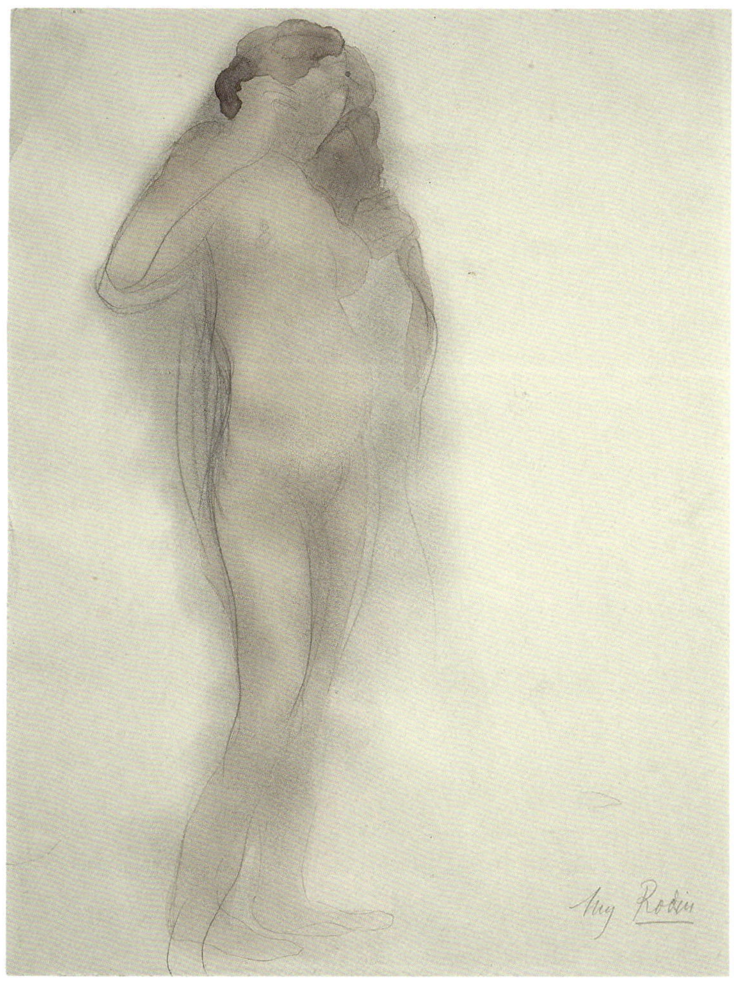

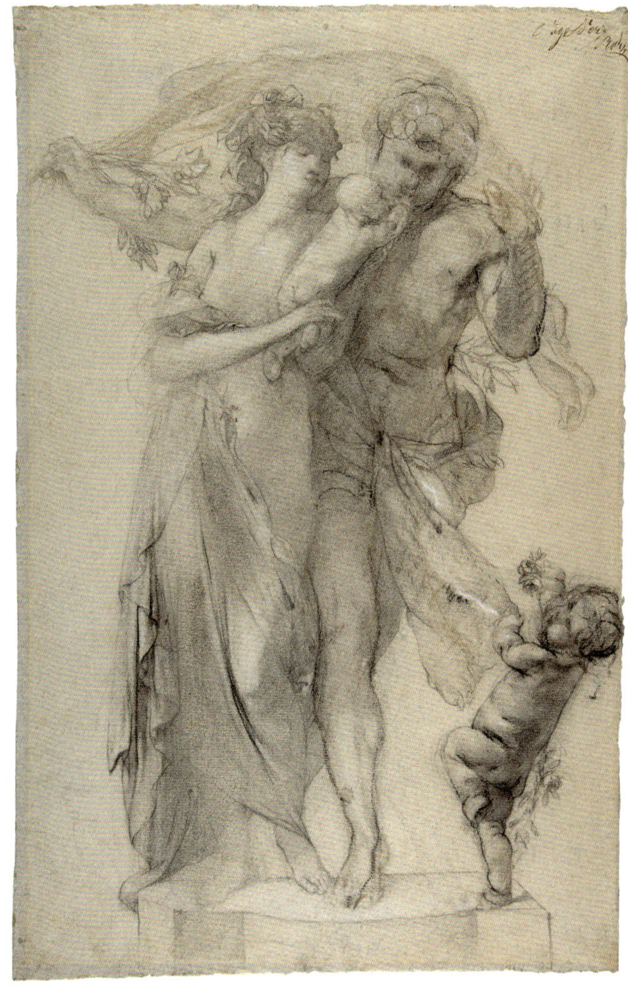

holds a remarkable drawing representing a synthesis of the engravings *Loves Leading the World* and *Spring*, dedicated to Rodin's friend Eva de Basily Callimaki. A *Cambodian Dancer* drawing, known only from a poor photograph taken before its dedication to Otto Grautoff, reappeared in 1981 thanks to a gift from Mrs. Richard Gimbel to the Baltimore Museum of Art. The many other significant works on paper in the United States include *The Genius of Sculpture* from the Cleveland Museum (cat. 102), and numerous drawings in private collections.

RODIN'S UNIQUE APPROACH TO DRAWING

More than a hundred years after Rodin's death, and despite their quantity, his drawings are still considered a secondary component of his practice: Rodin was and remains "a sculptor." Some critics of his time—Gustave Geffroy, for example—praised his graphic work for its sculptural qualities. To Rodin's detractors, however, the drawings were merely sketches or even indecent (overly erotic) and irrelevant records. As for the artist, he never stopped "pushing" them, with exhibitions and sales organized in Europe and the United States, beginning in 1896.[12] He also encouraged reproductions of his drawings in periodicals and luxury editions. If Rodin was trying to convince people to see his drawings as the equivalent of his sculptures or "elevate" them to the rank of paintings, his efforts indisputably failed.

How are we to explain Rodin's infatuation with drawing? How is it that around the age of sixty, after the major developments in his sculpture, Rodin found new fulfillment in drawing? Given that it required a sustained effort to master the anatomy of the human body, sculpture was, of course, not unrelated to this, as Rodin declared in 1903: "My drawings are the *result* of my sculpture."[13] At the École Impériale Spéciale de Dessin et de Mathématiques, where he studied from 1854 to 1857, as well as when he was competing to enter the École Supérieure des Beaux-Arts (which he failed to do three times), his talents as a draftsman won school prizes.[14] At the center of all academic instruction, drawing also played an essential role in the training of craftsmen, based on the same disciplines as those practiced by fine arts students: anatomy, perspective, and historical drawing. Analytical drawing from plaster casts (mostly of Classical sculpture) was regarded as an instrument of knowledge—"What I have not drawn, I have not seen," noted Goethe[15]—and provided the artist with a repertoire of models, drapery, and body parts (arms, legs, heads, feet). Drawing from memory allowed students to assimilate the styles of the masters. Rodin studied the ideal constitution of the human body by copying Classical statues at the Musée du Louvre (correcting nature by imitating great art). He did not have access to lessons with male live models or the anatomy lessons given by physicians at the École des Beaux-Arts using *écorché* casts (sculptures of flayed corpses) and woodcut illustrations. Rodin completed his education instead by drawing cadavers at the Paris morgue and by enrolling in classes at the Manufacture des Gobelins, where students drew from nude models. His *académies* (life drawings of models in standard academic poses) were created during this period (1857–60).

The series of "flayed" anatomical drawings—usually grouped under the headings of "black drawings," "drawings from imagination," "Dantesque," or even "Michelangelesque"—which date from the 1870s and continued until around 1889, launched Rodin's more personal studies during the six years he spent in Belgium, where he started painting. The black drawings show a great diversity of styles: from almost-naive linear sketches to overworked gouaches,

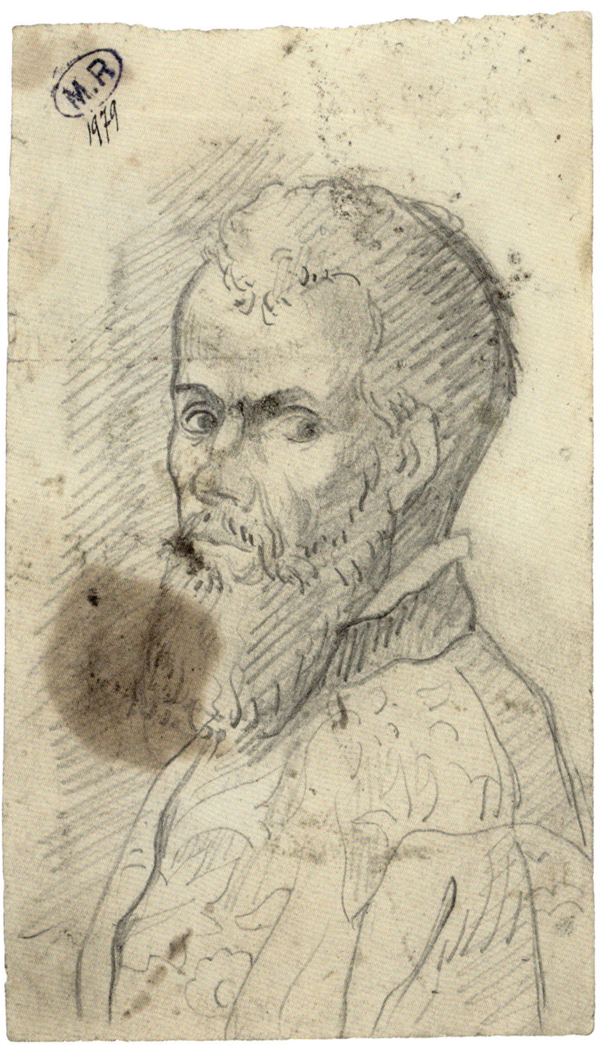

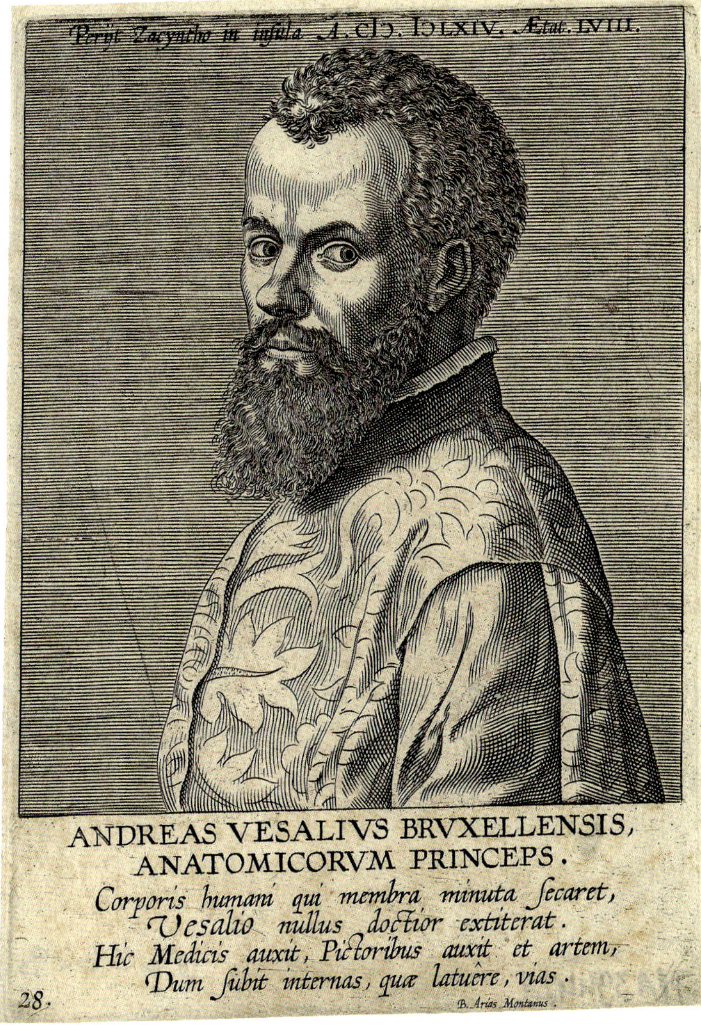

FIG. 3.3

Auguste Rodin, *Bust of Vesalius*, after an engraving (erroneously identified as a portrait of Michelangelo), c. 1870. Graphite on wove paper, 6 ¼ × 3 ¹⁵⁄₁₆ in. (15.9 × 9.9 cm). Musée Rodin, Paris. D. 1979.

FIG. 3.4

Philips Galle (Flemish, 1537–1612), *Portrait Bust of Flemish Anatomist Andreas Vesalius (1514–1546)*, c. 1572. Engraving after the title page for Andreas Vesalius, *De Humani Corporis Fabrica* by Jan Van Calkar (Northern Netherlandish, c. 1499–1546), 6 ⅞ × 4 ¹³⁄₁₆ in. (17.5 × 12.3 cm). The British Museum, London.

which Rodin completed in successive layers over time. There is a source for these drawings, never before identified, undoubtedly because Rodin never mentioned it: the most famous treatise of early modern anatomy, *On the Fabric of the Human Body* (*De Humani Corporis Fabrica*) (1543) by Andreas Vesalius, which Rodin must have consulted in nineteenth-century editions or through woodcut prints.[16] An undated sketch at the Musée Rodin in Paris, identified until now as a portrait of Michelangelo (fig. 3.3), confirms the Vesalius source. The sketch is actually a copy after a late print by Philips Galle (fig. 3.4) made by reversing a detail from the book's frontispiece, where Vesalius is seen dissecting a body in front of humanists and physicians. As is well known, the woodcut anatomical illustrations of the *Fabrica* (attributed to Jan Van Calkar, a pupil of Titian's) depict flayed men in action or in dramatic poses against landscape backgrounds. They shed light on Rodin's original approach before, during, and after his work on *The Gates of Hell*, commissioned in 1880. The theatricality of the flayed figures is evident in Rodin's engraving *La Ronde* (probably 1883), where characters observe a group of dancers in the middle of a hilly landscape (fig. 3.5).

As the Italian Renaissance author Leon Battista Alberti had recommended in his treatise *On Painting* (1450), Rodin first drew the muscles and bones *beneath* the flesh; but contrary to the classical tradition, he then dressed his flayed figures, not in skin and clothes but in shadows and light. The *Study for the "Gates of Hell": Shades Speaking to Dante* (fig. 3.6), a masterpiece in the Fogg Museum, is a good example of a drawing from the early 1880s where the *écorchés*

Auguste Rodin, *The Round* (*La Ronde*), probably 1883. Drypoint, 7 × 9 in. (17.8 × 22.9 cm). National Gallery of Art, Washington, DC. Rosenwald Collection, 1943.3.7402.

Auguste Rodin, *Study for the "Gates of Hell": Shades Speaking to Dante*, c. 1883. Black ink, gray wash, and white gouache over graphite on tan wove paper with ruled lines, 7 5/8 × 4 3/4 in. (19.4 × 11.8 cm). Harvard Art Museums / Fogg Museum, Cambridge, Massachusetts. Bequest of Grenville L. Winthrop, 1943.916.

Secunda musculorum tabula (diagram of muscles in a walking position), 1543. Woodcut engraving from Andreas Vesalius, *De Humani Corporis Fabrica* (*Seven Books on the Fabric of the Human Body*) (Basel: Johannes Oporinus, 1543). Cornell University Library, Ithaca, New York.

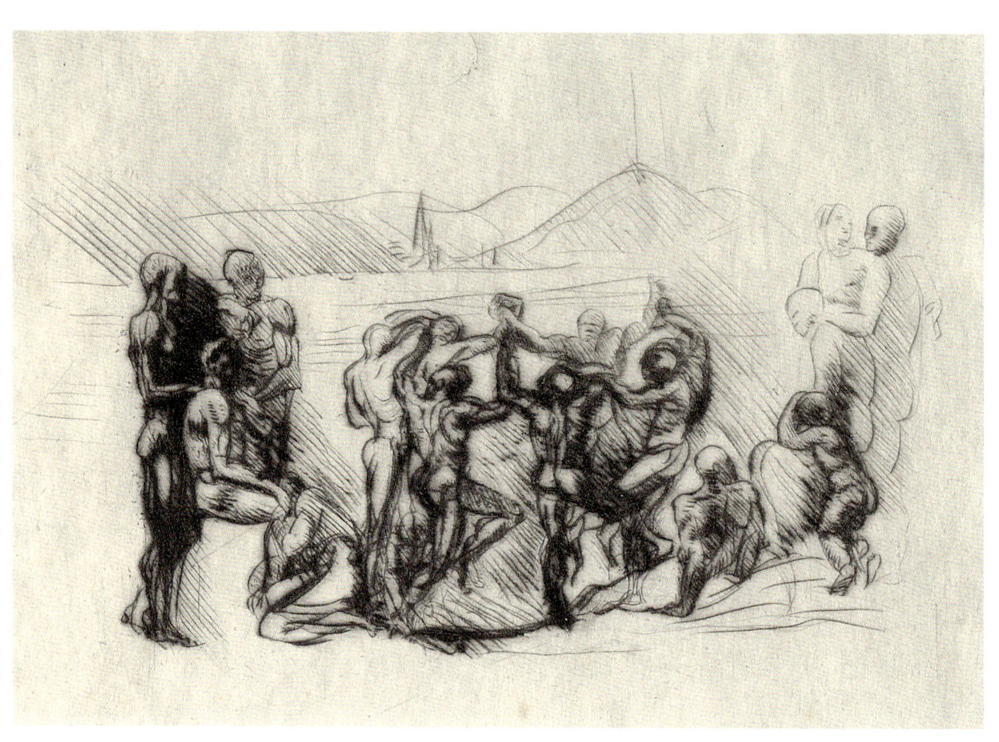

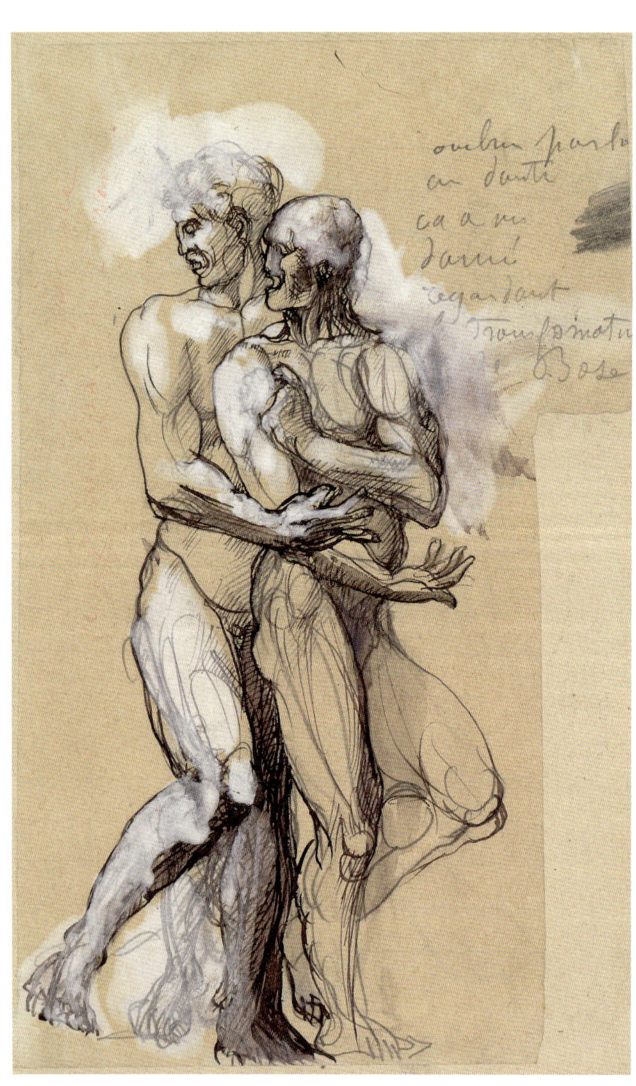

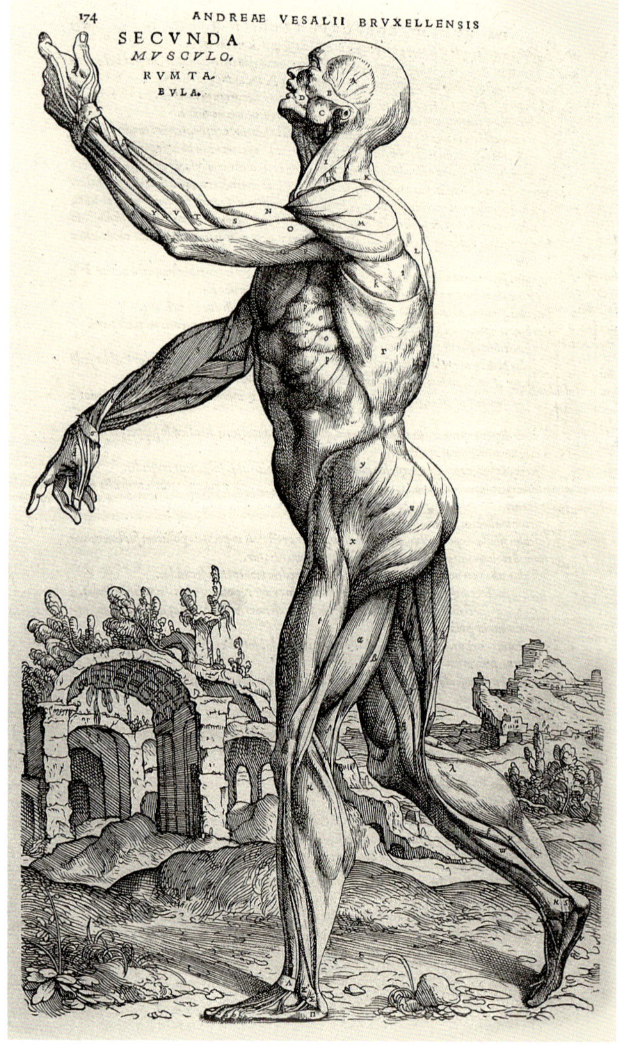

are heightened with pen hatchings, ink wash, and gouache. With fierce eyes and open hands, the figures' outraged expressions also refer to the *Fabrica*'s illustrations, even if Rodin did not copy a particular plate. It is known that Vesalius worked closely with his publisher and Van Calkar on the correlation between text and image, a dialectic observed in many of Rodin's black drawings.

The invisible scene taking place outside the frame of *Shades Speaking to Dante* is specified by an inscription in the upper-right corner, which the upturned hands of the two figures seem to be pointing to: "shades talking / to dante // seen / damned / looking at / the transformation / of Bose" (that is, the corrupt official Buoso Donati). This subtle link between figure and writing is also characteristic of the erudite design of Vesalius's plates, where the words "*Secunda Musculo / rum ta / bula*" (second plate of the stomach muscle) come out of the mouth of a flayed figure whose hand is pointing to the plate number, 174 (fig. 3.7). In the *Ugolino* series, Rodin's annotations, often quoting Dante, confer on his characters the quality of speech and sound. The partially erased vertical inscription on the left of the drawing in the Fogg ("do a sketch with bas-reliefs with 3 or 2 figures") shows that Rodin planned to use them for a bas-relief in the *Gates*. The focus on the hands is reminiscent of the *Monument to the Burghers of Calais* (see fig. 1.5). Finally, the two juxtaposed figures recall the repetition of the same body in the *Three Shades*.

Shades Speaking to Dante effectively sums up the role of drawing in relation to sculpture in Rodin's work: it is not a preparatory drawing for any recognizable work but a meditation encompassing all the elements of the genesis of his contemporaneous sculptures; this is the specific nature of drawing. The mind perceives in a different way a three-dimensional work—a sculpture finished on all sides—from a two-dimensional work where the line suspended by the edge of the sheet can be continued by the mind, offering a freedom of imagination that sculpture does not allow. Drawings can also be supplemented with captions, comments, or quotes, giving the images an audible dimension. Finally, there is the use of the white touches of gouache, which emphasize the muscles and simulate the effect of bronze surfaces highlighted by slanting light, capturing what the French art critic Paul Gsell would characterize as the "vision of a sculptor" on paper.[17]

In *Shades Speaking to Dante*, we observe another use of gouache in the vaporous form surrounding the shapes with a white cloud. These effects are often the result of *pentimenti* (Is Rodin trying to replace a wash that displeased him, and that we can still see underneath?) or by accidents that Rodin accepted as intrinsic to his works. Many black drawings already contain the aesthetic innovations of Rodin's most accomplished late drawings: saturation of matter, purification of lines, experiments with the medium's fluidity. Rodin plays with the transparency of ink, invariably dotted with drips, like the stigmata that mark bodies and charge them with meaning, indicating that something unusual is happening. Spots and stains echo the deliberate irregularities of the surfaces of bronzes and plasters; they challenge the coherence of a strictly figurative vision.

Art historians including Albert Alhadeff, Albert Elsen, and Kirk Varnedoe have rightly analyzed these drawings through the prism of Michelangelo, whom Rodin discovered during his trip to Italy in 1876.[18] Much has been made of this influence, particularly the anatomical characteristics of the bodies in his sculptures and drawings. Yet Rodin warned, "What should be admired in the drawing of Michelangelo is not the lines in themselves, the audacious foreshortenings and the skillful anatomy, but the thundering and desperate power of this Titan. The imitators of Buonarotti, who, lacking his soul, copied in painting his arched poses and tense musculatures, have fallen into ridicule."[19]

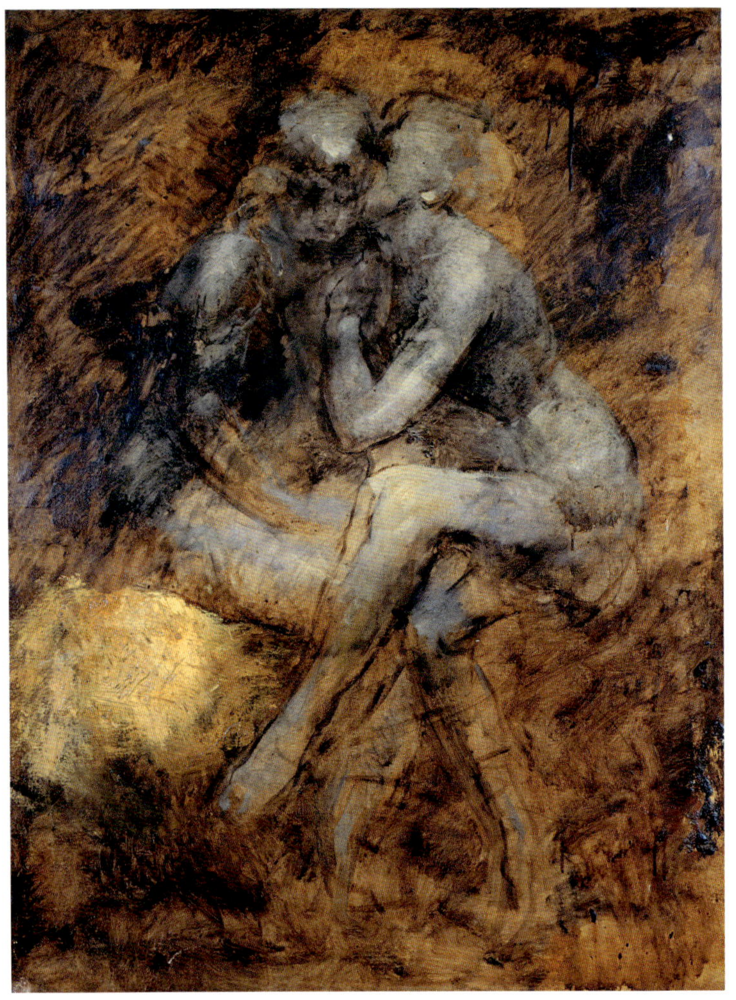

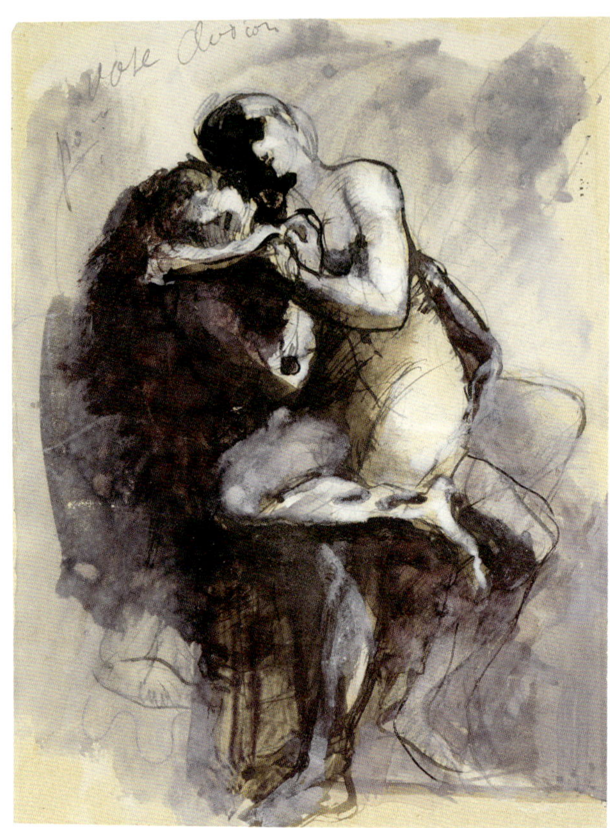

FIG. 3.8

Jean-Baptiste Carpeaux (French, 1827–1875), *Confidence*, 1873. Oil on canvas, 46 1/16 × 35 7/16 in. (117 × 90 cm). Petit Palais, Musée des Beaux-arts de la Ville de Paris. PPP3428.

FIG. 3.9

Auguste Rodin, *Vase Clodion (Lovers)*, before 1884. Black ink and gouache, with traces of graphite on tan wove paper, 7 7/16 × 5 11/16 in. (18.9 × 14.5 cm). Harvard Art Museums / Fogg Museum, Cambridge, Massachusetts. Bequest of Grenville L. Winthrop, 1943.914.

The drawings after Michelangelo or inspired by him (for example, the *Figure in Pose of Michelangelo's "Apollo"* at Maryhill, cat. 53) also show a more illusionistic treatment of the flesh and certain attention to morbidezza, or the delicate softness of the skin. Flavio Fergonzi finds this quality in the sculpture *The Shade* and attributes it to a drawing by Michelangelo, *Study for the Pietà*.[20]

We also see the indirect imprint of Michelangelo in the work of two artists who each left a deep mark on Rodin: Peter Paul Rubens, the "painter of flesh," and Jean-Baptiste Carpeaux, who, like Rodin, is known primarily as a sculptor despite his passion for painting. Carpeaux's *Confidence* (fig. 3.8), in which two lovers emerge from the shadows, is treated as an exercise in classical grisaille—the representation of the sculpture in monochrome painting: the bodies are modeled by shadows of gray glazing and more saturated touches of white, while an overall interlacing of brushstrokes, especially in the legs of the figures, lends a sketch-like quality. This astonishing canvas, in the Petit Palais in Paris, evokes an enlargement of Rodin's most pictorial black drawings. We find these same features in *Vase Clodion (Lovers)* (fig. 3.9), another drawing in the Fogg Museum, which Rodin gave to the painter John Singer Sargent.

Around 1890, Rodin underwent a profound stylistic revolution that would have consequences for the rest of his oeuvre. This change is usually explained as a break from his "sculptural" drawings. The paradigm shift was the culmination of over fifteen years of endeavor; it took place at the same time as his emerging interest in rapid life drawings of unposed female models. Rodin created small sculptures very quickly, but his new excitement with the speed of execution and exploration found its natural ally in graphite and paper.

During the years 1900 to 1914, Rodin expressed his ideas about art through articles, feature stories and interviews. This new form of introspection and emphasis on education coincided with his increasing appetite for drawing. Commentary by writers and journalists, which had appeared since Rodin's first public successes in the 1880s, was now replaced by "what the Master says" in his own words. Rodin engaged with the tradition of art history by referring to classical art historical disputes — unlike Claude Monet, who preferred "to leave these discussions to those who care about them and whose *métier* is writing."[21] In France, the status of sculpture was still the subject of a lively debate, dating back to the Renaissance *paragone*,[22] in which many intellectuals participated. In 1846, the poet Charles Baudelaire, who was also an influential art critic, elevated the status of painting over that of sculpture in a provocative publication, "Why Sculpture Is Boring," arguing that sculpture turned toward the past and was unable to renew itself and be modern. Rodin tried to prove him wrong.

In the *paragone*, one argument in favor of painting was that it could show a body simultaneously from several points of view on the same flat surface. Rodin was familiar with that proposition. In the drypoint *Henry Becque* (fig. 3.10), copied from a portrait bust he had modeled in clay, three different views of the head confront one another.[23] But Rodin's *Three Shades* (1881–86), separate casts of the same figure rotated in different positions (just like in the triple portrait of *Henry Becque*), demonstrate that sculpture can also accomplish

FIG. 3.10

Auguste Rodin, *Henry Becque*, 1885. Drypoint, 6 1/8 × 7 13/16 in. (15.6 × 19.9 cm). Cleveland Museum of Art. Gift of the Folio Club in honor of Henry S. Francis, 1967.164.

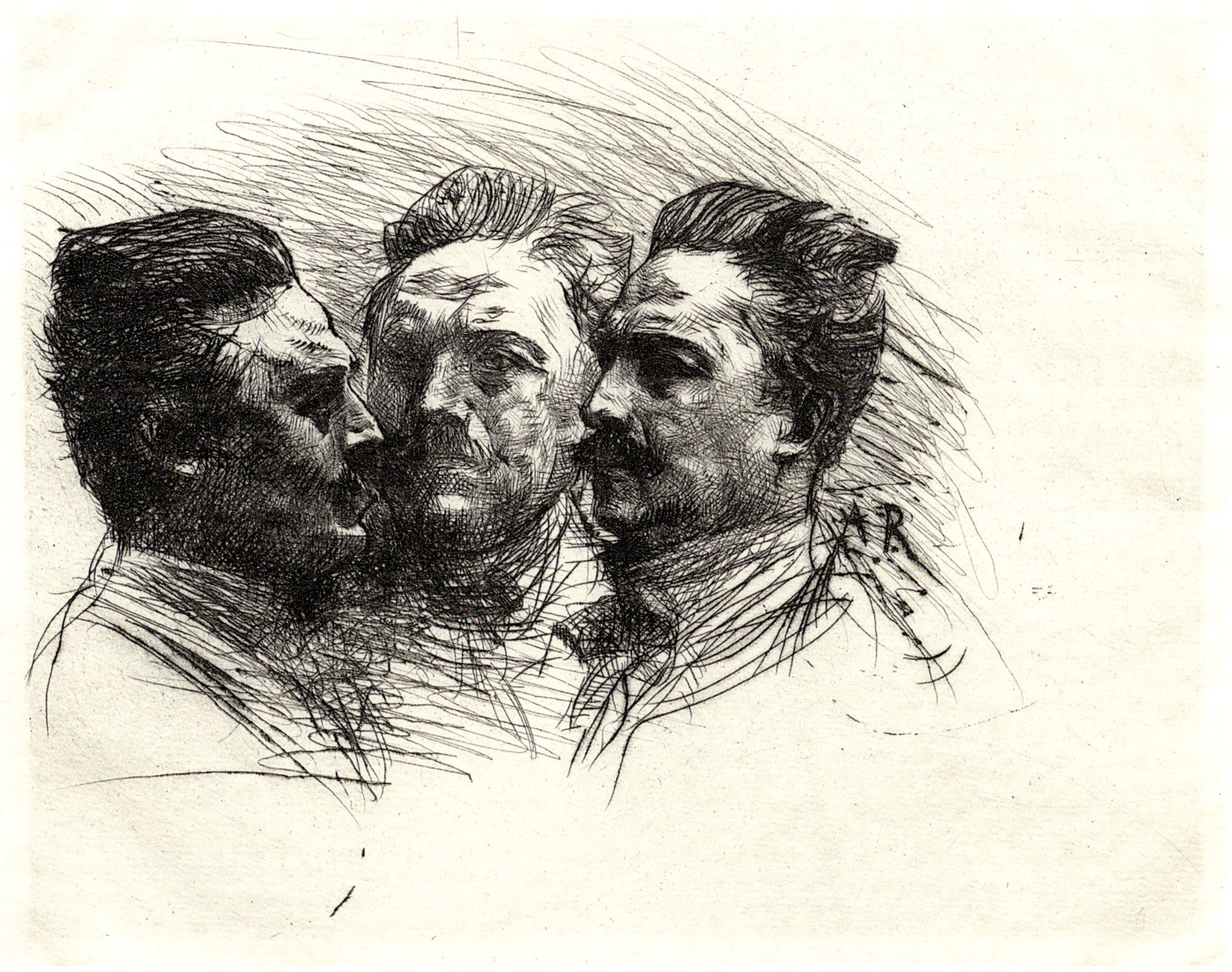

this feat, that it is not the prerogative solely of drawing and painting. The work also shows Rodin's interest in appreciating sculpture from a unique point of view: the *Three Shades* were destined to perch above the lintel of *The Gates of Hell* (see fig. 8.1), the monumental door imagined by Rodin in the 1880s for a proposed museum of decorative arts. One stands before the huge door in bas-relief, by nature a frontal composition, just as one does before a painting on a grand scale, and views the *Three Shades* from below.

In Rodin's lifetime, as Catherine Lampert has noted, the comparison of the *Gates* with painting was taken for granted, even if "in recent years the thematic source and sculptural achievements of the *Gates of Hell* have overshadowed its affinity to the logic and techniques of painting."[24] She explains: "It was in the art of Géricault and Delacroix that Rodin identified the contrast of harsh corporeality with a non-objective sense of matter (in other words, *impasto*), that he needed and sought after."[25] The later version of the *Gates* (the only one ever exhibited by the artist, in 1900), with all figures removed from the structure of the door, created a new "intangible space, modulated by light," which Antoinette Le Normand-Romain compares to Monet's *Cathedral* series.[26]

Rodin's interest in the *paragone* debate may be explained by the importance he placed on drawing. The terms of that debate were the framework Rodin's contemporaries used to judge his graphic work. Most of Rodin's own words on art are related to it, but also to the ancient "quarrel of color" (which erupted in the French Royal Academy of Painting and Sculpture in Paris in the seventeenth century) over the preeminence of *disegno* (drawing/conception) versus *colore* in the art of painting. In 1906, when painting seemed confirmed as the only mode of modern art, Rodin defended the idea that "sculpture is sister to painting and plays with shadow and light just as painting does. . . . Thus, the sculptor who is not a colorist is ignorant of the most important aspect of his profession."[27] Rodin speaks of color in sculpture as the "colorist" theoretician Roger de Piles understood it: the harmonious distribution of tones—light and shadow. This makes sense if we keep in mind that, in his youth, following the method of his teacher Horace Lecoq de Boisbaudran, Rodin drew after old master paintings in the Louvre, including works by Eustache Le Sueur (*Jesus Carrying His Cross*, c. 1651) and Nicolas Poussin (*The Childhood of Bacchus*, c. 1630). He would not draw in situ in the Louvre but instead memorized the compositions, then reproduced what he had recorded in his mind with tones and shades of graphite.

In his *Conversations* with Paul Gsell from 1911, when he favored the grays of graphite and pencil and the smudged effects seen in the *Reclining Nude Woman (Alda Moreno)* at the Philadelphia Museum of Art (cat. 83), Rodin again raised the question of color:

> "In your opinion, Gsell, is color a quality of painting or of sculpture?"
> "Of painting, naturally."
> "As paradoxical as it seems," Rodin says, "the greatest sculptors are as much colorists as the best painters or, rather, the best print-makers. They play so skillfully [with] all the possibilities of relief, they combine so well the boldness of light and the modesty of shadow, that their sculptures are as luscious as the most chatoyant etchings. Now color—this is the comment I was coming to—is like the flower of beautiful modeling. These two qualities always go together, and they are what give all masterpieces of sculpture the radiance of living flesh."[28]

A whole chapter of the *Conversations* is devoted to "Drawing and Color," the subjects par excellence of the *paragone*. Gsell characterizes Rodin's black drawings of the 1880s—which, as we saw with *Shades Speaking to Dante*, depict bones and muscles, bodies without flesh — as *visions of a sculptor*, while he describes the late watercolors, from around 1900, as "nudes overlaid with flesh-colored tints. These drawings are freer than the first ones. The poses are less fixed, more momentary. These are more the *visions of a painter*."[29]

By transforming his drawings into a "painter's vision," Rodin, through the voice of Gsell, raised them to the same rank as his sculptures, and at the same time shifted them over to the side of modernity. The flesh has its place in these later drawings, but Rodin eschewed the traditional technique of using touches of light in white gouache to convey its tones and volume; instead, his painted figures present a uniform, monochrome, almost abstract flesh, a *hue*, with pigment often deliberately applied outside the drawn lines (see, for example, the *Cambodian Dancers*, cats. 57, 65, 81, 97). Rodin insisted on these "fleeting impressions," "very rapid gestures," and "transitory bending and inflection." For him, "vagueness in flexibility allows the viewer's imagination to add something, thereby completing the artist's vision."[30]

Consider how relevant these words were in 1911, when Rodin himself described the drawings as having "Impressionist" qualities. Rodin may have become a "painter" by means of theory; however, he was certainly not an Impressionist sculptor, despite the efforts of the journalist Edmond Claris, who made this idea his leitmotif in 1902. In another published conversation, this time with Under-Secretary of State for Fine Arts Étienne Dujardin-Beaumetz, in 1913, Rodin confirmed that he was not an Impressionist, declaring in a chapter on "Color in Statuary": "Color! Trying to give color! That's an expression a sculptor should never use. In sculpture, there are no flaws; there are only exact forms."[31] Thus, what is important in sculpture is the precise form. And yet Rodin criticized Jean-Auguste-Dominique Ingres for his sculptural coldness, noting that Ingres's drawing "does not quiver," and his "pencil does not vibrate on the breast any more than on cloth. . . . He does not care. . . . For him, everything is dead."[32] This coldness was precisely the reproach that seventeenth-century "colorists" had leveled at painters who were too attached to antique models: they were criticized for painting "like sculptors."

Kirk Varnedoe's seminal scholarship identifies Rodin's drawings from his final twenty years as either Type I or Type II.[33] The first category, which Roger Marx describes as "snapshots of the female nude," are the drawings exclusively in graphite that inverted the traditional creative process, in which the artist constantly glances back and forth from the model to the sheet of paper.[34] Instead, Rodin introduced fortuity, developing a form of blind automatic drawing by concentrating his eyes on the model without looking at the paper. In refusing to watch his drawing evolve, he had no way of knowing what would be lost (hands, feet, heads, arms), focusing on what he saw rather than on what he was creating. *Figure Sketch* in the Smithsonian American Art Museum (cat. 1) and *Seated Woman* at the Museum of Modern Art, New York (cat. 36), are good examples of this practice. Rodin worked without preconceived ideas, exploiting whatever points of view the model proposed. As Maurice Guillemot observed in 1898, "He asks his models for a kind of animal presence and paradise in motion without the constraint of posing: *Do not pretend to do your hair — do your hair*."[35]

These first-draft drawings result from an instinctual gesture that Rodin would later develop in his Type II drawings, passing through various complex stages of tracing, adding watercolor, and finally using a pencil or even scissors (as in the cutouts at the Princeton University Library, cats. 88, 89). Another nuance in the Type II watercolors — again referring back to seventeenth-century academic debates — is the distance created between the work and the viewer, a question intimately tied to Rodin's definition of sculpture as being "nothing but drawing in all dimensions."[36] Rodin's *théorie des profils*, his thinking on the shared role of contours in sculpture and drawing, builds on a painter's concept, since it was Charles Le Brun, discussing Raphael's *Saint Michael*, who first spoke of "outlining even the smallest body limbs so that the figure can be seen with better detail, as I am certain that it is the circumscription of the lines . . . that gives cognizance of the true shape of the body."[37] The relationship between volume and *disegno esterno* (literally "external drawing," or outlining) had a particular impact on Rodin's two-dimensional rereading of his own sculptures: "In the human body, the contour is given by the place where the body ends; thus, it is the body that makes the shape. I place the model so that light, outlining it against a background, illuminates the contour."[38] The *profil*, the contour or border of the body defined by a backlight, is like a silhouette or a shadow. Against the light, the figure stands out from its context: its edges are perfectly clear, but all interior detail is lost. Rodin saw this contrast as constituting the silhouette's (or contour's) "material substance."

In an interview with the art critic Camille Mauclair in 1898, Rodin defined sculpture as a "drawing of movement in the air" and referred to "the dematerialization of all surroundings under the effects of twilight," when light is more penetrating and more *drawing* because the sun's rays are passing through the thickest layer of atmosphere:

> In order to understand this notion exactly, one should think about what one sees of a person stood up against the light of the twilight sky: a very precise silhouette, filled by a dark coloration, with indistinct details. The rapport between this dark coloration and the tone of the sky is the value, that is to say, that what gives the notion of material substance to the body. . . . All that we see essentially of a statue standing high in place, and all that carries, is its movement, its contour, its value.[39]

The sculptural problem of siting a work in the open air and the enhancement of its silhouette that results from placing it on a pedestal, at a distance from the viewer, had decisive consequences in drawing.[40] One of Rodin's intuitions was that he could impose on his drawn figures a law applicable to open-air monuments subject to natural light and atmospheric conditions. This principle is manifest in his drawings from around 1898, using a single simplified line heightened with a brown watercolor wash, known as his "terracotta-colored women." The transition from three dimensions to two imposes on these drawings a synthetic, compact look, abridging the figures to a silhouette and a gesture.

This effect had engaged Rodin since the 1880s, when he became interested in photography.[41] Unlike Degas, who used his own photos, Rodin used photographs of his works taken by others to nurture his reflections on drawing, painting, and sculpture. His close collaboration with the American photographer Edward Steichen was like that of a sculptor with his *praticien*.[42] Many of Rodin's drawings have qualities of sculptures viewed from a distance: exercises exploring the silhouette and the interior of the figure, which appears as a uniform shadow whose "material substance" has somehow been transposed into two dimensions. Here, too, we can see a late resurgence of Lecoq de Boisbaudran's representational method: drawings from memory, in charcoal or stumped graphite, giving flat, neutral results.[43] The drawing of a brown silhouette bathed in a light made of brushstrokes of very light blue watercolor, with openwork effects, yields results like those obtained by Steichen in *The Awakening* from 1901 (figs. 3.11, 3.12). A kind of inner shadow defines the figures in both images. Examining Rodin's drawing sheets closely, we see a delicate graphite outline, but these lines wane in favor of the full brown watercolor as we move farther from the paper (see, for example, *Sphinx*, cat. 98).

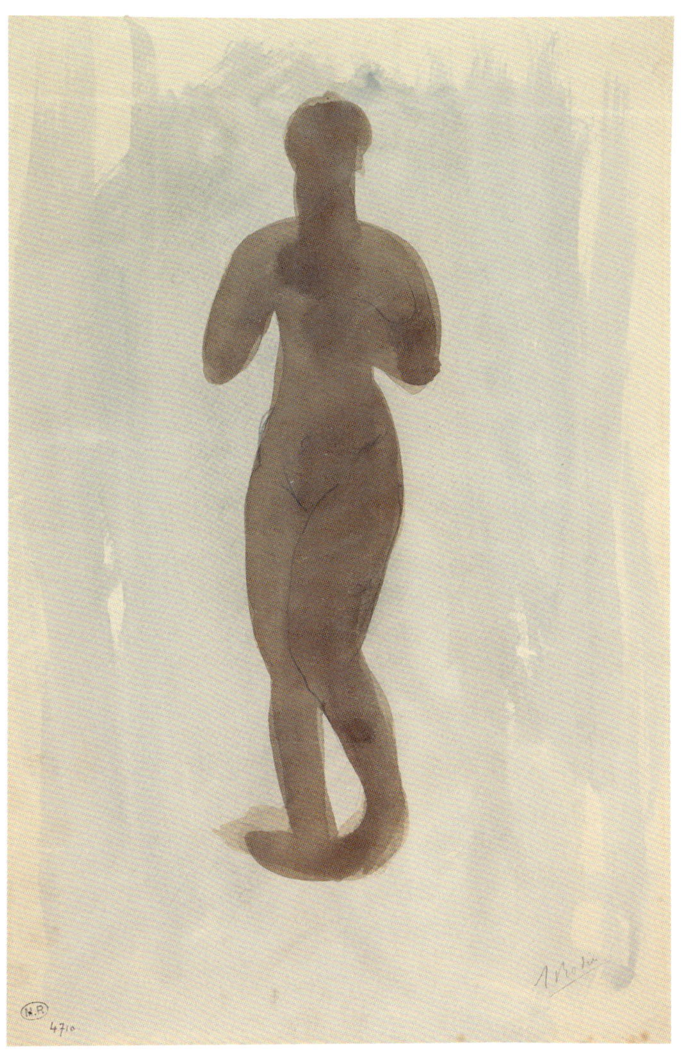

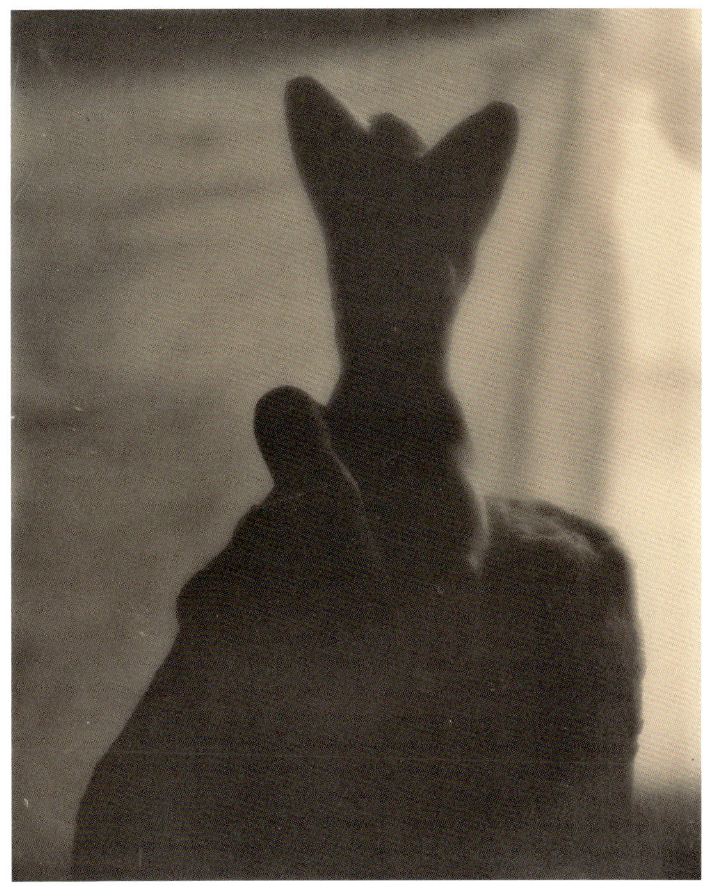

FIG. 3.11

Auguste Rodin, *Standing Nude*, c. 1898.
Graphite and watercolor on wove paper,
19 1/2 × 12 13/16 in. (50.7 × 32.5 cm).
Musée Rodin, Paris. D. 4710.

FIG. 3.12

Edward J. Steichen (American, 1879–
1973), *The Awakening*, 1901. Platinium
print, 9 13/16 × 7 7/8 in. (24.9 × 20 cm).
Musée Rodin, Paris. Ph. 684.

All these questions are closely linked to the gradual encroachment of color in Rodin's drawings from the mid-1890s until around 1906 (see the yellow ocher *Psyche*, which belonged to Malvina Hoffman, cat. 34, or the *Cambodian Dancer* in Boston's Museum of Fine Arts, with intense brown and blue watercolor, cat. 97). Large planes of color structure these compositions, sometimes surrounding figures that end up being lost within omnipresent brushstrokes (as in *Before Creation: Chaos*, cat. 54). Rodin exploits all the resources of watercolor, where abstract shapes appear as the accident of pigment concentrated on premoistened paper, suggesting marbling in the drapery (as in another drawing titled *Psyche*, in Maryhill, cat. 56). According to the classical concept of art, the medium used should disappear so the form can emerge, but in Rodin's work, the reverse occurs: accidental splashes, running effects, and fluid marks come to the fore. In this experimental approach, the jubilation of immediacy—usually reserved for drawing and painting—has a special resonance in sculpture. Take, for example, Rodin's relationship to time, space, hazard, materials—and especially his interest, noted by Rainer Maria Rilke, in the epidermis of his works as a place of deformations, scarifications, irregularities. His are *affected* bodies, a Spinozan term that seems relevant to Rodin; his watercolors, in particular, are part of this aesthetic. Rather than the formality and perfection of tradition, Rodin pursues a deformity of the human figure where the organic aspect of stains or marks takes precedence, evoking "natural images."

Through drawing, Rodin called into question the very nature of his sculpture. His work offers a synthesis between the arts in which sculpture, painting, drawing, and photography feed off one another. In his own way, he ended the debate over artistic hierarchies that French art theorists had pursued since the seventeenth century, in particular the argument of color versus drawing — in essence, the triumph that painting claimed over sculpture. By weaving analogies between these two principal forms, Rodin's sculpture emerged as a two-dimensional presence (through photography and drawing), and his drawing became the equivalent of sculpture by seizing its qualities of color and relief. In this way, he linked the nineteenth and twentieth centuries.

Art historian Natasha Ruiz-Gomez rightly points out the contradiction between "the persistent protestations of Rodin's faithfulness to nature" and the daring and innovative character of his art, which sought to create bodies, rather than re-creating them by faithfully imitating nature.[44] In the *paragone* debate, the eye — not the hand — was given primacy. The Academy banned the technique of stumping (blending charcoal or graphite to render contours and shading), not only on the grounds that it made things too easy, but also because it was done with the fingers, and touch belonged to the realm of sculpture. Roger de Piles rather audaciously correlated drawing and sculpture, based on the fact that the painter does not actually touch his canvas when he paints (except with his brushes), whereas the sculptor and the draftsman both touch their media with their hands. Rodin experienced a conspicuous pleasure in touching his sculpture, but equally in feeling the texture and grain of the papers he used. As an artist, he became increasingly modern — not because he drew modern life, but because he "insistently avoided imposing a moral value-scale of style,"[45] as his master Horace Lecoq de Boisbaudran had taught. He freed himself from the artificial hierarchies between the arts imposed by the French Academy. This is the most obvious sign of his art's longevity. More than a hundred years after his death, Rodin's drawings and sculptures have far from exhausted their ability to fascinate.

NOTES

Epigraph: Auguste Rodin to the sculptor Antoine Bourdelle, quoted in Elisabeth Chase Geissbuhler, *Rodin: Later Drawings* (Boston: Beacon Press, 1963), 2.

1. Catherine Lampert, "Rodin's Drawings and Late Works: 'What to Keep and What to Sacrifice,'" in *Rodin*, exh. cat., ed. Catherine Lampert and Antoinette Le Normand-Romain (London: Royal Academy of Arts, 2006), 157.

2. Since 2007, in preparing the catalogue raisonné of Rodin's drawings in France and in the rest of the world, I have undertaken to specify this body of work as objectively as possible, based on a systematic inventory of public and private collections. The figure of "more than 10,000" drawings often put forward is not supported by the data.

3. This chronology was proposed for the first time by Kirk Varnedoe, former curator at the Museum of Modern Art, New York, in his thesis on Rodin's drawings submitted to Stanford University in 1972.

4. For example, we recently identified the original drawing number D. 3857 of the Musée Rodin, considered "vanished" since the early 1920s, as the *Witches' Sabbath* (cat. 67), given to the Art Institute of Chicago by Robert Allerton. The Musée Rodin appears to have sold it. See Christina Buley-Uribe, "L'aliénabilité *de facto* de dessins du musée Rodin," *Cahiers d'histoire de l'art*, no. 19 (2021): 96–107.

5. Including, in Philadelphia, the Rodin Museum; in New York, the Metropolitan Museum of Art, the Museum of Modern Art, the Brooklyn Museum, and the Morgan Library and Museum; in Goldendale, Washington, the Maryhill Museum of Art; in New Haven, Connecticut, Yale University Art Gallery; in Chicago, the Art Institute; in Washington, DC, the National Gallery of Art and the Hirshhorn Museum and Sculpture Garden, Smithsonian Institution.

6. See, for example, Ashley Dunn, "Not Rodin: Misattributed Drawings in the Met Collection," *The Met* blog, November 28, 2017, http://www.metmuseum.org/blogs/now-at-the-met/2017/auguste-rodin-misattributed-drawings.

7. Dorothy Seiberling, "The Great Rodin: His Flagrant Faker," *Life*, June 4, 1965, 64–71; Rodolfo Paras-Perez, "Notes on Rodin's Drawings," *Art Quarterly* 30 (1967): 127–37; and J. Kirk T. Varnedoe, "True and False," in *The Drawings of Rodin*, ed. Albert E. Elsen and J. Kirk T. Varnedoe (New York: Praeger, 1971), 157–85.

8. Inventory numbers 1941.102, 1941.103, 1941.104, 1941.105, 1941.106, 1941.107, 1941.108, 1941.109, 1942.5, 1942.6, 1942.7, 1942.8, 1942.9, 1942.10, 1942.84, 1942.85, 1942.86, 1942.87, 1942.88, 1942.89, 1942.90, 1942.91, 1942.92, 1942.93, 1942.94, 1942.95, 1942.96.

9. Inventory numbers 1940.145.1, 1940.145.2, 1940.145.3, 1940.145.4, 1940.145.5, 1940.145.6, 1940.145.7, 1940.145.8, 1940.145.9.

10. To our knowledge, there are no other examples of sculpted works dedicated to a state or government.

11. J. Kirk T. Varnedoe, "Rodin as a Draftsman: A Chronological Perspective," in *The Drawings of Rodin*, ed. Albert E. Elsen and J. Kirk T. Varnedoe (New York: Praeger, 1971), 25–120; Jacques de Caso, "Rodin's Mastbaum Album," *Master Drawings* 10, no. 2 (Summer 1972): 155–61.

12. Rodin showed a selection of his drawings for the first time at a joint retrospective with Pierre Puvis de Chavannes and Eugène Carrière at the Musée Rath in Geneva.

13. See epigraph. Emphasis added here.

14. "At the age of fifteen and a half, he gained his first recompense, a bronze medal for drawing from the cast, and at seventeen a first bronze medal for modeling and a second class medal for drawing from the antique." Truman H. Bartlett, "Auguste Rodin, Sculptor," *American Architect and Building News* 25, no. 682 (January 19, 1889): 27. In his efforts to enter the École Supérieure des Beaux-Arts, Rodin was accepted in drawing, though not in sculpture.

15. "Was ich nicht gerechnet habe habe ich nicht gesehen." Johann Wolfgang Von Goethe, *Maxims and Reflections*, 1833.

16. In the mid-1870s, while in Brussels, Rodin made portraits of the well-known physician J. A. Thiriar and the pharmacist J. B. Van Berckelaer. It is possible that Rodin had access to some of the Vesalius plates thanks to them.

17. See Auguste Rodin, *Art: Conversations with Paul Gsell*, tr. Jacques de Caso and Patricia Sanders (Berkeley: University of California Press, 1984), 40. Originally published as *L'Art: Entretiens réunis par Paul Gsell* (Paris: Bernard Grasset, 1911).

18. See Albert Alhadeff, "Michelangelo and the Early Rodin," *Art Bulletin* 45 (December 1963): 363–67; Albert E. Elsen and J. Kirk T. Varnedoe, eds., *The Drawings of Rodin* (New York: Praeger, 1971); and Albert E. Elsen, *The Gates of Hell by Auguste Rodin* (Palo Alto, CA: Stanford University Press, 1985).

19. Rodin, *Art: Conversations with Paul Gsell*, 42.

20. The drawing was known to artists thanks to a widely distributed photograph. Rodin's *The Shade* was modeled after 1878, according to Antoinette Le Normand-Romain, *Rodin et le bronze: Catalogue des œuvres conservées au musée Rodin / The Bronzes of Rodin: Catalogue of Works in the Musée Rodin* (Paris: Éditions du musée Rodin / Réunion des musées nationaux, 2007), 2:569.

21. Monet's remark is in Edmond Claris, "De l'Impressionisme en sculpture," *La Nouvelle Revue*, 1902.

22. Known during the Italian Renaissance as the *paragone* (meaning "comparison" in Italian), this dispute centered on the relative merits of painting versus sculpture. On these questions, see Jacqueline Lichtenstein, *La tache aveugle: Essai sur les relations de la peinture et de la sculpture à l'âge moderne* (Paris: Gallimard, 2003).

23. See Victoria Thorson, *Rodin Graphics: A Catalogue Raisonné of Drypoints and Book Illustrations* (San Francisco: Fine Arts Museums of San Francisco, 1975), 44.

24. Catherine Lampert, *Rodin: Sculpture and Drawings*, exh. cat. (London: Arts Council of Great Britain, 1986), 74–76.

25. Lampert, *Rodin: Sculpture and Drawings*, 76.

26. Antoinette Le Normand-Romain, "Rodin et Monet: *La Porte de l'Enfer* comme une *Cathédrale*," in *La sculpture au XIXe siècle: Mélanges pour Anne Pingeot*, ed. Catherine Chevillot and Laure de Margerie (Paris: Nicolas Chaudun, 2008), 268–69. This is the first article devoted entirely to a comparison between sculpture and painting in Rodin's work.

27. "Rodin raconté par lui-même," *La Revue*, May 1, 1906.

28. Rodin, *Art: Conversations with Paul Gsell*, 26.

29. Rodin, *Art: Conversations with Paul Gsell*, 40, italics added.

30. Rodin, *Art: Conversations with Paul Gsell*, 35.

31. See Henri-Charles-Etienne Dujardin-Beaumetz, "Color in Statuary," in *Auguste Rodin: Readings on His Life and Works*, ed. Albert Elsen (Englewood Cliffs, NJ: Prentice-Hall, 1965), 170.

32. Rodin, quoted in J. E. S. Jeanes, "Souvenirs d'une époque heureuse: Rodin chez lui," *Candide*, December 6, 1934.

33. Varnedoe, "Rodin as a Draftsman."

34. Roger Marx, "Cartons d'artistes: Auguste Rodin," *L'Image*, 1897, 292–99.

35. Maurice Guillemot, "À travers la vie," *Le Gil Blas*, February 20, 1898.

36. Rodin, "Les dessins d'Auguste Rodin: Propos de Rodin rapportés par René Benjamin," in *Les dessins d'Auguste Rodin: Exposition, Paris, Salle des fêtes du Gil Blas*, exh. cat. (Paris: Gil Blas, 1910).

37. In his lecture at the first meeting of the Academy in 1667. See Max Imdhal, *Couleur: Les écrits des peintres français de Poussin à Delaunay* (Paris: Maison des sciences de l'homme, 1996), 52.

38. Rodin, quoted in Dujardin-Beaumetz, "The Contours," 11.

39. Camille Mauclair, "L'Art de M. Auguste Rodin," *Revue des Revues*, June 15, 1898, 597–99, 607.

40. See, on these questions, Antoinette Le Normand-Romain, ed. *La sculpture dans l'espace: Rodin, Brancusi, Giacometti . . .*, exh. cat. (Paris: Musée Rodin, 2005).

41. See J. Kirk T. Varnedoe, "Rodin and Photography," in *Rodin Rediscovered*, exh. cat., ed. Albert E. Elsen (Washington, DC: National Gallery of Art, 1981), 203–47.

42. A worker who executed commissions for others. For example, *The Man with the Broken Nose*, originally modeled by Rodin in 1864, was transposed into marble in 1875 by Léon Fourquet, one of Rodin's *praticiens*.

43. As Varnedoe, in "Rodin as a Draftsman," 27, remarks: "They display an undetailed, bland tonal facture, with little feel for line or volume."

44. Natasha Ruiz-Gomez, "Against the Grain: Rodin's Experiments with Paper," in *Ecstasies: Drawings by Auguste Rodin*, exh. cat., ed. Thomas Lederballe (Copenhagen: Statens Museum for Kunst, 2016), 171.

45. Varnedoe, "Rodin as a Draftsman," 27.

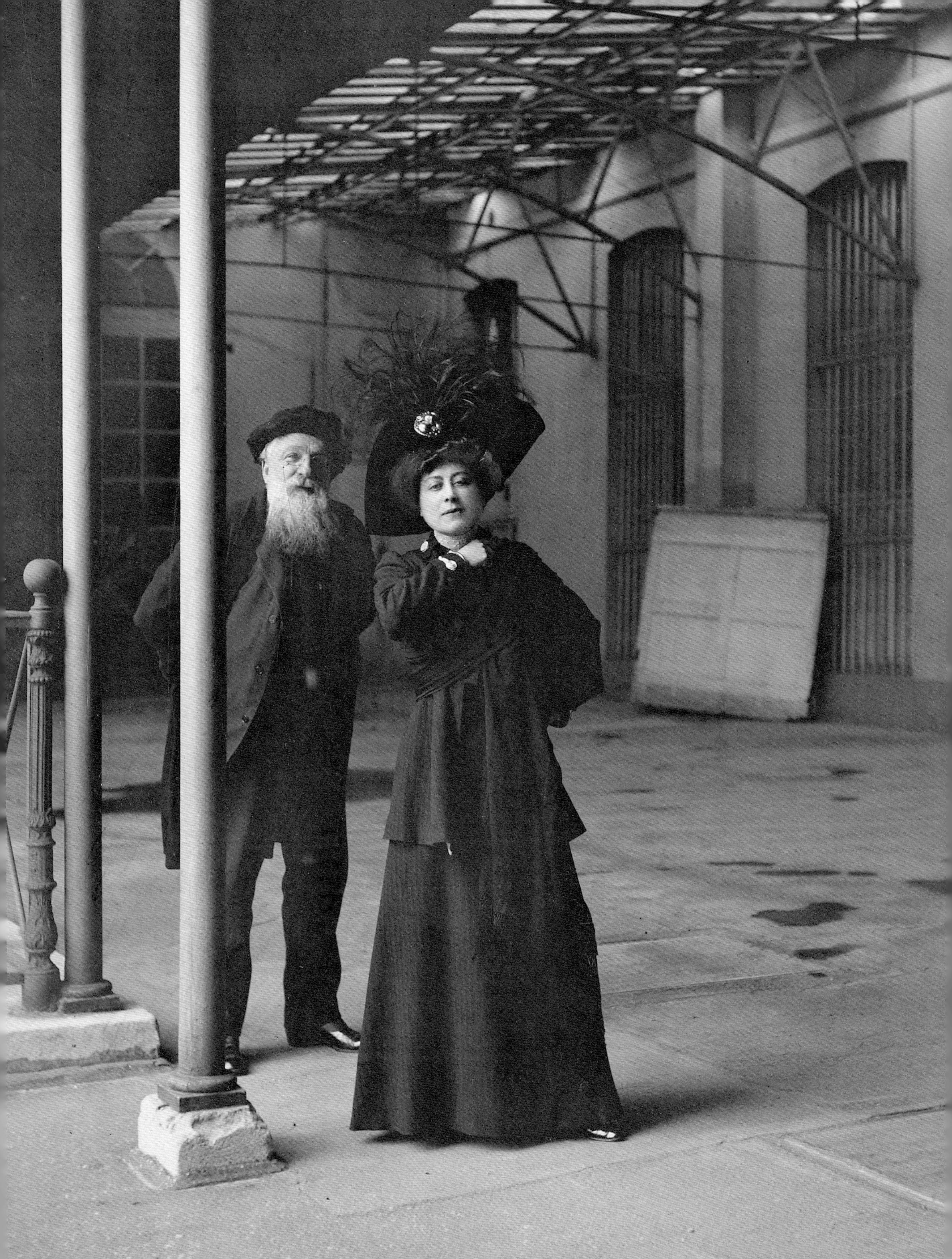

RODIN'S AMERICAN CIRCLE

VÉRONIQUE MATTIUSSI

I wish to send, through my friend Miss Seaton-Schmidt, greetings to all my friends in America, and to express my profound gratitude for their sympathetic appreciation of my art; it has been a great encouragement to me. I sincerely admire your young country, which possesses a veritable thirst for the beautiful, and which will in time grasp and comprehend all that is greatest in art.
— Auguste Rodin

Rodin's contacts with the United States and their decisive role in the artist's critical reputation and the dissemination of his work are already well studied.[1] Still, the rich, comprehensive archive kept by the sculptor, put in order by his secretaries, and donated to the French government in 1916 permits a number of different approaches to understanding their significance—chronological, quantitative, comparative. In addition, with its total of 8,473 correspondents, the archive invites us to reconsider the contours and specifics of a vast political, economic, social, artistic, and literary panorama, a web of late nineteenth-century international and cosmopolitan society—really, all of Paris and the entire world.

By considering the Americans in Rodin's entourage and enlarging the scope of our investigation to include both individuals peripheral to his orbit and evidence beyond the Rodin archive, we can understand the challenges confronting an artist who was all powerful in France but now facing an unknown situation with curiosity. He was attracted to this nation, paradoxically felt to be both barren and fertile, sensing the importance of its wild scent of power, progress, and emancipation. Forced to adapt to these new realities, Rodin ended up reinventing himself.

Henri Manuel (French, 1874–1947), *Portrait of Rodin and the Duchess of Choiseul*, c. 1909–10. Gelatin silver print, sheet: 8 7/16 × 6 in. (21.5 × 15.2 cm); mat: 13 × 9 15/16 in. (33 × 25.2 cm). Musée Rodin, Paris. Ph.00056.

A DECISIVE MEETING

The history of Rodin in the United States may have begun in Philadelphia in 1876, where Rodin showed eight of his works, but his first true encounter with America took place twelve years later. A series of visits by the sculptor Truman H. Bartlett in late 1887 and early 1888 marked the real beginning of Rodin's US connections. Our inquiry will conclude with Rodin's 1912 break with Claire de Choiseul (fig. 4.1), the artist's American-born lover, who contributed so much to the advancement of his career in the United States—and in general. While the full story exceeds these chronological limits, these two key moments involving two key figures essentially define Rodin's American relationships. Between these dates, who were the Americans interested in Rodin and viewing his works? When did this happen, and why?

The crucial encounter with Bartlett was a milestone, since Bartlett would publish, a year later, ten long and thoroughly documented articles in an art magazine called the *American Architect and Building News*, giving the essentials of the interviews he conducted with Rodin during his successive visits.[2] Bartlett's extensive time in Rodin's studio gave him unique and intimate access, inviting confessions from the sculptor, and his detailed records covered both Rodin's work and his life. Bartlett discussed the genesis of the sculptures—both their physical realization and their symbolic inspiration; the workings of Rodin's creative genius; and the personal qualities of the man himself. The articles, which gave pride of place to *The Gates of Hell*, offered unprecedented documentation of the beginnings of Rodin's career.

With this major, pioneering interview series, Bartlett helped construct the legend of the sculptor for his American readers. The Boston magazine in which he published the articles was in a large format and boasted a circulation of 7,500 copies around 1890—modest by American standards, but still respectable, even remarkable, for that type of periodical and given the quality of its contents.[3] With the serial publication of Bartlett's interviews—attracting major interest and academic enough in character to constitute, in effect, the first real monograph on the artist—Rodin crossed the Atlantic.[4] Despite a lukewarm and timid start, and battered throughout by cultural differences, each step of this crossing was a chance to elucidate Rodin's art further until it could win unparalleled and unwavering enthusiasm.

THE ARCHIVAL RECORD

A global and statistical approach to the artist's archive provides a broad, rich panorama of new lessons. Rodin's correspondents can be identified as coming from forty-four countries; France alone, unsurprisingly, accounts for almost half of the correspondents, but the United Kingdom, United States, and Germany are the three best-represented foreign countries, constituting five, four, and four percent of the correspondents, respectively. But the profile of these correspondents differs by nation.

In Germany, it was intellectuals, men of letters, and philosophers who took an early interest in Rodin, whereas in Italy, for example, it was the journalistic world, while many of his other correspondents were models. In England, Rodin was particularly appreciated, even adored, by the ruling class and intellectuals, in a society divided between an aristocracy with out-of-date but still powerful traditions and a flourishing upper-middle class. But above all, Rodin's many visits across the English Channel allowed him to cultivate bonds of friendship.

We should note that there were artists among the correspondents in all the countries where people were interested in Rodin. They figured among Rodin's main American correspondents, and many, like Lorado Taft, came to Paris to the sacred warehouse of marbles at 182 rue de l'Université, where Rodin received visitors every Saturday. The dancers Loïe Fuller and Isadora Duncan and the photographers Edward Steichen (figs. 4.2, 4.3) and Alfred Stieglitz rubbed shoulders with the sculptor there too. Primarily known for their art, some did not hesitate to boldly suggest business ventures and publicize the wealth at their disposal. But this mix of social activities with the rise of a new and unbridled economy around art surprised Rodin and sometimes created misunderstandings. From the outset, there were crucial differences between Rodin and the Americans simply because, as Bartlett complained of his compatriots, "Money is our God."[5] The uninhibited audacity of the business world, where one spoke openly of money and finance, clashed with Rodin's clearly disinterested vision and the amateurism of his business practices.

As more and more orders arrived from the United States, Rodin suddenly found himself needing to respond to new and unprecedented demand for his art. Loïe Fuller organized a showing of eighteen sculptures and seventeen of his drawings in 1903, at the National Arts Club in New York; in January 1908, Steichen and Stieglitz presented fifty-eight drawings at the Photo-Secession Gallery. In the latter case, the drawings, exclusively of female nudes with lascivious attitudes and very free poses, disconcerted a public that was traditionally puritanical and unprepared, to say the least, for this body of work. US artistic customs, values, and principles faced a challenge from Rodin's drawings; their sensuality was not considered appropriate by American tastes. But a shift was underway, a movement launched, leading to the Armory Show of 1913; if these exhibitions broke various codes of decorum, they also unquestionably charted the path toward a modern art on American soil.

FIG. 4.2

Edward J. Steichen (American, 1879–1973), *Self-Portrait with Brush and Palette*, 1902. Photogravure, 11 ¹⁵⁄₁₆ × 8 ¹⁄₁₆ in. (30.4 × 20.5 cm). Musée Rodin, Paris. Ph.02808.

FIG. 4.3

Edward J. Steichen, *Rodin—The Thinker*, 1902. Gum bichromate print, 10 ¼ × 12 ¹¹⁄₁₆ in. (26 × 32.2 cm). Musée Rodin, Paris. Ph.00217.

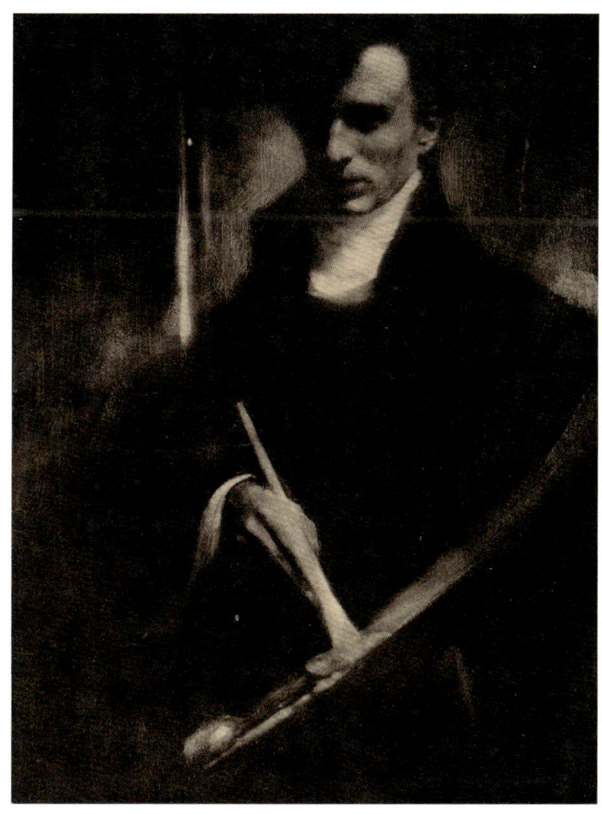

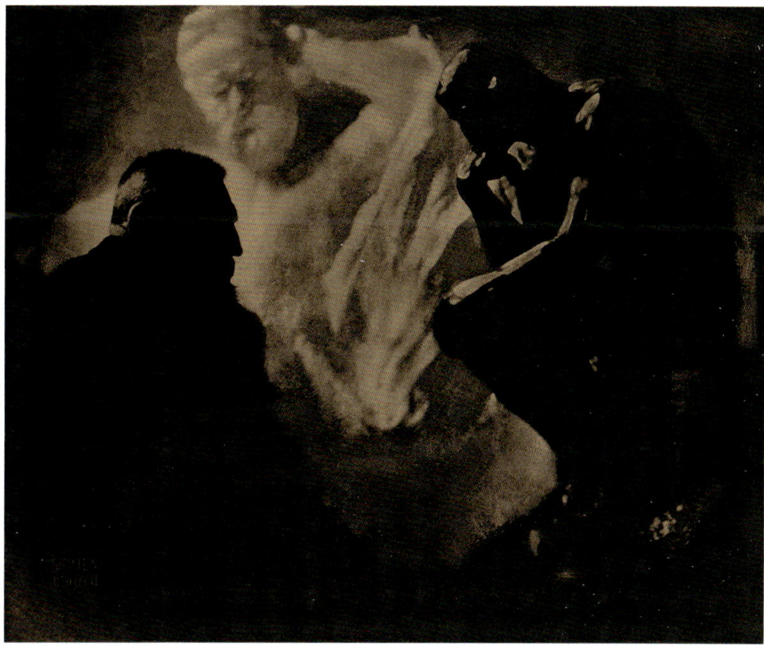

An artist's lucky star also encompasses the quality of the people around him. Rodin effortlessly attracted people of quality from every sphere, whether the most prominent or those with a promising future and whose commitment to him remained unflagging. The American collectors were essential here—first and foremost, they were the ones who defined a taste for Rodin's work and spearheaded that work's dissemination. In the 1890s, the possessors of the new fortunes created by industrialization saw Rodin as a way to symbolize their wealth and dignity. Initially, many of them commissioned portrait busts by the sculptor. At the turn of the century, and after his exhibition at the Pavillon de l'Alma on the sidelines of the Paris Exposition Universelle in 1900, Rodin's star continued to climb, and this first trend gave way to the acquisition of flagship works. Bertha Palmer, Thomas Fortune Ryan, Edward Henry Harriman, Katherine (Kate) Seney Simpson, and many others made this shift, along with fervent admirers and middlemen such as Sara Tyson Hallowell, Loïe Fuller, and the dealers Paul Durand-Ruel and Roland Knoedler. The close relationships between American museums and American private collectors naturally favored the American institutionalization of Rodin's works.

NEW PERSPECTIVES ON A LARGER SCALE

Rodin was now a world figure, traveling from one capital city to the next, receiving tributes, selling his works to the most important museums, and spending much—perhaps too much—of his time as his own agent.[6] He made more and more conquests, attracted by the easy pleasures of a worldly life, before falling for the impulsive American-born duchesse de Choiseul, who made him exchange his workman's tunic for the outfit of the perfect gentleman.[7]

During her involvement with Rodin, Claire de Choiseul noticed the emergence of these new clients and was the first to sense their full potential. Her grandfather had left France in 1824 to settle in New York and start a family. There, he raised his three sons, who would found the law firm Coudert Brothers in 1857; Charles Coudert, Claire's father, was a prominent New York lawyer. Claire had kept a valuable address book from her youth, and she used it to her partner's advantage, taking control of his business as a matter of course and quickly upending Rodin's slowly and laboriously established business methods, for instance by drastically raising the price of his sculptures.[8]

Rodin wondered about the prices other artists charged and asked the member of parliament Paul d'Estournelles de Constant (fig. 4.4), known for his efforts promoting French art abroad, for information: "Excuse my delay," d'Estournelles de Constant replied,

> but I was away, and then I wanted to make sure to get my information from a good source, because you are in an awkward situation. Here is what I have found out and what I think. First, you have to arrange everything properly, and for that you need to refer to your commissions while executing the projects. Second, you mustn't accept for a single bust any less than Chartran gets for a portrait!!![9] Now Chartran receives 25,000 francs; my American friends think you should get forty to fifty thousand francs, that is to say eight to ten thousand dollars, probably eight rather than ten for a large bust, six for a small one. If they ask you for a copy later, you can decide what to do, but I would say: My price is no less than 40,000 francs for a large bust. They don't care about paying one or two thousand dollars more, I think. And it's important that you not be demoted to a lower level of artist.[10]

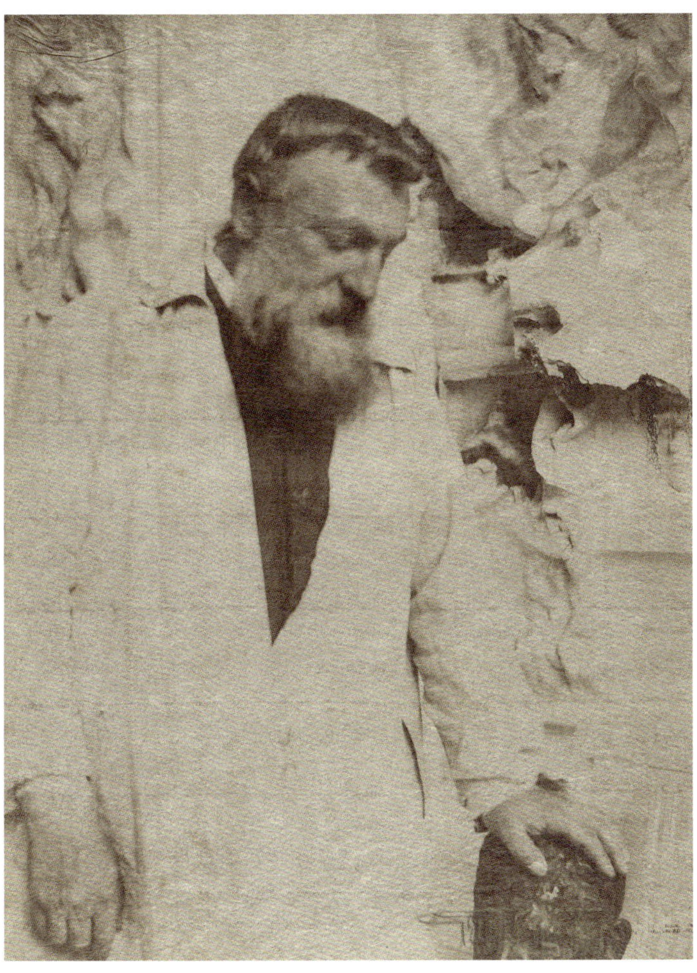

Gertrude Käsebier (American, 1852–1934), *Rodin with the Gates of Hell, His Left Hand Resting on the Bronze Bust of Baron d'Estournelles de Constant*, 1905. Photograph, sheet: 8 5/8 × 6 5/16 in. (22 × 16 cm); mat: 12 3/8 × 9 9/16 in. (31.5 × 24.3 cm). Musée Rodin, Paris. Ph.00241.

And so, in 1907, Joseph Pulitzer accepted without complaint or negotiation Rodin's terms for two versions of his bust, one in marble, the other bronze, for 35,000 francs, since the press magnate was, "like all American millionaires, . . . in a great hurry."[11] Ryan accepted the same terms in 1910, adding 10,000 francs for a second, greatly modified bronze version, and another 10,000 francs for a copy in silver. The vast fortune of Edward Henry Harriman, who owned a third of the railroads in the United States, certainly sufficed to convince Rodin to agree to make his bust, for the sum of 40,000 francs.[12] "Last week I went to see Rodin, who is still doing his Americans," Rainer Maria Rilke wrote in a letter, "and [he] really has a series of good strong portraits there now. How good it is that he has to do people . . . [staying] very close to the job, so that he has to graze around nearby, like a tightly tethered goat that has no choice farther afield."[13] Rodin permanently adopted Claire de Choiseul's inflated prices for works destined for the United States: "I was tempted to do portraits and nothing but portraits for enormous sums offered to me by American millionaires and their wives," Rodin admitted. "How do you say no to a man who hands you a blank check?"[14]

Through her connections, her family, and her perfect command of the English language, Claire de Choiseul easily ingratiated herself with ambassadors, industrialists and financiers, and numerous institutions and groups. And while the high-society invitations, honorary titles, and celebrations from the United States continued to multiply through her influence, they would also outlast her relationship with Rodin. The sales she orchestrated allowed him to reorganize his affairs and be assured of a comfortable income.

It was easy to convince Rodin of the economic advantages of these new arrangements, but he was even more intent on controlling his reputation. So when, in 1910, Paul Gsell planned to write an article devoted to French art in the United States,[15] Rodin became involved: "Before you publish your article in the *Journal*," Rodin wrote, "please come see me. I still have some names to give you and I hope you can read your finished article to me."[16] Gsell wrote back to reassure him the next day: "I praised Mr. Ryan for it [his involvement in defense of Rodin in the United States] and I emphasized the educational value that Americans see in the collection of your works. In short, I followed exactly the directions you so kindly gave me."[17]

During this same time, Gsell was actively working on publishing his own interviews with Rodin.[18] The artist was neither very interested in nor very helpful on that project, because, however eager he was to get media coverage, he did not yet see the signs of his success abroad. However, publishers in the same three countries listed above — the United Kingdom, Germany, and the United States — began planning translations as soon as the book was issued, scheduling publications and arranging numerous potential translators to take on the project.[19] A first German edition in February 1912 was followed at the end of the year by a second; at almost the same time, in November 1912, a British edition appeared, and the prestigious American publishing house Small, Maynard and Company published the book in Boston. They had bought the US rights and claimed, thanks to reproductions from the Metropolitan Museum of

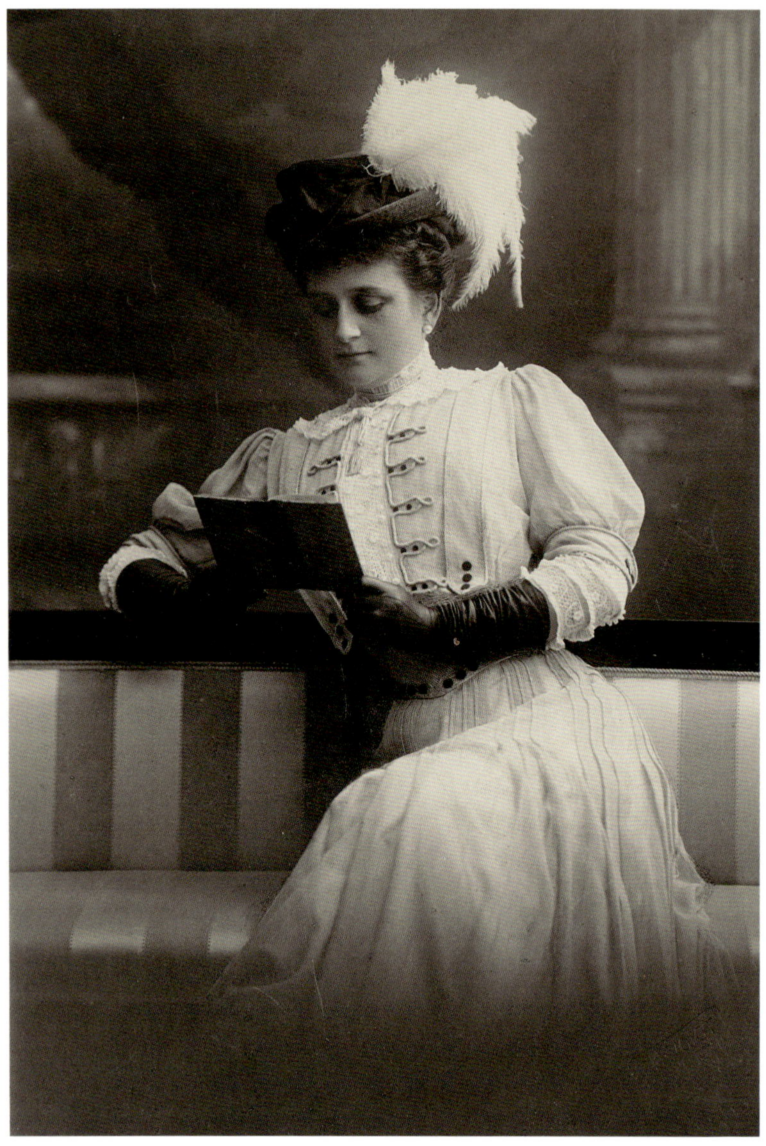

Art in New York, to be publishing "a more comprehensive edition of your book than either the English or the French edition."[20]

That same year, a New York publisher, Dodd, Mead and Company, put out another edition. Even more significant was the inexpensive third edition, published three years later in Boston,[21] "and [it] will we expect be much in demand for use by art students as well as lovers of art in general and admirers of your own work in particular."[22] Rodin used his book strategically, intending it for his professional, political, commercial, and social contacts without ever sending copies to his inner circle of friends. He sent it to the director of the Metropolitan Museum, Edward Robinson,[23] and to Francis Dawson,[24] a journalist and diplomat who was considering a similar publication for which he would share half the profits with the artist. Rodin's great admirer Sara Tyson Hallowell helped circulate the book, offering "countless copies to discerning friends."[25] Mary Hopkins, Malvina Hoffman, Kate Seeney Simpson (fig. 4.5), and others received autographed copies, and all were delighted to be getting such direct access to the master's thought.

Former First Lady Edith Kermit Roosevelt, who visited Rodin's home in Meudon in 1910, epitomizes the nature of his American connections, who were powerful and compelling figures on the whole, although his frequent correspondents were unusually diverse. There were admirers, artists, journalists, collectors, institutions, and a host of middlemen. Altogether, he exchanged letters with around four hundred individuals from the United States, enough to ensure Rodin's lasting influence in America, though there is nothing especially intimate in these letters. Despite some close relationships with Americans—mainly with artists[26]—geographical distance,[27] mutual ignorance of one another's languages, and cultural differences generally kept Americans out of Rodin's private circle. Rodin's relationship with the United States, while valuable to him, was modest and restrained, courteous rather than close. It would nonetheless prove faithful and lasting, continuing to deepen beyond his lifetime as Rodin became the best-represented French sculptor in the United States.

Epigraph: Auguste Rodin, "To the Venus de Milo," *Art and Progress* 3, no. 2 (December 1911): 409. Anna Seaton Schmidt (1859–1924), an American journalist and art historian, devoted numerous articles and lectures to Rodin. She proposed herself as a translator for Paul Gsell's book of interviews with Rodin, published in 1911, and repeatedly considered translating other books about him. It was she who translated the article by Rodin cited here, originally published as "A la Vénus de Milo" in *L'art et les artistes* (March 1910).

1. See Ruth Butler, *Rodin: The Shape of Genius* (New Haven, CT: Yale University Press, 1993); and Bernard Barryte, ed., *Rodin and America: Influence and Adaptation 1876–1936*, exh. cat. (Stanford, CA: Iris and B. Gerald Cantor Center for Visual Arts, Stanford University, 2011).

2. Truman H. Bartlett, "Auguste Rodin, Sculptor," *American Architect and Building News* 25, nos. 682–703 (January 19–June 15, 1889).

3. *American Architect and Building News* was the first American periodical devoted to architecture. The weekly was supported by the "Architects' lobbyist," a spokesman for the American Institute of Architects, which also contributed to the publication's success. In addition to architecture, the journal focused on art in general and aesthetics in particular, paying close attention to European innovations.

4. Truman H. Bartlett would also spread word of Rodin's work in a series of lectures in 1893. In 1903, he made a plan to gather his articles into a book illustrated with photographs of Rodin's works. Archives du musée Rodin, Paris.

5. Truman H. Bartlett to Auguste Rodin, June 3, 1905, Archives du musée Rodin, Paris.

6. William Rothenstein, *Men and Memories* (London: Faber and Faber, 1931–32), 2:45–46.

7. Born in the United States in 1864, Claire Coudert grew up in a wealthy family of French origin. In 1891, she married the Marquis Charles de Choiseul-Beaupré in New York; he would become duke (and she would obtain the title of duchess) in 1909. After their marriage, the Franco-American couple settled in France, where Claire proceeded to lead a life beguiled by various socialites but marred by the premature deaths of her children. She met Rodin in 1904 and became his mistress in 1907, remaining so until the summer of 1912.

8. "He [Rodin] is perfectly buzzy about his contracts; keeps no books or memoranda; forgets all he says, and has not the least idea of doing what is promised." Henry Adams to Henry Lee Higginson, July 12, 1902, in *The Letters of Henry Adams*, vol. 5, *1899–1905* (Cambridge, MA: Belknap Press of Harvard University Press, 1988), 390–91.

9. Théobald Chartran (1849–1907), a student of Alexandre Cabanel's, was a history and genre painter, recipient of many awards, and among the most fashionable portrait painters of his time. He epitomizes the painting of the Academic School.

10. Paul d'Estournelles de Constant to Auguste Rodin, September 26, 1906, Archives du musée Rodin, Paris.

11. Stephen MacKenna to Auguste Rodin, n.d., Archives du musée Rodin, Paris. For comparison, Rodin had asked 8,000 francs for a plaster and bronze of the bust of Arthur Jerome Eddy (cat. 7) in 1898.

12. At the request of Harriman's daughter Mary, shortly after his death on September 9, 1909.

13. Rainer Maria Rilke to Clara Rilke, November 3, 1909, in *Letters of Rainer Maria Rilke, 1892–1910*, tr. Jane Bannard Greene and M. D. Herter Norton (New York: W. W. Norton, 1945), 351.

14. Frank Harris, *Contemporary Portraits* (New York: M. Kennerley, 1915), 325, quoted in Frederic V. Grunfeld, *Rodin: A Biography* (New York: Henry Holt, 1987), 569.

15. "Un triomphe pour l'Art français aux États-Unis," *Le Journal*, September 5, 1910. Gsell describes his encounter with Thomas Fortune Ryan and his role in the development of the Rodin Galleries at the Metropolitan Museum of Art in New York.

16. Auguste Rodin to Paul Gsell, September 3, 1910, private collection.

17. Gsell to Rodin, September 4, 1910, Archives du musée Rodin, Paris.

18. Auguste Rodin, *L'art, entretiens réunis par Paul Gsell* (Paris: Bernard Grasset, 1911).

19. Kattarine Fedden would eventually be the translator. She had been recommended to Rodin by Alexander Harrison in late 1911 (Archives du musée Rodin, Paris). Fedden thanked Rodin on January 6, 1912, and sent the finished product to the artist via the publishing house in January 1913. It is now kept in the library of the Musée Rodin (Inv. 368).

20. Ralph Tracy Hale to Auguste Rodin, January 23, 1913, Archives du musée Rodin, Paris.

21. Also by Small, Maynard and Company.

22. Hale to Rodin, May 26, 1916, Paris, Archives du musée Rodin, Paris.

23. [The director's secretary] to Auguste Rodin, July 5, 1911, Archives du musée Rodin, Paris.

24. This copy is in the David M. Rubenstein Rare Book and Manuscript Library in Durham, North Carolina.

25. Sara Tyson Hallowell to Auguste Rodin, February 28, 1912, Archives du musée Rodin, Paris.

26. I am referring to contacts with Americans active in Paris or returning to the United States, such as Edward Steichen and Gutzon Borglum.

27. "Despite all the kind offers I have received, I really cannot have the pleasure of seeing you in Pittsburgh. I dare not undertake the trip because I am afraid it will be too physically tiring, because of the sea and the long crossing." Auguste Rodin to John Alexander, February 19, 1907, AM 16463, Princeton University, Alexander Autograph Collection.

**PART I
1885–
1915**

THE ERA OF
COLLECTORS

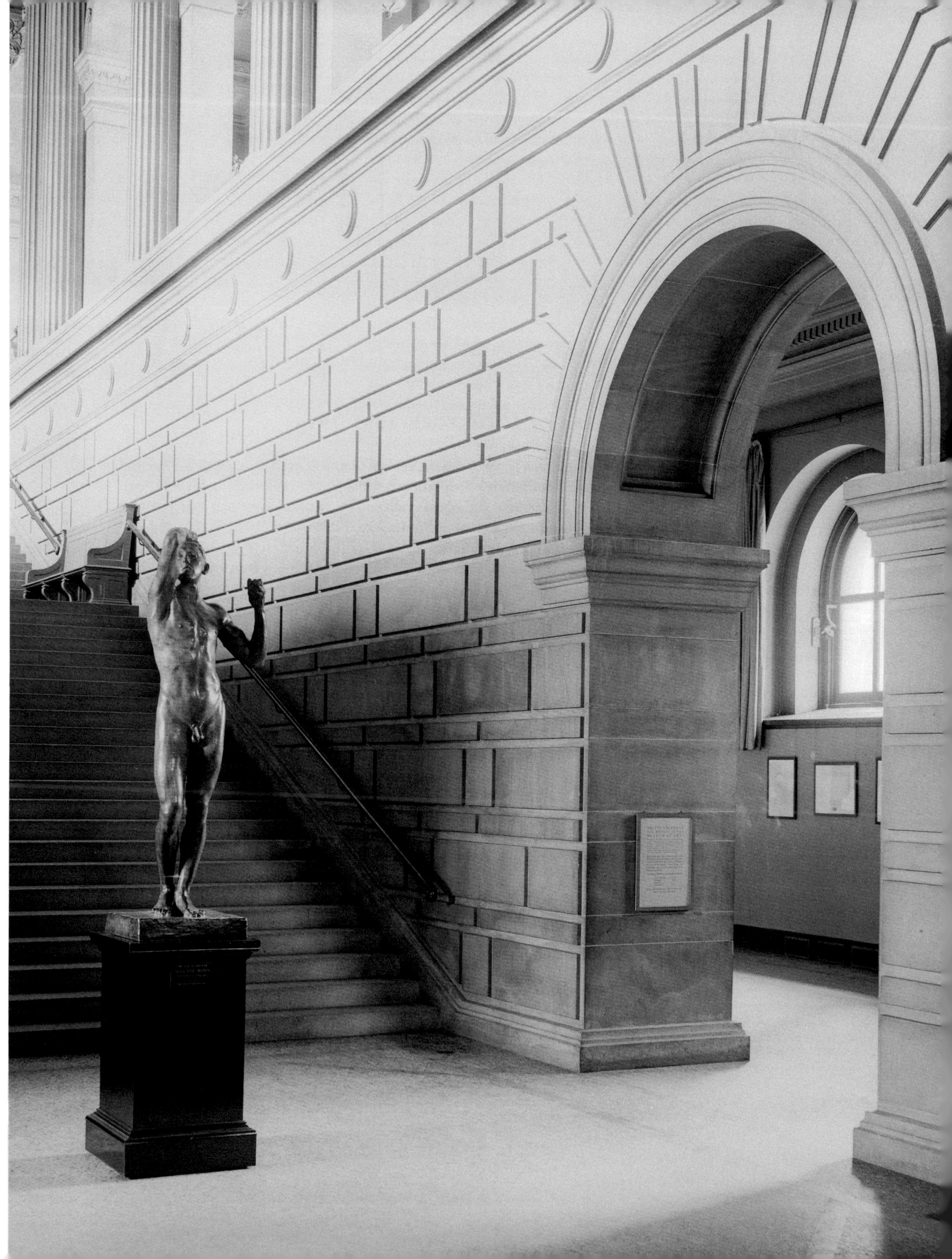

FIGURE SKETCH

c. 1898–1900
Graphite with stumping on wove paper
11 ½ × 7 ¼ in. (29.2 × 18.4 cm)
Dedicated and signed in graphite at lower right:
aux Etats Unis / Auguste Rodin / reconnaissance
Smithsonian American Art Museum,
Washington, DC
Gift of the Republic of France, 1915.11.70

The gift of *Figure Sketch* "with appreciation"
to the United States recalls the gift of Rodin's
bust *La France* (bronze, c. 1903–12) to
the American people in 1912 by the Comité
France-Amérique on the occasion of the
tercentenary of the discovery of Lake
Champlain. In the midst of the First World
War, *Figure Sketch* entered the collection of
the Smithsonian American Art Museum in
Washington, DC, together with three albums
containing a collection of eighty-two works
in crayon, pastel, charcoal, sanguine, pen
and ink, watercolor, and engraving, as well
as an album of letters by eminent French
statesmen and writers. These were "presented to the Government of the United
States by the citizens of the French Republic
as a token of their appreciation of the action
taken by American citizens toward relieving
the distress occasioned by the European
war," according to Acting Secretary of State
Alvey A. Adee. "Placing a high value on the
portfolios [. . .] the [State] Department has
determined that the most appropriate place
for their preservation and exhibition is the
National Gallery of Art [the Smithsonian
American Art Museum] in the Capital of the
United States."[1] Rodin's drawing is one of
the few works sent by a sculptor, along with
a drawing by Jean-Antoine Injalbert, a
somewhat-forgotten artist today who created
the allegorical figures on the Pont Mirabeau
in Paris. The collection mainly contains
sketches of various subjects (many landscapes and portraits) by painters, including
friends of Rodin such as Albert Besnard,
who dedicated his *Three Portrait Heads of
a Woman* "*à nos fidèles amis les Américains*"
(to our faithful friends the Americans).
Other artists in Rodin's circle called upon
for this diplomatic gesture included Charles
Cottet, Jean-Paul Laurens, Jean-François
Raffaelli, and Alfred Roll.
CBU

1. Alvey A. Adee, Acting Secretary of State, to
Richard Rathbun, Acting Secretary, Smithsonian
Institute, July 23, 1915. Document graciously
provided by Emily Conforto, Archives of the
Smithsonian American Art Museum.

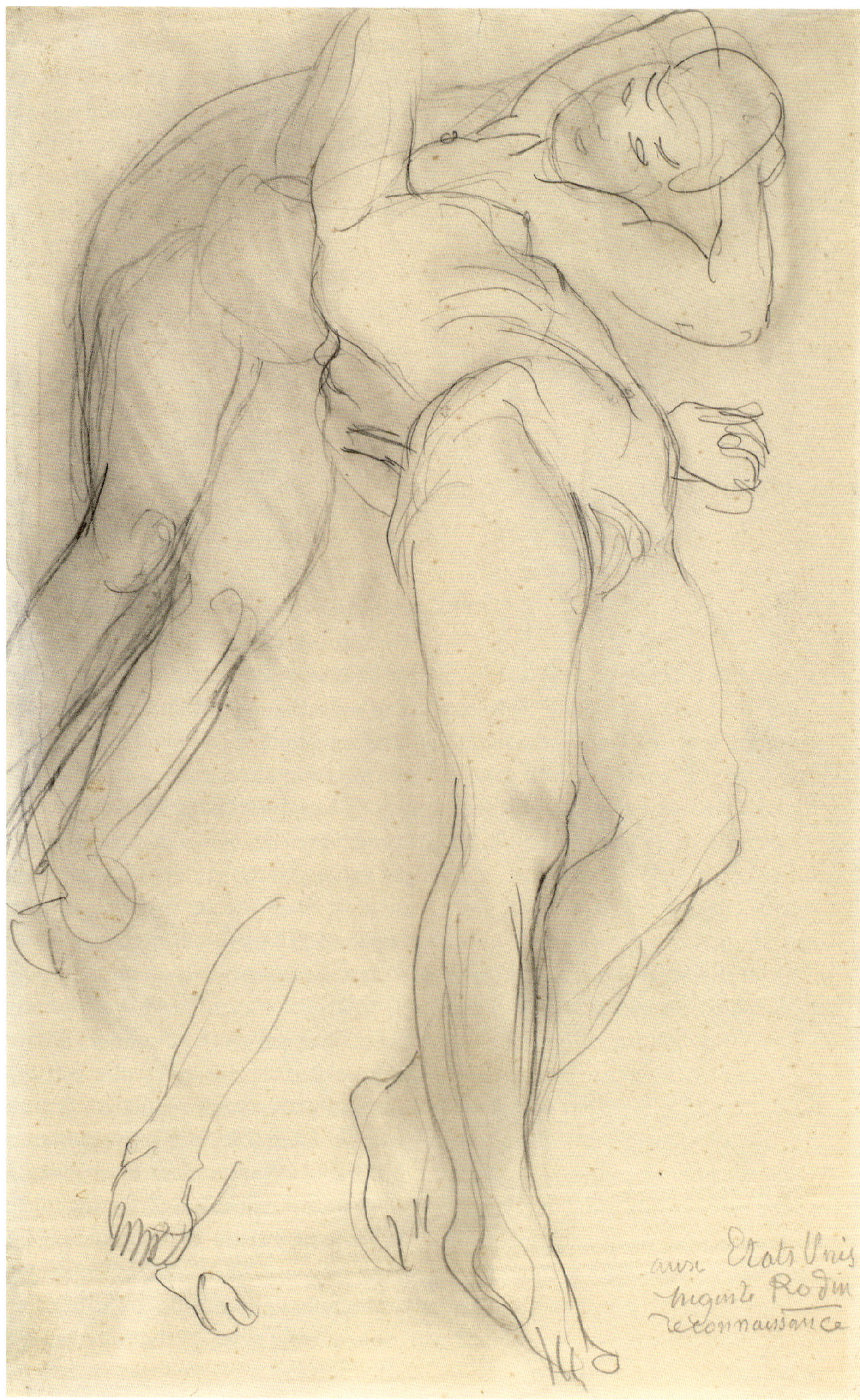

FALLEN CARYATID

Original model 1882
Marble, probably carved by Bozzoni, 1882–83
19 ¹¹⁄₁₆ × 12 × 10 ½ in. (50 × 30.48 × 26.67 cm)
Signed on base: *Rodin*
Museum of Fine Arts, Boston
Gift of the Estate of Samuel Isham through Julia Isham (Mrs. Henry Osborn Taylor), 17.3134

From the first time *Fallen Caryatid* was exhibited in Paris in 1883, the public interpreted this marble as an image of despair. When it was exhibited again in 1886, at Galerie Georges Petit, the journalist Émile Michelet suggested the title *Caryatid*, inspired by the first lines of Charles Baudelaire's poem "Le Guignon," which were inscribed on the base of the sculpture.[1] Michelet's title would be adopted about ten years later, for the Salon of 1897. This figure, overwhelmed by the weight of an ineluctable fate, would be positioned at the top of the left pilaster of the *Gates of Hell* around 1888.

This marble is probably the one that had belonged to the painter Jules Bastien-Lepage (1848–1884). On June 17, 1882, Rodin announced to Bastien-Lepage that "your marble is pretty much finished,"[2] and, in the *American Architect and Building News*, American sculptor Truman H. Bartlett later specified that Bastien-Lepage had acquired "a marble copy of the figure of *Sorrow* which he placed in his studio as the only piece of sculpture there."[3] One month later, he described the figure as "a young girl pressed down by a weight upon her shoulder."[4] The Museum of Fine Arts marble was a gift from the estate of New York painter and collector Samuel Isham (1855–1914), who was studying at the Academy Julian in Paris between 1885 and 1887. He undoubtedly acquired it at the time, which makes it the first artwork by Rodin to enter an American collection.

A receipt from the artisan Bozzoni, who carved the marble, suggests that the original project was likely modified during production to give the work a deeper meaning. On April 26, 1883, Bozzoni received 150 francs as "balance of payment for the crouching statue holding a vase."[5] But we know of no marble version of the *Fallen Caryatid* in which the figure is "holding a vase," and if we look closely at the Boston marble, we notice that unlike the other known versions, its stone is rounder and smoother at the bottom, while the upper part has been roughly chiseled to give it the appearance of raw material. Could there have originally been a vase here that gave the figure a

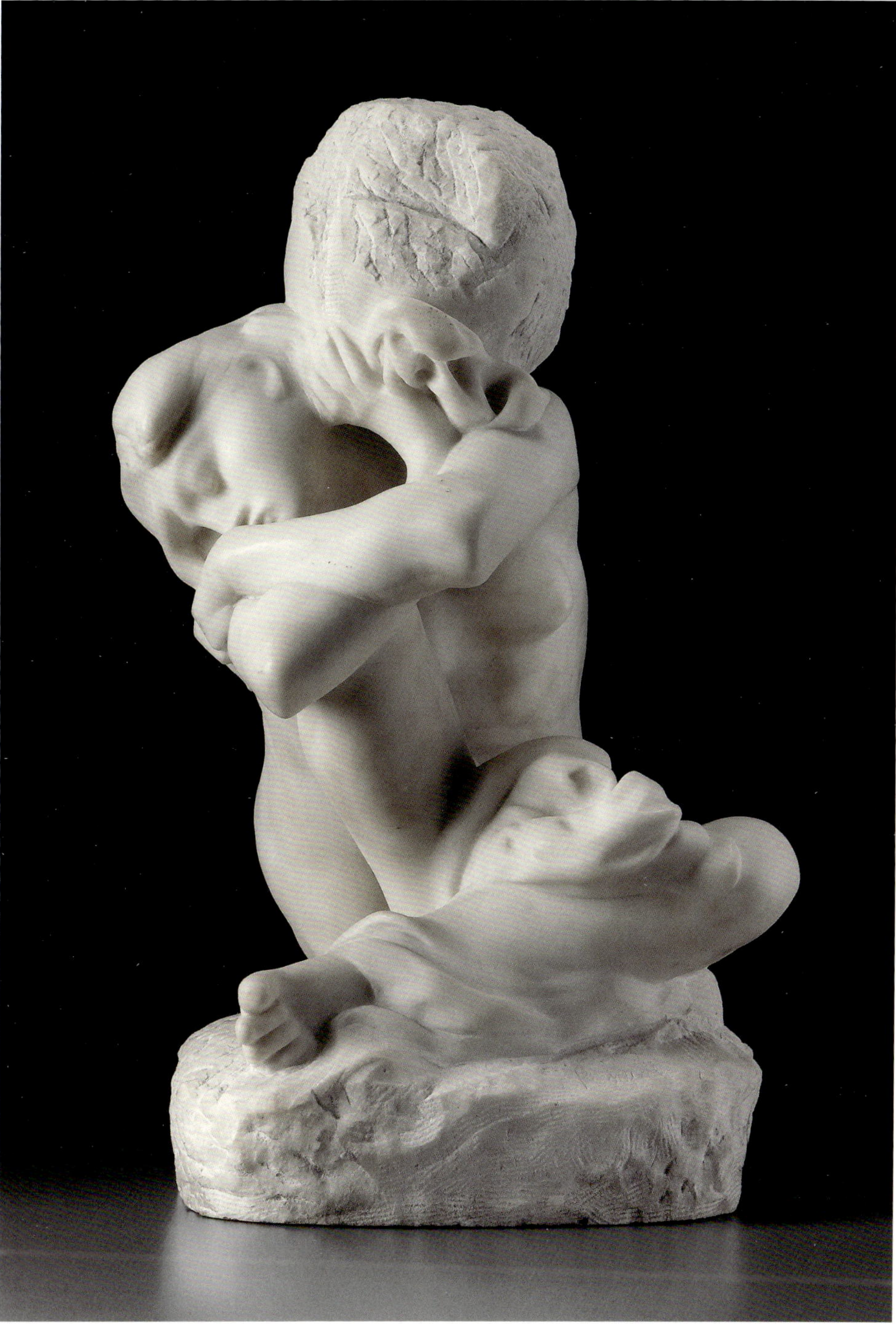

decorative aspect that Rodin wanted to eliminate?

Like the *Crouching Woman*, which it resembles, the *Fallen Caryatid* demonstrates the artist's knowledge of anatomy and modeling. Around 1881–82, in his enthusiasm for the commission of *The Gates of Hell*, Rodin produced a series of figures characterized by skillful composition and the representation of movement, which he used again later in assemblages. The *Fallen Caryatid* can, in fact, be recognized in *The Fallen Angel* (cat. 44).
ALNR

1. Émile Michelet, "Critique d'art: Le Salon de 1886, 2ème article," *La Jeune France*, July 1886, 772.
2. Auguste Rodin to Jules Bastien-Lepage, June 17, 1882, private collection.
3. Truman H. Bartlett, "Auguste Rodin, Sculptor," *American Architect and Building News* 25, no. 696 (April 27, 1889): 199.
4. Truman H. Bartlett, "Auguste Rodin, Sculptor," *American Architect and Building News* 25, no. 700 (May 25, 1889): 249.
5. Payment receipt addressed to Bozzoni, April 26, 1883, Archives du musée Rodin, Paris.

BUST OF ST. JOHN THE BAPTIST

Original model 1880
Bronze, cast by François Rudier (no marks), 1883
21 ³⁄₈ × 15 ³⁄₄ × 11 in. (54.3 × 40 × 27.9 cm)
Signed on base, under left shoulder: *A. Rodin*
Metropolitan Museum of Art, New York
Gift of Samuel P. Avery, 1893, 93.11

The first work by Rodin to enter an
American museum, this bronze bust of
St. John the Baptist was adapted from the
full-length figure, which is a bit larger than
life-size (height: 79 15/16 in. [203 cm]).
Based on an Italian peasant who had come to
Rodin's studio and posed naturally, the large
plaster model was shown at the Salon of
1880. The following year, Rodin exhibited
the bronze, which the French government
acquired for the Musée du Luxembourg.

That early bronze had been cast by
Charles-Adolphe Gruet, the first Parisian
founder whom Rodin called upon. Gruet also
produced a cast of the bust alone (today in
the Musée Rodin, Paris). A second cast, by
François Rudier, followed in 1883. This is
very likely the one that George A. Lucas,
an American dealer living in Paris, acquired
in 1888 (for 1,200 francs, whereas the cast
had cost only 250) and then sold to Samuel P.
Avery, who gave it to the Metropolitan
Museum of Art. Two more were produced
in 1891 and 1892, and one of these was
featured in the Second Annual Exhibition
of the National Sculpture Society in New
York in 1895 (see fig. 1.1). This bust offers
a good example of Rodin's policy toward
foundries. Rejecting the widespread practice
of producing unlimited editions among
foundries like Barbedienne or Thiébaut,
Rodin maintained control over the casts of
his works (with some exceptions, including
the reductions of the full figures *St. John
the Baptist* and *The Kiss*) and often changed
foundries between casts.

The *Bust of St. John the Baptist* is the
type of sculpture that pleased collectors.
The precise cast highlights the sculpture's
vigorous modeling and the artist's careful
attention to the beard and the hair, with
distinctly individualized strands of hair.
This work recalls bronzes from the Italian
Renaissance, which inspired Rodin very
directly at this time when his goal was
to establish himself in the Salon and obtain
commissions from the French government.
ALNR

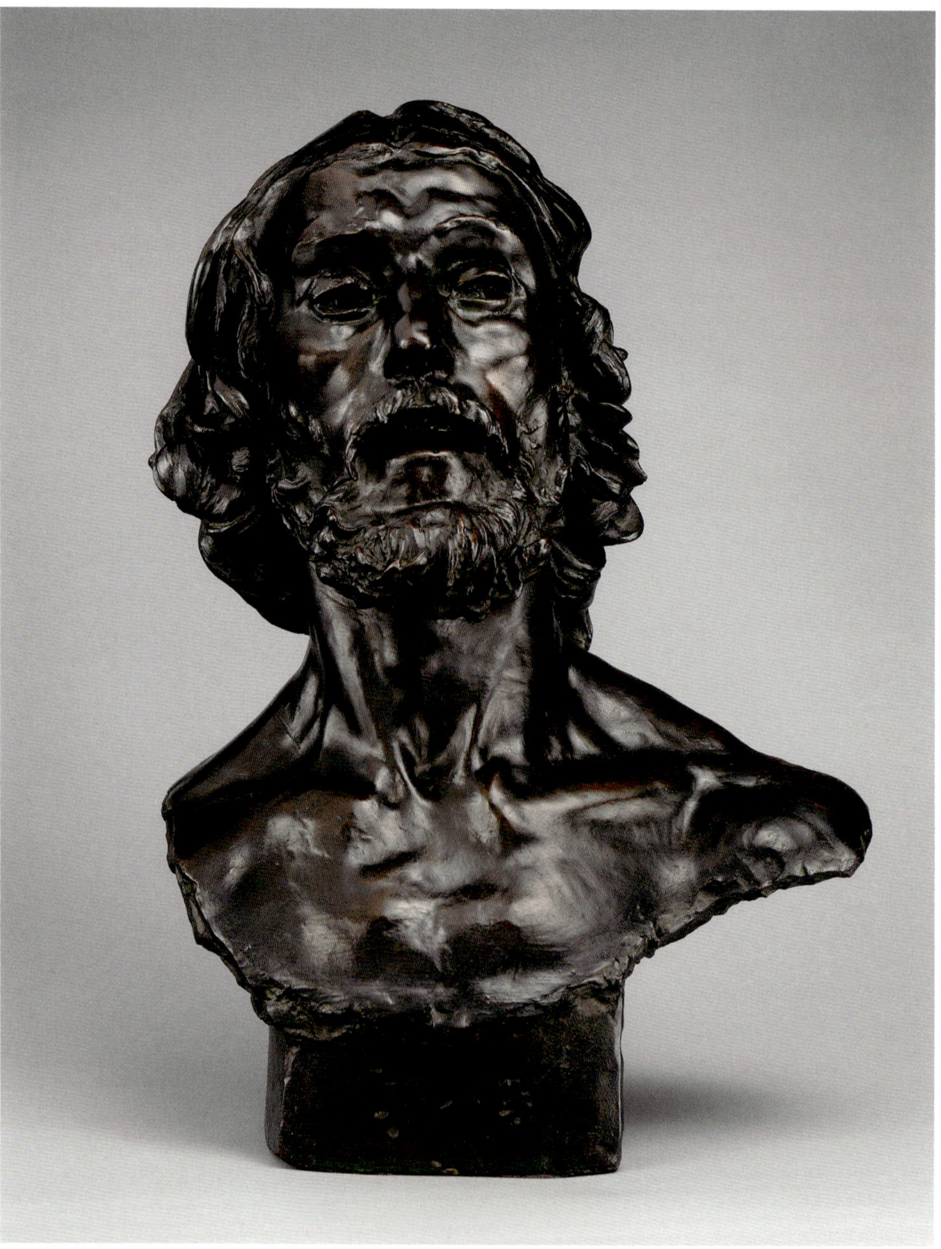

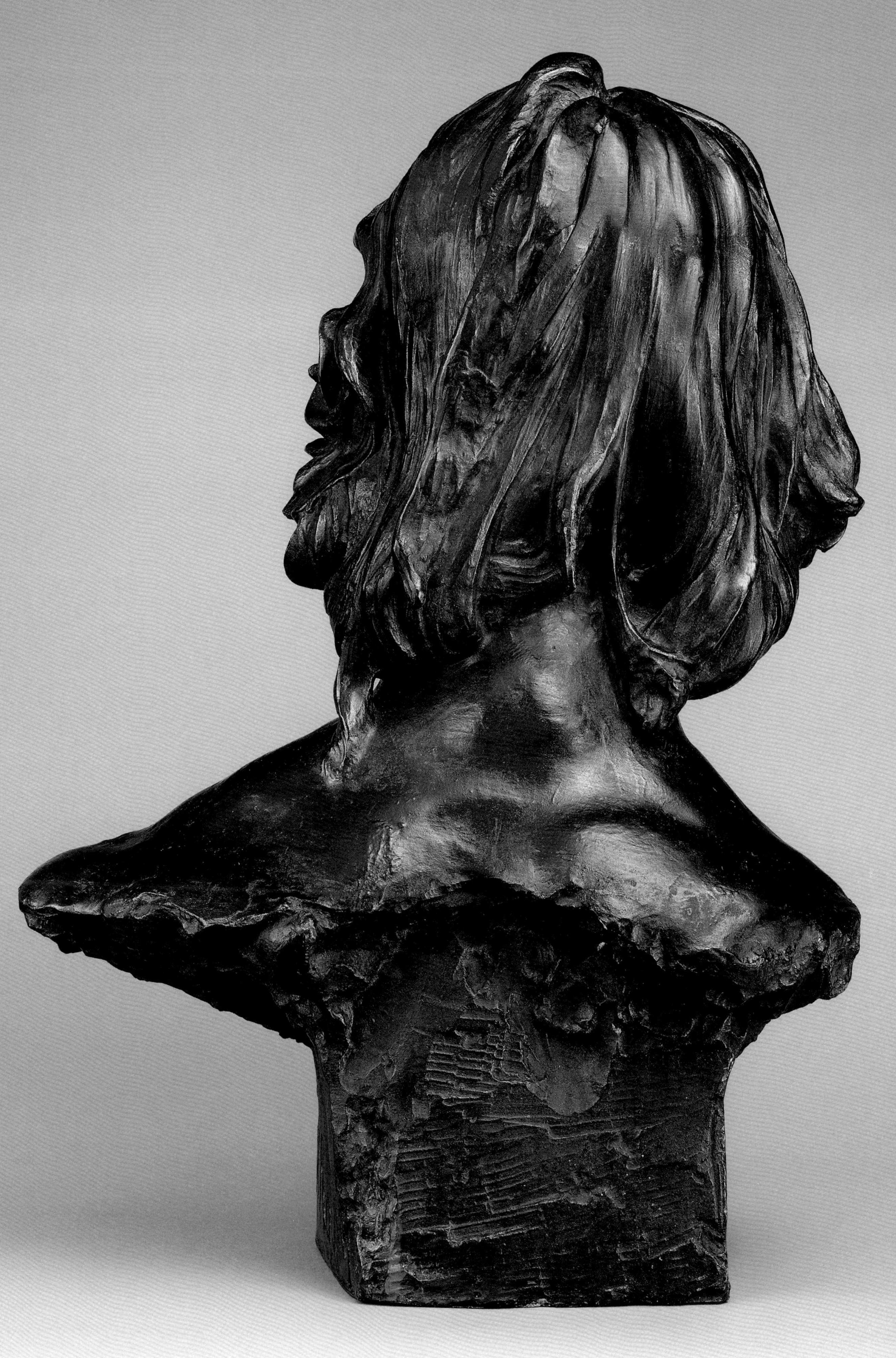

CUPID AND PSYCHE

Before 1886
Marble
With wooden base, 9 × 27 ½ × 17 ¾ in.
(22.9 × 69.9 × 45.1 cm)
Signed on side of base, near figures' feet:
A. Rodin
Iris Cantor Collection

Cupid and Psyche (or *Amour et Psyché*, sometimes also called *Psyché et Cupidon*), is one of three marbles exhibited during the 1893 Chicago World's Fair in *Loan Collection: Foreign Masterpieces Owned in the United States* and moved, after a few days on view, into a space that was accessible only upon request; they were considered too suggestive for the general public.[1] In the official catalogue, it was titled *Francesca and Paolo*,[2] as was the group known today as *Fugit Amor* (cat. 6). One reviewer interpreted these works as two successive stages in the story of the famous couple, with the first expressing the "illicit rapture of the lovers" and the second "their eternal torture and hopelessness."[3]

Connected to *The Gates of Hell*, the two groups date to the mid-1880s. An article published in 1886 by the journalist Gustave Geffroy, a great admirer of Rodin, makes it possible to identify *Cupid and Psyche* as one of the "marble sketches" exhibited at Galerie Georges Petit in Paris in 1886:

A couple is lying on bare ground that is sparsely sprinkled with a few leaves. Their cheeks touch, their hands move forward. The man, with one hand raised and his arm under the woman's head, while his other arm surrounds her torso, moves both abruptly and with delicate caution. The woman, as if sinking into the ground, one leg curved with instinctive, fleeting grace, draws her lover to her young breasts and throws her arms around his neck with ecstatic sweetness. The angular, hard lines, the powerful muscles, and the skin of both touch and blend together. They grasp each other with their entire arms, their entire bodies. It's the carnal intertwining of two beings who love and explore each other.[4]

Marbles of this type—exhibited at a commercial gallery and not at the official Salon—were intended for a clientele of private collectors who appreciated the quality of the execution as much as the passionate expression of the subject. Creating a connection with the elements of interior design they were called to be part of, they might be mounted on a finely crafted wooden base (as has fortunately been preserved, in this case). While we do not know what happened to the Chicago *Cupid and Psyche* after the exhibition in 1893, we can be sure that it quickly found its way to an art lover, leading Rodin to produce two more versions (Petit Palais, Paris; Metropolitan Museum of Art, New York).
ALNR

1. An anonymous account in the *Chicago Herald* describes the works as "wonderfully beautiful and executed with extraordinary delicacy" and laments that "the prudish and ignorant would have been revolted by their rigorous truthfulness." "Fought against Fate: The Struggle of the Sculptor Rodin," *Chicago Herald*, October 1, 1893.
2. The work, under the title *Francesca et Paolo*, was listed as "lent by Mr. Henry Sargent, New York" in *World's Columbian Exposition, 1893, Official Catalogue, Part X, Department K, Fine Arts* (Chicago: W. B. Conkey, 1893), 64, cat. 2,989. It appears under the same title, without mention of the lender, in the special catalogue *Loan Collection: Foreign Masterpieces Owned in the United States*, exh. cat. (Chicago: W. B. Conkey, 1893), cat. 123, http://archive.org/details /catalogueofunite00worl/page/8/mode/2up.
3. "Fought against Fate."
4. Gustave Geffroy, "Chronique Rodin," *La Justice*, July 11, 1886.

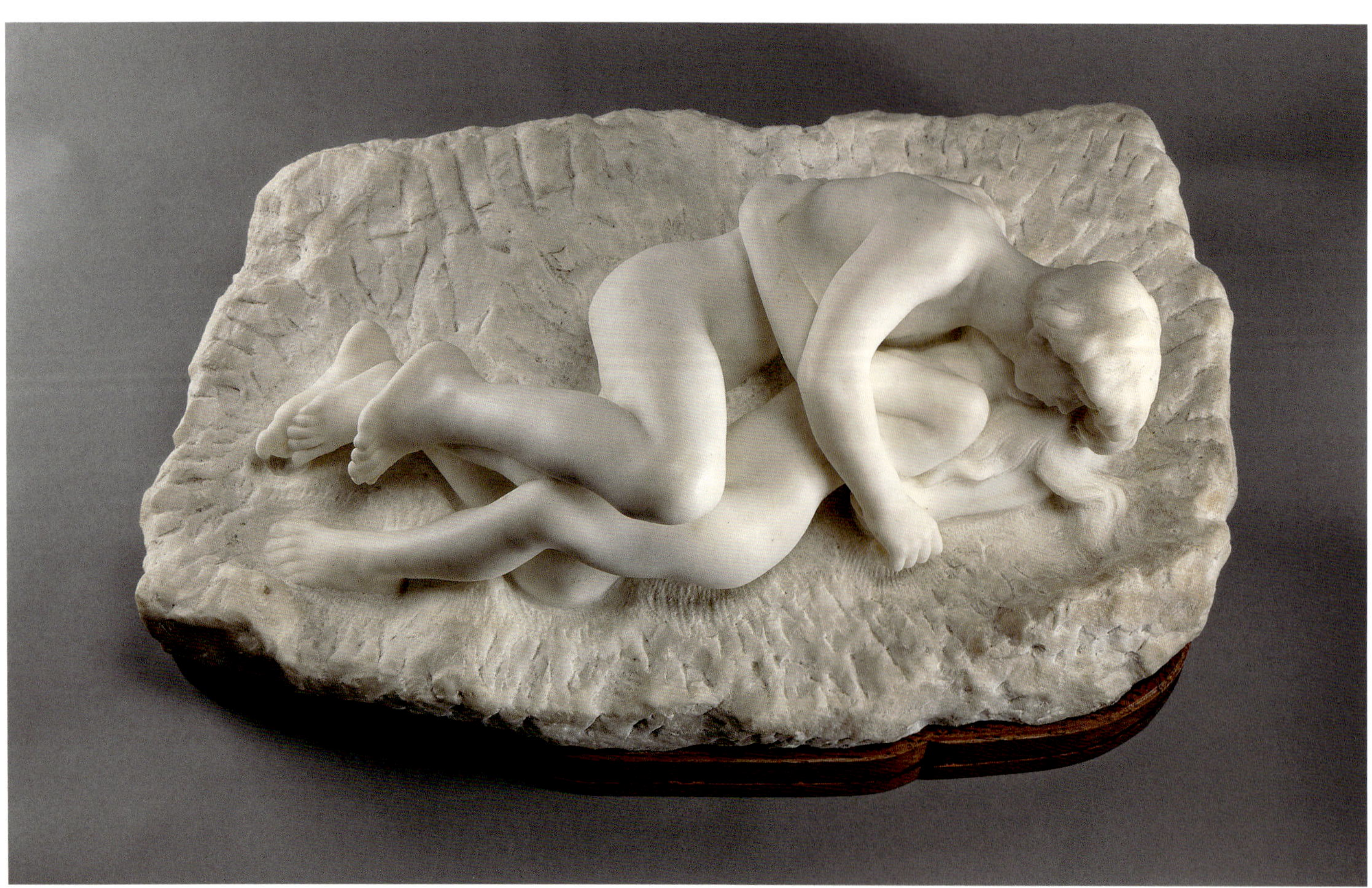

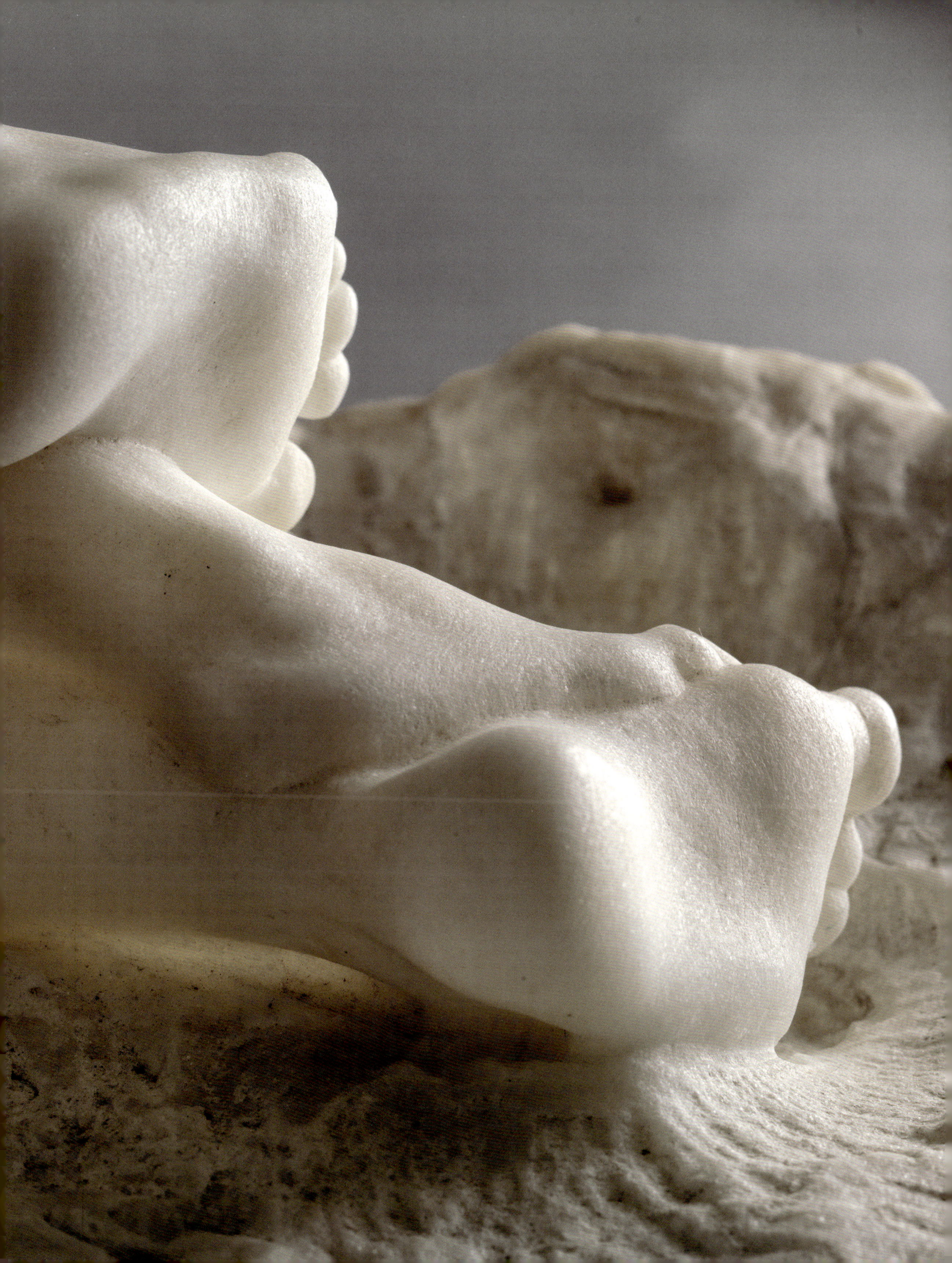

ASSEMBLAGE OF A WATCHMAN AND A SEATED BATHER, ALSO KNOWN AS THE CONFIDENCE

Assembled 1892
Bronze, perhaps cast by Adolphe Gruet, 1892
$5\,^{11}/_{16} \times 6\,^{1}/_{4} \times 3\,^{3}/_{16}$ in. (14.4 × 15.8 × 9.1 cm)
Dedicated and signed on rock: *épreuve unique /
en hommage a Miss Hallowell / Rodin*
Private collection

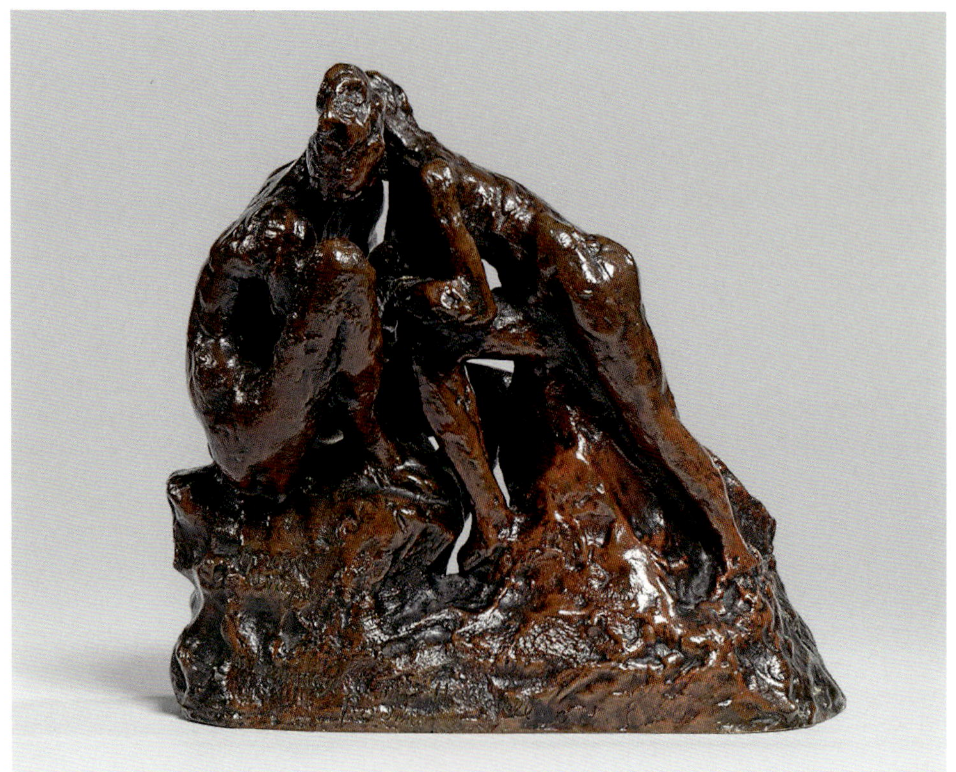

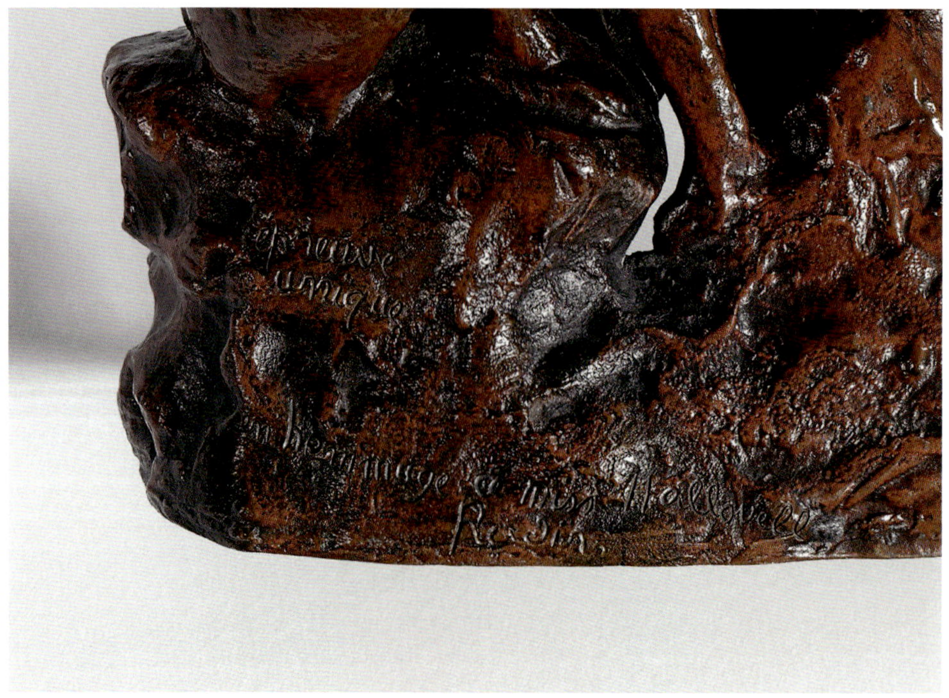

FUGIT AMOR, ALSO KNOWN AS THE SPHINX

Assembled before 1887
Bronze, probably cast by Griffoul and Lorge, 1892
14¾ × 17 ¹¹/₁₆ × 7 ¹¹/₁₆ in. (37.4 × 45 × 19.6 cm)
Inscribed and signed on base: *hommage respectueux / a Miss S. Hallowell / A. Rodin*
Private collection

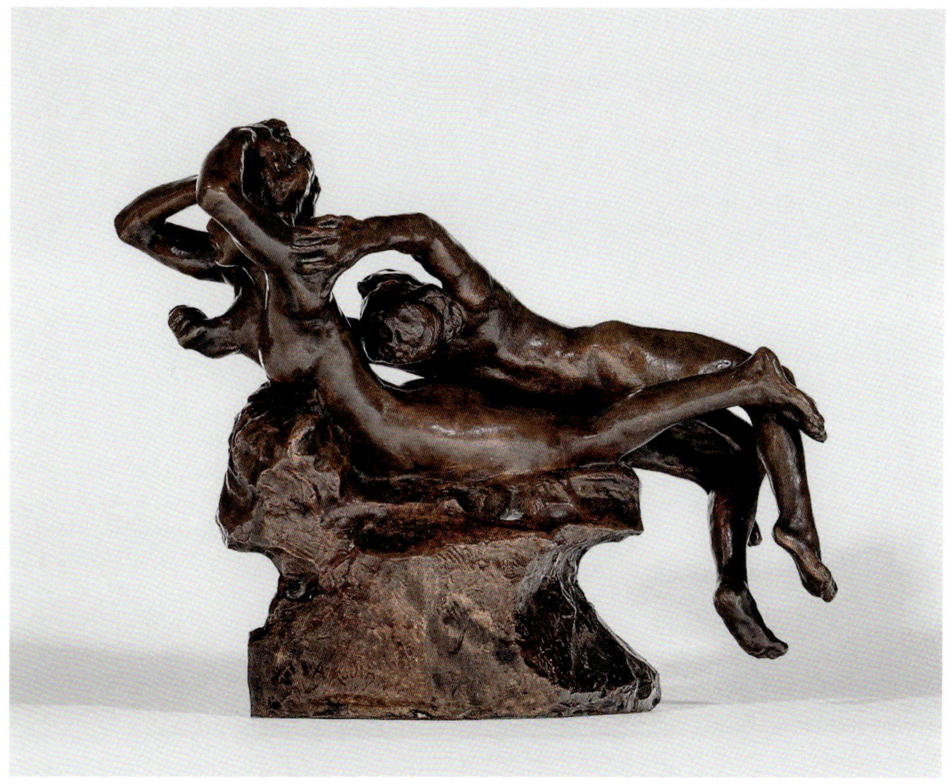

American art collector Bertha Palmer asked Sara Tyson Hallowell (1846–1924) to organize an exhibition of "Foreign Masterpieces Owned in the United States" for the World's Columbian Exposition in Chicago in 1893.[1] Hallowell arranged for Rodin to send three marbles. She presented them as belonging to an American collector — a "Mr. Henry Sargent, New York," according to the official catalogue of the exposition[2] — like the other works she had brought together. She was convinced Rodin's sculptures would find purchasers there. This proved not to be the case. Nevertheless, Rodin considered Hallowell a friend and was grateful. He gave her two bronzes that she bequeathed to her niece, Harriet Hallowell, who, like Sara, lived in Moret-sur-Loing, France, where they would perform exemplary relief work during World War I. Sara Hallowell thanked Rodin for the first work on January 2, 1893, and for the second on April 1, writing, "Another bronze statuette for me from the great sculptor. You are truly too generous and too kind to me."[3]

Like the marbles exhibited in Chicago, Hallowell's two bronzes are connected to *The Gates of Hell* very directly, for both consist of assemblages of figures from that work. The *Assemblage* (cat. 5) is the sole bronze cast of a group the artist reworked slightly in order to give it a certain homogeneity (unlike the *Death of Alcestis* [cat. 8] in which the component parts were assembled without great attention to unity). *Fugit Amor*, however, gave rise to multiple casts and many versions in bronze or marble, including one — perhaps the version located today at the Prefectural Museum of Art in Shizuoka, Japan — that was displayed in Chicago in 1893, under the title of *Sphinx*.

This group is made up of two figures, one of which is recognizable as one of the children from *Ugolino and His Sons* (cf. cat. 91). Stood upright, that figure would become *The Prodigal Son* (cat. 42). The *Fugit Amor* group is present on the right panel of the *Gates of Hell* and represents the agonized movement of two tortured beings in the second circle of hell in Dante's *Inferno*, where those who have yielded to lust are ceaselessly tormented. Both bronzes can be seen in a photograph of Sara Hallowell's home in Moret-sur-Loing from around 1920, with *Assemblage* on the desk and *Fugit Amor* atop an antique chest.[4]

The increasing volume of commissions had led Rodin to diversify the founders who worked for him. It is possible that the *Assemblage* was cast by Adolphe Gruet, who was the son of Charles-Adolphe Gruet and worked in turn for Rodin between 1891 and 1895. As for Griffoul and Lorge, they executed numerous casts for him between 1887 and 1894, including nine called "*groupe sphinge*" between 1887 and 1892 at the price of 250 francs, corresponding to this version of *Fugit Amor*, whose rocky, trapezoidal base skillfully highlights the unstoppable momentum that carries the group in its torturous race. Influenced by the anguish and pessimism of Baudelaire's *Fleurs du mal*, which Rodin was illustrating at the same time, this work thoroughly reflects the contemporaneous Symbolist movement. This timeliness explains its great success, as testified by the number of copies produced. ALNR

1. *Loan Collection: Foreign Masterpieces Owned in the United States*, exh. cat. (Chicago: W. B. Conkey, 1893), cat. 123, http://archive.org/details /catalogueofunite00worl/page/8/mode/2up.
2. *Francesca et Paolo*, in *World's Columbian Exposition, 1893, Official Catalogue, Part X, Department K, Fine Arts* (Chicago: W. B. Conkey, 1893), 64, cat. 2,989.
3. Sara Tyson Hallowell to Auguste Rodin, January 2, 1893, and April 1, 1893, Archives du musée Rodin, Paris.
4. The photograph is reproduced in Carolyn Kinder Carr, *Sara Tyson Hallowell: Pioneer Curator and Art Advisor in the Gilded Age* (Washington, DC: Smithsonian Institution Scholarly Press, 2019), 266.

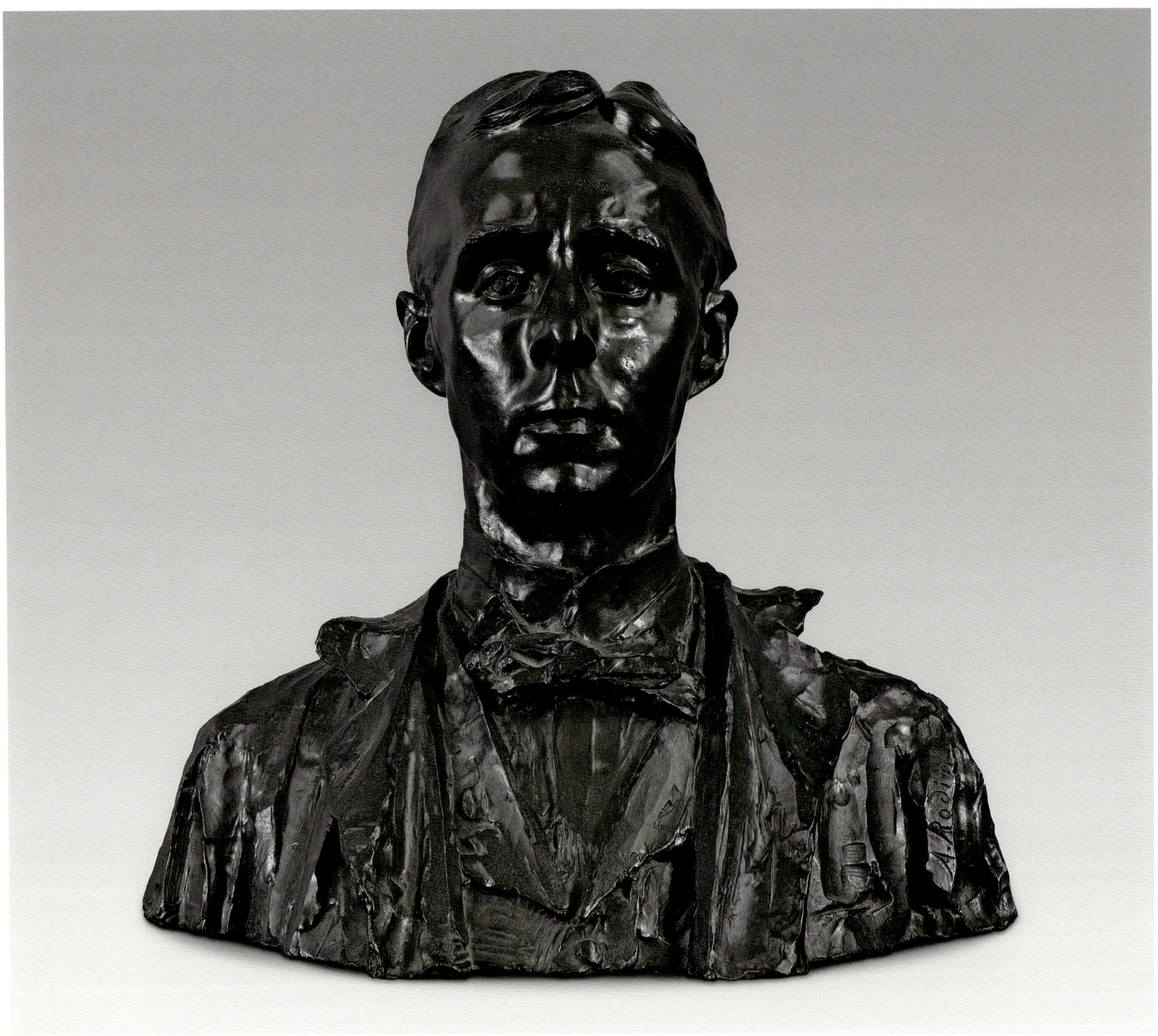

CAT. 7
ARTHUR JEROME EDDY

Original model 1898
Bronze, cast by Auguste Griffoul [no mark], 1898
17¾ × 19½ × 10¾ in. (45.1 × 49.5 × 27.3 cm)
Signed and dated, on left side of chest: *A. Rodin 1898*
Art Institute of Chicago
Arthur Jerome Eddy Memorial Collection, 1931.502

Arthur Jerome Eddy (1859–1920) was part of the cultured milieu of Chicago that discovered contemporary art at the 1893 World's Columbian Exposition. A lawyer and collector (according to Man Ray, he acquired the first Renoir in America[1]), Eddy became close to artists such as James Abbott McNeill Whistler, Wassily Kandinsky, and Francis Picabia. A great admirer of the Cubists, he wrote a book titled *Cubists and Post-Impressionism* in 1914. Shortly after the 1893 exposition, he went to Paris, where he posed for both Whistler (1894) and Rodin. He was the first American to commission a bust from Rodin, for what was then a high price of 8,000 francs, and went on to promote Rodin's work. On December 12, 1899, he gave a lecture at the Art Institute of Chicago titled "Hours with Rodin," accompanied by projected photographs provided by the artist.

In October 1898, founder Auguste Griffoul asked Rodin to stop by to see "the portrait bust of the American so you can judge the work for yourself."[2] Cast using the lost-wax method and skillfully executed so as to maintain the model's precise psychological expression, the bust was exhibited in Paris first at Galerie Georges Petit in late 1898 and then in Rodin's solo exhibition at the Pavillon de l'Alma in 1900. In 1930, Eddy's widow, Lucy Crao Orrell Eddy, gave the bust to the Art Institute, along with *Sleeping Muse* (1910) by Constantin Brancusi, which Eddy is said to have bought in 1913 or 1914.
ALNR

1. Man Ray, *Self Portrait* (Boston: Little, Brown, 1963), 60.
2. Auguste Griffoul to Auguste Rodin, October 17, 1898, Archives du musée Rodin, Paris.

DEATH OF ALCESTIS

Assembled c. 1899
Bronze, cast 1902
14 9/16 × 9 1/4 × 6 3/4 in. (37 × 23.5 × 17.2 cm)
Signed, left of figures, on side of base: *A. Rodin*
Museum of Fine Arts, Boston
Bequest of Major Henry Lee Higginson, 21.2521

Named after the opera by Bohemian-Austrian composer Christoph Wilibald Gluck, whose work Rodin greatly enjoyed, *Death of Alcestis* was shown in plaster at the Pavillon de l'Alma in Rodin's 1900 solo exhibition—as were most of the artist's sculptures, in expectation of commissions that would allow for bronze or marble versions. The bronze now in the Museum of Fine Arts, Boston, the sole cast of this group, is part of the selection commissioned by Henry Lee Higginson, founder and patron of the Boston Symphony Orchestra, who went to Rodin's studio in 1901 with Henry Adams to choose artworks for acquisition. But Rodin—whom Adams described in a letter to Higginson as "a peasant of genius [who] forgets all he says and has not the least idea of doing what is promised"[1]—forgot about the commission, and the four bronzes in question were sent to Boston only in the fall of 1902, and shortly afterward deposited at the museum. Rodin had brought *Death of Alcestis* to Adams in person on July 12, 1902, going on about his "admiration of the bronze, '*superbe*!,' '*exquis*!,' etc., etc., catching himself up every now and then to say that of course he referred only to the *patine*, when it was quite evident that he was admiring only his own work, which he liked in its bronze dress."[2]

In the eyes of a connoisseur like Adams, *Death of Alcestis* was "the Rodinniest thing" of the four, "and the most interesting, but it is not pretty and certainly neither sensual nor sensuous."[3] The plaster (Musée Rodin, Paris) had been sent, just as it was, to the foundry. It is made up of three figures that were assembled so quickly that one of them—in which we recognize one of the children of Ugolino from *The Gates of Hell* transformed into Mercury by wings at his feet—is suspended in the void, held up only by being attached to the side of his

neighbor. The same is true of the marble version (c. 1908–10, Thyssen-Bornemisza National Museum, Madrid), but the significant base and the rock on which the central figure is seated give the group a stable appearance that eclipses this astonishing detail.

ALNR

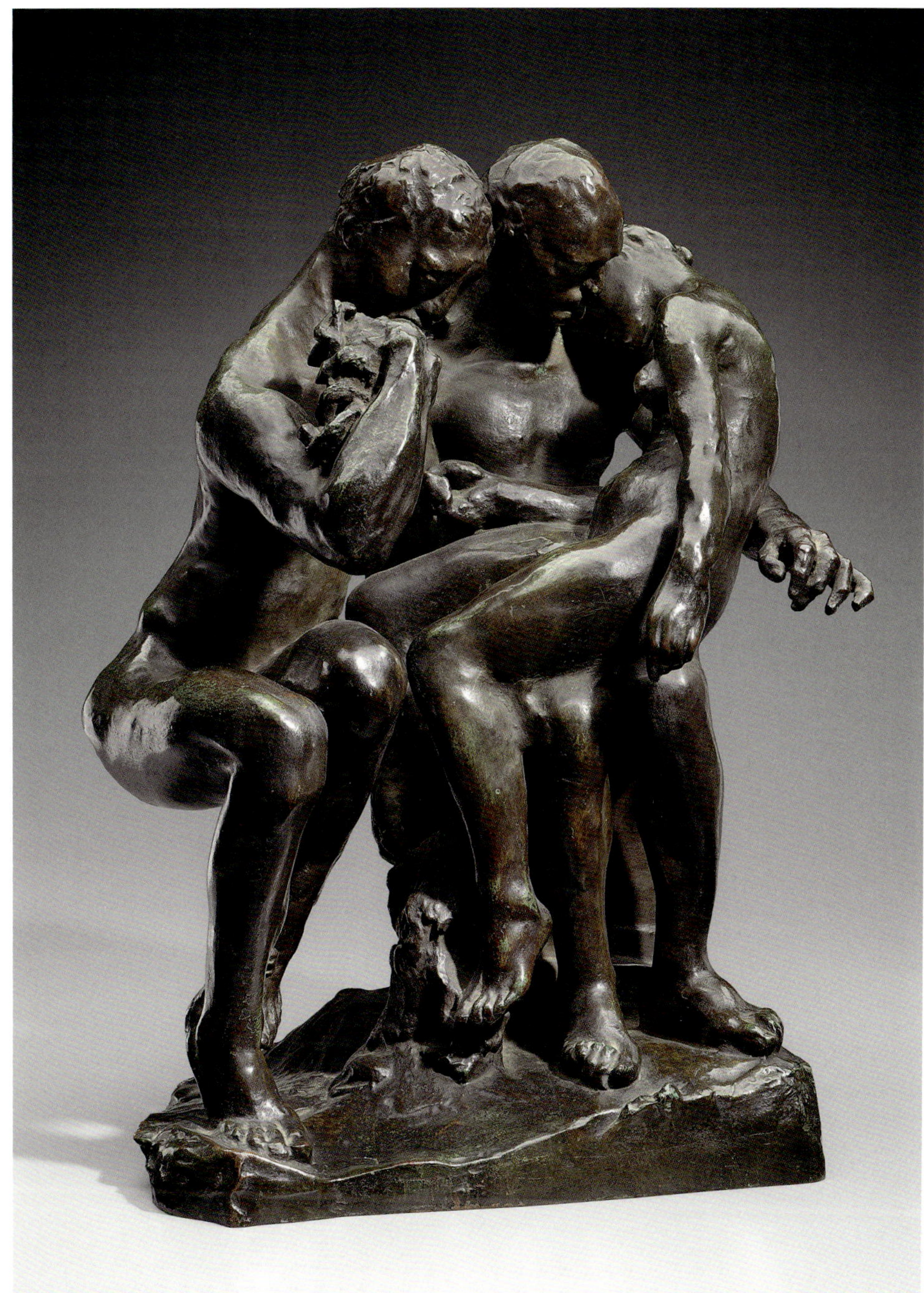

1. Henry Adams to Henry Lee Higginson, July 4, 1902, in *The Letters of Henry Adams*, vol. 5, *1899–1905*, ed. J. C. Levenson, Ernest Samuels, Charles Vandersee, and Viola Hopkins Winner (Cambridge, MA: Harvard University Press, 1989), 390.
2. Adams to Higginson, July 13, 1902, in *Letters of Henry Adams*, vol. 5, *1899–1905*, 393.
3. Adams to Higginson, October 23, 1902, in *Letters of Henry Adams*, vol. 5, *1899–1905*, 417.

CERES

1902
Marble
26 × 17 ½ × 13 ¾ in. (66 × 44.5 × 34.9 cm)
Signed, right side, edge of shoulder: *A. Rodin*
Museum of Fine Arts, Boston
Gift Major Henry Lee Higginson, 06.1910

When he visited Rodin in 1901, the Boston arts patron Henry Lee Higginson commissioned a marble version of the bust *Minerva*, the Roman goddess of wisdom, for whom marble versions of Rodin's 1888 portrait of Mariana Russell had been renamed. In October 1902, the artist considered the commission—this time titled *Ceres*, the goddess of agriculture—complete. He sent for Henry Adams, who described the work to Higginson: "After his manner, he had left it with as much appearance as possible of being unfinished, especially the base, which was not leveled down. He said that he liked it so, but would have it cut down if I wished. I did not wish. What worm am I to give orders to my masters?"[1] *Ceres* was thus sent to the United States without further modifications and immediately deposited at the Museum of Fine Arts, Boston, where it was shown with other works by Rodin before Higginson donated it to the museum in 1906.

Russell's classical features were a repeated source of inspiration for Rodin during the first decade of the twentieth century. He produced a dozen variations of *Minerva*, crowned with either hair, a helmet, or—in the manner of allegories for cities—with a small model of the Parthenon. But Russell's likeness could also be transformed into *Ceres* by draping a scarf over her shoulders. Rodin experimented with various approaches to the bust's costuming as well, from a martial cuirass, as in the fine *Minerva* in the Rodin Museum, Philadelphia (1901), to a rustic sheath, as suggested here through a distinctive treatment of the marble. The meticulously finished face contrasts with the roughly cut base, with the hair and draped fabric constituting intermediate areas that skillfully unite figuration and architectural element.

ALNR

1. Henry Adams to Henry Lee Higginson, October 2, 1902, in *The Letters of Henry Adams*, vol. 5, *1899–1905*, ed. J. C. Levenson, Ernest Samuels, Charles Vandersee, and Viola Hopkins Winner (Cambridge, MA: Harvard University Press, 1989), 408.

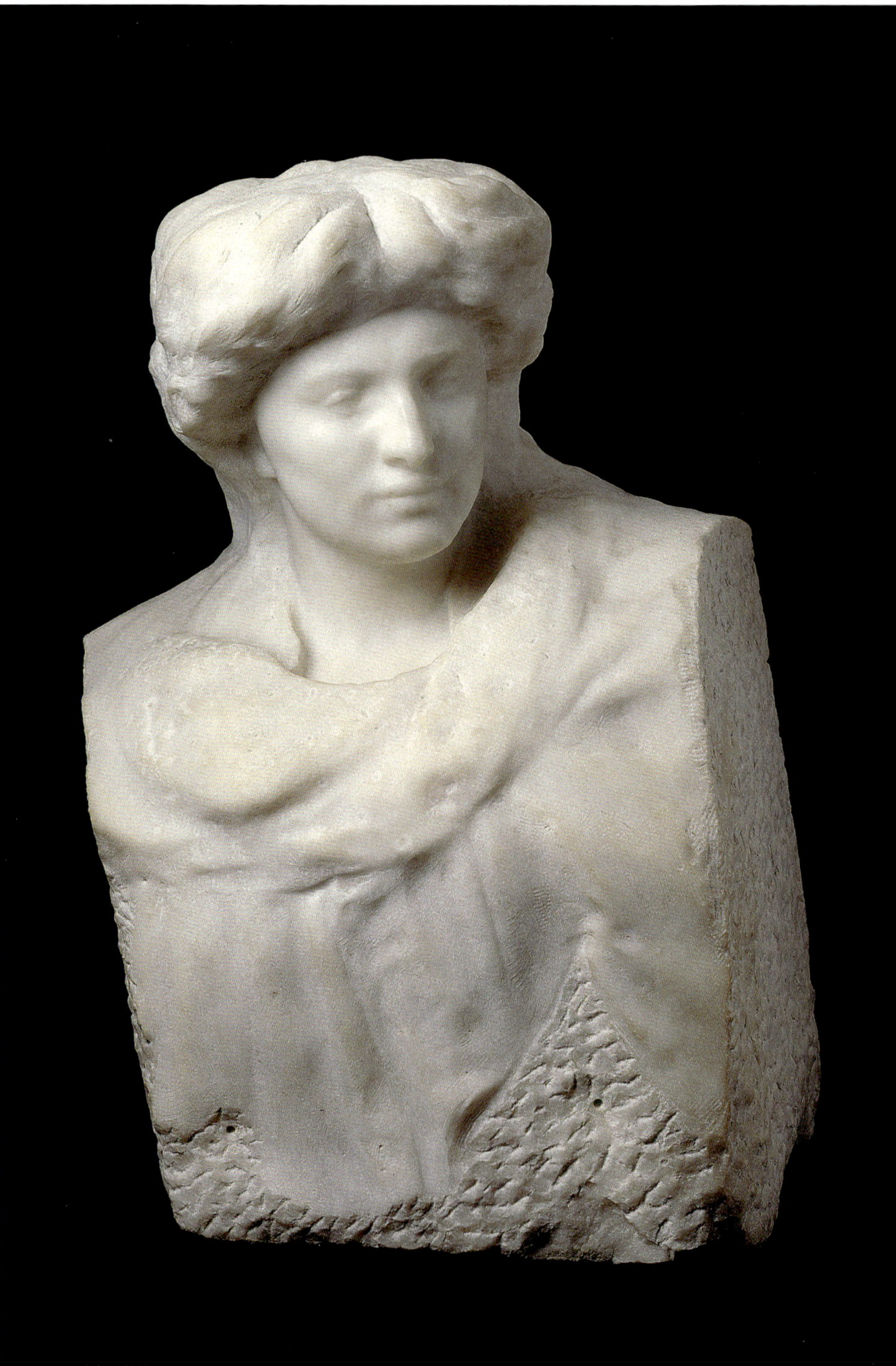

CAT. 10
THOUGHT

Original marble 1895
Marble, carved by Camille Raynaud, 1900–1901
29 1/8 × 17 1/16 × 18 1/8 in. (74 × 43.3 × 46 cm)
Signed, lower-right corner of pedestal: *A. Rodin*
Philadelphia Museum of Art
John G. Johnson Collection, cat. 1148

CAT. 11
THOUGHT

Original model 1895
Bronze, cast by Alexis Rudier, 1925
17 3/4 × 15 5/8 × 16 1/2 in. (45.1 × 39.7 × 41.9 cm)
Signed on top of base: *A. Rodin*
Rodin Museum, Philadelphia Museum of Art
Bequest of Jules E. Mastbaum, 1929, F1929-7-47

The painter Alexander Harrison (1853–1939) brought works by Rodin to Philadelphia well before the appearance of Jules Mastbaum, who would go on to establish the city's Rodin Museum. Harrison moved to France in 1879, where he studied with Jules Bastien-Lepage, and Rodin acquired several of the American's paintings. In 1901, Harrison convinced John G. Johnson (1841–1917), an important lawyer, to acquire this marble version of *Thought*. The Johnson collection, which contains some masterpieces, such as Rogier van der Weyden's *Crucifixion* (c. 1460), would become the foundation of the Philadelphia Museum of Art.

Like *Ceres* (cat. 9), this work is part of a series of Symbolist portraits based on the sculptor's favorite models, giving a much more personal dimension to what could have been a cold allegory.

This is the second marble version of *Thought*. The first (Musée d'Orsay, Paris) was exhibited at the Salon of the Société Nationale des Beaux-Arts in 1895 and then acquired by the Musée du Luxembourg, with Rodin promising to make no other versions. The face is a portrait of Rodin's student, assistant, and romantic partner Camille Claudel: Rodin made her portrait in 1882 when they became acquainted, and her memory haunted him for many years after they separated, around 1892. Here, the head seems to emerge from a block that has been roughly cut away, as if her mind might animate the inert stone.

Rodin did not care much to keep his promises and had a second marble executed by Camille Raynaud in 1900–1901. It arrived in Philadelphia in July 1901 and thrilled Johnson, who wrote, "You have made that coldest of all things—marble—warm with life."[1] He then decided to acquire two other works from Rodin: *Awakening: La Toilette de Venus* (stone; originally modeled c. 1890, carved by 1906) and *Despair* (marble; originally modeled 1890, carved 1906).

Jules Mastbaum, in turn, wanted a cast of *Thought*. When it was commissioned for Philadelphia, the decision was made, probably at the Musée Rodin in Paris (which had no director at the time, Léonce Bénédite being deceased and Georges Grappe not yet chosen), to leave off the lower half of the base, changing the relationship between the bust and its support and compromising the work's expressive power in this later version.
ALNR

1. John G. Johnson to Auguste Rodin, July 20, 1901, Archives du musée Rodin, Paris.

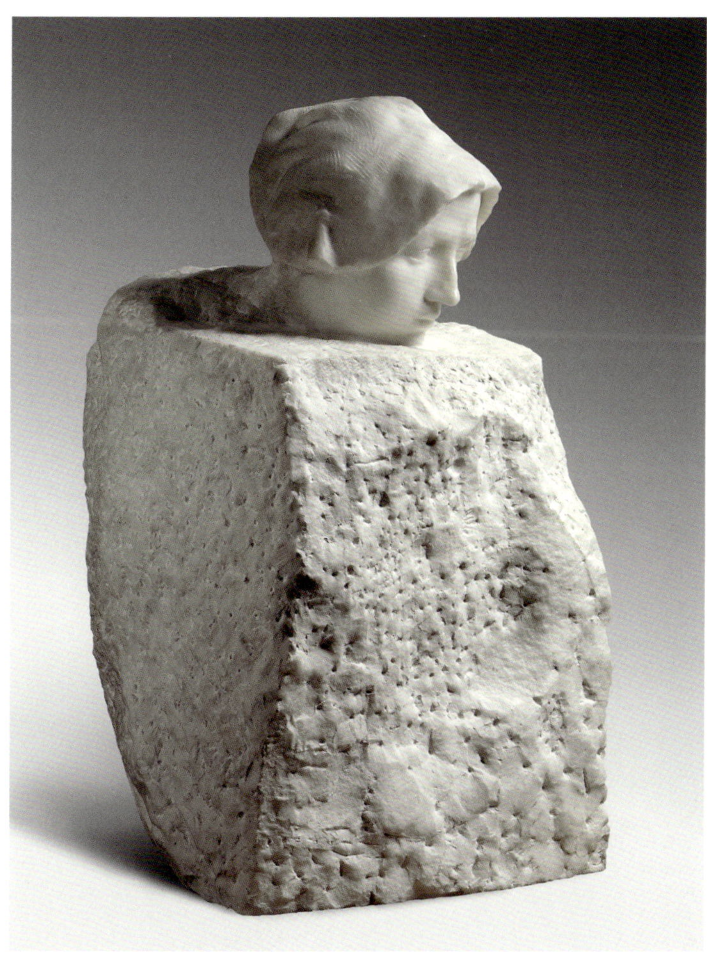

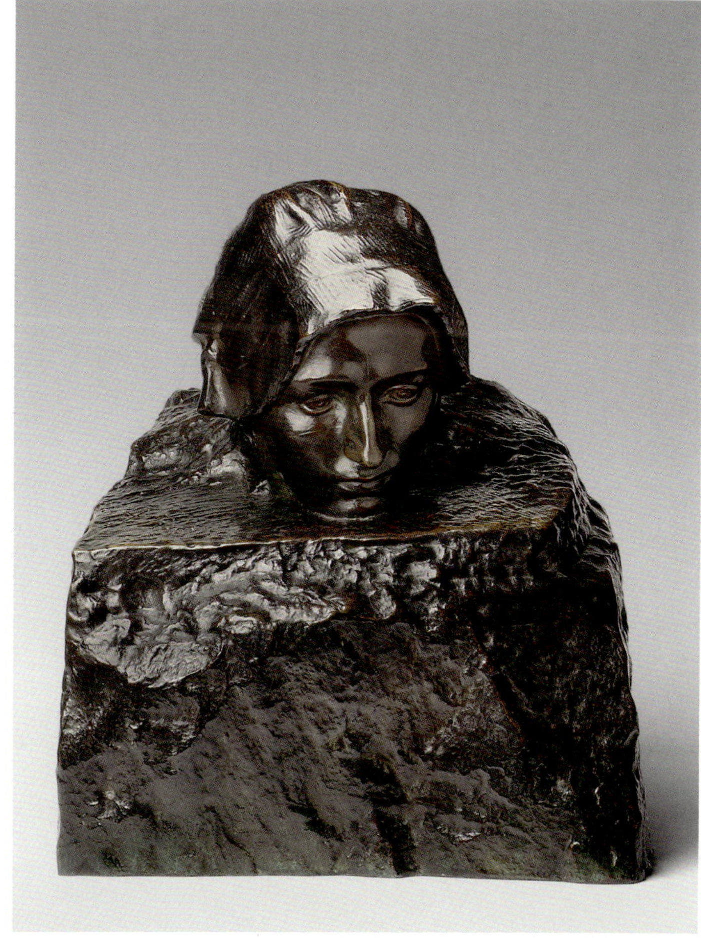

KATHERINE SENEY SIMPSON (MRS. JOHN W. SIMPSON)

1903
Marble
21 ¹³/₁₆ × 27 ³/₁₆ × 16 ⁵/₁₆ in. (55.4 × 69 × 41.5 cm)
Signed and dated on base: *A. Rodin / 1903*
National Gallery of Art, Washington, DC
Gift of Mrs. John W. Simpson, 1942.5.16

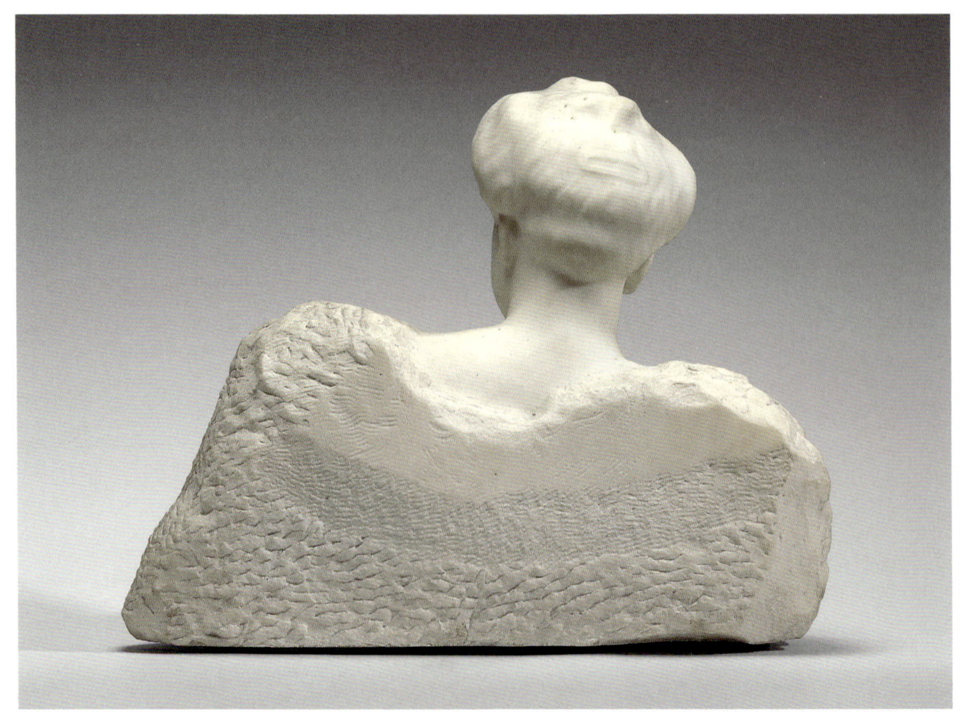

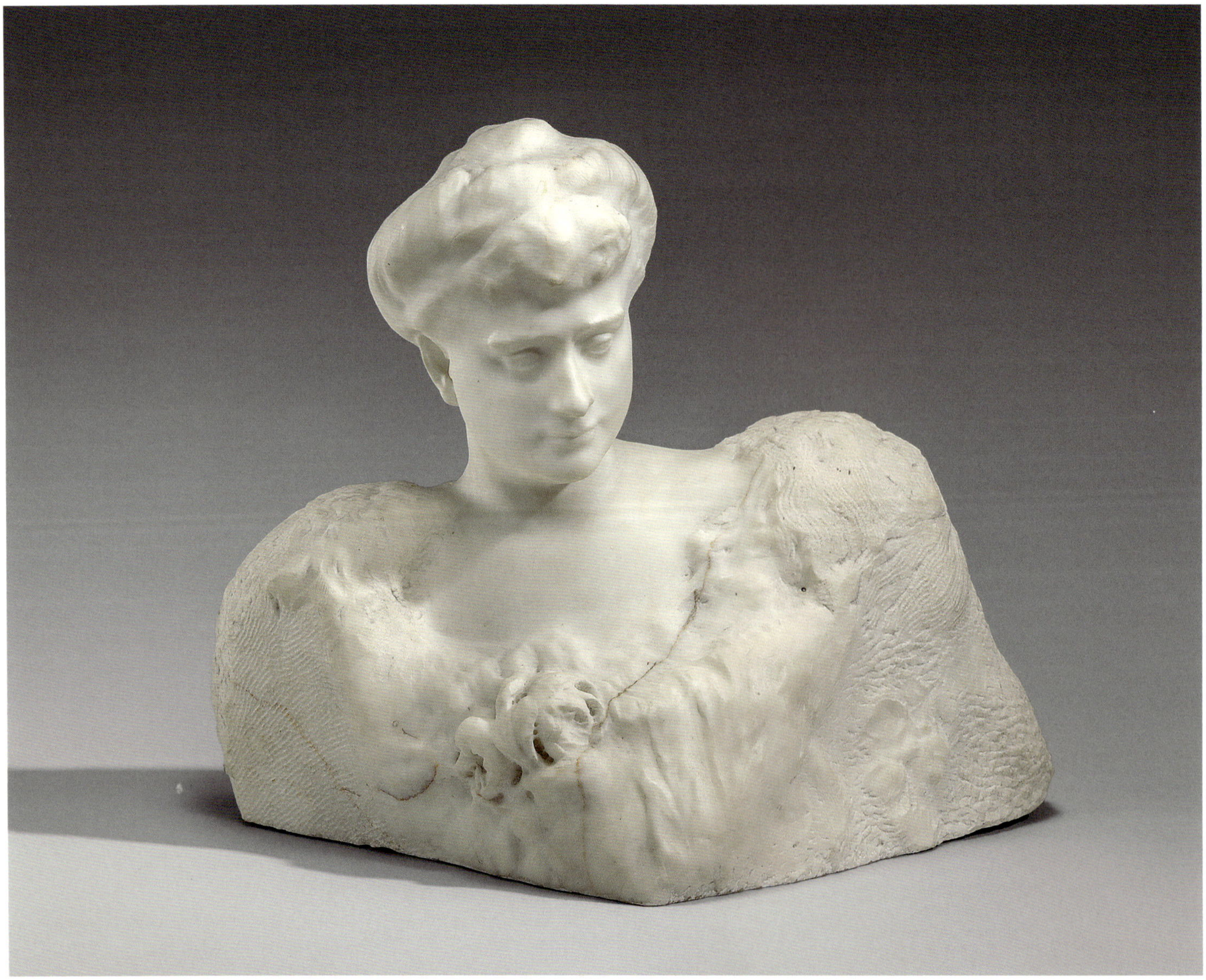

MASK OF KATHERINE SENEY SIMPSON (MRS. JOHN W. SIMPSON)

1902
Plaster
7 × 7 11/16 × 6 in. (17.8 × 19.5 × 15.3 cm)
Inscribed, dated, and signed, left side of chin, in graphite: *Mme K Simpson esquisse pour le portrait / 12 septembre 1909 / A. Rodin*
National Gallery of Art, Washington, DC
Gift of Mrs. John W. Simpson, 1942.5.21

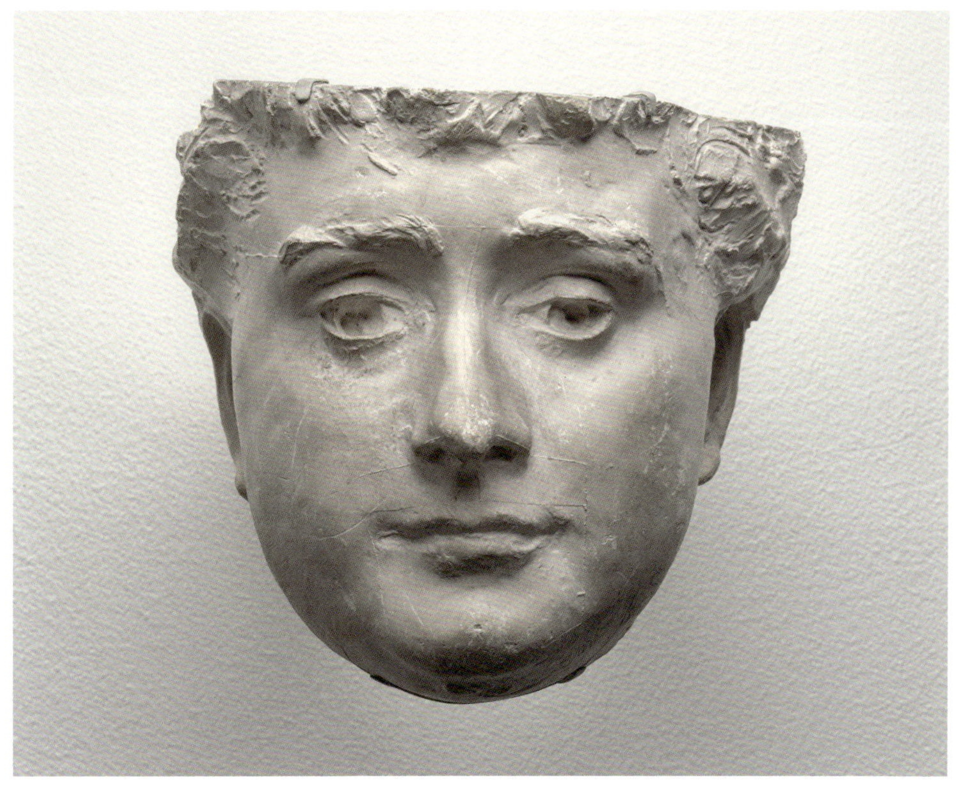

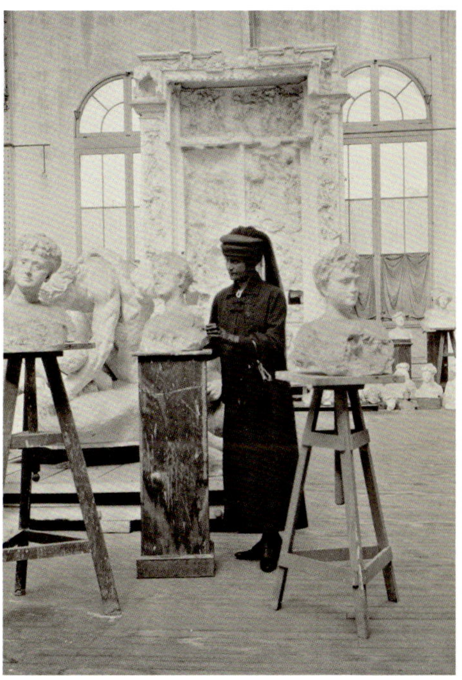

Photographer unknown, *Katherine Seney Simpson with the Studies for Her Portrait in Rodin's Studio at Meudon*, 1922. Gelatin silver print, 5 9/16 × 3 3/8 in. (14.1 × 8.5 cm). Iris & B. Gerald Cantor Center for Visual Arts, Stanford University, Palo Alto, California. Gift of the Iris and B. Gerald Cantor Foundation, 1987.69.

From the cultured milieu that founded the Metropolitan Museum of Art in New York, Katherine (Kate) Seney (c. 1869–1943) (see fig. 4.5) was among Rodin's most devoted American collectors—and friends. She had married a brilliant lawyer, John Woodruff Simpson (1850–1920), in 1889, and they often traveled to France. They met Rodin through Samuel Bing, a dealer whose clientele was both American and European. The Simpsons commissioned a portrait of Kate from Rodin in 1902.

From the first modeling in clay, Rodin captured the direct expression of her face, with her wide eyes. "Almost invariably," he told a journalist, "there is intelligence in the face of the women of this nation. But . . . there is, furthermore, kindness of heart evidenced in the countenance of this model. That is what I shall attempt to express. It is a difficult task."[1] During the course of sixty sittings (see fig. 7.1), he tried various positions of the head before settling on a frontal view of the face, and then the execution of the marble began. The nature of the block of marble was very important to Rodin. As if this contributed to his inspiration, he seemed to have a preference for irregular blocks, the original form of which he followed as much as possible. In this case, he selected a triangular block and positioned the face at the apex of one of the points, giving depth to the composition and, perhaps, also emphasizing that no particular viewpoint was favored. Even the

flaws in the marble did not bother him. The bust's striated back demonstrates three levels of carving, from rough to smooth stone.

The Simpsons were thrilled. "Of the bust, it is impossible to speak with moderation. It surpasses all expectation," John wrote to Rodin when the marble arrived in New York in 1903.[2] Kate sent a photograph of the bust to Rodin the next year, calling him "*mon sculpteur*" as if to underline the privileged relationship they had established. Rodin was also pleased with the work, to the point that he brought the marble back to Paris to display it at the Salon of the Société Nationale des Beaux-Arts in 1904 with the large model of *The Thinker*, shown for the first time. The two sculptures were unanimously admired.

A close friendship developed between the artist and the Simpsons—who returned to France every year, as evidenced by the many sculptures, such as Kate's plaster mask, and drawings dedicated to them during these visits, as well as the numerous letters and few photographs they exchanged over time. ALNR

1. Auguste Rodin, quoted in Jean Schopfer and Claude Anet, "Rodin," *The Craftsman*, March 1904, 532.
2. John Woodruff Simpson to Auguste Rodin, December 5, 1903, Archives du musée Rodin, translated in Ruth Butler, Suzanne Lindsay Glover, and Alison Luchs, *European Sculpture of the Nineteenth Century: The Collections of the National Gallery of Art Systematic Catalogue* (New York: Oxford University Press, 2001), 414.

STUDY FOR ST. JOHN THE BAPTIST, TODAY KNOWN AS THE SMALL WALKING MAN

Assembled c. 1899
Bronze, cast by Alexis Rudier [no mark], 1903
33 1/2 × 23 9/16 × 10 7/16 in. (85.1 × 59.8 × 26.5 cm)
Signed in incised letters on base between feet: *A. Rodin*; in raised letters on underside of base inside left foot: *A. Rodin*; in raised letters behind right heel, on underside of base: *A. Rodin*
National Gallery of Art, Washington, DC
Gift of Mrs. John W. Simpson, 1942.5.11

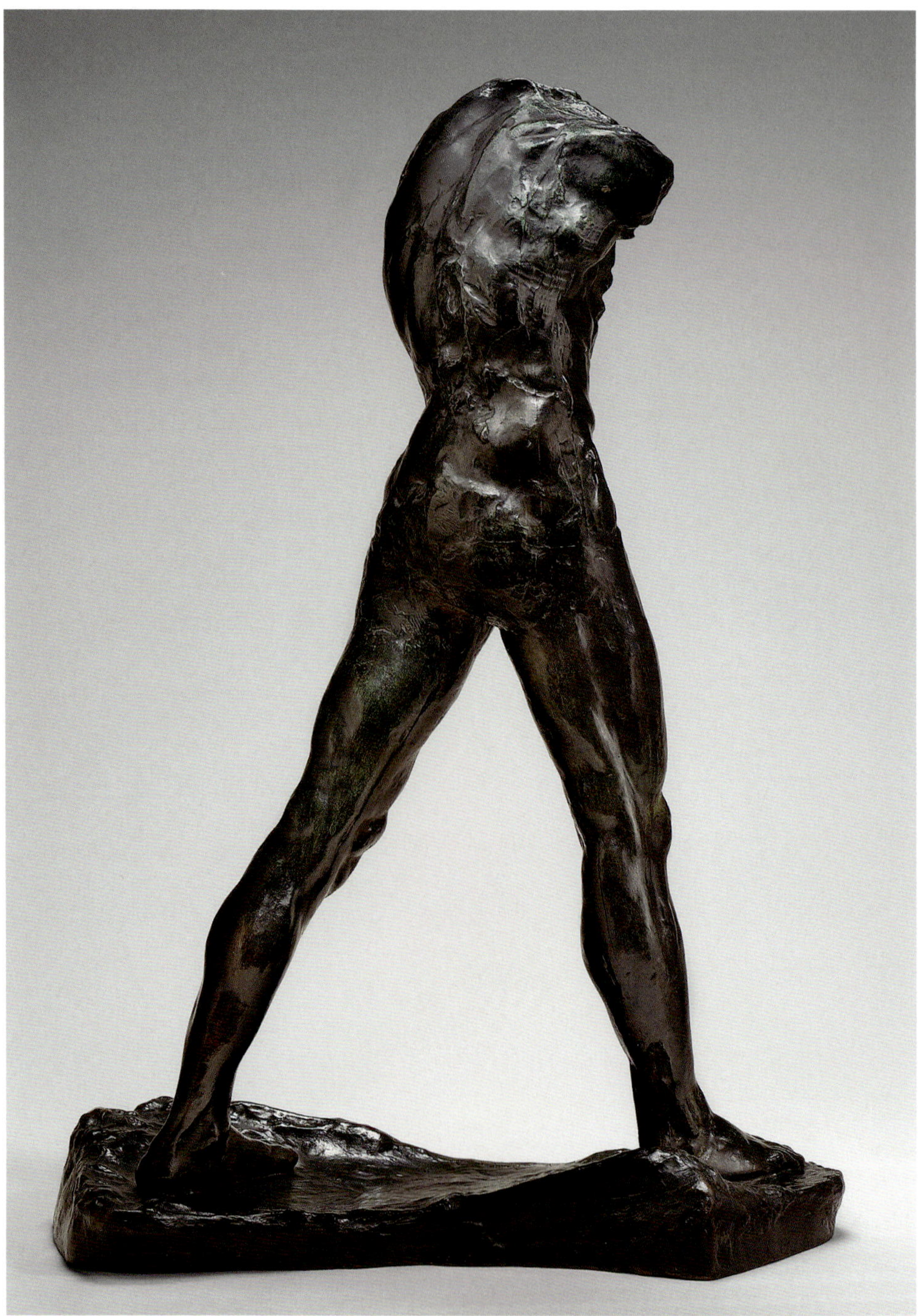

Rodin's portrait of Katherine Seney Simpson (cat. 12), commissioned by the sitter and her husband, John Woodruff Simpson, arrived in New York in late November or early December 1903 with the couple's first purchases from the artist, three recent bronze casts: this *Study for St. John the Baptist*, *The Thinker* (cf. cat. 21), and the *Head of Balzac* (cf. cat. 45), all of which are now in the collection of the National Gallery of Art in Washington, DC. The former two, cast in the models' original dimensions, were the first versions of these compositions to come to the United States. They were also the first casts of these models produced by Eugène Rudier (1878–1952), who worked under the name of his father, Alexis Rudier, and had just begun working as a founder for Rodin.

These acquisitions demonstrate the Simpsons' independent thinking. At the Rodin exhibition at the Pavillon de l'Alma, Paris, in 1900, the first and only time it had been exhibited, no one had paid any attention to the *Study for St. John the Baptist*. The figure, which received the title of *The Walking Man* in 1907 after it had been enlarged (cf. cat. 86), was originally named after the biblical figure because it came about from the assemblage of two much earlier studies, a damaged torso and a pair of legs, which were both studies for the large *St. John the Baptist* of 1880. We can imagine Rodin's joy at being encouraged by his new clients, and soon-to-be friends, in a direction that few understood. From this point forward, only form itself interested him—form whose meaning no longer depended on completion.

The Simpsons continued purchasing sculpture from Rodin until 1909. Their collection includes all media in which Rodin worked, from bronzes (all of excellent quality), marbles, terracottas, and plasters (with which Rodin parted more reluctantly) to drawings. After this date, they attempted above all to enhance the artist's reputation in the United States, generously lending from their collection and encouraging people in their circle to acquire Rodin's works. Kate survived her husband by over twenty years, and she decided to donate their Rodin collection (twenty-eight sculptures, eight drawings, and three drypoint prints) to the very young National Gallery of Art in Washington, DC, instead of to the Metropolitan Museum of Art in New York, which already had a beautiful and comprehensive collection of works by Rodin.
ALNR

A BURGHER OF CALAIS (JEAN D'AIRE)

Original model 1887, reduced 1895
Bronze, probably cast by François Rudier, 1904
18 ½ × 6 ⁵⁄₁₆ × 5 ½ in. (47 × 16 × 14 cm)
Signed on back of base: *A. Rodin*
National Gallery of Art, Washington, DC
Gift of Mrs. John W. Simpson, 1942.5.13

Commissioned by the city of Calais in January 1885, the *Monument to the Burghers of Calais* found its definitive form by 1889, at the *Claude Monet–A. Rodin* exhibition in Paris, when Rodin first grouped all six figures (cf. fig. 1.5).[1] The burghers, the elite of the city, had agreed to sacrifice their lives by carrying the keys to the city of Calais to the victorious king of England after a long siege. Wasted by hunger, brought low in defeat, and anticipating execution, they all suffered, but as imagined by Rodin, they experience this pain differently. Eustache de Saint Pierre, the oldest and the heart of the group, is resigned. Seen here, Jean d'Aire, "who would have lived for many years to come, but whose life is condensed into this sudden last hour,"[2] girds himself in order not to weaken. He is the image of firmness, while Pierre de Wissant is the very expression of drama, both in his face (cat. 46) and in his gestures.

Each of the six figures was modeled separately, and they were then reused individually as well. After the monument was inaugurated in Calais on June 3, 1895, Rodin had the figures reduced, starting with *Jean d'Aire* and *Pierre de Wissant*, the large models for which had also been among the first to be produced and exhibited in Paris, in 1887. These reductions were very popular with collectors, as evidenced by their numbers. US museums hold no fewer than ten small versions of *Jean d'Aire*. The version in Washington, DC, is one of the earliest, and probably one of three casts produced by François Rudier (uncle of Eugène Rudier), most likely that of 1904.

ALNR

1. *Claude Monet–A. Rodin*, exh. cat. (Paris: Galerie Georges Petit, 1889).
2. Rainer Maria Rilke, *Auguste Rodin* [1903], trans. Jessie Lamont and Hans Trausil (New York: Sunwise Turn, 1919), quoted in Albert E. Elsen, *Auguste Rodin: Readings on His Life and Work* (Englewood Cliffs, NJ: Prentice Hall, 1965), 138.

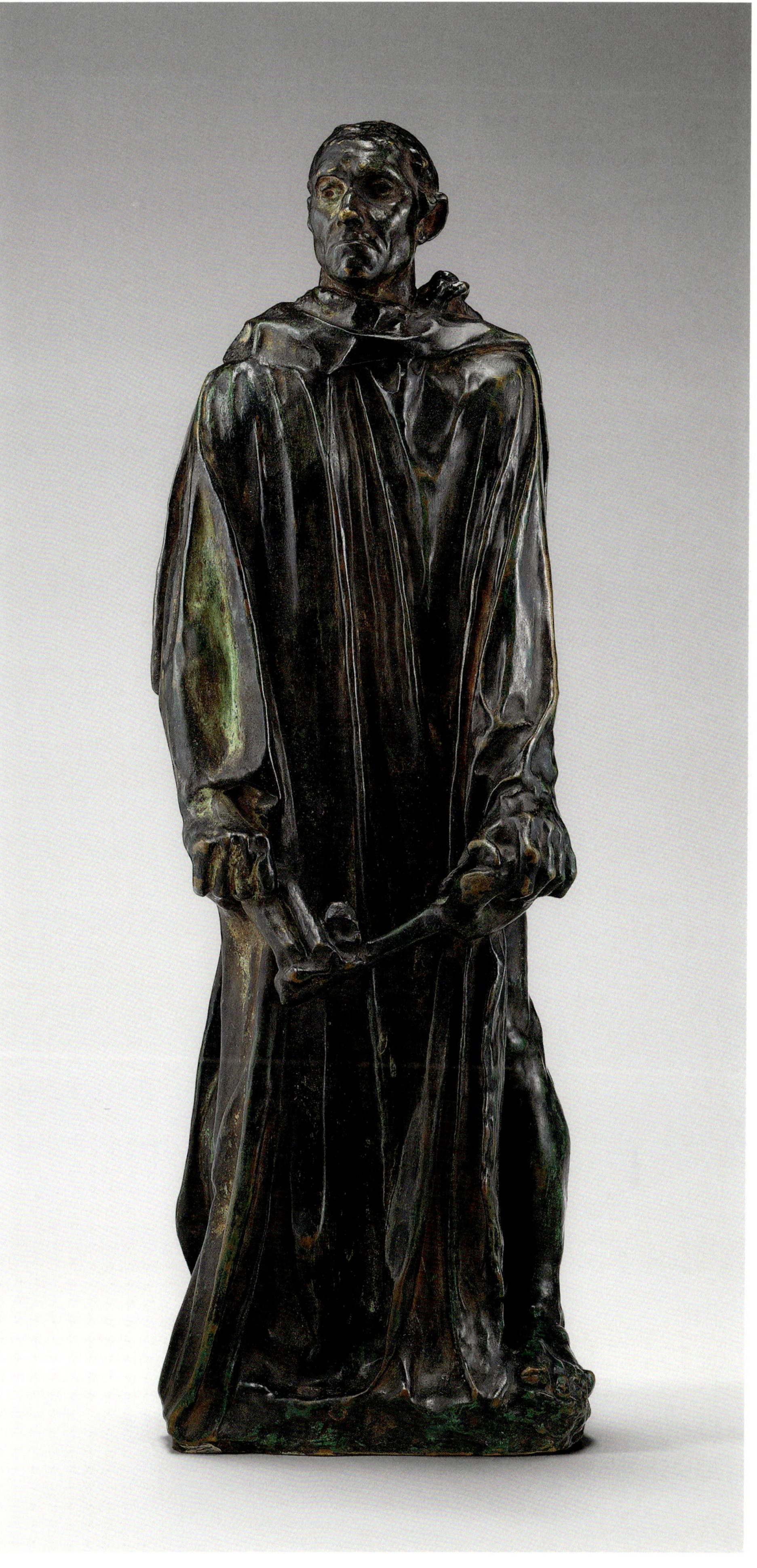

WOMAN AND CHILD (ORIGINALLY TITLED **FIRST IMPRESSION OF LOVE**)

Original model before 1893
Marble, carved 1902
17 × 17 1/2 × 13 1/16 in. (43.2 × 44.4 × 33.1 cm)
Signed, bottom left: *A. Rodin*
National Gallery of Art, Washington, DC
Gift of Mrs. John W. Simpson, 1942.5.19

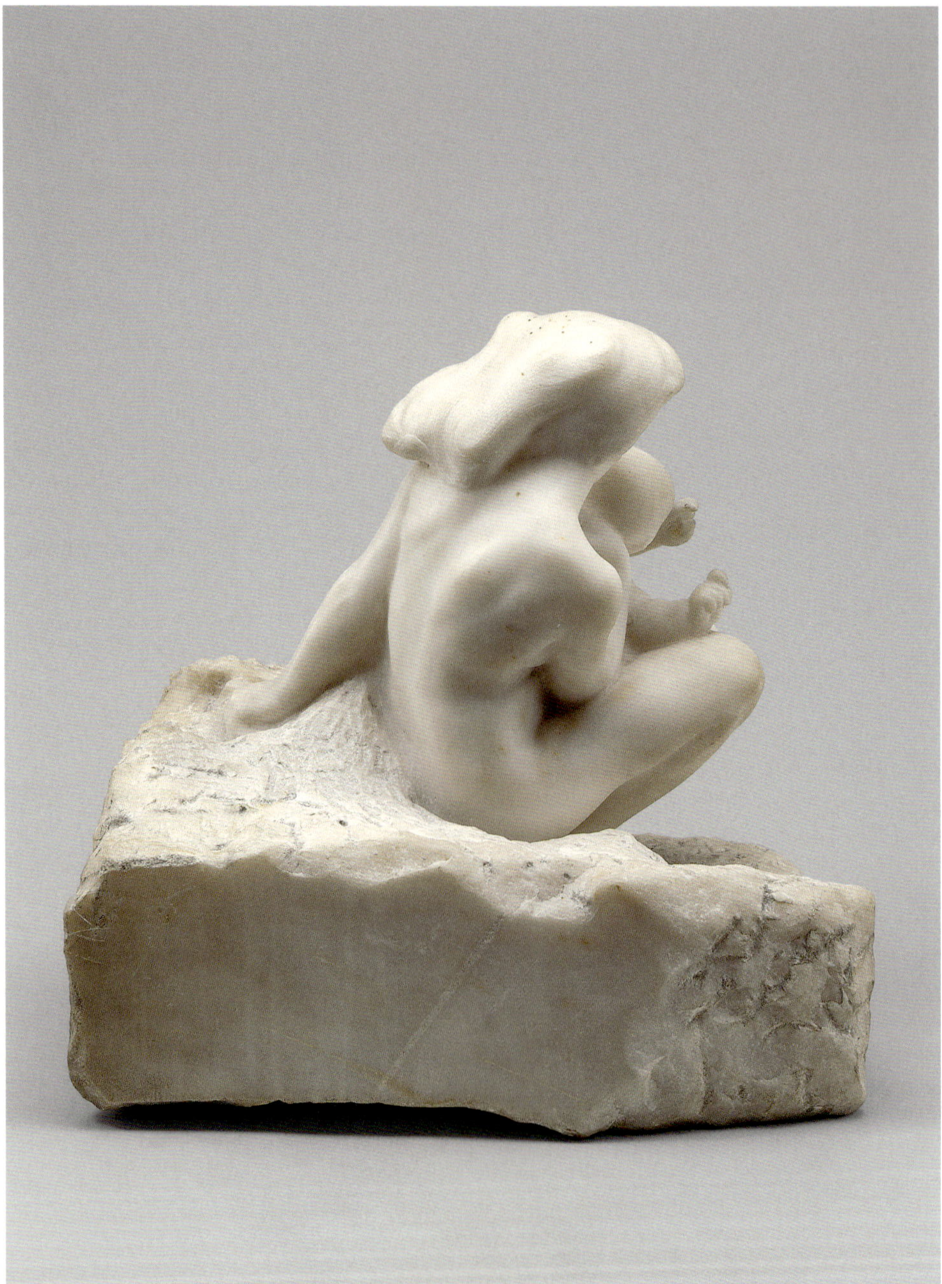

This charming composition illustrates the pleasure Rodin found in depicting children: they appear in numerous drawings and sculptures from the 1880s produced in tandem with his work on *The Gates of Hell*. Starting from the same young woman and child, he created three successful small groups on the theme of motherly love, all three of which would be rendered in bronze and marble versions.[1] The first two, compositions in high relief and in the round, reimagine a motif that initially appeared at the top of the left pilaster of the *Gates of Hell* before being replaced, after 1887, by the *Caryatid* (cf. cat. 2), which was more suited to the general theme. Rodin instead gave the grouping an independent existence, producing several related marbles, one of which joined the collection of the Rodin Museum in Philadelphia in 2010 (*Young Mother in the Grotto*, 1891). The third composition, seen in the marble *Woman and Child* in Washington, DC, presents a different child, who is lying down (rather than seated on the young woman's lap) and has been remodeled into a putto with the addition of two small wings. This alters the meaning of the group from an image of maternal love, characterized by great spontaneity in the expression of feeling, to an allegory of a love that seems more transitory.

Versions of this group were exhibited beginning in 1901 under the title *Fleeting Love*, but it seems that all the bronzes corresponding to this composition came from an initial marble version produced quite a bit earlier. That marble was acquired by the Scottish dealer Alexander Reid in January 1893 but has not been located. Although we know of three extant marble versions, they are different from the model used for the bronze casts, and all date to after 1900. The first of these marbles, which was exhibited as of 1903 in Boston, was part of the Higginson donation to the Museum of Fine Arts but was deaccessioned in 1961. With a new title

and a different treatment, particularly of the child who was completely separated from the rock, the National Gallery of Art *Woman and Child* is certainly slightly later. This was one of the first purchases by Katherine (Kate) Seney Simpson and John Woodruff Simpson, shortly after they commissioned a bust of Kate (cat. 12).[2] As Ruth Butler has shown, the couple paid the (very high) full price Rodin charged at the time, while later they benefited from the greatly reduced prices the artist offered to his friends.[3]

ALNR

1. Antoinette Le Normand-Romain, *Rodin et le bronze: Catalogue des œuvres conservées au musée Rodin / The Bronzes of Rodin: Catalogue of Works in the Musée Rodin* (Paris: Éditions du musée Rodin / Réunion des musées nationaux, 2007), 2:469–71.
2. As with the commissioned bust, they made the purchase through Samuel Bing. See bill of sale, January 24, 1903, Archives du musée Rodin, Paris.
3. Ruth Butler, Suzanne Lindsay Glover, and Alison Luchs, *European Sculpture of the Nineteenth Century: The Collections of the National Gallery of Art Systematic Catalogue* (Washington, DC: National Gallery of Art, 2001), 351–53.

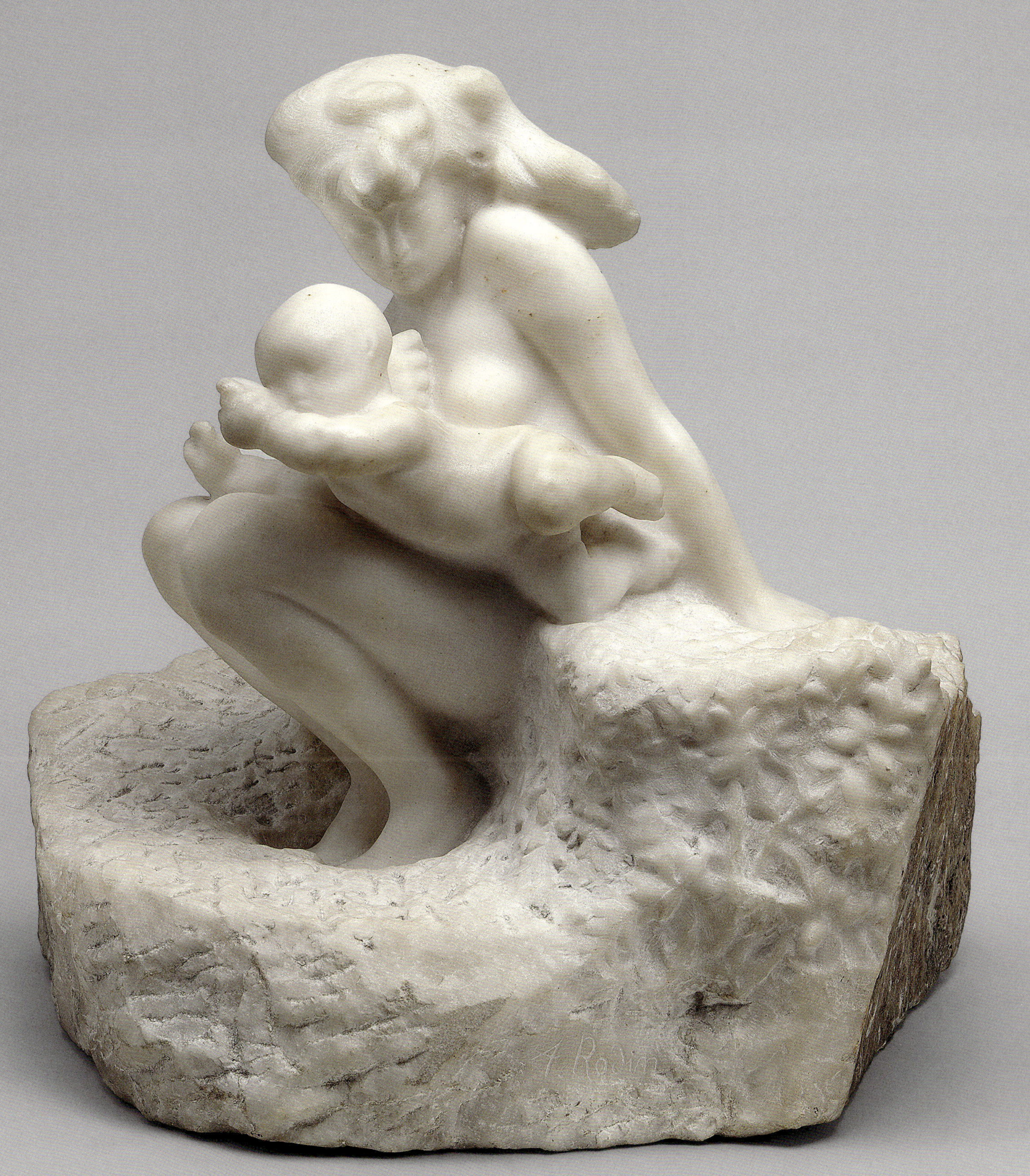

NUDE WOMAN CARRYING VASE ON HEAD (ANTIQUE VASE)

c. 1898–1900
Graphite with stumping and watercolor on wove paper
19 13/16 × 12 5/16 in. (50.3 × 31.2 cm)
Dedicated, signed, and dated in graphite on lower right: *à Madame K. Simpson amie / de mon art dès la première heure / Aug. Rodin 1909*
Inscribed upper left, in unknown hand: *1842*
National Gallery of Art, Washington, DC
Gift of Mrs. John W. Simpson, 1942.5.32

Rodin gave *Nude Woman Carrying Vase on Head* to Katherine (Kate) Seney Simpson as a tribute to "an early friend to his art," according to the inscription. When she visited Rodin in 1909, the date of the dedication of the drawing, he had already settled at the Hôtel Biron in Paris and was toying with the idea of establishing a Musée Rodin. His collection of antiques, which visitors like the Simpsons could admire at his home in Meudon, was made up primarily of Greco-Roman vases (no fewer than six hundred were inventoried after his death), which the artist had been incorporating into his own work for a long time. He would assemble his plaster figurines or even attach them to the small ancient vases, often of terracotta color. The drawing he gave to Simpson depicts a kneeling woman, her lower legs invisible and her raised arm echoing geometrically the curve of the vase she carries on her head, figure and vase merging in one synthetic whole, just like his assemblages of figurines and antique vases. Produced around 1898, it is contemporaneous with Rodin's watercolor series of "vase women," which developed toward a very Cycladic abstraction.[1] Rodin himself collected a couple of sculptures from this very ancient Bronze Age Mediterranean culture. Picasso would later adapt this motif in his *Bikini Vase* (1961, private collection).[2]

The year before Rodin dedicated this work to Simpson, it was shown, along with a hundred other of his drawings, at the French art exhibition of the Kunstverein in Leipzig, Germany, and reproduced as the frontispiece to an important article on his drawings by German art historian Otto Grautoff.[3] Those selected for publication and release in Germany would often later enter the United States. Indeed, several drawings included in Grautoff's publications on the artist were exhibited in New York in Alfred Stieglitz's Little Galleries of the Photo-Secession, later known as 291 (1908 and

1910), like the *Cambodian Dancer*—also reproduced in *Camera Work* in 1911—or *Kneeling Girl* (Art Institute of Chicago).[4] This concurrence is certainly not trivial and reflects the choice of the artist himself. The drawing given to Simpson, published by Grautoff under the title *Antique Vase* (undoubtedly the original title given by the artist), can be compared to another drawing of a "vase woman," *Origin of the Greek Vase* (c. 1900), acquired by the Metropolitan Museum of Art, New York, in 1913 through the gift of Thomas Fortune Ryan.

The Simpson collection (now mainly at the National Gallery of Art), gathered over several years, includes an impressive eighteen drawings, almost all of which were signed, dated, and dedicated to Rodin's American patrons. Only *Seated Female Nude Leaning to the Left* (1908), *Figure Bending Forward with Right Knee Raised* (n.d.), and *Two Figures* (c. 1905) have no dedication;

this may mean they were purchased at 291 in New York. Leaving aside rare exceptions where the drawings were given on the same day they were produced, most of them are dated well after their execution. They also constitute an ongoing display of friendship with Kate Simpson and her husband, John Woodruff Simpson, that is unique in the collecting history of the sculptor's drawings. CBU

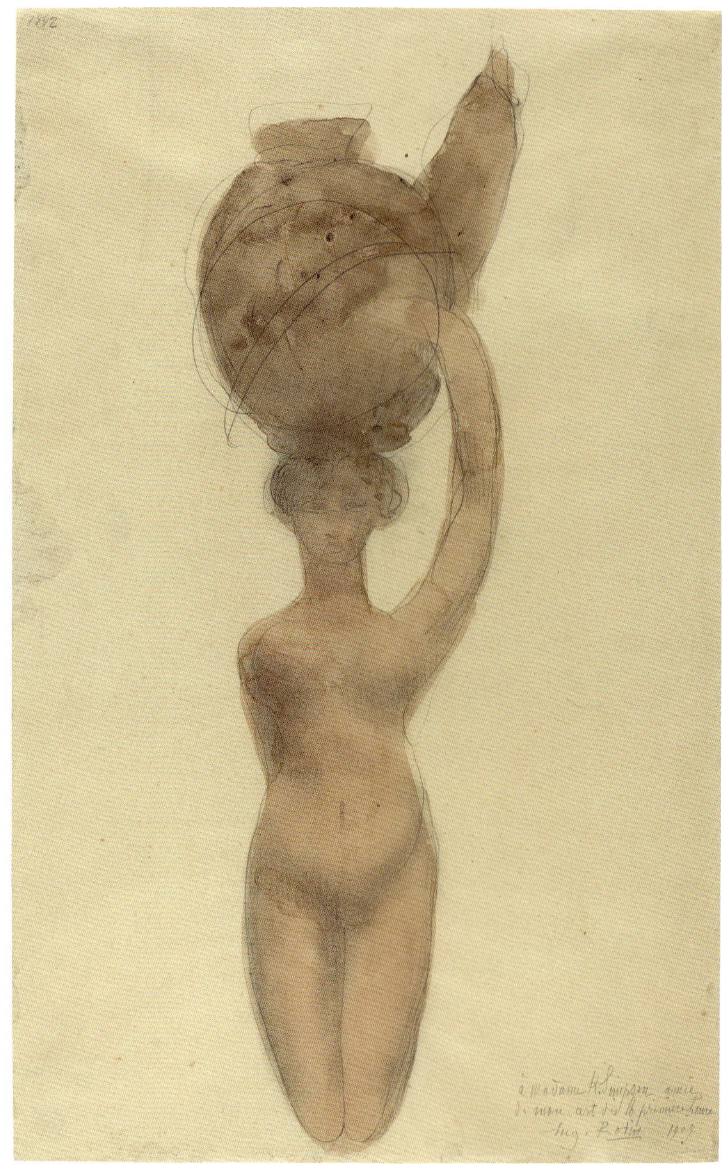

1. Claudie Judrin, "La femme-vase dans le dessin de Rodin," in *Naissance de la Modernité: Mélanges offerts à Jacques Vilain*, ed. Henry-Claude Cousseau, Christina Buley-Uribe, and Véronique Mattiussi (Paris: Relief, 2009), 107.
2. Christina Buley-Uribe, "Le dessin comme art," in *Rodin: L'Exposition du centenaire*, exh. cat., ed. Catherine Chevillot and Antoinette Le Normand-Romain (Paris: Grand Palais, 2017), 187.
3. Otto Grautoff, "Rodins Zeichnungen," *Kunst und Kunstler*, no. 11 (1908): 218.
4. Otto Grautoff, *Auguste Rodin* (Bielefeld: Velhagen and Klasing, 1908), 96, 100.

FIGURE FACING FORWARD (SERPENTINE?)

c. 1906
Graphite with stumping and watercolor on wove paper
12 13/16 × 9 15/16 in. (32.5 × 25.3 cm)
Signed in graphite, lower right: *A. Rodin*
Inscribed in later hand, center-right verso: *Mrs. Nelson Robinson / 23 E. 55*; lower-right verso: *38538*
National Gallery of Art, Washington, DC
Mrs. John W. Simpson, 1942.5.34

Figure Facing Forward, a drawing of a woman with visibly swaying hips and exaggeratedly long, curving arms, bears on the reverse the name "Mrs. Nelson Robinson." The style is very similar to the watercolors with soft lead pencil depicting the Japanese actress Hanako (born Ōta Hisa) in a kimono or the Cambodian dancers (like the drawing from Denman Waldo Ross in the Museum of Fine Arts, Boston) produced in 1906–7. Here, the extended arms and hands form the body of a snake stretching across the drawing. The young woman stares at the head that curves up toward her, while on the left of the sheet, its tail, which blends into the arm, wriggles downward. With its animated and undulating effect, this work may correspond to the drawing titled *Serpentine* acquired by Lillie R. Seney Robinson, Katherine Seney Simpson's sister, at the Rodin exhibition at the Little Galleries of the Photo-Secession in New York in 1908. The two sisters were close to Edward Steichen, who organized the exhibition with Alfred Stieglitz. Simpson wrote to Rodin in February 1908: "I was very pleased here in New York to see the exhibition of your drawings. They are so beautiful, and my sister Madame Robinson purchased two, *La Serpentine* and *L'homme qui marche*. Both are full of beauty and strength. From time to time I admire mine, and I never forget the gifts you have given me."[1] It could be tempting to suggest that the second drawing Simpson mentions is actually the sculpture *The Walking Man*,[2] but an exhibition review also describes a drawing like "the germ of *L'Homme qui marche*, the headless, armless torso on unfinished feet which appeared in plaster at the last Salon, this being a standing nude figure of a young woman holding a drapery of blue and white, but in such a manner that no detail of her figure is lost."[3] Rodin replied to his "very dear friend" Simpson: "It makes me very happy to hear that you think my drawings are beautiful and that Madame Robinson bought two of them."[4]
CBU

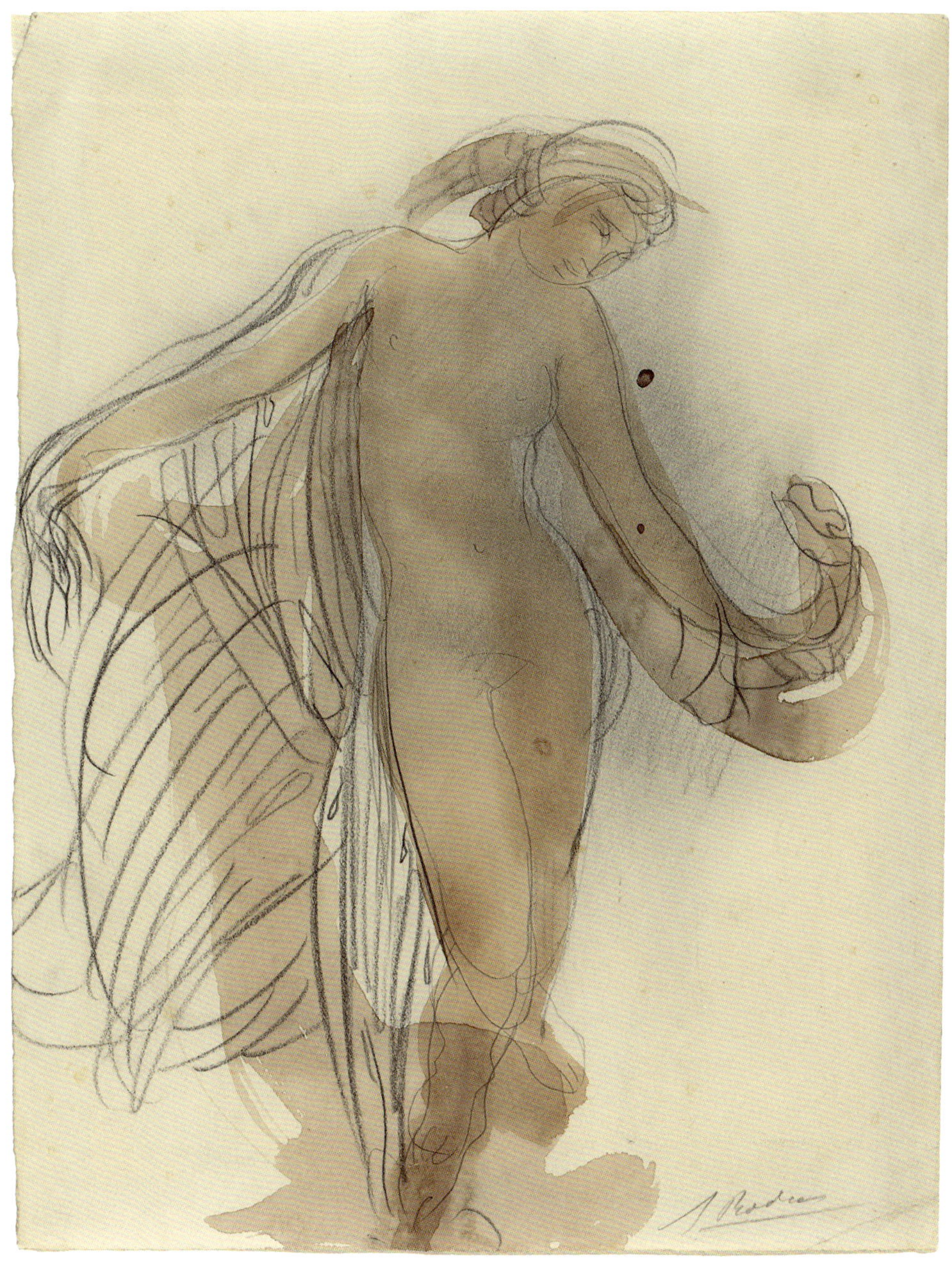

1. Katherine Seney Simpson to Auguste Rodin, February 2, 1908, Archives du musée Rodin, Paris.
2. Anna Tahinci, "Rodin's American Collectors in His Lifetime," in *Rodin and America: Influence and Adaptation, 1876–1936*, exh. cat., ed. Bernard Barryte and Roberta K. Tarbell (Palo Alto, CA: Cantor Arts Center, Stanford University, 2011), 331.
3. "Exhibition of Drawings by M. Auguste Rodin," January 2–January 21, 1908, newspaper transcriptions by Charles Brock, 1997, exhibitions file: New York, Archives du musée Rodin, Paris.
4. Auguste Rodin to Katherine Seney Simpson, February 17, 1908, Archives du musée Rodin, Paris.

MISS JEAN SIMPSON, SEATED

1903
Graphite and watercolor on wove paper
12 ¹³⁄₁₆ × 9 ⅞ in. (32.5 × 25.1 cm)
Inscribed and signed in graphite, upper right:
Mademoiselle Jean / 28 Sept. 1903 / A. Rodin
Signed in graphite, lower right: *A. Rodin*
Brooklyn Museum, New York
Gift of the Iris and B. Gerald Cantor Foundation,
87.94.4

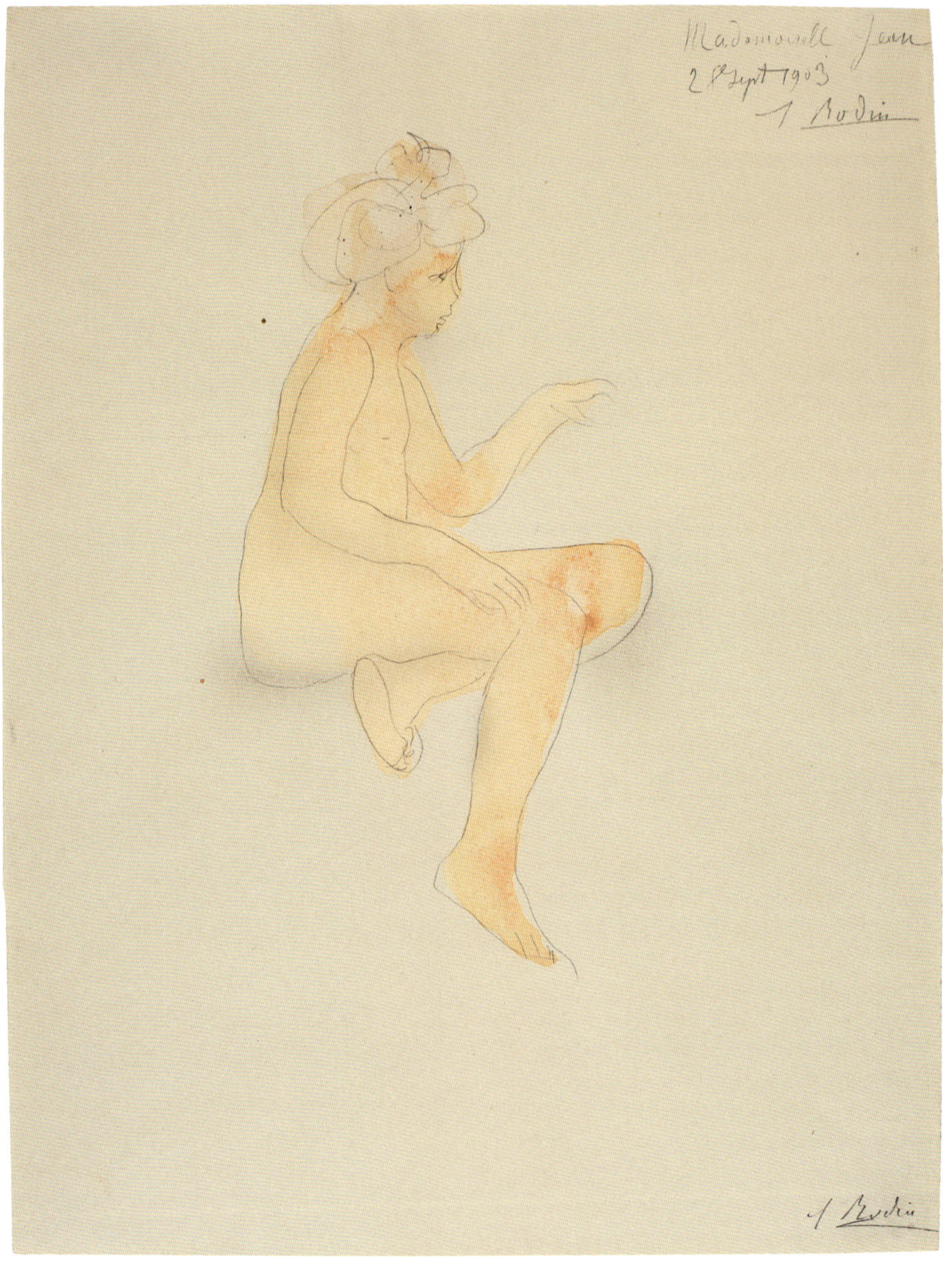

JEAN SIMPSON

1903
Graphite on wove paper
12 $\frac{15}{16}$ × 9 $\frac{13}{16}$ in. (32.9 × 24.9 cm)
Signed in graphite, lower right: *A. Rodin*
Brooklyn Museum, New York
Gift of the Iris and B. Gerald Cantor Foundation,
87.94.3

On September 28, 1903, Rodin made around twenty portraits of Jean Walker Simpson, the daughter of Katherine Seney Simpson, whose bust he was working on. He gave some of these drawings of the six-year-old girl to the Simpsons as a souvenir of that day. These are the only known drawings of children Rodin made after the 1880s. Before that time, Rodin's drawings—particularly those on the themes of Ugolino or Medea—were full of putti and toddlers. Unlike Rodin's usual female models, whom the artist asked to pose in unconventionally free positions, the little girl posed in academic nudity, as in cat. 19.

For this work the artist used the revolutionary method he had adopted in 1896: drawing "blind," without looking at the paper and without taking his eyes off the model posing in front of him, resulting in quick sketches in graphite, or *instantanés* (snapshots), as they were very soon called. Rodin then traced the model's silhouette in a continuous stroke onto thicker paper, recentering it, while maintaining the line of a spontaneous sketch. This is why most of the very pared-down drawings of Jean were preceded by primary life drawings that play the role of preparatory sketches, which Rodin kept for himself (the Brooklyn Museum drawings derive from D. 2210 and D. 1331, Musée Rodin, Paris).

Over the years, the Simpsons' annual visit to the sculptor's studio became the culmination of their summer trip to Europe. Photographs, especially those taken during their outings together to Versailles, reveal the family's sincere and ongoing friendship with Rodin. In December 1912, Rodin wrote to Jean after she sent a holiday card: "I thank Mademoiselle Jean for these thoughts and these little angels. This little watercolor in a pretty tone, by a lively hand. But above all this charming wish for Christmas has touched me deeply."[1] All of Jean's childhood watercolors sent to Rodin can still be seen in the Musée Rodin archives in Paris.
CBU

1. Auguste Rodin to Jean Simpson, Brooklyn Museum, Gift of the Iris and B. Gerald Cantor Foundation, 87.94.5.

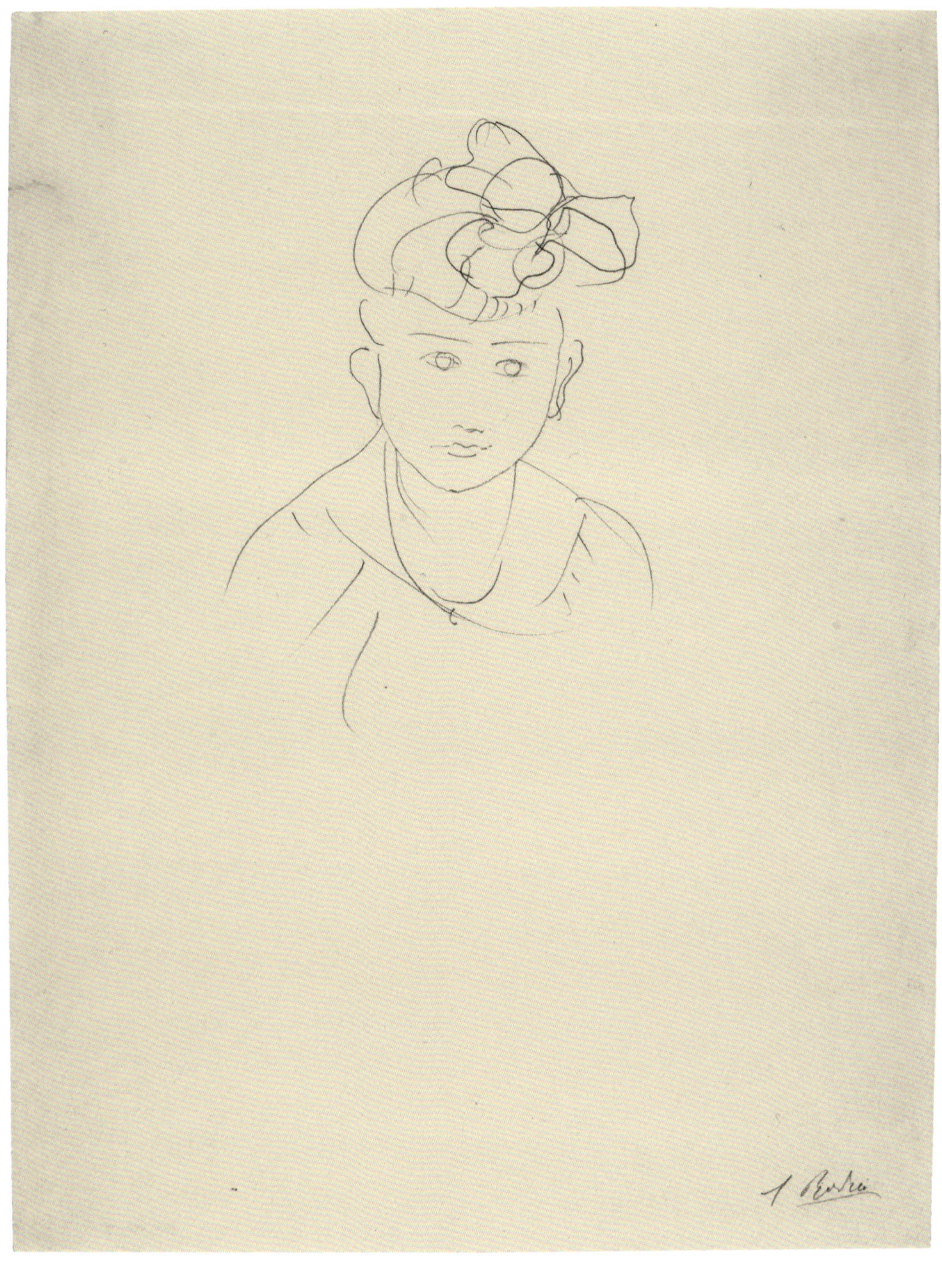

THE THINKER

Original model 1881–82
Bronze, probably cast by Alexis Rudier [no
marks], 1902 or 1906
20 × 21 ½ × 20 ½ in. (50.8 × 54.6 × 52 cm)
Signed on rock and to left of figure: *A. Rodin*
Dedicated, signed, and dated on base near right
foot: *à Loïe Fuller. A. Rodin / 1906*
Yale University Art Gallery, New Haven,
Connecticut
Bequest of Susan Vanderpoel Clark, 1967.82.4

On the tympanum of *The Gates of Hell*
(see fig. 8.1), *The Thinker* is at once Dante,
Victor Hugo, and Charles Baudelaire, the
three poets of significance for Rodin. In fact,
when the sculpture was first shown in
Copenhagen in 1888, it bore the title *The
Poet*.[1] Nude, detached from any context, but
in a pose that has always indicated medita-
tion, the figure has a universal dimension.
It quickly found its definitive form, which
resonates with multiple sources, such as
Michelangelo's *Portrait of Giuliano de' Medici*
(1526–34) in Florence or Albrecht Dürer's
Melancolia I (1514). These associations
contributed to the shift in its title first to
*The Thinker, The Poet: Fragment from the
Gates* at the Monet–Rodin exhibition at
Galerie Georges Petit in 1889, then simply to
The Thinker.

In Copenhagen, as in Paris, the figure was
exhibited in plaster, although a first bronze
had been cast in 1884. Beginning about
a decade later, various founders produced
new casts until Eugène Rudier, who went
on using his father's mark, "Alexis Rudier,"
came onto the scene in 1902. Thanks to
Katherine (Kate) Seney Simpson and John
Woodruff Simpton, a first *Thinker* (cast 1901,
National Gallery of Art, Washington, DC)
arrived on American soil in 1904 and was
shown at Alfred Stieglitz's 291 gallery
in 1910. "The dignified Penseur is like the
guardian angel of the exhibition," Kate
Simpson wrote to Rodin.[2] Yet it was only
after it was enlarged (cat. 69) that the *Thinker*
achieved the celebrity it enjoys today.

The version shown here has a nicely
shaded patina and is dedicated to the
American dancer Loïe Fuller, whose
Serpentine Dance was a great success in Paris
in the 1890s. Hoping to serve as Rodin's
agent in the United States, Fuller organized
an exhibition of about thirty sculptures and
drawings in New York in 1903.[3] It was a
failure, generating no sales, and led to
a falling out between Fuller and the artist,
but they reconciled quite quickly. Fuller
subsequently introduced Rodin to the

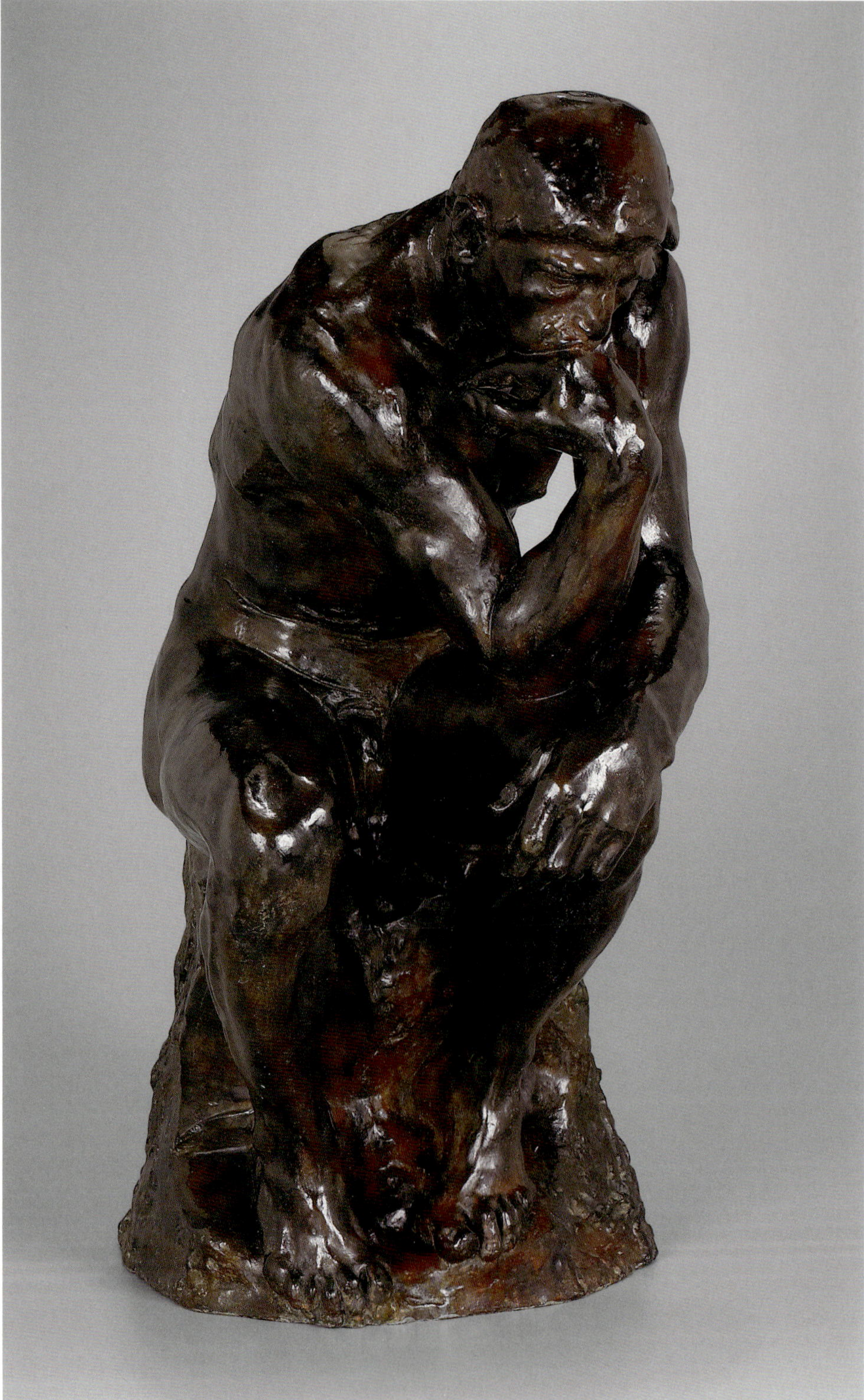

Japanese actress Hanako (cats. 26, 49). This
Thinker's dedication bears the date of 1906,
the year Rodin and Hanako met in Marseille.
The bronze displayed here may be either
the one that was featured in Fuller's 1903
exhibition or another cast of the same model
made in 1906.
ALNR

1. *Exposition française des Beaux-Arts*, Copenhagen,
summer 1888.
2. Katherine Seney Simpson to Auguste Rodin, April
1, 1910, Archives du musée Rodin, Paris; translated
in Ruth Butler, Suzanne Lindsay Glover, and Alison
Luchs, *European Sculpture of the Nineteenth Century:
The Collections of the National Gallery of Art
Systematic Catalogue* (Washington, DC: National
Gallery of Art, 2001), 423.
3. *Exhibition of Statuary and Paintings Belonging to
Miss Loïe Fuller*, National Arts Club of New York,
May 6–16, 1903.

THE HAND OF GOD

Original model 1895
Marble, carved by Louis Mathet, c. 1907
29 × 23 ¾ × 25 ¼ in. (73.7 × 60.3 × 64.1 cm)
Signed on base: *A. Rodin*
Metropolitan Museum of Art, New York
Gift of Edward D. Adams, 1908, 08.210

Several times during 1890s, Rodin used the many hands he had modeled while working on *The Gates of Hell* and the *Monument to the Burghers of Calais* as starting points for new compositions. *The Hand of God*, made beginning with the right hand of Pierre de Wissant, one of the *Burghers*, was much more than a simple assemblage. At a time when he was abandoning the traditional practices of sculpture, such as modeling, Rodin might have felt the need to reaffirm the role of the hand by equating the God of Genesis to a sculptor. Referring to a tradition that dates back to the Hebrew Bible, he had come to the idea, according to Judith Cladel, that the first thing "that God thought of in creating the world, if we can imagine the thoughts of God, was modeling. Isn't it amusing to make God a sculptor before all else?"[1]

In its original state, *The Hand of God* was exhibited in plaster (cat. 51) in Munich (*Vème Exposition International d'art ou Sécession*) in 1896, but only after it was crafted in marble did it attract the enthusiasm of collectors. The marble version at the Metropolitan Museum of Art, New York, one of the first works by Rodin to have entered the collection, was commissioned by Edward D. Adams in 1906 in order to strengthen his connection to Albert Kahn, his French friend, colleague, and fellow banker, for whom the first version (private collection) had been produced. Adams requested the work "through our joint ownership of your creation and by our sympathy with and appreciation of the products of your imagination and skill." And he said he was prepared to pay 15,000 francs for it, "upon the condition that M. Kahn would purchase the example now in your studio in Paris and that I would purchase a smaller example, these two constituting the sole production of your 'creation' design."[2] We know that this was not the case, however: two other marbles followed, one intended for American inventor and industrialist Samuel Colt (1916, Museum of Art, Rhode Island School of Design, Providence) and the other for the future Musée Rodin, Paris (1916–18). ALNR

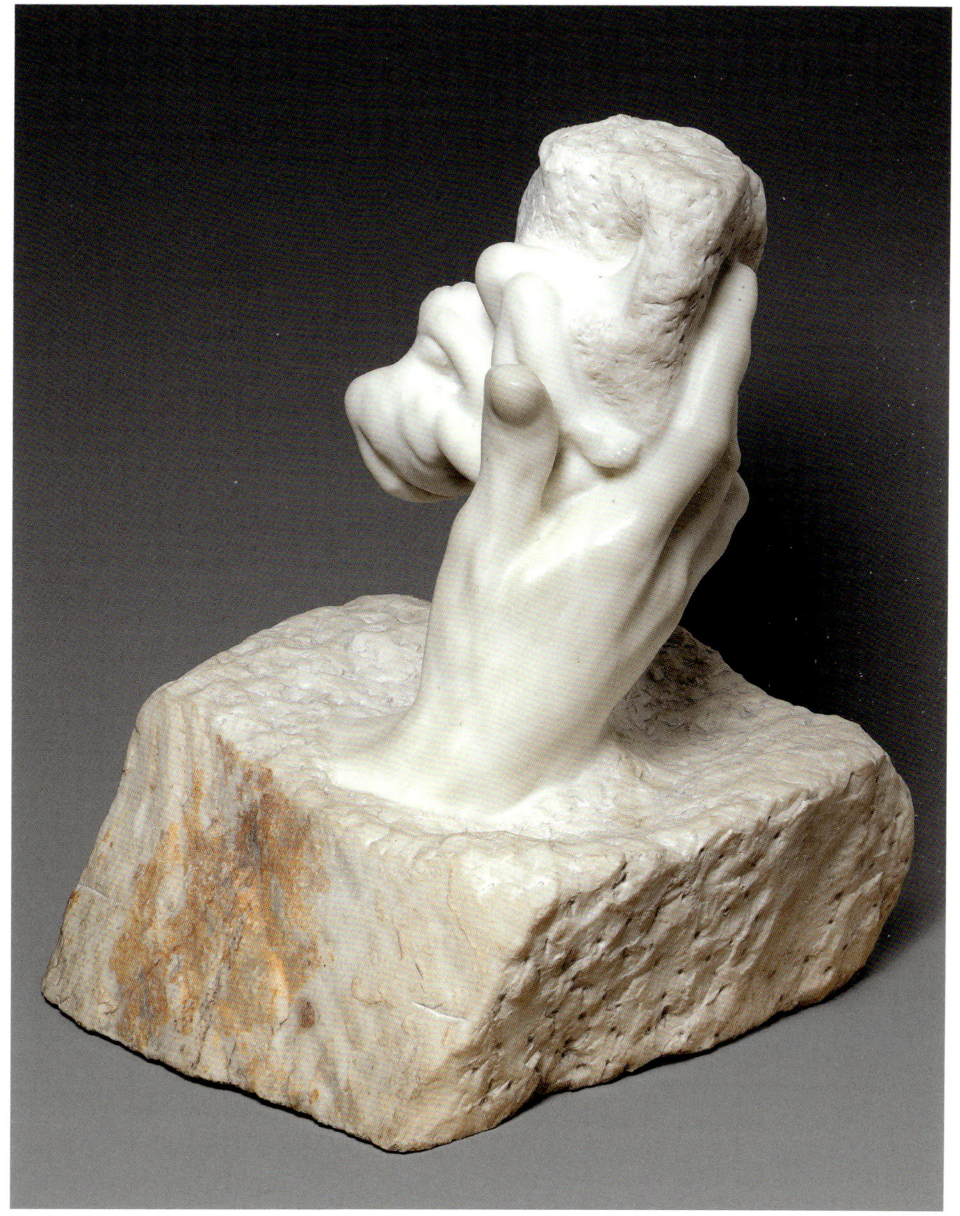

1. Judith Cladel, *Auguste Rodin, l'œuvre et l'homme* (Brussels: Librairie nationale d'art et d'histoire / G. Van Oest, 1908), 82.
2. Edward D. Adams to Auguste Rodin, November 2, 1906, Archives du musée Rodin, Paris.

SEATED NUDE

c. 1900–1908
Graphite with stumping, black crayon, and eraser
on wove paper
12 3/16 × 7 7/8 in. (31 × 20 cm)
Dedicated and signed in graphite, top right: *à
Monsieur Edward / Robinson / directeur du
Musée / Metropolitain / de New York / en
grande sympathie / Auguste Rodin*
Jonathan and Abby Freund, United States

Edward Robinson, who became the director
of the Metropolitan Museum of Art, New
York, in 1910, was instrumental in the
selection of the Rodin collection at the Met,
along with the museum's purchasing agent
John Marshall and the American sculptor
Daniel Chester French. Robinson discovered
Rodin's drawings during his visit to the
sculptor's studio in the summer of 1910.
The Met had just purchased some of Rodin's
drawings from the exhibition at Alfred
Stieglitz's 291 gallery in New York (see cats.
25, 26). In 1913, when sending the latest
sculptures acquired for the Met, Rodin told
Robinson he was very pleased with the
growth of the museum's Rodin gallery and
that he held back some drawings specially
for the Met—those would be the ones given
thanks to Thomas Fortune Ryan (see cats. 27,
28). We do not know how many drawings
Rodin sent to Robinson as a personal gift,
but *Seated Woman* was certainly among
them, with its formal yet amicable dedication
to the museum director. Rodin possibly
selected it for its classical appearance and its
virtuosity, yet the figure is radically different
from an academic nude. It is a life drawing
in keeping with the working method the
artist adopted as of 1896. The free use of the
pencil and strong calligraphic intensity give
it the appearance of a studio sketch that
was quickly made. The almost-abstract lines
forming the curly hair, like animated volutes,
join those tracing the back of the chair.
The mere presence of the chair is unusual. In
order to give his figures a timeless character,
Rodin seldom kept the furniture or objects
he drew in his preliminary drawings (a pared-
down variation of this drawing without the
chair exists [D. 2275, Musée Rodin, Paris]).
Here, the stumping, the white highlights
with the eraser, and the hatch marks do not
play their usual role of value markers in a
traditional way but contribute to the powerful
expression of the twisting back, the main
focus of the drawing. As revealed in a letter
from Susan Robinson, who bequeathed the

drawing to Katherine Lane, her husband
displayed the work until the end of his life
"on the mantel in his study" for his personal
enjoyment.[1]
CBU

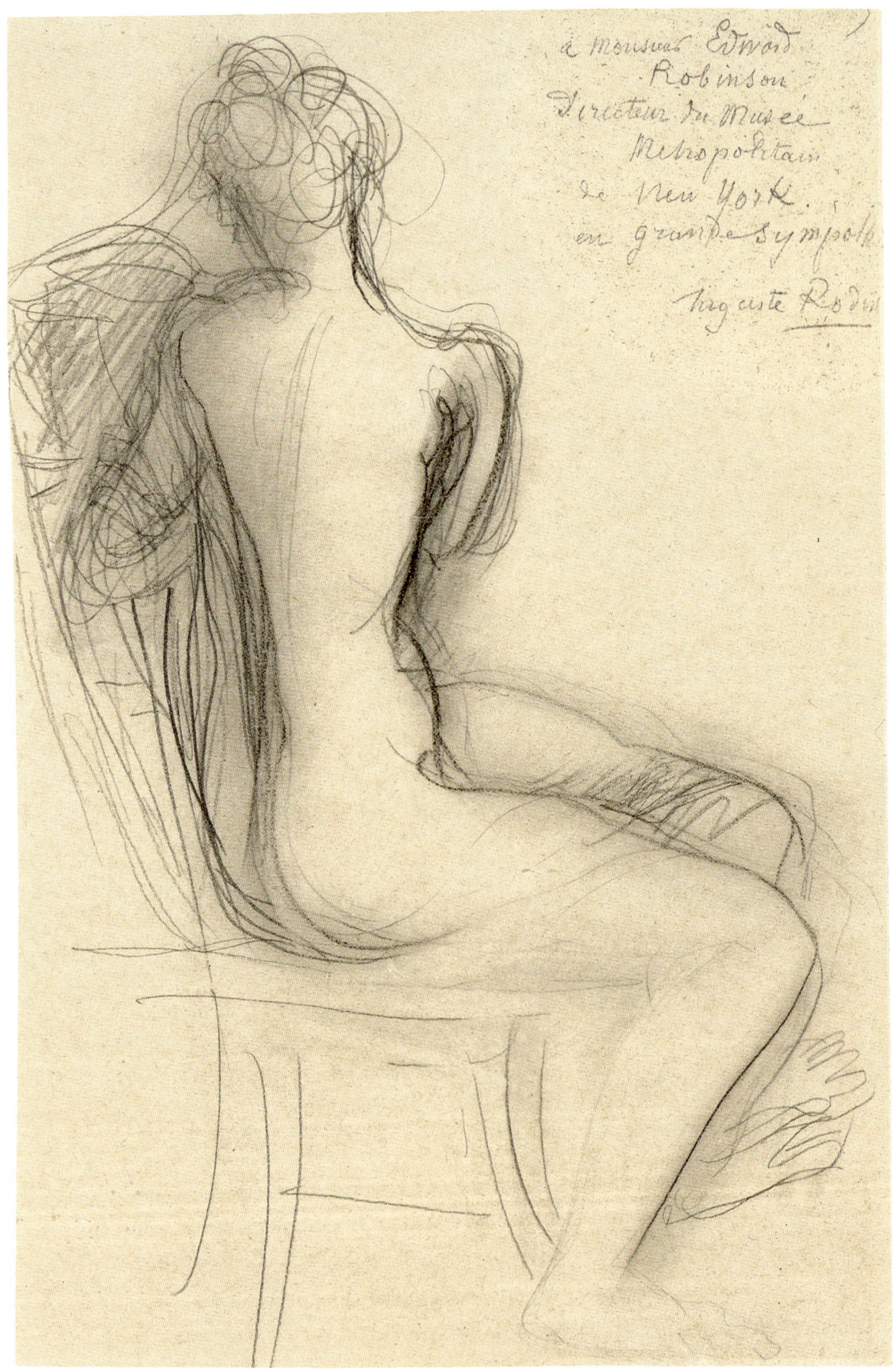

1. Susan Robinson to Katherine Lane, n.d.,
handwritten letter on verso of the mount for *Seated
Woman.*

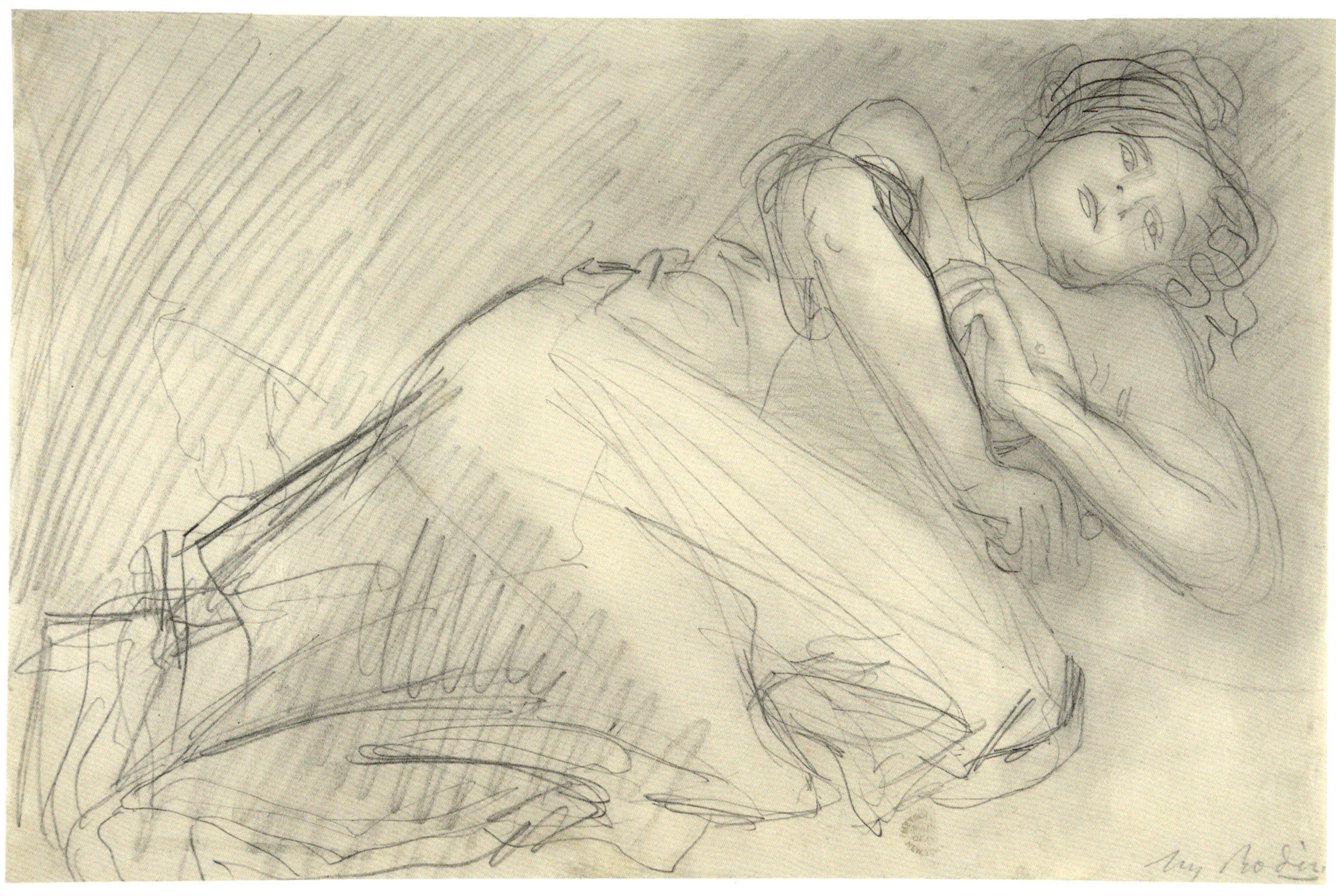

CAT. 24
THE ABANDONED (PSYCHE)

c. 1902
Graphite with stumping on wove paper
7 9/16 × 11 7/8 in. (19.4 × 30.4 cm)
Signed in graphite, lower right: *Aug. Rodin*
Metropolitan Museum of Art, New York
Rogers Fund, 1910, 10.45.20

This drawing was chosen for New York's Metropolitan Museum of Art by the British art critic Roger Fry, a painter in the Bloomsbury Group, who for a while was the curator of the museum's department of European paintings. It was the first Rodin drawing purchased for the Met through the bequest of businessman and patron Jacob S. Rogers. In May 1906, the same year he joined the museum, Fry, who had met Rodin at the home of William Rothenstein in London, visited Rodin's studio with his wife. Contrary to what has been asserted, it was not at this time that he acquired the drawing for the Met.[1] In fact, the artist kept *The Abandoned* until 1909, when Rodin himself put it up for auction at the Hôtel Drouot in Paris. The drawing is reproduced in the catalogue of this sale.[2] As indicated in the records of the sale, the dealer Percy Moore Turner acquired it for 380 francs, and he later offered it to Fry.[3]

The Abandoned, the title used in the catalogue, was chosen by the artist and should be understood as a reference to the myth of Psyche. After reading the *Metamorphoses* by Apuleius, Rodin devoted a series of drawings and watercolors to this subject, sometimes without making the connection explicit (see, for example, *Seated Woman [Psyche]*, cat. 36). The same figure, often reclining and draped in fabric, can represent different moments in the legend (see cats. 34, 36, 55, 56). Here, the melancholic expression of the model possibly refers to the theme of Psyche's abandonment to her gruesome fate. Beautiful Psyche, unknowingly a rival of Venus, was condemned to marry a monster and wait for him alone at the top of a ledge. She would later learn that her husband was none other than Cupid himself.

CBU

1. Roberta K. Tarbell, "Auguste Rodin's Drawings and Their Impact on American Artists," in *Rodin and America: Influence and Adaptation 1876–1936*, exh. cat., ed. Bernard Barryte and Roberta K. Tarbell (Stanford, CA: Iris and B. Gerald Cantor Center for Visual Arts, 2011), 171.
2. *Catalogue des peintures et dessins anciens et modernes*, Hôtel Drouot sale, Paris, May 6, 1909, cat. 119c.
3. Sales record, "6 Mai 1909. Vente de peintures et de dessins, Hôtel Drouot, salle 6. Requête de Me André Desvouges, Commissaire-priseur," Archives de Paris D60 E.

NERO

c. 1900–1910
Graphite with stumping, watercolor, and gouache
on wove paper
12 13/16 × 9 13/16 in. (32.5 × 24.9 cm)
Signed in graphite, lower right: *Aug. Rodin*
Inscribed in graphite, center right: *Néron*
Inscribed in later hand in graphite, lower left: *17*
Metropolitan Museum of Art, New York
John Stewart Kennedy Fund, 1910, 10.66.5

The seven Rodin drawings purchased by
the Metropolitan Museum of Art, New York,
at Alfred Stieglitz's 291 gallery in 1910[1] are
representative of the variety of the artist's
production at this time: life drawings in
pencil of female nudes (*Figure Disrobing*
and *Young Girl Kneeling*, both 1900–1910);
works whose models are known and that
are connected to his sculptural activity
(*Sketch for Figure on Whistler Monument*,
1905, posed for by Gwen John; the Japanese
actress *Hanako* [cat. 26]); and, finally,
masterfully executed drawings with layers
of gouache, watercolor wash, soft lead
pencil, and stumping (*The Embrace*, 1900–
1910; *Seated Female Nude*, 1900–1910).
Nero belongs to this last group.

There are only two known drawings by
Rodin annotated "Nero." As Victoria
Thorson has pointed out, both depict female
models.[2] Here, the model is kneeling, her
eyes crazed, surrounded by a halo of clouds
formed by a skillful interplay of hatch
marks, zigzags, and stumping. The figure
seems to exist outside the real world. In the
version held by the Musée Rodin, Paris,
the model, seated on a throne, appears as
an evanescent image whose face and asexual
body are difficult to make out. The Photo-
Secession exhibition notes in *Camera Work*
praise the drawing: "The bestiality of
[Rodin's] *Nero*, the Roman emperor, whose
square sensual head is crowned with foliage,
while the lower part of the figure is envel-
oped in an orgy of color suggestive of spilt
wine and blood, could hardly be surpassed."[3]
CBU

1. *An Exhibition of Recent and Early Drawings and
Watercolors by Auguste Rodin*, Little Galleries of the
Photo-Secession, March 1–April 1, 1910.
2. Victoria Thorson, "Symbolism and Conservatism
in Rodin's Late Drawings," in *The Drawings of Rodin*,
ed. Albert E. Elsen and J. Kirk T. Varnedoe (New
York: Praeger, 1971), 123.
3. Alfred Stieglitz, "Photo-Secession Notes: Rodin
Exhibition," in *Camera Work: The Complete
Illustrations 1903–1917*, ed. Pam Roberts (Cologne:
Taschen, 1997), 531 [no. 31, 1910].

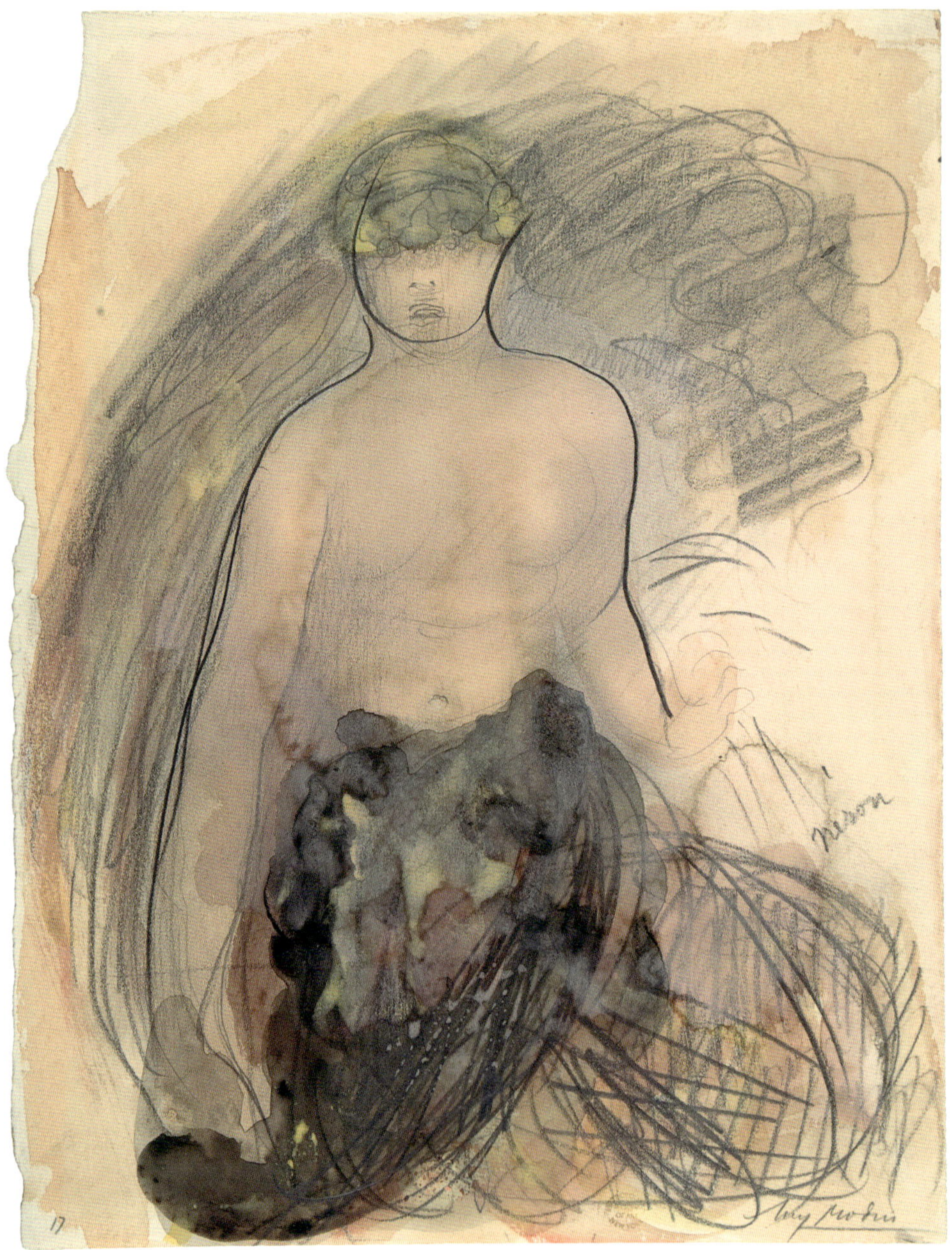

HANAKO

July 1906–7
Graphite, pen and ink, crayon, and gouache on wove paper
11 ¾ × 8 ⁷⁄₁₆ in. (29.8 × 21.4 cm)
Inscribed and signed in graphite, lower right: *Hanako / Aug. Rodin*
Inscribed by later hand in graphite, lower left: *9*
Metropolitan Museum of Art, New York
John Stewart Kennedy Fund, 1910, 10.66.2

We know of relatively few portrait drawings by Rodin in relation to the number of busts produced over the course of his career. *Hanako* is no exception. Compared to approximately fifty sculptures depicting this model, Ōta Hisa, a Japanese actress known as Hanako, we count only four known drawn portraits, including this one. The drawings, probably executed in July 1906 and reworked later, differ from the multiple expression heads modeled by Rodin during the years 1907–11 (cf. cat. 49).[1] After their first meeting, at the Colonial Exposition in Marseille in July 1906 (arranged by Loïe Fuller, who was Hanako's agent), Rodin asked Hanako to pose for him. He had discovered the actress in a performance with her company Arayama, adapted from traditional kabuki for the Western public. Hanako later related that Rodin first wanted to draw her in "her stage costume as a Jingoro doll, with her hairstyle and dress the same."[2]

Two portraits were perhaps produced on the spot. In one, held at the Musée Rodin in Paris (D. 2867), her hair is styled in the traditional geisha bun. In this second portrait, from the Metropolitan Museum of Art, New York, Hanako wears a stage wig with flowers and ribbons. The composition is striking, with the drawing arranged at the very top of a sheet left mostly white, like the untouched block of marble in the sculpture *Thought* (cat. 10). But here, Rodin has inverted the values of opposition between the polished skin tones and the roughly hewn block. The drawing's imperfections appear in the astonishing blue-gray wash defining Hanako's face and clasped hands. Flecked with something like a network of freckles, it recalls the air bubbles Rodin left on his plaster casts and his interest in surfaces with irregular textures. We find these effects in the artist's contemporaneous portraits of the young veiled Ottoman Turkish woman Nourye de

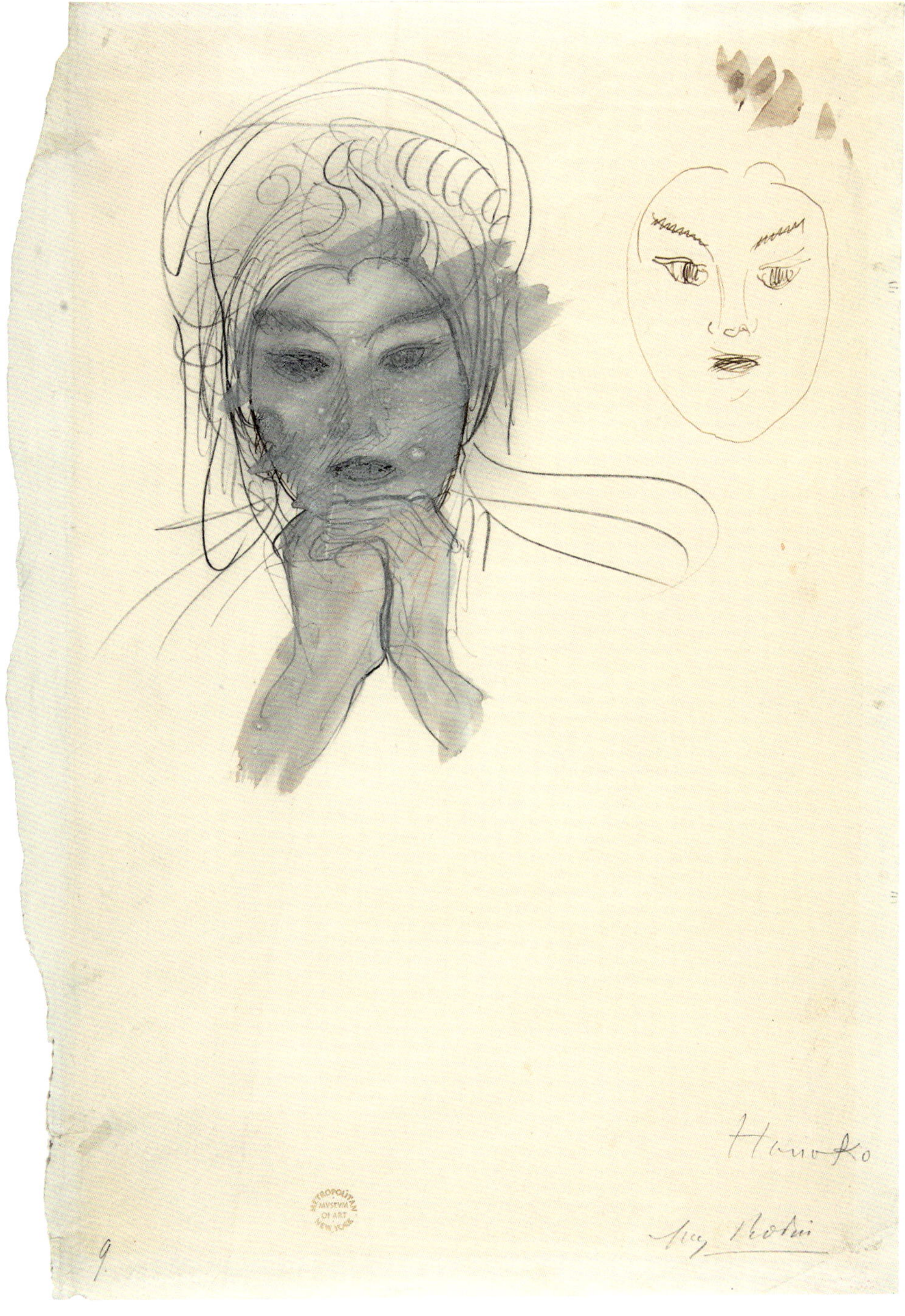

Rohozinska, whose features are suggested through transparent gouache. Exhibited in 1910 at Alfred Stieglitz's 291 gallery, the drawing of Hanako can also be read as a double portrait, with a bare face sketched to the right of the watercolor-pigmented one, like a photographic negative and its positive. The pared-down white face at right resembles a stylized Noh mask used in Japanese dance theater.
CBU

1. The versions of the very expressive portraits of Hanako are classified in a series of types, from type A to type G, recording different stages in various media (terracotta, plaster, plastiline) in the development of the heads.
2. *Gifu nichinichi shimbun*, January 6–7, 1925, cited by Miyuki Minami, "Rodin et Hanako," in *Rodin et le Japon*, exh. cat., ed. Claudie Judrin (Shizuoka: Prefectoral Museum of Art, 2001), 17.

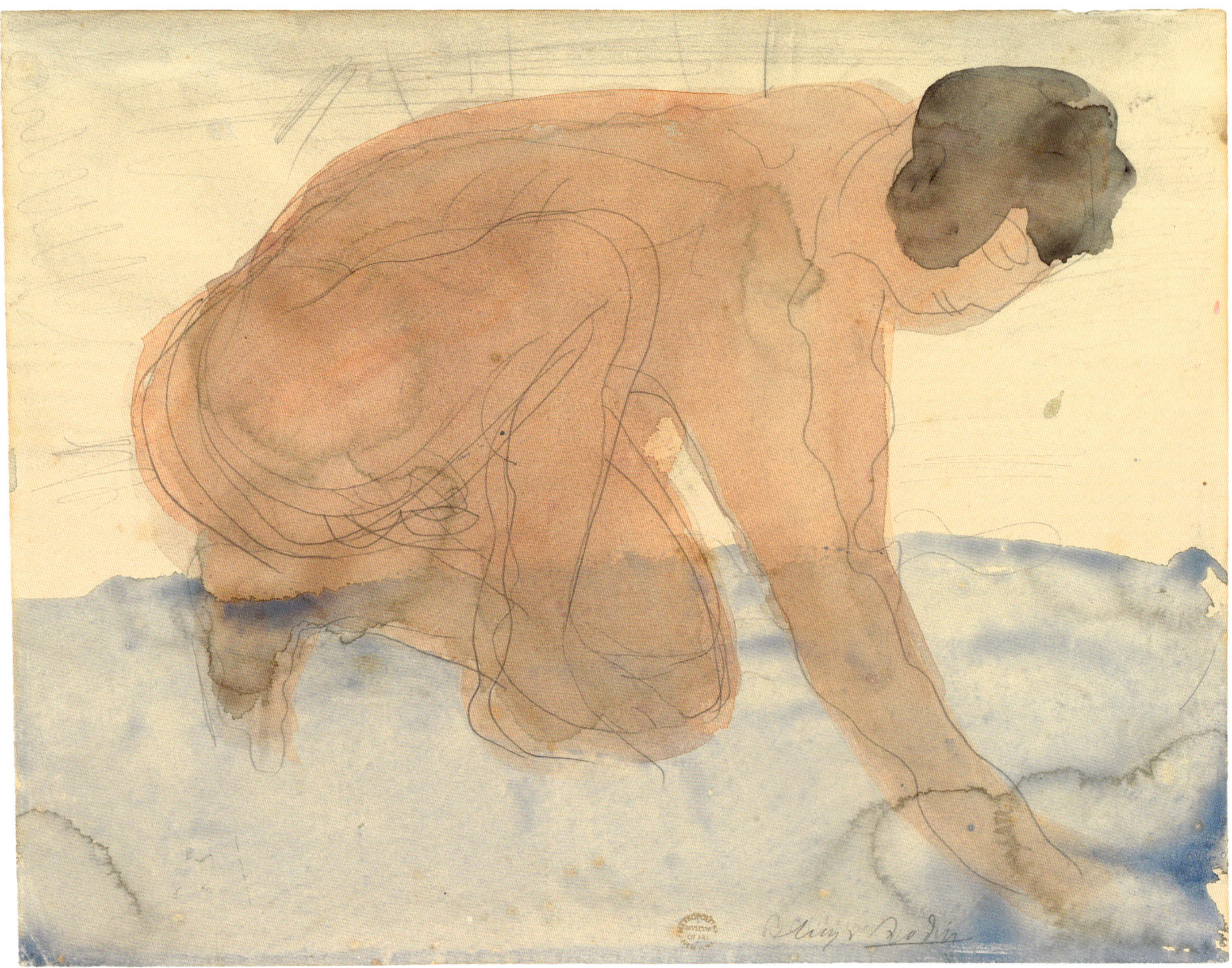

NUDE FIGURE ON HANDS AND KNEES (EXECUTIONER)

c. 1898–1900
Graphite with stumping and watercolor on wove paper
9 3/4 × 12 13/16 in. (24.8 × 32.5 cm)
Signed in graphite over inscription, lower right: *Aug. Rodin*
Inscribed in graphite, lower right: *Bourreau*
Metropolitan Museum of Art, New York
Gift of Thomas F. Ryan, 1913, 13.164.1

Nude Figure on Hands and Knees, which can be dated to about 1898–1900, is linked to a companion piece (the primary life drawing of the same model in the same pose), *Kneeling Nude Male*, labeled a "bas-relief" in the Rodin Museum in Philadelphia (cat. 82). The two drawings reveal how Rodin might respond to the same theme with either sculptural—using hatchings and effects of stumping for volume—or pictorial perception. Around 1900, color assumed an increasingly dominant place in his works on paper as watercolor tended to invade the page and transform Rodin's drawings into paintings. Often, a complex, abstract mass creates an environment around the figure, sometimes evoking a landscape. The body then becomes a hill, mountain, moon, or planet. Many of Rodin's figures seem to be immersed in watercolor, which he sometimes confirms by adding a tiny boat on the edge of the color wash (see cats. 76, 95).

In *Nude Figure on Hands and Knees*, the blue watercolor tentatively suggests the sea or a cloudy sky, though the horizon is not completely level. Undoubtedly, both are possible, as in a drawing of a woman floating in the waves that Rodin annotated *Nuage* (Cloud) and *Naufrage* (Shipwreck) (D. 4081, Musée Rodin, Paris). Here, the muscled arms of the young man, with undefined extremities, seem to penetrate into an area of spots that the highly aqueous watercolor spontaneously forms on the paper. Rodin often used these effects to draw the aquatic plant world. Some contemporaneous drawings, such as *Apollo in the Sea* and *Apollo in the Clouds*, are similar to *Nude Figure on Hands and Knees*, and the few lines bursting forth behind his back could depict rays of light for the god of the sun. As often in Rodin's work, the watercolors are polysemous, and the word *bourreau* (executioner), barely legible under the signature, refers to the novel 1899 *Le jardin des supplices* (*The Torture Garden*) by Octave Mirbeau. Rodin created twenty drawings to illustrate the second edition of this baroque text centering on the atrocities of colonialism, published by Ambroise Vollard in 1902 (for the first edition, see cat. 96).

CBU

FEMALE NUDE RECLINING

c. 1909–10
Graphite with stumping on wove paper
14 3/16 × 9 1/4 in. (36 × 23.5 cm)
Signed in graphite, lower right: *Aug Rodin*
Metropolitan Museum of Art, New York
Gift of Thomas F. Ryan, 1913, 13.164.4

Among the six drawings that entered the Metropolitan Museum of Art, New York, in 1913 through the financial gift of Thomas F. Ryan, *Female Nude Reclining* should be set apart. Executed around 1909–10, at a time when Rodin was beginning to focus on the exclusive use of graphite, the drawing depicts a recumbent model dressed in a wide-open robe. Only her arms, quickly sketched, are covered, while her face, torso, and thighs are offered up to the viewer's gaze. Rodin oriented the sheet vertically, which makes the twisting body more expressive, and he signed it in this direction. The unusual vertical orientation for a reclining nude gives the viewer a looming vantage point that makes the figure seem closer, nearly palpable. Two other drawings at the Musée Rodin in Paris likely depict the same model at the same time: *Female Nude Reclining with Open Garments* (D.2963), annotated "Steichen/photo/antique"; and *Female Nude Sitting with Her Bathrobe Half Open* (D. 5097), which bears the label "Photo-Secession." It is tempting to recognize in her the features of Claire Coudert, the duchesse de Choiseul, Rodin's "muse" from 1909 to 1912, whom he also called his "little bacchante." Different from Rodin's usual nudes, these three drawings have nothing synthetic or distanced about them. Here, the gesture is extended through attentive observation, almost as if this were a portrait. Rarely was Rodin so intimate. The closeness to the model reaches a climax through the astonishing use of contrasts— as between the rapid lines of the arms and hands and the subtle treatment of the flesh— that reflect Rodin's increasing interest in photography, in particular the work of the American Pictorialists. The stringy hatch marks, the doubled breasts, and the navel create a blurred effect, as in a photograph, contrasting with the clear focus on the nose and mouth, drawn with a sharp pencil.
CBU

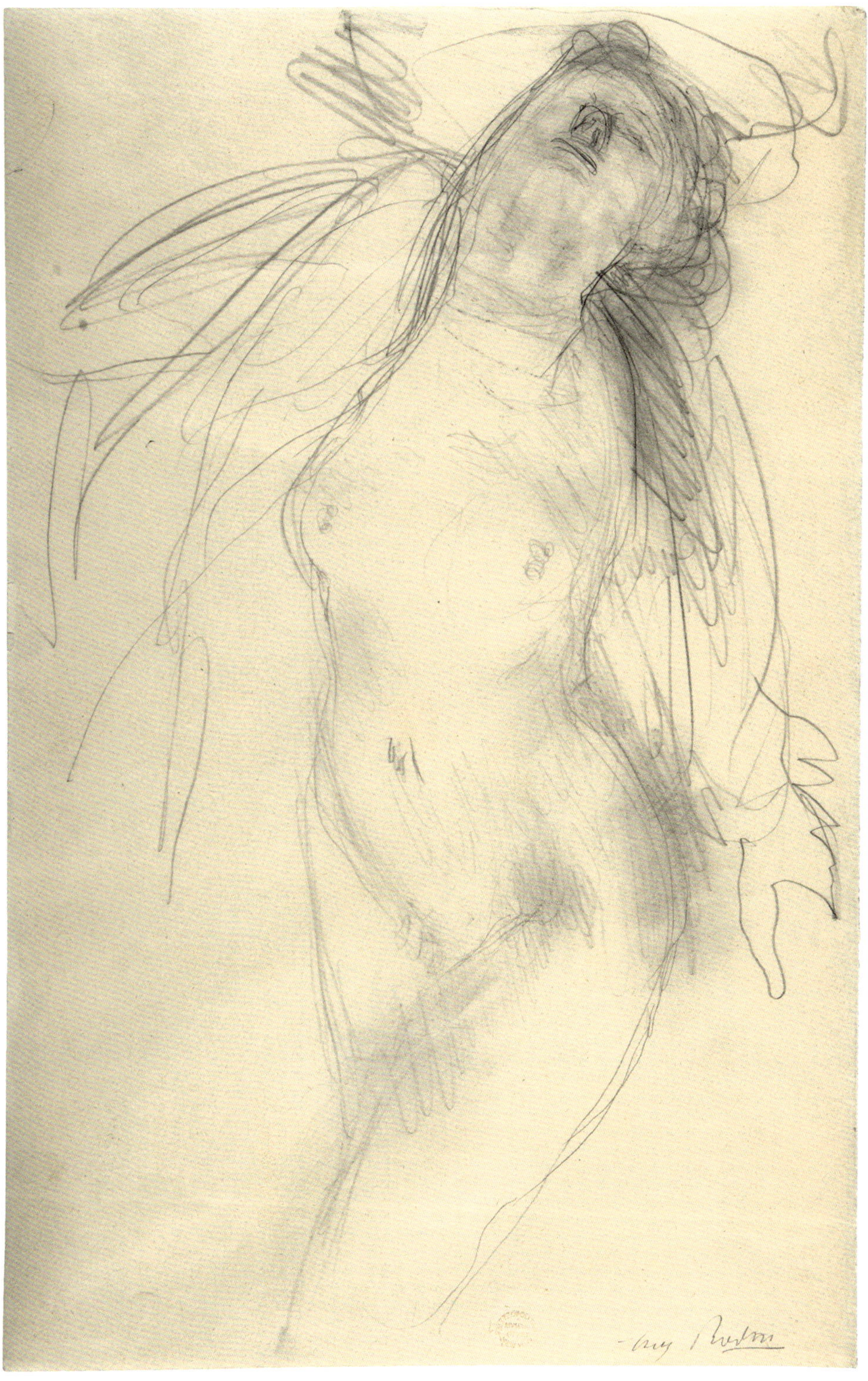

HONORÉ DE BALZAC

1891
Terracotta
With base: 15 × 5 × 5 in. (38.1 × 12.7 ×
12.7 cm)
Signed on back of neck: *A. Rodin*
Metropolitan Museum of Art, New York
Rogers Fund, 1912, 12.11.1

Purchased directly from the artist's studio,
this head study dates to the very beginning
of the long genesis of Rodin's monument
to the novelist Honoré de Balzac (1799–1850),
the first president of the Société des Gens
de Lettres. Before even receiving the official
commission on August 14, 1891, Rodin
began work, gathering an abundance of
documentation (written and artistic) and
traveling across Touraine, where Balzac was
born, seeking a model who looked like the
writer. He found one in Tours: a cart driver
by the name of Estager, who is well known
through a series of photographs.

Estager posed for Rodin in fall 1891
while the sculptor was staying with Camille
Claudel at the Château de l'Islette near
Azay-le-Rideau. From the many sittings he
required of Estager, whom Rodin asked to
grow out his hair so that the resemblance
would be perfect, there remain two studies:
a mask held at the Musée Rodin, Paris, and
this head from the Metropolitan Museum
of Art, New York. This terracotta bears
all the signs of direct modeling, such as a
flattened lump of clay on the upper lip,
incisions indicating the mustache, and the
fact that it was hollowed out for firing.
The eyes of both studies are the same, but
the artworks differ in expression; the mask
in the Musée Rodin is more smiling. Both
were cast in bronze. Through a series of
subsequent moldings, following adjustments
and changes made by adding material, the
mask allowed Rodin to finish the bust called
Smiling Head (Musée Rodin, Paris, S. 764),
which ended the first phase of his work,
around 1893, before being enlarged around
1899. The definitive head used in the
completed monument (cat. 85), modeled
in 1898, belongs to a different type.
ALNR

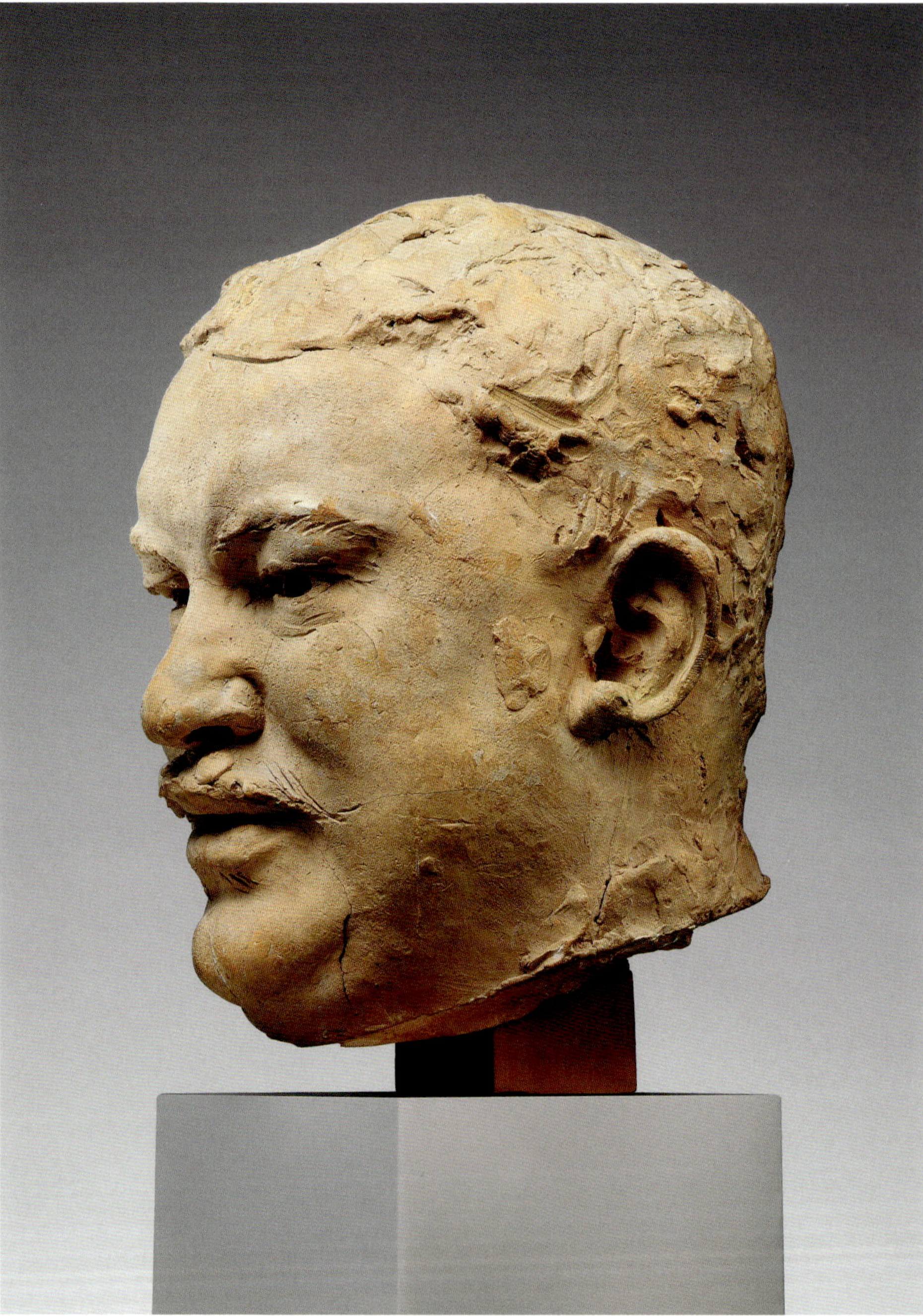

YOUNG WOMAN KNEELING

Original model late 19th–early 20th century
Plaster
8 1/8 × 6 5/16 × 4 in. (20.6 × 16.8 × 10.2 cm)
Signed vertically on the figure's back: *Rodin*
Metropolitan Museum of Art, New York
Gift of Auguste Rodin, 1912, 12.12.3

Rodin was very pleased with the purchases
that New York's Metropolitan Museum of Art
made from him in 1911 through a financial
gift of Thomas Fortune Ryan. To show his
gratitude, he added a bust of Ryan (1909),
which was a strong image of a powerful man;
the superb *Torso (A Study for Ariane without
Arms)* in terracotta, influenced by recollec-
tions of Michelangelo; and several studies in
plaster, including *Head of Mrs. Russell* and
Gwen John (Study for a Muse) as well as small
figures such as this example and studies
of hands, arms, and legs. This led the Met
to elect him Honorary Fellow for Life.[1]

Some of Rodin's plaster casts can be
related to well-known works, but this is not
the case for all of them. It is impossible to
date this *Young Woman Kneeling*, a simple
study from life.
ALNR

1. *Annual Report of the Trustees of the Metropolitan
Museum of Art*, 1911, Archives, Metropolitan
Museum of Art, New York.

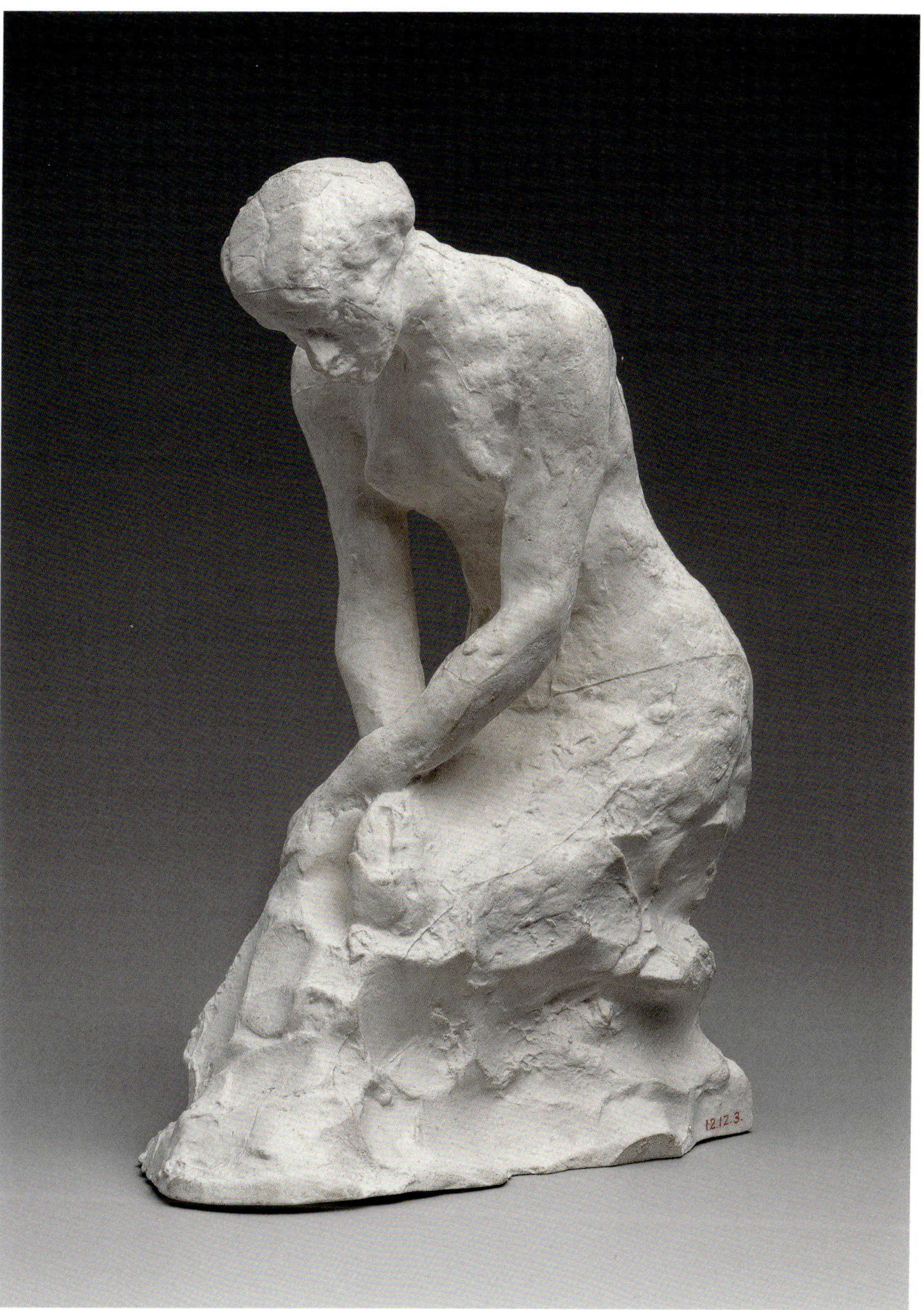

STUDY OF THE LEFT HAND AND ARM OF "MEDITATION"

Original model c. 1894
Plaster
4⅛ × 9⅛ × 6⅛ in. (10.5 × 23.2 × 15.6 cm)
Signed around opening of base: *A. Rodin*
Metropolitan Museum of Art, New York
Gift of Auguste Rodin, 1912, 12.12.9

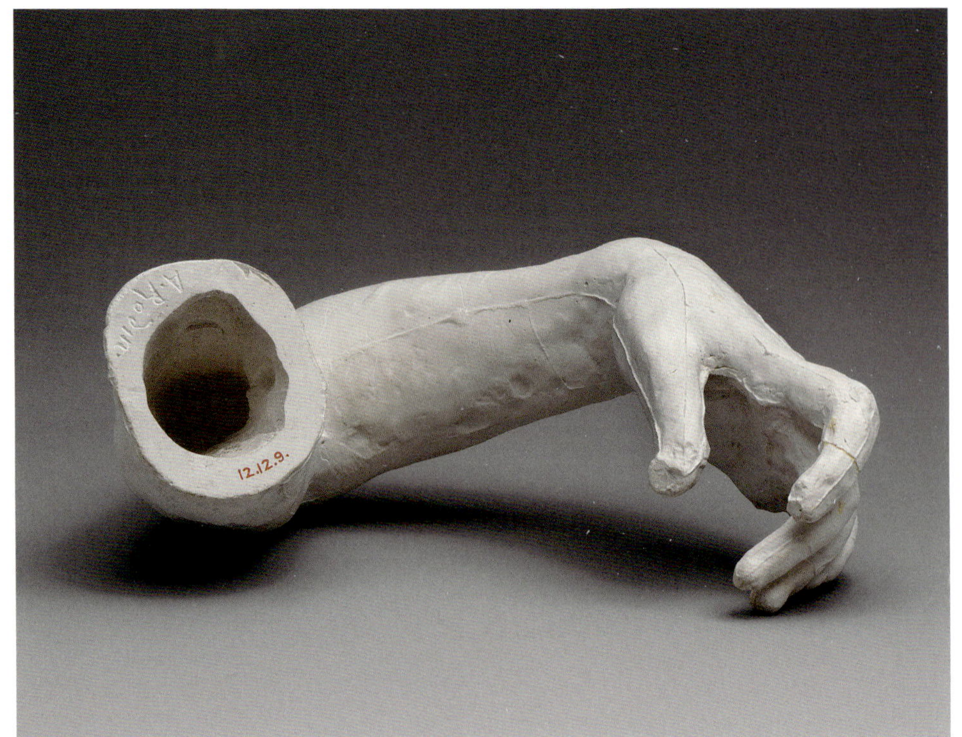

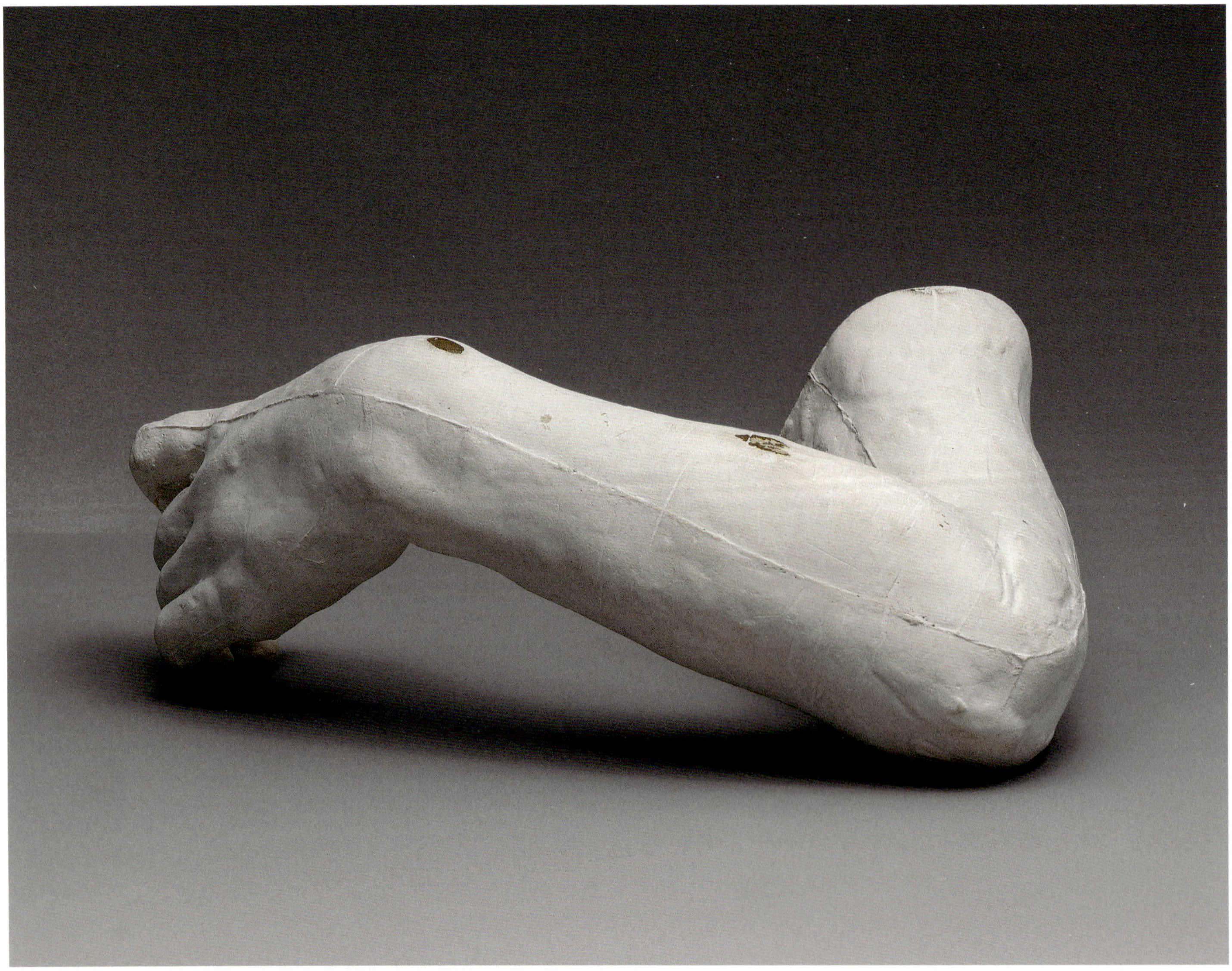

STUDY OF A HAND

Original model late 19th–early 20th century
Plaster
4 ¾ × 2 × 1 ¼ in. (12.1 × 5.1 × 3.2 cm)
Signed under base: *A. Rodin*
Metropolitan Museum of Art, New York
Gift of Auguste Rodin, 12.12.16

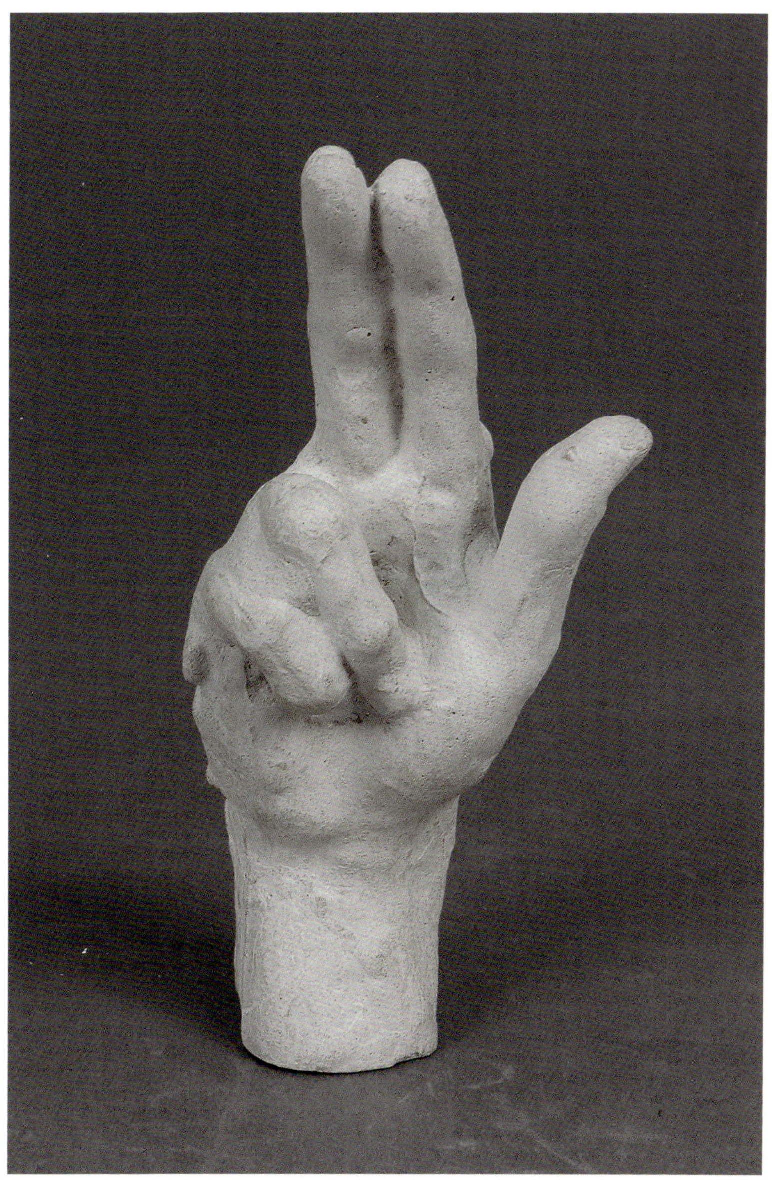

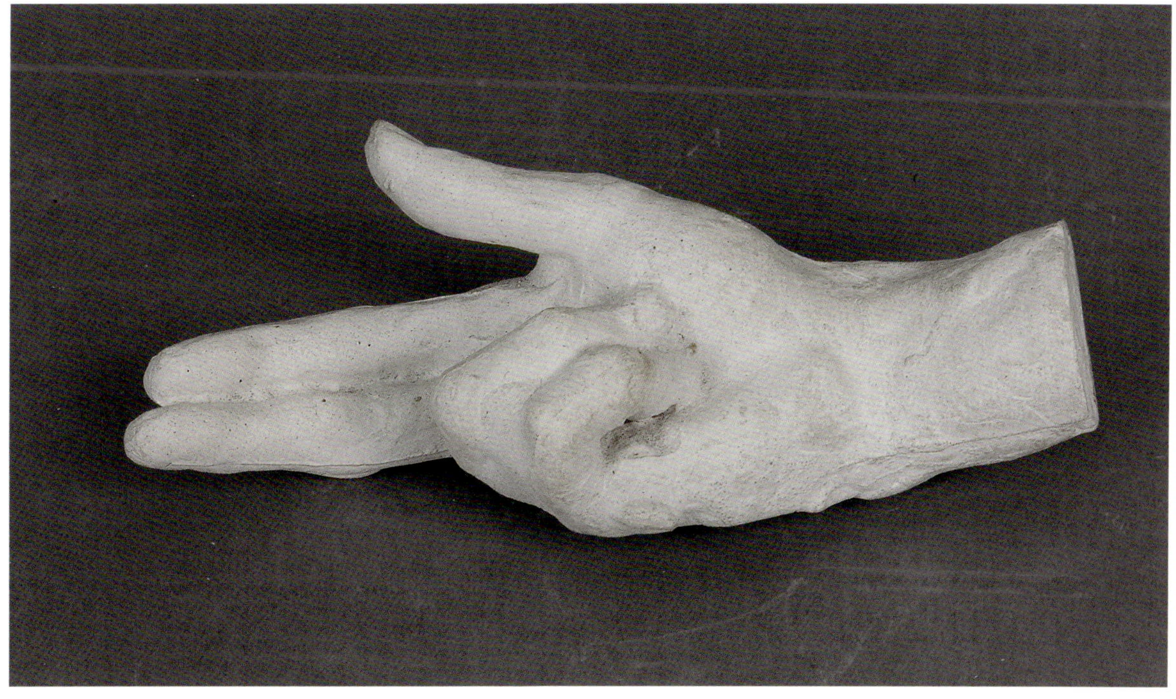

STUDY OF A HAND

Original model late 19th–early 20th century
Plaster
6 3/8 × 2 1/2 × 3 3/4 in. (16.2 × 6.4 × 9.5 cm)
Signed under base: *A. Rodin*
Metropolitan Museum of Art, New York
Gift of Auguste Rodin, 1912, 12.12.10

Beginning in the 1880s, Rodin established a supply of hands and arms, feet, and legs, multiplied through casting, into which he could delve according to his needs, without having to go through all the steps involved in modeling. These *abattis* (body parts: limbs and heads), of which the Musée Rodin, Paris, has dozens of copies of all sizes, are part of his studio materials, freeing the creative act from the delays inherent in the sculptor's craft. Even if the first ones were simple fragments intended for the figures in *The Gates of Hell*, Rodin gave each one, however small, an expressiveness that allowed them to become autonomous artworks. In fact, he exhibited some of them or had them cast in bronze, and he also had them photographed. For his images, Eugène Druet staged Rodin's plasters on a white woolen blanket, the hand becoming in Druet's lens a kind of monster, "which seems to crawl, violent, furrowed with cracks, with a forced movement of tentacles, with a movement like a driven animal, crippled, still marching toward an invisible enemy."[1] Rodin was encouraged in this direction by the ancient fragments he collected, and also by a long sculptural tradition of making the hand almost a separate individual. Some hands also served as the starting point for assemblages, such as the *The Hand of God* (cat. 22), or for enlargements.

He did not like to part with these studies, yet he did give away sets of them on a few occasions to show his gratitude or friendship. The set of small hands, arms, and legs given by the artist to the Metropolitan Museum of Art, New York, at the time of the opening of the museum's Rodin gallery in 1912 was completed in 1966 by five small hands bequeathed by the sculptor and his former student Malvina Hoffman, to whom he had also given them. We find others in the National Gallery of Art, Washington, DC; in the Legion of Honor, San Francisco; and at the Maryhill Museum in Goldendale, Washington, thanks to avid collectors Katherine Seney Simpson, Alma Spreckels, and Loïe Fuller.
ANLR

1. Gustave Kahn, "Les mains de Rodin," *La Plume*, no. 266 (May 15, 1900): 316.

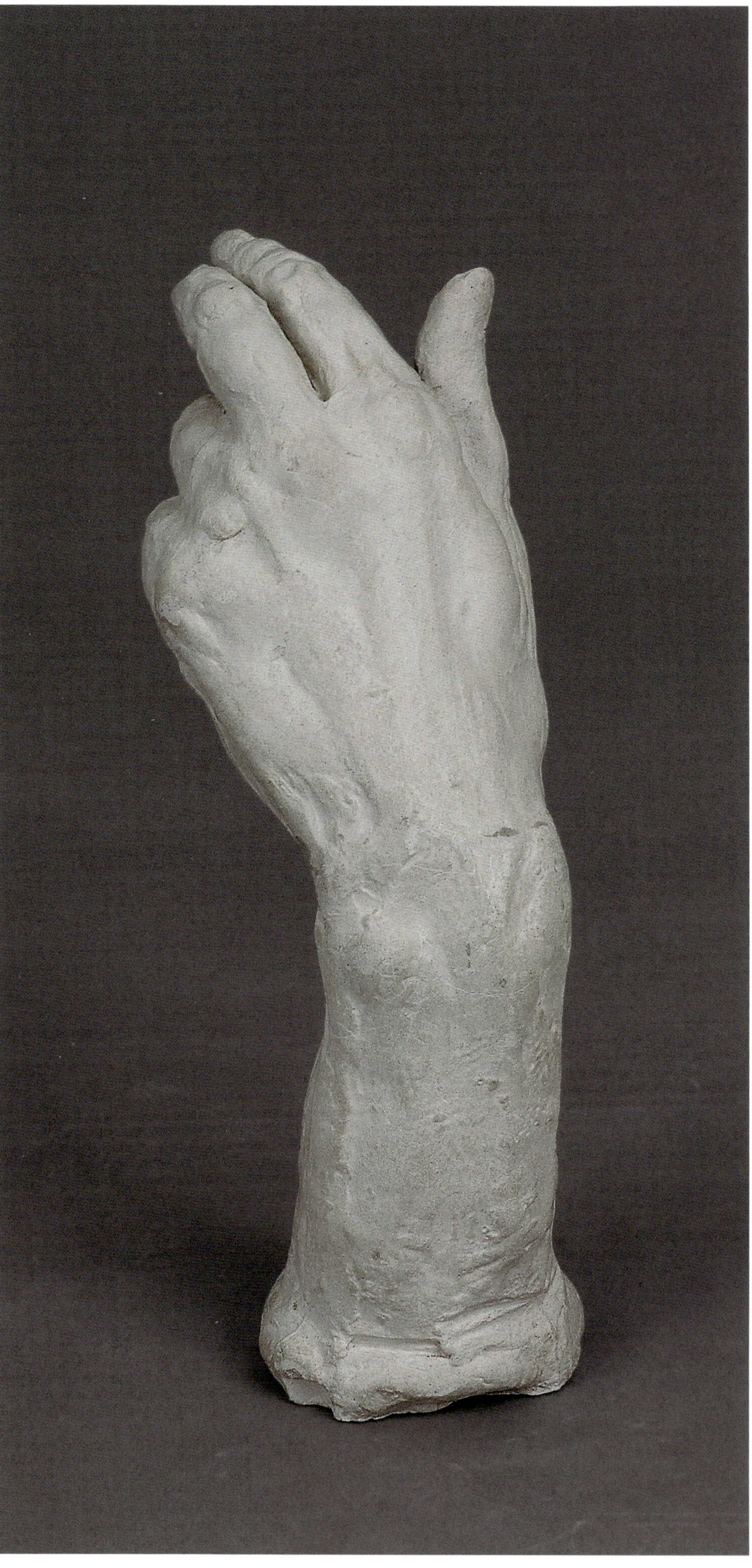

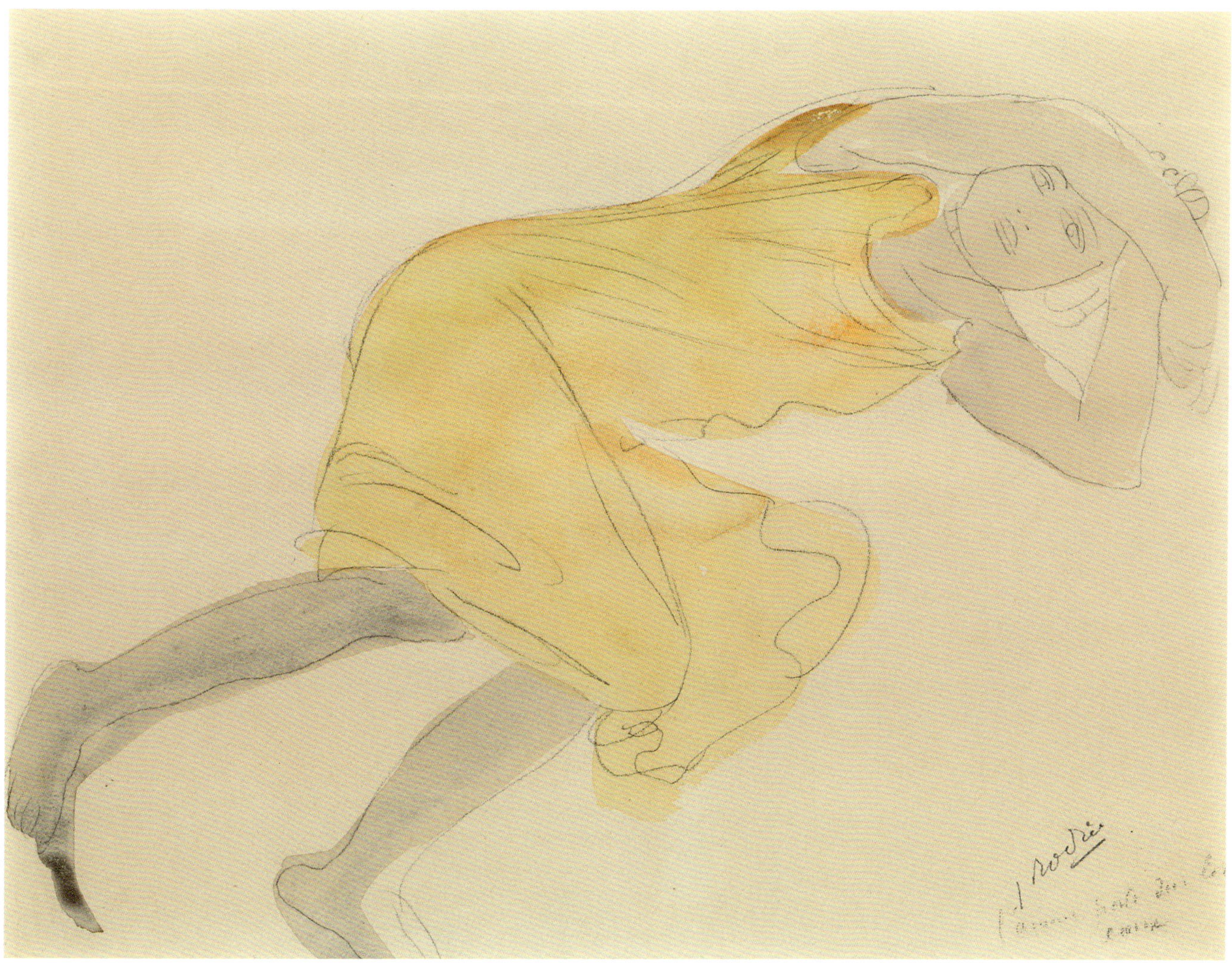

CAT. 34
PSYCHE (LOVE OVER THE WATERS)

c. 1902
Graphite and watercolor on wove paper
9¾ × 12¾ in. (24.7 × 32.4 cm)
Signed and inscribed in graphite, lower right:
A. Rodin / l'amour porté sur les eaux
Private collection, courtesy of Nicholas Sands &
Company Fine Art, New York

American artist Malvina Hoffman (1885–1966), known for the statues of "racial types" that she produced in the early 1930s for the Hall of Man at the Field Museum of Chicago, was one of Rodin's last students. Admitted to his studio for an entire year, between 1910 and 1911, she completed her training during numerous trips to Paris and continued to correspond with the artist until his death. Trained by American sculptor Gutzon Borglum as a teenager, she had moved to France to meet Rodin, whom she had discovered through Katherine Seney Simpson's collection in New York. Simpson wrote her a letter of introduction. Hoffman described the trusting friendship she shared with Rodin in her memoir *Heads and Tales* in 1936, and their vast correspondence is preserved today at the Musée Rodin, Paris, and the Getty Research Institute, Los Angeles. Her diary and a play, both at the Getty, describe the oppressive atmosphere at the Hôtel Biron, the Paris home and studio Rodin shared with other artists at the time, due to the supposed tyrannical personality of Rodin's lover Claire Coudert, the duchesse de Choiseul.[1] The lessons in drawing, modeling, and carving marble were given in the ground-floor salons, which were turned into studios.

Beginning in 1913, Hoffman served as an intermediary for the sale of Rodin's works in the United States and helped him settle many practical questions as the First World War approached. In particular, she helped him sort his drawings. It was perhaps to thank her that Rodin gave her this drawing of Psyche, one of the most beautiful versions on this theme of the confusion of love. The rippling folds of the yellow-ocher dress evoke Psyche being carried off by Zephyr's breath into the kingdom of Love. The sky-blue wash that extends her right foot is not the effect of chance and refers to the inscription *l'amour porté sur les eaux* (love carried on the waters) at the bottom of the paper. In a passage from the *Romance of the Rose*, a medieval French poem inspired by an ancient Roman novel by Apuleius, the hero is carried by a river to the wall that protects the orchard of Love. Another drawing by the same title (c. 1900, Fine Arts Museums of San Francisco), which depicts a nude man floating on the waves, supports this interpretation.

CBU

1. Malvina Hoffman, *Diary* and play titled *Paris*, Getty Research Institute, Los Angeles, 850042.

CAT. 35

STRETCHING FIGURE (THE ANGEL THROWN DOWN TO EARTH OR TRAPEZE)

c. 1898–1900
Graphite and watercolor on wove paper
13 × 9¾ in. (33.0 × 24.9 cm)
Inscribed and signed in graphite, lower right:
enfer / devant l'effroy / A. Rodin;
center right: *rebelle / l'ange précipité /*
sur la terre / enfer; upper right: *trapeze*
Museum of Modern Art, New York
Bequest of Mina Turner, 254.1976

CAT. 36

SEATED WOMAN (PSYCHE)

c. 1902
Graphite on wove paper
12 ¼ × 8 in. (31.2 × 20.2 cm)
Museum of Modern Art, New York
Bequest of Mina Turner, 251.1976

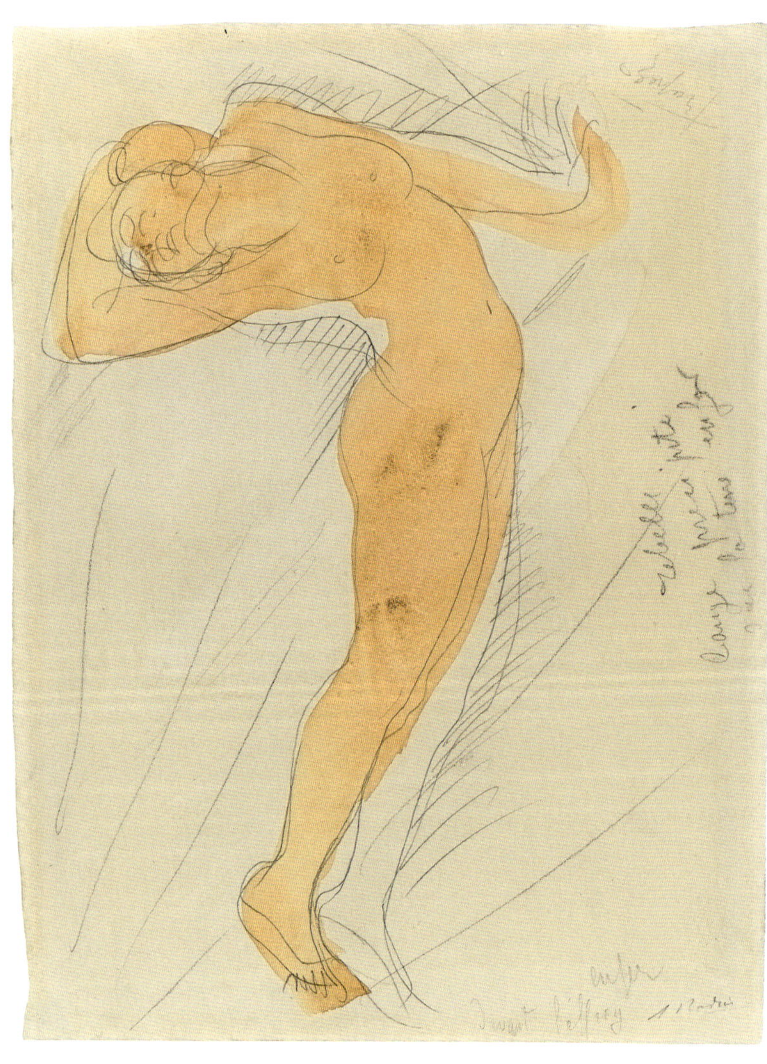

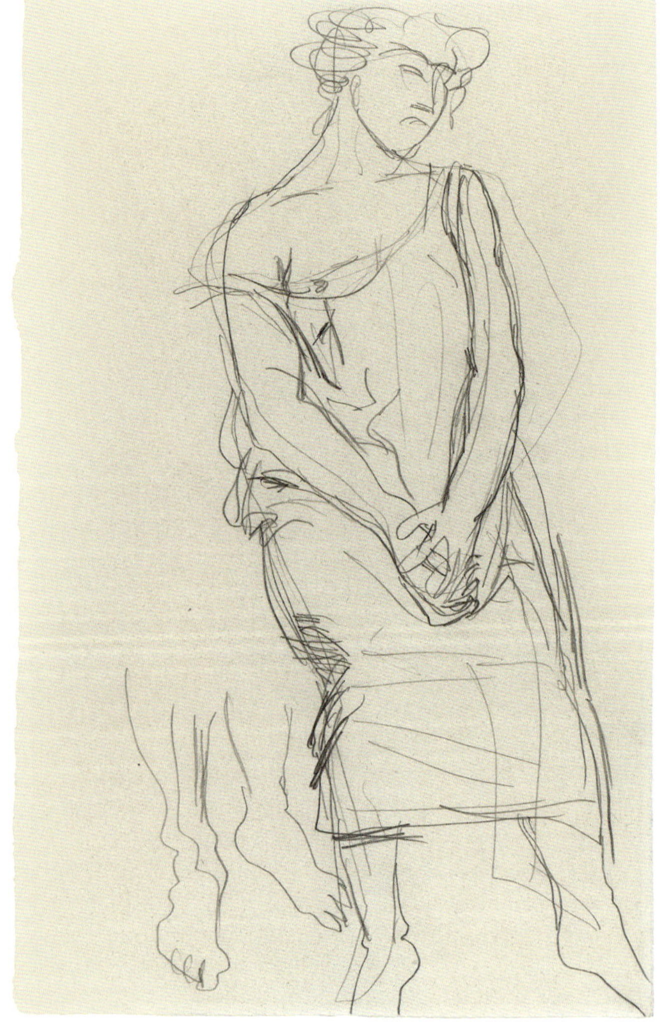

Rodin treated Gertrude Käsebier (1852–1934) as an equal. A pioneering photographer, she was the only woman to photograph Rodin. Adolf de Meyer, founder of fashion photography and famous for his portraits of Vaslav Njinski, introduced her to the sculptor in September 1905 as "perhaps the greatest photographer in America, certainly in her own way the equal of Mr. Steichen."[1] At Rodin's home in Meudon, where she was invited to stay, they developed a wordless friendship, as neither mastered the other's language. From 1906 to 1913, the two artists regularly gave each other artworks. To thank her for a series of photographs sent in April 1906, Rodin wrote to her: "Let me kiss your dear hands effusively. I have never received such a delightful gift. My portrait makes me very happy, but I see that you spent a lot of time and study to do it. It's so nice to receive it from so far away, from America. This is the proof that friendship travels and does not perish. . . . With all my artist's heart to another artist."[2] At the end of the same year, as a Christmas present, Rodin sent her four drawings—a very generous gift, as the sculptor usually gave away his work very sparingly. She thanked him enthusiastically: "You remembered me! The precious drawings are in my keeping. Words cannot express my delight. They will inspire me as long as I live. . . . Thank you, thank you, thank you!"[3]

While the number of drawings belonging to the photographer remains uncertain, she seems to have owned three others, according to the catalogue of the 1913 Armory Show organized by the Association of American Painters and Sculptors. Rodin was represented only by artworks belonging to Käsebier: the catalogue listed "Seven drawings. Lent by Mrs. G. Kasebier" and a bronze, *Figure of Man*, then a recent gift from Rodin in December 1912.[4] However, as Anne McCauley has observed, curiously, "two of the drawings were apparently sold from the show, which suggests they weren't Käsebier's."[5] Whatever the case may be, between the gift for Christmas 1906 and the exhibition in 1913, Käsebier may have added other purchases to her collection that have not yet been identified. We cannot state with certainty that the four drawings bequeathed to the Museum of Modern Art (MoMA) in 1976 by her granddaughter Mina Turner

correspond to the gifts from Rodin, even if it is a likely hypothesis. If the four works—including *Seated Woman* and *Stretching Figure*—are indeed those bestowed by Rodin, they should be appreciated as exemplars of his art.

Seated Woman (Psyche) (cat. 36), a figure with her hands clasped and a pouting expression, also exists in a pared-down version with watercolor, titled *Perrette (and the Pot of Milk)*, alluding to the fable by Jean de la Fontaine (Musée Rodin, Paris, D. 4722). Rodin selected for his friend the first draft in pencil, with the two feet at left rapidly redrawn, and not its finished version. This choice can be explained by the importance that Rodin accorded at this time to vigorous expression in his "blind" sketches, which he drew without looking at the paper, and where chance played a decisive role. *Reclining Woman*, known as *Pompei* (c. 1900–1906, MoMA), which Rodin gave to Käsebier at the same time, is an erotic companion piece to this drawing, related to the series of *Psyches*. *Stretching Figure* (cat. 35), produced earlier, around 1898, along with the fourth drawing from this gift, *Kneeling Woman* (c. 1900–1906, MoMA), seems to correspond more to the taste of the Pictorialist photographers, especially Edward Steichen.

Stretching Figure attests to the role of *The Gates of Hell* as a framework for generating figures that were constantly renewed, even long after Rodin had abandoned the original commission. The paper can be viewed in three different directions (Rodin also made a cutout version that can be turned in every direction, which is today at the Musée Rodin in Paris and may be the starting point for the variation in viewpoints of *Stretching Figure*): vertically, the figure depicts a woman bent with fear, annotated *l'enfer* (hell); horizontally, an *ange rebelle précipité depuis l'enfer sur la terre* (rebel angel thrown from hell to earth); diagonally or upside-down, an acrobat flying on a trapeze. The lines form sorts of rays that are part of the energy of the scene and evoke those in the *Sun Series*, works later exhibited at Stieglitz's 291 gallery in New York.
CBU

1. Adolf de Meyer to Auguste Rodin, September 1905, Archives du musée Rodin, Paris.
2. Auguste Rodin to Gertrude Käsebier, April 1906, Gertrude Käsebier Papers, New York Public Library.
3. Käsebier to Rodin, n.d. [late December 1906], Archives du musée Rodin, Paris.
4. Association of American Painters and Sculptors, *International Exhibition of Modern Art*, exh. cat. (New York: Association of American Painters and Sculptors, 1913), cats. 1,016 and 1,015.
5. Anne McCauley, "Auguste Rodin, 1908 and 1910: The Eternal Feminine," in *Modern Art and America: Alfred Stieglitz and His New York Galleries*, exh. cat., ed. Sarah Greenough (Washington, DC: National Gallery of Art, 2001), 71–78, 492n23. Roberta J. M. Olson identifies Wilhelm R. Valentiner, founder of *Art in America*, as one of the purchasers (*The Muse and the Poet*), while a drawing with watercolor "a green one" was sold to Lydia S. Hays. Roberta J. M. Olson, "Drawings at the Armory: The Currency of Change and Modernism," in *The Armory Show at 100: Modernism and Revolution*, exh. cat., ed. Marylin Satin Kushner, Kimberly Orcutt, and Casey Nelson Blake (New York: New-York Historical Society, 2013), 457.

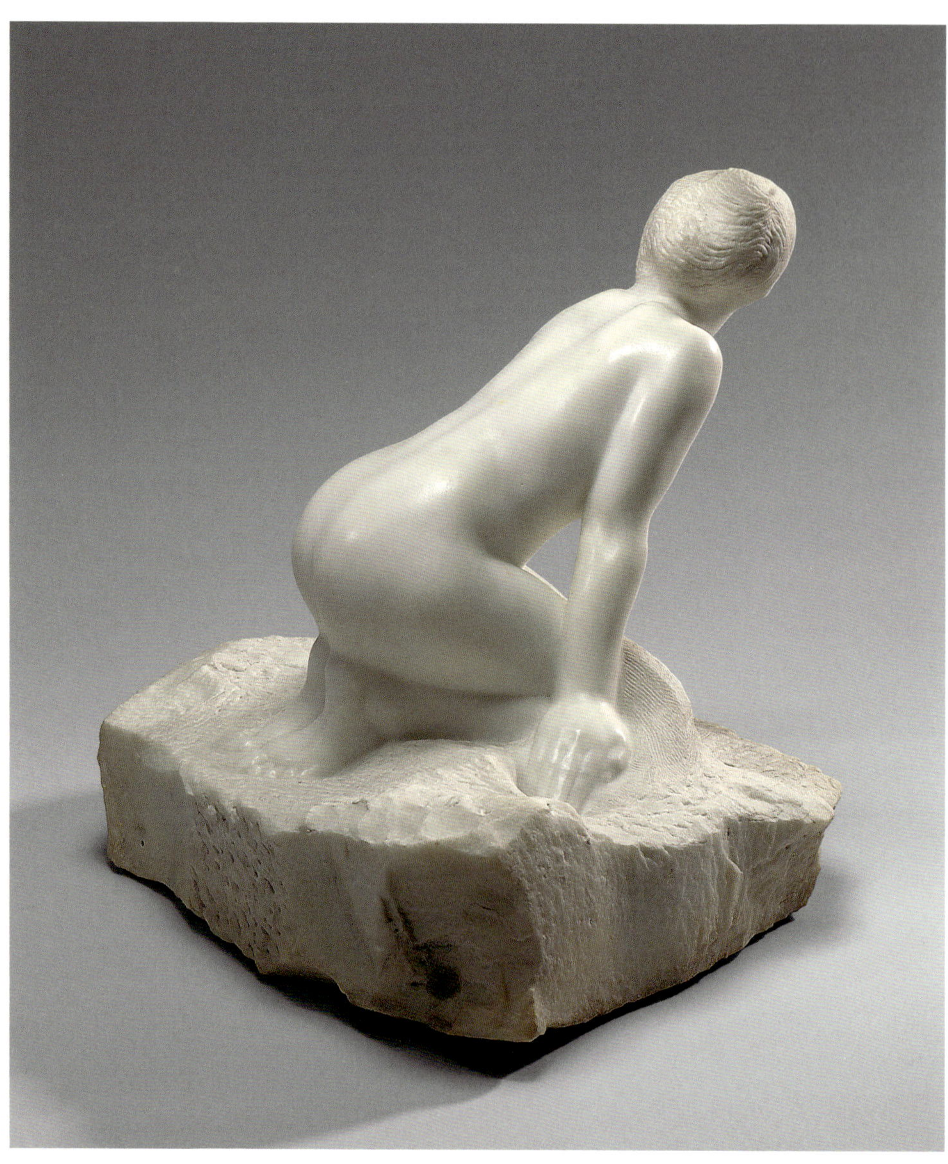

FIGURE OF A WOMAN, "THE SPHINX"

Original model before 1888
Marble, carved 1909
23 ¼ × 24 ⁷⁄₁₆ × 22 ¹⁵⁄₁₆ in. (59 × 62.1 × 58.3 cm)
Signed on base, near fingers: *A. Rodin*
National Gallery of Art, Washington, DC
Gift of Eugene and Agnes E. Meyer, 1967,
1967.13.6

Visiting Europe, the young journalist Agnes Ernst (1887–1970), who would marry Eugene Meyer, a banker and later the owner of the *Washington Post*, at the beginning of the following year, met Rodin several times in 1909. As she recalls in *Out of These Roots*, her 1953 autobiography, "A curiously warm friendship sprang between us which I had to defend now and then against his sensual attitude toward all women."[1] Back in New York, she supported Alfred Stieglitz's 291 gallery and was keenly interested in contemporary artists.

In its original size (height: 7 ¹⁄₁₆ in., 18 cm), *The Sphinx*, exhibited in 1889 at Galerie Georges Petit, is one of a series of crouching figures. Yet this one is distinct due to a kind of animal curiosity that makes her stretch or lift her head, depending on the direction from which she is viewed. She can be recognized in various assemblages, of which one of the most poetic, with a terracotta bowl, is *The Little Water Fairy* (marble, 1903, Musée Rodin, Paris). After 1900, *the Sphinx* was enlarged, and two marble versions were made. When purchasing one of them at a high price, 10,000 francs, Agnes and Eugene Meyer let Rodin choose whichever one he thought better to send to them. The marble sculpture now in the National Gallery of Art in Washington, DC, had indeed been executed with particular care, and while Rodin played, as usual, on the contrast between

the base, left untouched, and the more finished figure (even if the right knee seems to have been rapidly carved), the polished surface is of a quality that is rare for Rodin, especially at that time.

The Sphinx was waiting for the Meyers in New York upon their return from their honeymoon. Agnes Meyer gave it to the National Gallery in Washington at the same time she donated her portrait by Constantin Brancusi. In 1910, she had planned to have her husband's portrait done by Rodin, but this did not take place.
ALNR

1. Agnes E. Meyer, *Out of These Roots: The Autobiography of an American Woman* (Boston: Little, Brown, 1953), 84–85.

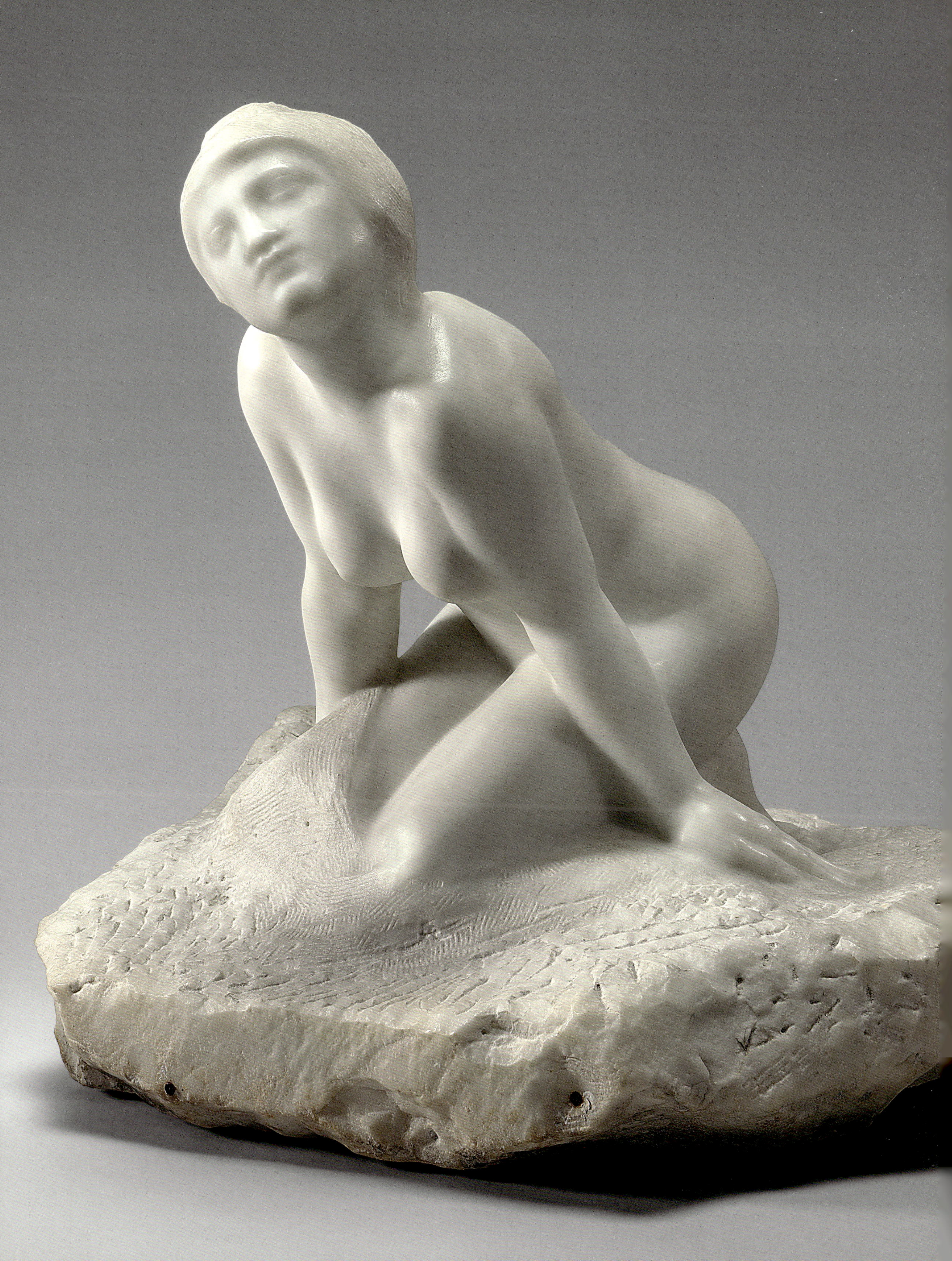

HORSEMAN (RECTO);
HORSE AND RIDER (VERSO)

c. 1886–89
Graphite, pen and ink, gouache, and traces of
faded ink; graphite (verso) on wove paper, tipped
onto wove paper
8 9/16 × 6 7/8 in. (21.7 × 17.4 cm)
Dated and signed, lower left, on paper support:
1889 / Aug. / Rodin
Art Institute of Chicago
Alfred Stieglitz Collection, 1949.580

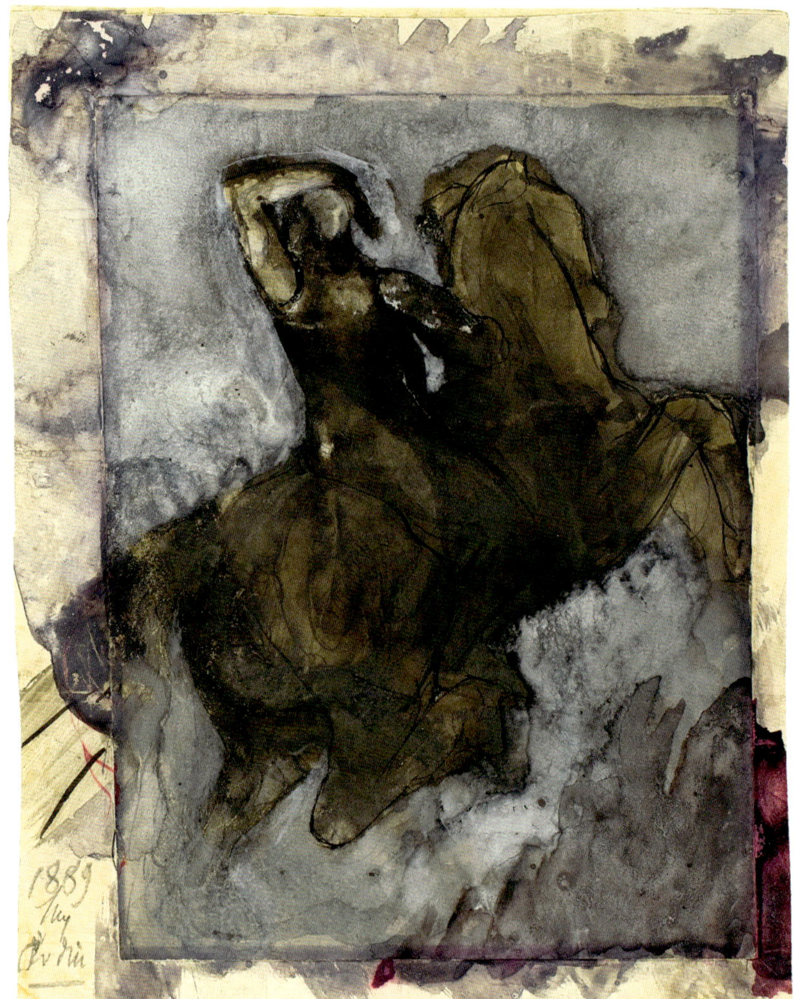

A gift from Rodin to American photographer
Edward Steichen, *Horseman* was included
in the two Rodin exhibitions organized by
photographer and gallerist Alfred Stieglitz
in New York, in 1908 and 1910.[1] Produced in
the 1880s, over thirty years earlier, this
gouache sheet must have had particular
value for the two photographers, because
they decided to publish it first among eight
watercolors by Rodin in a single issue of
Stieglitz's journal, *Camera Work*.[2] Most
of these works date to 1898–1900, the latest
being *Cambodian Dancer*, purchased by
French American photographer and art critic
Paul Haviland and dating to 1906 (private
collection), and *Standing Female Nude
Bending*, executed c. 1908 (also from the
Stieglitz collection and today at the Art
Institute of Chicago). This selection corresponds both to the types Rodin chose to
publish and release in the foreign press and
magazines and to the taste of Steichen, who
had met Rodin in 1901. Having come to
Europe at the age of twenty-two to make a
series of portraits of famous artists, Steichen

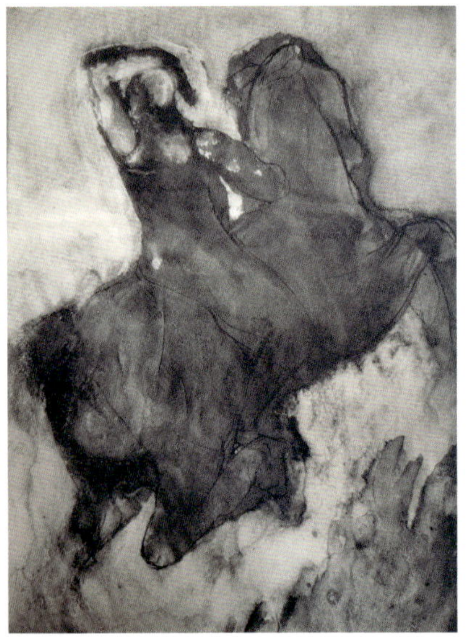

Reproduction of Rodin's *Horseman* (c. 1886–89)
in *Camera Work: A Photographic Quarterly*,
no. 33 (January 1911).

regularly visited Rodin's studio for almost
a year. Throughout his stay, he became
familiar with the drawings that Rodin had
recently shown during the Paris Exposition
Universelle of 1900: many were still mounted
in their frames and scattered in his studio
of La Goulette and in the former Pavillon de
l'Alma, which Rodin had taken apart and
reconstructed at his home in Meudon after
the world's fair. It is also likely that Rodin
showed Steichen the *Album Fenaille* (1897),
which contained 142 lavish facsimiles of
"black" imaginative drawings for *The Gates
of Hell*, among which are images of centaurs
and rearing horses.

Stylistically close to the "blacks" with
intense dramatic effects, *Horseman* was likely
produced around 1886, at a time when Rodin
was working on the plans for an equestrian
monument to the Chilean general Patricio
Lynch. It is a good example of the way
the artist exploited early pencil sketches to
provide the basis of new, more elaborate
drawings. Rodin left visible the two-layer
construction of the work (a pencil sketch
was glued onto a larger sheet in order to give
more breadth to the composition). The date
of 1889 and signature at the bottom left are

undoubtedly later additions, perhaps in
anticipation of the New York exhibition.
A true hymn to expression, it is somewhat
reminiscent of the rearing horses in the lost
Battle of Anghiari by Leonardo da Vinci,
known through copies and prints. It should
be noted that when *Horseman* appeared in
Camera Work, following Steichen's photograph of the sculptor's *Balzac* (see p. 198),
the monochrome photo-engraving purposefully eliminated all the effects of relief in
the drawing. Like Steichen's *Balzac*, the
rider is a back-lit silhouette, "fronting the
spiritual immensity of the sky."[3]
CBU

1. In their note to the reader, "Our Illustrations,"
the editors explain that "the nine other plates in the
number are reproductions of Rodin's drawings,
the original of which were exhibited in the two
Rodin exhibitions held at the Photo-Secession
Galleries." Alfred Stieglitz, *Camera Work: A
Photographic Quarterly*, no. 33 (January 1911): 69.
2. *Camera Work: A Photographic Quarterly*, nos.
34–35 (April–July 1911): 25.
3. Charles H. Caffin, "Prints by Eduard J.
Steichen — of Rodin's 'Balzac,'" in *Camera Work: The
Complete Illustrations 1903–1917*, ed. Pam Roberts
(Cologne: Taschen, 1997), 486 [no. 28, 1909].

LIGHTLY DRAPED DANCING FEMALE NUDE

c. 1900
Graphite with stumping on card laid down on
wove paper
12 1/16 × 7 3/4 in. (30.6 × 19.7 cm)
Dedicated and signed in graphite on lower right:
hommage / affectueux à madame /
C. Steichen / Aug. Rodin
Art Institute of Chicago
Alfred Stieglitz Collection, 1949.898

Lightly Draped Dancing Female Nude
depicts a woman whose arms and hands are
exaggeratedly deformed by her movement.
As a result of Rodin's "blind" life-drawing
technique, it is "a record of a form in
transition."[1] It reflects Rodin's wish to banish
the professional model's fixed or traditional
poses and to seize on the natural movement
that the artist expected of her. The stretching movements of the limbs and the clothing,
which blend together, produce a kind of
dissolution of the body. This type of work
reveals what early twentieth-century
avant-garde movements owe to Rodin (see,
for example, Umberto Boccioni and his
sculpture *Unique Forms of Continuity in
Space*, 1913, Museo de Arte Contemporáneo
de la Universidad de São Paulo). Rodin gave
the drawing to Edward Steichen's wife, Clara.
A friend of the sculptor since 1901, Steichen
encouraged Rodin to adopt a new way
of seeing his art. Steichen's *Balzac* series of
photographs by moonlight (see p. 198),
executed at Rodin's request, but with an
energy and aesthetic entirely characteristic
of Steichen, is the strongest expression of
their symbiotic dialogue. In 1908, when
Alfred Stieglitz and Steichen started
exhibiting works in other media than
photography, Rodin was naturally chosen
for the first major exhibition of a French
modernist artist (followed by Henri Matisse
and Paul Cézanne), with a substantial
selection of fifty-eight drawings.[2] According
to Marius de Zayas, "Steichen must have seen
in them all the elements needed to stir up
things in New York. And they did. With this
exhibition the Photo-Secession became the
key which opened the doors of New York to
modern art."[3] That same year, the relationship
between Steichen and Rodin became even
more personal. Clara Steichen gave birth to
their child Kate, baptized "Rodina" in
homage to the sculptor, who offered her a
version of *The Walking Man* (cf. cat. 86).
It may also be on the occasion of Kate's birth
that this drawing was dedicated to Clara.
CBU

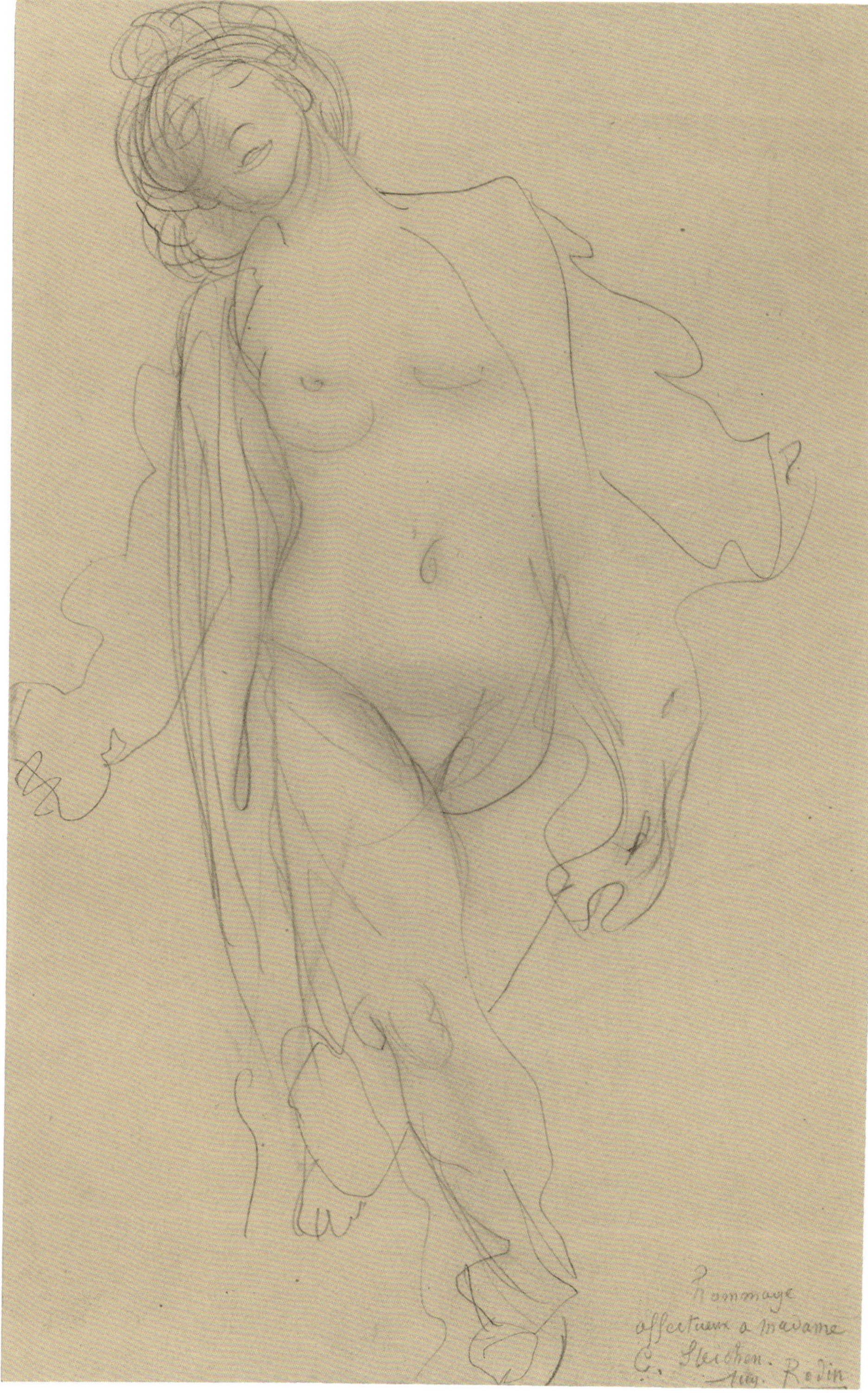

1. Kirk Varnedoe puts it well: "Rodin sought to
register, almost seismographically, rather than
to invent." J. Kirk T. Varnedoe, "Rodin as a
Draftsman—a Chronological Perspective," in *The
Drawings of Rodin*, ed. Albert E. Elsen and J. Kirk T.
Varnedoe (New York: Praeger, 1971), 84.
2. Rodin's show was not the first. Ruth Butler pointed
out "the Rodin show took longer to assemble than
anticipated. While Steichen was in Paris, Stieglitz
hung drawings and watercolors by Pamela Coleman
Smith." Ruth Butler, "Rodin and His American
Collectors," in *The Documented Image: Visions in Art
History*, ed. Gabriel P. Weisberg and Laurinda S.
Dixon (Syracuse, NY: Syracuse University Press,
1987), 109n36.
3. Marius de Zayas, *How, When and Why Modern Art
Came to New York*, ed. Francis M. Naumann
(Cambridge, MA: MIT Press, 1996), 2.

RECLINING NUDE

c. 1900
Graphite with stumping on wove paper
12 ⅛ × 8 ¹⁄₁₆ in. (30.8 × 20.4 cm)
Signed in graphite, lower right: *A. Rodin*
Art Institute of Chicago
Alfred Stieglitz Collection, 1949.899

This astonishing foreshortened figure seems intensely energetic despite its reclining position, as if drawn simply under the impulse of the line. It is a good example of the works critics noticed at the two exhibitions of Rodin's drawings organized by the Photo-Secessionists Alfred Stieglitz and Edward Steichen in New York in 1908 and 1910. Stieglitz wrote to Rodin on January 17, "I can only say to have been given the opportunity to live with them constantly for four weeks is the greatest spiritual treat I have ever had."[1] John Nilsen Laurvik of the *New York Times* wrote:

> In these swift, sure, stenographic notes a mastery of expressive drawing is revealed—a sculptor's mastery—which is seldom beautiful, according to accepted standards of beauty, but that never fail to be interesting and imbued with vital meaning. They have a separate, individual beauty of their own—the beauty of all expressive, characteristic things.[2]

The presence of a signature on this kind of quick drawing indicates that Rodin had the intention of exhibiting it or giving it to someone, and that he considered it finished. An inscription on the back reveals that Rodin gave it to the British American critic Charles H. Caffin, though we do not know under what circumstances. A friend of Steichen and Stieglitz, Caffin gave this drawing to Stieglitz in 1909. He regularly published in *Camera Work* during the entire run of the journal, from 1903 to 1917. In the first issue, he established a parallel between Rodin's work and that of Steichen, who "enjoyed the privilege of frequent and intimate relations with the great artist, and came under the inspiration of his grand and independent mentality and of his extraordinarily subtle perception of beauty. These influences lit upon a young nature that has within it the capacity for corresponding qualities."[3]
CBU

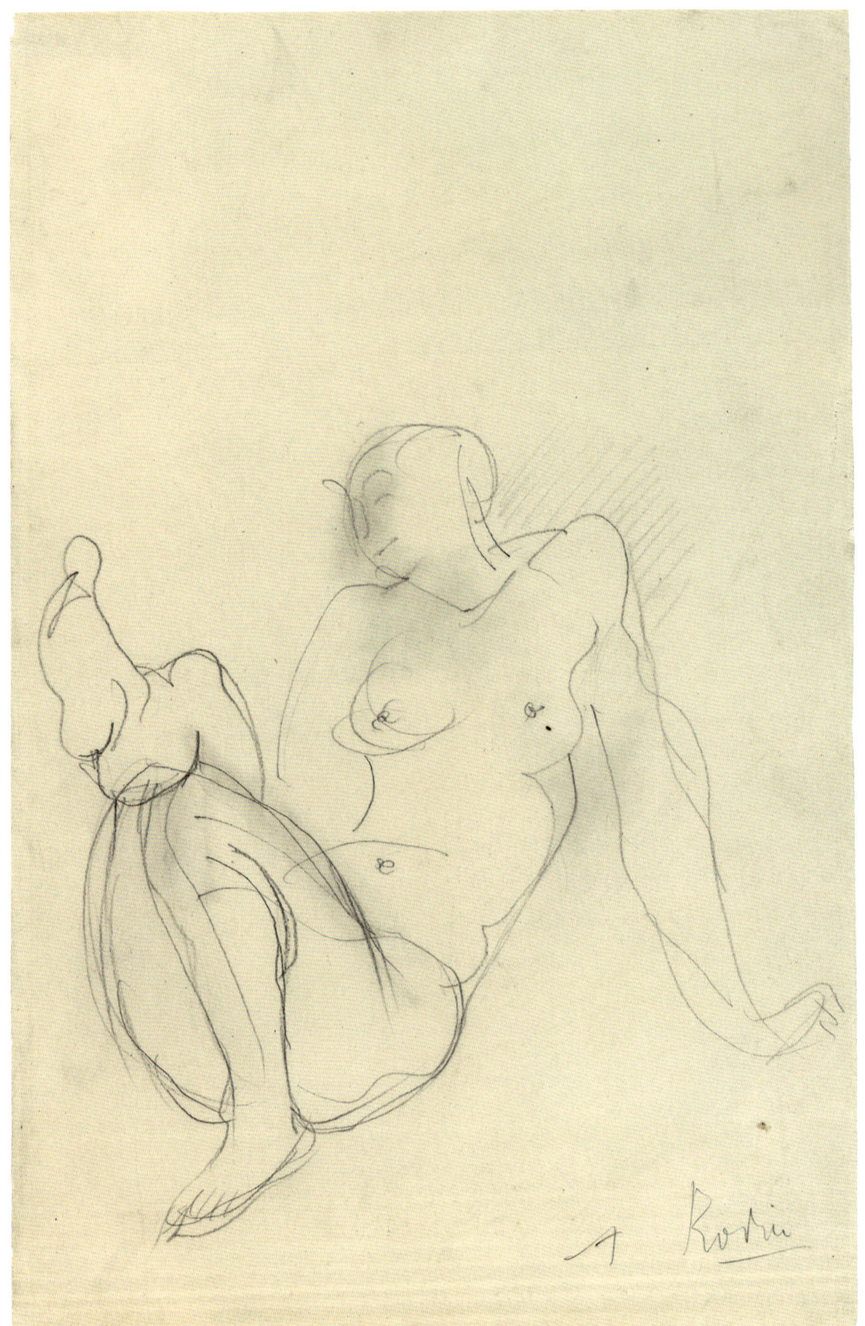

1. Alfred Stieglitz to Auguste Rodin, January 17, 1908, Archives du musée Rodin, Paris.
2. "The Rodin Drawings at the Photo-Secession Galleries," press reviews, in *Camera Work: The Complete Illustrations 1903–1917*, ed. Pam Roberts (Cologne: Taschen, 1997), 403 [no. 22, 1908].
3. Charles H. Caffin, "Eduard J. Steichen's Work— An Appreciation," *Camera Work: A Photographic Quarterly*, no. 1 (January 1903): 23.

WITCH'S SABBATH

c. 1900–1905
Watercolor, gouache, and graphite on wove paper
12 ¹³⁄₁₆ × 9 ¾ in. (32.6 × 24.8 cm)
Inscribed and signed in graphite, lower right:
sabbat / Aug. Rodin
Metropolitan Museum of Art, New York
Gift of Georgia O'Keeffe, 1965, 65.261.1

The theme of the witches' Sabbath that had developed since the Renaissance, especially in Northern Europe (see Albrecht Dürer's and Hans Baldung's woodcuts), is longstanding in Rodin's work. Already established in the 1880s and connected to that of centaurs and Bacchic dancing processions—as in *Dawn: Return from the Sabbath* at the Rodin Museum in Philadelphia (cat. 77) or *The Witches' Sabbath* at the Art Institute of Chicago (cat. 67), these works depict the dancing ride of a nude woman, a witch, carried on the back of a centaur instead of the traditional goat. In his modern renderings of the subject, Rodin is more explicit. *Witch's Sabbath*, given to the Metropolitan Museum of Art, New York, by Georgia O'Keeffe in 1965, belongs to a small group of erotic watercolors from Rodin's mature period. These are generally young women with open garments, revealing their bodies, to whom the artist gives a broom and incongruous features, as seen here, such as the round eyes and mouth (or in Musée Rodin, Paris, D. 3980). In this version, the figure appears in a halo of pink and blue-gray watercolor wash that may suggest the dawn, when the revelers return from the feast of Sabbath. A reviewer for the *New York Times* considered some of the drawings exhibited at Alfred Stieglitz's gallery in 1908—despite their "unusual artistic interest"—to be "a challenge to the prurient prudery of our puritanism. As one looks at these amazing records of unabashed observations of an artist, who is also a man, one marvels that this little gallery has not long since been raided by the blind folly that guards our morals."[1]
CBU

1. "The Rodin Drawings at the Photo-Secession Galleries," press reviews, in *Camera Work: The Complete Illustrations 1903–1917*, ed. Pam Roberts (Cologne: Taschen, 1997), 403 [no. 22, 1908].

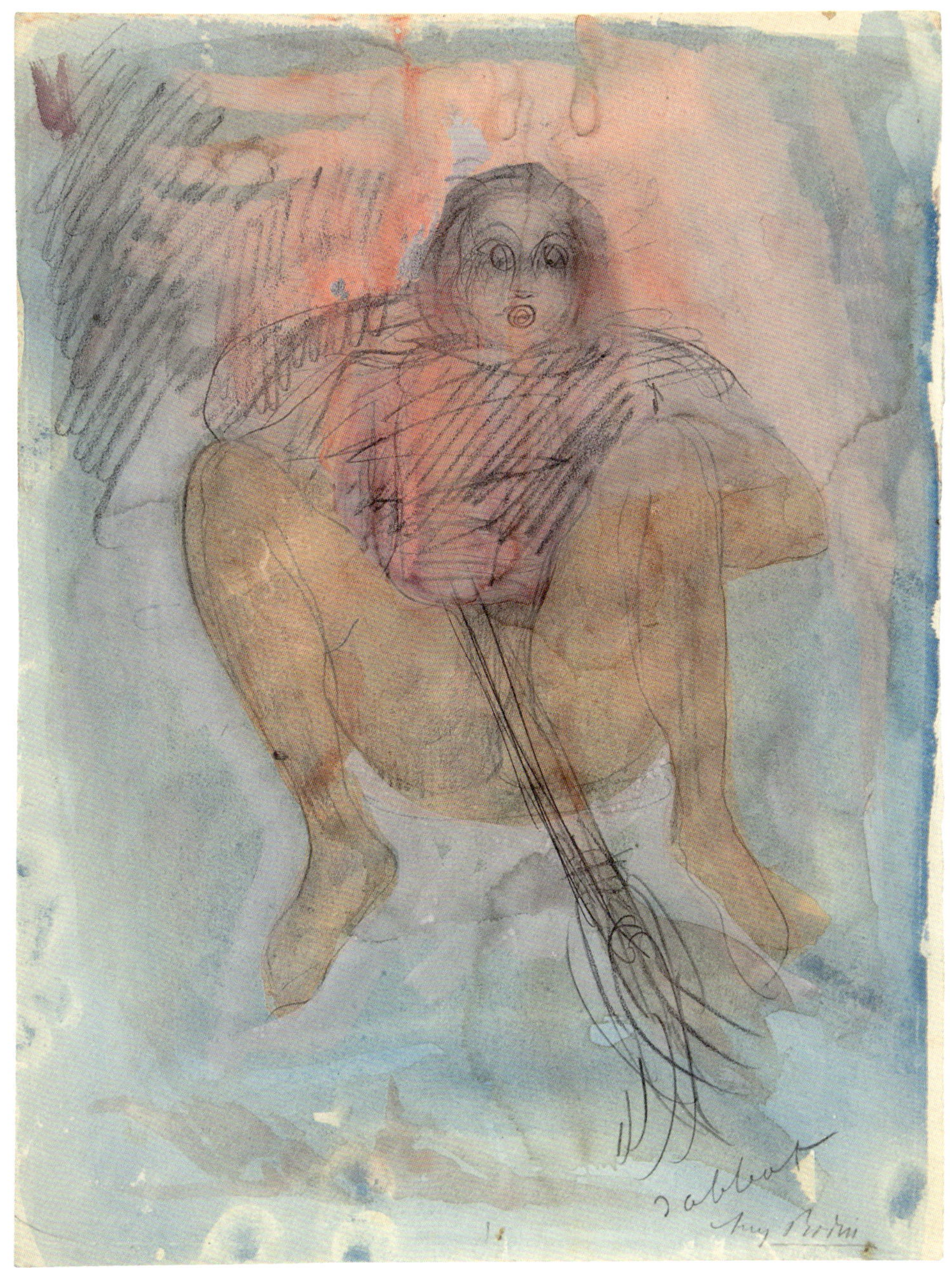

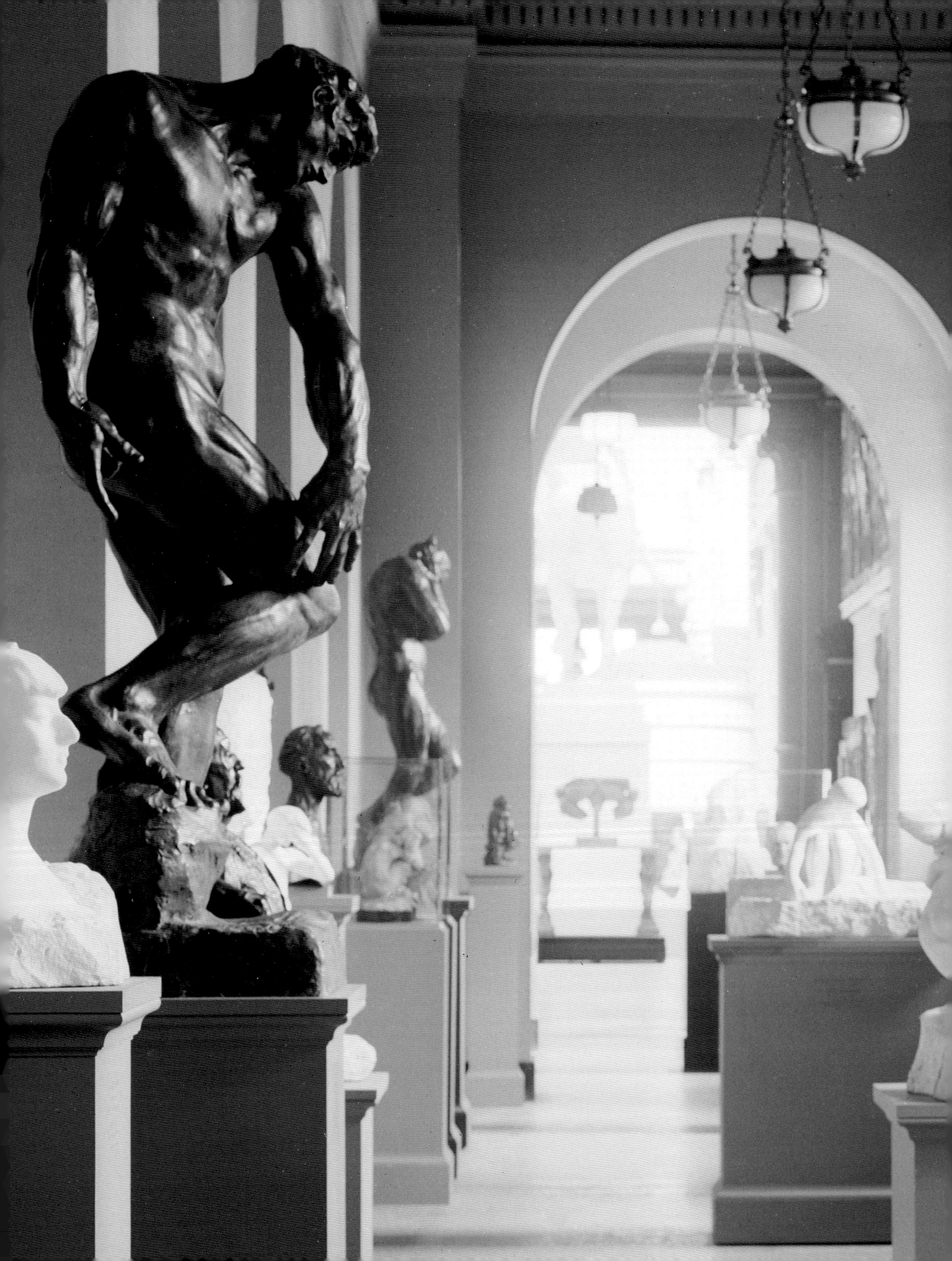

MAKING THE "LITTLE RODIN GALLERY"

THE RODIN COLLECTION AT THE MET

ELYSE NELSON

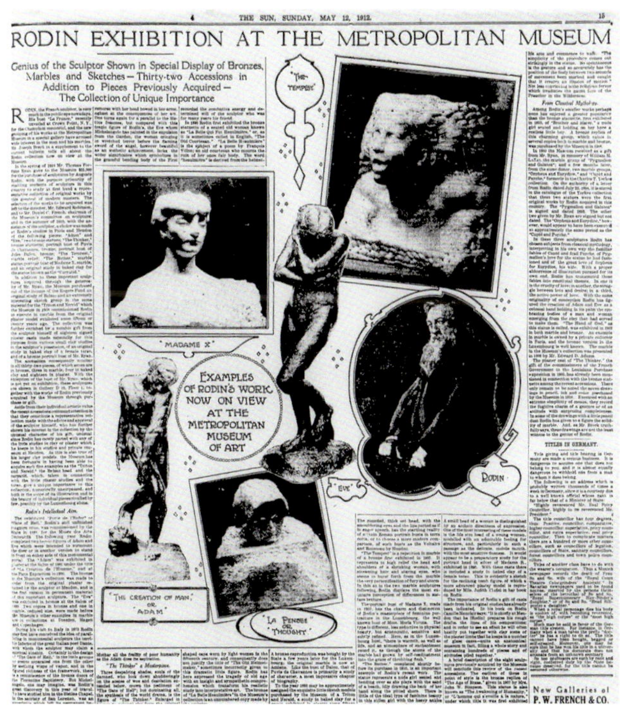

"Rodin Exhibition at the Metropolitan Museum," *Sun* (New York), May 12, 1912.

On May 2, 1912, a gallery devoted to the art of Rodin opened at the Metropolitan Museum of Art in New York (the Met). The inauguration of the new collection was a major event in the city's art world, where, in the years before the founding of the Museum of Modern Art, the acquisition and exhibition of works of living artists by cultural institutions was still rare. A full-page spread in the *Sun* announced the gallery's opening, calling its contents a "collection of unique importance" and drawing attention to Rodin's involvement in its assembly, as the majority of the works came to the museum through the artist by gift or by sale (fig. 5.1).[1] This "little Rodin gallery," as another newspaper called it, contained over thirty marbles, bronzes, terracotta and plaster sketches, and drawings, altogether composing the most significant body of works by Rodin to enter an American museum during his lifetime.[2]

The formation of the Met's Rodin collection, which culminated in the opening of the Rodin gallery, is a fascinating chapter in the history of the institution's European sculpture acquisitions. Dating back to the early 1900s, in the final decades of the artist's life, this process involved a number of museum-affiliated collectors, philanthropists, trustees, and agents who endeavored to bring Rodin's art to an American audience. The first of these advocates to make her ambitions for the broader reception of Rodin in the United States apparent was Katherine (Kate) Seney Simpson, daughter of a Brooklyn banker and art collector, George I. Seney. In 1902, while summering in Europe, Simpson sat for a portrait by Rodin. This occasion marked the beginning of a long period of patronage and friendship that would last until the sculptor's death in 1917. In the years following her portrait, Simpson and her husband, New York lawyer John Woodruff Simpson, would transform their residence at 926 Fifth Avenue into a small Rodin museum. In her correspondence with Rodin, dating from 1903 until his death, Simpson expressed the reverence with which she viewed the artist's work: "In every room of my house I have some beautiful works by you, and it is truly a part of my life to admire them."[3] But Simpson was not content to keep her passion for the art of Rodin a private affair, and it was under her enthusiastic instruction that several American museums came to acquire his work.

Her campaign at the Met began in 1903 when, following a conversation with the museum's director, Louis Palma di Cesnola, she penned a letter to the trustees, dated May 23, remarking that the existing collection of sculpture was "noticeably deficient" and "would be greatly improved by the addition of one of the masterpieces of Auguste Rodin." She further advised to "make haste to secure a good piece by him," as the bronze *Bust of St. John the Baptist*, given by Samuel P. Avery in 1893 (cat. 3), was "far too small and unimportant to represent the greatest living master of sculpture." She concluded, "Rodin is now an old man and the time is limited in which it will be possible to command his services."[4]

Three years later, the Met's trustees heeded this call. On January 15, 1906, the Committee on Sculpture, a standing committee of the Board of Trustees chaired by the prominent American sculptor Daniel Chester French, published a report counseling the museum to acquire and display "the best works of modern sculpture," including "the work of living artists" and that of Rodin in particular. According to the committee, this shift in acquisitions focus from ancient to modern sculpture had both practical and artistic benefits, for "the expenditure of a sum equal to the cost of one work of antiquity, of historic or archaeological value, would create a collection of popular interest and would tend to stimulate this important art."[5] With the *Bust of St. John the Baptist* and an enlarged plaster cast of Rodin's *Thinker* (made originally for the Louisiana Purchase Exposition, known as the St. Louis World's Fair, of 1904) already in the collection, the committee's report indicated a clear intention to significantly deepen its holdings of Rodin's work.[6]

In the subsequent months, Simpson acted to support the new collecting mandate by offering her counsel to Edward Robinson, vice director of the Met between 1905 and 1910, regarding the acquisition of works by Rodin, and by commissioning as a gift the first bronze cast of *The Age of Bronze* (original model 1876, cast c. 1906; cf. cat. 87), also the first full-length bronze by Rodin to enter the collection.[7] In a letter from 1908, Simpson conveyed to Rodin the pride she felt in finally seeing the sculpture prominently installed at the foot of the museum's grand staircase (fig. 5.2).[8] Around the same time, a trustee and fellow member of French's Committee on Sculpture, Edward D. Adams, commissioned a marble version of *The Hand of God* (cat. 22), stipulating that Rodin refrain from allowing additional versions of the sculpture to be produced, to ensure its rarity.[9] The second version of the composition to be executed in marble, Adams's commissioned piece was carved by one of Rodin's assistants, Louis Mathet, and given to the museum upon its completion in 1908.

The Met promptly sought to make two additional acquisitions: a small bronze edition of *Brother and Sister* (original model 1890–91, cast 1908) and a marble group to be carved after the virtuoso composition *Triton and Nereid* (before 1908). The latter never came to fruition, at least in part due to Rodin's reluctance to make restorations to the original plaster model, which had become damaged. The museum would instead acquire an exquisite terracotta sketch for the marble

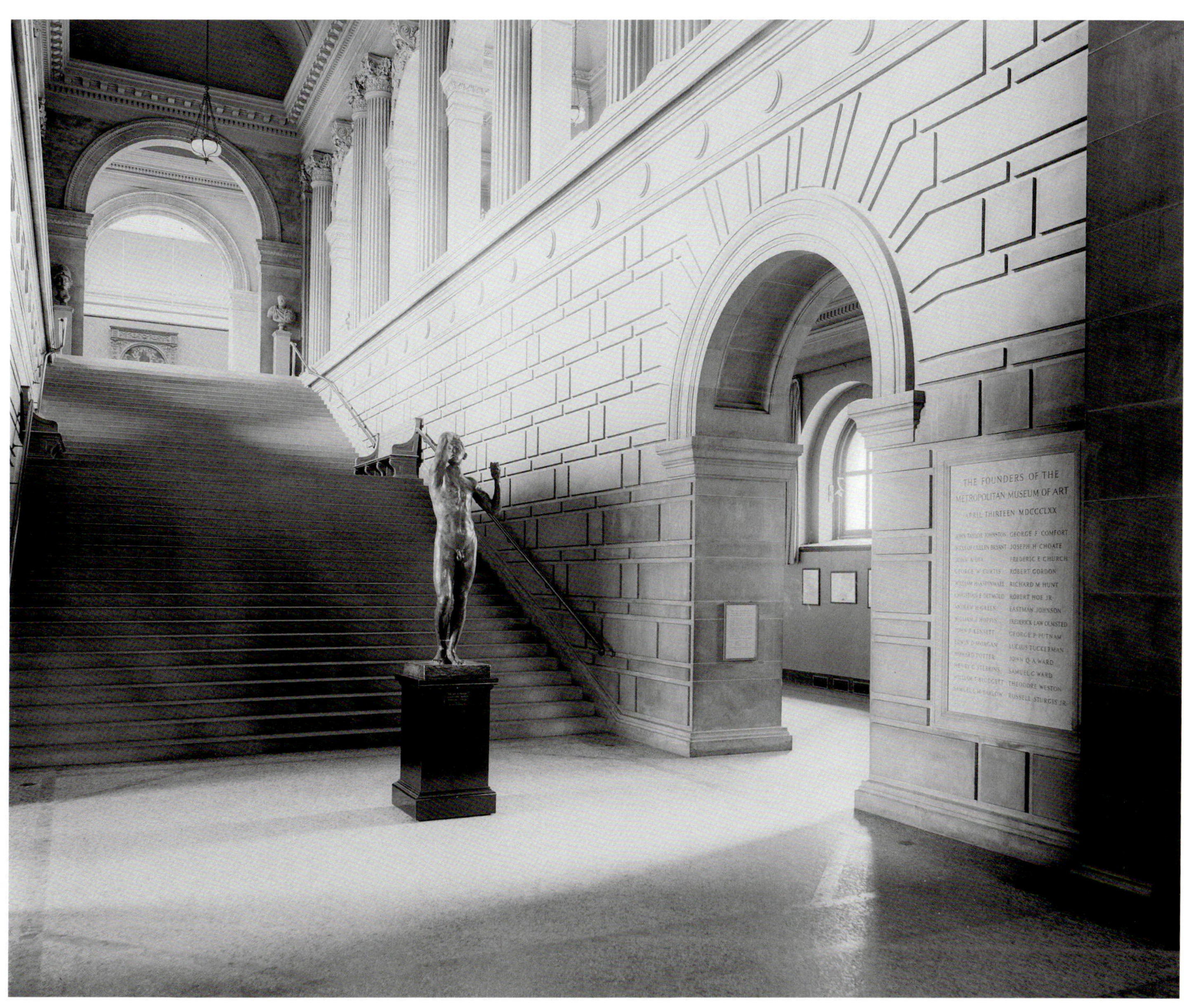

FIG. 5.2

The Age of Bronze (bronze, original model
1876, cast c. 1906) installed at the base
of the Great Hall steps, photographed
in 1919, just left of the arched entrance to
the Rodin installation, Wing D, Room 1
(Great Hall), Metropolitan Museum of Art,
New York.

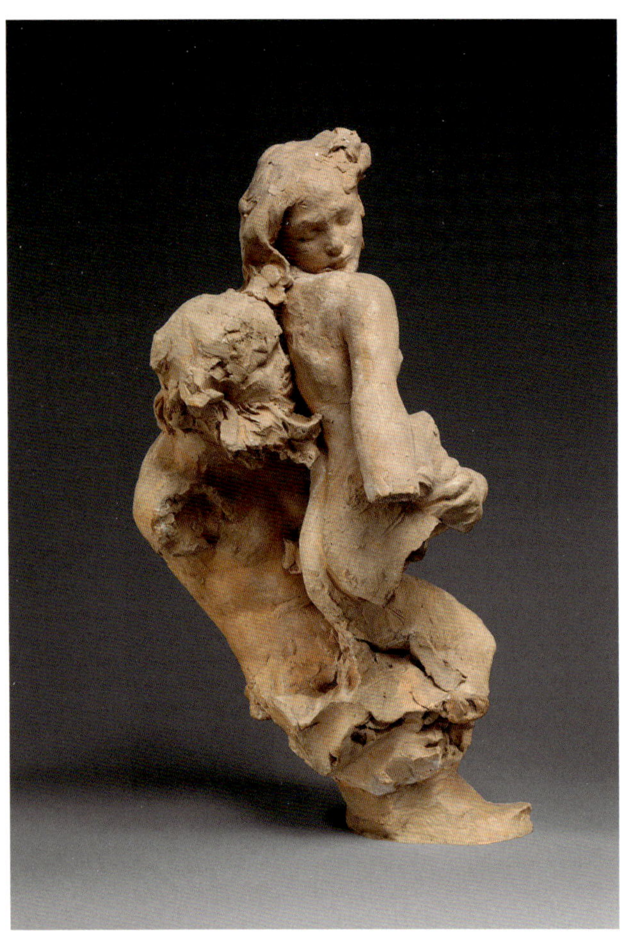

FIG. 5.3

Auguste Rodin (French, 1840–1917), *Triton and Nereid*, c. 1886–93. Terracotta, 15 ½ × 9 × 9 ¾ in. (39.4 × 22.9 × 24.8 cm). Metropolitan Museum of Art, New York. Rogers Fund, 1912, 12.11.2.

FIG. 5.4

Auguste Rodin, *Orpheus and Eurydice*, modeled c. 1887, carved 1893. Marble, 48 ¾ × 31 ⅛ × 25 ⅜ in. (123.8 × 79.1 × 64.5 cm). Metropolitan Museum of Art, New York. Gift of Thomas F. Ryan, 1910, 10.63.2.

group a few years later (fig. 5.3).[10] The pursuit of these acquisitions in 1908 came at the recommendation of John Marshall, a Classical sculpture connoisseur who acted as the Metropolitan Museum's purchasing agent. Working under the direction of Robinson, Marshall visited Rodin's Paris studio in late 1907 or early 1908 and made an initial selection of twenty-four recommended works for acquisition, which he catalogued, with pricing and photographs, in a detailed letter to Robinson, dated January 6, 1908.[11]

Following these initial acquisitions, however, the Met's negotiations with the artist stalled for want of funds. On May 20, 1908, Robinson wrote apologetically to Simpson regarding the purchasing lull, which he attributed to the "shrinkage in our purchasing funds and the great demands upon them."[12] It would take the involvement of a dedicated patron, the New York financier Thomas Fortune Ryan, to help the museum to fully realize the Committee on Sculpture's plans. An avid collector of Italian Renaissance sculpture—as well as paintings, enamels, majolica, rare books and prints, and furniture—Ryan also owned nineteenth-century bronzes and several works by Rodin, to whom he was likely introduced by the sculptor's lover Claire Coudert, duchesse de Choiseul. Criticized by Rodin's inner circle for the way she allegedly micromanaged and manipulated the aging artist over the course of their relationship, the duchess was nonetheless an influential intermediary who helped to introduce Rodin's work to wealthy American collectors.

In 1909, Rodin modeled Ryan's portrait in Paris during a series of sittings that, according to a contemporary account, proceeded in silence due to the language barrier between them.[13] The result was a rather rigid and unflattering likeness that displeased Ryan, so much so that it was excluded from the patron's gifts to the Met and was instead among the works given by the artist himself. Despite disliking his portrait, Ryan admired Rodin's work and was also receptive to the idea, proposed by the museum, that he be the sole benefactor to help expand the Met's holdings by the sculptor. In 1910, Ryan presented three sculptures by Rodin to the Metropolitan: *Pygmalion and Galatea* (original model 1889, carved 1909), which he purchased from the artist, and *Orpheus and Eurydice* (fig. 5.4) and *Cupid and Psyche* (carved 1893), two works from the Charles T. Yerkes sale of January 22, 1910. In addition, he made a gift of $25,000 for the museum to acquire other works by the artist. The gift came with few stipulations, and only a gentle suggestion that "there ought to be a room of Rodin's works at the Museum."[14] Ryan was apparently pleased to hand the selection process over to Robinson and French. He wrote to Claire Coudert: "I have placed $25,000 at the disposal of the Museum and Mr. Robinson and Mr. French are going to Paris soon to buy as many pieces by the Great Master as they can get for the money."[15]

Robinson and French identified ten sculptures for purchase using Ryan's funds: *The Thinker* (original model c. 1880, cast by 1910), *Adam* (original model 1880–81, cast 1910), and *Eve* (original model 1881, cast 1910), busts of sculptor Jules Dalou (original model 1883, cast 1910) and painter Puvis de Chavannes (original model 1891, cast 1910), and *The Old Courtesan* (original model 1885–87, cast 1910), all in bronze; *Madame X* (c. 1907), *Beside the Sea* (original model c. 1895–1900, carved 1906), and the so-called *Tempest* (carved before 1910) in marble; and the *Caryatid* (original model 1883) in terracotta. Two additional terracottas—*Honoré de Balzac* (cat. 29) and the aforementioned *Triton and*

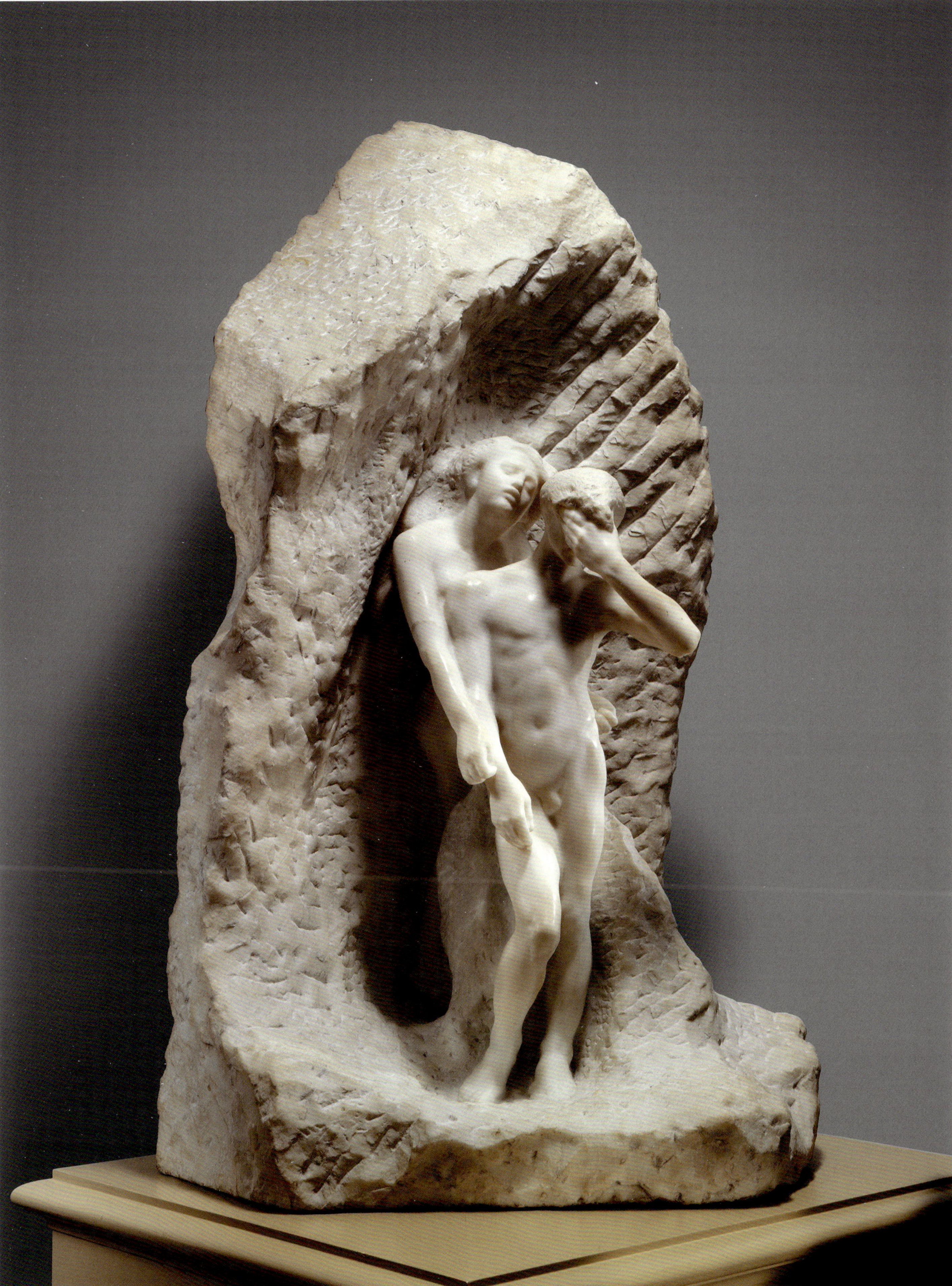

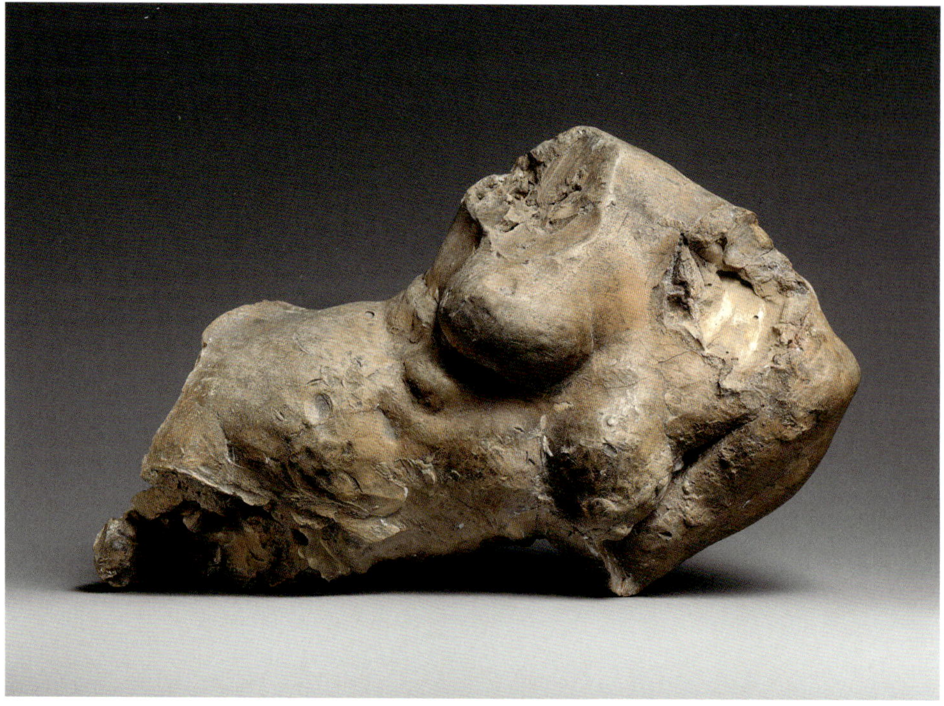

FIG. 5.5

Auguste Rodin, *Torso (A Study of Ariane without Arms)*, c. 1900–1905. Terracotta, 7 × 11 ⅝ × 4 ¼ in. (17.8 × 29.5 × 10.8 cm). Metropolitan Museum of Art, New York. Gift of Auguste Rodin, 1912, 12.13.1.

FIG. 5.6

Michelangelo Buonarroti (Italian, 1475–1564), *The Atlas Slave*, c. 1530–34. Marble, height: 109 in. (277 cm). Accademia, Florence.

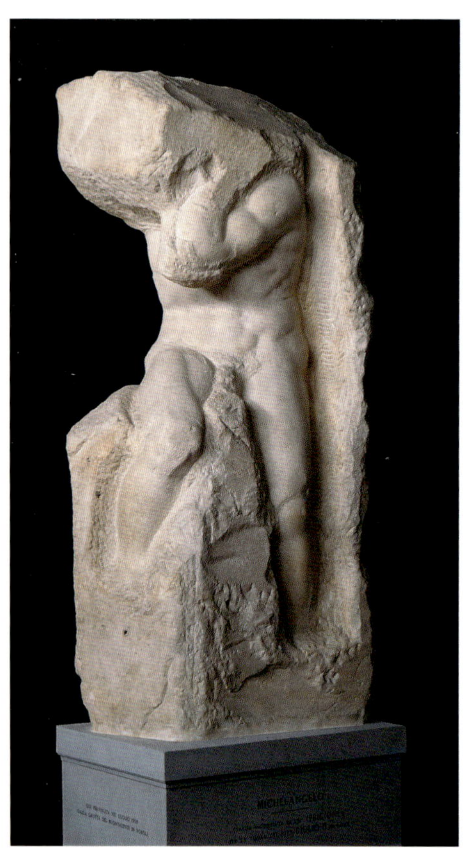

Nereid—were also acquired using separate museum funds.[16] The latter two terracottas were unique and original sketches unrelated to the processes of replication, involving the hands of many assistants, through which the other Rodin works acquired by the Met were made. The sensitivity of the modeling— seen in the flowing locks of the Triton's hair and puffed flesh around Balzac's eyes, for instance—indicates that these intimate works were, in fact, produced by Rodin's own hand. Their inclusion in the collection ensured that the Met would have sculptures representing every stage in Rodin's creative process, from initial sketch to bronze replica. In July 1910, Robinson wrote to Rodin with a final list of the works to be acquired by the museum enclosed.

To this list, Rodin added the "bronze bust of Mr. Thomas F. Ryan" (original model 1909, cast before 1911) and some "small drawers with hands, feet, etc."—plaster studies of limbs used in his process of composing figures from various individually modeled parts (cats. 31–33)—offered as gifts to the Metropolitan.[17] By the mid-1880s, he had begun to extract many of the figures (or parts of figures) from the reliefs of *The Gates of Hell*, enlarging or transfigur- ing them to create independent sculptures. Sometimes he left these parts unfin- ished or fragmented. In *Triton and Nereid*, for instance, the female figure's upper thigh and Triton's embracing arm have been ripped away, the trace of such violence preserved in baked clay. Rodin's final gift to the Met also included a vibrantly modeled fragment of a reclining torso with its head and limbs inten- tionally removed (fig. 5.5). Displayed on a simple wooden base that was once in the artist's studio, the sculpture reflects his interest in the expressive potential of sculptural fragments, which he gleaned from the remains of ancient Greek and Roman sculpture, as well as from the *non finito* (unfinished) aesthetic culti- vated by Michelangelo (fig. 5.6).

While the assortment of plaster body parts began as working models, Rodin also recognized these compositional fragments as works of art in their own right. For Robinson, however, their pedagogical value was most resonant: "Your gift of the small studies of details will be much appreciated by students of sculpture and they will be of inestimable importance as a lesson to show that the master of Impressionism in sculpture obtains his success through the close and laborious study of nature."[18] Indeed, much of the discourse on the collection in the period

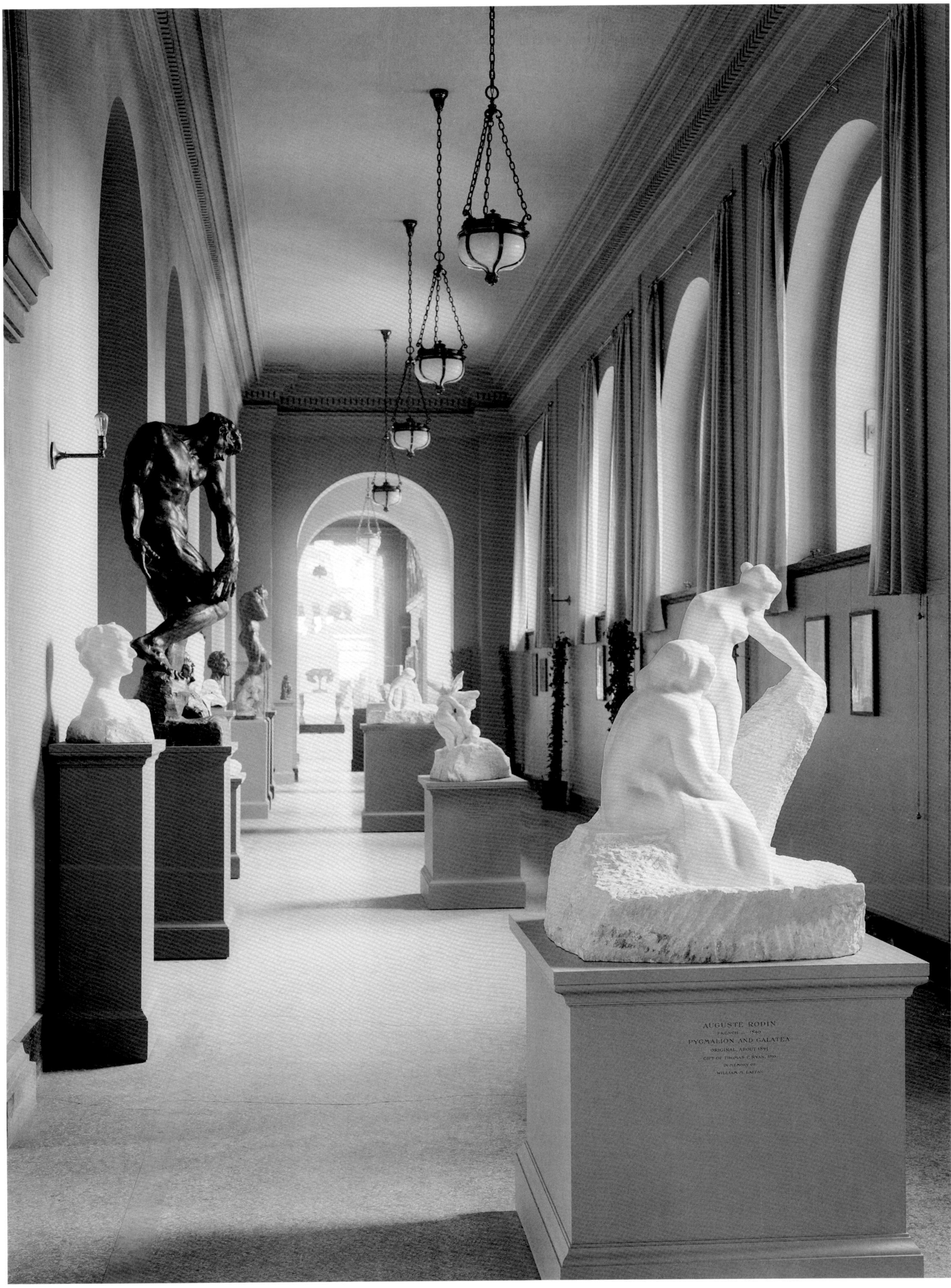

AUGUSTE RODIN
FRENCH — 1840
PYGMALION AND GALATEA
ORIGINAL, ABOUT 1893
GIFT OF THOMAS F. RYAN, 1910
IN MEMORY OF
WILLIAM M. LAFFAN

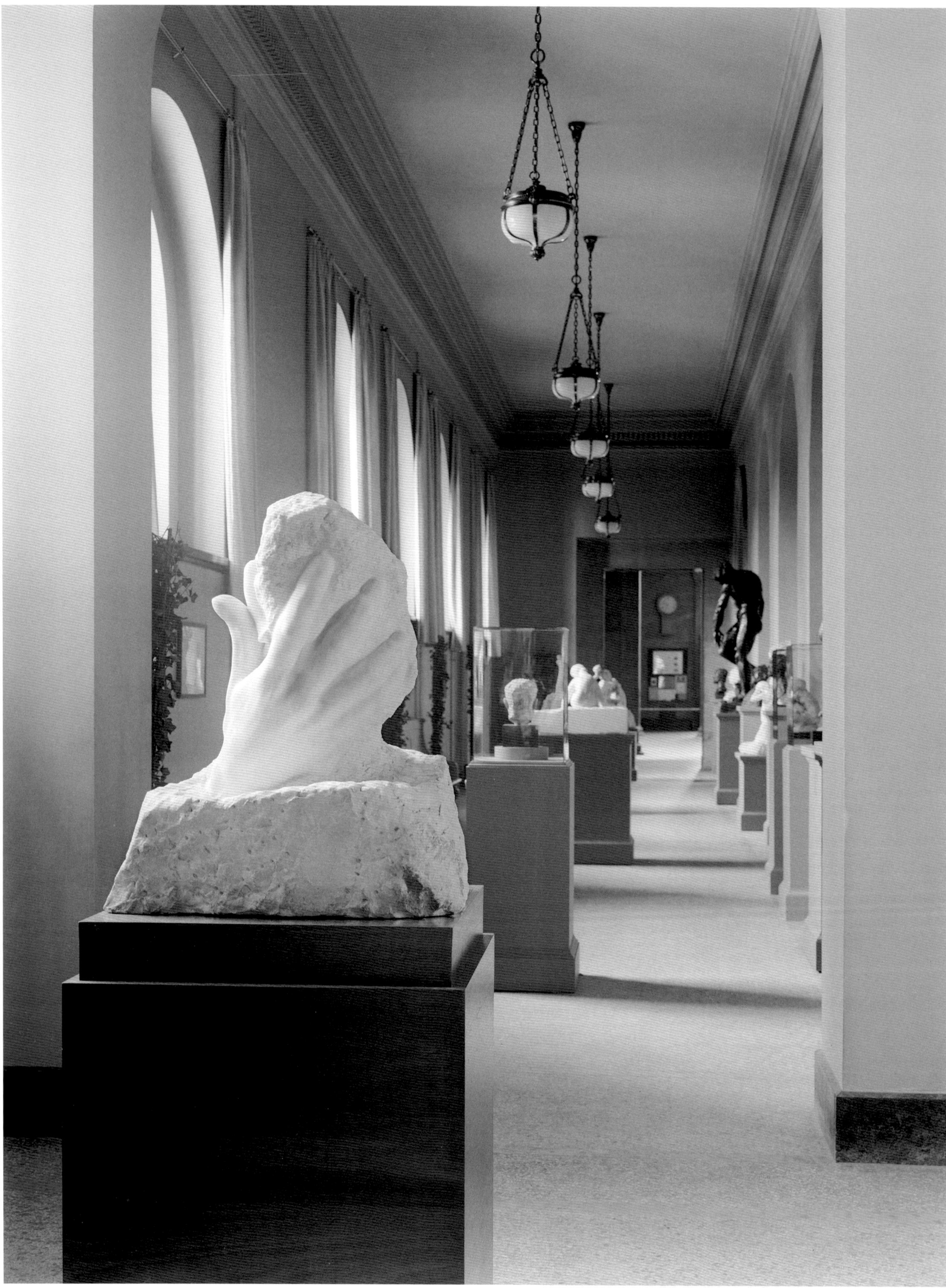

surrounding the opening of the "little Rodin gallery" in 1912 had to do with its potential to enlighten and inspire a new generation of artists. The Met publication written by Joseph Breck, then assistant curator of decorative arts, to accompany the collection's debut strongly emphasized the new acquisitions' educational significance. The purpose of the Rodin installation, Breck explained, was to enable "students of sculpture in this country to study at first hand a representative collection of original works by this greatest of modern masters."[19] However, the Met's presentation rejected the informal display then typical of study collections; Rodin's works were instead exhibited in an elegant manner that underscored their status as fine art (figs. 5.7–8).

In the Committee on Sculpture's report six years earlier, French had argued that the Met should reorganize its sculpture displays "so as to present a coherent and orderly collection." He emphasized that "a certain space [should] be set aside expressly for aesthetic purposes, so that separate works may be exhibited with appropriate surroundings tending to enhance their artistic effect."[20] The 1912 inauguration of the Rodin collection exemplified the committee's new approach to the presentation of sculpture as an aesthetic experience. By mixing sculptural media and pedestal heights, and by showcasing Rodin's sculpture alongside newly acquired drawings by the artist, the curators established a syncopation of form across the stately gallery.

In the years immediately following the Rodin gallery's inauguration, acquisitions from his oeuvre continued in the form of sporadic gifts, from Watson Dickerman's gift of the first bronze cast of *The Martyr* (original model 1885, cast 1913) in 1913 to Isaac Dudley Fletcher's bequest of *Eternal Spring* in 1917 (original model c. 1881, carved 1907). However, the sculptures on view in 1912 remain the core of the Metropolitan Museum's Rodin collection today, built on the transformative gifts and passion of patrons Kate Seney Simpson and Thomas Fortune Ryan.[21]

NOTES

This text is indebted to the research of Clare Vincent, who provided the earliest account of this history. I should also like to thank James Moske, Melissa Bowling, Sophia Feist, Denise Allen, Thayer Tolles, and Dana Pilson for their assistance with archival research. I am grateful to Antoinette Le Normand-Romain and Esther Bell for their invitation to participate in this project and for their insights.

1. "Rodin Exhibition at the Metropolitan Museum," *Sun (New York)*, May 12, 1912.

2. R. C., "Auguste Rodin at the Metropolitan Museum," *New York Tribune*, May 19, 1912.

3. Katherine Seney Simpson to Auguste Rodin, February 2 [1908?], Archives du musée Rodin, Paris.

4. Katherine Seney Simpson to the Director's Office, Metropolitan Museum of Art, May 23, 1903, Metropolitan Museum of Art Archives, New York (hereafter MMA Archives), folder Si5861, fols. 1–4.

5. *Sculpture Committee—Reports and Correspondence, 1906–1907*, January 15, 1906, Office of the Secretary Records, MMA Archives.

6. The plaster cast of *The Thinker* was offered to the Metropolitan Museum in a letter from André Saglio, commissioner of fine arts of the French government, to Daniel Chester French, dated December 13, 1904, folder SA18, fols. 1, 2, 4, MMA Archives. See also Clare Vincent, "Rodin at the Metropolitan Museum of Art: A History of the Collection," *Metropolitan Museum of Art Bulletin* (Spring 1981): 15.

7. The MMA Archives contain detailed records of this gift, which arrived in New York on May 7, 1907: folder Si5861, fols. 9, 11, 19–29, 37, 39–43, 54.

8. *The Simpson Correspondence*, letter 18, Kate Simpson to Rodin, February 2, 1908, reproduced in Ruth Butler and Suzanne Glover Lindsay, *European Sculpture of the Nineteenth Century* (Washington, DC: National Gallery of Art, 2000), 419.

9. This history is recounted at length in Anna Tahinci, "Rodin and His American Collectors," in *Rodin and America: Influence and Adaptation, 1876–1936*, ed. Bernard Barryte and Roberta K. Tarbell (Milan: Silvana Editoriale, 2011), 322–23. Documents relating to Adams's gift and Rodin's agreement not to produce other examples of *The Hand of God* are in folder Edward Dean Adams, fols. 1, 8–10, MMA Archives. Despite this arrangement, Rodin went on to produce other versions in marble.

10. On the history of the *Triton and Nereid* commission, see Vincent, "Rodin at the Metropolitan Museum of Art," 19. Records of the commission are in folder Scu480, fols. 1–4, 6–7, MMA Archives.

11. John Marshall to Edward Robinson, January 6, 1908, folder R9582, fols. 1–8, MMA Archives.

12. Edward Robinson to Katherine Seney Simpson, May 20, 1908, MMA Archives.

13. See Vincent, "Rodin at the Metropolitan Museum of Art," 21, 24.

14. As recounted in a letter from Daniel Chester French to Frederick S. Wait, January 10, 1910, received copy, Daniel Chester French Papers, Manuscript Division, Library of Congress, Washington, DC.

15. Thomas Fortune Ryan to Claire Coudert de Choiseul, April 9, [1910], Archives du musée Rodin, Paris.

16. Robinson recorded his impressions of the visit and artist in letters to Harriet French Hollis (July 21, 1910) and to his brother William M. R. French (August 13, 1910). See Vincent, "Rodin at the Metropolitan Museum of Art," 30.

17. List of Rodin Sculptures, July 22, 1910, folder R617, fol. 4, MMA Archives.

18. Edward Robinson, as quoted in Vincent, "Rodin at the Metropolitan Museum of Art," 20.

19. Joseph Breck, *The Collection of Sculptures by Auguste Rodin* (New York: Metropolitan Museum of Art, 1913), 3.

20. *Sculpture Committee—Reports and Correspondence, 1906–1907*, January 15, 1906, Office of the Secretary Records, MMA Archives.

21. Only in the 1980s would new American patrons emerge to rival Simpson's and Ryan's role in shaping the Rodin collection at the Met. For the story of collectors Iris and B. Gerald Cantor, see Patrick R. Crowley's essay in this volume, "Staging *The Gates of Hell*," pp. 221–27.

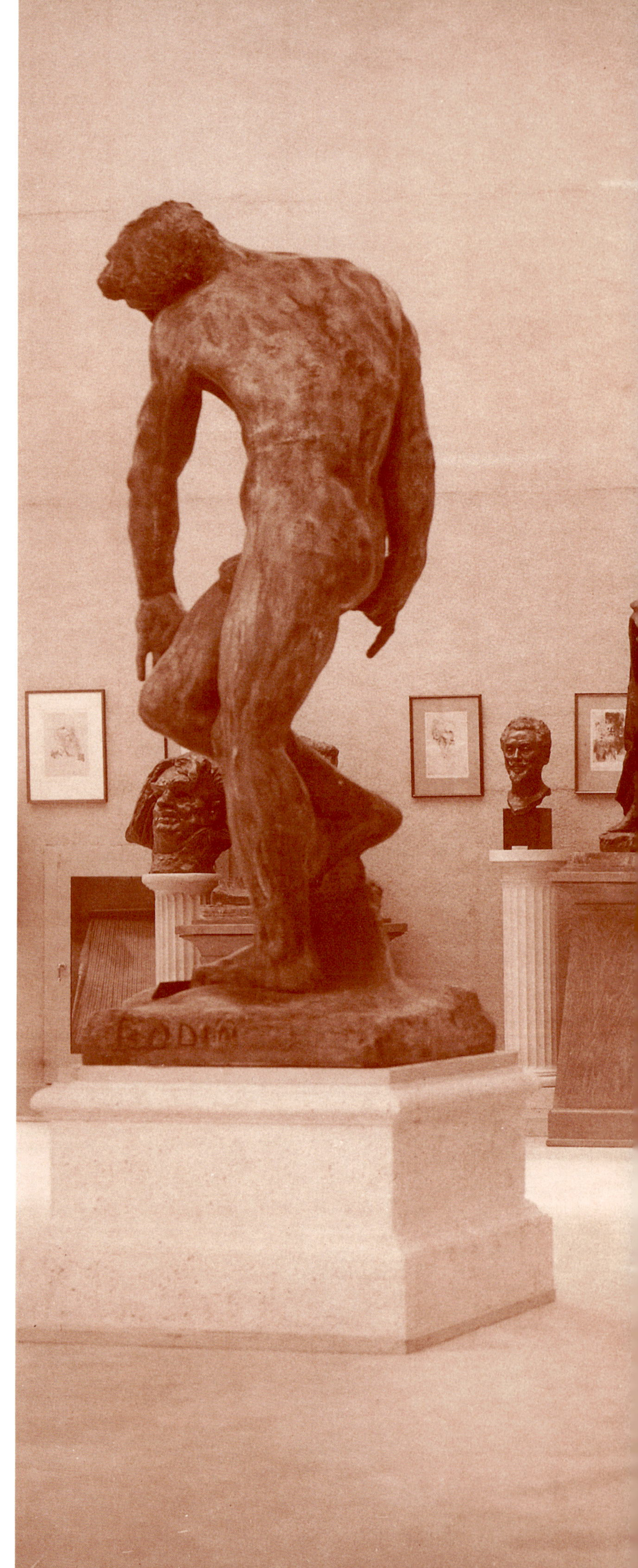

PART II
1915–1950

FROM PRIVATE COLLECTIONS TO MUSEUMS

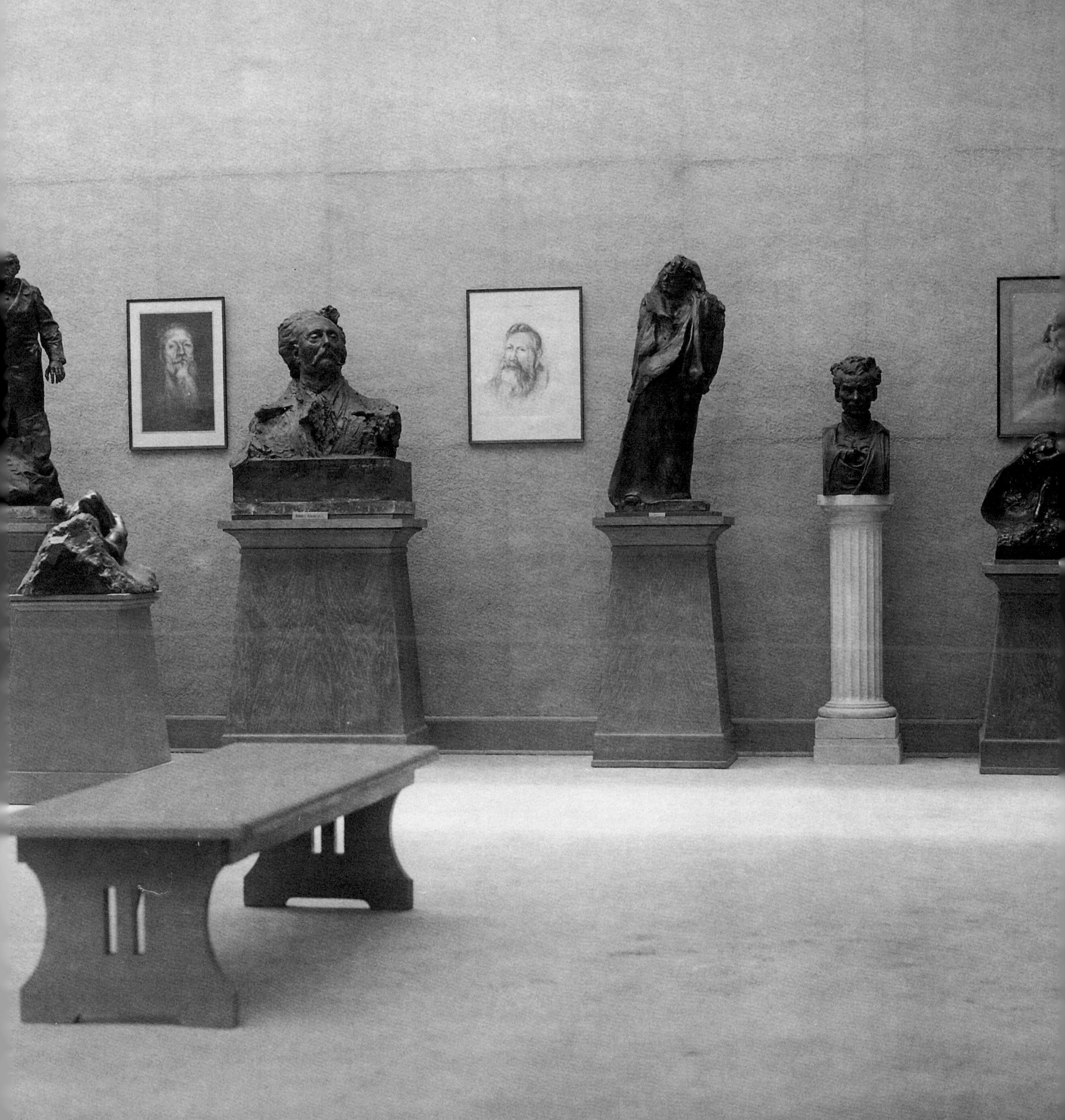

FROM PRIVATE COLLECTIONS TO MUSEUMS, 1915–1950

Auguste Rodin died in 1917. He had been weakened for some time, and Léonce Bénédite, the executor of his will and the first curator of the Musée Rodin in Paris, guarded Rodin carefully during the last months of his life, distancing those who might constitute a threat to the future museum. This was also the case with Loïe Fuller, who became an intermediary on the West Coast for two collectors, Samuel Hill, who had made his fortune building roads in the Pacific Northwest, and sugar heiress and philanthropist Alma de Bretteville Spreckels. At the end of Panama-Pacific International Exposition in San Francisco in 1915, where a selection of works that formed the nucleus of her collection were on view, Spreckels donated the large *Thinker* to the city of San Francisco. Then, in 1924, she deposited thirty-one works in her possession at the newly built Palace of the Legion of Honor. Later, she gave her entire collection to the museum, in several stages. The works acquired after 1915 probably came, for the most part, from Alexis Rudier, Rodin's primary founder after 1902, who simultaneously worked as a dealer, combing the studio and art market in Paris.[1]

However, Spreckels was hard headed and sometimes refused what Fuller offered her, deeming the prices too high. Thus, a group of drawings acquired by Fuller, who had intended to sell them to Spreckels, would ultimately end up in Hill's collection. Fuller left them as a loan guarantee in Cleveland, where Hill purchased them. He would go on to found the Maryhill Museum of Art in Goldendale, Washington, which opened in 1940, after its founder's death, through the support of Alma Spreckels. With only one life-size figure, the Hill collection is more modest than that of Spreckels. But it has a large number of plaster casts, including the life-size *Eve* (cat. 48), which bears an exceptional system of guiding marks for its execution in marble.

Rodin's death ended the possibility of acquiring artworks directly from him, and the generation of collectors who had been in direct contact with him was gradually dying out. While sculptures and drawings that had belonged to John G. Johnson, Arthur Jerome Eddy, Henry Lee Higginson, Agnes and Eugene Meyer, Alfred Stieglitz, Gertrude Käsebier, Robert Allerton, William A. Clark, and Katherine Seney Simpson joined public institutions,[2] a new generation turned to the art market or the Musée Rodin to acquire posthumous bronze casts. Opened in 1919, the museum had received from the artist the right and even the mission to issues new bronzes, both to finance its operations and to contribute to the knowledge of his oeuvre by producing permanent versions of artworks that for various reasons had not been completed, starting with *The Gates of Hell*. Casts of his most famous subjects multiplied, particularly large *Thinkers* (Cleveland, 1917; Detroit, 1922; Philadelphia, 1928; Baltimore, 1928; New York, Columbia University, 1930) and *The Age of Bronze* (San Francisco, 1915; Cleveland, 1918; Buffalo, 1925; Philadelphia, 1925). These posthumous casts are considered original bronzes.

Philadelphia collector Jules Mastbaum, "the king of cinema," understood that bronzes from the Musée Rodin afforded a way to obtain original works.[3] This allowed him to create an American version of the Paris museum, displaying what was considered the essential oeuvre of Rodin at that time, namely works from the first part of his career. This included the first cast of *The Gates of Hell* (1925), originally commissioned by Kojiro Matsukata, a businessman who intended to create a museum of occidental art in Tokyo, but which ultimately went to Mastbaum through a twist of fate, and the *Monument to the Burghers of Calais*. The Rodin Museum in Philadelphia was inaugurated in 1929, and it was certainly this example that encouraged wholesale magnate Jacob Epstein of Baltimore to acquire a fine collection of bronzes, including a large *Thinker* (cat. 69), at the same time.

Another American Rodin collector bears mentioning: Grenville L. Winthrop (1864–1943), though the present exhibition does not include any examples from his holdings because the conditions of his bequest to Harvard University prohibit the works from leaving its museum. Taking advantage of sales that followed the deaths of friends and admirers of Rodin, he was able to acquire very important works, such as a marble *Eternal Idol* (see fig. 1.6) that had belonged to Eugène Carrière and the sole bronze cast of *A Study for Romeo and Juliet*, given by Rodin to Jacques-Émile Blanche in exchange for his portrait in 1904. Winthrop bequeathed all his collections, ranging from ancient art to works of the twentieth century, to Harvard, his alma mater.

Immediately prior to World War II, the United States offered a broad vision of Rodin's work and his creative processes, although it was very classical: missing were the large, innovative figures such as *Monument to Balzac* (see cat. 85) or *The Walking Man*, which reveal his role as the originator of twentieth-century sculpture.

ALNR

1. After Rodin's death, Eugène Rudier went on casting bronzes on behalf of the Musée Rodin, Paris, under the mark of his father Alexis Rudier. He was the museum's near-exclusive founder until his death in 1952.

2. For more on private collectors' contributions to the Rodin collection at the National Gallery of Art, Washington, DC, specifically, see the essay in this volume by C. D. Dickerson III, "Sculpture at the National Gallery of Art: From Andrew W. Mellon to Katherine Seney Simpson to Today," pp. 185–91.

3. For a detailed account of Mastbaum's collection activity, see the essay in this volume by Jennifer A. Thompson, "Collecting with High Ideals and Enjoyment: Jules and Etta Mastbaum and the Rodin Museum in Philadelphia," pp. 177–83.

THE PRODIGAL SON

Original model before 1887, enlarged 1893
Bronze, cast by Alexis Rudier, 1914
64 × 28 × 34 ½ in. (162.6 × 71.1 × 87.6 cm)
Signed on base, top-right front corner: *A. Rodin*
Stamped inside: *A. Rodin*; stamped rear of base,
right: *Ais. Rudier Fondeur Paris*
Fine Arts Museums of San Francisco, Legion of
Honor
Gift of Alma de Bretteville Spreckels, 1940.137

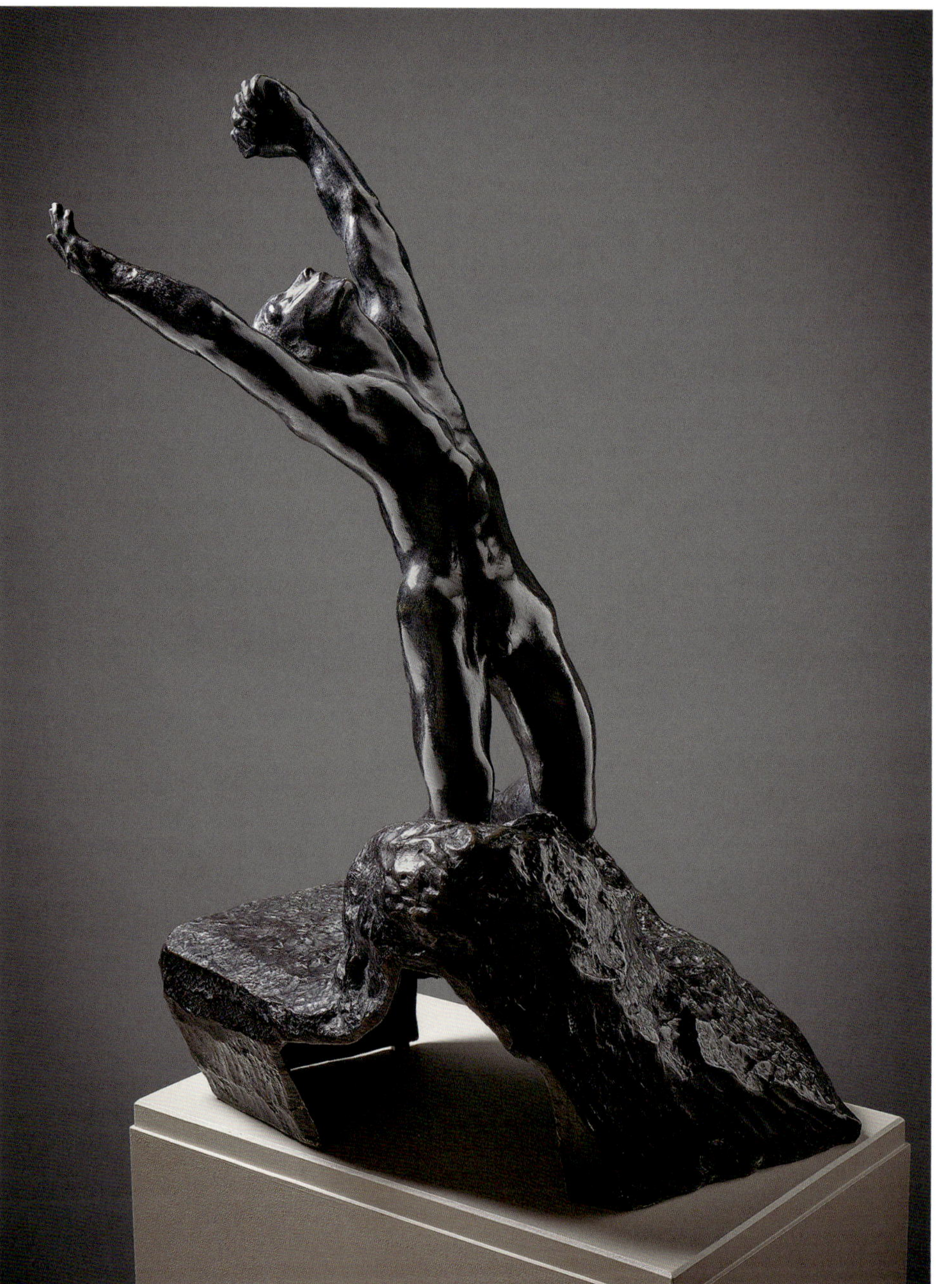

At an unspecified date, Rodin separated the
two figures of *Fugit Amor* (cat. 6) without
bothering to eliminate the traces of their
assemblage, which are quite visible here on
the young man's back. Positioned vertically
and enlarged in 1893, this figure received
the title *Prodigal Son* in reference to the
parable from the Gospel of Luke. Rodin
had reworked the model to make it more
expressive, as interviewer Paul Gsell reported:
"'Look!' Rodin told me, 'I have accentuated
the swelling of the muscles that express
distress. Here, here, there—I have exaggerated the distance between the tendons that
reveal the outburst of prayer.'"[1]

The stone version (1893, Ny Carlsberg
Glyptotek, Copenhagen), executed by
François Pompon, was exhibited in Paris at
the Salon d'Automne of 1905. It led to a
bronze edition starting in 1913. The initial
casts, including those now in the Victoria &
Albert Museum in London and the Fine
Arts Museums of San Francisco, which was
the third to be produced, are characterized
by a base that is open in front and back,
strengthening the impression of suspension
in space that the figure produces. Typical
of the dramatic expression in the artist's
work in the 1880s, the *Prodigal Son* appears
in December 1914 on the list of works that
Rodin planned to send to the Panama-
Pacific Exposition in 1915, after Loïe Fuller
convinced him to complete the selection to
be sent by the French government.[2] At the
end of the exposition, Spreckels purchased
the bronze as planned. Like cats. 43 and 44,
it was probably deposited in the Palace of
the Legion of Honor by 1924 but given to
the institution only later, as Alma preferred
to keep "her children," as she called them,
under her authority.
ALNR

1. Auguste Rodin, *Art: Conversations with Paul Gsell*
[1911], trans. Jacques de Caso and Patricia B. Sanders
(Berkeley: University of California Press, 1984), 12.
2. Rodin's correspondence includes multiple lists of
the works he planned to send to the Panama-Pacific
Exposition in 1915. See, for example, Auguste Rodin
to Loïe Fuller, December 1914, in Auguste Rodin,
Correspondance, vol. 4, *1913–1917* (Paris: Éditions du
musée Rodin, 1992), nos. 128–30, 132.

FEMALE FIGURE, HALF-LENGTH

Original model c. 1910
Bronze, cast by Montagutelli, 1913
29 ¼ × 12 ¼ × 23 ⅝ in. (74.3 × 31.1 × 60 cm)
Signed: *Rodin*
Stamped: *Montagutelli Fres Paris Cire Perdue*
Fine Arts Museums of San Francisco, Legion of
Honor
Gift of Alma de Bretteville Spreckels, 1942.36

Like *Prodigal Son*, this astonishing *Female
Figure, Half-Length* appeared (hors catalogue)
at the Panama-Pacific International
Exposition of 1915. "Now your works from
the Luxembourg will be in another room
with things from the government—also the
torso of a woman," Loïe Fuller wrote to
Rodin June 10. She continued, "M. Guiffrey
tells me the torso is for sale. I've asked him
not to sell it before I can ask you to sell it to
me, for me. I don't want people here to
think that things by you can be sold at the
exposition and I love this torso, it's really so,
so beautiful. I'll make any sacrifice to get
it."[1] Next to earlier figures such as *The Age
of Bronze* (cat. 87) or the large *St. John
the Baptist*, these two works displayed the
boldest and most recent side of Rodin.
Always concerned with making his work
known, he was in the habit of showing his
newest pieces as soon as possible. He had
two casts of this torso made by Montagutelli
in February and March 1913 so that he could
keep one available (Musée Rodin, Paris) and
show the other.

The point of departure for this work was
the torso of *The Martyr*, modeled around
1885 in connection with *The Gates of Hell*,
and then enlarged in 1899. The first bronze
cast of the large version, immediately
acquired by Watson B. Dickerman to be
given to the Metropolitan Museum of Art
in New York, was produced in 1913, thus
at the same time as that of the torso.
The original torso had been subjected to
two further modifications. First, before 1900,
Rodin reduced the torso to a minimum,
greatly opening the upper part by removing
the head, neck, and part of the left shoulder.
He arranged the figure upright and tipped
it backward with a wedge placed under the
thighs, as seen in a photograph by Eugène
Druet (Musée Rodin, Paris, Ph 310). Later,
almost certainly around 1910, Rodin decided
to add the head of a girl with long hair and
to remove the wedge. The work titled *Female
Figure, Half-Length* thus lost the character of
pure sculpture, verging on abstraction, that
it had before. It nonetheless found increased
energy through its forward angle and the

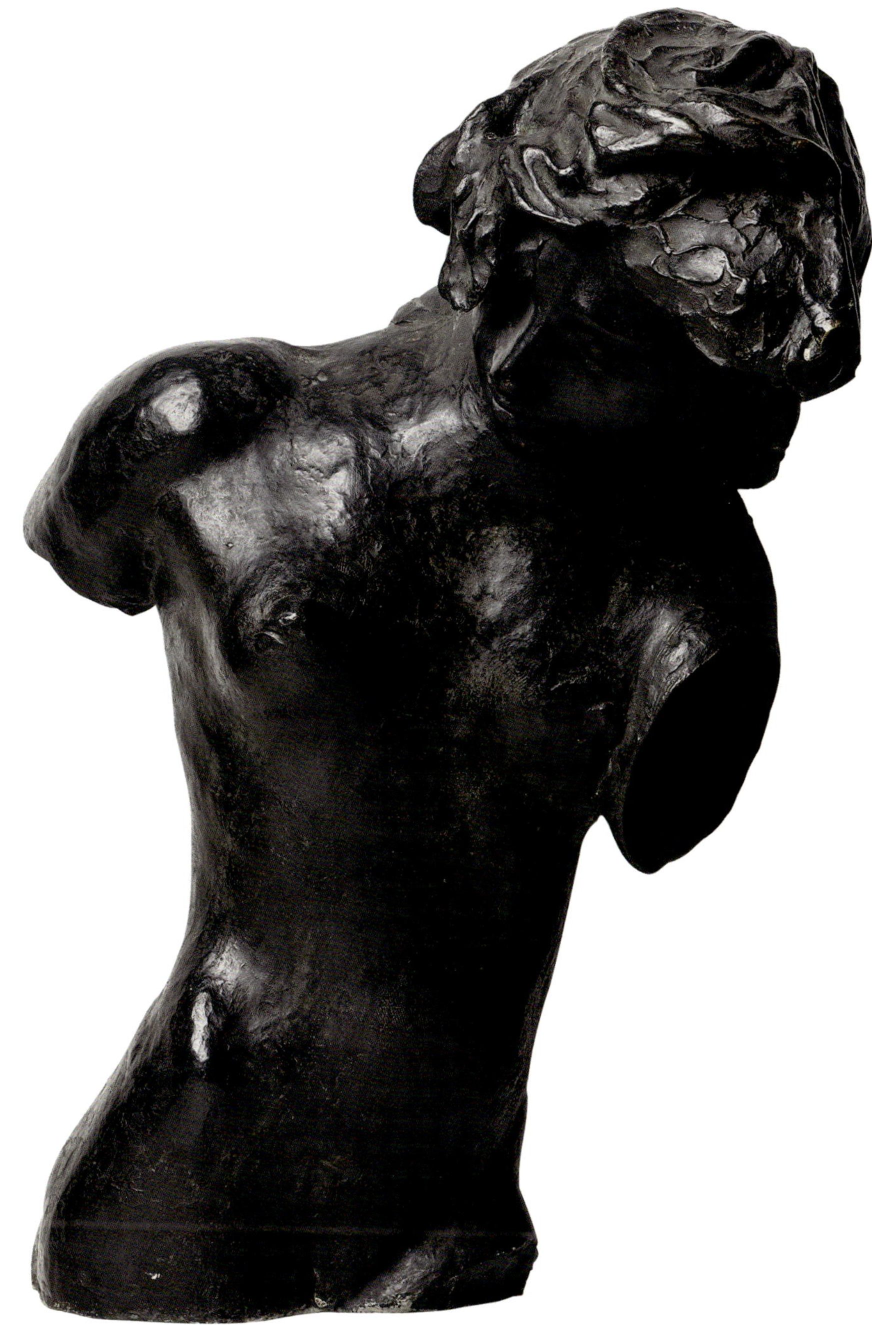

movement of the head, which twists away
from the pelvis.
ALNR

1. Loïe Fuller to Auguste Rodin, June 10, 1915,
Archives du musée Rodin, Paris.

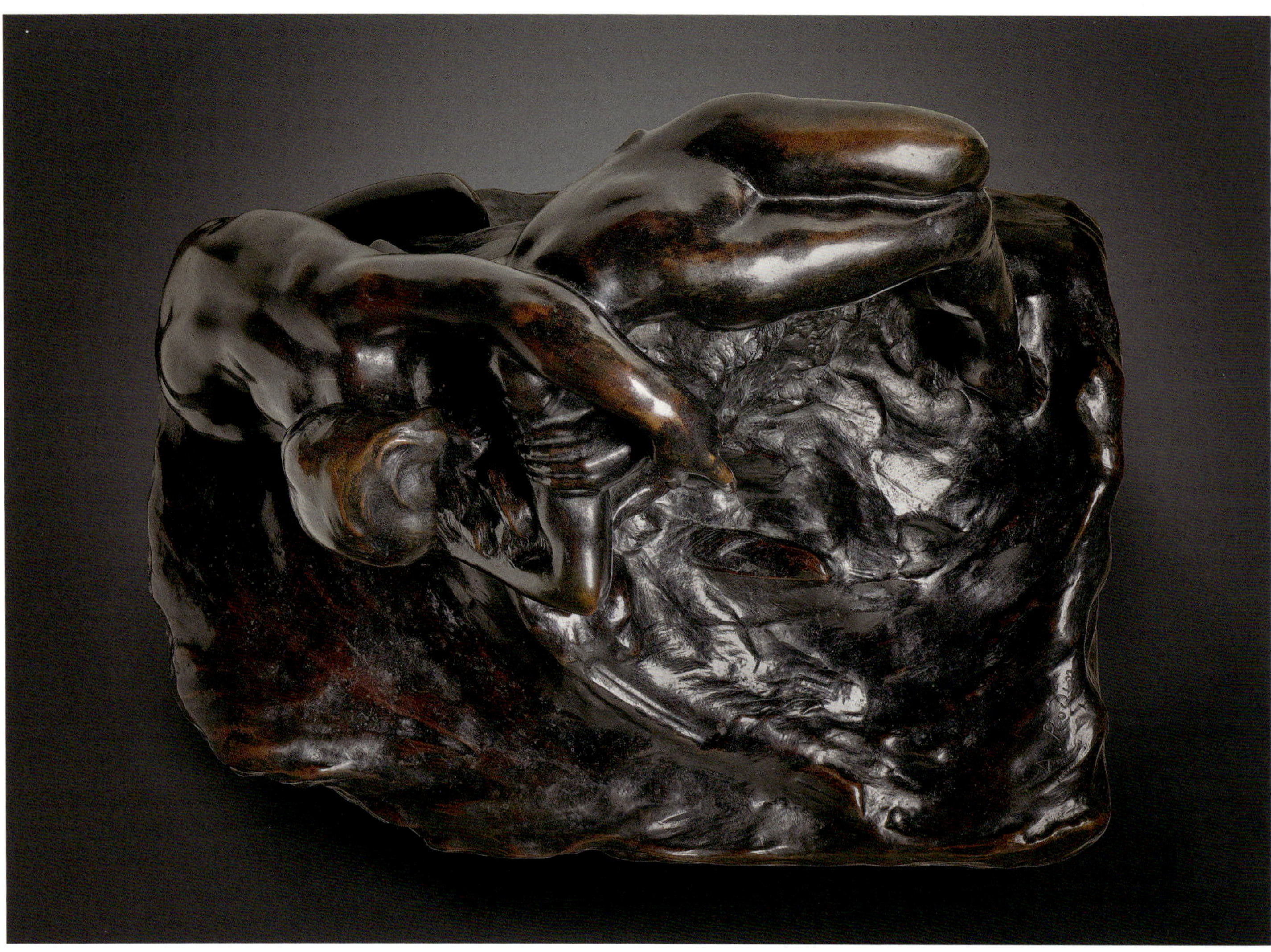

CAT. 44
THE FALLEN ANGEL

Original model c. 1895–1900
Bronze, cast by Alexis Rudier, probably 1915
Signed, top of base, right: *A. Rodin*
Stamped on back: *A. Rudier Fondeur Paris*
20 ⅛ × 21 ½ × 32 in. (51.1 × 54.6 × 81.3 cm)
Fine Arts Museums of San Francisco, Legion of Honor
Gift of Alma de Bretteville Spreckels, 1940.139

Produced by the assemblage of two figures from the 1880s, *Fallen Caryatid* (cat. 2) and the *Torso of Adele*, *The Fallen Angel* is a good example of the way in which Rodin availed himself of the repertoire he had created. It shows his enormous skill at combining forms — in this case, two bodies, one hunched over while the other is expansive, voluptuously stretched and arched. Joined by a kiss, they form a semicircle that unfolds horizontally. Sometimes titled *Illusions Received by the Earth*, this group, along with works such as *The Sirens* and *Christ and Mary Magdalene*

(cat. 101), shows Rodin's connection to the Symbolist movement.

We know this work had three states. This one, the second, produced around 1900, with the left arm of a crouching figure thrown over the body of a second figure, is the most influenced by the fin-de-siècle context. The angel's broken wing, which covers the base, transforms into a kind of wave, while the various elements — hair, wing, ground — blend into one another. Its starting point is a marble (private collection, Japan), originally acquired by the English collector Edmund Davis for 15,000 francs in 1903, from which a number of bronze casts were made. Around 1912–14, Rodin's attention had once again returned to the work, and he displayed it several times. The San Francisco bronze cast does not seem to have been displayed at the Panama-Pacific International Exposition, although *Fallen Angel* does appear on the lists drawn up for (and almost certainly by) Loïe Fuller in

December 1914.[1] Rodin had specified that the bronzes would be shipped to California as they were delivered by Rudier,[2] but it seems that this bronze was not ready in time to be part of the shipment that left France in late 1914. Indeed, it could be identified as one of the two copies of the "large Icarus group" cast by Rudier in January and June 1915,[3] as the composition perfectly justifies that new title of mythological rather than Symbolist inspiration.
ALNR

1. Rodin's correspondence includes multiple lists of the works he planned to send to the Panama-Pacific Exposition in 1915. See, for example, Auguste Rodin to Loïe Fuller, December 1914, in Auguste Rodin, *Correspondance*, vol. 4, *1913–1917* (Paris: Éditions du musée Rodin, 1992), nos. 128–130, 132.
2. Rodin to Fuller, December 16, 1914, in Rodin, *Correspondance*, vol. 4, *1913–1917*, no. 128.
3. Rudier bill, 1915, Archives du musée Rodin, Paris.

HEAD OF BALZAC
(LAST STUDY)

Original model c. 1897
Bronze on tall marble base, cast before 1915
Signed, lower-left side: *A. Rodin*
16¾ × 7½ × 8½ in. (42.6 × 19 × 21.6 cm)
Fine Arts Museums of San Francisco, Legion of Honor
Gift of Alma de Bretteville Spreckels, 1941.34.5

In the long history of Rodin's *Monument to Balzac* (cf. cat. 85), this version is close to the definitive head, with medium-length hair; however, the planes formed by the hair are simpler and the neck more exposed here than in the final monument. Here, Rodin no longer looks for any resemblance to the studies he previously produced from the model Estager (cat. 29), which are similar to life portraits made of the writer himself. A plaster cast from this later series was used to produce the enlargement for the full-scale monument.

This particular head quickly became a success. Bronze casts were featured in various exhibitions, particularly at the National Arts Club in New York in 1903, and Rodin himself offered some of them as gifts to individuals like the writer and journalist Camille Mauclair. In March 1901, Mauclair thanked Rodin for having sent him this "extraordinary mask, an animated rock, the synthesis of expression, true with true truth, that of the soul, that of inner meanings. . . . The obsessiveness of this face, which is elemental instead of human, is unforgettable."[1] Other bronzes were acquired by collectors or friends of the artist, such as Mariana Russell, who modeled for his mythological subjects (cat. 9), or Anglo-German count and modern art patron Harry Graf Kessler.

At least two examples of this *Head of Balzac*, both predating Rodin's death in 1917 and belonging to Arsène Alexandre and Alma de Bretteville Spreckels, respectively, were mounted on tall marble bases formed from a rough block. Its simplified conical form directs the viewer's attention to Balzac's face, just like the writer's cloak, stripped of all detail, in the *Monument to Balzac* (cf. cat. 85), of which the base seems to be an abstract transposition. Could this be a way for Rodin to take his thinking on the simplification of the clothing to the extreme? ALNR

1. Camille Mauclair to Auguste Rodin, March 1901, Archives du musée Rodin, Paris.

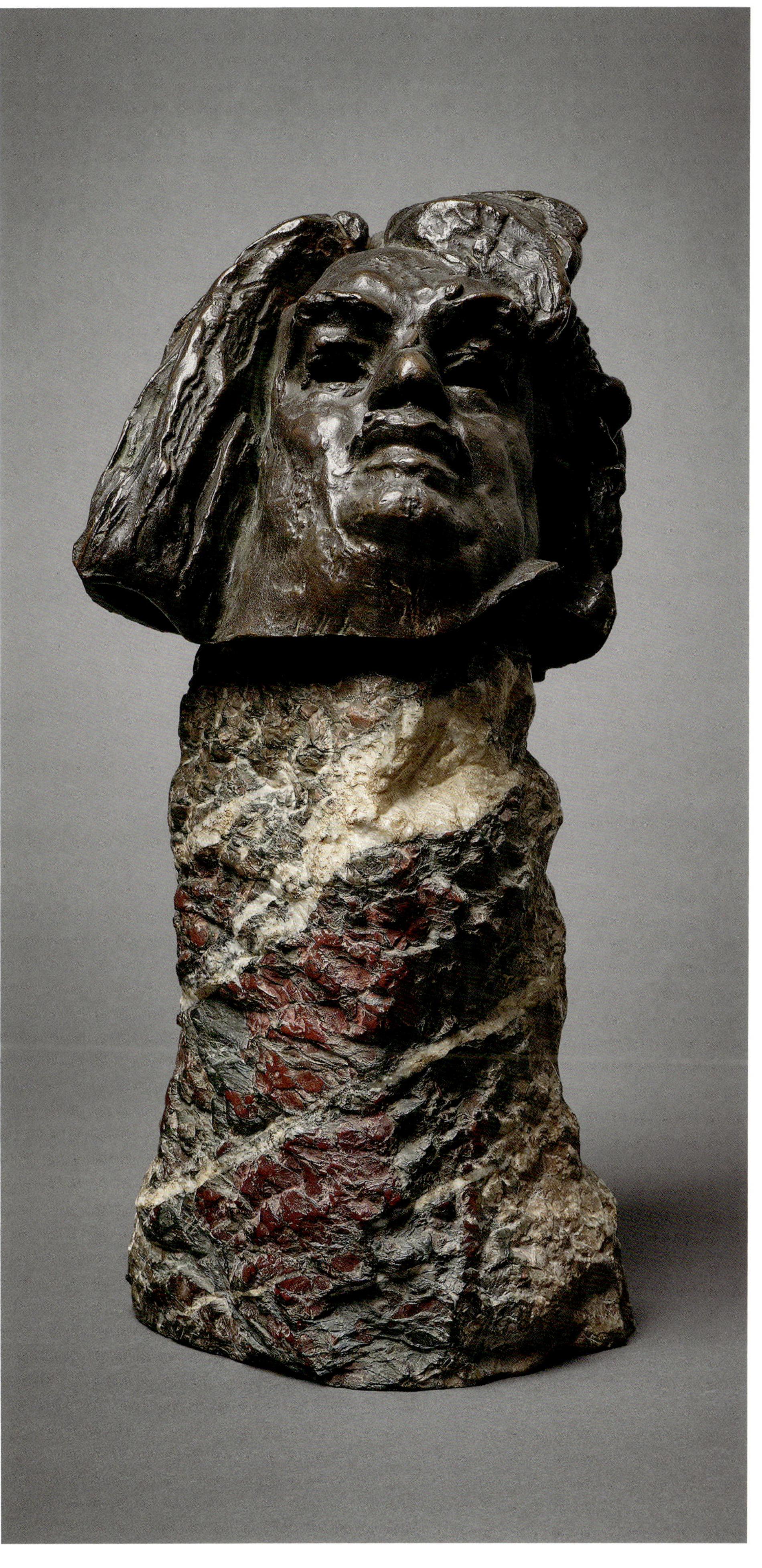

HEROIC HEAD OF PIERRE DE WISSANT, ONE OF THE BURGHERS OF CALAIS

Original model 1887, enlarged 1908
Bronze, cast by Alexis Rudier, 1916; patinated by
Jean Limet
32 ⅞ × 18 ½ × 21 ¾ in. (83.5 × 47 × 55.2 cm)
Signed on neck, at left: *A. Rodin*
Inscribed, lower back: *Alexis Rudier /
Fondeur-Paris*
Cleveland Museum of Art
The Norweb Collection, 1920.120

Hailing from a family of collectors involved
in the founding of the Cleveland Museum of
Art and subsequently the first woman
president of its Board of Trustees, Emery
May Holden Norweb met American dancer
Loïe Fuller in France through the Red Cross
during World War I. In Paris in 1917,
probably influenced by the suffering she
witnessed at the time, Norweb acquired the
Heroic Head of Pierre de Wissant, which
she gave to the Cleveland Museum of Art in
1920. The museum already had a plaster
version of the sculpture, given by Fuller.

Rodin modeled the six *Burghers of Calais*
individually while completing the first phase
of *The Gates of Hell*. He sought forms
directly in the clay, inspired by live models,
attempting to express the passions that move
human beings. The expressive face and hands
of *Pierre de Wissant* (modeled 1887) — who,
of the six *Burghers*, most strongly conveys
the drama these men experienced — were
used elsewhere by Rodin (see *The Hand of
God*, cat. 22). Reflecting the subject's extreme
suffering, that plaster head gave rise to
bronze casts, both in its original size and in
colossal dimensions that, faithfully reproducing even the smallest details of the model,
emphasize its intensity. The large plaster
model was shown in 1908 in the Salon de
Gand, Belgium, and cast the following year
for the city's museum. The Cleveland cast
is the second bronze version of this head.
ALNR

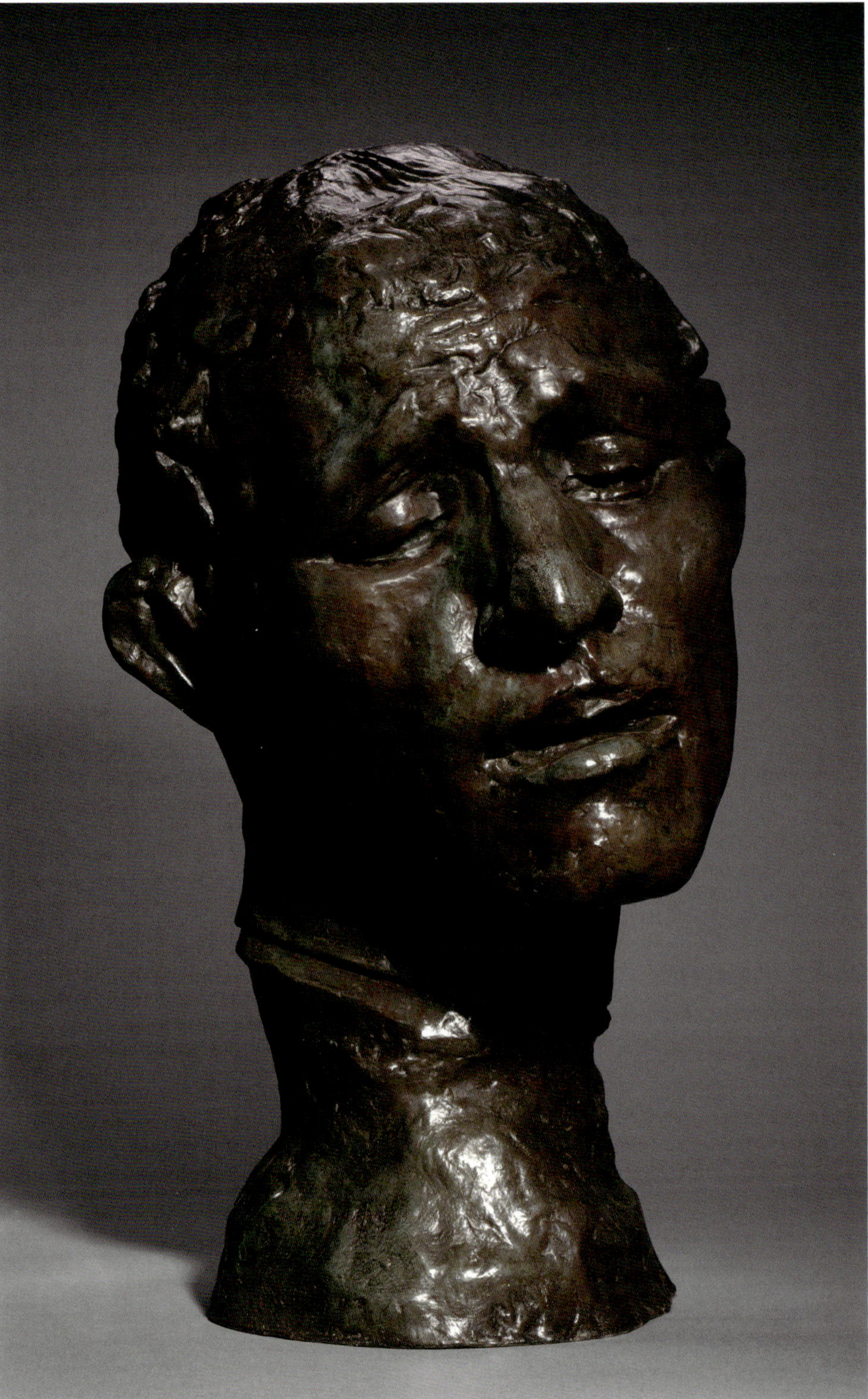

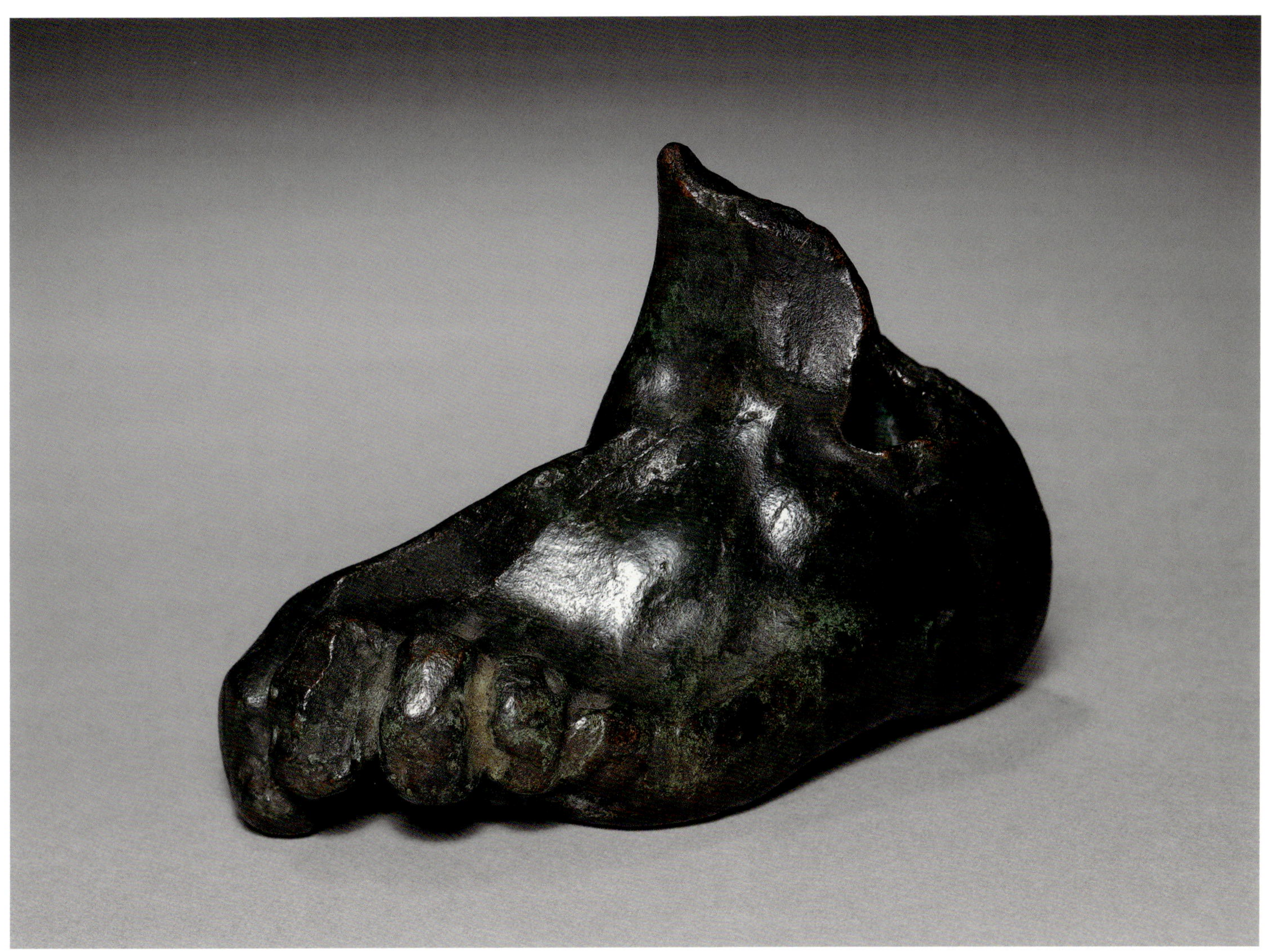

CAT. 47

MODEL OF A FOOT
(LEFT FOOT)

Original model late 19th–early 20th century
Bronze, cast before 1917
2 ¹³⁄₁₆ × 1 ¾ in. (7.2 × 4.4 cm);
length (toe to heel): 4 ⁵⁄₁₆ in. (11 cm)
Signed over heel: *A. Rodin*
Cleveland Museum of Art
Gift of Loïe Fuller, 1917.372

Less than a year after its opening on June 6, 1916, the Cleveland Museum of Art already had eight sculptures by Rodin, including a large *Thinker* given by local collector Ralph King on the advice of the artist's friend and patron Katherine Seney Simpson. The following year, *The Age of Bronze* joined the museum's collection. Encouraged by the friendship of Emery May Holden Norweb, the first woman president of the museum's Board of Trustees, and taking advantage of

interest in the artist, Loïe Fuller (who unsuccessfully tried to become Rodin's US agent) left at the museum a set of drawings that she had acquired in France and originally hoped to sell to Alma de Bretteville Spreckels. The drawings served as collateral for a loan of $9,000. When the sale to Spreckels fell through, Fuller turned to the Cleveland Museum and—most likely to smooth negotiations—she herself donated the *Heroic Head of Pierre de Wissant* in plaster (cf. cat. 46), this foot, and a small *Jean d'Aire* (one of the *Burghers of Calais*) in bronze. It was likely Fuller, hoping to strengthen her negotiating position, who convinced Rodin to give a seventeenth-century ivory *Christ* from his own collection to Norweb so that she could donate it to the Cleveland Museum on his behalf (1917.290). The museum retained

the ivory's original presentation in a wicker frame with a period silk lining. Ultimately, the drawing was purchased by Samuel Hill and left Cleveland.

The Rodin sculptures belonging to the museum, with the addition of some other artworks made available by local collectors, as well as the drawings owned by Loïe Fuller, were shown in December 1917 at an exhibition that had originally been planned for spring 1918 but was moved up because of Rodin's death.

We know nothing about the original model for this plaster foot, which seems too large to be simply a study when compared to the studies preserved in storage at the Musée Rodin. It could be a fragment recovered after a faulty cast or following an accident.
ALNR

EVE

1881/82–99
Plaster with graphite guiding marks
67 × 18 ⅛ × 23 ¼ in. (170 × 47 × 59 cm)
Maryhill Museum of Art, Goldendale, Washington
Bequest of Samuel Hill, 1938.01.0162

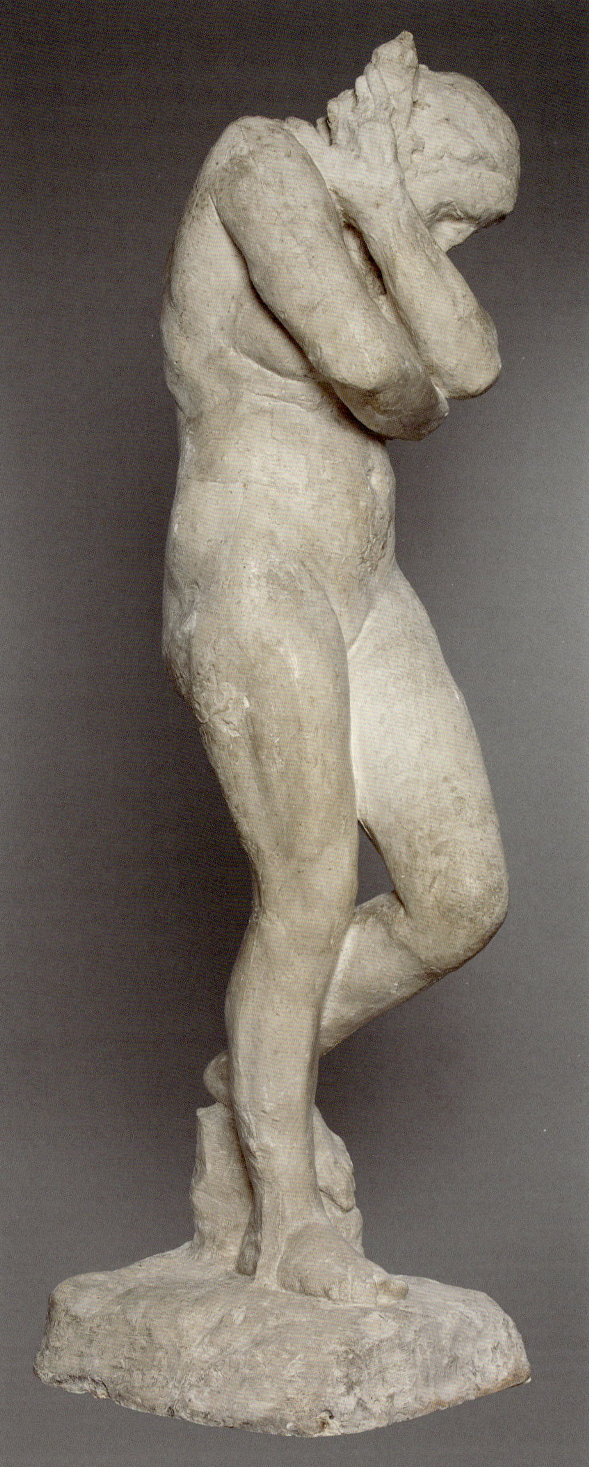

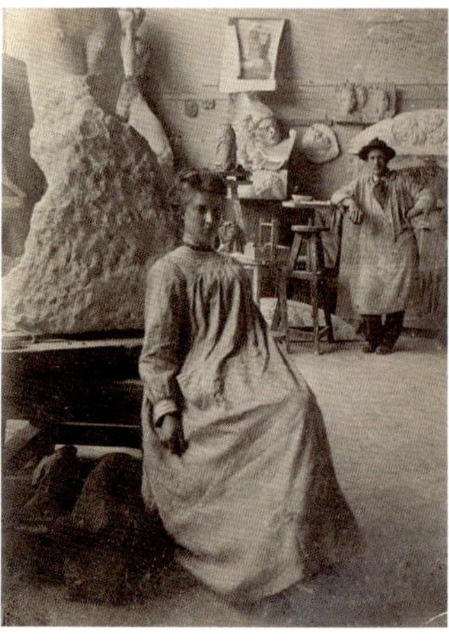

Unknown photographer, Emile-Antoine Bourdelle's workshop, with a German student in front of the large *Eve* in progress, c. 1905. Paris, Musée Bourdelle.

Rodin began working on *Eve* in 1881 as a companion piece for *Adam*, from *The Gates of Hell*, but he abandoned the figure after a few months when the young woman who posed for Eve, Maria Abbruzzesi, became pregnant; the presence of a model was essential for Rodin. Instead, he reworked the large version into a small one, which encountered great success in both marble and bronze beginning in 1883. But in 1897, he decided to cast the original large figure, in two copies, and to show it in Paris and Brussels in 1899. He had not modified the plaster since the modeling sessions with Abbruzzesi ceased, as revealed by the framework around the ankles and irregular sculpting, particularly of the stomach, left hand, and head. Yet the back, with its deeply indented central groove, is a magnificent demonstration of his sculpting talent. *Eve* thus represents two different stages in Rodin's artistic process, separated by fifteen years and combined in a single sculpture. Rodin understood that leaving the signs of time visible, as well as the marks of the work's production, gave it greater strength and significance, harnessing its duration as a sign of its vitality.

The plaster cast seen here has the unusual characteristic of being covered with a network of guide marks, indicated with pencil, of which we know few equivalents. It comes from the workshop of an artisan whom Rodin asked to execute a stone or marble version — probably Antoine Bourdelle (1861–1929), who between 1901 and 1906 executed the limestone sculpture today at Ny Carlsberg Glyptotek in Copenhagen.[1] Indeed, the guide marks visible in a photo of the stone version in process in Bourdelle's studio are placed on the buttocks in exactly the same place as on the plaster.[2] Instead of returning the plaster to Rodin, who asked for it several times, Bourdelle may have kept it and then passed it on to Loïe Fuller. It would be tempting to connect it with a 1928 letter in which Queen Marie of Romania complained to Alma Spreckels that some plaster casts — including a "large life-sized figure of one of the three guardians of the Gates of Hell [*The Three Shades*]," for which

she had paid 200,000 francs — had ended up at Maryhill.[3] Marie, who was undoubtedly writing several years after the fact about works she had never seen, may have remembered only the link with the *Gates of Hell*, which *Eve* and the *Shades* share. ALNR

1. Bourdelle's version (height: 72 ¹⁵/₁₆ in., 175 cm) is closer in size to this plaster cast from the Maryhill Museum of Art than to the two known marbles (height: 54 ¹¹/₁₆ in., 139 cm; and 58 ¼ in., 148 cm), both in the Musée Rodin, Paris, which remain unfinished.
2. I am grateful to François Blanchetière for sharing this information with me.
3. Marie of Romania to Alma de Bretteville Spreckels, October 1928, quoted in Bernice Scharlach, *Big Alma, San Francisco's Alma Spreckels* (San Francisco: Scottwall Associates, 1990), 174.

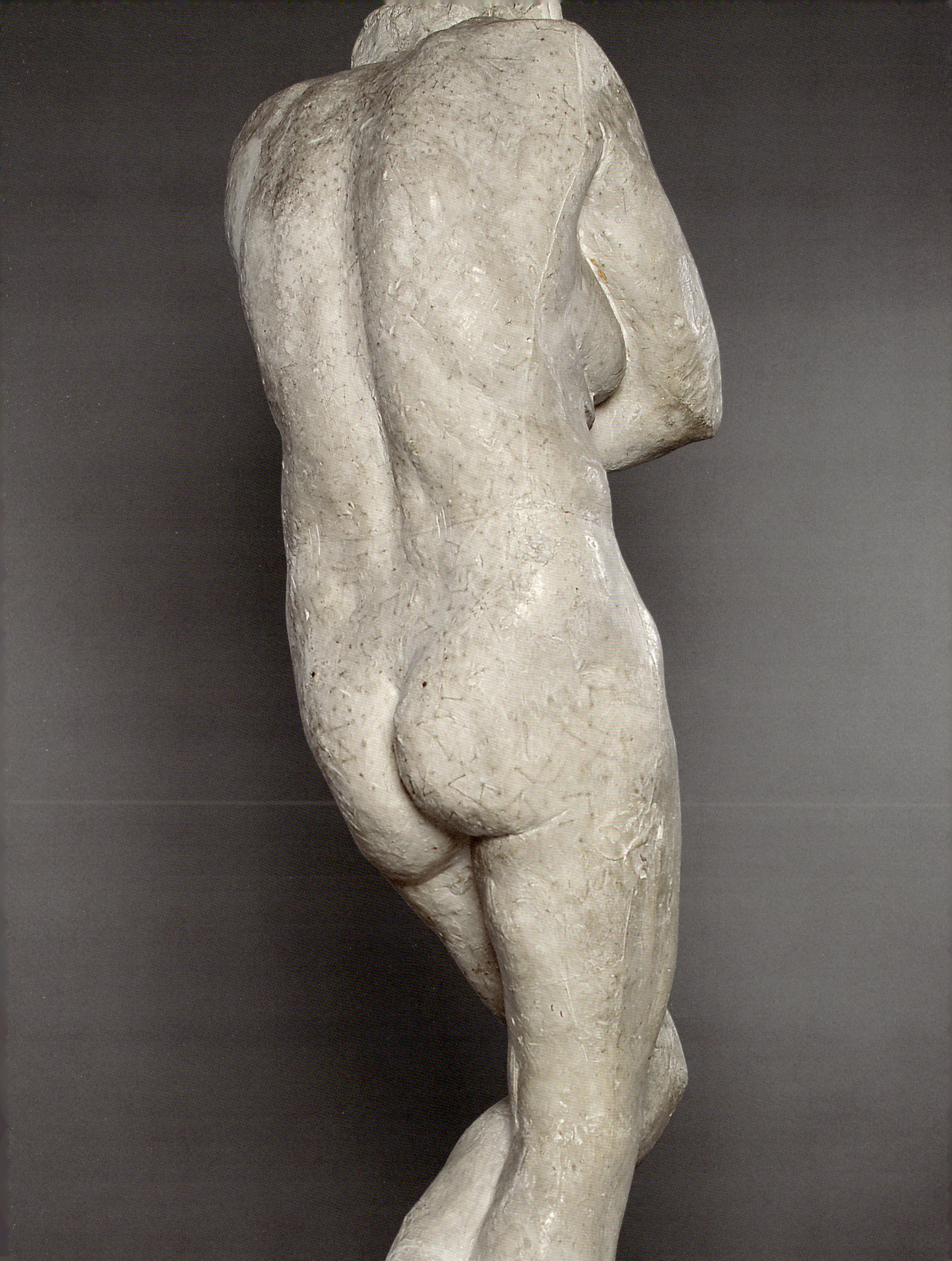

HANAKO (TYPE A)

1907
Gilded bronze on wood base
6 ½ × 5 × 5 ⅝ in. (16.5 × 12.7 × 14.3 cm)
Dedicated at back on bottom: *A-l'admirable et /
Geniale artiste / Loïe-fuller / A. Rodin*
Fine Arts Museums of San Francisco, Legion of
Honor
Gift of Alma de Bretteville Spreckels, 1941.34.7

Rodin first saw Ōta Hisa (1868–1945), the
Japanese actress better known by her stage
name, Hanako, in Marseille in 1906, where
she performed in a play titled *The Revenge of
the Geisha*, which ended with the heroine's
death. Her acting fascinated him. According
to Loïe Fuller, "Her face became immovable,
as if petrified, but her eyes continued to
reveal intense animation . . . with great
wide-open eyes she surveyed death, which
had just overtaken her."[1] He wanted to make
a portrait of her, and Fuller, who had taken
the actress under her wing, served as
intermediary and arranged for the sittings
(cf. cat. 26).

From the beginning, Rodin had been
interested in rendering an expression
marked by anguish, expressed by knitted
eyebrows, squinting, and a partially open
mouth. "Hanako did not pose like other
people. Her features were contracted in an
expression of cold, terrible rage. She had
the look of a tiger, an expression thoroughly
foreign to our Western countenances."[2]
Rodin modeled several studies,[3] resulting
in a version (called type A[4]) of which he gave
copies to Loïe Fuller and Hanako herself,
as the actress related in 1925.[5] The artist's
agenda for December 4, 1907, notes: "Have
Hanako head signed to take to Loïe Fuller."[6]
He probably added at that moment the
inscription "*A l'admirable et géniale artiste
Loïe Fuller*," which can be seen on very
few copies.

A number of plaster casts are known,
including one conserved at the Maryhill
Museum in Goldendale, Washington, which
comes from Loïe Fuller and bears the same
inscription as the San Francisco bronze.

Many bronzes were produced beginning
in 1913. Several, including one located in
the Musée Rodin, Paris, have a gilded patina
like the one in San Francisco and also bear
the same inscription, indicating the essential
role Fuller played in the connections that
developed between Rodin and the United
States, especially on the West Coast.
ALNR

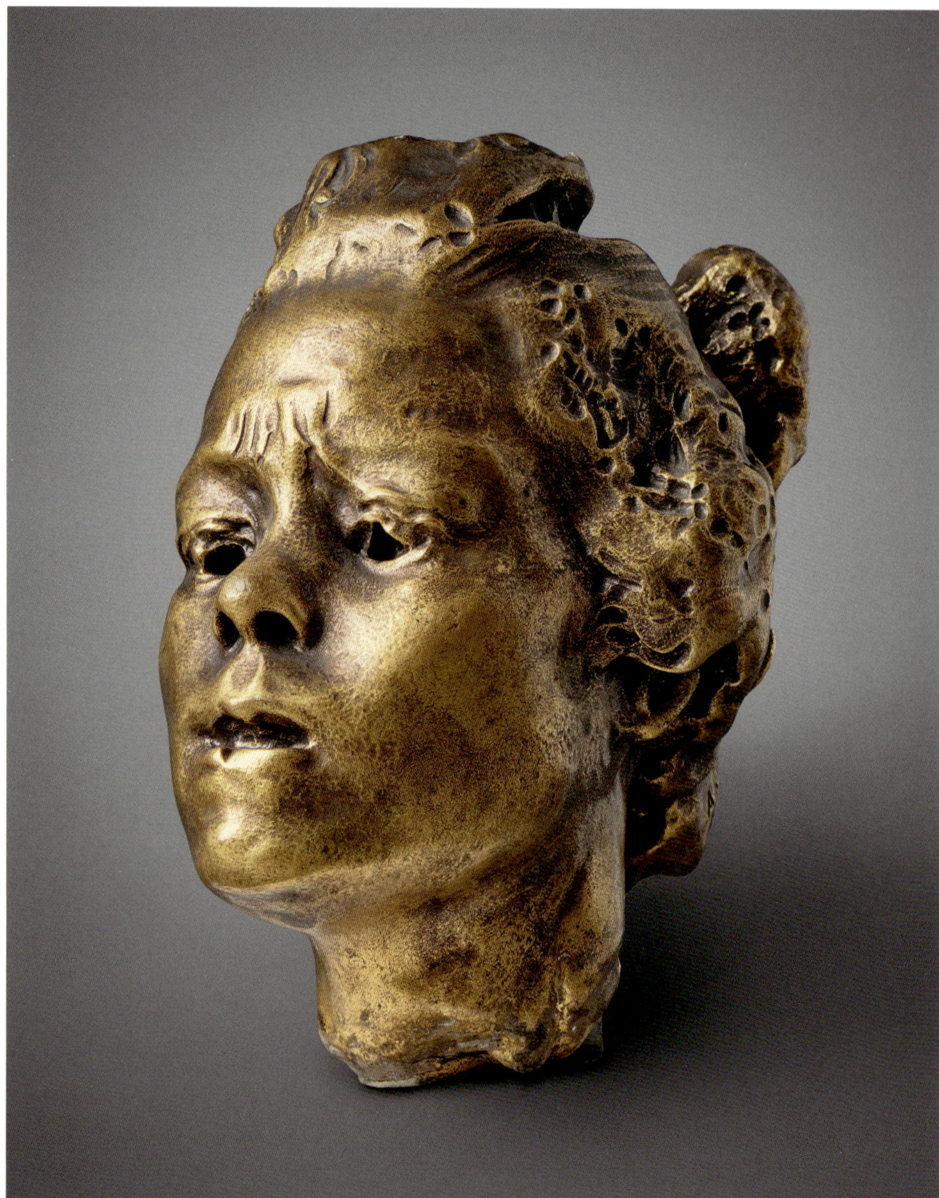

1. Loïe Fuller, *Fifteen Years of a Dancer's Life*
(London: H. Jenkins, 1913), 215.
2. Judith Cladel, *Rodin: The Man and His Art
with Leaves from His Notebook*, trans. S. K. Star
(New York: Century 1918), 162.
3. Chloé Ariot, Agnes Cascio, and Guylaine Mary,
"In Search of Hanako: Fifty Portraits by Rodin,"
Burlington Magazine, no. 162 (October 2020): 851–59.
4. The versions of the very expressive portraits of
Hanako are classified in a series of types, from type A
to type G, recording different stages in various media
(terracotta, plaster, plastiline) in the developments of
the heads.
5. *Gifu Daily News*, January 6, 1925, quoted in
Suketaro Sawada, *Little Hanako* (Nagoya: Chunichi
Publishing Company, 1987), 106.
6. Quoted in François Blanchetière and Bénédicte
Garnier, eds., *Rodin: Le Rêve japonais*, exh. cat.
(Paris: Musée Rodin, 2007), 130.

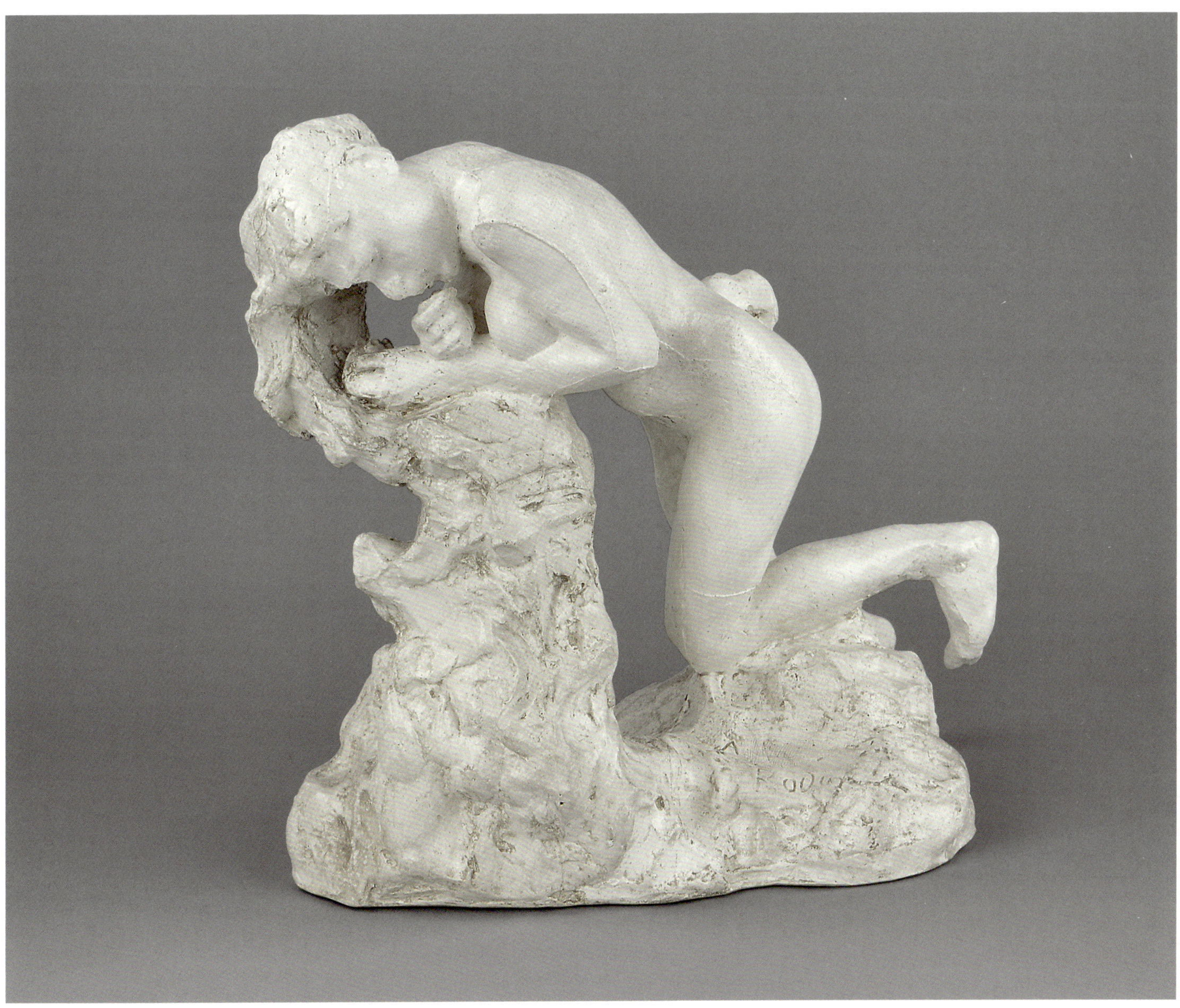

CAT. 50
EVE EATING THE APPLE, KNOWN AS DAWN

Original model c. 1887
Plaster
10 ½ × 6 × 10 ¼ in. (26.7 × 15.2 × 26 cm)
Signed on base: *A Rodin*
Maryhill Museum of Art, Goldendale, Washington
Bequest of Samuel Hill, 1938.01.0164

This small plaster, like *The Hand of God* (cat. 51), was among the works Loïe Fuller obtained either from Rodin himself or, after his death, from one of his plaster molders, bronze founders, or collectors. The plaster cast of *Eve Eating the Apple* now in the Maryhill Museum of Art, Goldendale, Washington, was made from a small terracotta original that Rodin gave to Katherine Seney Simpson (c. 1885, National Gallery of Art, Washington, DC). This female nude, similar to the small figure known as *Sorrow No. 2*, is among those he reused most freely. He sometimes combined it with other elements, such as the left hand of a *Burgher of Calais* (*Hand of the Devil*, 1907, Musée Rodin, Paris). Elsewhere, he also used only the torso, which he ultimately enlarged to three times its original size. Cut diagonally across the pelvis (the legs excised completely) and placed vertically on a base that widens slightly toward the bottom, the torso gave rise to a softer, almost abstract shape in one of the last works by Rodin, showing him at his most modern (*Torso of a Woman*, c. 1914, Victoria & Albert Museum, London).

This kneeling figure, which can be dated to the late 1880s by a fragment corresponding to the head and torso that appears on the right panel of the *Gates of Hell*, belatedly received the title *Eve Eating the Apple*, while the plaster made from it is often titled *Dawn* (*L'Aube*) based on a misreading of a dedication to the sculptor Jean-Paul Aubé (1837–1916) on the copy at the Musée Rodin, Paris. The tuft of hair visible on the figure's lower back is more characteristic of a female faun than of Eve. *Faunesse, Eve, Dawn*: these works all share a strong element of sensuality.
ALNR

THE HAND OF GOD

Original model before 1895
Plaster c. 1900
13 ½ × 11 × 10 ½ in. (34.3 × 27.9 × 26.7 cm)
Dedicated and signed in graphite on base:
A Loïe. Rodin
Maryhill Museum of Art, Goldendale, Washington
Bequest of Samuel Hill, 1938.01.186

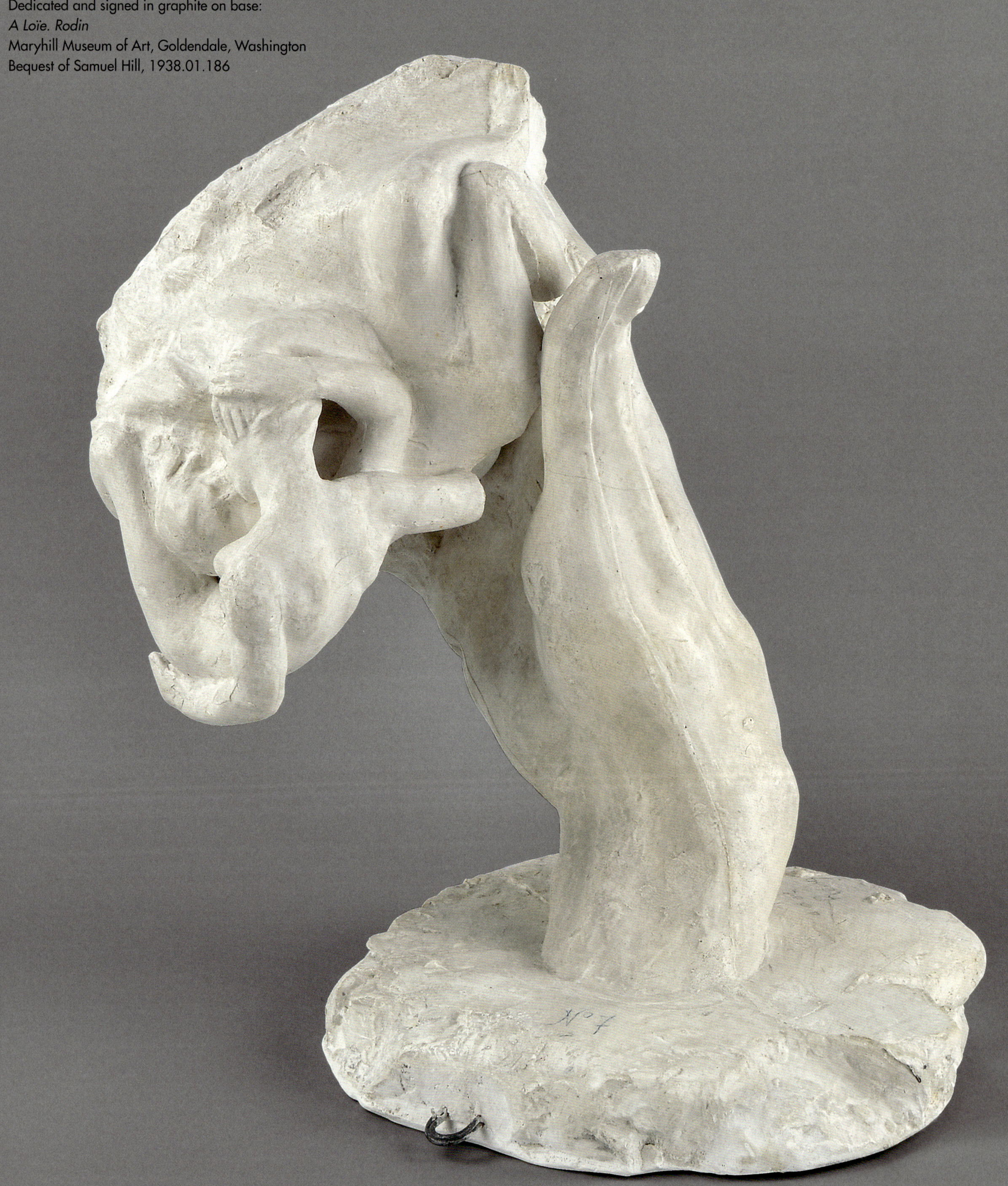

THE HAND OF GOD

Original model before 1895
Bronze, cast by Alexis Rudier, before 1908
38 × 24½ × 17 in. (96.5 × 62.2 × 43.2 cm)
Signed on base: *A. Rodin*
Carnegie Museum of Art, Pittsburgh
Purchase, 20.14.5

On May 2, 1908, the banker and collector Albert Kahn authorized Rodin to accept the request from the French government for a bronze copy of *The Hand of God*, noting that it "is quite understood that there are only three copies of this work: the first . . . in bronze, which is intended for the Luxembourg; the second a reproduction of this group that was sold to Mr. Ed. Adams [cat. 22], and the third that is mine. No other copy can be made without my permission."[1]

Seemingly the only bronze produced from the first marble and in the same dimensions, the Pittsburgh *Hand of God* boasts—like the San Francisco *Prodigal Son* (cat. 42), but well before it—the unusual characteristic of an open base cut diagonally in the back. This allows for a reduction in the footprint of the piece, but it raises the question of how Rodin wanted the work to be seen (of course, vertical presentation of a marble requires the work to be supported by a prop). He may have planned to display the work horizontally— as when it was first shown in Munich in 1896, and as it appeared in Rodin's solo exhibition in Paris in 1900[2]—with the fingers stretched toward the viewer, making the open side of the base more or less invisible.

Cast by Alexis Rudier, the bronze was acquired in 1909 for the Musée du Luxembourg (the inventory mark *LUX 158* is quite visible) and then transferred to the Musée Rodin in Paris after it was founded in 1919.[3] The following year, it was sent to Pittsburgh for the Carnegie Institute's *Nineteenth Annual International Exhibition of Paintings*[4] and then acquired by the institution, satisfying the wish of one of its former directors. On February 24, 1906, John Beattie, who had met Rodin at a lunch at Alexander Harrison's residence in Paris, had sought to convince him to send "a group of your masterly works for exhibition in the Carnegie Institute at the time of the dedication of the enlarged building."[5] That arrangement did not take place, for Rodin wanted the institution to commit to purchasing the works, pointing out that sending them constituted a significant expense for him.

A metaphor for the creative impulse, to which Rodin attached such tremendous importance, *Hand of God* was well received, as the four marbles and the number of

plaster and bronze versions attest. Of various dimensions, but always smaller than the marbles, the plaster and bronze versions (in heights of 5⅞ in., 15 cm; 13 in., 33 cm; and 28¾ in., 73 cm) came, for the most part, from the molding of the first marble. This is not the case for the plaster cast in the Maryhill Museum of Art, which also differs from the others in its unique size. Moreover, a hook placed on the side allows it to be displayed like it was in Paris in 1900, with the hand turned toward the viewer and not toward the sky. This arrangement, which the marble versions forsook, leads us to believe that the cast was made around 1900. ALNR

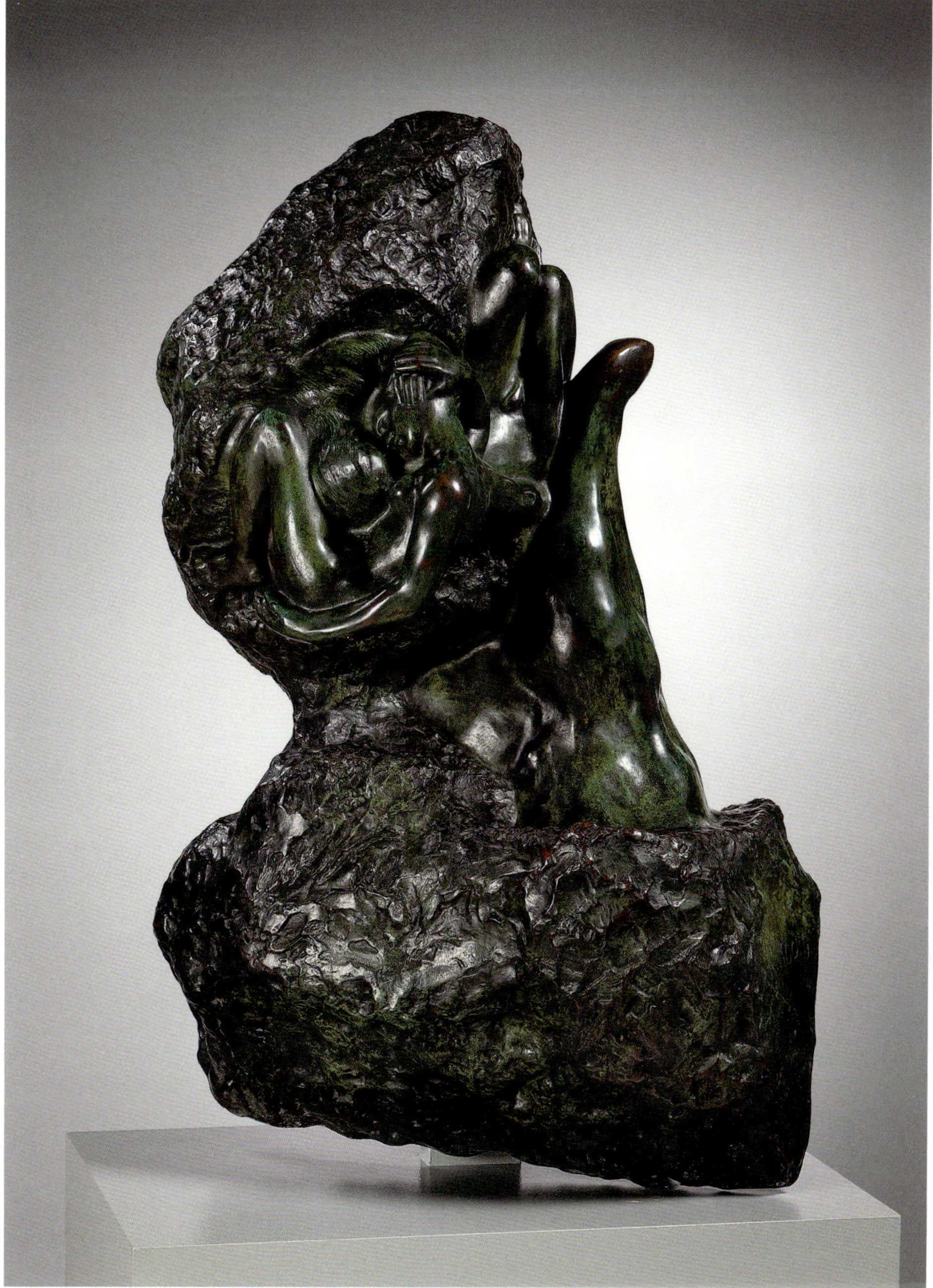

1. Albert Kahn to Auguste Rodin, May 2, 1908, Archives du musée Rodin, Paris.
2. *Exposition Rodin*, exh. cat. (Paris: Palais de l'Alma, 1900), cat. 67.
3. See Anne Pingeot, "Rodin au musée du Luxembourg," *48/14. La revue du musée d'Orsay*, no. 11 (Autumn 2000): 69.
4. *Nineteenth Annual International Exhibition of Paintings* (Pittsburgh: Carnegie Institute, 1920), cat. 377.
5. John Beattie to Auguste Rodin, February 24, 1906, Carnegie Museum of Art Museum Archives, Pittsburgh.

FIGURE IN POSE OF MICHELANGELO'S "APOLLO"

c. 1876
Charcoal, watercolor, and gouache on wove
paper
13 ¾ × 9 ¼ in. (34.9 × 23.5 cm)
Maryhill Museum of Art, Goldendale, Washington
Bequest of Samuel Hill, 1938.01.0094

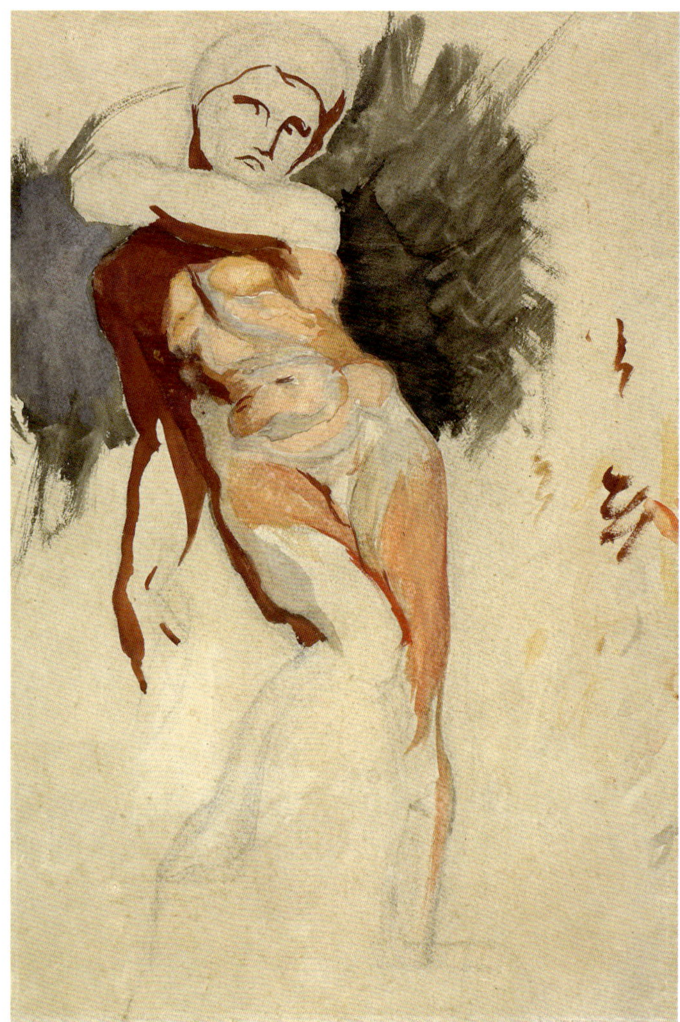

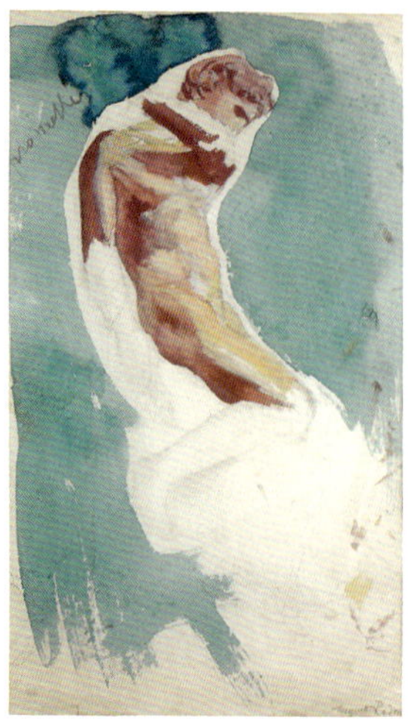

Auguste Rodin, *Prometheus*,
c. 1876. Charcoal, watercolor,
and gouache on wove paper,
16 ¹⁵⁄₁₆ × 9 ⅝ in. (43 ×
24.5 cm). Collection of André
Bromberg, France.

The *Figure in Pose of Michelangelo's "Apollo"* (after the Italian sculptor's work in the Bargello National Museum, Florence) has no equivalent in the collections of the Musée Rodin in Paris, which attests to the exceptional nature of this drawing from the Maryhill Museum of Art in Goldendale, Washington. We can probably situate it after the artist's first trip to Italy, in 1876.[1] Only one other drawing, titled *Prometheus* (c. 1876, collection of André Bromberg, France), has the same unusual format, depicts the same subject (the same marble, but seen in profile), and is treated with the same brush technique. The two drawings illustrate the way in which Rodin developed his thinking on contrapposto, the twisting of hips, shoulders, and head in opposing directions, which led in particular to the figure of *The Shade*.

The large size of the two sheets is very unusual. At this time, Rodin focused on small sketches in red ink that he preserved in albums. A more painterly work, the *Apollo* at the Maryhill Museum, features the addition of gouache and watercolor. The partial coloring, concentrated on the bust, recalls the artist's early interest in the fragmentary aspect of ancient art, while the right hand with the finger pointing to the ground, as in Rodin's *Adam*, one of the figures planned for *Gates of Hell*, is a direct reference to Michelangelo. The treatment of the pink flesh of the stomach reveals Rodin's interest in Peter Paul Rubens at the time, whose work he had discovered at the Royal Museum of Fine Arts in Antwerp.

The Maryhill Museum has one of the most important American collections of Rodin's works on paper: twenty-three drawings of major interest for our understanding of the artist. Loïe Fuller, who hoped to serve as the artist's US agent, received permission to acquire them in Rome in 1915:

It was in Rome at a great dinner party in honor of Rodin at the Villa de Medicis, given by [Albert] Besnard, at which he said he was going to give a set of drawings for an Album to be created for the soldiers and I spoke up and said: But the

Master had just promised the same thing, haven't you Master? He replied: Oui. And afterwards I asked him to prepare a document to that effect and to give me the order for the pictures. He dictated and signed the paper and gave the order for the Inspecteur des Beaux-Arts [Armand Dayot] to choose the pictures—those are the drawings—I afterwards bought them of the Master. . . . I suppose the museum in Cleveland has ceded theirs to Mr. Samuel [Hill].[2]

Fuller originally hoped to sell the drawings to Alma de Bretteville Spreckels on behalf of the Legion of Honor in San Francisco, but after Spreckels declined, she deposited the drawings at the Cleveland Museum as collateral for a personal loan of $9,000 from the Cleveland Trust Company. When Fuller was unable to pay back the loan, Samuel Hill paid off her debt and

became owner of the drawings in 1921, intending them for his planned Maryhill Museum of Art. Hill died prematurely, and Spreckels took charge of opening the Goldendale museum in 1940. That same year, she offered nine drawings from her own collection to the Legion of Honor in San Francisco, not knowing they were all by the most formidable forger of Rodin in the United States, Ernest Durig (1894–1962).[3]
CBU

1. J. Kirk T. Varnedoe, "Rodin as a Draftsman— A Chronological Perspective," in *The Drawings of Rodin*, ed. Albert Elsen and J. Kirk T. Varnedoe (New York: Praeger, 1971), 48, fig. 25.
2. Loïe Fuller to Alma de Bretteville Spreckels, draft, c. 1924?, New York Public Library.
3. For more on Durig's forgeries, see the essay in this volume by Christina Buley-Uribe, "The Role of Drawing in the Art of Rodin," p. 47.

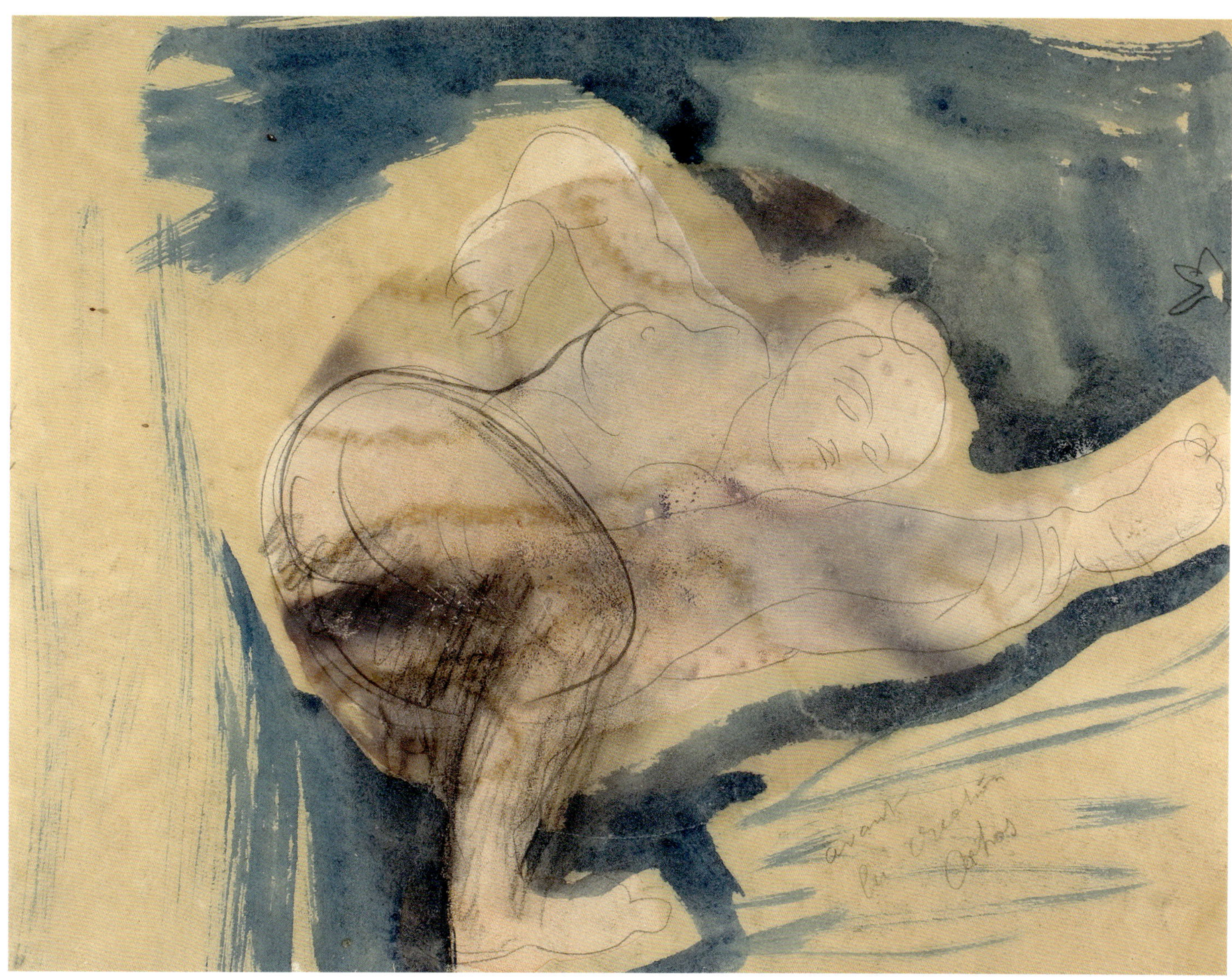

CAT. 54
BEFORE CREATION: CHAOS

c. 1898–1900
Graphite and watercolor on wove paper
9 ¾ × 12 ¾ in. (24.8 × 32.4 cm)
Inscribed in graphite, center right: *avant /
la creation / Cahos* [*sic*]
Maryhill Museum of Art, Goldendale, Washington
Bequest of Samuel Hill, 1938.1.116

Works like Rodin's *Before Creation: Chaos*
had a marked impact on early twentieth-
century American artists, particularly on
Georgia O'Keeffe,[1] and later on the Abstract
Expressionists. *Chaos* can be understood
as an abstract work in that the elements of
the body appear on their own terms, without
any claim to the unity of a figure. Rodin
crossed out the right thigh here before
soaking it in a purplish-blue wash. The ring
of blue watercolor that redefines and offsets
the contours of the figure contrasts with
the fluid paint covering the body and gives
a sculptural appearance to the whole. This

disparate assemblage perhaps led to the
work's evocative title. A sketch of a little star
on the right side of the sheet, surrounding
a white square left blank, recalls the general
form of the figure. It has the effect of a burst
of light in the dark. A drawing of very
similar design, probably developed at the
same time, titled *Moon* (D. 4240, Musée
Rodin, Paris), depicts a woman lying on her
back with her legs spread.
CBU

1. See Roberta K. Tarbell, "Auguste Rodin's Drawings
and Their Impact on American Artists," in *Rodin
and America: Influence and Adaptation 1876–1936*,
exh. cat., ed. Bernard Barryte and Roberta K. Tarbell
(Stanford, CA: Iris and B. Gerald Cantor Center for
Visual Arts, 2011), 161–205.

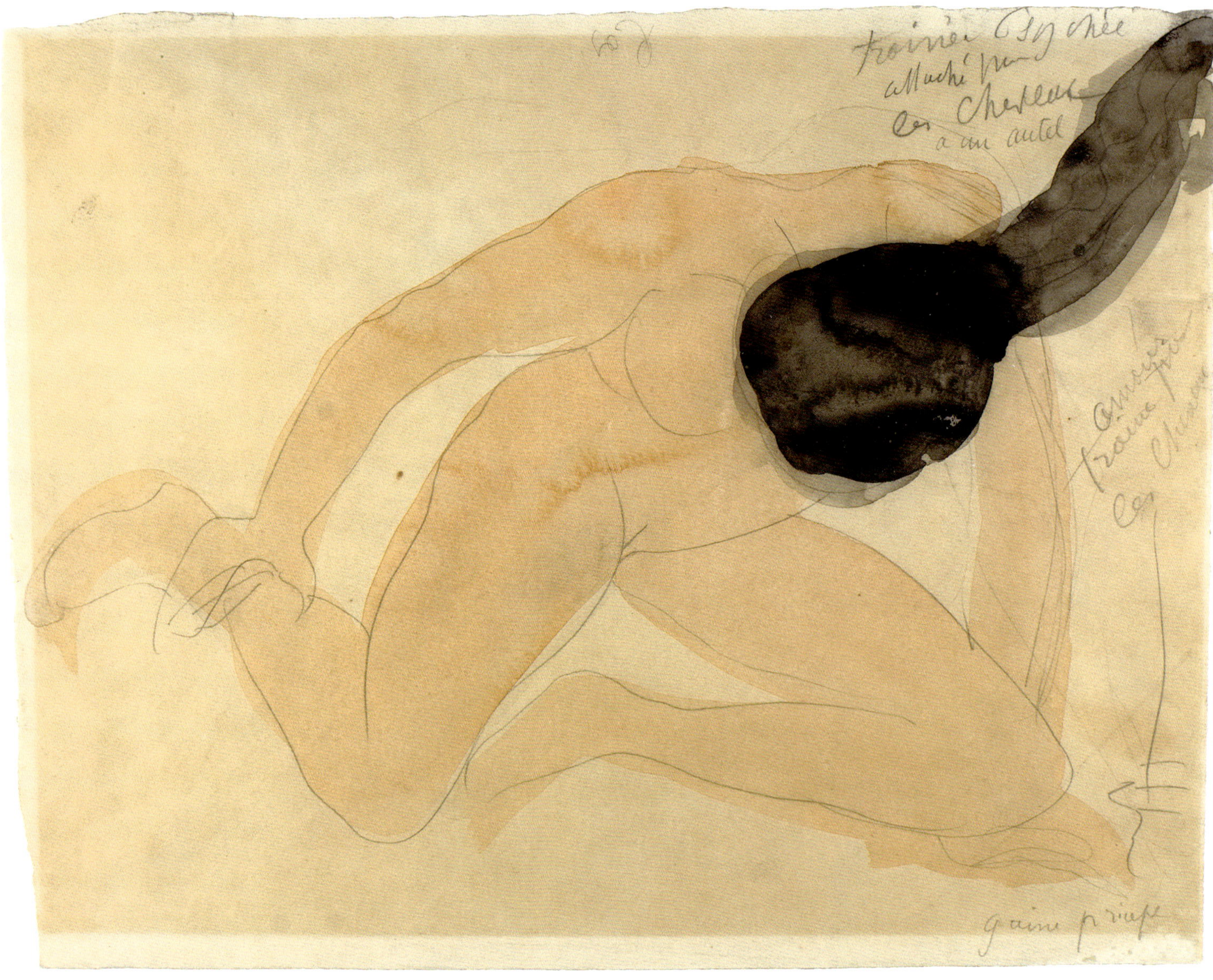

CAT. 55

PSYCHE

c. 1902
Graphite and watercolor on wove paper
10¾ × 12½ in. (27.3 × 31.8 cm)
Inscribed in graphite, upper right: *trainée Psychée
[sic] / attachée par / les cheveux / à un autel*;
center right: *amour / traine par / les cheveux*;
lower right: *gaine priape*; upper middle: *bas*
Maryhill Museum of Art, Goldendale, Washington
Bequest of Samuel Hill, 1938.1.107

CAT. 56

PSYCHE

c. 1902
Graphite and watercolor on wove paper
17 × 14 in. (43.2 × 35.6 cm)
Signed in graphite, bottom right: *Aug. Rodin*
Maryhill Museum of Art, Goldendale, Washington
Bequest of Samuel Hill, 1938.1.104

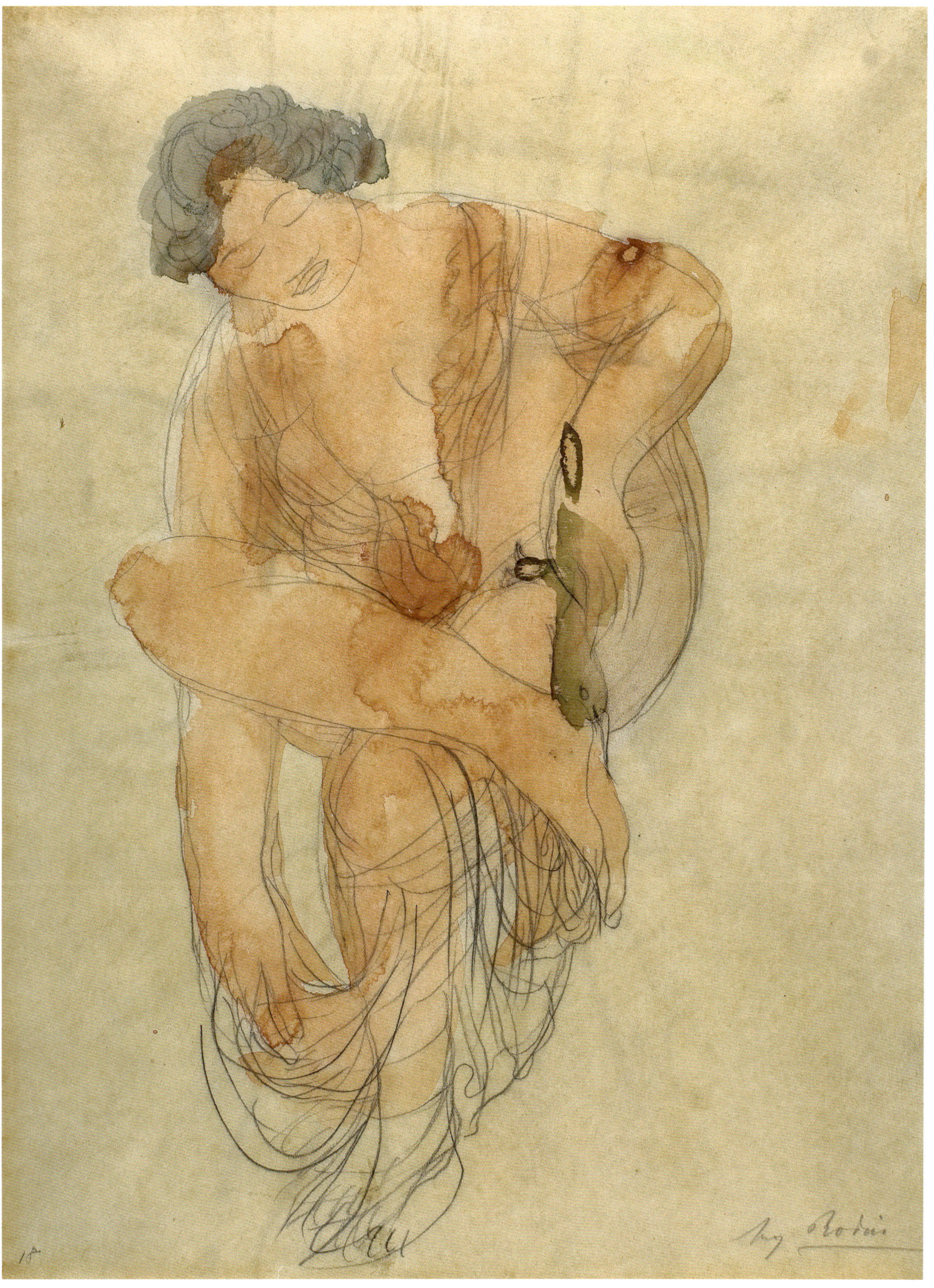

CAMBODIAN DANCER IN YELLOW, AT THE END OF A RAINBOW

c. 1906–7
Graphite and watercolor on wove paper
12¾ × 9⅞ in. (32.4 × 25.1 cm)
Signed in graphite, bottom right: *Aug. Rodin*
Maryhill Museum of Art, Goldendale, Washington
Bequest of Samuel Hill, 1938.01.0099

The Maryhill Museum of Art owns a set of six *Psyches* as well as two *Cambodian Dancers*, reflecting the importance of these two motifs, which were curiously merged in Rodin's mind. The *Psyches* form a serial portrait of the same model, nude or draped, whose various moods he depicted. We see this in a group of drawings he exhibited at the Hugo Heller Gallery in Vienna in 1908.[1] Rodin described the drawings in a letter to Rainer Maria Rilke, suggesting that the poet write a new version of the tale of Cupid and Psyche, from Apuleius's *Metamorphoses*: "I should also tell you about all the drawings of Psyche that I sent to Vienna. I have more here or elsewhere. I thought of you to recreate such a beautiful myth. I've made drawings from it that lead me beyond everything. It's a very delightful story of woman and the beginning of her life."[2] In the ancient Roman novelist's text, Psyche believes she must marry a monster and weeps in despair at the top of a rock (cat. 24) before being carried off into the air (cat. 34). Apuleius's description of Psyche's flight corresponds to Rodin's artistic preoccupations; he moves his heroine as if she were weightless from one sheet to the next on the white, neutral space of the paper. Turning this into a celestial image, as Rodin did in 1906, was quite simple. When he discovered the royal dancers of Cambodia in their performances at the colonial exhibition in Marseille, he immediately associated them with an ancient "animated nature" (cat. 65).[3] The *Cambodian Dancer* labeled "*Danse de Psyché au ciel*" (D. 4496, Musée Rodin, Paris) and *Cambodian Dancer in Yellow at the End of a Rainbow* from the Maryhill collection exemplify these drawings of Khmer dancers whom Rodin found "just like Psyches"—glorious, pure, angelic—as he wrote to Rilke, "because, despite my impetuous desire, I could not enter this very beautiful, profound dance, and my expression of it is a bit eighteenth century. But this fusion has grace. The Cambodian dancers are beyond the beauty we are capable of, or that I was able to grasp."[4]

CBU

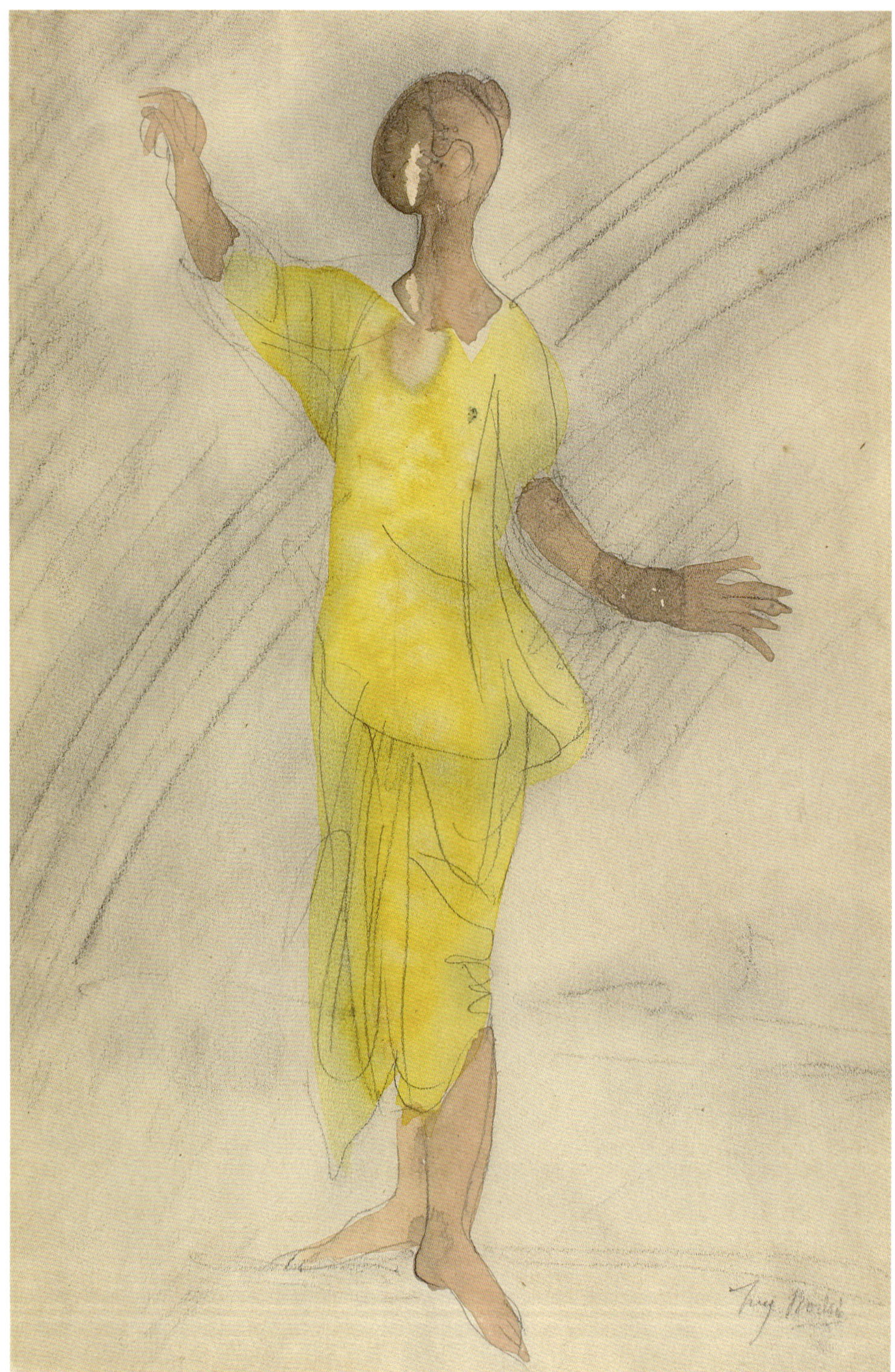

1. Rodin titled these works *Douleur de Psyché* (*Suffering of Psyche*), *Songe inquiet de Psyché* (*Psyche's Anxious Dream*), *Tristesse* (*Sadness*), and *Égarement de Psyché* (*Bewilderment of Psyche*), all Musée Rodin, Paris.
2. Auguste Rodin to Rainer Maria Rilke, November 8, 1907, Archives, Musée Rodin, Paris.
3. See Christina Buley-Uribe, "The Drawings of the Cambodians," in *Rodin and the Cambodian Dancers: His Final Passion*, exh. cat., ed. Jacques Vilain (Paris: Musée Rodin, 2006), 69.
4. Rodin to Rilke, November 8, 1907.

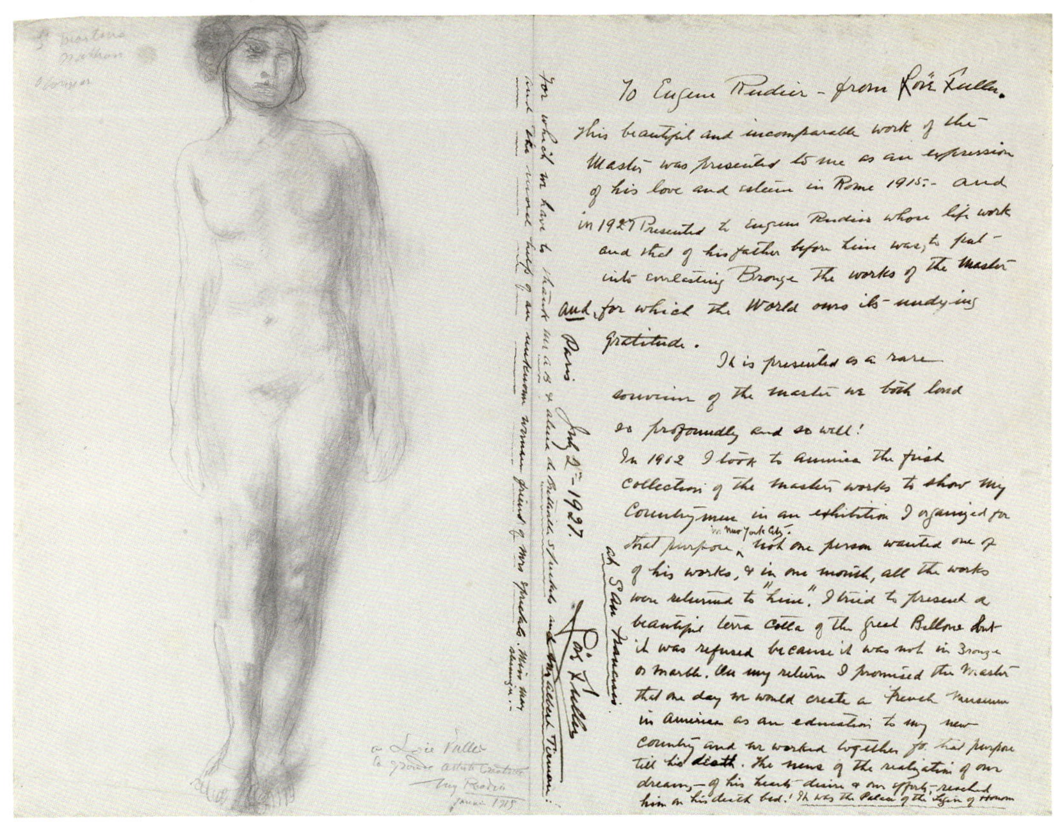

CAT. 58
FEMALE FIGURE (ASSUNTA PETRICCA)

1915
Graphite with stumping on wove paper
17⁵⁄₁₆ × 23 ¼ in. (44 × 59 cm)
Left page inscribed in graphite in Rodin's hand, top left: *S Martino / Nathan / O Conner*
Dedicated, signed, and dated, bottom right: *à Loïe Fuller / la grande artiste créatrice / Aug Rodin / janvier 1915*

Right page inscribed, signed, and dated in pen and brown ink in Loïe Fuller's hand: *To Eugène Rudier from Loïe Fuller. / This beautiful and incomparable work of the Master was presented to me as an expression of his love and esteem in Rome 1915, and in 1927 Presented to Eugene Rudier, whose life work and that of his father before him was to put into everlasting Bronze the works of the master and for which the world owes its undying gratitude. It is presented as a rare souvenir of the master we both loved so profoundly and so well! In 1902 [actually 1903] I took to America the first collection of the master's works to show my countrymen in an exhibition I organized for that purpose in New York City. Not one person wanted one of his works, + in one month, all the works were returned to "him." I tried to present a beautiful terra cotta of the great Bellone but it was refused because it was not in bronze or marble. On my return I promised the master that one day we would create a French Museum in America as an education to my new country and we worked together for that purpose till his death. The news of the realization of our dream, — of his heart's desire and our efforts — reached him on his death bed! It was the Palace of the Legion of Honor at San Francisco / for which we have to thank Mr. AB & Alma de Bretteville Spreckels and Mr. Albert Tirman: and the moral help of an unknown woman friend of Mrs. Spreckels, Miss May Slesinger. Paris, July 2nd 1927. Loïe Fuller.*

Fine Arts Museums of San Francisco, Legion of Honor
Museum purchase, gift of Mrs. John N. Rosekrans Jr., in memory of her husband, grandson of Alma de Bretteville Spreckels, 2007.49

Rodin was seventy-four years old when he drew this standing female nude during his trip to Rome in winter 1914–15. Traveling from London, where he had sought refuge with Rose Beuret at the outbreak of the war, Rodin had intended to make a bust of Pope Benedict XV. Loïe Fuller joined them to discuss the Panama-Pacific International Exposition in San Francisco planned for June 1915. They stayed with a friend of Rodin's, John Marshall, an antiquities dealer and agent for the Metropolitan Museum of Art, New York, who had selected the original nucleus of works for the Met's Rodin gallery in 1910. Dissatisfied with his sittings with the pope, the sculptor seems to have consoled himself by improvising a studio in the back of a bakery, where he made several sketches of a young Italian woman. We know her name, Assunta Petricca, from an inscription on one of the drawings given to Marshall as a Christmas present (D. 7693, Musée Rodin, Paris). Petricca posed standing up, her legs together, with her arms alongside her body or lifting her hair. The soft, blended forms express the personality of the young woman, whose portrait Rodin sketched at the same time. The version in San Francisco was given to Loïe Fuller a few days later, in January. The inscription at the top left, "O'Conner," might refer to Eleanor O'Connor, the secretary of the Comtesse de Greffulhe, who was present in London in 1914 when Rodin was attending the opening of an exhibition at Grosvenor Gallery. The long inscription by Loïe Fuller to Eugène Rudier, dated 1927, shows her efforts to establish the artist's reputation in the United States and advocates for her planned Rodin museum in San Francisco.[1]

CBU

1. See Christina Buley-Uribe, "Assunta Petricca," in *Mes sœurs divines: Rodin et 99 femmes de son entourage* (Paris: Relief, 2013), 306–7, ill. fig. 74.

FEMALE TORSO

Original model c. 1889–90
Plaster on plaster base
5 ¼ × 3 ¹⁵⁄₁₆ × 3 ¹⁵⁄₁₆ in. (13.3 × 10 × 10 cm)
Fine Arts Museums of San Francisco, Legion of
Honor
Gift of Adolph B. Spreckels Jr., 1933.12.10

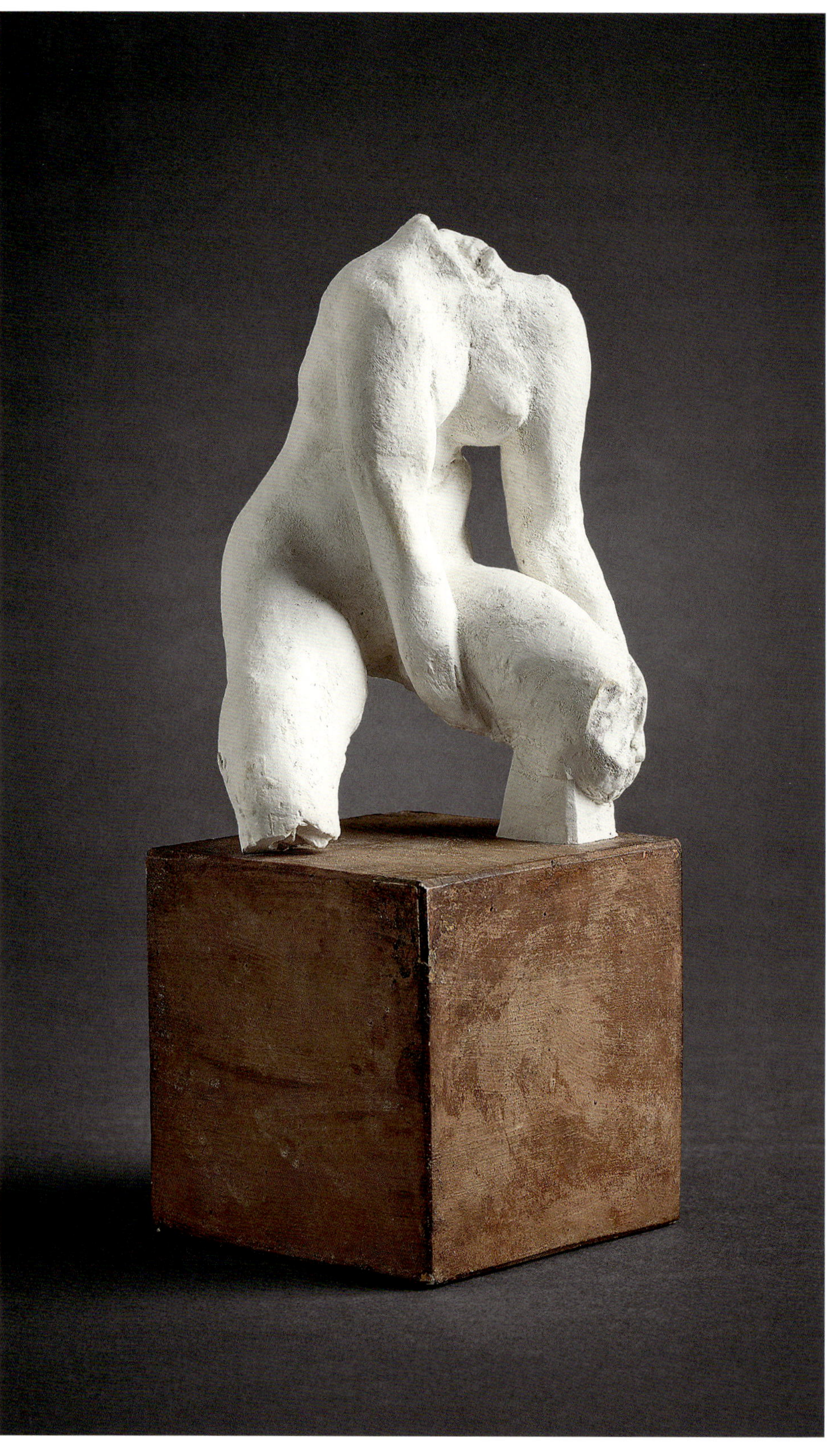

CAT. 60
FEMALE TORSO WITH A SLAVIC WOMAN'S HEAD

Original models c. 1905
Plaster on marble base
8 × 2¾ × 4 in. (20.3 × 7 × 10.2 cm)
Fine Arts Museums of San Francisco, Legion of Honor
Gift of Adolph B. Spreckels Jr., 1933.12.14

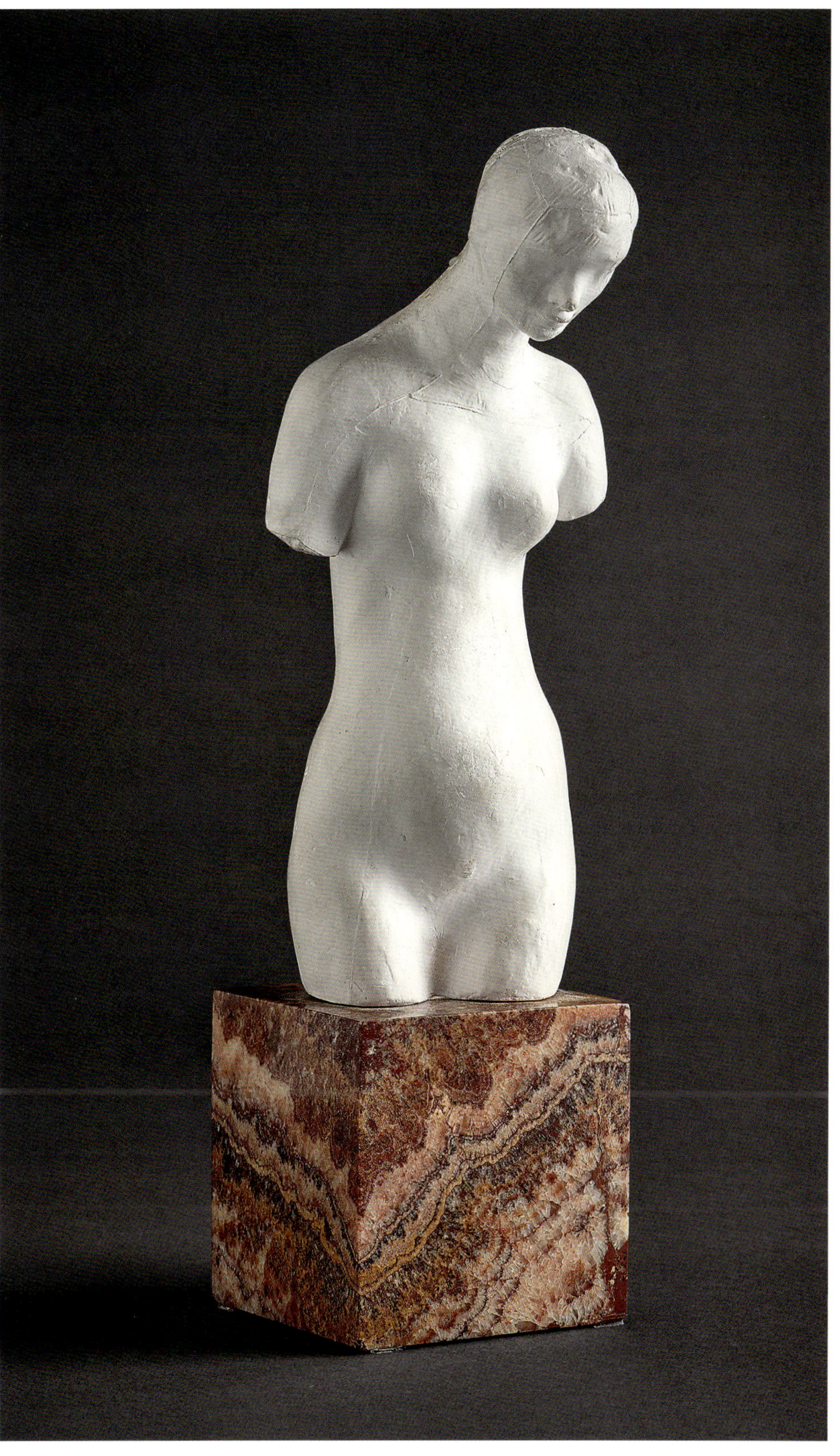

TWO HANDS

Assembled c. 1900
Plaster on marble base
4 ⅛ × 3 × 2 ¼ in. (10.5 × 7.6 × 5.7 cm)
Fine Arts Museums of San Francisco, Legion of
Honor
Gift of Adolph B. Spreckels Jr., 1933.12.12

The twenty-four Rodin plaster casts that
entered the San Francisco Palace of the
Legion of Honor in 1933, three of which are
shown here, represent two-thirds of what we
know of the Rudier Collection in New York.[1]
Previously, much of the museum's Rodin
collection had been assembled by socialite
and philanthropist Alma de Bretteville
Spreckels, working closely with Loïe Fuller,
who acted as the artist's self-appointed
agent. It seems likely that Malvina Hoffman
(and not Fuller, who died in January 1928)
served as intermediary between Rudier and
the Spreckelses in this case and convinced
Adolph Spreckels Jr. to take the reins from
his mother, who always complained that the
prices were too high.

As displayed at the inauguration of the
Palace of the Legion of Honor in 1924,
the museum's Rodin collection originally
contained mainly bronzes or marble sculptures, or plaster casts of completed works
such as *Christ and Mary Magdalene*. This set
of plaster studies from Rudier, which are
representative of the studio materials that
were the basis of Rodin's art, provided a
very direct vision of his work, making them
a vital addition to the museum's holdings.
The two small *Female Torsos* are a very good
example. The first, with no head (cat. 59),
was exhibited in Geneva in 1896[2] as a plaster
cast belonging to Mathias Morhardt, who
was a staunch defender of Rodin. Enlarged,
this "fragment, torso of a woman in the
ancient style," as it was described in the
catalogue of Rodin's 1900 solo exhibition at
the Pavillon de l'Alma,[3] shows the freedom
of form that characterizes the artist's work
from about 1895 onward. The sensuality
of the elegant *Female Torso with a Slavic
Woman's Head* (cat. 60) made it one of Rodin's
favorite figures, and he used it several times
for assemblages, including with vases from
various sources, around 1900.

Some of the plaster casts acquired by the
Legion of Honor in 1933 gave rise to bronze
casts during Rodin's lifetime. For instance,
the artist widely circulated bronze casts of
the penultimate study for the *Head of Balzac*
(part of the 1933 acquisition), along with the
last study (cat. 45, a bronze cast of which
Alma Spreckels had purchased earlier). After
the artist's death in 1917, the Musée Rodin

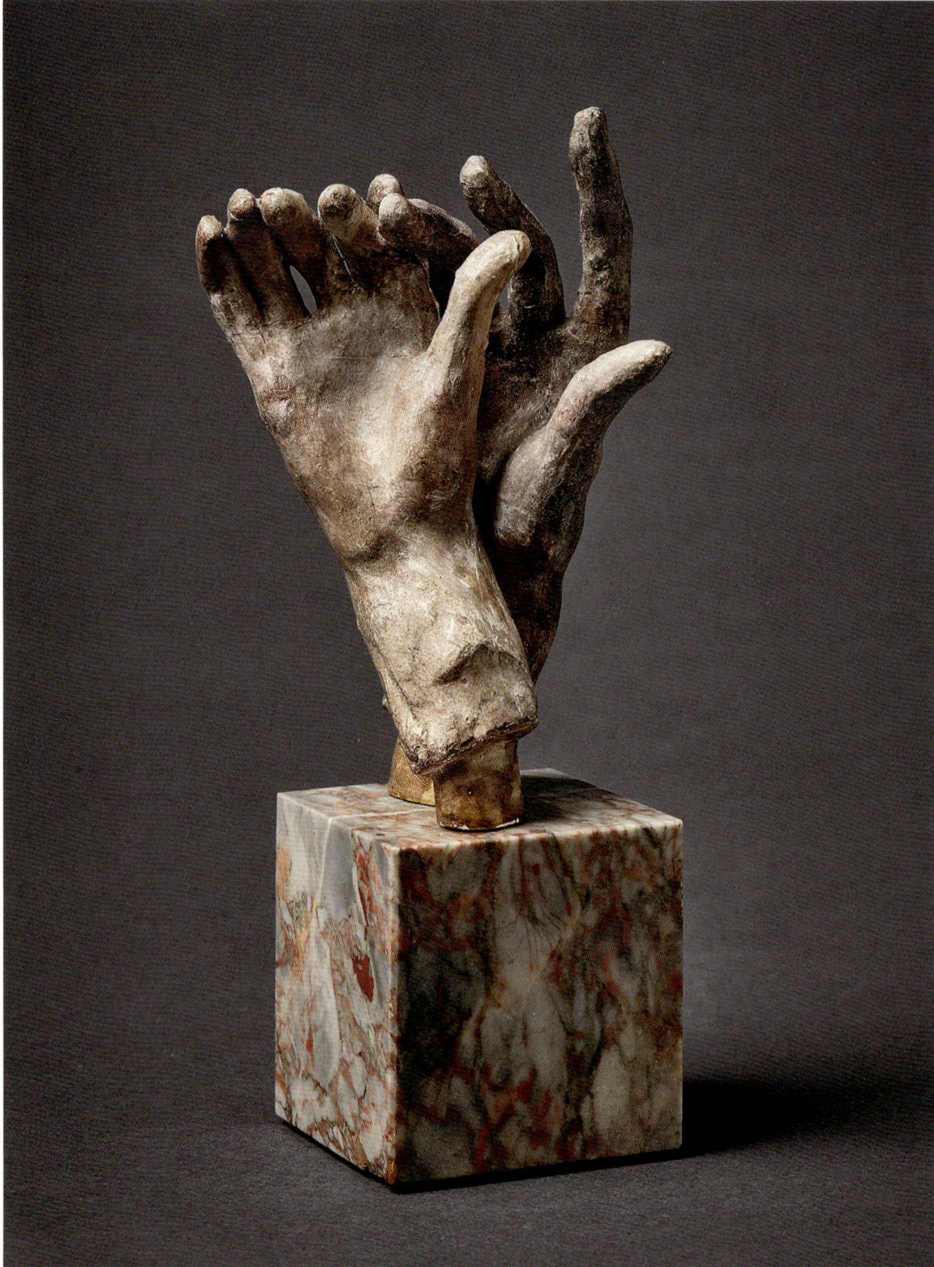

developed the editions of the *Hands*, as the
chairman of the board of directors saw these
as an easy source of income: "People would
buy them as gifts for various ceremonies
where it is difficult to find the right thing to
give," he pointed out.[4] The Rudier collection
included several of these hands, including
this composition of two right hands, which
Jacques de Caso compared to "a pair of
delicate butterflies."[5] The Musée Rodin has
a bronze version.
ALNR

1. From undated photos, prints held in the Fine Arts
Museums of San Francisco and the Hoffman archive
at the Getty Research Institute, Los Angeles;
negatives on glass at the Musée Rodin, Paris. We can
identify these three small plaster casts (cats. 59–61),
with their cube-shaped bases, both in individual
prints and in a photograph of a glass case housing
some of the collection.

2. *Exposition des œuvres de MM. P. Puvis de
Chavannes, Auguste Rodin, Eugène Carrière* (Geneva:
Musée Rath, 1896), cat. 120. See also Antoinette Le
Normand-Romain, *Rodin et le bronze: Catalogue des
œuvres conservées au musée Rodin / The Bronzes of
Rodin: Catalogue of Works in the Musée Rodin* (Paris:
Éditions du musée Rodin / Réunion des musées
nationaux) 2:686.

3. *Exposition Rodin*, exh. cat. (Paris: Palais de l'Alma,
1900), cat. 112.

4. Baron Chassériau, board of directors, November
18, 1926, Archives du musée Rodin, Paris.

5. Jacques de Caso, catalogue entry, in *Rodin's
Sculpture: A Critical Study of the Spreckels Collection,
California Palace of Legion of Honor*, Jacques de Caso
and Patricia B. Sanders (San Francisco: Fine Arts
Museums, 1977), 331.

Camille Claudel
French, 1864–1943
BUST OF AUGUSTE RODIN

Original model 1892
Bronze with marble base, probably cast by
François Rudier, c. 1900
16 ¼ × 9 ¾ × 11 ¼ in. (41.3 × 24.8 × 28.6 cm)
Signed on back: *CClaudel*
Fine Arts Museums of San Francisco, Legion of
Honor
Gift of Alma de Bretteville Spreckels, 1968.26.7

Rodin made several portraits of Camille
Claudel (1864–1943), his student and lover.
As would be expected, she also made a
portrait of him—still young, with a drawn
face whose wide forehead and strong nose
are the very image of the will and power
to create. This work, characterized by a
meticulous analysis of the features, was
begun in 1888–89, abandoned and picked
up again, and finally finished with a first cast
(Musée Rodin, Paris) financed by Rodin
and executed by Adolphe Gruet in time to
be exhibited at the Salon of the Société
Nationale des Beaux-Arts of 1892. Serving
as the artist's official portrait until 1902,
the bust was displayed frequently—for
instance, in Chicago in 1893 and in New York
in 1903, in the exhibition of Loïe Fuller's
collection at the National Arts Club.[1]

   When the two artists separated in 1892,
years of difficulty began for Claudel. In
a strange twist of fate, this bust was one of
the few works that she managed to sell.[2]
She received from the newspaper *Mercure de
France* an order for fifteen copies, which
were to be cast by François Rudier and on
which she would do the chasing herself,
marking each with a caduceus as a distinctive sign.[3] But this represented a great
deal of work for minimal profit, and Rodin
counseled her to do as little as possible:
"It should remain without caduceus, without
its seams removed—that should not concern
you."[4] The present bronze is probably one
of the fifteen. It may have been acquired
by Loïe Fuller in 1900, a date on which
Emilia Cimino, who was close to both Rodin
and Fuller, mentions an "affair" (without
further details) between Claudel and Fuller.
But it is mounted on a type of base of which
we know almost no equivalent outside the
San Francisco collection (cf. *Head of Balzac*,
cat. 45). Given that Fuller played a decisive
role in the development of this collection,
it is tempting to attribute these distinctive
bases to her initiative.
ALNR

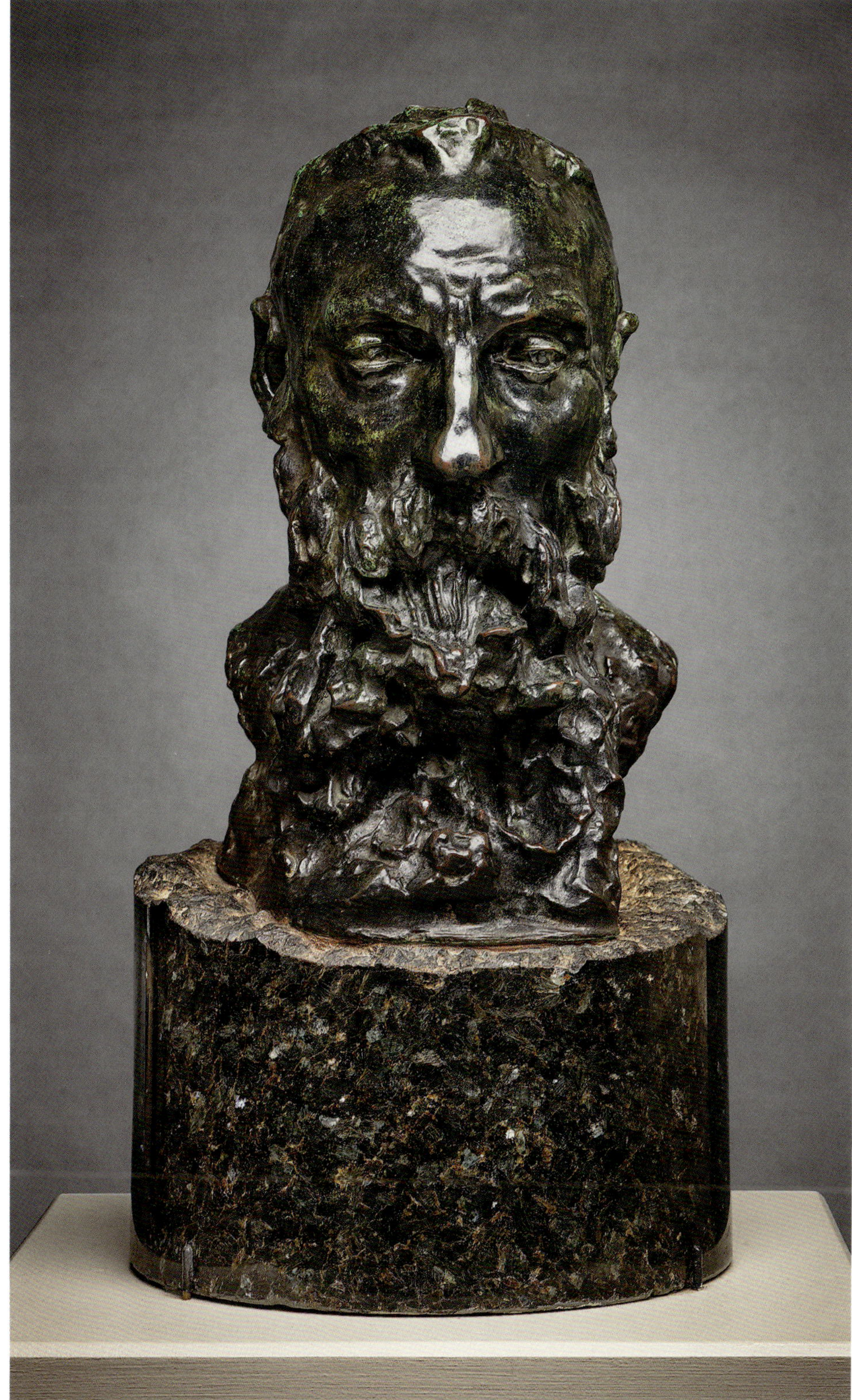

1. *World's Columbian Exposition, 1893, Official
Catalogue, Part X, Department K, Fine Arts* (Chicago:
W. B. Conkey, 1893), 93; *Exhibition of Statuary and
Paintings Belonging to Miss Loïe Fuller*, National Arts
Club of New York, May 6–16, 1903.
2. Antoinette Le Normand-Romain, *Rodin and
Camille Claudel: Fateful Encounters*, exh. cat. (Detroit:
Institute of Art, 2006), 75–78.
3. Anne Rivière, Bruno Gaudichon, and Danielle
Ghanassia, *Camille Claudel* (Paris: Société nouvelle
Adam Biro, 2000), 85–88.
4. Auguste Rodin to Camille Claudel, December 2,
1897; see *Camille Claudel, 1864–1943* (Madrid:
Fundación Mapfre, 2007), 129–30.
5. Emilia Cimino to Auguste Rodin, March 22, 1900,
Archives du musée Rodin, Paris. I thank Anne
Rivière for alerting me to this document.

MAN WITH SERPENT

1885
Plaster
27 1/2 × 22 × 11 7/8 in. (69.9 × 55.9 × 30.2 cm)
Clark Art Institute, Williamstown, Massachusetts
Acquired by Sterling Clark, 1923, 1955.1023

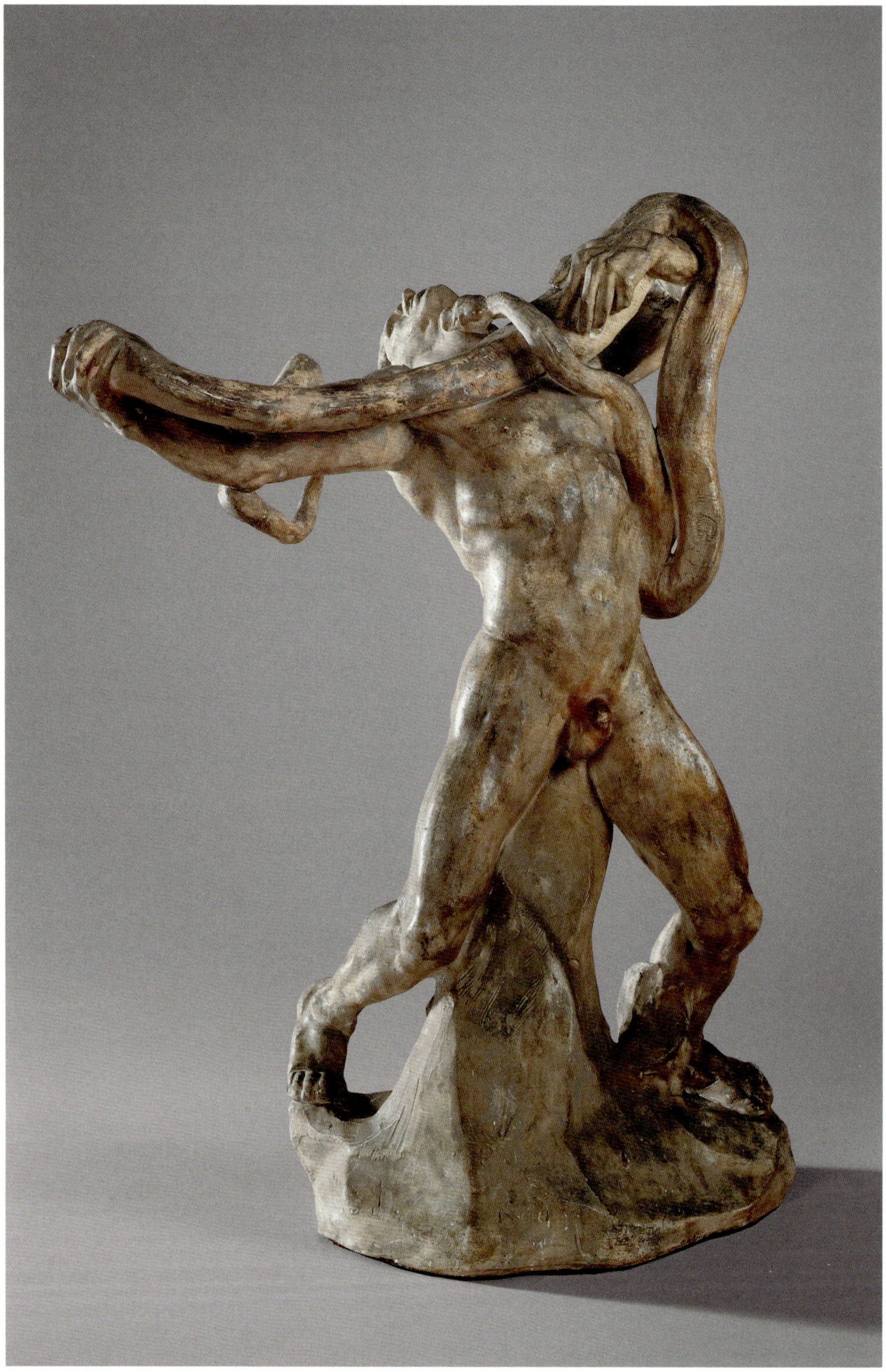

Man with Serpent derives from a figure
originally modeled for *The Gates of Hell*,
seen dramatically hanging on to the lintel of
the left panel in the oldest photographs
of the *Gates* (1887). Rodin's *Falling Man*
certainly dates to 1881–82, when so many
figures for the *Gates* were modeled. *Man
with Serpent* is mentioned for the first time in
September 1885, when Georges Bracquemond
confirmed to Rodin the interest of collector
Antony Roux in it.[1] In this composition,
a snake, wrapped around the figure's new
arms, bites the erstwhile *Falling Man* on
the neck. Roux had probably demanded that
Rodin make some changes to the figure,
almost certainly to echo the ancient marble
group *Laocoön* in the Vatican, and following
several drawings for the *Gates*. "It's agreed,"
Rodin confirmed, "only my study will
remain unchanged for me. . . . It's to reflect
the subject, the man fighting with a snake,
that I will change the arms."[2]

As was his practice, Roux specified that
his had to be the only version of that specific
composition made, and he took the precau-
tion of acquiring the plaster at the same time
as the bronze. Indeed, Roux's bronze, cast
by Griffoul and Lorge in 1887 for the price of

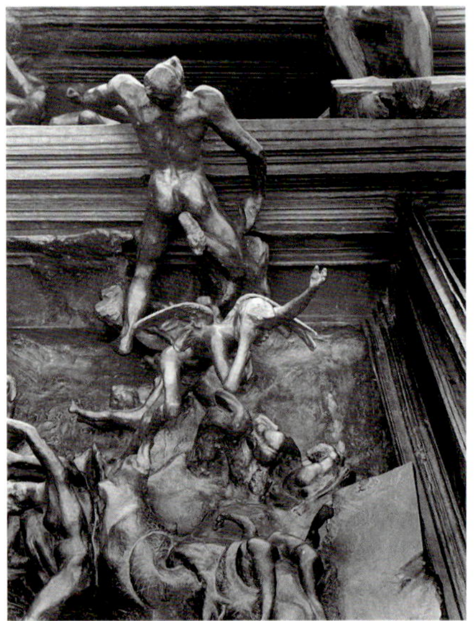

Auguste Rodin, *The Gates of Hell* (detail),
1880–c. 1900, cast in 1981. Bronze, 250 3/4 ×
158 × 33 3/8 in. (636.91 × 401.42 × 84.77 cm).
Iris & B. Gerald Cantor Center for Visual Arts at
Stanford University. Gift of the B. Gerald Cantor
Collection, 1986.85.

300 francs (today in the Musée Cantonal
des Beaux-Arts in Lausanne), was unique.
Rodin had nonetheless maintained the right
"to use the figure of the man, but with
changes to the pose and without the snake."[3]
The *Falling Man* served as a starting point
for several assemblages, the most famous of
which is *I Am Beautiful*, which was shown
in 1886 at Galerie Georges Petit in Paris.
ALNR

1. Georges Bracquemond to Auguste Rodin,
September 22, 1885, Archives du Musée Rodin, Paris.
2. Auguste Rodin, quoted in the sale catalogue
Collection Antony Roux (Paris: Galerie Georges Petit,
May 19–20, 1914), 101.
3. Antoni Roux to Auguste Rodin, June 28, 1887,
Archives du Musée Rodin, Paris.

MASK OF THE MAN WITH THE BROKEN NOSE

Original model 1864–65
Bronze, probably cast by Charles-Adolphe Gruet, 1881
12 ¼ × 7 ¾ × 6 ½ in. (31.1 × 19.7 × 16.5 cm)
Museum of Art, Rhode Island School of Design, Providence
Gift of Mrs. Gustav Radeke 1921, 21.341

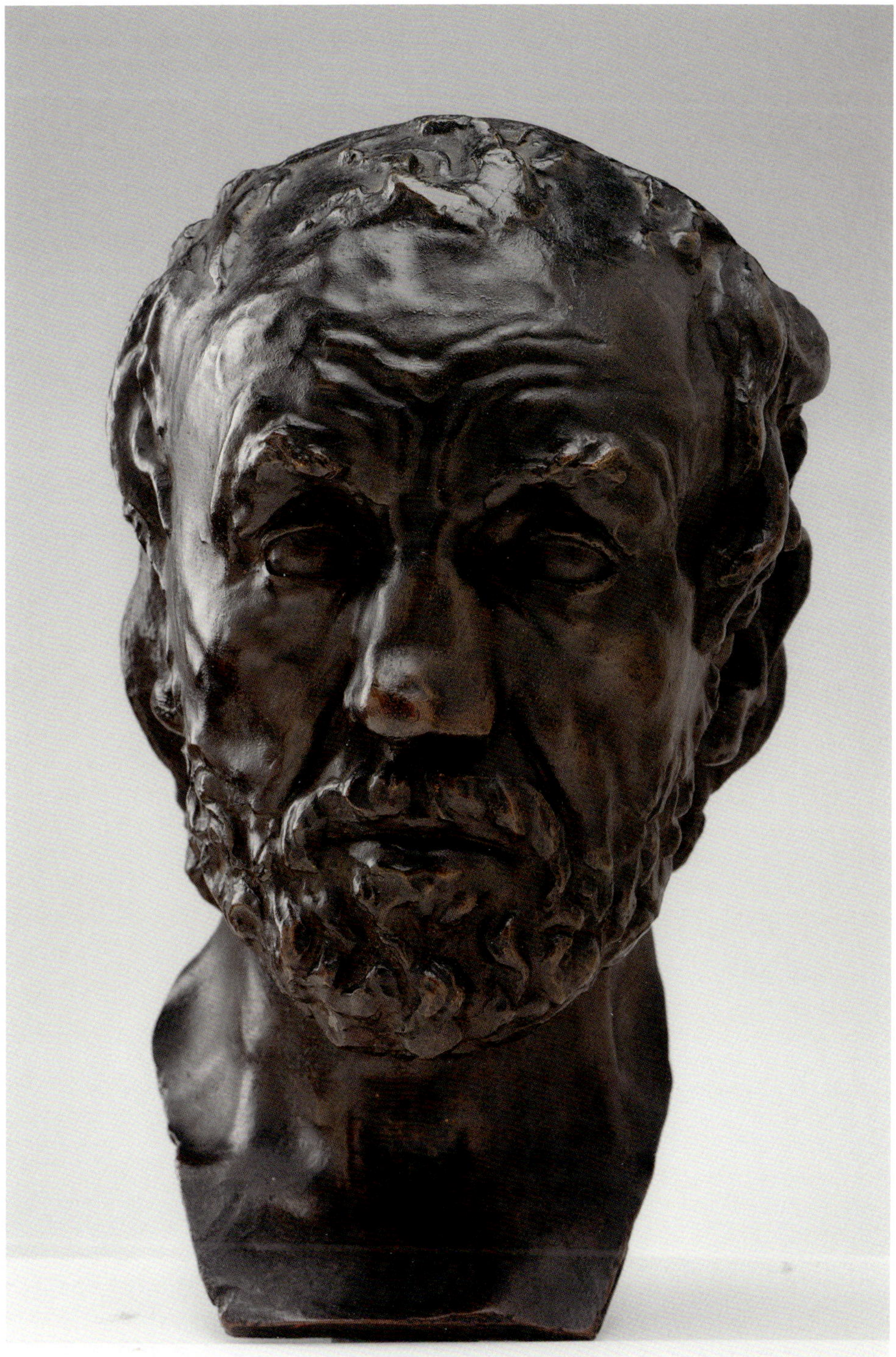

"This mask determined all my future work," Rodin told American journalist Truman H. Bartlett in a series of interviews published in 1889. "It is the first good piece of modeling I ever did. . . . In fact, I have never succeeded in making a figure as good as the *Broken Nose*."[1] A prime example from Rodin's early career, this mask had as its starting point a portrait of Bibi, a handyman working at artists' studios, and was probably executed in 1864. The following winter was very cold, and the back of the head of the clay bust froze, came loose, and broke into pieces. Rodin saved the mask and sent it as it was to the Salon of 1865. But at that date, an incomplete work was not acceptable, and it was refused. However, Rodin carefully preserved it, made a bust in marble from it (1875, Musée Rodin, Paris), and finally exhibited a first bronze cast at the 1878 Salon. At that time, a reviewer noted its resemblance to the portrait of Michelangelo by Daniele de Volterra,[2] and the title *Man with the Broken Nose* was established.

So many versions were made, beginning in 1881, that after 1900 it became necessary to make a new model, which can be recognized in particular by the neck cut horizontally at the base, whereas the first version, on which this cast is modeled, showed the top of the chest extending from the neck. This is one of the very first bronze casts, and like the plaster cast preserved at the Musée Rodin bears a growth over the left eyelid and two very visible accidents, small gaps at the top of the mustache and under the chin, as well as the strands of hair above both ears. It was acquired in 1882 by Constantine Ionides (1833–1900), a banker of Greek origin living in London, who collected art by naturalist artists who were friends of Rodin, such as the painters Jules Bastien-Lepage, Léon Lhermitte, and Alphonse Legros and the sculptor Jules Dalou.

It then belonged to Eliza Greene Metcalf Radeke (1854–1931), president of the Rhode Island School of Design, to which she left her collection (including this bust and the two drawings that follow, donated in 1921) for philanthropic and educational purposes. The school is comparable to the École Spéciale de Dessin et de Mathématiques, the forerunner of the École Nationale Supérieure des Arts Décoratifs, where Rodin studied, and which was founded to train artists for the industrial arts.

ALNR

1. Truman H. Bartlett, "Auguste Rodin, Sculptor," *American Architect and Building News* 25, no. 682 (January 19, 1889): 29.
2. Louis Ménard, "La sculpture au Salon de 1878," *L'Art* 14 (1878): 277.

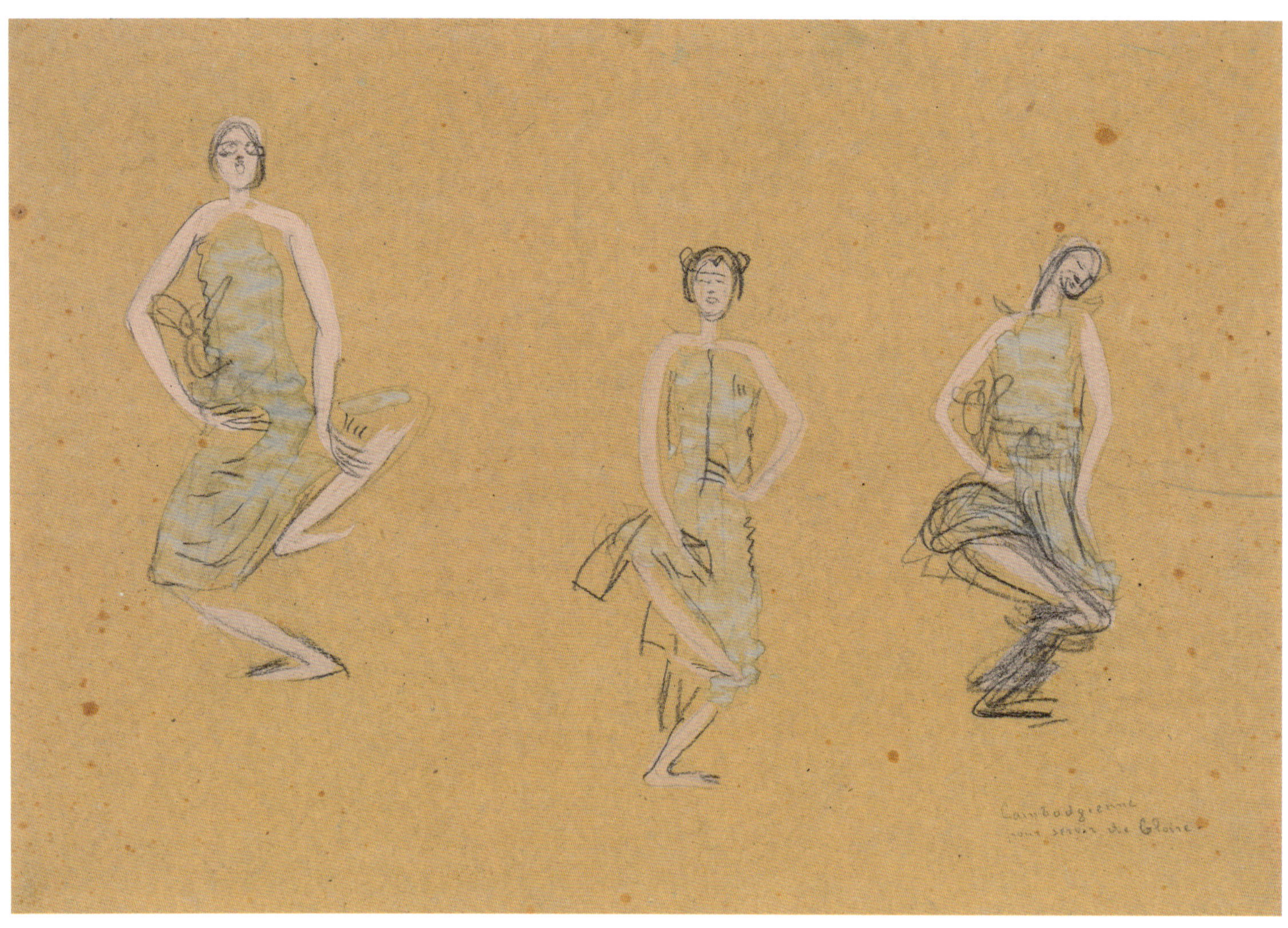

CAT. 65

CAMBODIAN DANCERS

c. 1906–7
Graphite, watercolor, and gouache on wove
paper mounted to cardboard
7 ¾ × 11 ⅜ in. (19.7 × 28.9 cm)
Inscribed by René Chéruy (Rodin's secretary) in
graphite, lower right: *Cambodgienne pour servir
de gloire*
Museum of Art, Rhode Island School of Design,
Providence
Gift of Mrs. Gustav Radeke, 21.128

THE MERMAID

c. 1898–1900
Graphite and watercolor on wove paper mounted to cardboard
13 ⅛ × 10 ½ in. (33.3 × 26.7 cm)
Inscribed in graphite, middle right: *bas / marine* [?]
Museum of Art, Rhode Island School of Design, Providence
Gift of Mrs. Gustav Radeke, 21.476

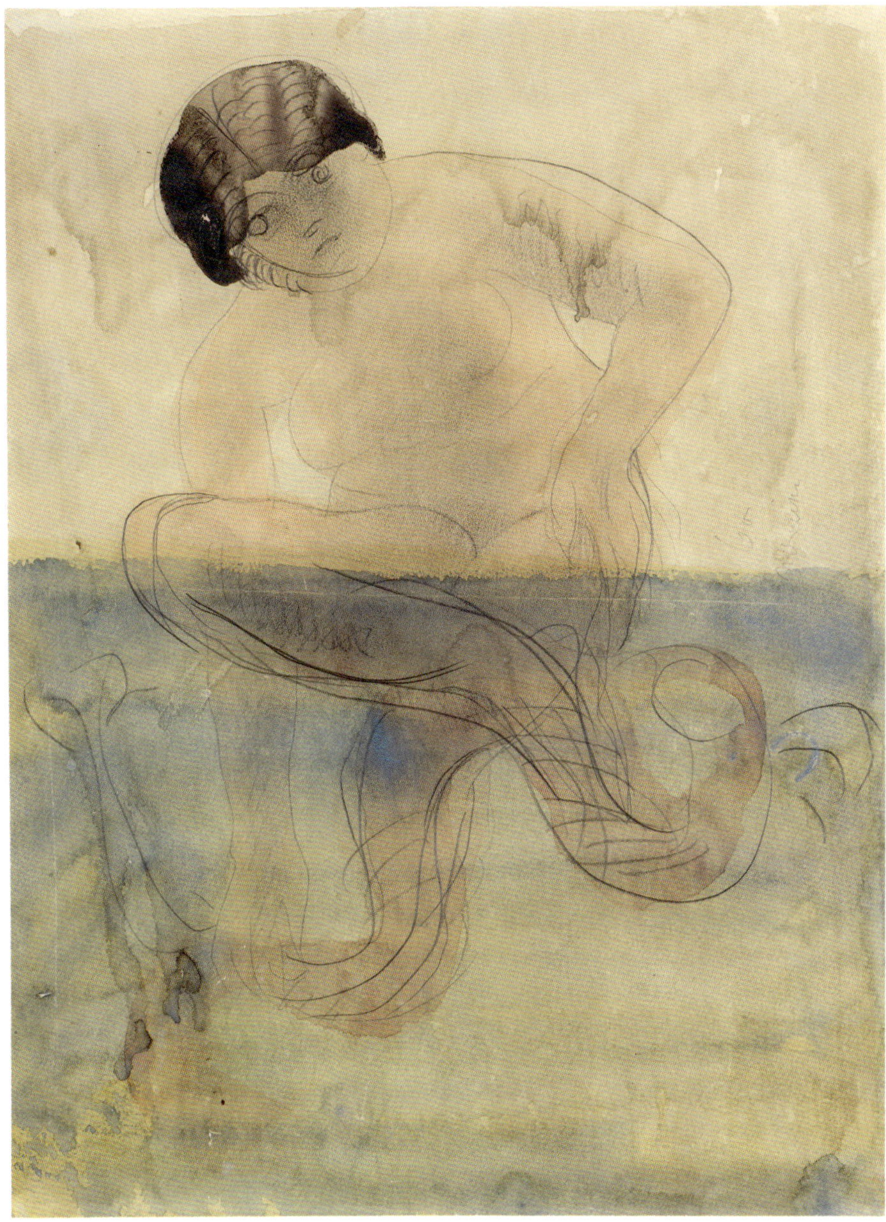

The two drawings that Eliza Greene Metcalf Radeke gave to the Rhode Island School of Design are representative of the variety of Rodin's drawings. *The Mermaid*—with a double tail, a symbol of lust—is typical of medieval iconography, especially of Romanesque art, which may have inspired Rodin, particularly in the naive treatment of the face. The drawing is not part of a particular illustration project but belongs to a series with titles related to aquatic and Mediterranean themes, *Female Bather*, *Greek Islands*, *Ulysses*—titles given by the artist when he showed them for the first time in 1900 in Paris, at the Pavillon de l'Alma. A *Mermaid Coming out of the Water* (Musée Rodin, Paris, D. 5060) was also included in the exhibition.

Here, Rodin began by quickly drawing his model, seated and holding one foot, without finishing the legs, which he converted into a double fish tail. Transformations of the body are common in his work, as in *Figure Facing Forward* (cat. 18). In this example, the use of blue watercolor on the lower half of the sheet identifies her as a bather. Rodin plays with the transparency of watercolor and the combination of spots, as in several drawings of women-as-rocks emerging from muddy waters. Oriented vertically, the drawing's water line perfectly divides the human legs and the tail of the mermaid: in the water, the fantastic world; in the air, the real world. The inscription on the right side, *bas* (down), indicates that Rodin suggests another direction for interpreting the drawing, which shifts the whole into a more abstract representation.

The second drawing Radeke donated is equally interesting. This c. 1906 *Cambodian Dancers* is a rare drawing on Fabriano paper, which Rodin used only one other time in the entire series (Musée Rodin, Paris, D. 5064). The two works similarly depict several dancers in a frieze. The poet Rainer Maria Rilke, upon seeing one such sheet, compared Rodin's Cambodian dancers to "the most tender flowers having bloomed on the happy soil of your immense labour, . . . preserved for ever as in a herbarium, where plants, carefully dried, have taken a definitive gesture which contains in essence the fragile and yet eternal rhythm of their life."[1] The inscription "Cambodgienne pour servir de gloire" by Rodin's secretary René Chéruy (see the cutouts from Princeton, cats. 88, 89) indicates that these are preparatory drawings depicting angels for a planned fresco of Paradise in the chapel of the seminary of Saint-Sulpice, where the Musée du Luxembourg was slated to move. Rodin was supposed to decorate a room devoted to his work, but the project never materialized (see the *Cambodian Dancer* acquired by Jules Mastbaum, cat. 81).
CBU

1. Rainer Maria Rilke to Auguste Rodin, November 3, 1907, in Rainer Maria Rilke, *Lettres à Rodin*, preface by Georges Grappe (Paris: Éditions Émile-Paul Frères, 1931), 73.

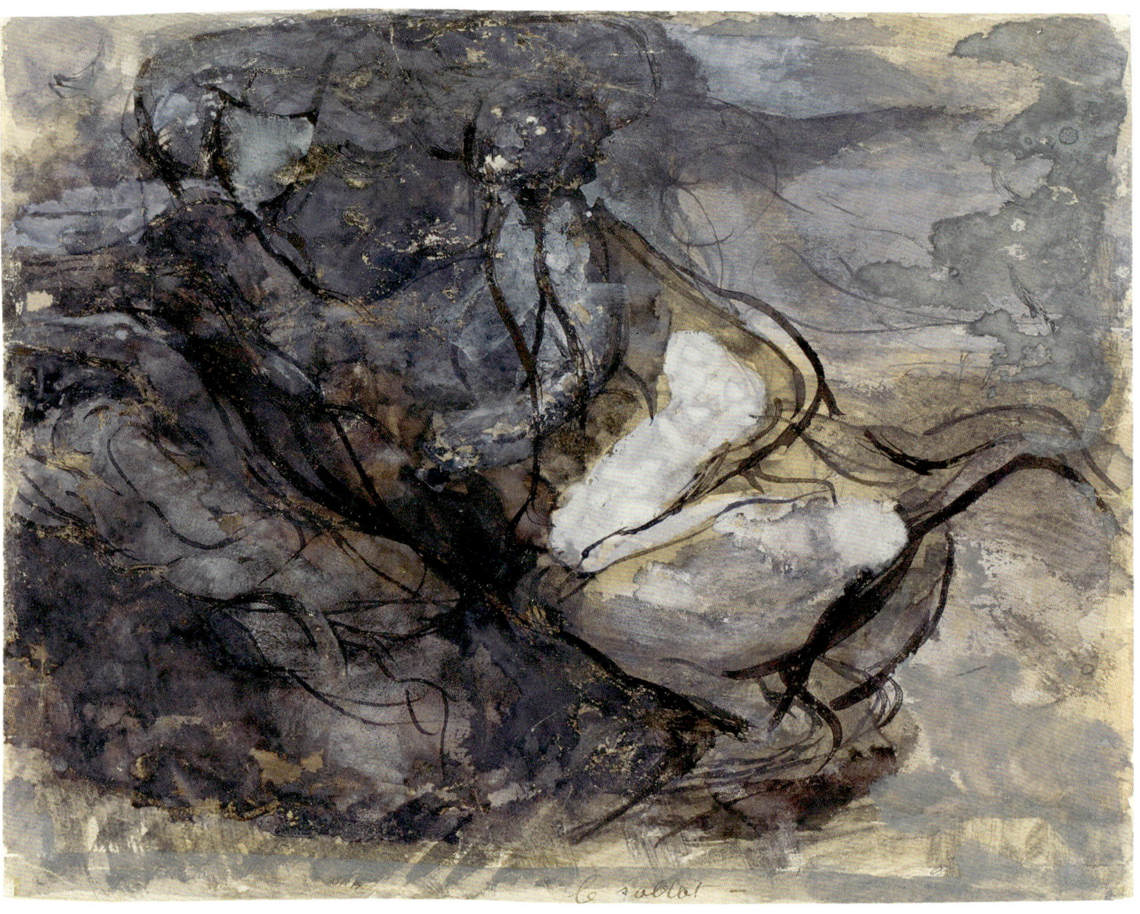

CAT. 67

THE WITCHES' SABBATH (RECTO); SKETCHES OF CENTAURS (VERSO)

c. 1883–89
Graphite, pen and ink, gouache (recto), and
graphite (verso), on wove paper
5¾ × 7 ½ in. (14.6 × 19.1 cm)
Inscribed with pen and brown ink, lower center
(recto): *le sabbat*
Art Institute of Chicago
Gift of Robert Allerton, 1923.943

The Witches' Sabbath, the reverse side of
which depicts a sketch of a centaur, dates to
the time of the maturation of *The Gates of
Hell*, around 1883. It is thus linked to the
sculptor's ideas on incorporating such motifs
into his great bas-relief. Rodin had brought
together a repertoire of centaurs—around
fifty drawings—inspired by reading Dante's
Divine Comedy. Even if these are not strictly
preparatory drawings for sculptures but
rather free explorations, they are designed
as drafts of bas-reliefs and sculpture in the
round. The reliefs *Mask of a Weeping Woman*
and *Centaurs* temporarily occupied the
bottom of the two panels of the *Gates*, but
then the sculptor restricted the theme to
a rearing figure at the top of the left pilaster.

The Witches' Sabbath was part of this line of
thought, probably until 1889, as Rodin often
reworked sketches after years had passed.
Thomas Lederballe suggests Rodin picked up
the theme in Charles Baudelaire's poems
Les fleurs du mal (*The Flowers of Evil*, 1857),
a known source for the *Gates*, where the
witch figures as a diabolical muse.[1]

Here, the fantastic procession unfolds in
dramatic lighting that recalls the lithograph
Bon Voyage from Goya's *Caprichos*, with
its "spotlights" on some parts of the body.
As suggested by the title, the figure kneeling
on the back of a bull is going to a ritual
gathering of witches (we can make out a
crescent moon in the top left corner of the
paper), closely followed by a roughly
sketched bird (an owl?) whose head and
wing we can identify. We may wonder about
the choice of a bull in this drawing, as in
its companion piece: *Man on a Bull* (Musée
Rodin, Paris, D. 2003), a cutout by Rodin
that poet Rainer Maria Rilke compared to
a Rembrandt. In both cases, a figure with
powerful muscles and indeterminate sex
is transported by a bull by moonlight, in a
representation that is more somber than
the idyllic *Dawn: Return from the Sabbath*
(c. 1885) of the Rodin Museum in Philadelphia
(cat. 77). Did Rodin have in mind the tale
from the seventh circle of Hell in Dante's

Inferno, where Dante and Virgil witness the
torture of the violent, including the Minotaur
killed by Theseus and Ariadne, before being
escorted by the centaur Nessus? *Witches'
Sabbath* had originally been part of Rodin's
donation to the French government in 1916,
under the number 3857 (replaced in 1926),
as confirmed by the recent discovery of its
original mounting paper.[2] The philanthropist
Robert Allerton (1873–1964) must have
acquired it at the same time as the bronzes
purchased from the Musée Rodin, which
immediately entered the collection of the Art
Institute of Chicago. Allerton began donating
works by Rodin to the Art Institute, of which
he was honorary president and trustee, in
1922. In addition to three late watercolors,
he gave *Sabbath* and completed this series of
Rodin works in 1925 by giving a *Portrait
of Rodin* by William Rothenstein.
CBU

1. Thomas Lederballe, "Ecstasies: Drawings by
Auguste Rodin," in *Ecstasies: Drawings by Auguste
Rodin*, exh. cat. (Copenhagen: Statens Museum for
Kunst, 2016), 45.
2. Christina Buley-Uribe, "L'aliénabilité *de facto* de
dessins du musée Rodin?," *Cahiers d'histoire de l'art*,
no. 19 (2021): 96–107.

THE KISS

Original model c. 1881–82
Bronze, cast by Griffoul and Lorge (no mark),
1888
34 × 19 ½ × 20 ¾ in. (86.4 × 49.5 × 52.7 cm)
Signed on back of base: *Rodin*
Baltimore Museum of Art
Jacob Epstein Collection, 1951.128

This high-quality cast bronze did not escape
the attention of Loïe Fuller when it became
available on the Parisian market after the
death of the bronze's first owner, the painter
Alfred Roll (1846–1919): "There is an old
friend of the Master who has a 'Kiss' one of
the first made. Rodin gave it to him and
before his death he said to him: your group
[*The Kiss*] is worth 7,500 francs now and after
my death it will be 150,000. Tokyo [that is,
Kojiro Matsukata, who wanted to found
a museum of Western art in Tokyo] is now
offering him 800,000 for it!"[1]

This was one of the first bronze casts
produced from the original model of the Paolo
and Francesca group created for *The Gates of
Hell*, where it occupied the center of the left
panel until sometime prior to 1887. Exhibited
in Paris and then in Brussels in 1887, this
"adorable group of lovers, naked as jay-
birds"[2]—despite the fact that Paolo and
Francesca were historical figures who would
traditionally be depicted fully clothed—had
been enthusiastically received by critics,
who remarked on its refreshing simplicity.
A Belgian journalist, Lucien Solvay, suggested
replacing the original title, *Françoise de
Rimini*, with "*The Kiss*, or nothing at all,"
thus emphasizing the universal dimension of
the work.[3]

The large marble (Musée Rodin, Paris)
commissioned by the Fine Arts administration
to appear in the Paris Exposition Universelle
of 1889 was not ready by that date. It was
shown at the 1898 Salon of Société Nationale
des Beaux-Arts, with the *Monument to Balzac*,
and again in 1900 at the Pavillon de l'Alma.
Rodin had made no changes—and had not
even bothered to sign the marble—but it
enjoyed considerable success, to the point
that two copies were made immediately
and another one after Rodin's death, for
Philadelphia, where it was deemed essential
to complete the Rodin Museum. The foundry
Barbedienne had signed a contract with
Rodin as early as 1898 to produce reduced
versions of the marble (four different sizes),
all in smaller dimensions than the original
terracotta model, over which Rodin maintained control. While there are dozens of
the Barbedienne *Kiss* (Rodin gave one of the
smallest versions to his friend and avid

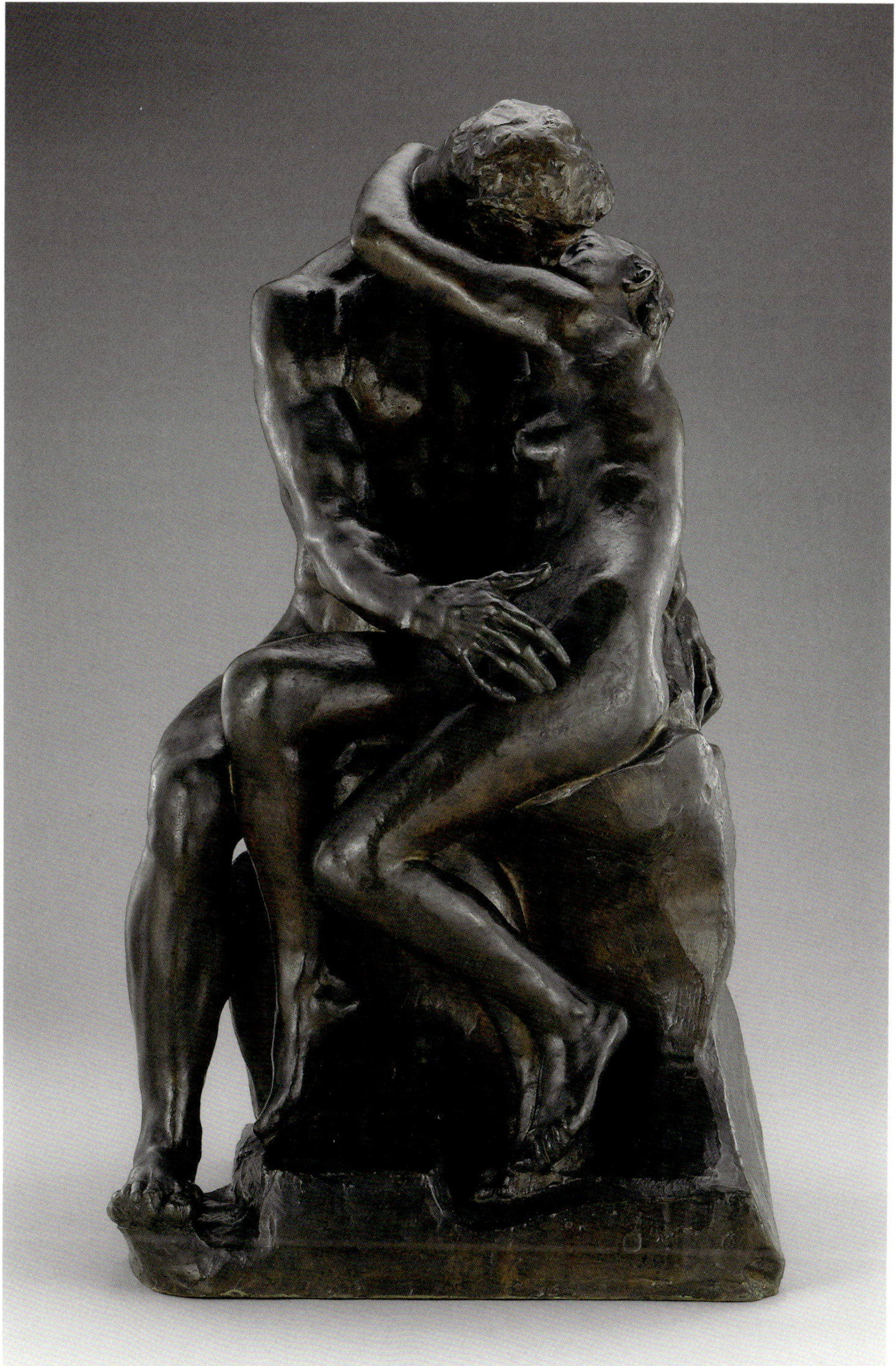

collector Katherine Seney Simpson, inscribed
"in memory of the hours in the studio"),
casts from the original model, like this one
from the Baltimore Museum of Art, are rare.
ALNR

1. Loïe Fuller to Alma de Bretteville Spreckels,
c. 1920, C9-46-2, 3, New York Public Library. Fuller
may have meant 80,000 francs for *The Kiss*, given that
Jules Mastbaum was quoted a price of 700,000 francs
for *The Gates of Hell* in 1925 (see p. 178).
2. Untitled press clipping from an article by Lucien
Solvay in *La Nation*, September 27, 1887, Archives
du musée Rodin, Paris.
3. Solvay, 1887.

THE THINKER

Original model 1881–82, enlarged 1903
Bronze, cast by Alexis Rudier, 1928
79 × 37¾ × 59 in. (200.7 × 95.9 × 149.9 cm)
Inscribed right side, near back: *A. Rodin*; back
left: *Alexis Rudier, Fondeur, Paris*
Baltimore Museum of Art
Jacob Epstein Collection, 1930.25.1

The Thinker is one of few figures in Rodin's
oeuvre that underwent only insignificant
modifications of minor details after the
original model, beyond its enlargement in
1902–3. In 1904, the large model was
displayed at the International Society of
Sculptors, Painters and Gravers in London
and then at the Salon of the Société Nationale
des Beaux-Arts in Paris, where it proved
so popular that a subscription was launched
to give the work "to the people of Paris."
Amid political and social crisis, the sculpture
was seen as a symbol of democracy.

Versions of this figure, the success of
which derived from its combination of
physical strength and intellectual prowess,
multiplied quickly, in three different sizes.
Eight bronze casts of the enlarged model
were made during Rodin's lifetime, and more
followed after his death. Ten large-scale
bronzes are located today on American soil
(Louisville, San Francisco, Cleveland, Detroit,
Philadelphia, Baltimore, New York, Kansas
City, and Pasadena and Palo Alto, California).
France sent the first, made with the lost-wax
method by A. A. Hébrard, to the Louisiana
Purchase Exposition in 1904. But Rodin
was not satisfied with it, and a plaster cast
replaced it in Saint Louis. Nevertheless,
Henry Walters acquired the Hébrard bronze
for the Walters Art Gallery in Baltimore. The
subsequent bronze casts were all produced
with sand by Alexis Rudier.

The Rudier *Thinker* in Baltimore today,
the fourteenth bronze produced, was
commissioned from the Musée Rodin, Paris,
by Jacob Epstein, a patron and philanthropist who had made a fortune through mail-
order catalogues. He was in contact with
Albert Rosenthal, advisor to Jules Mastbaum,
who established the Rodin Museum in
Philadelphia. Following Mastbaum's example,
The Thinker was placed — as in Cleveland,
Detroit, and, later, Louisville — on a tall
base in front of the neoclassical façade of
the museum. Its presence in Baltimore in
this very visible position led Henry Walters
to part with his version, which went to
Louisville in 1949.

ALNR

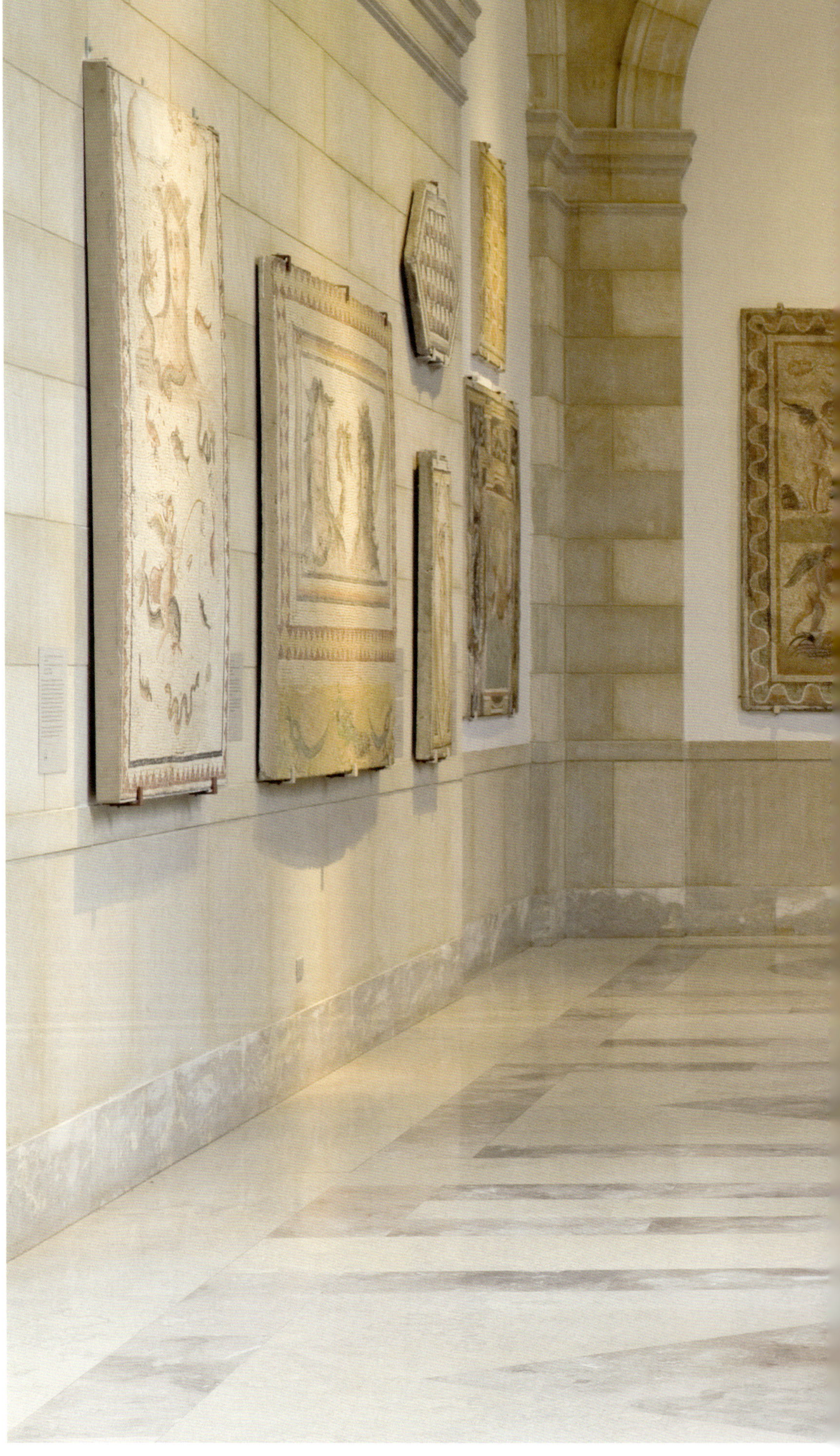

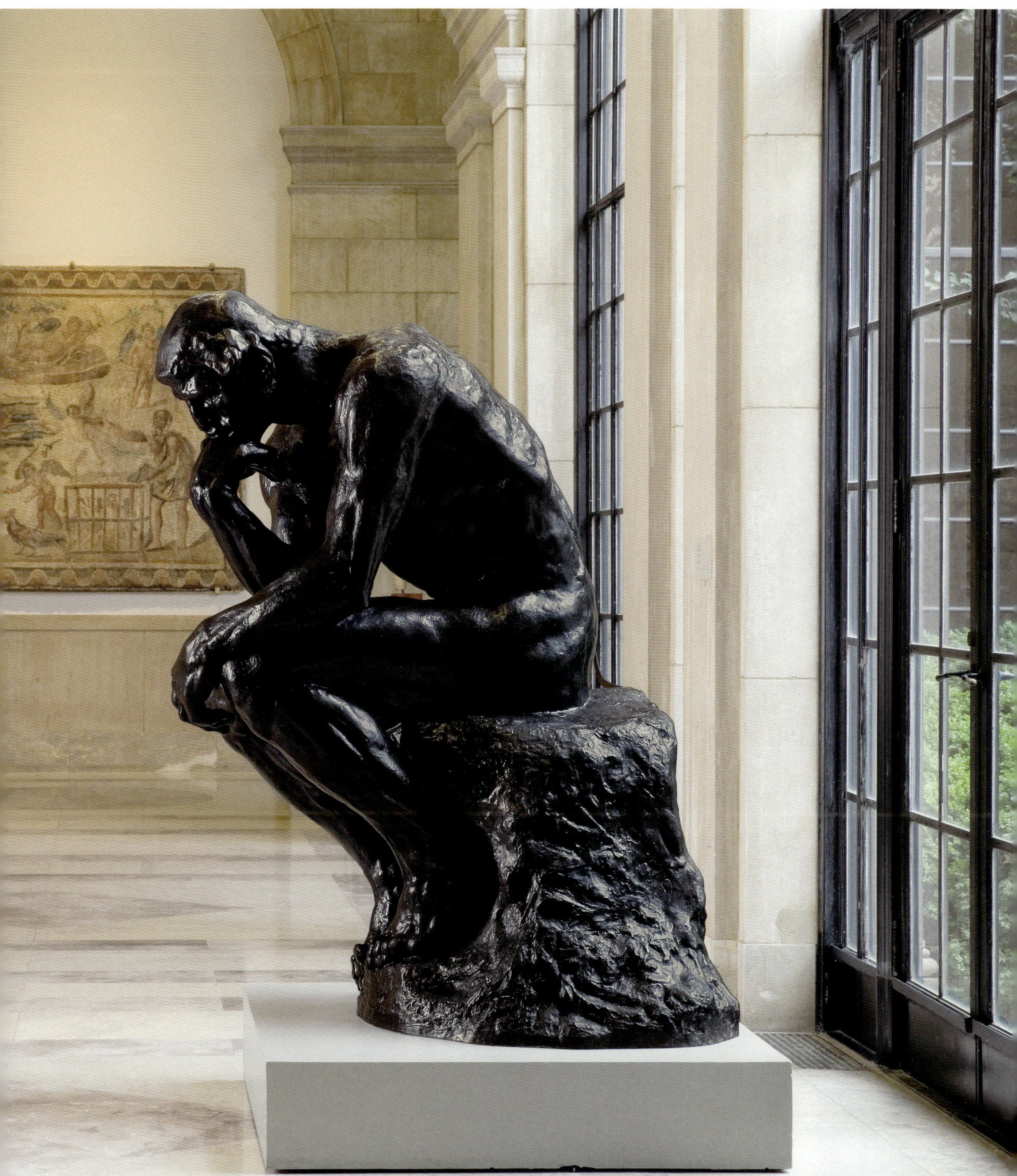

THE BENEDICTIONS

Original model before 1896, version on a round
base probably enlarged 1898
Bronze, cast by Alexis Rudier, by 1926
31 ½ × 23 ¼ × 25 in. (80 × 59.1 × 63.5 cm)
Signed, front of base, at right: *A. Rodin*
Rodin Museum, Philadelphia Museum of Art
Bequest of Jules E. Mastbaum, 1929, F1929-7-11

Evincing a lyricism that is rare in the artist's
work, this group does not seem to have
been composed by assemblage but instead
modeled from scratch in the early 1890s—
although Rodin did not know at the time
what meaning to give to these two, winged
figures, who are intertwined like seaweed
pulled along in the current. In Geneva in
1896, he titled them *The Glories*, and the title
of *The Benedictions* only appeared in connection with the Pavillon de l'Alma exhibition
in Paris, in 1900. As Arsène Alexandre
explained in the exhibition catalogue, "Two
female figures, like great beneficent birds,
have just landed on the summit, graceful and
serious, closely grouped, spreading over the
world their prayers and the refreshing shade
of their wings."[1]

The group was an immediate success:
three marble versions were produced, differing
in the distance separating the two bodies:
their legs were left relatively independent
in the first (1900, Gulbenkian Foundation,
Lisbon) and were close together in the
versions in Copenhagen and Paris. From the
sketch to the large model, there are bronzes
in three different sizes, with the casts of the
large model themselves divided into two
groups depending on whether they correspond to the Lisbon marble (with a rectangu-
lar base, the most common) or the plaster
model (with a round base), such as the one
in Philadelphia, described as "2nd proof or
bronze cast,"[2] and followed in 1927 by a
third cast commissioned by Jacob Epstein for
Baltimore. Produced by Rodin's assistant
Henri Lebossé in 1898, the enlargement had
been shown at the exhibition that took place
in Brussels and the Netherlands in 1899,[3]
the work then finding the size that suited it
best. It seems, however, that a new enlargement to twice the original size was undertaken in 1911, probably in connection with
plans for producing an unrealized *Monument
to Labor*, conceived as a tower (plaster model
c. 1899, Musée Rodin, Paris).
ALNR

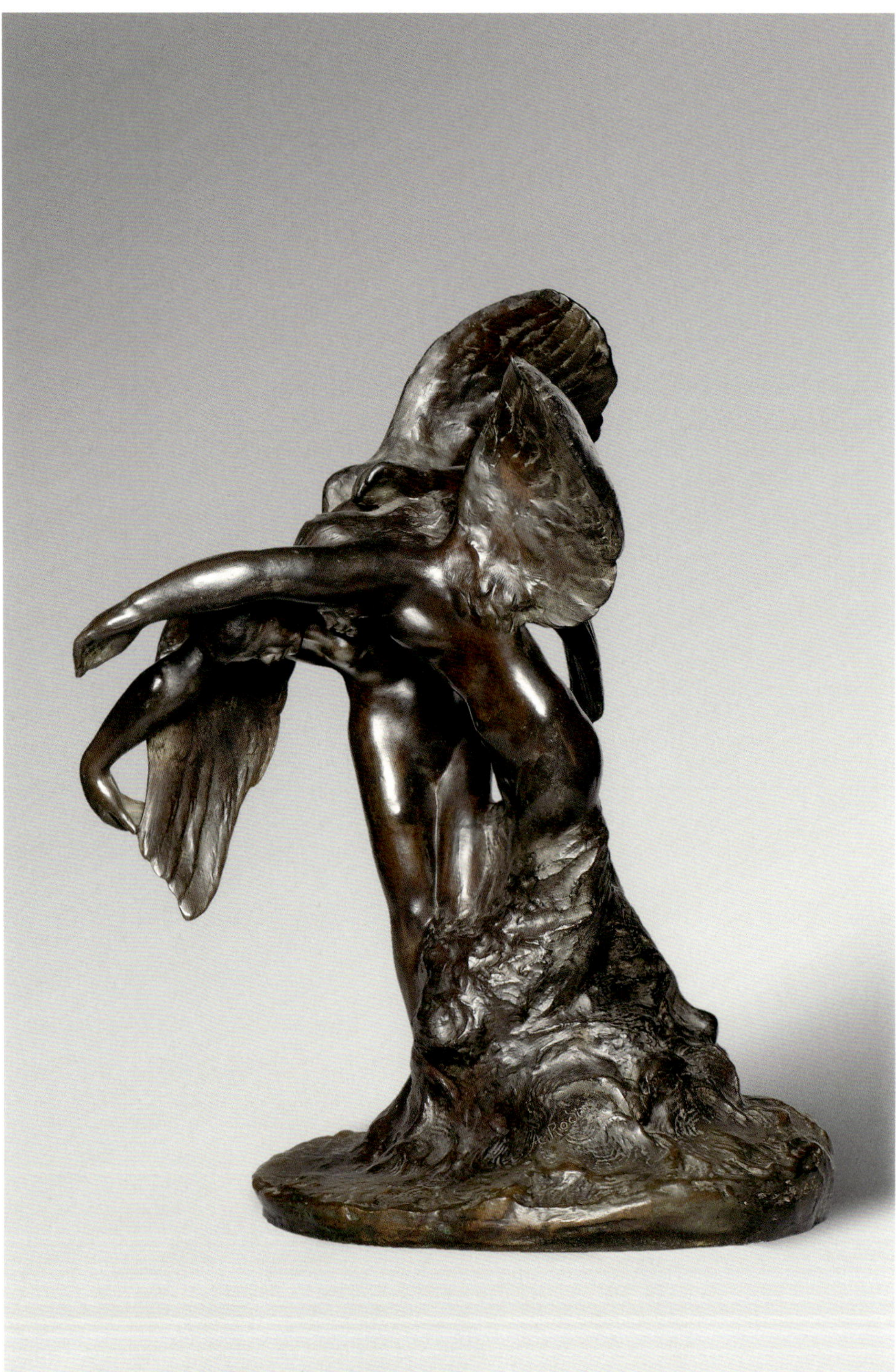

1. *Exposition Rodin*, exh. cat. (Paris: Palais de l'Alma,
1900), cat. 125.
2. Third order from Jules E. Mastbaum, August 27,
1925, Archives du musée Rodin, Paris.
3. *Tentoonstelling van Beeldhouwwzerken door
A. Rodin*, Maison d'Art, Brussels; Rotterdamsche
Kunstkring, Rotterdam; Maatchappij Arti &
Amicitae, Amsterdam; and Haagsche Kunstkring,
The Hague, May 8–November 5, 1899.

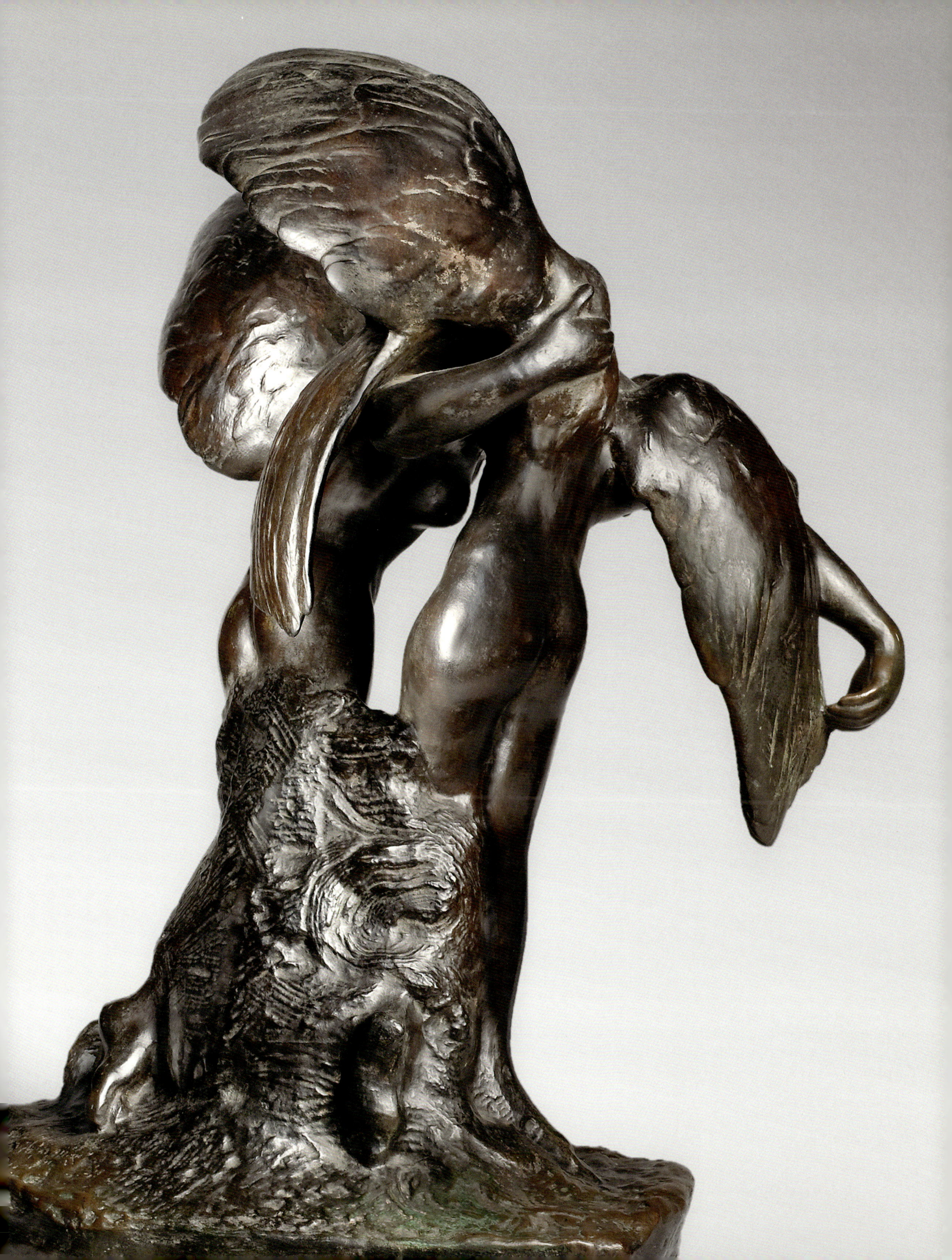

SHAME (ABSOLUTION)

Original model c. 1895–1900
Bronze, cast by Alexis Rudier, 1925–26
25¾ × 15 × 12½ in. (65.4 × 38.1 × 31.8 cm)
Signed on base: *A. Rodin*
Inscribed beneath left foot of seated figure:
la pudeur; on top of base: *absolution*
Foundry mark, center rear of base: *Alexis Rudier /
Fondeur Paris*
Rodin Museum, Philadelphia Museum of Art
Bequest of Jules E. Mastbaum, 1929, F1929-7-16

Shame or *Absolution* is an assemblage of two
figures. The seated main figure is a much earlier study that received the title *Cybele* after
1904. Posed for by Adèle Abbruzzesi, Rodin's
favorite model in the early 1880s, this piece
originated in 1887 as a half-figure at the bottom of the right pilaster of *The Gates of Hell*.
It was often exhibited and used in assemblages, and it was finally enlarged in the early
twentieth century. The second figure was
adapted from a little huddled nude, known
as *Andromeda* or *Danaid* (around 1888). A
marble version of this second figure was displayed at the World's Columbian Exposition
in Chicago in 1893. From her back, to the
movement of her head turned to the left, to
the way her arms are attached to the torso,
everything in the second *Shame* figure corresponds to *Andromeda*. Rodin simply tight-
ened the bend of the knee to press the right
tibia against the thigh. As for the principal
figure, as can be seen in the Musée Rodin
plaster, her original right forearm has been
modified to better accommodate the second
figure, and she has received a head that was
attached rather abruptly. Meanwhile, the
hair that spreads to the left of the *Danaid* now
flows to the right of the second figure. The
two figures were joined at an unknown date.

This type of assemblage made of figures
that were mostly modeled in connection with
the *Gates of Hell*, of which *Fugit Amor* (cat. 6)
is a famous example, multiplied throughout
the 1890s. The relationship of the figures
to each other is what interested Rodin,
but he also had to think of his clientele.
Consequently, when they were realized in
marble, his compositions received titles
referring to the Symbolist movement at
the end of the century, sometimes inscribed
directly on the plaster model. *Shame
(Absolution)*, the date of which is not known,
remained a model and was never exhibited,
nor mentioned in any reviews. Perhaps Rodin
hesitated and ultimately preferred another
assemblage that suggests the same meaning
of protection or pardon, *Youth Triumphant*
or *The Fate and the Convalescent*, the marble
version of which (1896, MAK, Österreisches

Museum für angewandte Kunst, Vienna) was
exhibited in Paris at the Salon de la Société
Nationale des Beaux-Arts in 1896.

In addition to classic works such as *The
Age of Bronze* or *St. John the Baptist*, Jules
Mastbaum also obtained bronzes, some
of which are unique casts, produced from
molding the marbles; models for monuments,
such as *Claude Lorrain* and *Victor Hugo*;
and plaster casts that were undoubtedly

selected with the Musée Rodin curator
Georges Grappe, including *Shame (Absolution)*.[1]
This is what gives the Rodin Museum in
Philadelphia its unique character.
ALNR

1. Fourth order from Jules E. Mastbaum, November
7, 1925, Archives du musée Rodin, Paris.

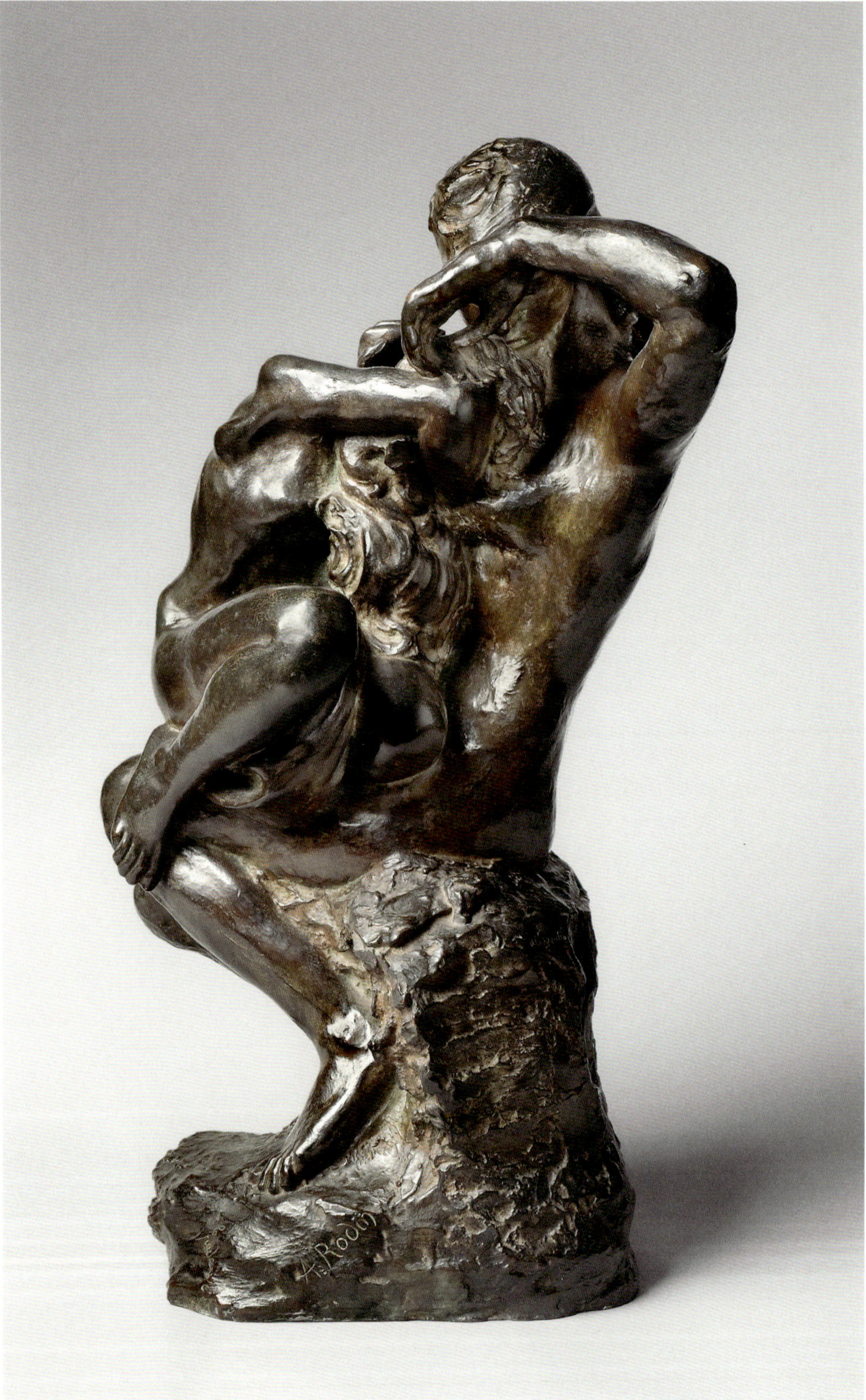

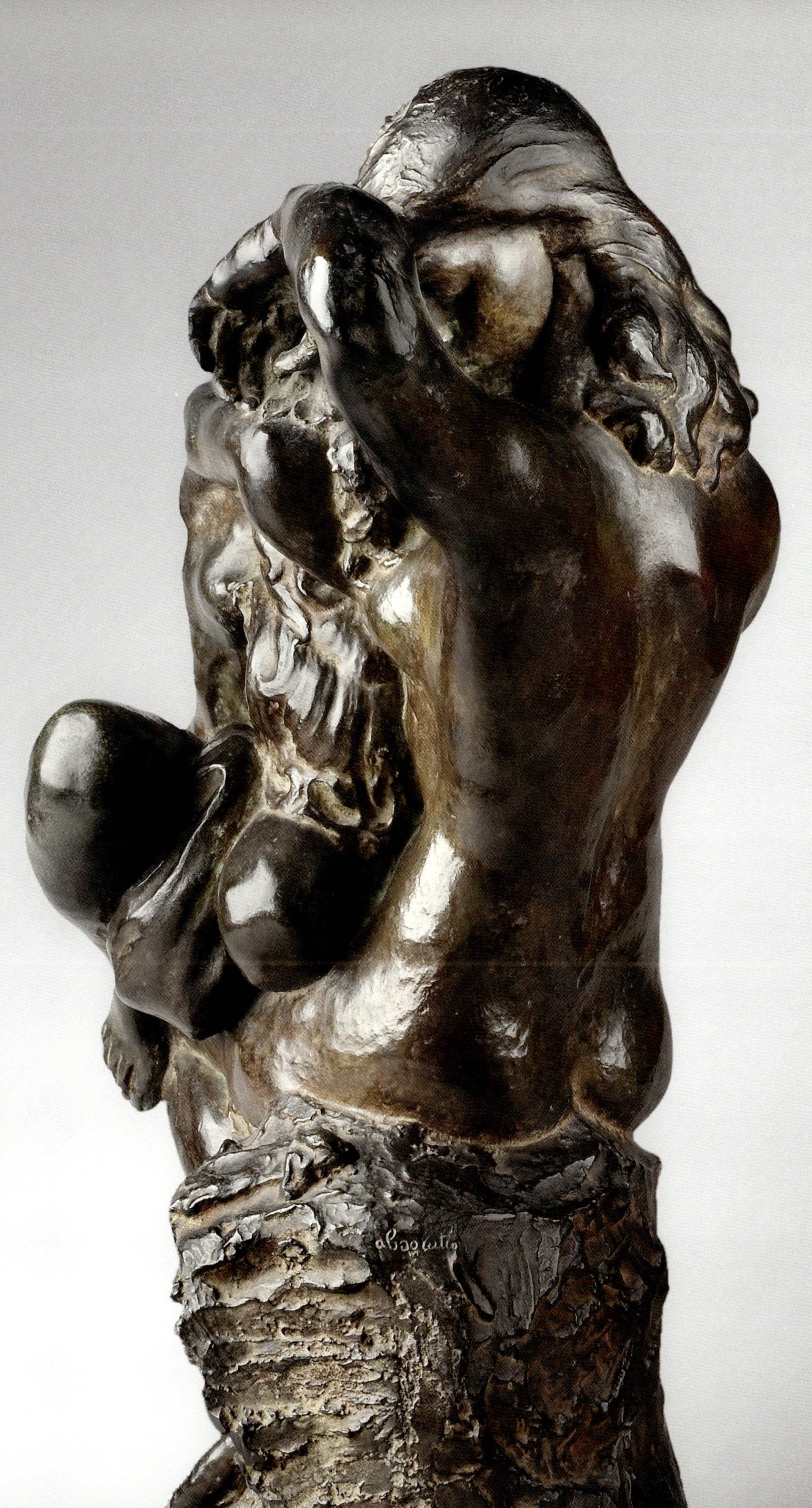

MEDEA

Original model c. 1880
Plaster
23 ½ × 12 ½ × 9 ½ in. (59.7 × 31.8 × 24.1 cm)
Rodin Museum, Philadelphia Museum of Art
Bequest of Jules E. Mastbaum, 1929,
F1929-7–100

A lesser-known work by Rodin, this plaster shows his admiration for the Romantic painter Eugène Delacroix. The pyramidal composition and the position of Medea, who seems to turn away from her children before killing them to avenge herself on their father, Jason, directly echo a painting of the same title exhibited by Delacroix at the Salon of 1838 (Lille, Palais des Beaux-Arts).

In Rodin's composition, the figure seems almost buried in magnificent drapery that was molded directly on a piece of fabric laid over the plaster figure's body. This makes it unusual in Rodin's oeuvre, which consists essentially of nudes. He must have seen it as a companion piece to *Ugolino and His Sons* (cat. 91), since the two compositions were both fully developed in the late 1870s. Like Ugolino, Medea was originally seated, but an ink sketch annotated "Ugolin Médée" (Musée Rodin, Paris, D. 00153) shows that Rodin then planned a composition in which the principal figure crawls over the bodies of his children. This is the arrangement that he adopted for *Ugolino*, while Medea seems to soar up over the course of the drawings in ink wash and gouache (D.02056) or watercolor (D. 04196 and D. 04955), which were made over an extended period.

The Musée Rodin in Paris has two plaster casts of *Medea*, one reworked by Rodin and the other a cast that differs from that of Philadelphia by the addition of a narrow base. This plaster, then titled *Femme drapée funéraire*, appears along with *Ecclesiastes* on a list of twenty-two "original sketches" selected by Etta Wedell Mastbaum during her visit to the museum on July 29, 1927.[1] She was continuing the work to establish Philadelphia's Rodin Museum following the death of her husband, Jules Mastbaum. She had arranged for the Paris museum to donate the plasters to her, and she would then have molds made on them. According to the Musée Rodin conservator Georges Grappe, "these plaster casts are very precious and all first casts."[2] This implies that the plaster casts from Rodin's studio were sent to Philadelphia, with the Paris museum replacing them with versions produced in new molds.
ALNR

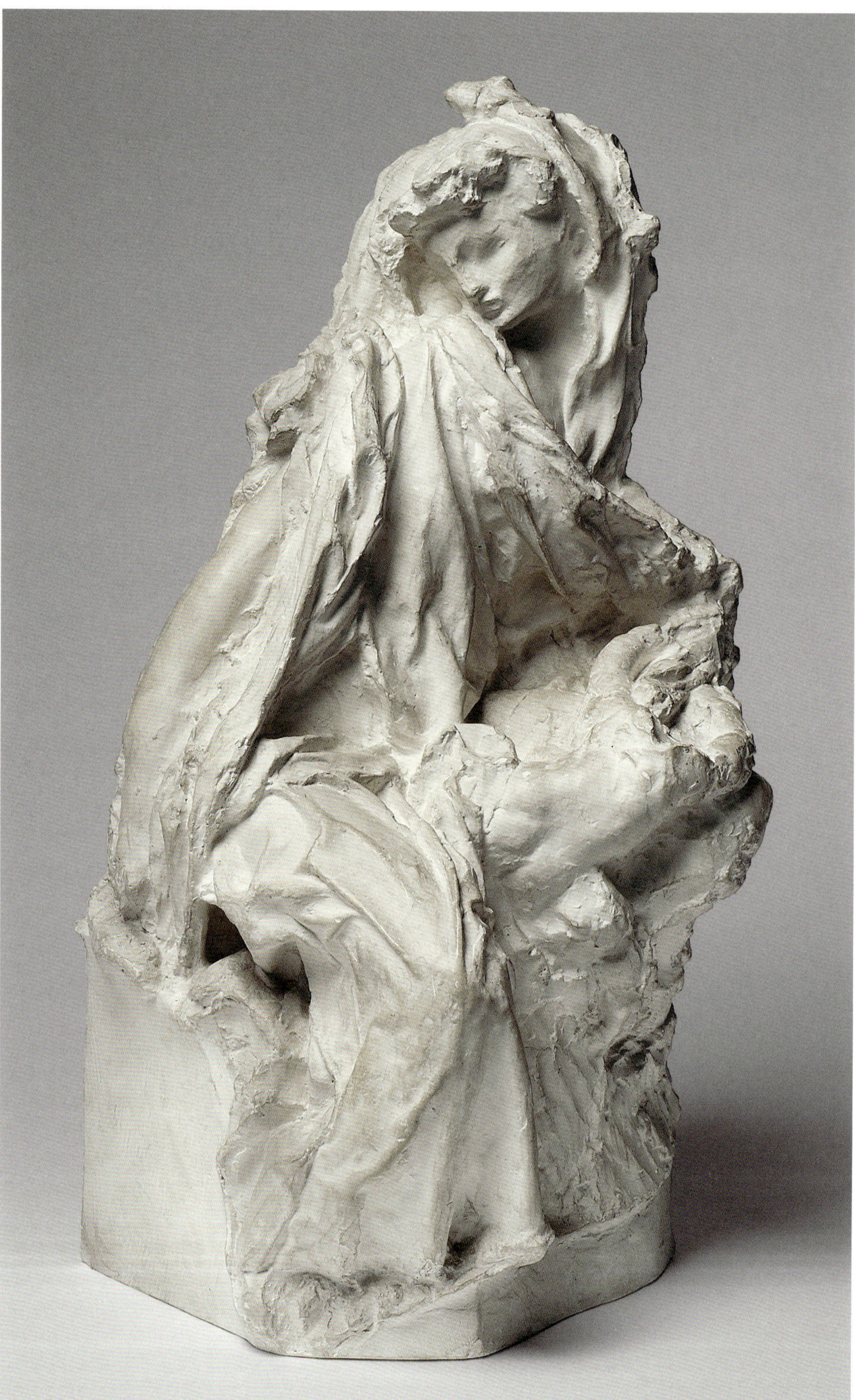

1. "Désignation et notes relatives aux esquisses originales . . . désignées par Madame Mastbaum lors de sa visite à Meudon le vendredi 29 juillet 1927," February 15, 1929, Archives du musée Rodin, Paris.
2. Georges Grappe to Guérin (transport agent), February 21, 1929, Archives du musée Rodin, Paris.

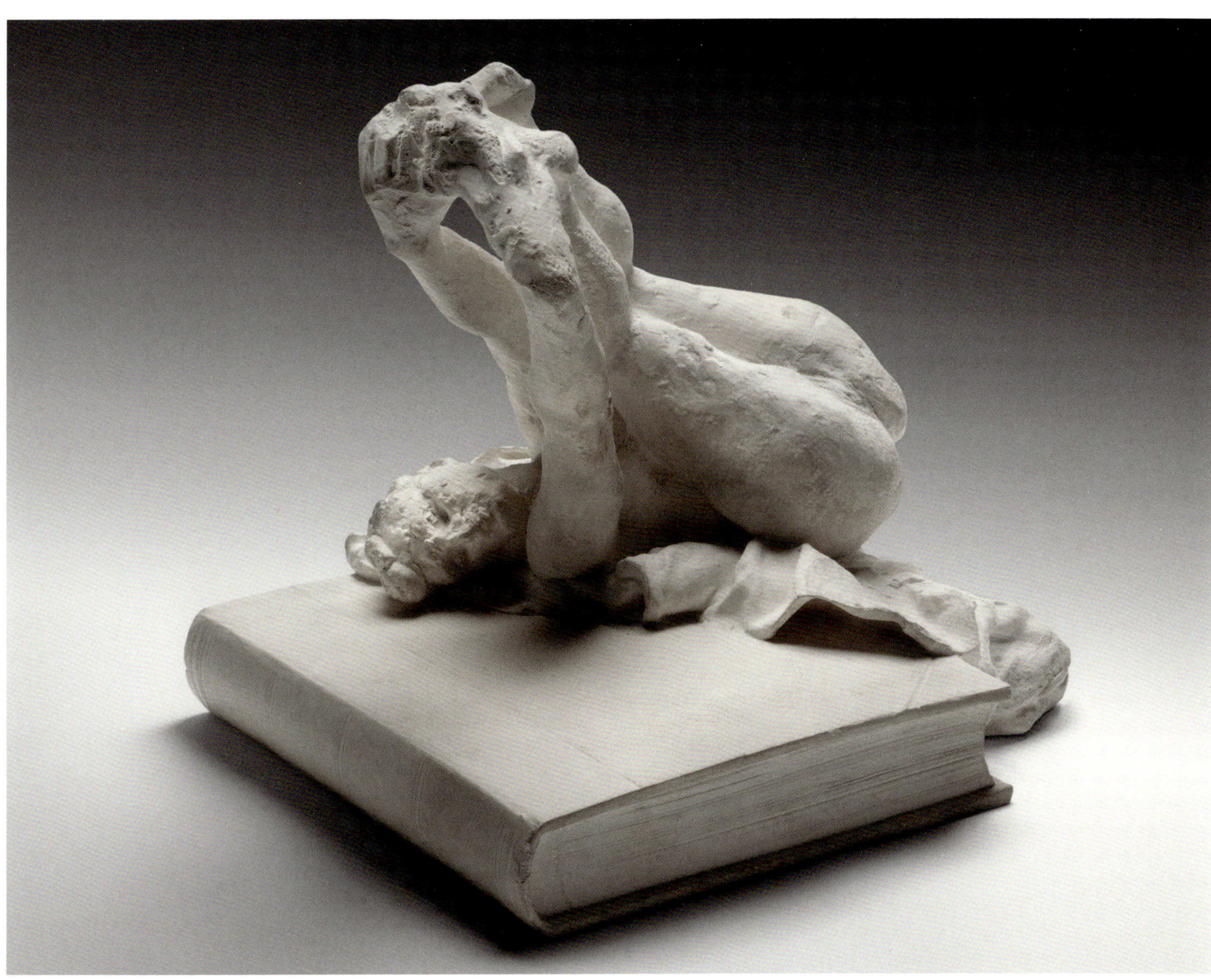

CAT. 73
ECCLESIASTES

Original model before 1899
Plaster
10 × 11 × 10 in. (25.4 × 27.9 × 25.4 cm)
Rodin Museum, Philadelphia Museum of Art
Bequest of Jules E. Mastbaum, 1929,
F1929-7-117

Displayed in the Rodin exhibition that traveled in Belgium and the Netherlands in 1899,[1] the *Woman with a Book*, as it was still called in 1900, took the title *Ecclesiastes* in Düsseldorf in 1904. This assemblage is a good example of the way in which Rodin's works received titles, doubtless suggested by members of the artist's circle. The new title refers to the Hebrew Bible book of Ecclesiastes, in which the son of King David preaches, "Vanity of vanities! All is vanity. What does man gain by all the toil at which he toils under the sun?" The preacher then

goes on to list various aspects of human activity, dismissing them one after another, before renouncing wisdom to indulge in pleasure—the moment evoked here. In time, he will reject pleasure, declaring, "This also is vanity and a striving after wind."[2]

The bold position and the plump body of the model connect this figure to other female nudes Rodin made prior to 1899. However, the way Rodin used the figure here is particularly audacious. Before 1899, he had the idea of positioning the figure on its back, in a pose as erotic as Jean-Honoré Fragonard's *La Gimblette, Girl with a Dog* (1770, Alte Pinakothek, Munich), and then attaching it to a cast of a book that was much larger than the figure. It is clear that Rodin's creative process embraced chance, and that he never started with a preconceived idea. However, one of his main concerns was to

save time—as he did here by using a cast of a book as a base—which led him to practices that appear completely innovative in the context of his time. Taking his approach to its logical conclusion, he did not hesitate to consider this a completed work, showing *Ecclesiastes* several times and rendering it in marble. The book was then transformed into a cushion, which brings us back to the erotic, but more conventional, world of Fragonard, an eighteenth-century painter known for his joie de vivre.
ALNR

1. *Tentoonstelling van Beeldhouwwzerken door A. Rodin*, Maison d'Art, Brussels; Rotterdamsche Kunstkring, Rotterdam; Maatchappij Arti & Amicitae, Amsterdam; and Haagsche Kunstkring, The Hague, May 8–November 5, 1899.
2. Ecclesiastes 1:2–3; 2:36, English Standard Version.

MASK OF ROSE BEURET, LATER MME RODIN

Original model c. 1882
Ground glass refired in a mold (*pâte de verre*),
executed by Jean Cros, c. 1911
9 ½ × 6 ¼ × 7 ⅛ in. (24.1 × 15.9 × 18.1 cm)
Rodin Museum, Philadelphia Museum of Art
Bequest of Jules E. Mastbaum, 1929, F1929-7-43

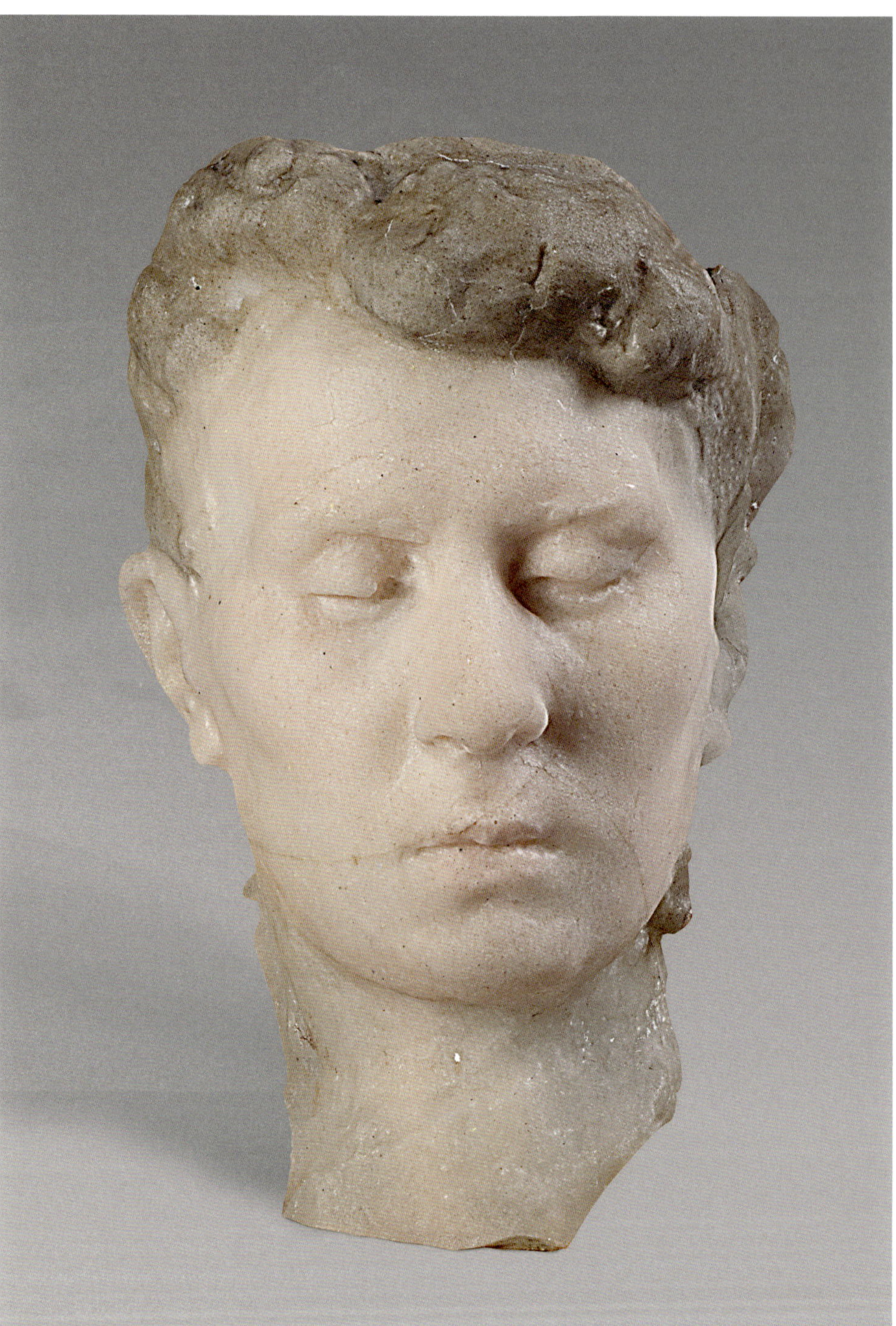

Rose Beuret (1844–1917) was Rodin's loyal
lifelong partner from the early 1860s on, and
together they had a son, Auguste, born in
1864. They married in January 1917, shortly
before their deaths (hers on February 14
and his on November 17 of that year).
She posed for him repeatedly and inspired
several allegorical busts, such as *Mignon*,
Bellona and *The Alsatian Woman*, to which
we can compare the mask shown here.

This c. 1882 *Mask of Rose Beuret* is a
severe image, with the eyes almost closed,
and it was exhibited for the first time in
plaster in 1900.[1] Yet, before this date,
in 1898, it had served as the starting point
for the bust carved in marble by Antoine
Bourdelle (Musée Rodin, Paris), in which
Rodin played with the contrast between
an almost raw background and a face that
was much more finished.

First cast in bronze in 1903 and displayed
in several exhibitions, starting at Dusseldorf
(International Exhibition of Fine Arts) in
1904, this portrait met with success, as
demonstrated by the large number of copies,
including this one in *pâte de verre*, executed
by Jean Cros, the son of Henry Cros, the
developer of the *pâte de verre* technique,
in which a paste made from ground glass is
brushed onto a mold and fired. Rodin's
desire to take advantage of the possibilities
offered by various types of materials found
its culmination in this precious material,
which could give the illusion of life by
introducing color in his sculpture. Rodin
called on Cros in 1911 for the portraits
of four women who were close to him: Rose
Beuret, whom everyone already considered
his wife; Camille Claudel, his student and
former lover; Hélène de Nostitz, a German
socialite and close friend of Rodin; and the
Japanese actress Hanako, who also modeled
for him. As with the mask of Hanako (cat. 49),
which is also part of the collection of the
Rodin Museum in Philadelphia, the mask
of Rose Beuret was described as a "single
cast retouched by the artist" on a bill dated
August 27, 1925.[2]
ALNR

1. *Exposition Rodin*, exh. cat. (Paris: Palais de l'Alma,
1900), cat. 17.
2. Order of August 27, 1925, Archives du musée
Rodin, Paris.

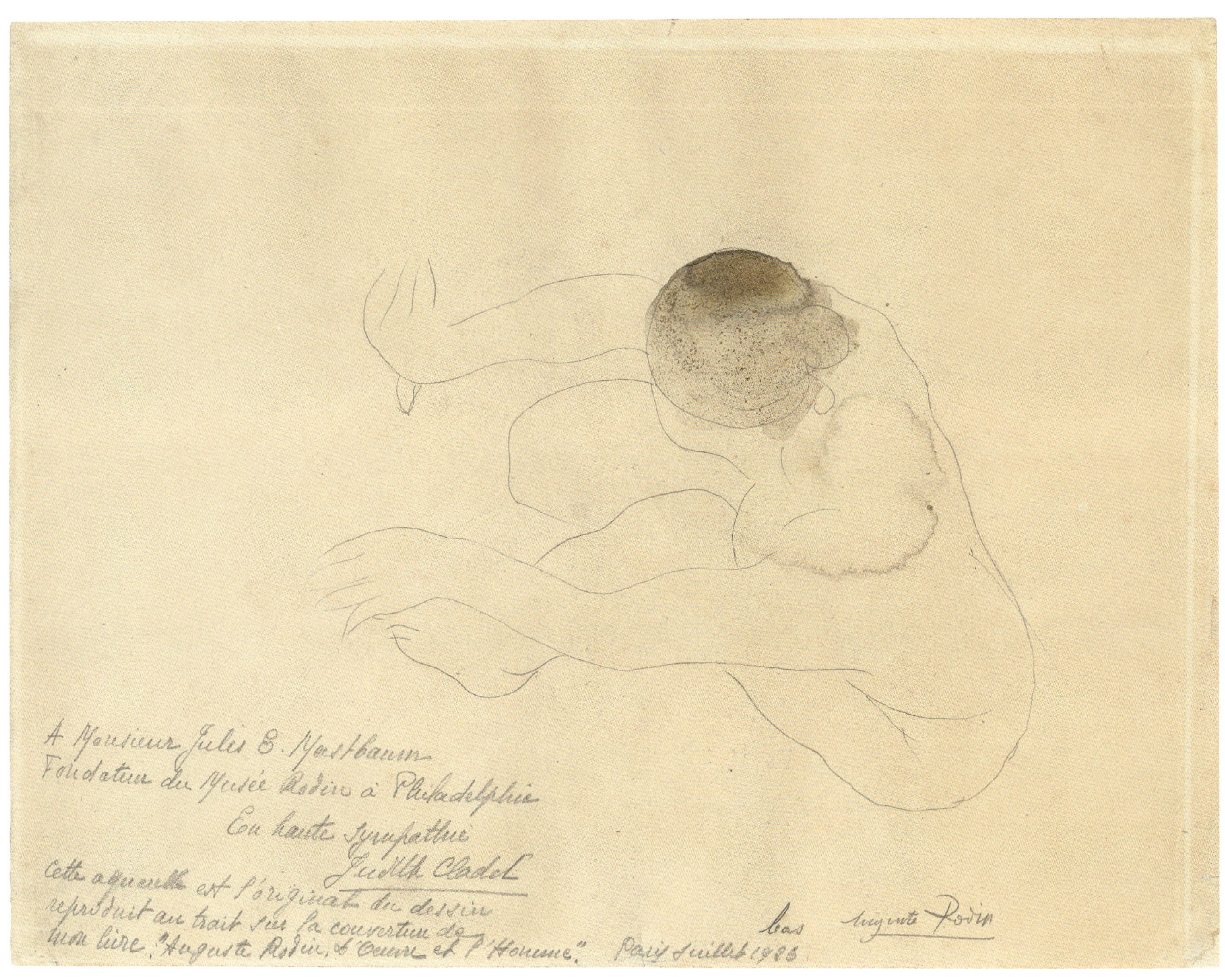

CAT. 75
SEATED WOMAN

c. 1900
Graphite and watercolor on wove paper
9 11/16 × 12 7/8 in. (24.6 × 32.7 cm)
Signed in graphite, lower right: *bas / Auguste Rodin*
Inscribed in graphite, lower left, in the hand of Judith Cladel: *À Monsieur Jules E. Mastbaum / Fondateur du Musée Rodin à Philadelphie / En haute sympathie / Judith Cladel / Cette aquarelle est l'original du dessin / reproduit au trait sur la couverture de / mon livre: "Auguste Rodin. L'œuvre et l'homme." Paris. Juillet 1926*
Rodin Museum, Philadelphia Museum of Art
Bequest of Jules E. Mastbaum, 1929,
1929-7-197

Seated Woman was bequeathed in 1929 to the Philadelphia Rodin Museum after the premature death of its founder, while a second drawing, *Female Nude with Raised Leg* (1900–1905), went to Jules Mastbaum's nephew Richard Gimbel and is now in the Baltimore Museum of Art. Both feature a dedication to Mastbaum by Rodin's friend Judith Cladel (1873–1958). A journalist and novelist, Cladel was a key figure in the establishment of the Musée Rodin in Paris and an early supporter of Mastbaum's project for the museum in Philadelphia. The author of *L'œuvre et l'homme* (1908; a comprehensive biography of Rodin with this watercolor on the cover), Cladel understood and appreciated the encyclopedic nature of Mastbaum's vision, as he sought to create a museum that was devoted not only to Rodin's genius but to his life as an artist. For this reason, he gathered a significant quantity of documents, archival materials, and books from friends and relatives of the late artist, as well as his Parisian collectors. Cladel's book *L'œuvre et l'homme* shared this ambition to present the totality of the artist's life and work, and this is probably why she gave the two drawings to Mastbaum.
CBU

WOMAN AND TWO CHILDREN

c. 1883
Graphite, pen, ink, and gouache on wove paper
Sheet: 7 1/16 × 5 1/4 in. (17.9 × 13.3 cm)
Rodin Museum, Philadelphia Museum of Art
Bequest of Jules E. Mastbaum, F1929-7-168

Jules Mastbaum's collection, the core of
Philadelphia's Rodin Museum, contains the
most complete set of drawings by Rodin
in the United States, beginning with what is
called the "Mastbaum Album," a rare example
of a youthful notebook belonging to Rodin,
of which the Musée Rodin in Paris has no
equivalent. Mastbaum also had nine so-
called black drawings, named for their dark
tonality and subject matter, inspired by
Dante's *Divine Comedy*. No fewer than five
of these were published in the *Album
Fenaille* in 1897, a true bibliophilic undertaking: *Castor and Pollux* (F1929-7-169),
Dante (F1929-7-165), *Dawn: Return from the
Sabbath* (cat. 77), and *Faun and Fauness*
(F1929-7-167), as well as the drawing shown
here, *Woman and Two Children* (*Album
Fenaille* plate 93). The latter represents a
recurring theme in Rodin's work in the
1880s. It is often associated, either surrepti-
tiously or more overtly, with a sea motif and
a horizon (here on the left with a small boat,
which is more visible in the reproduction
in the *Album Fenaille*), as if the two figures of
the woman and child appear in the context
of a dense sky and river/sea. In other
drawings, this mother and child are presented directly on the boat, which in Dante's
Inferno is Charon's ferry on the River Styx,
leading from life to death. This association
between the child and death is not limited to
the themes of woman/child/river. We find
it in the drawings depicting Ugolino, who in
the *Inferno* is condemned to devour his
children, and in mythical figures of infanti-
cide, Medea (cf. cat. 72) and Niobe.[1]

Remarkable throughout this entire series
is Rodin's insistence on shadows and light,
which gives these drawings a sculptural
quality, and his use of ink and gouache,
which transforms them into little paintings
of great intensity. The opaque grisaille is
very similar to the paintings of Jean-Baptiste
Carpeaux (see fig. 3.8). The artist visited
the Musée du Louvre religiously all his life.
Here, the recollection of Leonardo da Vinci's
The Virgin and Child with St. Anne is
striking: we see a figure supporting her
children, who are solidly planted on
her draped thighs, and a protruding foot.
CBU

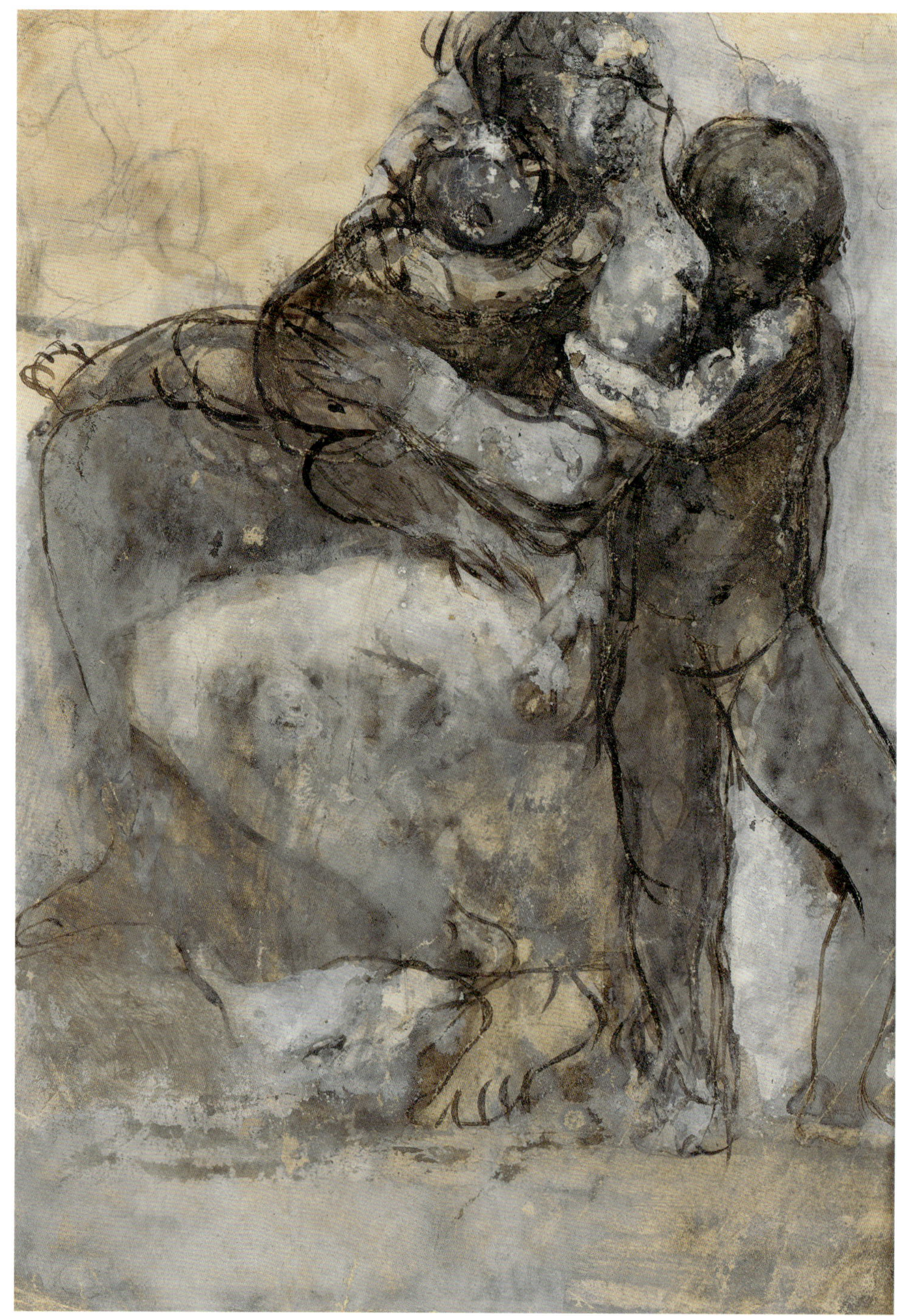

1. On this subject, see Jacques de Caso, "Forme
plastique et imagination: L'album Fenaille de Rodin,"
in *Figures d'ombres: Les dessins de Auguste Rodin: Une
production de la maison Goupil*, ed. Annick Bergeon,
exh. cat. (Bordeaux: Musée Goupil, 1996), 9–18.

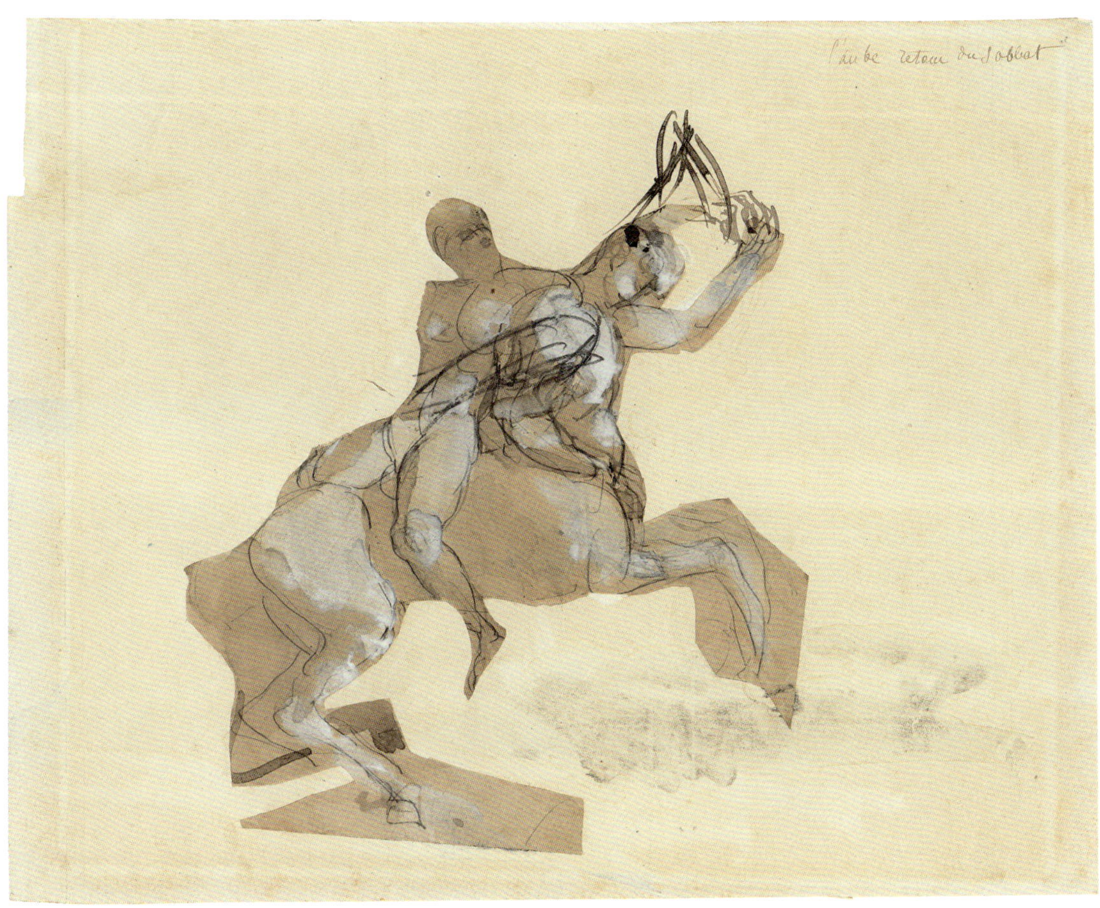

CENTAUR CARRYING A WOMAN (DAWN: RETURN FROM THE SABBATH)

c. 1883–85
Pen and ink, wash, gouache on cutout and
mounted paper
Sheet (irregular): 7 7/8 × 9 15/16 in. (20 × 25.2 cm)
Inscribed with pen and brown ink, upper right:
l'aube / retour du sabbat
Rodin Museum, Philadelphia Museum of Art
Bequest of Jules E. Mastbaum, 1929,
F1929-7-166

Dawn: Return from the Sabbath is a reinter-preted cutout silhouette of one of Rodin's "black drawings" representing a centaur carrying a woman. Rodin glued the cutout onto a larger sheet of paper to give it a sort of landscape background, even if it is barely suggested. Like the *Witches' Sabbath* at the Art Institute of Chicago (cat. 67), the drawing does not in any way present a stereotypical image of an unsightly, evil witch, such as those imagined by Shakespeare in *Macbeth* or by Hans Baldung, Albrecht Dürer, or Francisco de Goya, to cite only the best-known examples. Although this work evokes the pagan, orgiastic celebration that is traditionally depicted, Rodin associates it

with the motif of the centaur, which became increasingly important to the artist in the 1880s. Traditional symbols of violence and vice, the centaurs drawn by Rodin are closer to Dionysian figures and are found, in particular, in his creations for the Sèvres national porcelain factory, where he worked as a designer from 1879 to 1882.[1] Bacchanalian dancing processions with ecstatic centaurs and satyrs drawn to drunkenness and sex were familiar themes, as seen in the frieze of the *Seau de Pompei*, a large cup decorated by Rodin (1882–83, Musée Rodin, Paris). The same eighteenth-century ornamental spirit can be found in this drawing from the Rodin Museum in Philadelphia, where the dancing ride of a naked woman carried on a centaur's back is transformed into a witches' proces-sion. Victoria Thorson sees the position of the woman straddling the centaur as evoking the excessive sexual appetite of the witch (for a later erotic version, see cat. 41).[2]

Here, the first rays of sunlight are master-fully suggested by the touches of gouache on the bodies. Originally, the background of the sheet was heightened with broad strokes of gray ink wash, evoking an unfolding of shadows at dawn. With time, the wash has faded away, but it is visible in the facsimile of the drawing, first published in 1897.[3] As always in Rodin's work, the figure was not

initially defined, but the title inscribed on the upper right and later modifications provide the keys to the interpretation of the work. By adding energetic strokes of pen and brown ink, like the lashings of a whip, in the continuation of the centaur's tilted head, Rodin emphasizes the two arms joined overhead "en couronne" (as it is called in ballet). Notwithstanding a recent comment about the "abrupt correction" of the arms to "move them higher,"[4] which would create an anatomical aberration, Rodin transformed the arms into the mouth of an impressive animal with erect, pointed horns or ears — probably a bull, as in the version in Chicago. CBU

1. From 1883 until as late as 1892, he collaborated with the manufacturer from the outside. See François Blanchetière, "Un franc-tireur inspiré: Rodin et la manufacture de Sèvres," in *Rodin: Les arts décoratifs*, exh. cat., ed. François Blanchetière and William Saadé (Paris: Musée Rodin, 2009), 120–31.
2. Victoria Thorson, "Symbolism and Conservatism in Rodin's Late Drawings," in *The Drawings of Rodin*, ed. Albert E. Elsen and J. Kirk T. Varnedoe (New York: Praeger, 1971), 132, 172.
3. See *Les dessins de Auguste Rodin*, known as the "Album Fenaille" (Paris: Maison Goupil, Boussod, Manzi, Joyant, 1897), plate 115.
4. Sophie Biass-Fabiani, *Rodin: Dessiner, Découper* (Paris: Hazan, 2020), 35.

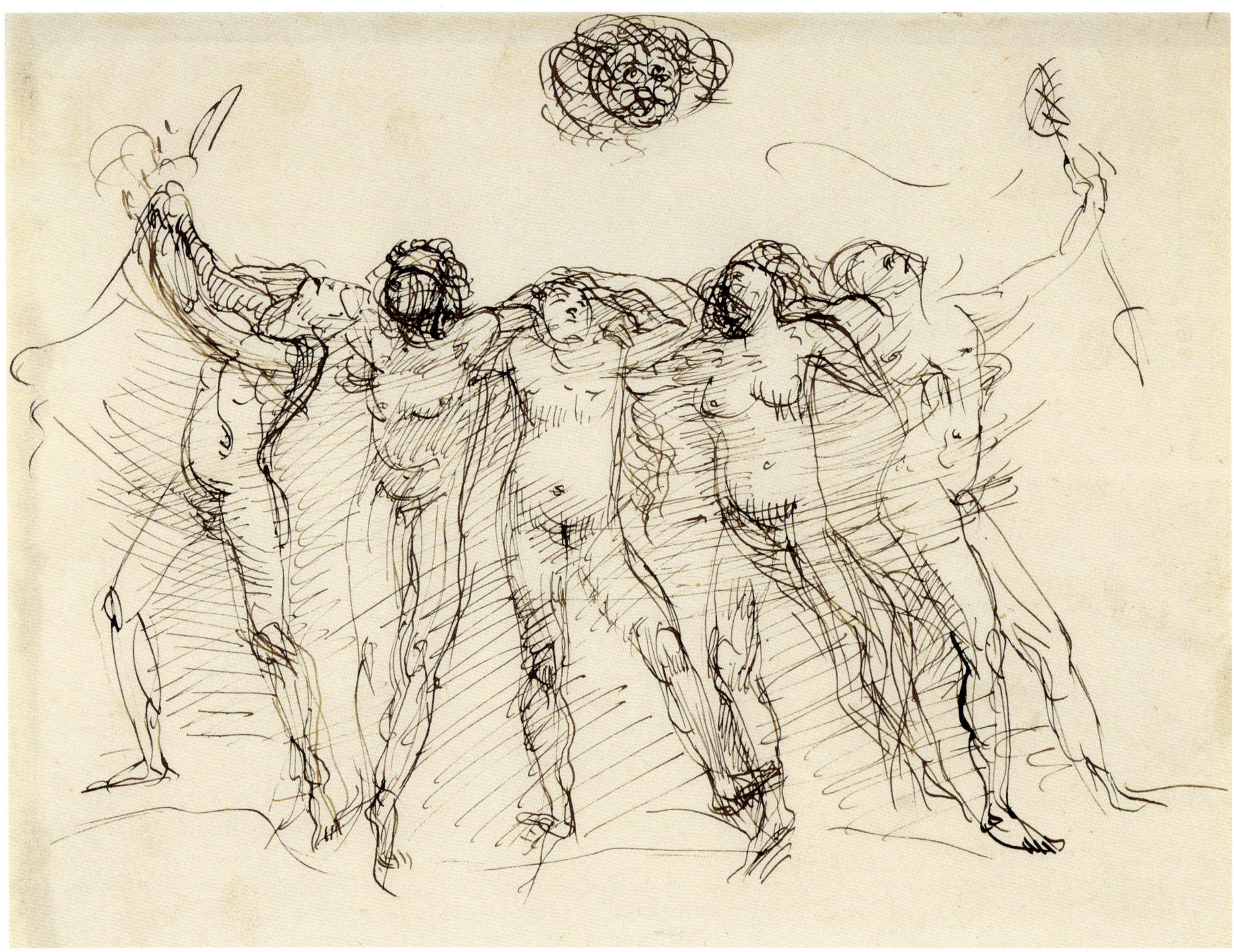

CAT. 78

DANCE (DRAWING RECONSTRUCTED FROM MEMORY BY RODIN, AFTER A DESTROYED VASE)

c. 1887–1907
Pen and ink on wove paper
7 ⅛ × 9 in. (18.1 × 22.9 cm)
Collector's stamp of the Musée Rodin collection (?) on left edge: *AR* (not identified by Lugt)
Collector's stamp of the R.M collection on verso, lower left (not identified by Lugt)
Mr. Hugh Justin Seto and Mrs. Amy T. Seto

Dance can be dated at the earliest to around 1887, when Rodin was collaborating with Jules Desbois at the Manufacture Nationale de Sèvres on several vases, and at the latest to 1907, when the drawing was reproduced in *Auguste Rodin céramiste* by Roger Marx.[1] The style of the drawing and the technique are characteristic of the 1880s, a time when Rodin was working on his sketches for *The Gates of Hell*. It also coincides with the years when he collaborated with the Manufacture

de Sèvres, beginning in 1879. Rodin used a sheet of letterhead with his address at the Dépôt des marbres, which is not unusual. This may be a drawing commissioned by Roger Marx himself to illustrate his book. Regarding the vase created in collaboration with Jules Desbois in 1887, which was destroyed during firing and for which the drawing was made, Marx wrote: "A fourth vase from the same collaboration was Rodin's favorite; he had depicted a dancing procession of nude bacchantes who evoked in his eyes *The Song* and *The Dance*; the piece shattered during firing and it survives only in memory."[2] The drawing depicts dancing maenads or bacchantes and recalls Rodin's vivid pen sketches from the late 1880s, his illustrations for Charles Baudelaire's poem *Les fleurs du mal* (1887–88), and his drypoints from the same period (a technique

Rodin mastered with great expertise). A noteworthy example is *La Ronde* (drypoint, 1883–84, see fig. 3.5). On the back of this drawing, the stamp "R.M." does not correspond to the mark of a known collection; it has not been identified or listed by Frits Lugt in his reference book on collector's marks. Our hypothesis is that it is a "Rodin Museum" mark created by Jules Mastbaum for his future museum in Philadelphia. The mark is found on the back of the drawing depicting Alda Moreno from the same collection (cat. 83).
CBU

1. Roger Marx, *Auguste Rodin céramiste* (Paris: Société de propagation des Livres d'Art, 1907), 47.
2. Marx, *Auguste Rodin céramiste*, 28–29.

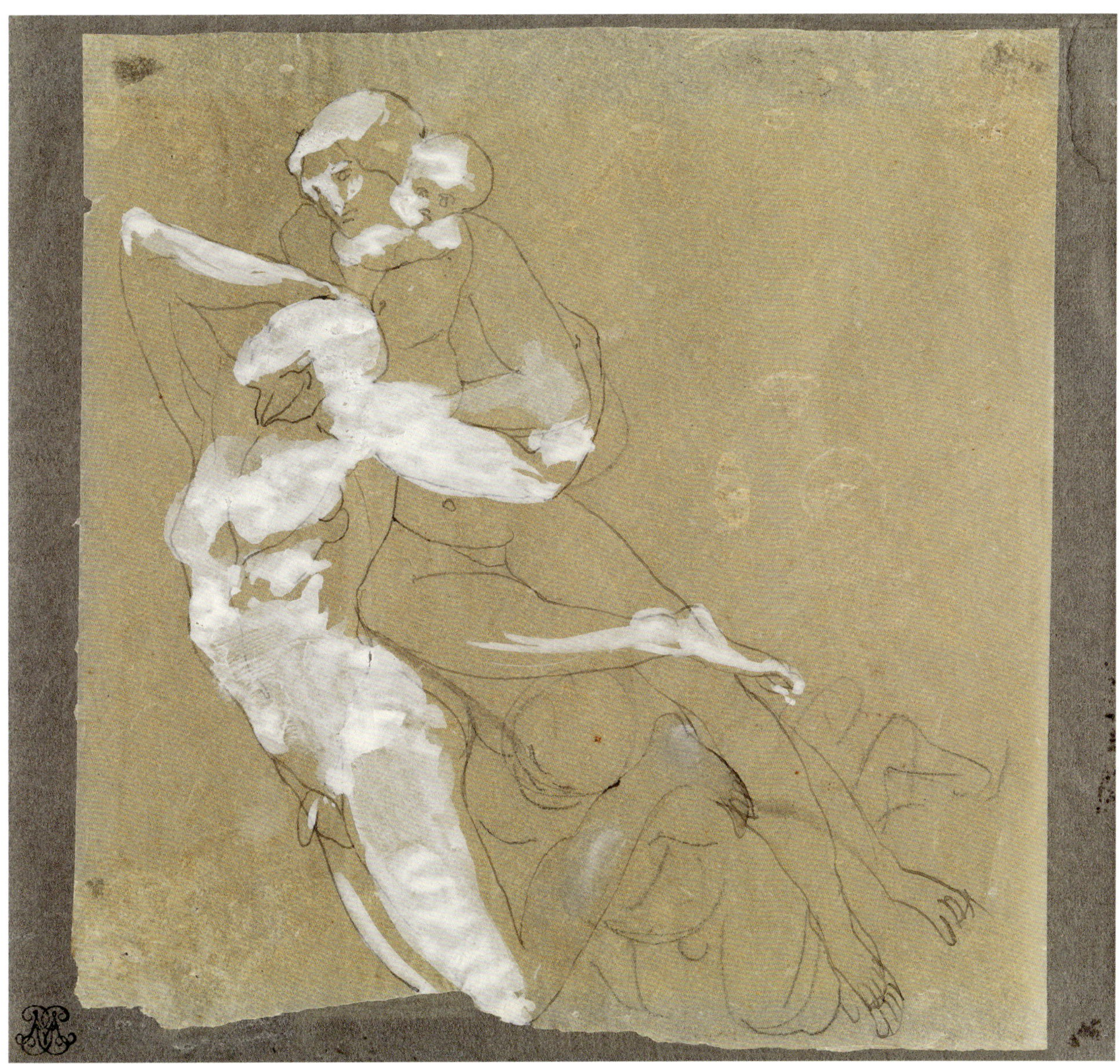

CAT. 79
GROUP OF FIGURES (TIME)

c. 1885–90
Graphite, pen and ink, and gouache on tracing
paper mounted to a gray sheet
5⅜ × 5⅜ in. (13.7 × 13.7 cm)
Collector's stamp of Marcel Louis Guérin on the
mount (Lugt 1872b)
Private collection, courtesy of Nicholas Sands &
Company Fine Art, New York

Before entering the collection of the
Mastbaum family, this drawing belonged to
Marcel Guérin (1837–1948), a great connoisseur of Rodin's work and a member of the
board of directors of the Musée Rodin, Paris,
from 1923 until his death in 1948. Guérin
put together the essential part of his
collection in 1913, as attested by the artist's
list of payments received.[1] Jules Mastbaum,
the founder of the Rodin Museum of
Philadelphia, certainly must have appreciated

such an unusual artwork—as well as its
noteworthy provenance. It is representative
of the way in which the artist prepared for
his decoration of porcelain, even if it is not
directly linked to a known vase or ceramic
object. Between 1879 and 1882, Rodin
completed many decoration projects for the
Manufacture Nationale de Sèvres. *Group
of Figures* was traced using a drawing held
at the Musée Rodin (D. 2072) annotated
"le Temps." The fine lines of the drawing,
adopted beginning around at this time,
are intended to be easily transposable when
incised on a vase. The daubs of white
gouache that lighten certain parts of the
bodies left blank evoke the highlights Rodin
made using a brush and liquid white engobe,
or clay slip, on his decorated porcelain.
We find rare examples of his ceramics in
the United States, particularly at the Cantor

Center for Visual Arts at Stanford (glazed
ceramic tiles titled *Springtime* and
Composition with Children, 1879–82) and at
the Los Angeles County Museum of Art
(*Mother and Child*, c. 1880–81). Mastbaum's
choice to acquire this uncommon drawing
can be explained once again by his desire
to cover the entire spectrum of Rodin's
artistic creation.
CBU

1. "Répertoire des chèques reçus et sommes
encaissées," Archives du Musée Rodin, Paris.

STANDING FEMALE NUDE WITH DRAPERY

c. 1909–15
Graphite with stumping on wove paper
12 × 7 3/8 in. (19.7 × 29.8 cm)
Inscribed in graphite, top left: *le/de soleil . . .*
[unclear inscription]
Rodin Museum, Philadelphia Museum of Art
Bequest of Jules E. Mastbaum, 1929,
F1929-7-191

In this late drawing of a draped woman, acquired by Jules Mastbaum, the stumping is combined with a dense network of hatch marks employed to highlight a part of the model's body. According to Paul Gsell, "The silvery gray rubbing envelops the forms like a cloud; it renders them lighter and seemingly unreal,"[1] just like the atmospheric effects in Rodin's late marble sculptures. This technique has been seen as reflecting the influence of the evanescent *camaïeu* figures, with hazy contours, painted by Rodin's great friend Eugène Carrière.[2] Furthermore, Pictorialist photography, especially the work of Americans Edward Steichen and Gertrude Käsebier, also influenced the sculptor, particularly their photos of his own sculptures (see figs. 3.12, 4.2–4, and p. 198). Several drawings in this style are annotated "to be made in marble" or have annotations connected to the idea of transposition in stone. Some were dedicated and dated by Rodin in 1910, 1914, and 1915 (see cat. 58). Here, the figure seems to hold a scythe at the tips of her fingers, which transforms the vertical lines of the fore-ground into tall grass—perhaps a reference to Ceres, the goddess of the harvest.
CBU

1. Paul Gsell, "Le dessin et la couleur," *La Revue*, October 1, 1910, 724.
2. See Mina Oya, Antoinette Le Normand-Romain, and Rodolphe Rapetti, eds., *Auguste Rodin, Eugène Carrière*, exh. cat. (Tokyo: National Museum of Western Art, 2006).

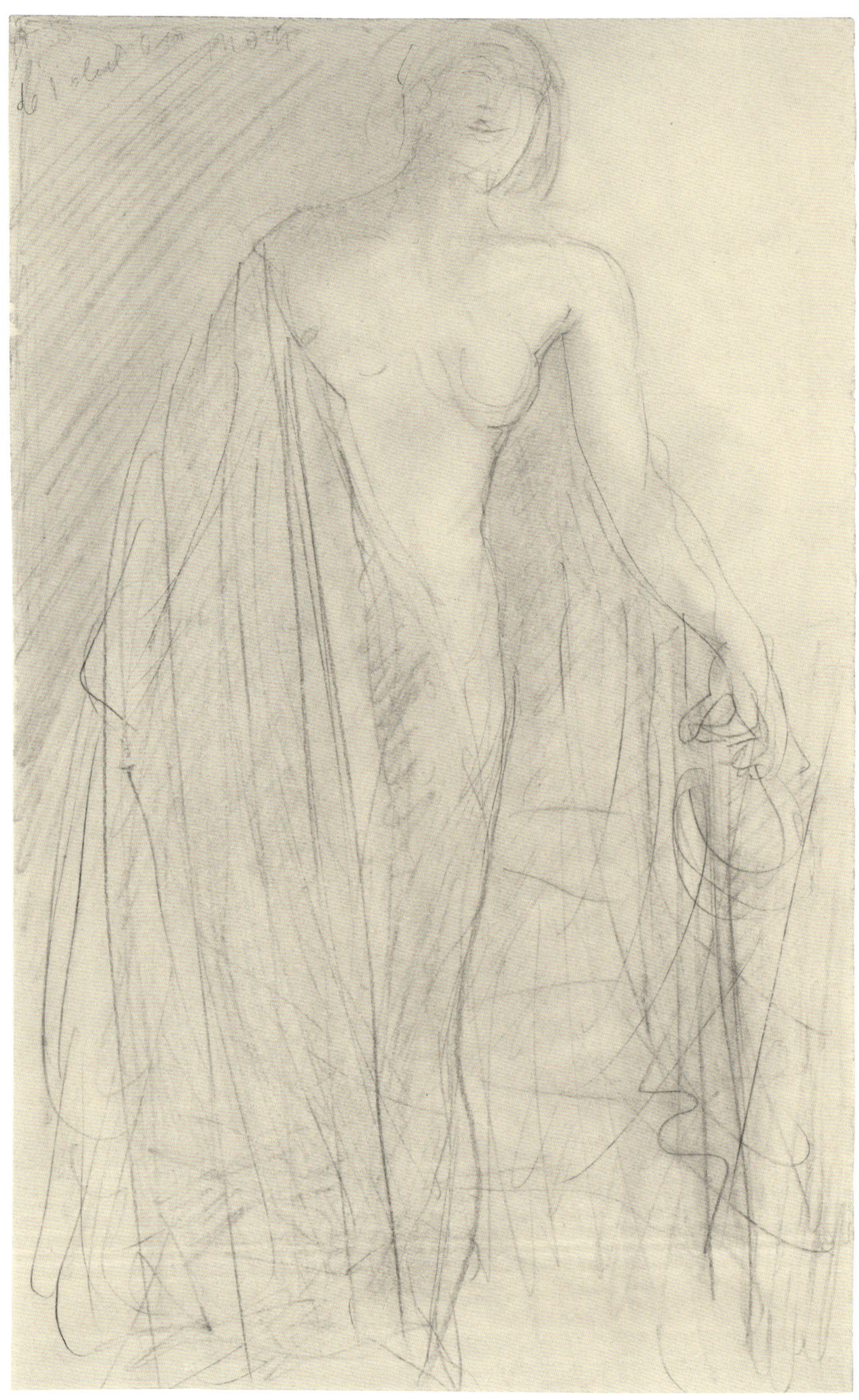

CAMBODIAN DANCER WITH SWIRLING DRAPERY

c. 1906–7
Graphite and watercolor on wove paper
12 3/16 × 8 in. (31 × 20.3 cm)
Inscribed in graphite, lower right, by Rodin's
secretary, René Chéruy: *Cambodgienne pour
servir de gloire*
Rodin Museum, Philadelphia Museum of Art
Bequest of Jules E. Mastbaum, 1929,
F1929-7-196

In July 1906, Rodin attended a performance
in Paris of the royal dancers of Cambodia,
who had accompanied King Sisowath I on an
official visit to France.[1] When the company
left for Marseilles to be part of the Colonial
Exposition, Rodin, thrilled by their performance, decided to follow them. He made
about 150 watercolors, which were immediately recognized as the pinnacle of his art.
Some drawings, such as this one, were
reworked in order to be incorporated into
a fresco intended for the museum of living
artists in Paris (called the Musée du
Luxembourg). In 1907, Étienne Dujardin-
Beaumetz, undersecretary of state for fine
arts, tasked Rodin with decorating an
extension of this museum in the former
seminary of Saint-Sulpice. Rodin was very
attached to this project because an entire
room was to be devoted to his sculptures.
The idea was to display a bronze of *The
Gates of Hell* surrounded by a fresco of
Paradise including multiple angels. Curiously,
Rodin chose to depict these angels "of
Glory"—as Rodin's secretary René Chéruy
indicated on numerous drawings (see cat.
65)—as Cambodian Dancers. Rodin often
transformed the wing tips of the serpent
Naga in Khmer mythology, observed on the
back of the dancers' costumes, into angels'
wings, which the artist associated with
ancient Greek winged Victories, as in this
example. We see that the dancer carries
in her right hand an object that has been too
quickly sketched to be identified but is
clearly defined in other drawings: a statuette
of *Nike*, a Victory, like that held by the
Athena-Nike of the Parthenon. In these
exotic dances, Rodin discovered other
worlds that had preserved authenticity, a
vital sense of the sacred, and the universal
beauty of ancient statues.
CBU

1. See Jacques Vilain, "The Cambodian Dancers Are
My Youth: I Would Have Followed Them All the Way
to Cairo," in *Rodin and the Cambodian Dancers:
His Final Passion*, exh. cat., ed. Jacques Vilain (Paris:
Musée Rodin, 2006), 11–14.

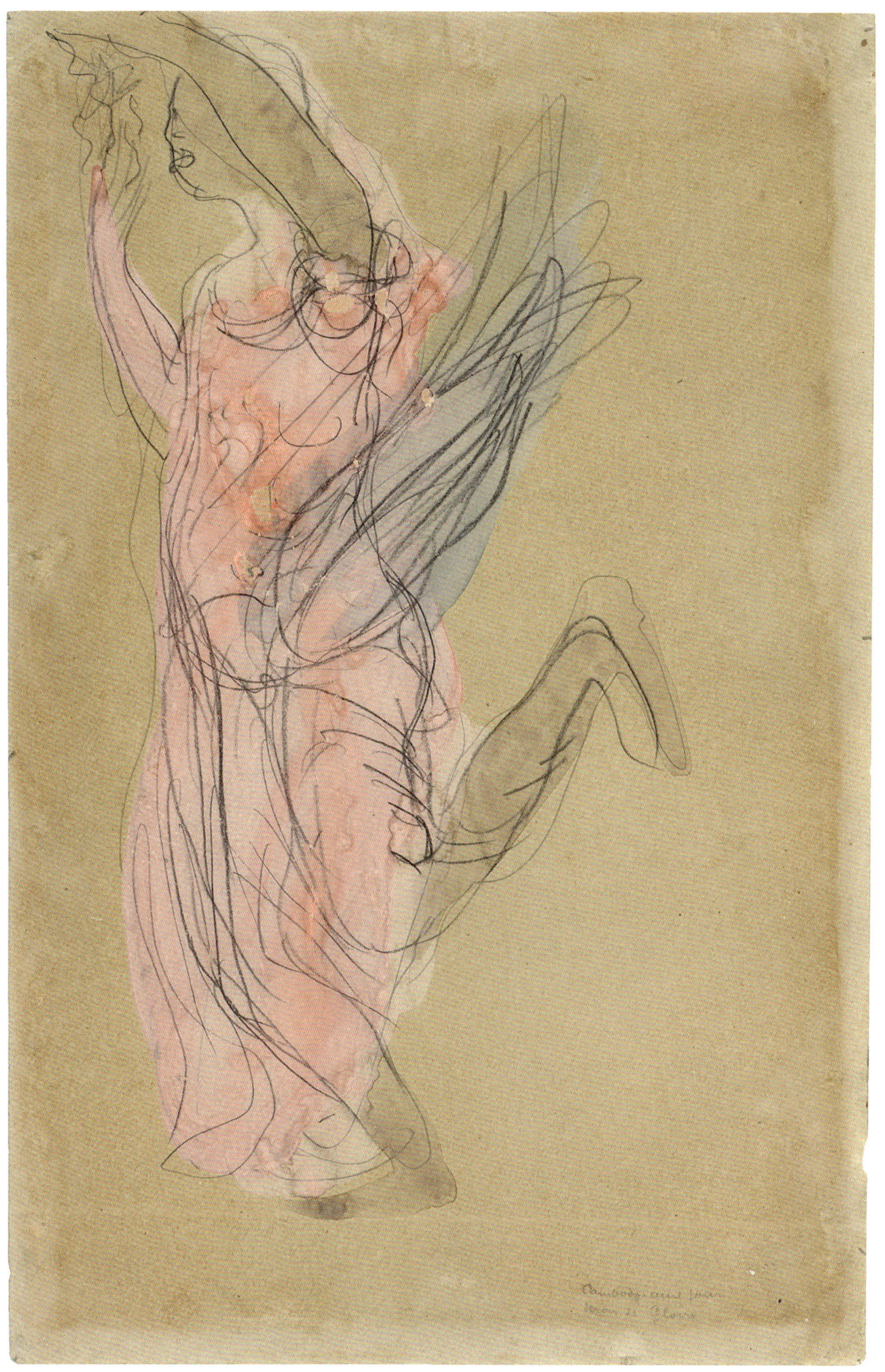

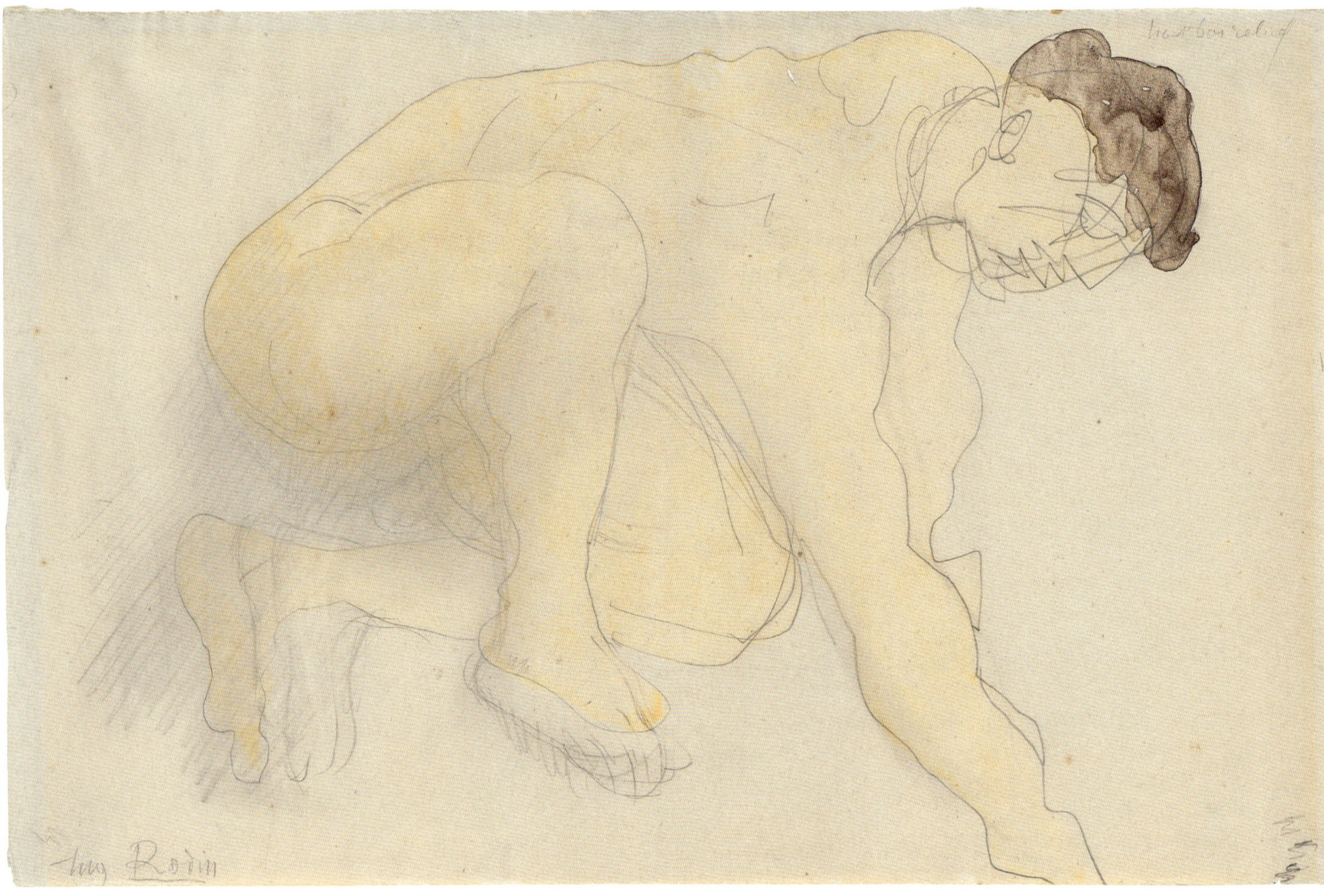

CAT. 82
KNEELING NUDE MALE

c. 1900–1905
Graphite with stumping and watercolor on wove
paper
7⅞ × 12¼ in. (20 × 31.1 cm)
Signed in graphite, lower left: *Aug. Rodin*
Inscribed in graphite, top right: *haut bas relief*
Rodin Museum, Philadelphia Museum of Art
Bequest of Jules E. Mastbaum, 1929,
F1929-7-185

Kneeling Nude Male is one of the few life
drawings in Jules Mastbaum's collection
illustrating the process of "blind" sketching
that Rodin developed in the mid-1890s.
"What is this drawing?" the artist asked:

> Not once describing the shape of that
> mass did I shift my eyes from the model.
> Why? Because I wanted to be sure that
> nothing evaded my grasp of it. Not a
> thought about the technical problem of
> representing it on paper could be allowed
> to arrest the flow of my feelings about it,
> from my eye to my hand. The moment
> I drop my eyes that flow stops. That
> is why my drawings are only my way of
> testing myself. They are my way of
> proving to myself how far this incorpora-
> tion of the subtle secrets of the human
> form has taken place within me. I try to
> see the figure as a mass, as volume. . . .
> My object is to test to what extent my
> hands already feel what my eyes see.[1]

The result was a drawing executed with
great calligraphic freedom, which Rodin did
not hesitate to present as a completed work.
Despite the distortions of the limbs and
the hand cut off by the edge of the paper as
he continued to draw, Rodin colored the
drawing and signed it. The addition of hatch
marks and stumping as well as the annotation "bas-relief" at the top right emphasize
the quality of the drawing, which cannot be
seen as merely a draft. He used an equivalent
process in sculpture by deliberately leaving
the seams of the piece molds visible in his
bronzes. *Kneeling Nude Male* is the primary
life drawing related to *Nude Figure on Hands
and Knees (Executioner)* (cat. 27). It demonstrates the extensive developments that Rodin
gave to a single motif.
CBU

1. Auguste Rodin, quoted in Anthony Ludovici,
Personnal Reminiscences of Auguste Rodin (London:
John Murray, 1926), 138–39.

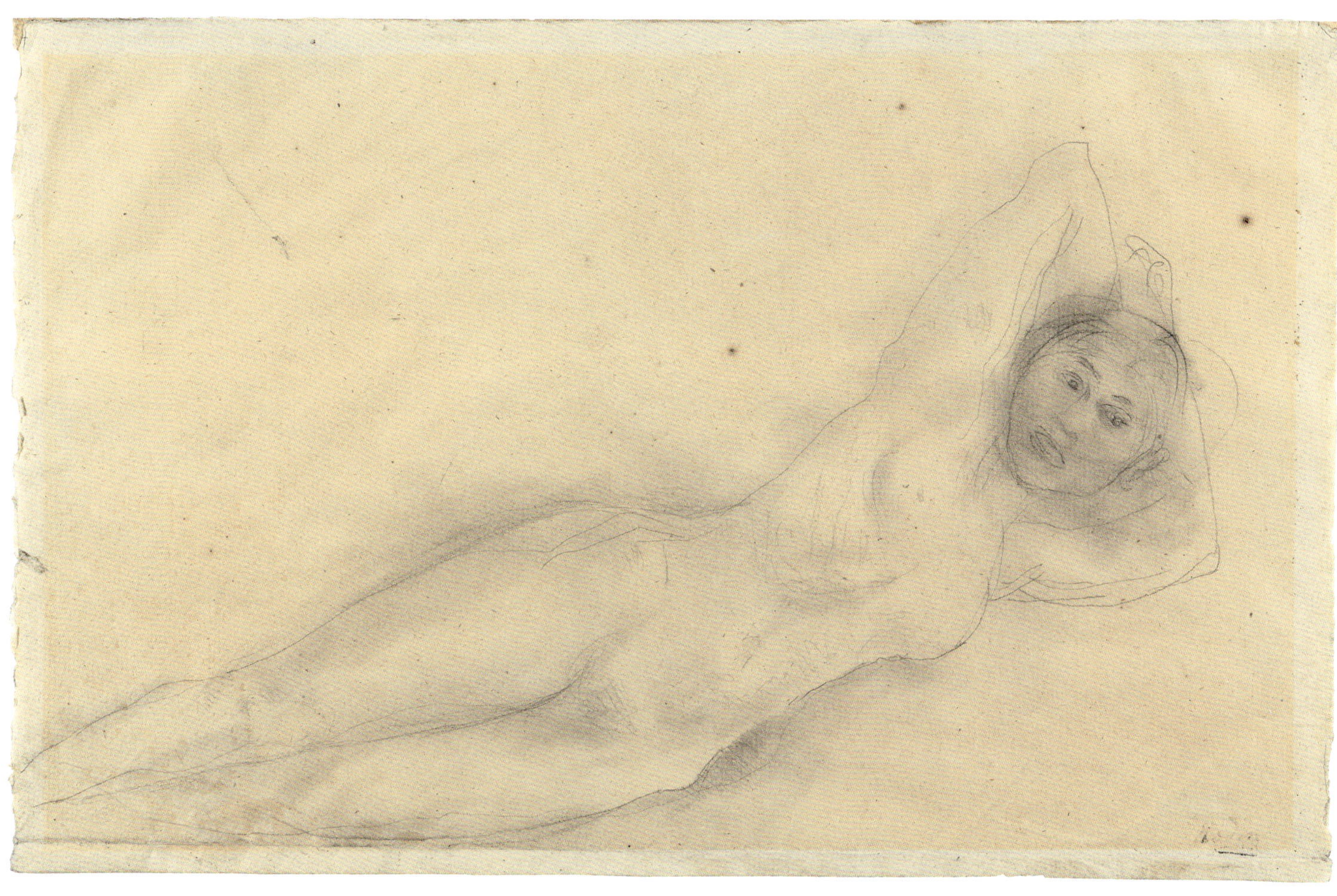

CAT. 83
RECLINING NUDE WOMAN (ALDA MORENO)

c. 1910
Graphite with stumping on laid paper with watermark (Drey . . . K)
9 7/16 × 15 1/16 in. (24 × 38.3 cm)
Collector's stamp of the musée Rodin collection (?) lower right: *Rodin* (Lugt. 2142)
Collector's stamp of the R.M collection on verso (not identified by Lugt)
Rodin Museum, Philadelphia Museum of Art
Bequest of Jules E. Mastbaum, 1929,
F1929-7-176

Reclining Nude Woman demonstrates once again the range of Jules Mastbaum's selection of works in his desire to construct a complete collection of Rodin's art. It likely depicts Alda Moreno, a professional acrobat of the Paris Opéra Comique who was able to achieve the most extreme contortioned postures.[1] Moreno was the companion and muse of Jules Desbois (1840–1935), one of Rodin's close collaborators. She posed for the famous *Dance Movements* modeled by the sculptor, as well as for about fifty drawings created during two separate periods: 1903–1905 (watercolors of her dancing) and 1910–1913 (drawings of her in varied attitudes, in graphite pencil with stumping). In Mastbaum's version of Moreno resting, Rodin emphasized the expression on her face. Like in many drawings by Rodin, the orientation of the sheet of paper is unclear. It reads equally well upside-down or even vertically.[2] The ''Rodin'' signature at the bottom right suggests the artist chose his preferred orientation. However, it is not autograph: it is a signature mark stamped with ink, created around 1916 by Léonce Bénédite, the first curator of the Musée Rodin in Paris.[3] Bénédite actively collaborated on establishing the Paris museum as well as the future museum in Philadelphia.
CBU

1. John Tancock proposes to identify the model as Hanako; however, the known sketches of the Japanese actress in the nude differ stylistically and are not executed on laid paper as in this example. See John L. Tancock, *The Sculpture of Auguste Rodin* (Philadelphia: Philadelphia Museum of Art, 1976), 546. Thanks to Lisa Morra from the Philadelphia Museum of Art, we can confirm the drawing is Moreno because of its special paper bearing the watermark ''Drey . . . K.'' Paper historian Claude Laroque identifies this as a Könige Drey Mill paper, which Rodin exclusively used for the Alda Moreno series (see drawings D. 1769, 1775, 1781, 1790, 1791, 1812, 4919, 5096, and 5099, Musée Rodin, Paris).
2. See Tancock, *The Sculpture of Auguste Rodin*, 550, ill. no. 97-98-I.
3. Frits Lugt lists it as number L. 2142 in *Les marques de collection de dessins et d'estampes* (1921), available online, http://www.marquesdecollections.fr. We recently discovered that there are three different ''Rodin'' stamps; this one corresponds to our stamp no. 2. Christina Buley-Uribe, ''L'aliénabilité *de facto* de dessins du musée Rodin?,'' *Cahiers d'histoire de l'art*, no. 19 (2021): 96–107.

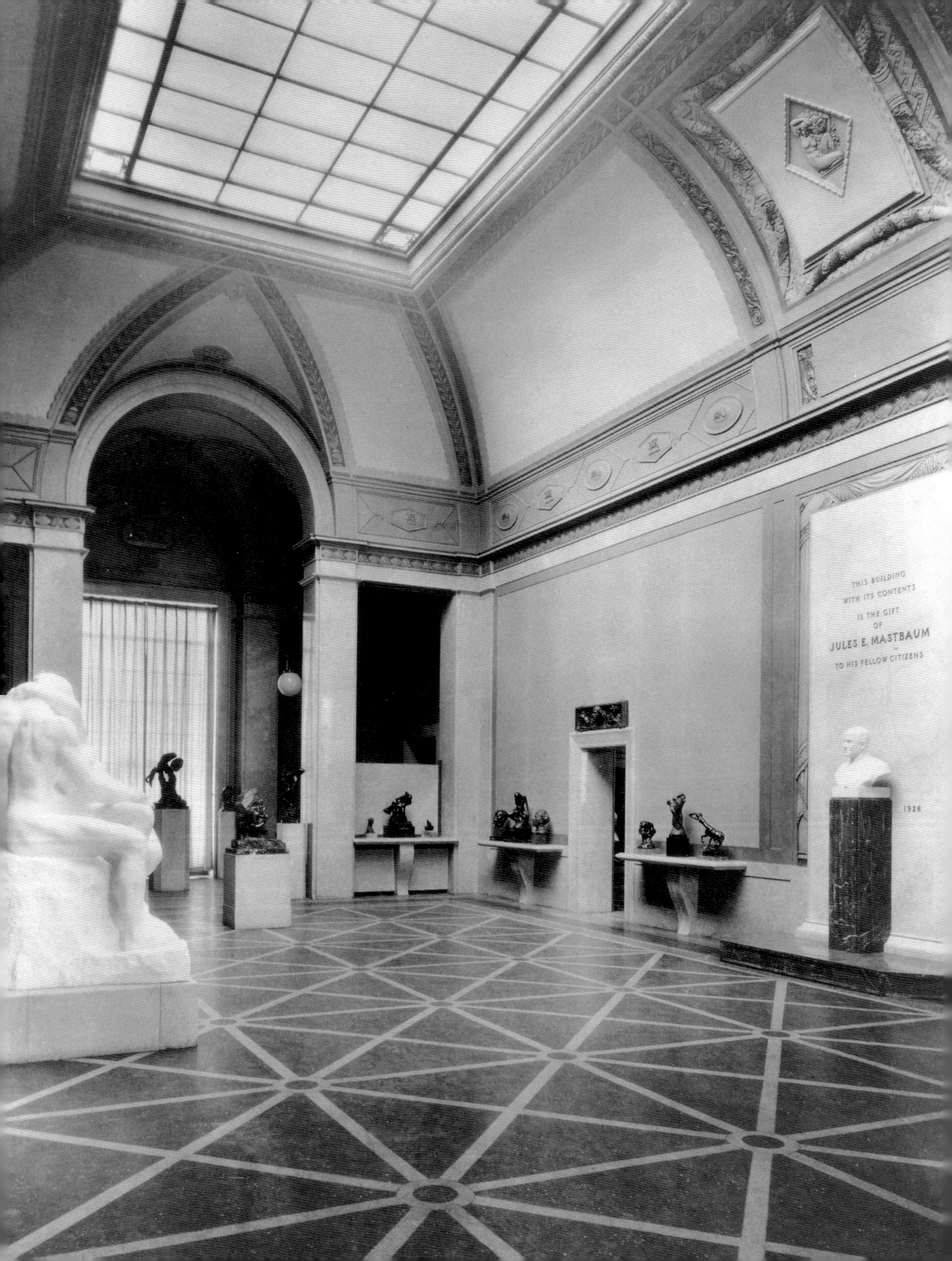
THIS BUILDING
WITH ITS CONTENTS
IS THE GIFT
OF
JULES E. MASTBAUM
TO HIS FELLOW CITIZENS
1926

COLLECTING WITH HIGH IDEALS AND ENJOYMENT

JULES AND ETTA MASTBAUM AND THE RODIN MUSEUM IN PHILADELPHIA

JENNIFER A. THOMPSON

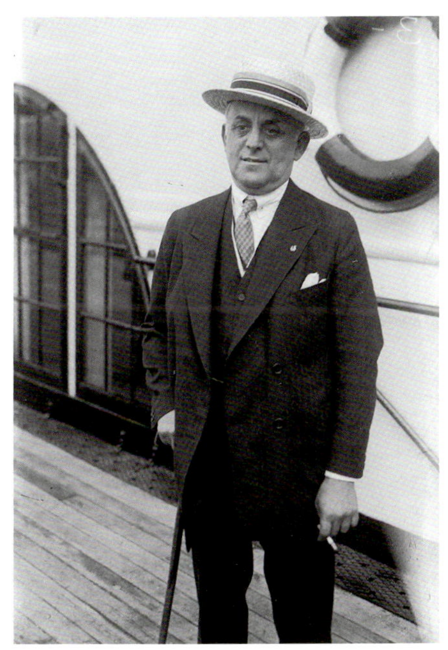

On September 16, 1924, Jules Mastbaum made his first visit to the Musée Rodin in Paris. Accompanied by the American painter Gilbert White and welcomed by the museum's director, Léonce Bénédite, the Philadelphia businessman was captivated by the sculptures he encountered there. He left with a small bronze in his pocket and a promise that seven more would be cast by the Rudier foundry and shipped to him in Philadelphia.[1] Over the next two years, Mastbaum's personal fascination with Rodin became public as he acquired hundreds of sculptures and drawings by the artist and turned his attention to creating a Rodin museum in Philadelphia, a project guided by, in his words, "high ideals and enjoyment."[2]

Jules Ephraim Mastbaum (1872–1926, fig. 6.1) was born in Philadelphia and attended local schools prior to studying at the Wharton School of Finance at the University of Pennsylvania. In 1904, he married Etta Wedell (1866–1953), whose mother, Rachel Lit, was one of the founders of Lit Brothers department store, where Etta served as personnel director before her marriage.[3] Following an early career with Gimbel Brothers department store, Mastbaum and his brother Stanley formed a real estate company that branched into the burgeoning motion picture business around 1905. After Stanley's untimely death in 1918, Mastbaum ran the business—renamed the Stanley Company of America—with acumen, demonstrating a talent for mergers and delivering quality entertainment. By 1926, the Stanley Company owned more than 250 cinemas in Pennsylvania, New Jersey, New York, Maryland, and Delaware.[4] Stanley Theatres were well regarded for their lavish interiors, comfortable seats, air conditioning, and full orchestras that accompanied the latest silent films from First National Pictures. Contemplating a European expansion, Mastbaum traveled with his wife Etta to Paris in 1924, taking in the Olympic Games and visiting the Musée Rodin in the days before his departure.[5]

It was likely not Mastbaum's first encounter with Rodin's work; he may have seen the artist's exhibition at the Pavillon de l'Alma in 1900 (see fig. 1.8), when he was in Paris as a buyer for Gimbel's.[6] Philadelphia newspapers regularly covered the sculptor's work from 1890 onward, and Mastbaum could see Rodins at the Pennsylvania Academy of the Fine Arts, which acquired a plaster *Age of Bronze* (see fig. 6.8) in 1898 and a marble *Danaid* (original model 1885, enlarged 1889, carved before 1902, now Philadelphia Museum of Art), in 1902 and exhibited forty-six drawings by the artist in 1908.[7] Three works belonging to Philadelphia lawyer John G. Johnson (cf. cat. 10) were on display in the collector's home on Broad Street in 1924. Mastbaum might also have spoken about Rodin with Samuel Stockton White III, a prize-winning bodybuilder who posed for Rodin's sculpture *American Athlete* in 1901–4 and later was a prominent Philadelphia businessman and member of Mastbaum's sporting club. The sculptor's studio also lured Philadelphia artists to Paris: Giuseppe Donato joined the atelier briefly in 1904, while Meta Vaux Warrick benefitted from Rodin's advice and support, exhibiting the work she did "in Paris under Rodin" at the Pennsylvania Museum and School of Industrial Art in January 1905.[8]

The winner of a school award for drawing and sketching, Mastbaum began collecting small French bronzes in 1922–23 with the help of artist Albert Rosenthal.[9] The emotions and human stories Mastbaum discovered in Rodin's sculptures in September 1924 profoundly affected him, perhaps because they spoke a language comparable to the drama, immediacy, and power of motion pictures. Indeed, the cinema magnate made a link between Rodin and the theater just ten days after visiting the Musée Rodin. Announcing to reporters on his arrival in New York that he had ordered seven Rodin bronzes, Mastbaum added: "When they arrive in this country—and I expect they will be here in about two months—I shall have them displayed publicly at the Stanley Theatre and later I may distribute them in various Stanley houses."[10]

Mastbaum followed this purchase in February 1925 with an order for nineteen bronzes, "for the theatres and my home," including *The Hand of God* (original model 1898, cast 1925; cf. cat. 22), *Adam* (modeled 1880–81, cast 1925), and portraits of Jules Dalou (original model 1883, cast 1925), George Bernard Shaw (original model 1906, cast 1926), and Victor Hugo (original model 1883, cast 1925).[11] Over the summer, Mastbaum ordered full-size versions of the *Monument to the Burghers of Calais* (original model 1884–95, cast 1919–21; cf. fig. 1.5), *The Thinker* (original model 1880–81, enlarged 1902–4, cast 1919; cf. cat. 69), and *The Age of Bronze* (original model 1875–77, cast 1925; cf. cat. 87), and he and his family made their first visit to Rodin's grave and home at Meudon, a place that moved them deeply (fig. 6.2). Mastbaum cabled Philadelphia with the news that he had acquired ninety-eight Rodins for display at the upcoming Sesquicentennial Exposition and hinted that the collection would be given to the city one day.[12]

The decision to create an American museum devoted to Rodin was bolstered in December 1925 when Mastbaum made his largest and most ambitious acquisition: *The Gates of Hell* (cf. fig. 8.1). The collector had explored the idea of acquiring the monumental bronze doors—previously known only in plaster—a year earlier, when discussion of the *Gates* had consumed his correspondence. Nevertheless, he waited until the last minute to place his order; he had been offered *The Gates of Hell* for 700,000 francs with the understanding that the price would rise to a million francs in 1926. Mastbaum was disappointed to learn that it would take two years to cast and ship the doors, the capstone of his collection, to Philadelphia.[13]

While over one hundred pieces from Mastbaum's collection were on view at the Sesquicentennial from June to December 1926 (fig. 5.3), he announced his intention to construct a Rodin museum on the Benjamin Franklin Parkway,

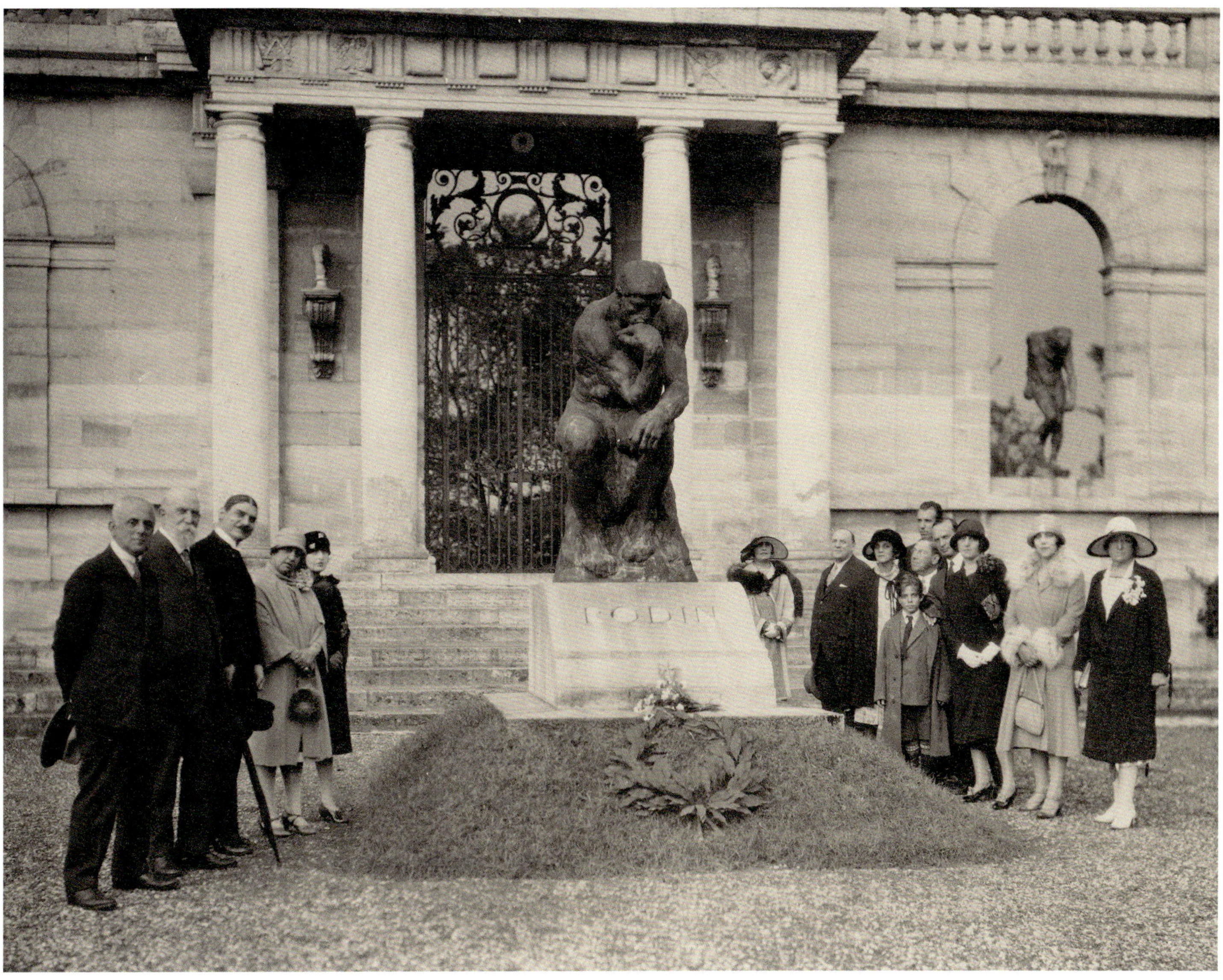

FIG. 6.2

Jules Mastbaum, Arthur Chassériau, Georges Grappe, Etta Wedell Mastbaum, and members of the Mastbaum family in front of Rodin's grave at Meudon, July 1926. Archives du musée Rodin, Paris. PH. 6633.

Philadelphia's Champs Élysées. The two French architects hired for the project, Jacques Gréber and Paul Philippe Cret, had been involved in planning the tree-lined parkway (fig. 6.4) extending from City Hall to the Philadelphia Museum of Art, and Cret had just designed galleries for the Detroit Institute of Arts and Albert Barnes.[14]

As conceived by Gréber, Cret, and Mastbaum, the museum was to be an ensemble of architecture, gardens, and sculpture. Mastbaum stipulated that the entrance should faithfully recreate Rodin's grave at Meudon, where the artist was buried under a cast of *The Thinker* in front of reassembled fragments from the late seventeenth-century Château d'Issy-les-Moulineaux (fig. 6.5). Passing through this proscenium-like structure, visitors would encounter a sculpture-filled garden containing a reflecting pool and a museum building with *The Gates of Hell* installed in its central portico (fig. 6.6). Beaux-Arts principles of symmetry and clarity would dominate the building's light-filled interior, which was divided into elegant galleries decorated with ornamental plasterwork and richly patterned terrazzo floors (fig. 6.7).

With architectural plans underway, Mastbaum focused on building a museum-worthy collection. From the Musée Rodin, which was authorized by the artist to oversee the production of new bronze casts, Mastbaum acquired several

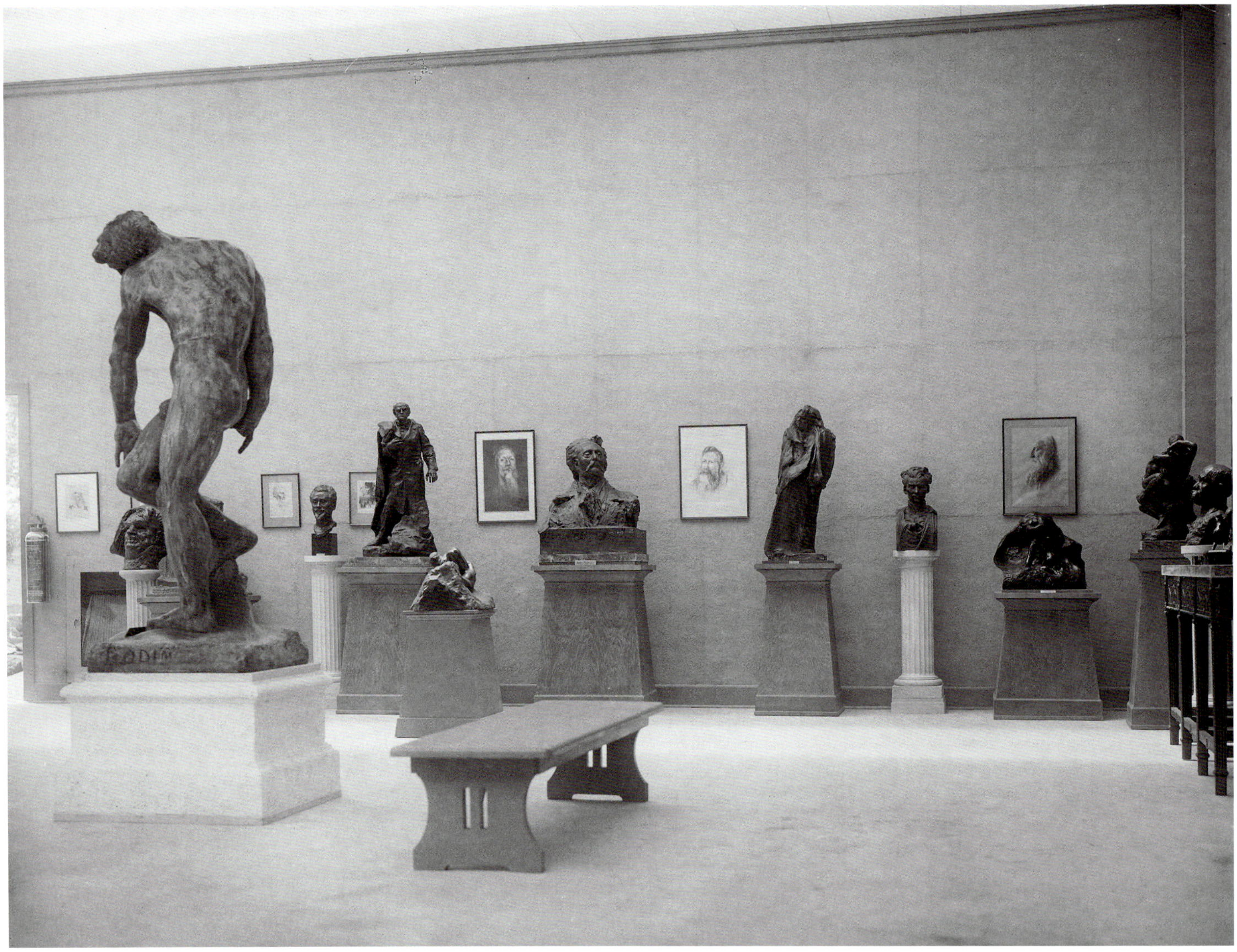

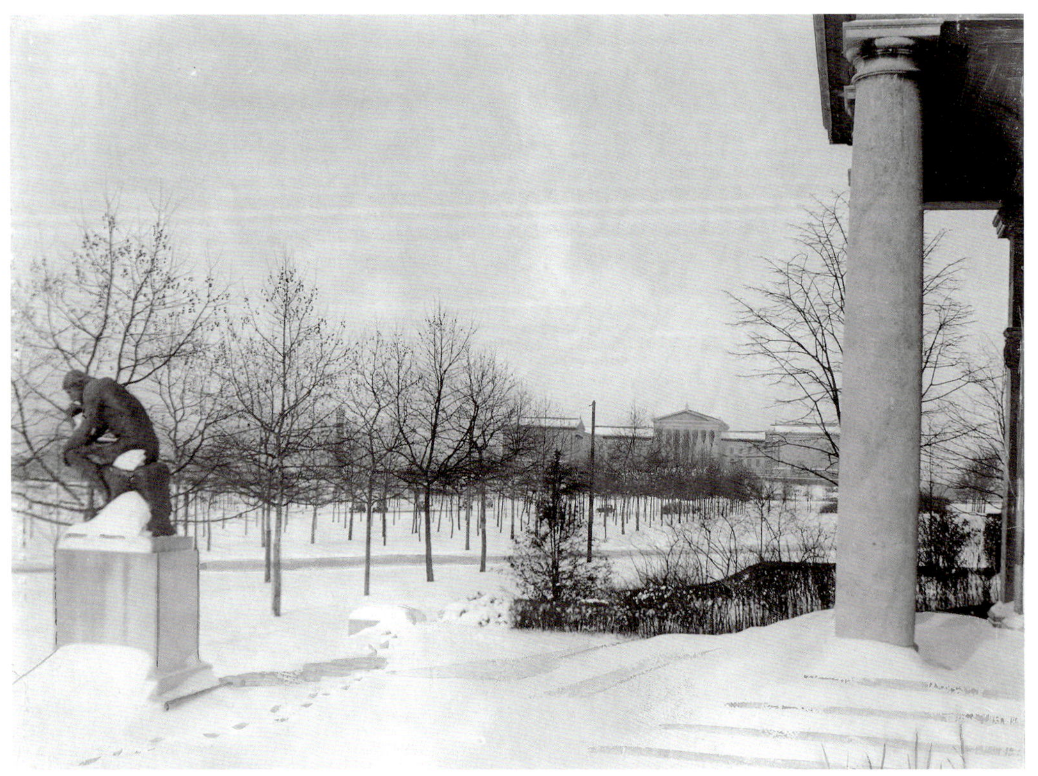

FIG. 6.3
The Jules E. Mastbaum Collection in
Gallery 25 of the Sesquicentennial
Exposition, Philadelphia, June–December
1926. Photograph by W. Coulbourn
Brown. Curatorial files, Department
of European Painting and Sculpture,
Philadelphia Museum of Art.

FIG. 6.4
The Thinker at the entrance to the Rodin
Museum on the Benjamin Franklin
Parkway, 1930s. Temple University
Library, Urban Archives, Philadelphia.

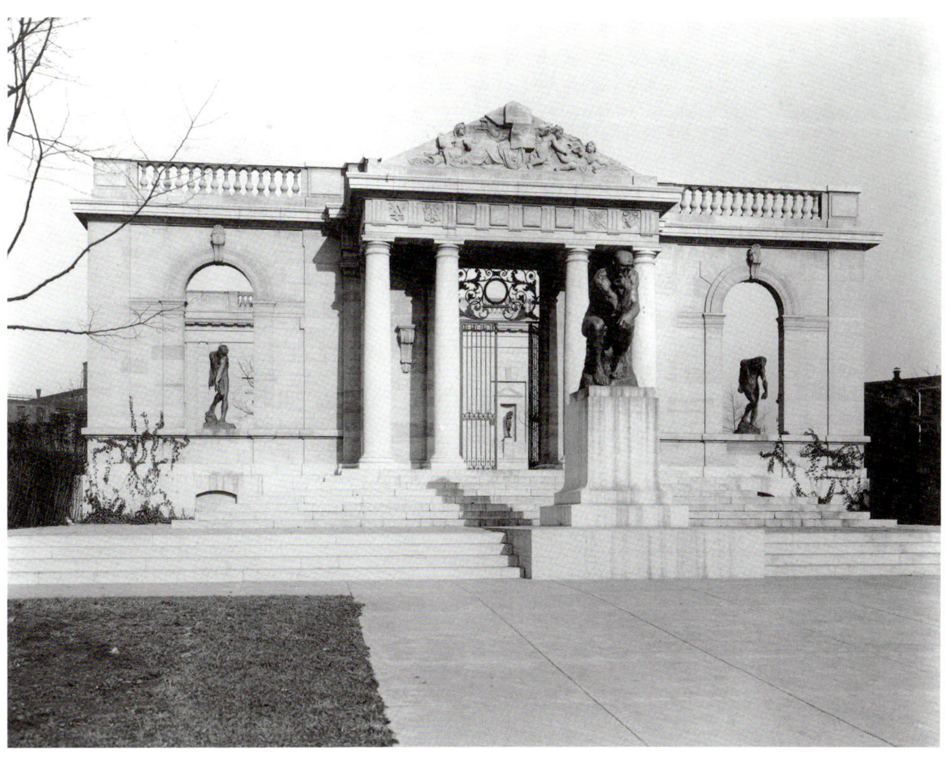

FIG. 6.5

Entrance to the Rodin Museum, Philadelphia, c. 1930. Photographs, Rodin Museum Records, Library and Archives, Philadelphia Museum of Art.

FIG. 6.6

Exterior of the Rodin Museum, Philadelphia, c. 1930. Photographs, Rodin Museum Records, Library and Archives, Philadelphia Museum of Art.

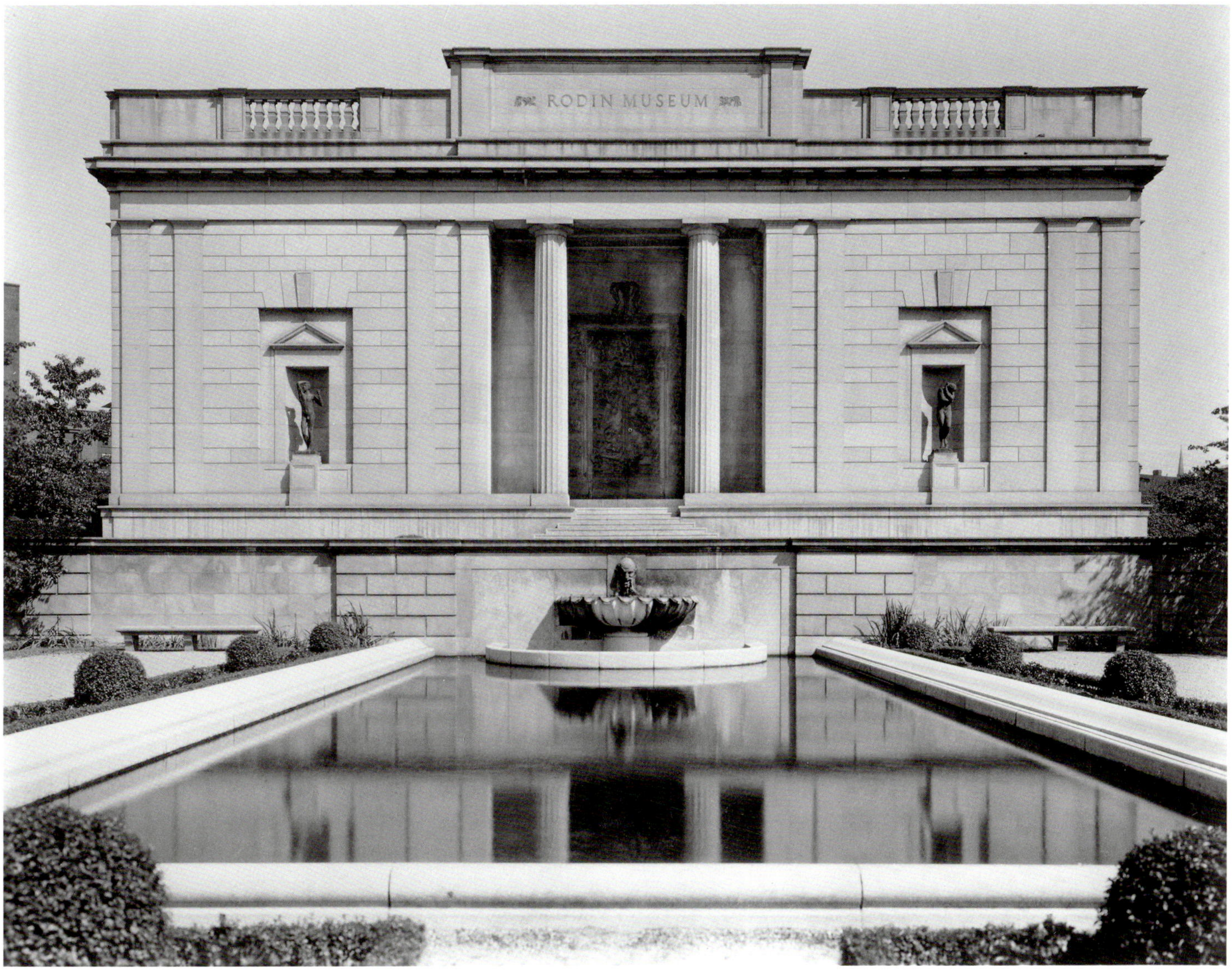

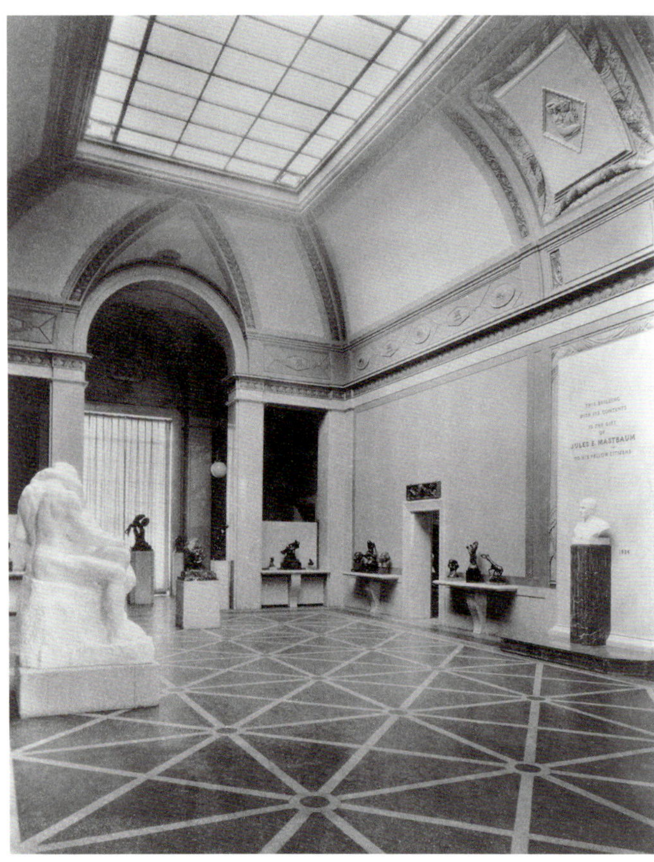
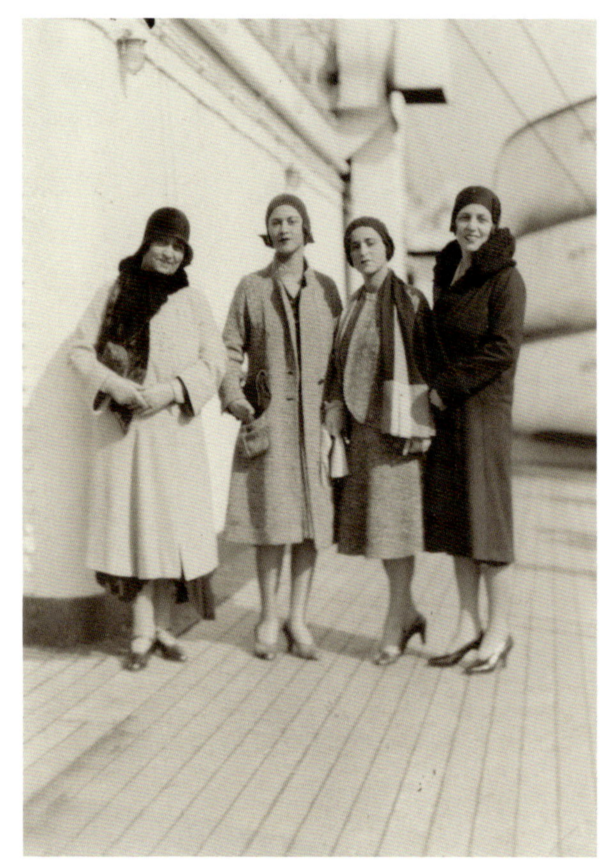

Interior of the Rodin Museum, Philadelphia, with Henri Gréber's copy of *The Kiss* opposite his marble memorial bust of Jules Mastbaum, c. 1930. Photographs, Rodin Museum Records, Library and Archives, Philadelphia Museum of Art.

Etta Wedell Mastbaum with her daughters Elizabeth, Louisette, and Margery on the SS *Leviathan*, October 10, 1929. The George D. McDowell Philadelphia Evening Bulletin Photographs, Temple University Library.

unique works, among them *The Hand of the Devil Holding Woman* (original model 1903, cast 1925), *Two Hands* (original model 1904, cast 1925), and a pâte-de-verre portrait of Rodin's partner, Rose Beuret (cat. 74). These sculptures, probably suggested by the Musée Rodin, broadened the collection beyond Rodin's best-known and iconic works, though the Philadelphian still shied away from the sculptor's bolder and more erotically charged pieces. Mastbaum was convinced that his museum needed plasters to explain Rodin's working process, and in this he was undoubtedly inspired by the Metropolitan Museum of Art.[15] Through conversations with Bénédite, Mastbaum understood that several plasters would be shipped with the bronzes "as a mark of appreciation for my purchases."[16] Bénédite's successor, Georges Grappe, was surprised to learn of these promises and worked to convince the museum's Board of Governors to approve them. In spring 1926, Grappe and Mastbaum came to an amicable agreement in which the Musée Rodin presented six works as gifts to the Philadelphia museum.[17]

Mastbaum also worked with the F. & J. Tempelaere Gallery and enlisted the help of Judith Cladel and Loïe Fuller to purchase marbles, plasters, drawings, and ephemera including photographs, books, and letters. With their assistance, he bought marbles of *Andromeda* (original model 1885, carved 1886) and *Minerva* (original model c. 1898, carved 1901), an early sketchbook, trial proofs for *Les Cathédrales de France*, and hundreds of drawings.[18] One of the last pieces Mastbaum sought was a large marble by Rodin. Frustrated by their scarcity on the art market, he approached Grappe in August 1926 with a request to copy *The Kiss* (carved 1888–98, Musée Rodin, Paris, cf. cat. 68), arguing that the architects Gréber and Cret felt a large marble "necessary for the interior to our Museum and the 'Le Baiser' . . . is perhaps Rodin's finest group in marble."[19] Knowing Jules and Etta Mastbaum's fondness for the piece, the Paris museum granted permission, provided that the copy, carved by Henri Gréber (visible in fig. 6.7), be labeled as such.

With the collection nearly complete and designs finalized, Mastbaum was planning a ground-breaking ceremony when he died on December 7, 1926, from complications following abdominal surgery. Museum plans were halted while the family and city mourned, but in 1927, Mastbaum's widow and his three daughters (fig. 6.8) resolved to continue the project. Etta went to Paris to make the final payment for *The Gates of Hell* and fulfill Mastbaum's promise to contribute funds toward a new exhibition building at Meudon. In return, she persuaded the Paris museum to present twenty-two plasters to Philadelphia (among them, cats. 72, 73), works she and her advisors believed had been promised to her husband.[20]

The Rodin museum envisioned by Mastbaum formally opened on November 29, 1929, with a ceremony involving 2,000 guests. New York Mayor James Walker, a close friend, spoke at the event and described Mastbaum's endeavor:

> As he loved Rodin, he was unhappy until he could share this stupendous joy in Rodin's work. There were those who, because of limited circumstances, would never have learned of the works of Rodin if they had remained over there in France. And Mr. Mastbaum felt that because there were some who could not go abroad to see these things he would bring Rodin to them here.[21]

Honoring her contributions to French art and substantial efforts to realize the museum, French Ambassador Paul Claudel presented Etta Mastbaum with the prestigious Legion d'Honneur at the museum's opening. The award held especial significance, since Etta had given the building and its contents to the city on the eve of the museum's inauguration.[22] In its first year, the museum welcomed nearly 400,000 visitors, and it continues to realize the Mastbaums' goal of making Rodin's work "freely available for the study and enjoyment" of their fellow citizens today.[23]

NOTES

1. For accounts of this visit, see Jules Mastbaum to Oscar Stern, September 27, 1924, Rodin Museum Records, Philadelphia Museum of Art (PMA) Library and Archives; and Ruth Butler, "Rodin's Legacy: Bronzes for the World," in *Naissance de la modernité: Mélanges offerts à Jacques Vilain*, ed. Henry-Claude Cousseau, Christina Buley-Uribe, and Véronique Mattiussi (Paris: Relief, 2010), 211.

2. Mastbaum to Stern, February 18, 1926, Rodin Museum Records, PMA Library and Archives.

3. For more on the history of Lit Brothers and the Lit and Wedell families, see Steve Minor, "Lit Brothers Building (1891), view04, 701–739 Market St, Philadelphia, PA, USA," accessed December 9, 2021, http://www.flickr.com/photos/sminor/33706336433.

4. Jennifer A. Thompson, *Rodin Museum, Philadelphia* (Philadelphia: Philadelphia Museum of Art, 2012), 13–21.

5. "Jules Mastbaum to Build Picture Palace in Paris," *Jewish Exponent*, September 19, 1924, 17.

6. *Philadelphia Inquirer*, June 17, 1900, 11.

7. *Philadelphia Inquirer*, November 22, 1908, 2.

8. *Philadelphia Inquirer*, October 23, 1904, 1; and Renée Ater, *Remaking Race and History: The Sculpture of Meta Warrick Fuller* (Berkeley: University of California Press, 2011), 18–23.

9. *Philadelphia Evening Bulletin*, December 9, 1926, and handwritten reminiscences, Albert Rosenthal, Papers, Archives of American Art.

10. "Jules E. Mastbaum Returns from Foreign Trip," *Jewish Exponent*, September 26, 1924.

11. Mastbaum to Stern, February 6, 1925, Rodin Museum Records, PMA Library and Archives. Except where otherwise indicated, all works mentioned throughout this essay are presently in the collection of the Rodin Museum, Philadelphia.

12. "Jules E. Mastbaum Purchases 98 Rodins," *Jewish Exponent*, September 25, 1925.

13. In 1920, Japanese collector Kojiro Matsukata placed an order for *The Gates of Hell*, but high import duties prohibited him from taking possession of it until 1959. Unknowingly, Mastbaum obtained some casts originally intended for Matsukata. Akiko Mabuchi, "Rodin's Gates of Hell: The First Four Bronzes and Their Destinies," *The Matsukata Collection: A One-Hundred-Year Odyssey*, exh. cat. (Tokyo: National Museum of Western Art, 2019), 308–17.

14. For more on the architectural collaboration, see David Brownlee, *Building the City Beautiful: The Benjamin Franklin Parkway and the Philadelphia Museum of Art* (Philadelphia: Philadelphia Museum of Art, 1989), 77–81.

15. See Elyse Nelson's essay in this volume, "Making the 'Little Rodin Gallery': The Rodin Collection at the Met."

16. Mastbaum to Stern, February 1, 1926, Rodin Museum Records, PMA Library and Archives.

17. Georges Grappe to Jules Mastbaum, April 12,

1926, Rodin Museum Records, PMA Library and Archives; and Antoinette Le Normand-Romain, *Rodin et le bronze: Catalogue des œuvres conservées au musée Rodin / The Bronzes of Rodin: Catalogue of Works in the Musée Rodin*, 2 vols. (Paris: Éditions du musée Rodin / Réunion des musées nationaux, 2007), 1:42.

18. To Mastbaum's disappointment, some of the drawings would prove to be forgeries. Mastbaum to Stern, February 18, 1926, Rodin Museum Records, PMA Library and Archives.

19. Mastbaum to Grappe, August 30, 1926, Archives du musée Rodin.

20. Adeline Foulon, "La donation de Jules Mastbaum au musée Rodin de Meudon" (MA thesis, Université Paris 1 Panthéon-Sorbonne, 2017), 82–88, 120–21.

21. "Mastbaum Lauded as Rodin Museum Is Given to Phila," *Philadelphia Inquirer*, November 30, 1929.

22. On the same day, the city asked the Philadelphia Museum of Art to administer the Rodin Museum, an arrangement that continues today.

23. Mastbaum to Commissioners of Fairmount Park, April 15, 1926, Rodin Museum Records, PMA Library and Archives.

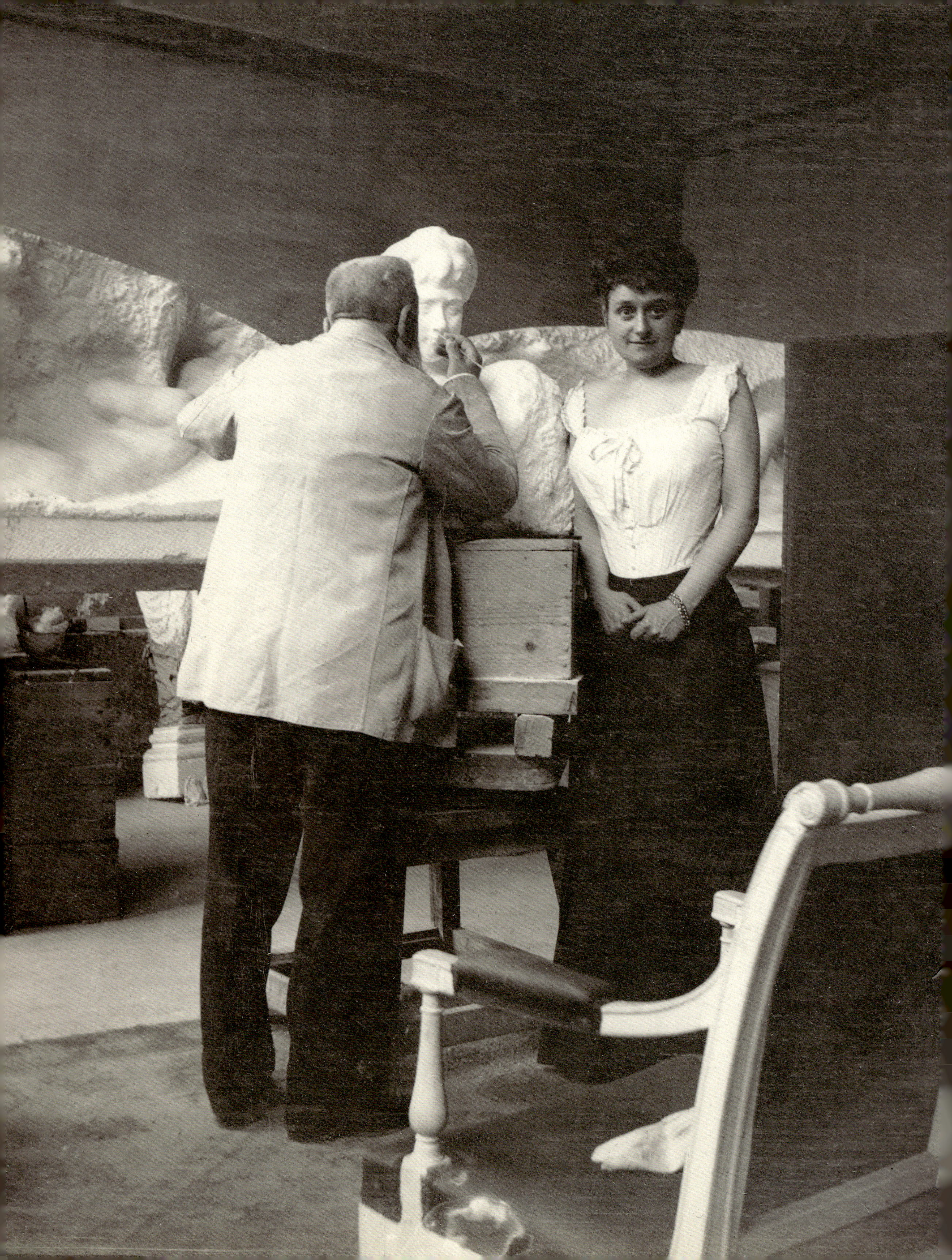

SCULPTURE AT THE NATIONAL GALLERY OF ART

FROM ANDREW W. MELLON TO KATHERINE SENEY SIMPSON TO TODAY

C. D. DICKERSON III

The National Gallery of Art was barely a year old when Katherine (Kate) Seney Simpson (fig. 7.1), in the spring of 1942, agreed to give her formidable collection of works by Auguste Rodin to the nation. It was an unexpected decision in many ways. Until that moment, her loyalties as a museum patron had run decisively toward the Metropolitan Museum of Art in her native New York. There are no indications at all that she had strong connections with Washington, DC. The gallery was also an unusual choice in that its collection of sculpture was still extremely young — decades away from achieving the world-class stature it enjoys today. Among the many holes needing to be filled was nineteenth-century French sculpture, of which there was not a single example in 1942. The gallery's first director, David E. Finley, was quick to help Simpson see the opportunity in the absence: he made the case that while her gift would be largely duplicative at the Met, it would be transformative for the gallery, which was still struggling to show its commitment to collecting sculpture. Simpson's gift would prove an important part of why this all changed over the next couple of years.

Andrew W. Mellon (fig. 7.2) founded the National Gallery of Art in 1935.[1] According to his original vision for the nation's art museum, there was to be no sculpture — only paintings. This reflected his personal priorities as a collector. Born in Pittsburgh in 1855, he had turned to collecting in middle age after becoming wildly successful as a businessman. From the start, his passion was for paintings. Unsurprisingly, his preference in museums was for pure picture galleries like the National Gallery in London, one of his favorite places to relax while serving as the US ambassador to England between 1932 and 1933. As he began to contemplate "his" gallery in Washington, he looked to England's as his model. Over a two-year period, however — between 1935 and his death in 1937 — his attitudes changed. He came to relax his objections

FIG. 7.1

Ouida B. Grant (American, 1880–1983), *Mrs. Katherine Seney Simpson Posing for Rodin in His Studio*, 1902 (detail). Collodion aristotype proof, 3 9/16 × 3 9/16 in. (9 × 9 cm). Musée Rodin, Paris. Ph. 678.

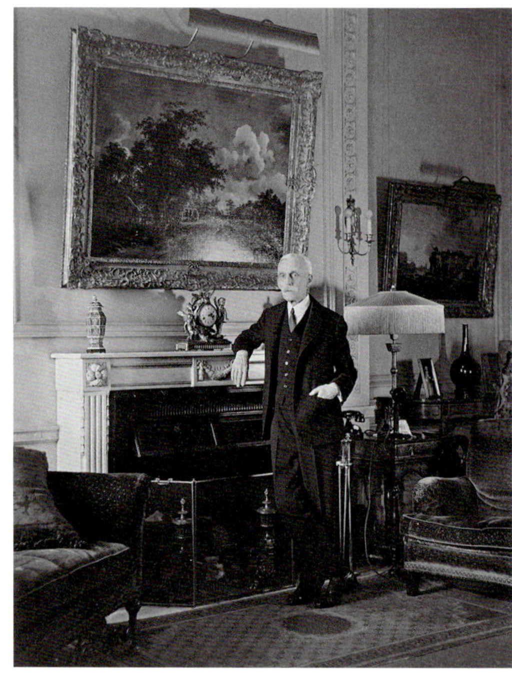

Andrew W. Mellon in his apartment at
1785 Massachusetts Avenue, NW,
Washington, DC, in 1928. National Gallery
of Art, Washington, DC, Gallery Archives.

FIG. 7.3

View of rotunda, National Gallery of Art,
Washington, DC, with bronze *Mercury* after
Giambologna (Flemish, 1529–1608),
c. 1780 / c. 1850. National Gallery of Art,
Washington, DC. Andrew W. Mellon
Collection, 1937.1.131.

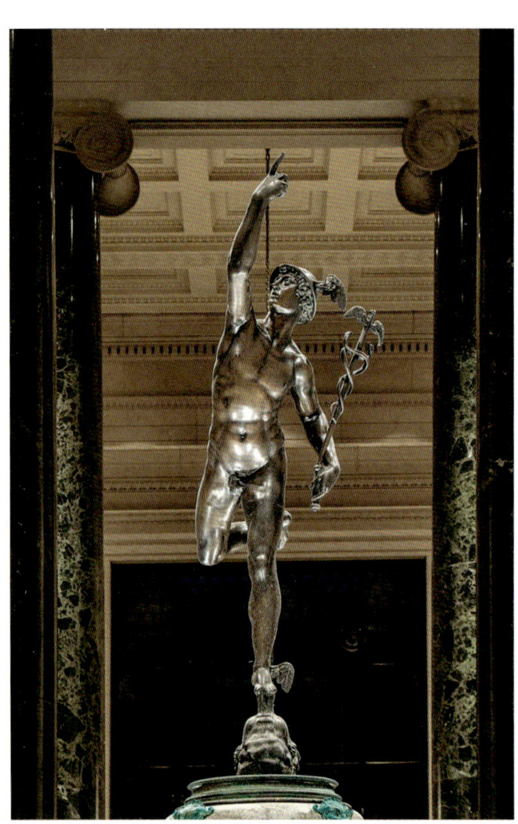

to sculpture, which he ultimately admitted into the gallery's collecting program.

In January 1935, Mellon acquired his first work of sculpture, a marble relief of the Madonna and Child then attributed to the Florentine artist Agostino di Duccio. What prompted the purchase is unclear. He may have been attracted to the work because of its distinguished provenance; it was formerly owned by the financier John Pierpont Morgan, whose collection had drawn Mellon's interest when it was on view at the Met in 1913. Almost two years would pass before Mellon purchased any more sculptures—this time a group of twenty from the London-based dealer Joseph Duveen. The sudden acquisition of so many almost certainly reflected where the designs for the gallery's building stood in early 1936. Mellon's chosen architect, John Russell Pope, was convinced that the interior should be organized around several monumental spaces, including the domed rotunda. He planned for these spaces to be filled with sculpture.[2] When Mellon learned of Pope's intentions, he must have expressed some alarm: Where were all those sculptures going to come from?

An important part of the answer would soon reveal itself. While in London that summer, Mellon visited Duveen, with whom he had a longstanding relationship. Duveen told him about a major group of Italian Renaissance paintings and sculptures that he had recently secured from the Parisian collector Gustave Dreyfus. Because the works had already been shipped to New York, Mellon agreed to see them in the fall, a visit he was forced to postpone due to illness. In his place, he sent Finley, who was instructed to select the best and have them sent to Washington. By October, twenty-four paintings and twenty sculptures had been installed in the apartment beneath Mellon's on Massachusetts Avenue. On December 16, he agreed to buy them all, bringing his collection of sculpture to twenty-one works.

Three of the newly acquired sculptures could not have been better chosen for the vast interior spaces that Pope had designed. A bronze version of Giambologna's *Mercury*, now known to be a later cast, would become the focal point of the rotunda (fig. 7.3). Two other life-size bronzes, a Venus and a Bacchus, later discovered to have come from a princely villa near Milan, would become the centerpieces of the west sculpture hall. Mellon's death on August 27, 1937—just a week after the gallery's groundbreaking—meant he was never able to appreciate how beautifully the sculptures blended with Pope's interior.

When the gallery opened to the public on March 17, 1941, more than forty sculptures were available for viewing. In addition to Mellon's twenty-one, the gallery's trustees acquired four works in 1940: a pair of French fountains for the east and west garden courts, as well as two monumental urns in the style of Clodion (Claude Michel) for the east

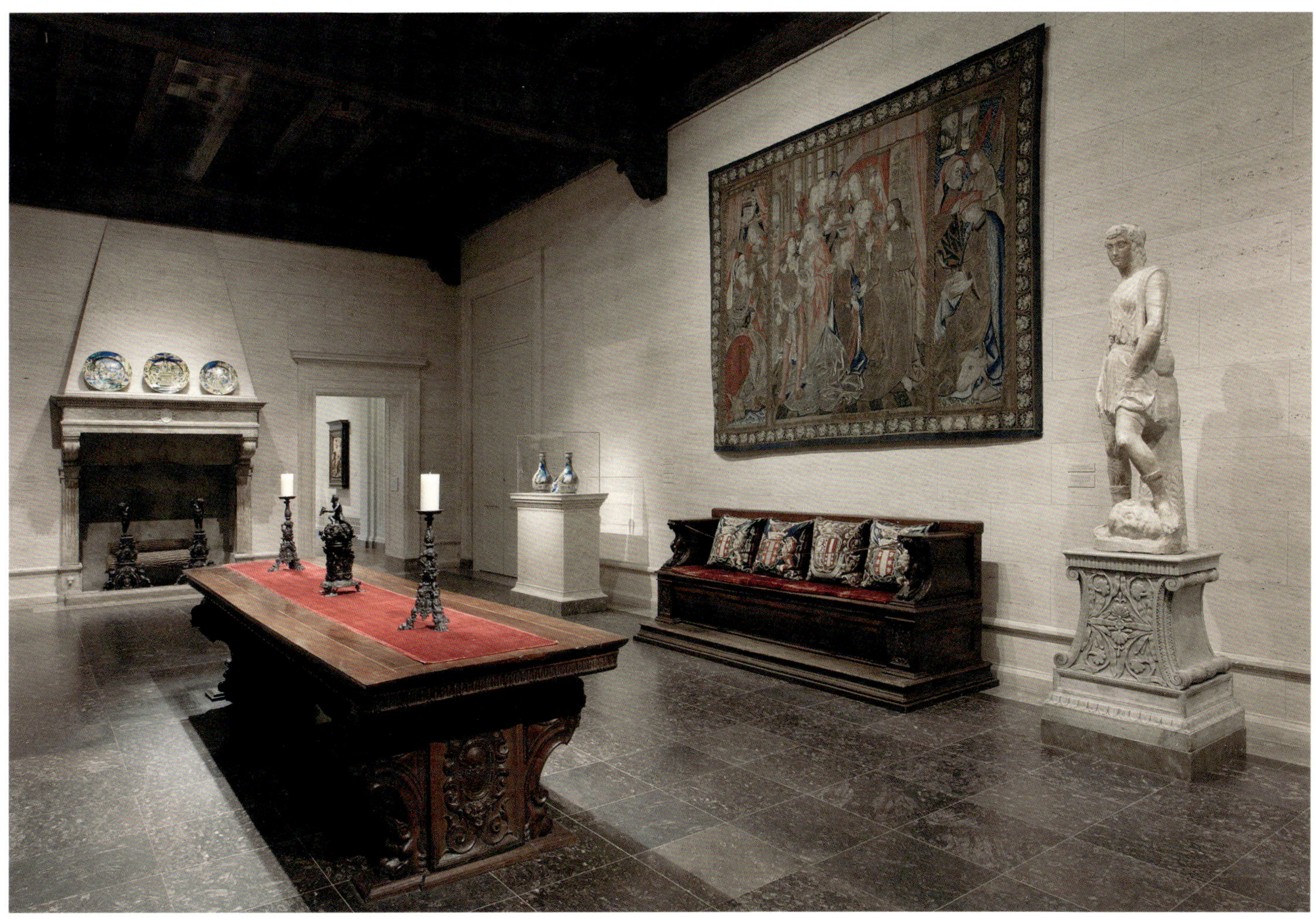

West Building ground-floor sculpture gallery (original "Widener" galleries), National Gallery of Art, Washington, DC.

sculpture hall. The remainder, which totaled nineteen, were gifts from Samuel H. Kress, all sculptures from the Italian Renaissance. Although Kress was a New Yorker and had given serious thoughts to founding his own museum, Finley had succeeded in convincing him to follow Mellon's example and donate his vast collection of Italian and French paintings, sculptures, and decorative arts to the nation. Kress signaled his agreement by transferring a first group of 133 works—including the nineteen sculptures—to the gallery in 1939.

As the gallery was being built, Finley and the trustees eyed a second major target: the collection assembled by Peter A. B. Widener and his son, Joseph, housed at Lynnewood Hall, their palatial home outside Philadelphia. Andrew Mellon had coveted the collection for years because of its fabulous riches in Renaissance and Baroque European paintings. He was less enamored with the collection's sculpture and decorative arts, even though many of the objects could not be rarer, as with the chalice made for Abbot Suger of Saint-Denis. Joseph Widener had pledged to his father that he would never break up the collection, which posed a quandary for Mellon, who was uneasy taking so many three-dimensional works, especially small ones. His son, Paul, eventually brokered a deal that brought the entire collection to the National Gallery of Art. It hinged on an agreement to install all the decorative arts and small sculptures on the museum's ground floor in special galleries meant to evoke Lynnewood Hall—thus sequestered from the paintings on the main floor (fig. 7.4). Although the gift had been finalized before the gallery's opening in 1941, legal complications prevented any of the art from arriving until the end of 1942.

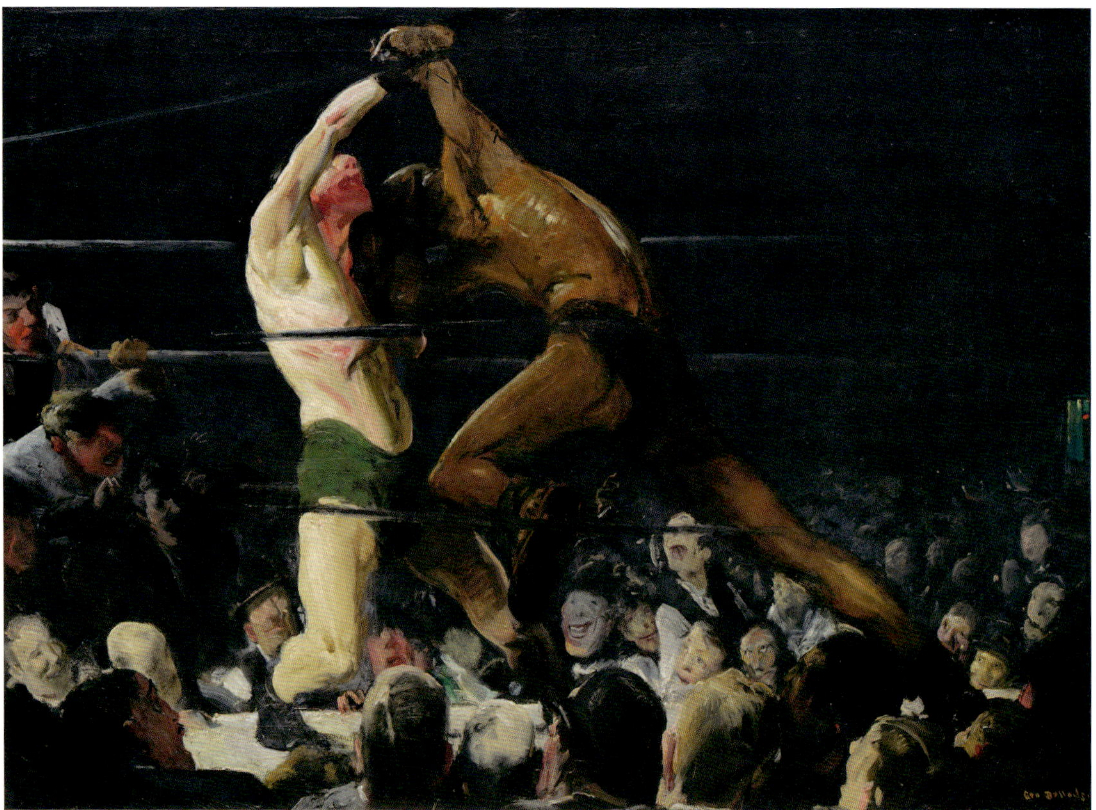

George Bellows (American, 1882–1925), *Both Members of This Club*, 1909. Oil on canvas, 45 ¼ × 63 ³⁄₁₆ in. (115 × 160.5 cm). National Gallery of Art, Washington, DC. Chester Dale Collection, 1944.13.1.

Thus, to summarize the situation at the moment when Kate Seney Simpson pledged her Rodins to the gallery in the spring of 1942, there were barely forty sculptures on view, as compared with the hundreds of paintings. These sculptures were almost uniformly from the Italian Renaissance—nothing from later than the eighteenth century. Simpson is likely to have understood that, thanks to Kress and the Wideners, many more works of sculpture would be joining the collection in the years ahead, although still none that might suggest the gallery was prepared to make a true commitment to collecting nineteenth- or twentieth-century sculpture. She had to have known that her twenty-five Rodins would be decided outliers in a collection of sculpture that was as yet unabashedly "old master."

Furthermore, Simpson's Rodins would be entering a collection with no examples of painting from the same period. By the time of her gift, the gallery had made barely any inroads into nineteenth-century painting—let alone twentieth-century painting. The few exceptions were from the Wideners, including two landscapes by Camille Corot.[3] Although more and more nineteenth-century paintings would find their way into the collection from 1943 on, the great gifts of Impressionist and modern painting from Chester Dale and others were still well in the gallery's future.[4] This also points up another way the Rodins were radical: they were as close to modern art as the gallery would come with its collecting before 1944, when Dale donated George Bellows's *Both Members of This Club* (fig. 7.5), painted in 1909. Maybe the fact that the gallery had already accepted the Rodins, which dated to the same decade, played a role in encouraging Dale to give the painting. What is certain is that he resented the gallery's policy against collecting works by living artists—a policy he succeeded in overturning as an eventual trustee.

Whatever reservations Kate Seney Simpson might have had about the lack of appropriate company for her Rodins, she was able to put them aside and focus

Edgar Degas (French, 1834–1917), *Little Dancer Aged Fourteen*, 1878–81. Pigmented beeswax, clay, metal armature, rope, paintbrushes, human hair, silk and linen ribbon, cotton faille bodice, cotton and silk tutu, and linen slippers, on wooden base, 38 15/16 × 13 11/16 × 13 7/8 in. (98.9 × 34.7 × 35.2 cm). National Gallery of Art, Washington, DC. Collection of Mr. and Mrs. Paul Mellon, 1999.80.28.

on the exciting future they foretold for the gallery's sculpture collection. In a giant leap forward, the gallery received more than 1,400 works of sculpture from the Samuel H. Kress Foundation in 1957. Although roughly eighty-five percent were small bronzes, medals, and plaquettes from the Renaissance — one of the world's great collections of this material — there were also important examples of eighteenth- and early nineteenth-century French sculpture, which helped provide more of a context for the Rodins.[5]

Almost simultaneously, Paul Mellon was finalizing an acquisition that, in due course, would completely recalibrate where the gallery's strengths in sculpture lay — a shift in the direction of French Impressionism and the Rodins. On May 25, 1956, he purchased sixty-nine of Edgar Degas's original wax sculptures. The waxes had been presumed destroyed during the 1920s when Degas's heirs cast bronze copies of them. In fact, a large group had been saved, including the artist's unquestioned masterpiece as a sculptor, *Little Dancer Aged Fourteen* (fig. 7.6), which he exhibited in 1881 at the sixth Impressionist exhibition. In

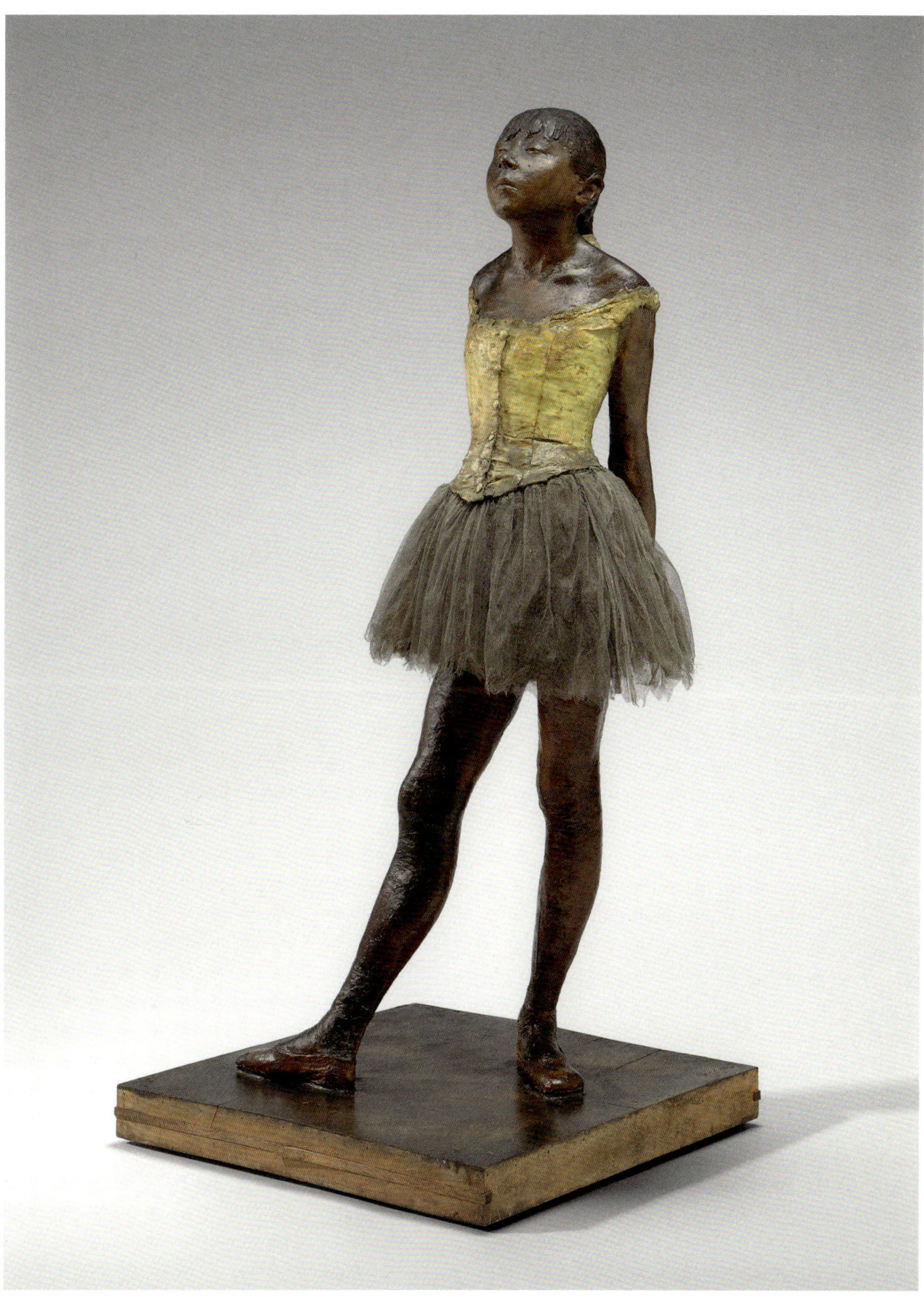

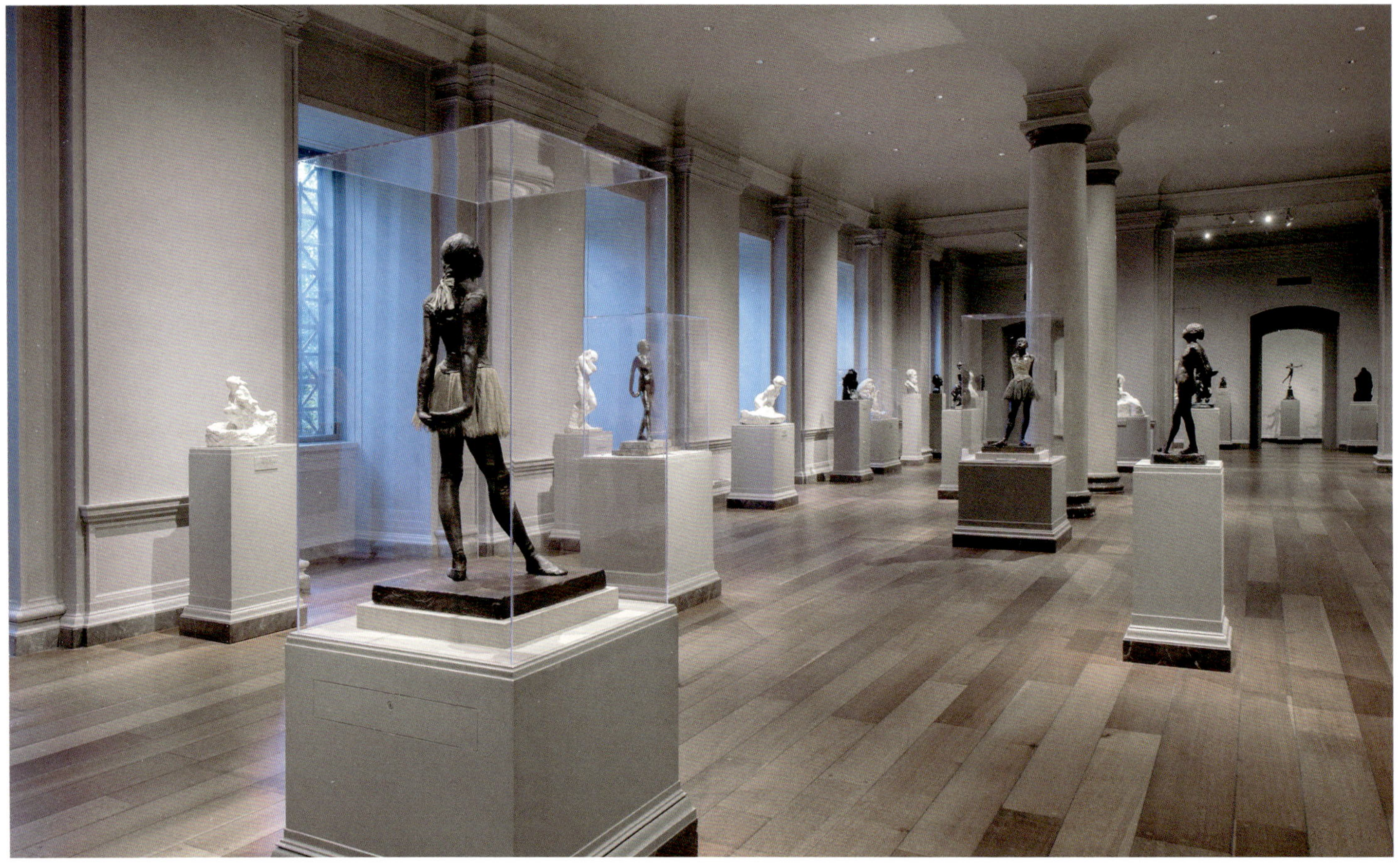

FIG. 7.7

West Building ground-floor sculpture gallery, National Gallery of Art, Washington, DC, with wax and plaster versions of Degas's *Little Dancer Aged Fourteen*, 1878–81, and sculptures by Rodin.

FIG. 7.8

Paul Gauguin (French, 1848–1903), *Eve*, 1890. Glazed ceramic, 23⅞ × 11 × 10¾ in. (60.6 × 27.9 × 27.3 cm). National Gallery of Art, Washington, DC. Ailsa Mellon Bruce Fund, 1970.30.1.

FIG. 7.9

Auguste Rodin (French, 1840–1917), *The Age of Bronze*, model 1875–76, cast 1898. Plaster, 70⅞ × 28 × 23 in. (180 × 71.1 × 58.4 cm). National Gallery of Art, Washington, DC. Gift of Iris and B. Gerald Cantor, in Honor of the 50th Anniversary of the National Gallery of Art, 1991.183.1.

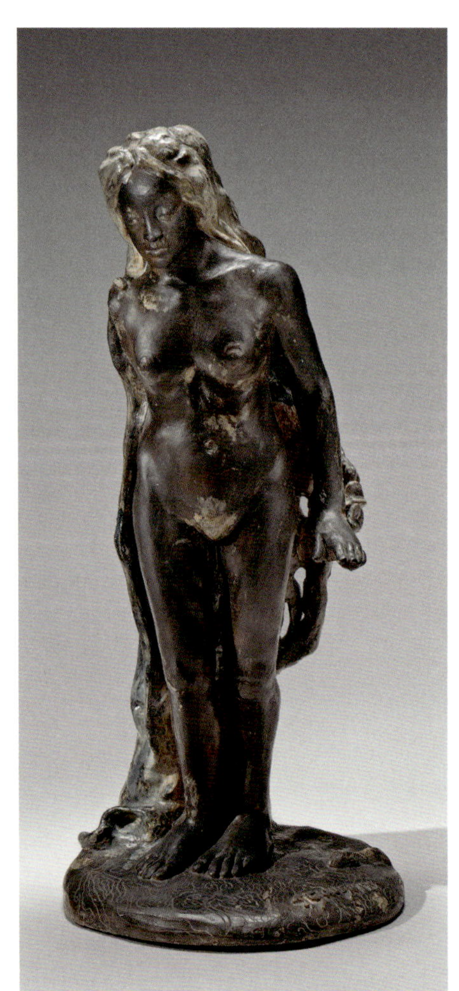

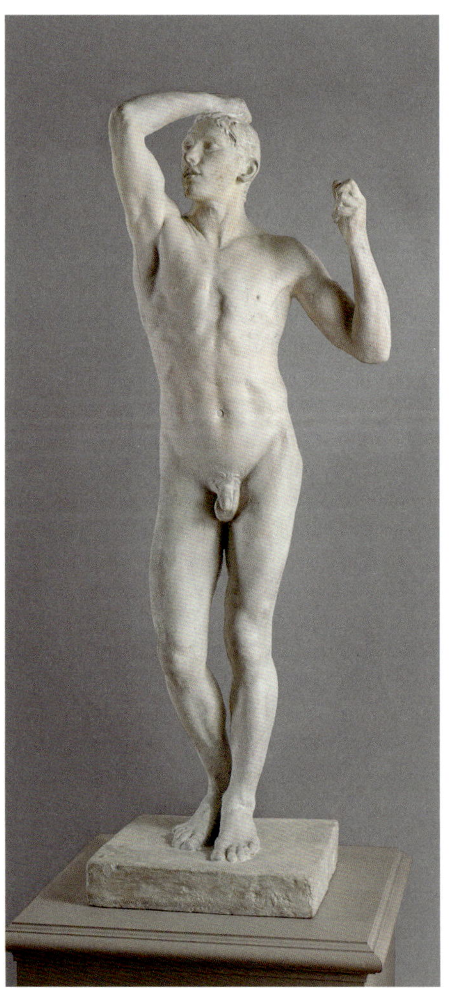

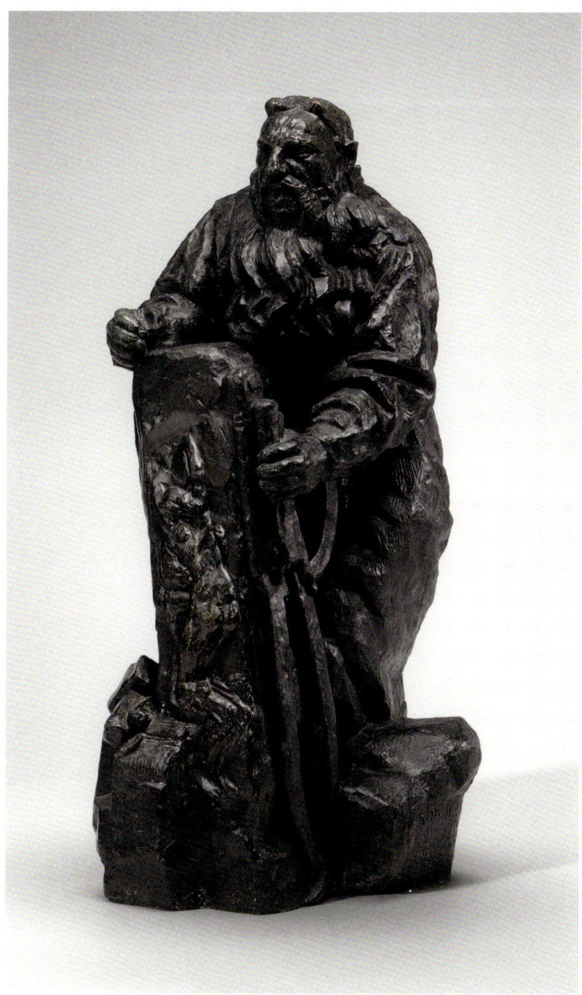

FIG. 7.10

Émile-Antoine Bourdelle (French, 1861–1929), *Rodin Working on His "Gates of Hell,"* model 1910, cast before 1929. Bronze, height: 27 in. (68.6 cm). National Gallery of Art, Washington, DC. Gift of Alfredo Halegua and Dr. Raquel Halegua, 2014.4.1.

1955, M. Knoedler and Company displayed the waxes in New York, where Mellon saw them and became transfixed. On being told they were for sale, he tasked the gallery's director, John Walker, with vetting their authenticity. No problems emerged, and Mellon made the purchase.

Eventually, he would donate the lion's share of the waxes to the gallery: in 1985, Mellon made a first gift of seventeen, with the remaining thirty-five coming as a bequest after his death in 1999. In addition to donating these works made during Degas's lifetime (including the *Little Dancer*), Mellon gave ten of the posthumous bronzes in three gifts, in 1985, 1995, and by bequest. Edith G. Rosenwald, wife of the distinguished collector Lessing J. Rosenwald, added two more bronzes in 1989, bringing the number of Degas works in the gallery's collection to sixty-four.

Today, these sculptures are paired with the Rodins in a sequence of spacious ground-floor galleries that are as important a place as any (certainly in the United States) for the study of French sculpture from the 1860s through the 1910s (fig. 7.7). This has not been lost on collectors, who have continued to augment the National Gallery of Art's holdings over the years. Among the many important French artists of the period whose sculptures can now be viewed at the gallery are Jules Dalou, Honoré Daumier, and Paul Gauguin (fig. 7.8). There have also been significant gifts of work by Rodin, including a plaster version of *The Age of Bronze* (fig. 7.9) from Iris and B. Gerald Cantor. Two important marbles by Rodin, *Eve* (original model c. 1881, carved 1890/91) and *Paolo and Francesca* (c. 1909), a massive relief, further enriched the gallery's holdings in 2014, coming with the collections of the Corcoran Gallery. Importantly, the gallery has continued to respect the scope of Simpson's collection by not admitting any Rodins that do not date to the artist's lifetime—a unique situation among the many repositories of Rodin in the United States. Now totaling fifty-eight works, the collection of Rodins has also gained depth with the purchase of two sculptures by (or made in collaboration with) his instructor Albert-Ernest Carrier-Belleuse, as well as with the 2014 gift by Alfredo and Raquel Halegua of a bronze image of Rodin sculpting *The Gates of Hell* (fig. 7.10) by one of his most trusted assistants, Émile-Antoine Bourdelle.

While Kate Seney Simpson had various motives for making her gift to the National Gallery of Art in 1942, above all, she wanted her collection to remain intact and to make a difference where it was going. How profound a difference that would be—surely one even greater than she would ever have imagined.

NOTES

1. For what follows concerning the history of the gallery's sculpture collection, I have drawn on my essay "The Sculpture Collection: Shaping a Vision, Expanding a Legacy," *National Gallery of Art Bulletin*, no. 56 (Spring 2017): 2–43. I am grateful to Anne Halpern and Alison Luchs for their assistance in piecing together how the collection developed.

2. The primary evidence is a perspectival drawing by Pope's partner, Otto R. Eggers, showing the west sculpture hall installed with many works of classicizing sculpture.

3. The two landscapes are *View near Epernon* (1850/60; 1942.9.13) and *The Forest of Coubron* (1872; 1942.9.12). There was a third Corot from the Wideners: *Corot's Studio: Woman Seated before an Easel, a Mandolin in Her Hand* (c. 1868; 1942.9.11).

4. Although Dale began lending his paintings to the gallery, as well as making occasional gifts, during the late 1940s, his bequest, which included 240 paintings and seven sculptures, came at his death in 1962. It was celebrated with an exhibition in 1965. For Dale's history with the gallery, see, most recently, Kimberly

Jones and Maygene Daniels, *The Chester Dale Collection* (Washington, DC: National Gallery of Art, 2009).

5. It should be noted that two of the most important nineteenth-century sculptures from the Kress collection had already been donated in 1943: Jean-Baptiste Carpeaux's *Neapolitan Fisherboy* (1863–67; 1943.4.89) and his *Girl with a Shell* (1863–67; 1943.4.90).

PART III
1950–2014

THE REVIVAL

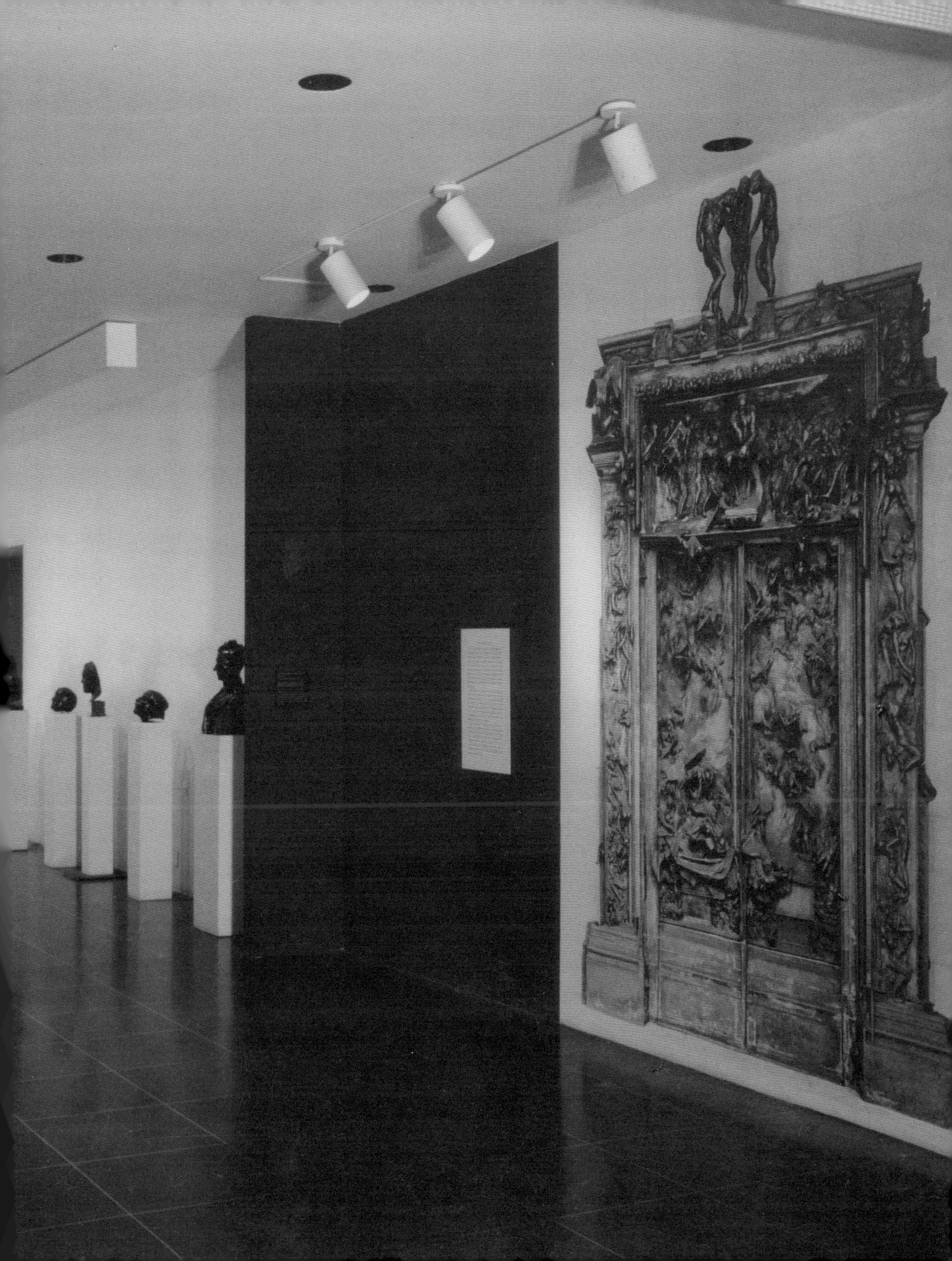

THE REVIVAL, 1950–2014

Following World War II, Auguste Rodin fell out of fashion among avant-garde artists and critics. Museums put most of his work in storage, and sculptor Jacques Lipchitz declared in 1954, "Rodin is still an unknown man."[1] Yet, on May 3, 1955, the Museum of Modern Art in New York (MoMA) acquired a bronze cast of the large *Balzac* (cat. 85) in memory of gallerist Curt Valentin, an enthusiastic admirer of Rodin who contributed to the artist's recognition through a series of exhibitions in his New York gallery.[2] As MoMA director Alfred Barr explained to Marcel Aubert, then director of the Musée Rodin in Paris, *Balzac* stood out to him "as one of the very great sculptures in the entire history of Western art."[3] A 1952–53 traveling exhibition organized by Andrew C. Ritchie, *Sculpture of the Twentieth Century*, had paved the road for Rodin's return to favor, declaring Rodin "the father of modern sculpture, and probably the greatest sculptor of our day."[4] Above all, Leo Steinberg and Albert E. Elsen led the rediscovery of Rodin. In 1963, MoMA tasked Elsen with organizing the artist's first large-scale US exhibition, while at the Charles E. Slatkin Galleries, Steinberg made Rodin the departure point for twentieth-century sculpture.[5]

Meanwhile, Cécile Goldscheider, director of the Musée Rodin, Paris, realized that championing the sculptor's modernity represented a key strategy to stimulate sales of bronzes, which financed the institution. She highlighted Rodin's most innovative works, of which few bronze casts had been made previously, particularly *The Walking Man* (cf. cat. 86) and *Monument to Balzac*. She also emphasized lesser-known aspects of Rodin's work, including preparatory studies; sketches, such as *Dance Movements* and *Nijinsky* (cf. cats. 90, 100); and fragments from the museum's storeroom, revealed in the exhibitions *Balzac et Rodin* (Musée Rodin, 1950) and *Rodin inconnu* (Louvre, 1962–63). Through Elsen, several of these bronzes entered American collections. Nearly all ten casts of the *Walking Man* made between 1958 and 1969 were acquired by American museums or collectors. At the same time, B. Gerald Cantor, founder, president, and director of Cantor Fitzgerald Incorporated, an innovative stock brokerage, developed a passion for Rodin. Strongly committed to the artist, he offered crucial support to the Musée Rodin in Paris and, with the help of Elsen, he founded the Iris & B. Gerald Cantor Center for Visual Arts at Stanford University in California, which serves as a companion to the Rodin Museum in Philadelphia. Like its East Coast precursor, the center's key work was *The Gates of Hell* (see fig. 8.1), the first in a new series of bronzes cast using the lost-wax process. Other American museums benefited from Cantor's generosity, as well. To the Metropolitan Museum of Art, New York, he donated the eleventh bronze cast of the *Monument to the Burghers of Calais*, made in 1989, and two Rodin terracottas in Greek and Renaissance styles (*Greek Sculpture* and *Renaissance Sculpture*), which the artist had given to Gertrude Vanderbilt Whitney in 1911. This period, essential in cementing the artist's status, culminated in the ambitious exhibition *Rodin Rediscovered* at the National Gallery of Art in Washington, DC, in 1981, organized and inspired by Elsen, whose goal was to present "the latest Rodin research."[6]

One final aspect of Rodin's work had, however, remained neglected: the marbles. The pretext was that they had been executed by assistants—as was always the case among sculptors in the late nineteenth century. Recently, scholars have recognized their importance, and the Rodin Museum in Philadelphia has acquired two marbles, while the J. Paul Getty Museum in Los Angeles purchased the second marble version of *Christ and Mary Magdalene* (cat. 101) in 2014.

American public and private collections have continued to incorporate more works by Rodin throughout the twentieth and twenty-first centuries: marbles; bronzes not previously shown or made exceptional by their prestigious provenance, such as the first bronze cast of *Ugolino and His Sons* (cat. 91), produced for painter Henri Lerolle and on loan at the Clark from an English collector; rare terracottas; and numerous drawings, which had sometimes vanished after leaving Rodin's studio. These works, which surfaced after remaining in the shadows for decades, have increased knowledge of Rodin and helped to distinguish authentic works from forgeries—especially in the case of the drawings, a task begun by art historian and curator Kirk Varnedoe.[7] The acquisition and exhibition history of the objects is also a significant area of research. By demonstrating the extent of the artist's influence, the histories of these works show that American collectors like Katherine Seney Simpson and John Woodruff Simpson or Loïe Fuller and, later, Jules Mastbaum and B. Gerald and Iris Cantor attained their goal: Rodin's reputation is fully established in the United States.

ALNR

1. Quoted by Leo Steinberg, "Rodin," in *Other Criteria: Confrontations with Twentieth-Century Art* [1972] (Chicago: University of Chicago Press, 2007), 324.
2. *From Rodin to Brancusi*, 1941; *Homage to Rodin*, 1942; *Auguste Rodin: Watercolors and Drawings*, 1946; *The Heritage of Rodin: An Exhibition Assembled in Honor of the Diamond Jubilee of the Philadelphia Museum of Art*, 1950; and the landmark *Auguste Rodin* (comprising forty-four sculptures and thirty-seven drawings), 1954–55, on view in New York before traveling to Minneapolis; Des Moines; Portland, Oregon; Santa Barbara, California; St. Louis; and Cincinnati.
3. Alfred Barr to Marcel Aubert, March 8, 1954, Archives du musée Rodin, Paris.
4. Andrew C. Ritchie, *Sculpture of the Twentieth Century*, exh. cat. (New York: Museum of Modern Art, 1952), 3.
5. Steinberg, "Rodin," 322–403; originally published as the introduction to *Rodin: Sculpture and Drawings*, exh. cat. (New York: Charles E. Slatkin Galleries, 1963).
6. Albert E. Elsen, ed., *Rodin Rediscovered*, exh. cat. (Washington, DC: National Gallery of Art, 1981), 11.
7. Albert E. Elsen and J. Kirk T. Varnedoe, eds., *The Drawings of Rodin* (New York: Praeger, 1971).

IRIS, MESSENGER OF THE GODS

Original model 1895
Bronze, cast by Alexis Rudier, probably c. 1950
32 ½ × 34 × 14 ¾ in. (82.5 × 86.3 × 37.5 cm)
Signed under left foot: *A. Rodin*
Hirshhorn Museum and Sculpture Garden,
Smithsonian Institution, Washington, DC
Gift of Joseph H. Hirshhorn, 1966, 66.4330

Iris appears as the very symbol of the new direction Rodin embarked on in the last decade of the nineteenth century. It came about from a study for the *Monument to Victor Hugo* that was almost surely damaged, which had the effect of strengthening the suggestive power of the elements that survived. Positioned vertically and enlarged, the figure appears to run through air like the messenger of the gods. Rodin often visited London in the 1880s and probably got the idea for naming this figure from his memory of the *Iris* on the western pediment of the Parthenon marbles at the British Museum. (He had initially titled it, simply, *Woman with Spread Legs*.) Rodin had never gone so far or been so overt, at least in sculpture, for he had mostly explored erotic imagery on paper, encouraging his models to pose in ways that broke with studio practices.

Publicly shown for the first time in 1898, at the sixth Munich Secession, "the admirable *Iris*," in the words of critic Gustave Geffroy,[1] soon found success with private collectors, who were clearly receptive to this explosive examination of female sexuality. In 1908, Edward Perry Warren, a collector of antiquities and friend of John Marshall, who was interested in the sculpture's new treatment of an ancient theme, gave his bronze version to the Museum of Fine Arts in Boston, which, deciding the work could not be shown, traded it to art dealer Curt Valentin in 1953 for several small bronzes by Rodin, Aristide Maillol, Henry Moore, and Henri Matisse.

By the following year, Valentin was selling two examples of *Iris*, the second a recent cast that came directly from the Musée Rodin in Paris. One attracted the attention of Edgar J. Kaufmann Sr., a generous patron who was especially involved in architecture (Frank Lloyd Wright's 1939 Fallingwater; Richard Neutra's 1946 Desert House); it is located today at the Fondation Beyeler in Basel. The other was acquired August 10, 1955, by Joseph H. Hirshhorn. Rodin — especially

twentieth-century Rodin — plays a large role in the collection that Hirshhorn built, with the sculptor's later artworks establishing a thread that runs throughout the century. Also in Hirshhorn's namesake collection at the Smithsonian Institution, the painting *Nude with Leg Up (Leigh Bowery)* (1992) by Lucian Freud, who admired Rodin, offers an echo of *Iris* with a male subject.

Although the documents do not allow for definite identification of the *Iris* that was formerly in Boston, it seems likely that it is the one now in the Fondation Beyeler. The Beyeler cast has a signature in relief under the foot, which is identical to that in the Musée Rodin, suggesting that the two casts are more or less contemporaneous and were both produced during the artist's lifetime. ALNR

1. Gustave Geffroy to Auguste Rodin, February 12, 1907, Archives du musée Rodin, Paris.

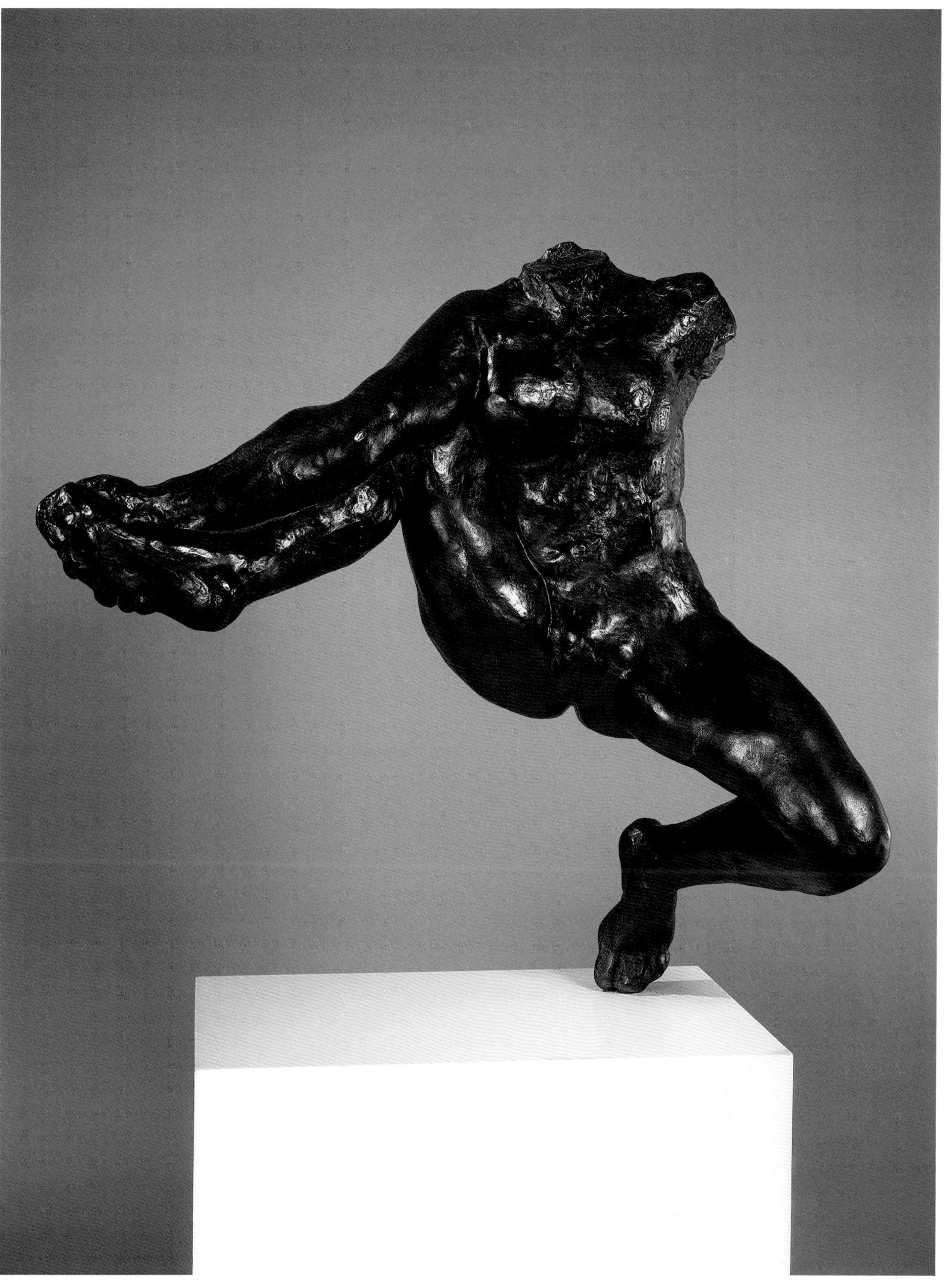

MONUMENT TO BALZAC

Original model 1897, enlarged 1898
Bronze, 4th cast, cast by Georges Rudier, 1954
111 × 48 ¼ × 41 in. (282 × 122.5 × 104.2 cm)
Signed behind figure's left foot, top of base:
A. Rodin
Museum of Modern Art, New York
Presented in memory of Curt Valentin by his
friends, 1955, 28.1955

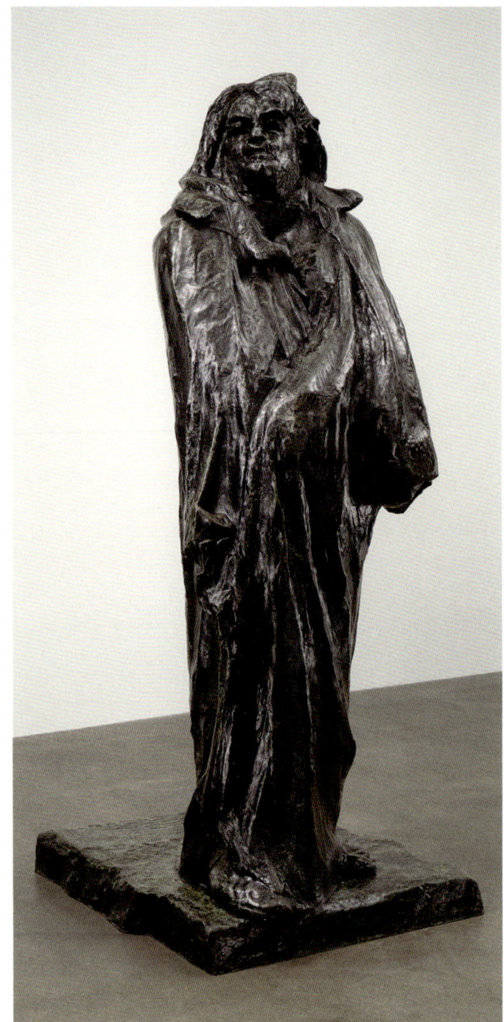

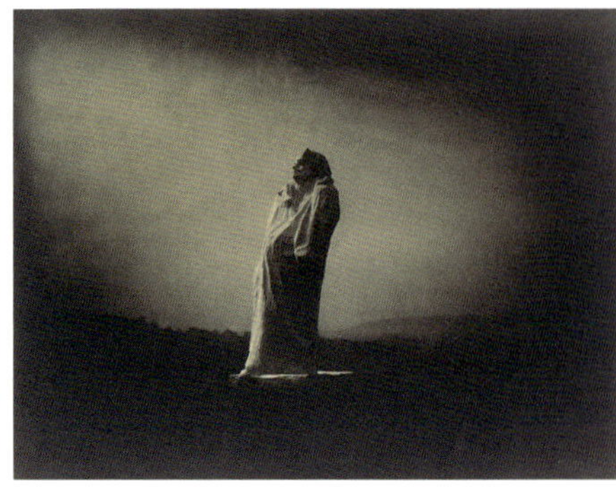

Edward J. Steichen, *Balzac, Towards the Light, Midnight*, 1908. Direct carbon print, 14 ⅜ × 19 in. (36.5 × 48.2 cm). Metropolitan Museum of Art, New York. Alfred Stieglitz Collection, 1933, 33.43.38.

"Finally, it is done," Charles Chincholle declared of the *Monument to Balzac* on March 19, 1898. "It exists. I've seen it, from the front, from behind, on the right, on the left. . . . It is three meters high. Balzac stands, draped in his famous dressing gown. With his strong head thrown back, he proudly looks at humanity, which, when he was flesh and blood, was sometimes so harsh to him."[1] Shown at the Salon of the Société Nationale des Beaux-Arts in 1898, the long-awaited statue immediately became the main attraction, unleashing criticism and caricatures, while *The Kiss* (cf. cat. 68), the large marble version of which was on view (Musée Rodin, Paris), received only praise. On May 9, the Société des Gens de Lettres, which had commissioned the monument, informed the artist that it could not accept a work in which it "did not recognize" Honoré de Balzac (1799–1850).[2]

As he conducted his research, Rodin had distanced himself from existing portraits, dismissing most physical details and keeping only the essential elements, which he exaggerated in order to express the novelist's creative power: the bull's neck; the lion's mane; the large, ironic, sensual mouth; and, especially, the fiery eyes that had made such an impression on Balzac's contemporaries. This approach appeared to be the logical end point of the artist's development at this time: the Rodin of the 1890s was an artist who, after devoting himself to exploring move- ment as a means of expressing the passions, then turned toward a more pared-down style of sculpture, reduced to the essential.

Those who defended or represented modernity in art—Claude Monet, Paul Cézanne, Paul Gauguin, and Camille Claudel—did not hide their enthusiasm for the sculpture. But Rodin was afraid of the connection that could be made between his *Balzac* and the Dreyfus Affair, which was tearing apart French society at the time. (Émile Zola, then-president of the Société des Gens de Lettres, had used his influence to secure the commission for Rodin. In 1898, Zola defended Captain Alfred Dreyfus, who had been falsely convicted of betraying France, in an article famously titled

"J'accuse . . .!"[3]) At the end of the Salon, the plaster was brought back to his studio and only shown once more during his lifetime, in Rodin's solo exhibition of 1900 at the Pavillon de l'Alma in Paris.[4] However, in 1908, as Balzac's house in Paris was being opened to the public, Rodin had the statue photographed by American Pictorialist Edward Steichen. He produced a series of famous images at night moving his camera according to the path of the moon and ending at dawn with a final full-length image, which allowed him to record the statue standing out "like a silhouette against the setting moon," in his own words. Steichen added that Rodin could not hide his emotion upon seeing the photo series, telling him, "You will make the world understand my Balzac through your pictures."[5]

It would take thirty more years before a bronze was finally cast for exhibition in the public space of Paris (installed 1939, carrefour Vavin on the boulevard du Montparnasse). In 1955, a group of friends from the art world offered the fourth cast,

seen here, to the Museum of Modern Art, New York, in memory of gallerist Curt Valentin, who had been a staunch defender of Rodin. Of the eight bronzes still to be cast, three entered American collections (Hirshhorn Museum and Sculpture Garden in Washington, DC; Norton Simon Art Foundation in Pasadena, California; and Los Angeles County Museum of Art). ALNR

1. Charles Chincholle, "La statue de Balzac," *Le Figaro*, March 19, 1898.
2. Charles Chincholle, "La Vente de la statue de Balzac," *Le Figaro*, May 12, 1898.
3. Émile Zola, "J'accuse . . .!," *L'Aurore*, January 13, 1898.
4. *Exposition Rodin*, exh. cat. (Paris: Palais de l'Alma, 1900), cat. 90; see also Antoinette Le Normand-Romain, ed. *Rodin en 1900: L'Exposition de l'Alma* (Paris: Musée du Luxembourg, 2001), cat. 68.
5. Edward Steichen, dictated to Grace Mayer, Museum of Modern Art, New York, 1972–89; quoted in Malcolm Daniel, *Stieglitz, Steichen, Strand: Masterworks from the Metropolitan Museum of Art* (New York: Metropolitan Museum of Art, 2010), 16.

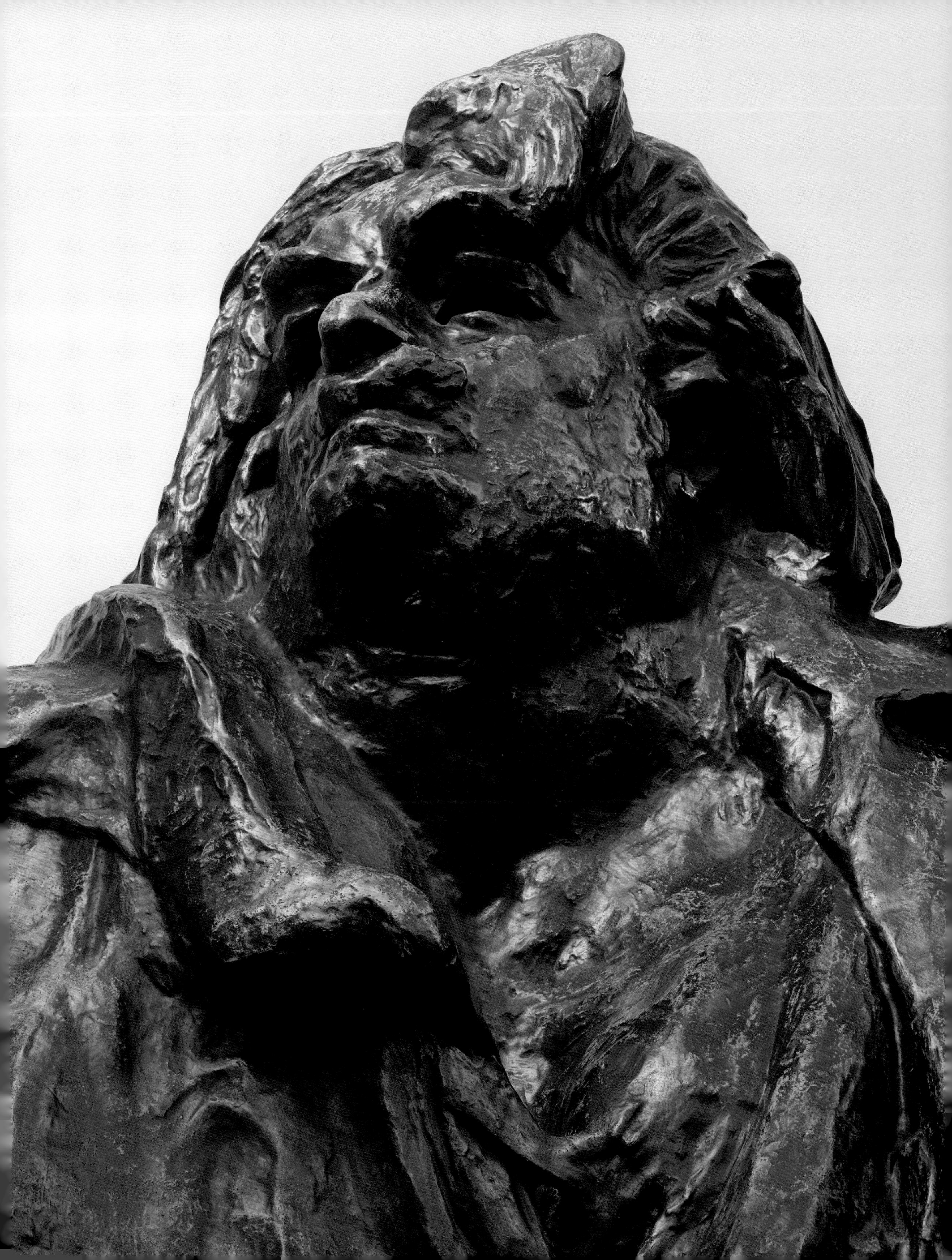

THE WALKING MAN

Original model 1907
Bronze, cast by Georges Rudier, 1965
Numbered 9, but actually the 11th cast
Signature and date incised in base: *A. Rodin ©
by Musée Rodin. 1965*
Incised on figure's right, in base: · *Georges Rudier
· / · Fondeur · Paris*
88 3/16 × 29 1/2 × 53 1/8 in. (224 × 75 × 135 cm)
Smith College Museum of Art, Northampton,
Massachusetts
Purchased 1965, SC 1965.30

Perhaps the most spectacular of the partial
figures from the last part of Rodin's career,
The Walking Man found its full power only
after being enlarged and shown at the 1907
Salon of the Société Nationale des Beaux-
Arts. In its original size, it had hardly been
noticed, except by American collectors
Katherine Seney Simpson and John Woodruff
Simpson, who purchased one of its first
bronze casts (cat. 14). As for the large version,
it remained misunderstood for a long time,
though a group of amateurs donated the first
bronze to the French state to be placed in the
courtyard of the Palazzo Farnese, site of
the French Embassy in Rome.

Very receptive to chance, which was a
part of life in artists' studios, Rodin had been
dazzled by a forgotten clay study of a torso,
a study for the 1880 *St. John the Baptist*,
damaged by time, that he rediscovered in his
studio before 1887. He then had a plaster
cast made of it, photographed it, and showed
it in 1889 through an initial bronze cast. Ten
years later, he attached it to a pair of legs,
also a study for *St. John the Baptist*, that had
been perfectly preserved. In that form, the
artwork seemed satisfactory to him, and it
was indeed perfectly in line with his artistic
approach in 1895–1900.

As with other figures, Rodin had it
enlarged to almost three times its size, in
1905–6. At the 1907 Salon, the large plaster
model was received with excitement by the
public, who saw a resurrection of ancient
sculpture in this "companion to the Winged
Victory of Samothrace created by a genius
of the twentieth century."[1] In fact, the
composition had been better understood by
the molders of the plaster, who transported
it from Rodin's studio to the Salon and gave
the work its new title, *The Walking Man*.
Rather than reproduce a single moment, the
figure offers a reinterpretation of the process
of walking. Rodin suggests the gradual
unfolding of the action through a shift
between the axes of the various parts of the
body, with the whole being recombined
visually so as to compress a series of moments
into a single pose. The artwork thus becomes
pure movement, making time and space
constituent elements of sculpture. The simple
descriptive title *Walking Man* is sufficient,
as the form no longer depends on any
literary, religious, or historical reference; its
own dynamic energy gives it meaning.
ALNR

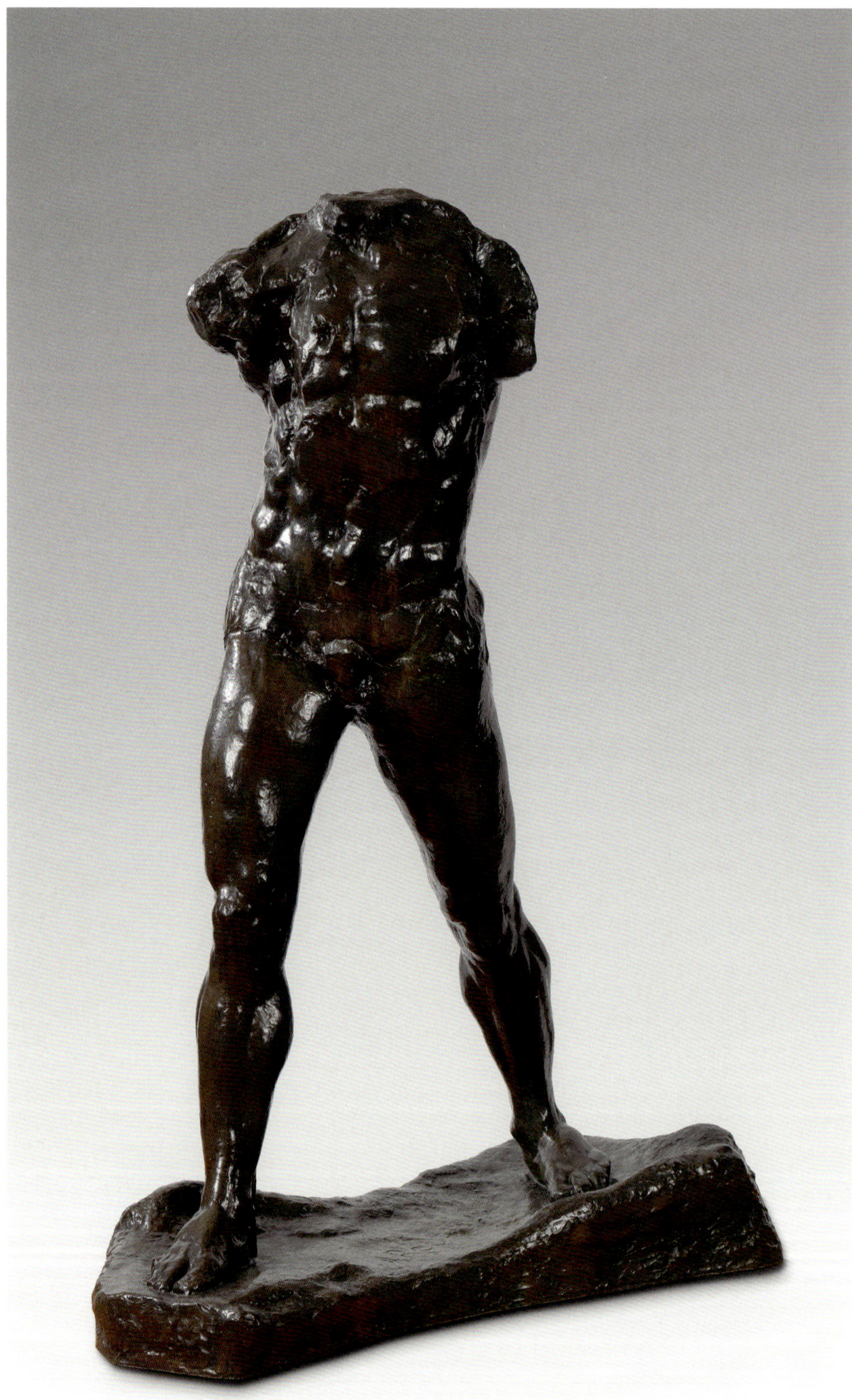

1. Antoni Roux to Auguste Rodin, April 24, 1907,
Archives du musée Rodin, Paris.

THE AGE OF BRONZE

Original model 1876
Bronze, cast by Alexis Rudier, c. 1910–20
71 × 20 × 20 in. (180.3 × 50.8 × 50.8 cm)
Signed on base: *A. Rodin*
Inscribed on back: *Alexis Rudier Fondeur Paris*
Stamped in relief, inside: *A. Rodin*
Iris & B. Gerald Cantor Center for Visual Arts,
Stanford University, Palo Alto, California
Gift of the B. Gerald Cantor Foundation,
1983.300

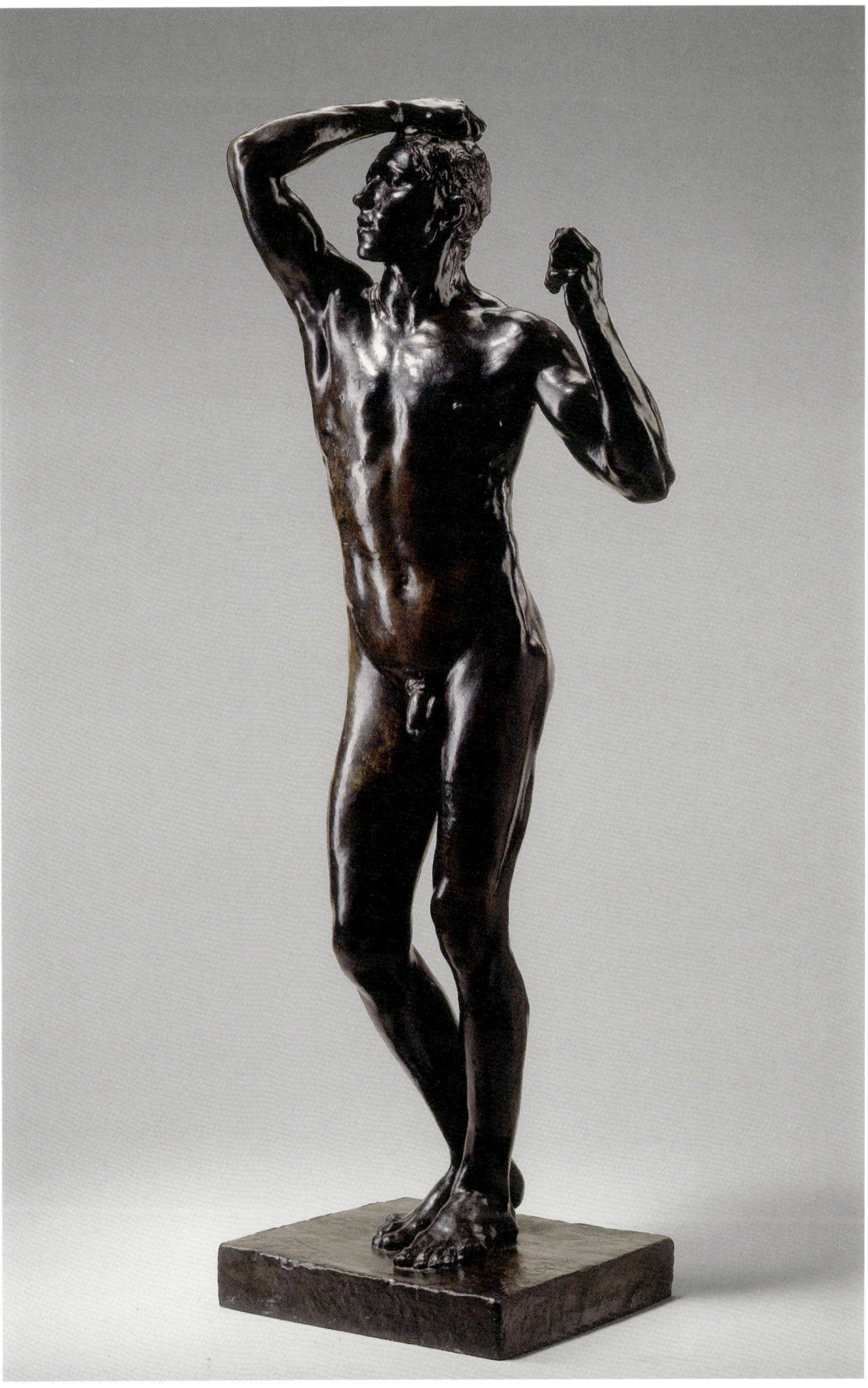

Modeled in 1876, *The Age of Bronze* represents the completion of the long period of research and struggle that constituted Rodin's early career. At this time, his sole goal was to study the nude. He thus rejected traditional models, who offered him only prescribed, conventional positions, and in October 1875, he turned to a young soldier, Auguste Neyt, with whom he collaborated to choose this figure's ideal pose. Rodin's first trip to Italy, in spring 1876, confirmed for him this new direction for sculpture. The *Age of Bronze*, first shown in Brussels, at Cercle artistique in 1877, and then at the Salon in Paris, was noticed for "a quality that is as precious as it is rare: life,"[1] but it surprised the public because it had no title. As one critic put it, "The artist only forgot one thing: to baptize his plaster in order to reveal its subject."[2] It was therefore suspected that it was the result of casts from life—a mere mechanical copy—rather than modeled by the sculptor's own hand. In 1880, once Rodin had managed to prove his good faith, with the help of other sculptors who sent a letter to Director of Fine Arts Edmond Turquet,[3] the Fine Arts Administration commissioned a first bronze (Paris, Musée d'Orsay). Many others followed, as bronze editions had no limit before 1968 (after which editions of bronze sculpture were limited to twelve copies by law). The Rudier foundry cast twenty-nine copies of the *Age of Bronze* before 1918 and fourteen more between 1918 and 1943!

The first example of this figure on American soil was the plaster acquired by the Pennsylvania Academy of the Fine Arts in 1897 (now National Gallery of Art, Washington, DC) on the advice of sculptor Paul Wayland Bartlett to serve as a model for young artists who did not have access to a live model.[4] This was the best possible praise of an anatomical study that had become a perfect illusion. In 1907, Kate Simpson gave a bronze, the first in North America, to the Metropolitan Museum of Art in New York in an effort to convince the museum to put together a collection of the artist's work. B. Gerald Cantor was lucky enough to acquire a cast that can be dated to the early twentieth century by the raised stamp on the interior. The presence of this bronze in a Rodin collection of such importance was essential for showing the development of Rodin's work.

ALNR

1. Untitled article, *L'Étoile belge*, January 29, 1877.
2. Jean Rousseau, "Revue des arts," *Echo du Parlement belge*, April 11, 1877. The work's subsequent title, *Age of Bronze*, derives from the Greek poet Hesiod's "Works and Days" (8th–7th c. BCE); we do not know who suggested it to Rodin.
3. Letter to Edmond Turquet, February 5, 1880, F21/4338, Archives nationales, Paris.
4. A decade earlier, Barlett's father, Truman H. Bartlett, had published an important series of interviews that introduced the artist to American audiences: "Auguste Rodin, Sculptor," *American Architect and Building News* 25, nos. 682–703 (January 19–June 15, 1889).

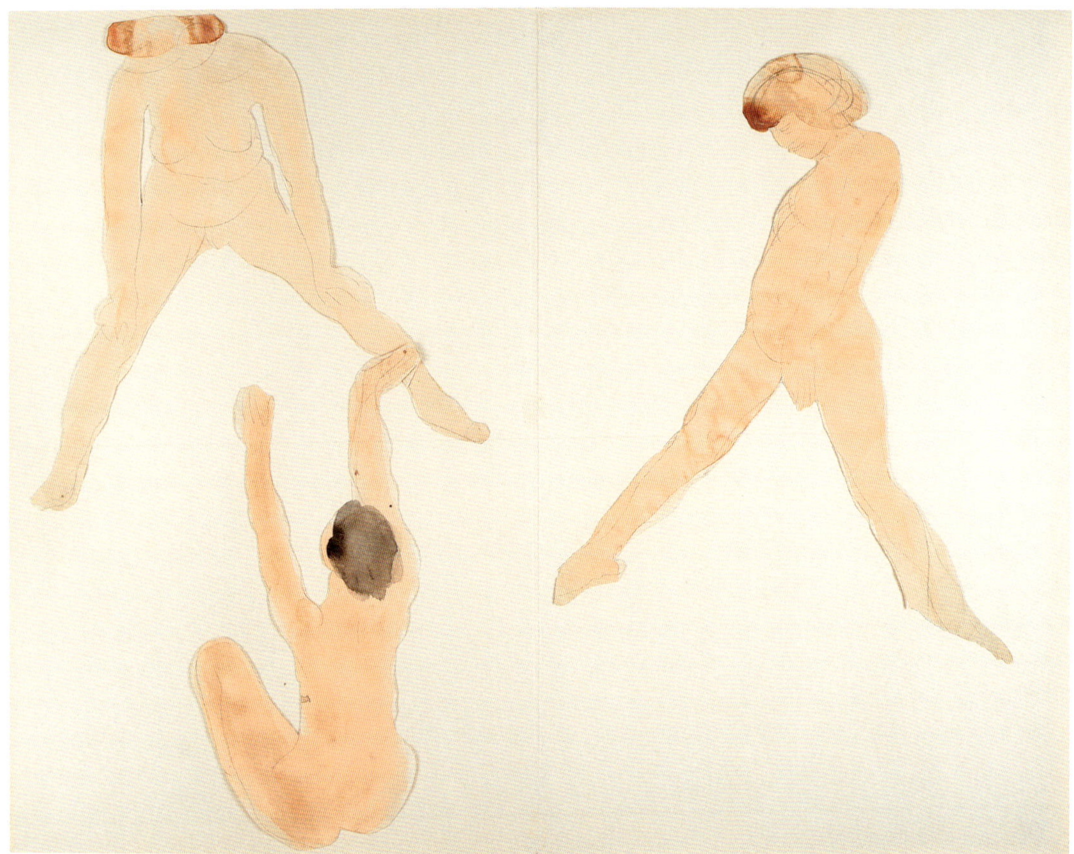

CAT. 88
THREE FEMALE NUDE CUTOUT FIGURES

c. 1900–1906
Graphite and watercolor on wove paper,
cut out and mounted to wove paper
22 ½ × 28 ½ in. (57.2 × 72.4 cm)
Graphic Arts Collection, Princeton University,
Princeton, New Jersey
Gift of René Chéruy's students, HSV / 7 I /
GA 2006.01573, 2006.01574, 2006,01575

In 1965, Princeton University Library cataloger Howard C. Rice Jr. described a recent acquisition of ephemera related to Rodin, "including several letters, notes, and sketches in his autograph" obtained from the artist's former secretary, René Chéruy (1880–1965), who had subsequently taught French in Connecticut. Thomas S. Brush enhanced an initial gift of materials with "several pencil and watercolor drawings by Rodin, as well as examples of his dry points . . . which also belonged to Mr. Chéruy." Rice indicates that these documents and drawings "evoke mainly the years 1902–1908, when Chéruy, then in his twenties, was performing numerous secretarial chores for 'the Master,' who was in his sixties and at the peak of his contemporary fame."[1]

Chéruy's archives preserve even the slightest mementos, such as drafts of letters and apparently insignificant sketches. The cutout watercolors at Princeton are of particular interest. They are a unique set outside the Musée Rodin in Paris and exemplify an intimate practice of the artist; he almost never showed them. The cutout figures, sometimes assembled in pairs, are today considered one of the most innovative aspects of his art and predate the Cubist *papier collés* of Pablo Picasso, Henri Matisse, Paul Klee, and Hans Arp. Rodin initially drew models from life, without looking at the paper, then simplified and reworked the resulting figure with watercolor. As Albert Elsen noted, the first step for revolutionizing art with drawing was that Rodin "stressed expressiveness over anatomical beauty and correct proportions."[2] By using intermediate tracing paper, he would create two or three versions of the same figure on thick paper. Some watercolored figures were intended to become two-dimensional paper-cutout silhouettes, like these. In 1908, Rodin and other artists, including Matisse, rented workshops in the Hôtel Biron in Paris. As Elsen has demonstrated, the discovery of Rodin's work, both drawings and sculpture, was decisive for the development of Matisse's famed paper-cutout technique.[3] Just like Matisse—but fifty years earlier—Rodin played with the arrangement of his cutout, watercolored pieces: he would *sculpt* with scissors. Matisse, who used mechanically colored paper, turned to cutout as a way of accessing solid swathes of color: he would *paint* form with scissors rather than with a brush.[4] Rodin used the cutout technique in a manner comparable to that of casting and assembling in sculpture. Even if many artists before Rodin made cutouts for experimental purposes, particularly painters such as Peter Paul Rubens and Jean-Auguste-Dominique Ingres, Rodin's "paper sculptures" as such are the first in art history. His attempt at collaging three figures on a single sheet preserved at Princeton, of which there is no equivalent at the Musée Rodin in Paris, is the only example of seeking an artistic composition in this form, where the figures interact together.

CBU

1. Howard C. Rice Jr., "Glimpses of Rodin," *Princeton University Library Chronicle* 27, no. 1 (Autumn 1965): 33.
2. Albert Elsen, "Rodin's Drawings and the Mastery of Abundance," in *The Drawings of Rodin*, ed. Albert Elsen and J. Kirk T. Varnedoe (New York: Praeger, 1971), 24.
3. Albert Elsen, "Rodin's Drawings and the Art of Matisse," *Arts Magazine* 61, no. 7 (March 1987): 32–39.
4. For further reading on Rodin's early influence on Matisse, see Dorothy Kosinski, Jay McKean Fisher, and Steven Nash, eds., *Matisse: Painter as Sculptor*, exh. cat. (Baltimore: Baltimore Museum of Art, 2007).

FEMALE NUDE CUTOUT FIGURE

c. 1900–1906
Graphite and watercolor on wove paper
mounted to a later support
13 × 8⅞ in. (33 × 22.5 cm)
Graphic Arts Collection, Princeton University,
Princeton, New Jersey
Gift of René Chéury's students, 2006.01560
HSV / 71 / GA

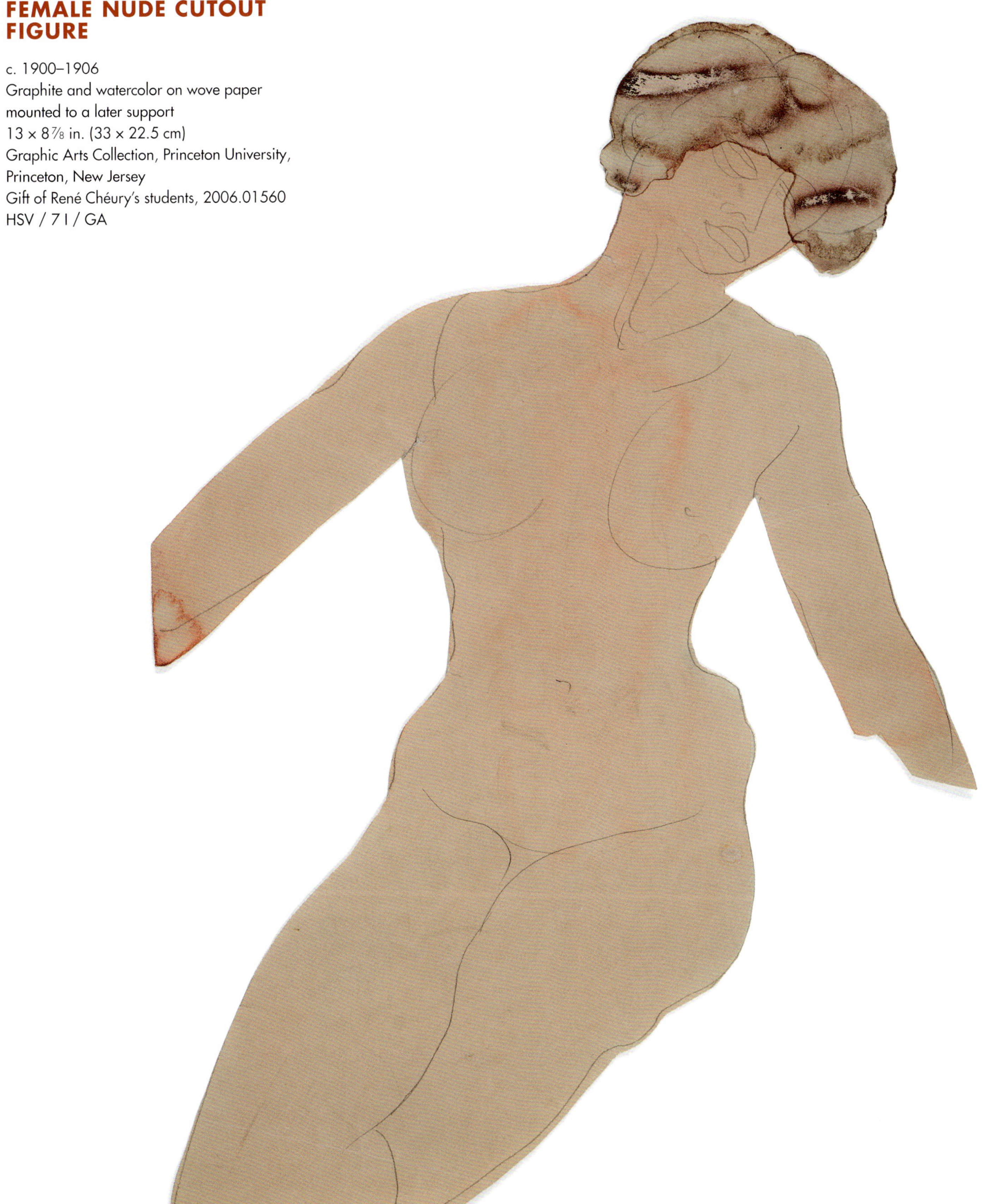

DANCE MOVEMENT H

c. 1911
Bronze, cast by Georges Rudier, 1965
11 ¼ × 3 × 4 ¼ in. (28.6 × 7.6 × 10.8 cm)
Signed on right arm: *A. Rodin*
Inscribed on right ankle: *Georges Rudier Fondeur Paris*; below: *No. 11 / © by Musée Rodin 1965*
Iris & B. Gerald Cantor Center for Visual Arts, Stanford University, Palo Alto, California
Gift of the Iris & B. Gerald Cantor Foundation, 1975.84

On May 27, 1911, Anglo-German count and modern art collector Harry Graf Kessler noted in his journal that he had seen in Rodin's studio "a window full of little clay figures . . . with surprisingly new lines and movements, closer to his *drawings* than the sculptures that he has made up until now."[1] Kessler saw them again on June 2, 1912, and noted what Rodin said: "There are people," he told his visitors, "who found it obscene. Yet it's almost pure mathematics. It's not passionate."[2]

Unlike Edgar Degas, Rodin was not as interested in classical ballet as in various types of dance that he deemed more authentic or more modern, such as the dancing of the female Cambodian dancers of King Sisowath, but also that of Loïe Fuller, Isadora Duncan, Vaslav Nijinsky, or Alda Moreno, an Opéra Comique dancer whom he discovered in 1905 but who posed for him mostly between 1910 and 1913.[3]

His series of nine *Dance Movements* constitutes, along with the small *Nijinsky*, the last true demonstration of his creativity. This artist, who had been turned toward the future for his entire life, tried to capture the essence of form in movement in these clay statuettes where the relationship to the material is decisive. While the related plasters are soaked in whitewash that erases their details, traces of the hand and knife marks are vividly present in the clay sculptures. The nature of the clay's proportions, size, and elasticity controls the organization of the forms, which pays no heed to traditional anatomy. They can all be viewed either head up or down, or combined differently. For example, *Dance Movement C*, shown vertically at the Musée Rodin in Paris, is sometimes turned over and put on a pedestal with its head at the bottom. A mold also revealed a variation of *Dance Movement C* with the arm and left leg on a different axis and completed by the right leg from *Dance Movement G*.

For a long time, the series remained unknown to the public, and bronze casts were made beginning only in 1945, under the influence of Cécile Goldscheider, then director of the Musée Rodin. As the modest dimensions of the *Dance Movements* and their modernity made them very desirable to private collectors, galleries competed for them, and the first series of bronzes sold out quickly. Casts of the last two figures (*Dance Movements H* and *I*) were made in 1963 as Leo Steinberg and Albert E. Elsen were developing a new vision of a "modern" Rodin in whose work material played a decisive role.
ALNR

1. Harry Graf Kessler, May 27, 1911, entry in *Journal: Regards sur l'art et les artistes contemporains (1889–1937)*, translated from German by Jean Torrent, ed. Ursel Berger, Julia Drost, Alexandre Kostka, Antoinette Le Normand-Romain, Dominique Lobstein, and Philippe Thiébaut, 2 vol. (Paris: Maisons des sciences de l'homme, 2017), doi: http://doi.org/10.4000/books.editionsmsh.10922.
2. Kessler, June 2, 1912, entry in *Journal*.
3. See Alexandra Gerstein, "Flight, Arabesque and Cantilever in Rodin's Movement Studies," in *Rodin and Dance: The Essence of Movement*, exh. cat., ed. Alexandra Gerstein (London: Courtauld Gallery, 2017), 25–39.

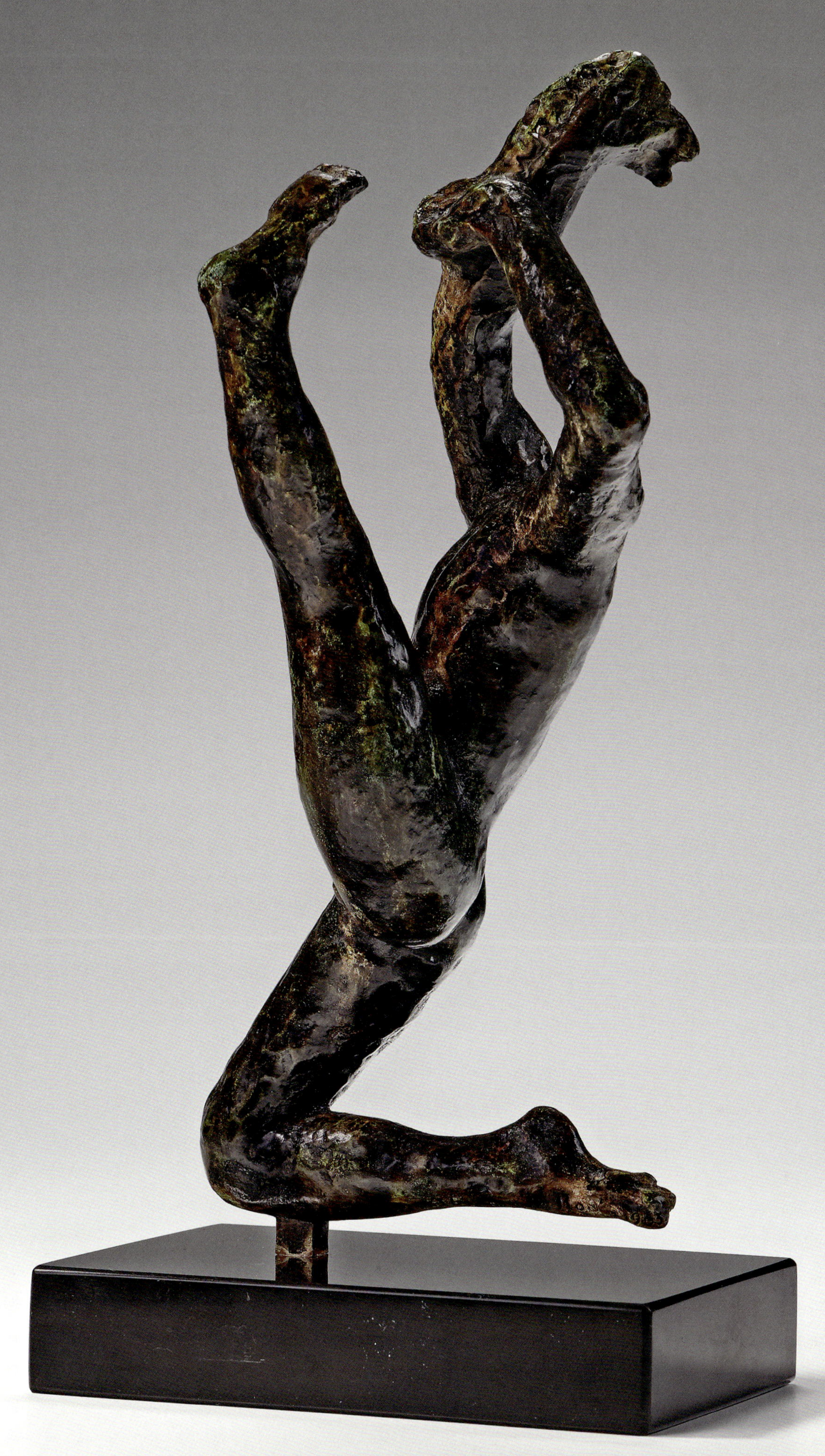

UGOLINO AND HIS SONS

Original model c. 1881–82
Bronze, cast by Eugène Gonon, 1883
15⅞ × 16³⁄₁₆ × 25⅜ in. (40.3 × 41.1 × 64.5 cm)
Signed on base: *Rodin*
Inscribed on base: *E. GONON FONDEUR*
Private collection, London, on loan to the Clark Art Institute

Ugolino, an Italian nobleman featured in Dante's *Divine Comedy (Inferno)*, is one of the most developed characters in the drawings Rodin made as part of his research for *The Gates of Hell*. Dante describes the morbid punishment of Ugolino della Gherardesca (c. 1220–1289), the tyrant of Pisa, who watches his children and grandchildren die one by one and ends up devouring them.

Mentioned in documents for the first time in 1882, the "terrible Ugolino"[1] seems to have been present in Rodin's earliest studies for the *Gates of Hell*. Led by a search for expressiveness similar to that of the Vatican's ancient *Laocoön* marble group, the artist followed Dante's text closely to show this character in the final moments of his torture. Guilty of having betrayed his city during the battles between Italian city-states in the thirteenth century, he was imprisoned in a tower, the key to which was thrown into the Arno River. He was sentenced to die of hunger, as were his two sons and two grandsons, who succumbed before him.

We know that Rodin had initially thought of depicting Ugolino seated, as in the sculpture by Jean-Baptiste Carpeaux (*Ugolino*, 1863, Musée d'Orsay), a pose found in Rodin's drawings and in the *Third Maquette of the Gates of Hell* (c. 1880). This is the case for the two drawings on the next spread (cats. 92, 93). *Ugolino and His Sons: Fifth Day*, an important acquisition for the Metropolitan Museum of Art, New York, was until now known only through a reference in the medical journal *Archives de Thérapeutique*. "Each gesture is a painful contraction," the author emphasized. "Each expression is a horrible grimace. And always there is such knowledge and concern for anatomy and myology. The figures have abnormal attitudes, poses of torture, yet Rodin makes these movements acceptable by the precise attachment and possible flexion of all the muscles."[2] The drawing was produced at a much earlier date, surely around 1875, when Rodin was still living in Belgium. During this time, he considerably deepened the knowledge of anatomy that he had acquired during his training at the École Impériale Spéciale de Dessin et de Mathématiques. The instruction he received there from Ornamentalists, which was hardly different from that of the École des Beaux-Arts, was entirely based on the study of the human body—from life, plaster casts, and cadavers at the morgue.

The Stanford drawing (cat. 93) is undoubtedly related to the *Third Maquette* and marks a turning point in the development of the composition of the *Gates of Hell*. This was the moment when the composition became unified, with *Paolo and Francesca* (which would be known in the future as *The Kiss*) and the *Ugolino* group placed as companion pieces below the door panels. As in the maquette, and like the statue by Carpeaux, Stanford's *Ugolino* is seated facing the viewer and holds his son, probably Gaddo, who died on the fourth day. The composition is rather like Michelangelo's *Pietà* (1498–99, Vatican), except that Rodin's Ugolino is nothing like the *Mater Dolorosa* and is, on the contrary, threatening, like a Medea. The work was published for the first time by F. J. Pillet in the *French Magazine* in April 1899, with a few other previously unpublished drawings.[3]

In its definitive state, the sculpture group shows the final moments of Ugolino's torture. With the fourth child on the verge of dying, his gaze mad, Ugolino seems to want to bite the neck of the child who has fallen into his arms. "I saw all three of them fall one by one, before the sixth day; and, already blind, I then began to crawl over each of them, calling them for two days after their death. And then hunger did what grief could not," Ugolino tells the poet when they meet in hell.[4] According to Truman H. Bartlett, whose series of interviews with the artist introduced him to a wide US audience, Rodin "made a figure of a man walking on his hands and knees. A friend seeing it said: 'That would [have] made a good Ugolino.'"[5] We know what close attention Rodin paid to the suggestions of others, and this may explain the shift from a figure represented vertically, and thus still possessing human dignity, toward this poor being reduced to an animal state.

Like many of the sculptures from the *Gates*, this group exists in two forms: complete or with modifications—in particular, with the rear part removed in order for the work to be integrated in the panels of the *Gates of Hell*. It was, of course, the complete version that gave rise to the bronze castings—few in number, no doubt due to the frightening subject matter. The first is shown here. It was made for painter Henri Lerolle by Eugène Gonon, who asked for 1,200 francs to produce it "in a single cast. . . . This group," he continued, "is very difficult. I don't want this price to scare you. I couldn't do it for less but not right away since I have a lot to do right now."[6]

"Certainly, I would have preferred to pay him only 1,000 francs as you said at first," Lerolle told Rodin. "But since I don't want to give up your group on account of 200 francs, I ask you to do your best. . . . I'm very eager to have it."[7] The resulting bronze seems more finished than the two subsequent casts by Griffoul and Lorge in 1889 (Musée Rodin, Paris, and Cantor Center, Stanford, with the inscription "2ème épreuve"): the hands of Ugolino's children, for example, are more precise and detailed. We can also note the thick strand of hair that falls over Ugolino's forehead. Still present in the plaster cast corresponding to the fragment of the *Gates*, it has disappeared from the other plaster and bronze casts.

The bronze shown here, which can be recognized in a self-portrait photo of Degas (Paris, Musée d'Orsay) in the company of Christine and Yvonne Lerolle, was displayed in Brussels in 1887 along with the future *Kiss*. Unlike the latter, *Ugolino* had no success with collectors, but for Rodin it was an important work, and he decided to enlarge it after 1900. Moreover, he often reused elements from the group, particularly the head and torso of the child standing near his father (as in *Female Centaur* and *The Prodigal Son* [cat. 42]).
ALNR and CBU

1. "Art Notes," *Magazine of Art*, 10 (1882): 1.
2. André Mycho, "Quelques dessins d'Auguste Rodin," reproduced without inscriptions, *Archives de Thérapeutique* (December 1899): 312.
3. F. J. Pillet, "La technique du dessin," *Le Moniteur du dessin*, July 25, 1900.
4. Dante, *Inferno*, XXXIII, 67–75.
5. "Anecdotes," manuscript, Ms. Fr. 126, Bartlett Papers, Houghton Library, Harvard University, Cambridge, Massachusetts.
6. Eugène Gonon to Auguste Rodin, July 17, 1883, Archives du musée Rodin, Paris.
7. Henri Lerolle to Auguste Rodin, [July 1883?], Archives du musée Rodin, Paris.

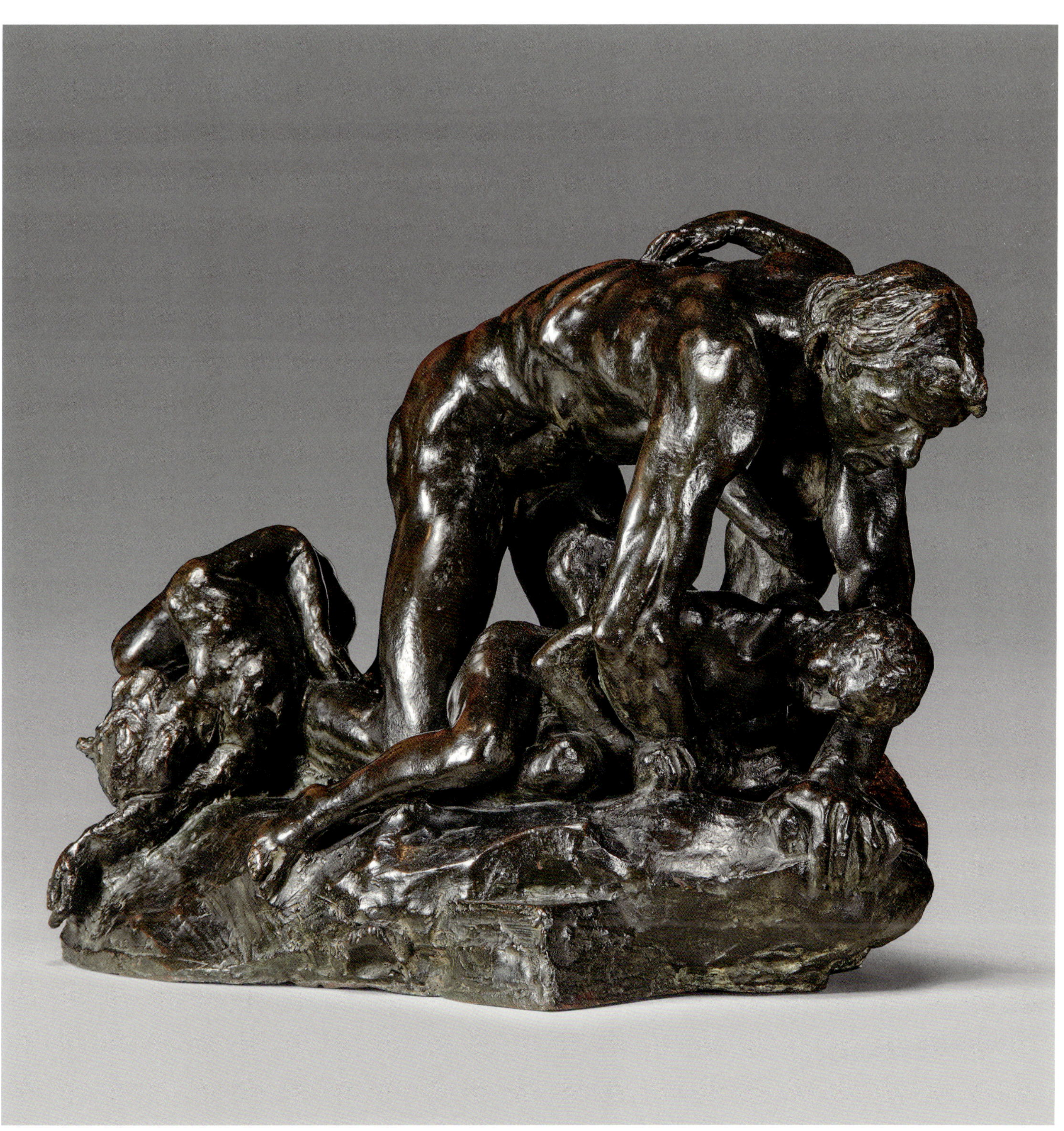

UGOLINO AND HIS SONS: FIFTH DAY (RECTO); DANTE AND VIRGIL: ANATOMICAL STUDIES (VERSO)

1876–80
Graphite and pen and ink on graph paper
6 1/8 × 3 3/4 in. (15.6 × 9.6 cm)
Inscribed in pen and ink, top left: *5*; top right:
ugolin 5ᵉ jour
Inscribed by another hand in red pencil, right
margin: *9 cent 1/2*; in blue pencil, top left:
1338/68
Metropolitan Museum of Art, New York
Anonymous Gift, 2012, 2012.222.2 a, b

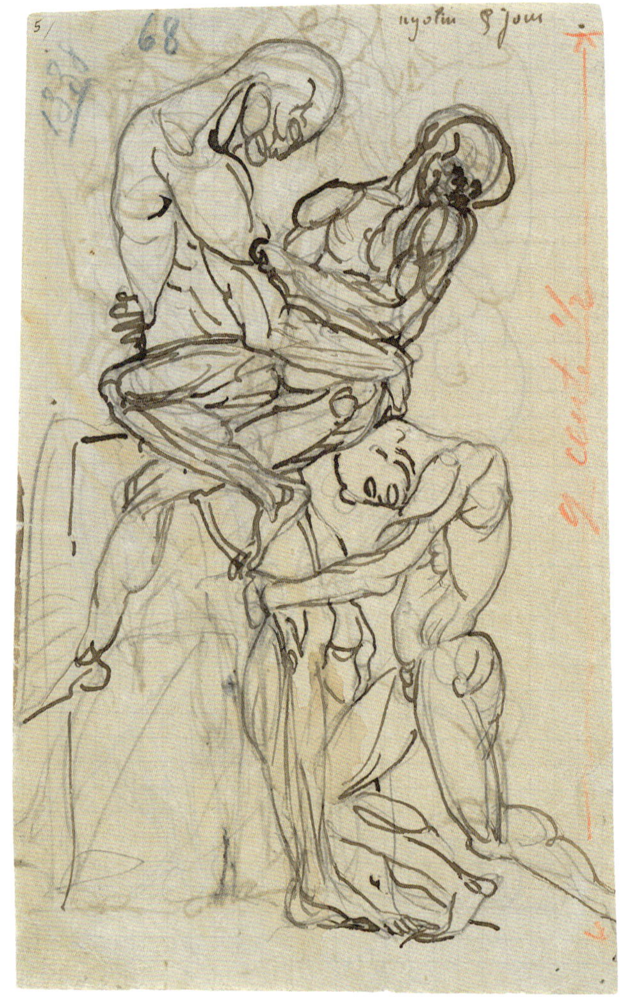

STUDY FOR UGOLINO AND HIS SONS (RECTO); SKETCH OF UGOLINO AND SON (VERSO)

c. 1876–80
Graphite and pen and ink on graph paper
5 5/8 × 3 11/16 in. (14.3 × 9.3 cm)
Inscribed with pen and ink, at bottom right:
Ugolin; at top left (verso): *planche*
Unauthenticated initials in graphite, lower right:
A.R.
Iris and B. Gerald Cantor Center for Visual Arts,
Stanford University, Palo Alto, California
Gift of the Iris & B. Gerald Cantor Foundation,
1987.39

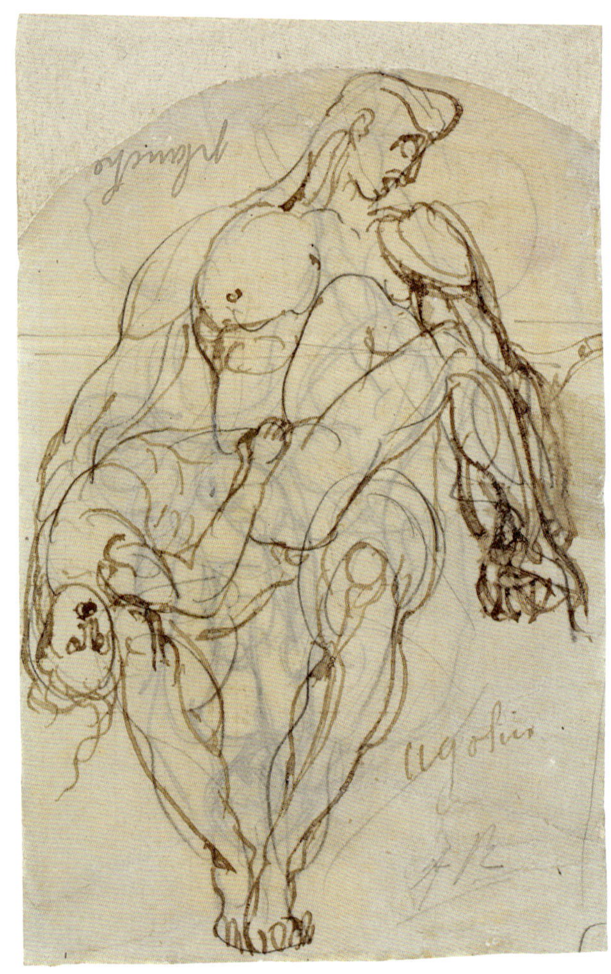

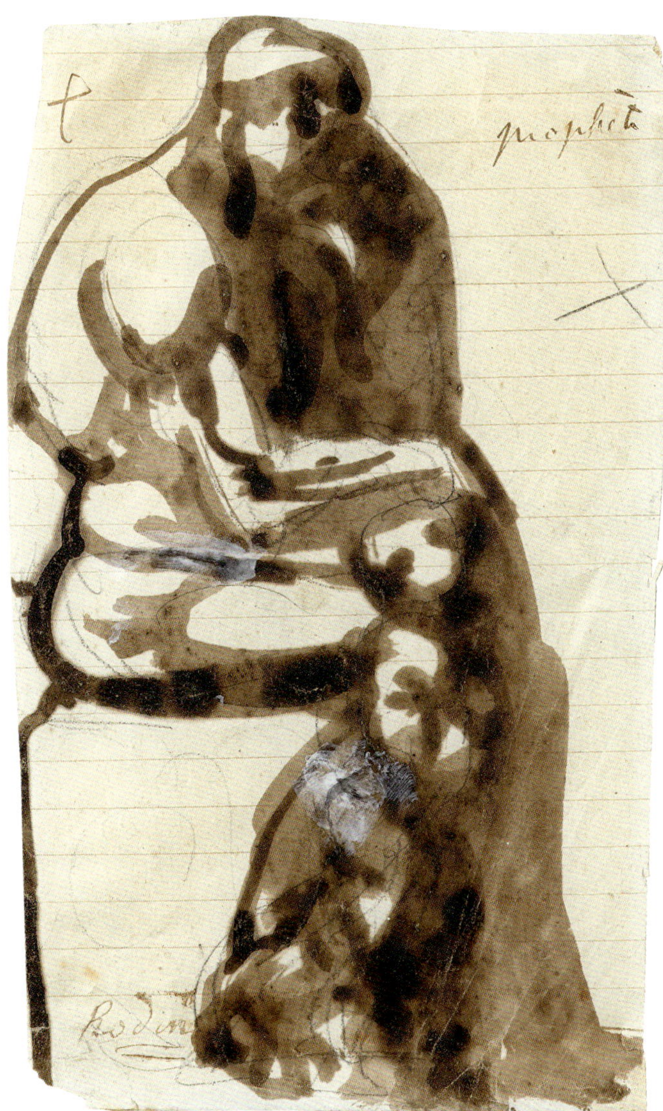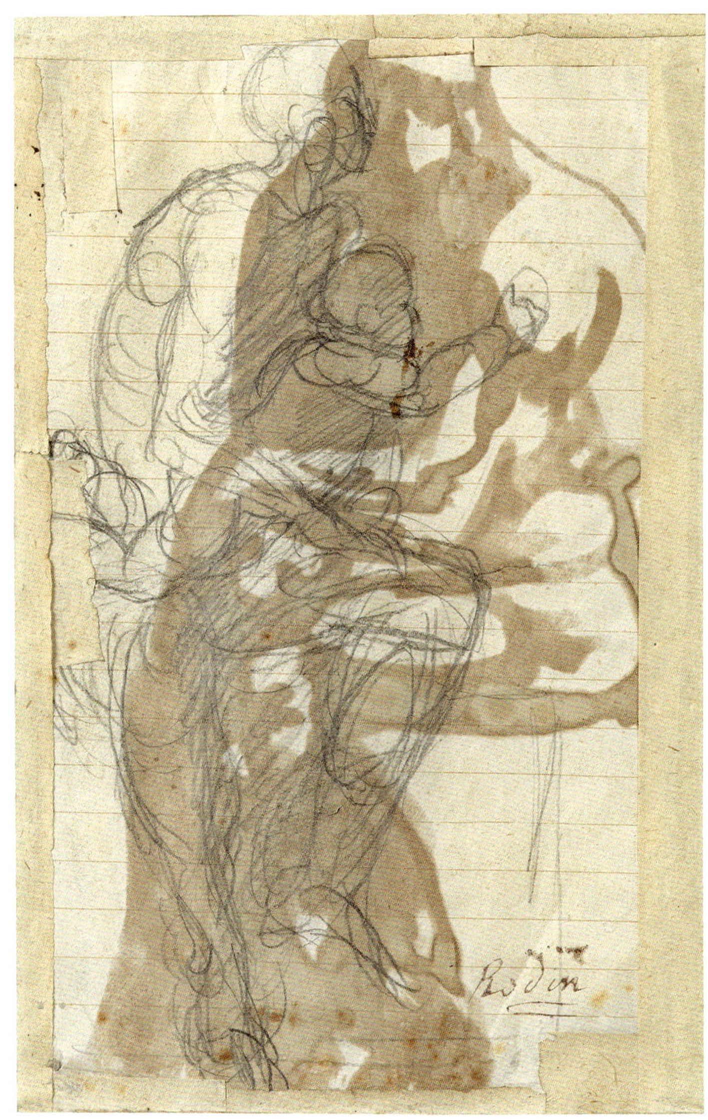

CAT. 94

THE THINKER (THE PROPHET OR UGOLINO) (RECTO); STUDY FOR UGOLINO (VERSO)

c. 1880
Graphite, ink, and gouache (recto) and graphite (verso) on lined paper
7 1/2 × 4 5/16 in. (19 × 11 cm)
Inscribed in pen and ink, upper right: *prophète*
Collector's stamp of the Musée Rodin collection(?), recto and verso: *Rodin* (Lugt. 2142)
Rappaport Rodin Collection

A powerful image of *The Thinker* seated on a pedestal, this drawing is the only known study on paper for the artist's most famous sculpture. Modeled by 1880–81 to occupy the center of the tympanum of the *Gates of Hell*, the seated athlete represents a meditation on creation. This is undoubtedly the meaning of Rodin's inscription of the word "prophète" on the sheet, an allusion to a line from Victor Hugo's famous poem "The Function of the Poet." The drawing lets us trace the development of the artist's creative process: the starting point was a sketch of Ugolino, which recalls how much Rodin's *Thinker* owes to the *Ugolino* by Jean-Baptiste Carpeaux (1863, Musée d'Orsay). On the recto, the figure leans his right arm on the head of a standing toddler who blends in with his leg, while on the verso, an écorché (a figure drawing without skin, displaying the muscles) with a bent back, close to Carpeaux's figure, seizes a child. Almost certainly produced in Belgium in 1876 while Rodin was working on a torso of *Ugolino*, the drawing includes additions made with large brush strokes and a brown ink wash we can date to 1880, when the *Gates* was commissioned.

The signature stamp "Rodin," present on both sides of the sheet, is connected to the origins of the Musée Rodin in Paris, opened in 1919 through the artist's donation of all his work to the French state. Ownership of some drawings previously in the museum was transferred under circumstances not yet clarified.[1] We know that this exceptional work was shown in 1932 to the Paris expert Jean Cailac, who then presented it to Georges Grappe, conservator of the Musée Rodin.[2]
CBU

1. Christina Buley-Uribe, "L'aliénabilité *de facto* de dessins du musée Rodin?," *Cahiers d'histoire de l'art*, no. 19 (2021): 96–107.
2. Manuscript note, Archives du Musée Rodin, Paris.

CHARYBDIS

c. 1883
Graphite, ink, watercolor, and gouache on wove
paper, cut out, torn, and glued on support
8 ¼ × 3 ⅜ in. (21× 8.6 cm)
Inscribed and signed in ink, upper left: *Charybe*
[*sic*] / *A. Rodin*
Private collection, courtesy of Nicholas Sands &
Company Fine Art, New York

This drawing of *Charybdis* after Rodin's
Eve belonged to the American sculptor Leo
Lentelli (1879–1961), who participated in the
decoration of the Panama-Pacific International
Exposition in San Francisco in 1915. It is
related to a series of preparatory studies
produced for a commissioned illustration
of a play, *Enguerrande*, published in 1884
by Émile Bergerat. The plot recounts the
shipwreck of the queen of Corsica whose
boat washes up on an unknown island.
Enguerrande swims to the coast and finds
refuge in a cottage, where she removes her
wet clothes. The prince of Sicily falls in love
when he sees the queen through a dormer
window, like "Aphrodite eternally nude."[1]
Like the figures in two other drawings after
Eve made in preparation for his *Enguerrande*,
Charybdis brings her right arm to her face.[2]
In his new interpretation of Eve/Enguerrande,
Rodin transforms the gesture of a pudic
"Venus" (alias Eve or Enguerrande) into an
expression of horror. On the horizon, on
the right, we see a rough sketch of a ship.
Is this an allusion to Homer's *Odyssey*,
in which Odysseus orders his men to avoid
the whirlpool of Charybdis? Or perhaps
Rodin already had in mind the image of
the beautiful Enguerrande in distress
from her shipwreck when he sketched the
distant vessel.
CBU

1. Emile Bergerat, *Enguerrande* (Paris: Bibliothèque
des Deux Mondes, Franzine, Klein, 1884), 91.
2. See Victoria Thorson, *Rodin Graphics: A Catalogue
Raisonné of Drypoints and Book Illustrations* (San
Francisco: Fine Arts Museums of San Francisco,
1975), 79–81; and Christina Buley-Uribe, "D'Ève à
Enguerrande," in *Naissance de la Modernité*, ed.
Henry-Claude Cousseau, Christina Buley-Uribe, and
Véronique Mattiussi (Paris: Relief, 2009), 89–101.

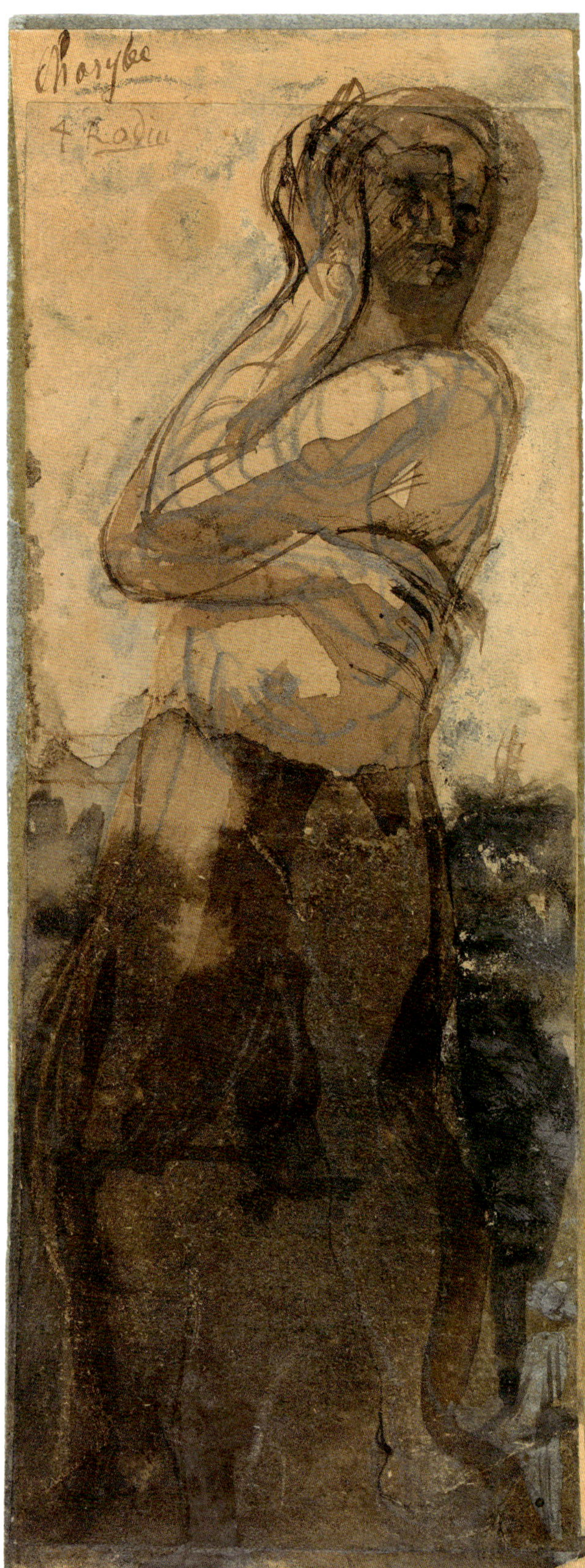

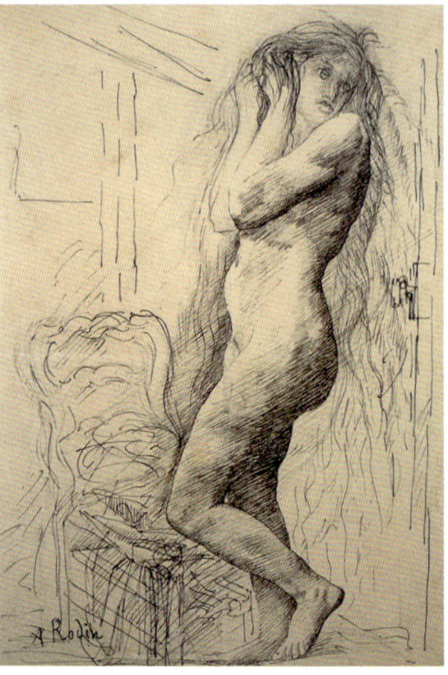

Auguste Rodin, *Enguerrande in
the Fisherman's Cabin*, 1884. Pen
and ink on wove paper, 8 ¼ ×
6 1/16 in. (21 × 15.3 cm). Private
collection.

SALOME

c. 1895
Graphite, pen and ink, watercolor, and gouache
on laid paper
6⅞ × 4⁷⁄₁₆ in. (17.4 × 11.2 cm)
Private collection

"The same feeling of brotherhood, the same
love of art, has made us friends for always . . .
I still have the same admiration for the artist
who helped me to understand light, clouds,
the sea, the cathedrals that I already loved
so much, but whose beauty awakened in the
dawn by your expression touched me so
deeply."[1] This excerpt from an 1897 letter
from Rodin to Claude Monet expresses the
substance of the friendship between the two
artists. Beginning in 1886 and 1887, they
participated in group exhibitions with other
Impressionist painters at Galerie Georges Petit,
particularly with Pierre-Auguste Renoir,
before organizing a joint exhibition of their
work in the summer of 1889 — "only you and
me," Monet said.[2]

The two friends gave each other artworks
as signs of their mutual admiration. Rodin
owned one of the thirty-nine views of
Belle-Île,[3] while Monet's collection featured
three sculptures by Rodin including the
plaster *Minotaur* in the Musée Marmottan
as well as this drawing, of which only the
title, *Salome*, was known until now. Sent
to Monet in April 1897, in response to the
painter's support for his *Victor Hugo*, exhibited at the Salon, the drawing remained
in the Monet family for a long time. A letter
from Rodin that reappeared at the sale of
Claude Monet's archives led to its clear
identification as the model for the lithograph
of the frontispiece for *Le jardin des supplices*
by Octave Mirbeau, published by Ambroise
Vollard in 1899: "Here, my friend, while
waiting for something better, this little Salome.
If Mirbeau needs it, we'll take a photograph."[4] The model's gesture of removing her
chemise and creating a sort of tray perhaps
reminded Rodin of the daughter of Herod
receiving the head of Saint John the Baptist.
The only drawing by Rodin known to have
belonged to Claude Monet, it entered a
private collection in the United States in 2017.
CBU

1. Auguste Rodin to Claude Monet, September 22,
1897, Archives du musée Rodin, Paris.
2. *Claude Monet–A. Rodin*, exh. cat. (Paris: Galerie
Georges Petit, 1889). Monet to Rodin, February 28,
1889, Archives du musée Rodin, Paris.
3. Claude Monet, *Belle-Île*, 1886, oil on canvas, Paris,
Musée Rodin, P.7329.
4. Rodin to Monet, [late April 1897], Paris, Artcurial
sale, December 13, 2006, *Archives Claude Monet*, no.
1207, lot 284.

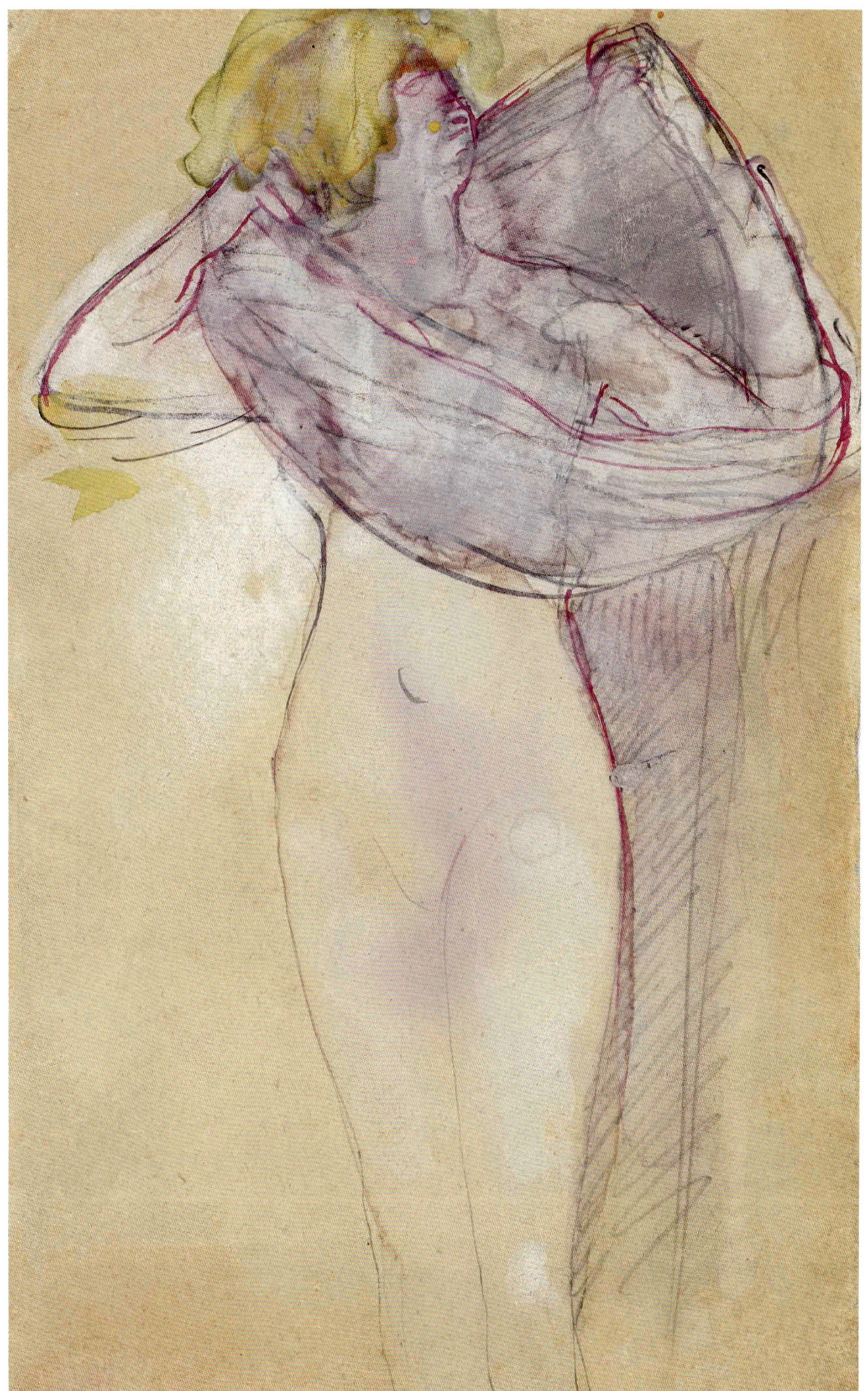

CAMBODIAN DANCER

1906
Watercolor over graphite pencil on paper
11 7/16 × 7 11/16 in. (29 × 19.6 cm)
Museum of Fine Arts, Boston
Bequest of John T. Spaulding, 48.851

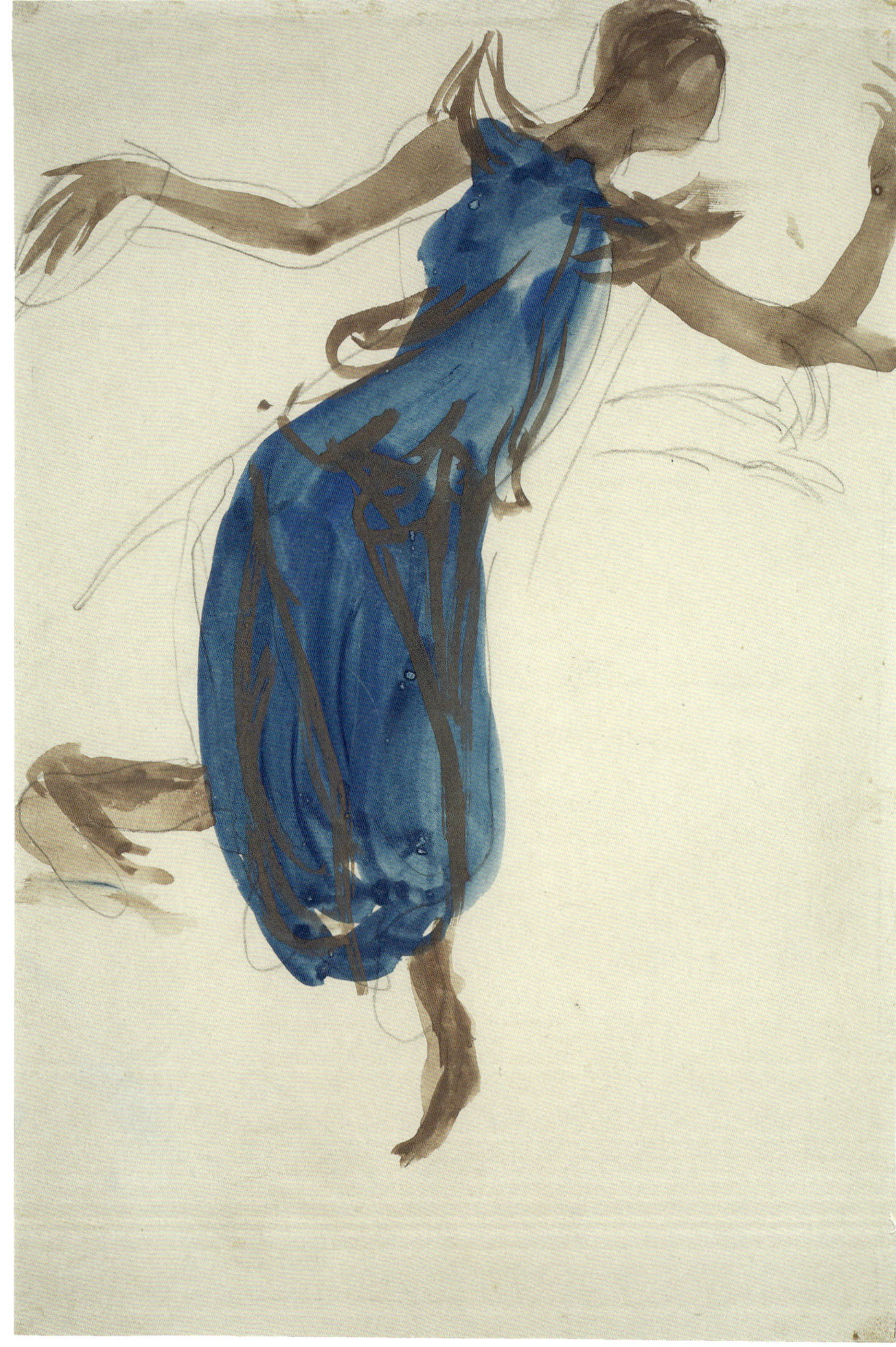

John Taylor Spaulding was one of the major donors to the Museum of Fine Arts, Boston. As a connoisseur of Asian art, he must have been interested in Khmer dances, but it was surely the spontaneous style of this Cambodian dancer by Rodin that attracted the collector, more than the subject itself. In his book *The Evolution of Taste in American Collecting*, René Brimo compares Spaulding's taste to that of three other American art aficionados and philanthropists: Adolph Lewisohn, Chester Dale, and Albert C. Barnes.[1] Spaulding could also be compared to Denman Waldo Ross (1853–1935). Like Ross, Spaulding was an obsessive collector of Japanese prints and an admirer of Impressionist painting. Ross also owned the first drawings by Rodin to enter an American museum. In 1907 and 1908, the Museum of Fine Arts received his gift of three watercolors, including another *Cambodian Dancer* (08.187).

Rodin discovered Asian dances in the context of universal and colonial expositions, yet the sculptor did not consider them specifically in terms of their exoticism. He transcribed Khmer dance with his own unique way of seeing, focusing on grace and elegance. Just like the Javanese dancers he admired in Paris in 1889, the Cambodian dancers Rodin sketched in Marseille in 1906 gave him a feeling of rapture: "I contemplated them in ecstasy. . . . When they left, I thought they took the beauty of the world with them," he said.[2] For Rodin, they paradoxically embodied a concept of Western antiquity. He felt he had found the authenticity and flawlessness of that era in these young female dancers from the Far East. The artist did not strive to reproduce the traditional costumes in detail, and the sampot (a long cloth tied at the waist, like a sarong) became in his pencil lines a kind of Greco-Roman toga. In Spaulding's blue version, as in the pink version owned by Ross, the color wash evokes the shimmering elegance of Cambodian silk. The contrast between the underlying drawing, the watercolor, and the dynamic modifications, either with a brush (Spaulding) or a soft-lead pencil (Ross) gives an impression of speed to the slow movements of these ritual choreographies. It should be recalled that the dancers' costumes were sewn close to the body for each show, and we can see that Rodin added quick blue strokes to this *Cambodian Dancer*, with the same brush used for the brown wash, in order to redraw the limbs and certain elements of the costume. In this way, he emphasizes the harmony between the costume and the body. The body and the hands, with their delicate, slender fingers, as well as the curved feet, echo the sinuous folds of fabric and the curve of the shoulder pads. Despite their similar themes, Spaulding's drawing appears more experimental than the masterful and classic *Cambodian Dancer* acquired by Ross. All that counts here are the fluid lines, like a watercolor by Edouard Manet or James McNeill Whistler.

CBU

1. René Brimo, *The Evolution of Taste in American Collecting* [1938], trans. Kenneth Haltman (University Park, PA: Penn State University Press, 2017).
2. Auguste Rodin, quoted in Louis Vauxcelles, *Les dessins de Rodin* (Paris: Galerie Devambez, 1908), 6.

SPHINX

c. 1898–1900
Graphite with stumping and watercolor on wove paper
19 3/16 × 12 3/4 in. (48.7 × 32.4 cm)
Signed, lower right: *Aug. Rodin*
Inscribed in graphite, upper right: *sphinx*; on right toward middle: *noir draperie*
J. Paul Getty Museum, Los Angeles
2008.60

Although he never traveled to Egypt, in his late years Rodin collected more than 900 antique Egyptian sculptures and artifacts. Shortly before 1900, he produced a small series of watercolors related to ancient Egypt, based on his life drawings after models posing in his atelier: *Cleopatra*, *Memnon*, *Simeon in the Desert*, *Isis*, and *Egypt*,[1] to which we must add this impressive drawing titled *Sphinx*. The drawing does not literally depict the Egyptian mythical lion creature with a human head; only the title suggests an enigma in this figure with crossed arms. Its large round eyes look up to the right of the page, where Rodin has inscribed the word "Sphinx." References to Egypt in Rodin's work do not convey the degree of Orientalist fascination or exoticism seen in that of his contemporaries. His images include little exoticizing specificity and very few Egyptian attributes or emblems—only titles referring to the ancient civilization that Rodin had discovered at the Musée du Louvre in his youth. His drawings are never, as it were, illustrations; rather, Rodin's starting point was always a living model, the human body. "Nature," for him, was the "truth" of a pose. Here, only a few hints evoke the land of the pharaohs: the rough sketch of a pyramid on the horizon that is glimpsed behind a palm tree and the flat orange-pink watercolor tints from a brush with little water, suggesting dry soil. In a terracotta shade, the figure itself evokes the brown silhouettes of ancient Egyptian paintings, which were concise and compact. The annotation *noir draperie* (black drapery) next to the lines and stumping surrounding the figure suggests that the clue to the enigma is the goddess Isis. Always depicted veiled in black, Isis symbolizes Nature in the Western iconographic tradition; the artist must follow her, but her face is always hidden from him.

CBU

1. *Cleopatra* (D. 5000), *Memnon* (D. 3924), *Isis* (D. 4236), and *Egypt*, (D. 4719), all Musée Rodin, Paris; *Simeon in the Desert*, Musée Fabre, Aix-Les-Bains. See Christina Buley-Uribe, "Dessiner l'Antique," in *Rodin: La lumière de l'antique*, exh. cat., ed. Pascale Picard (Paris: Gallimard, 2013), 217.

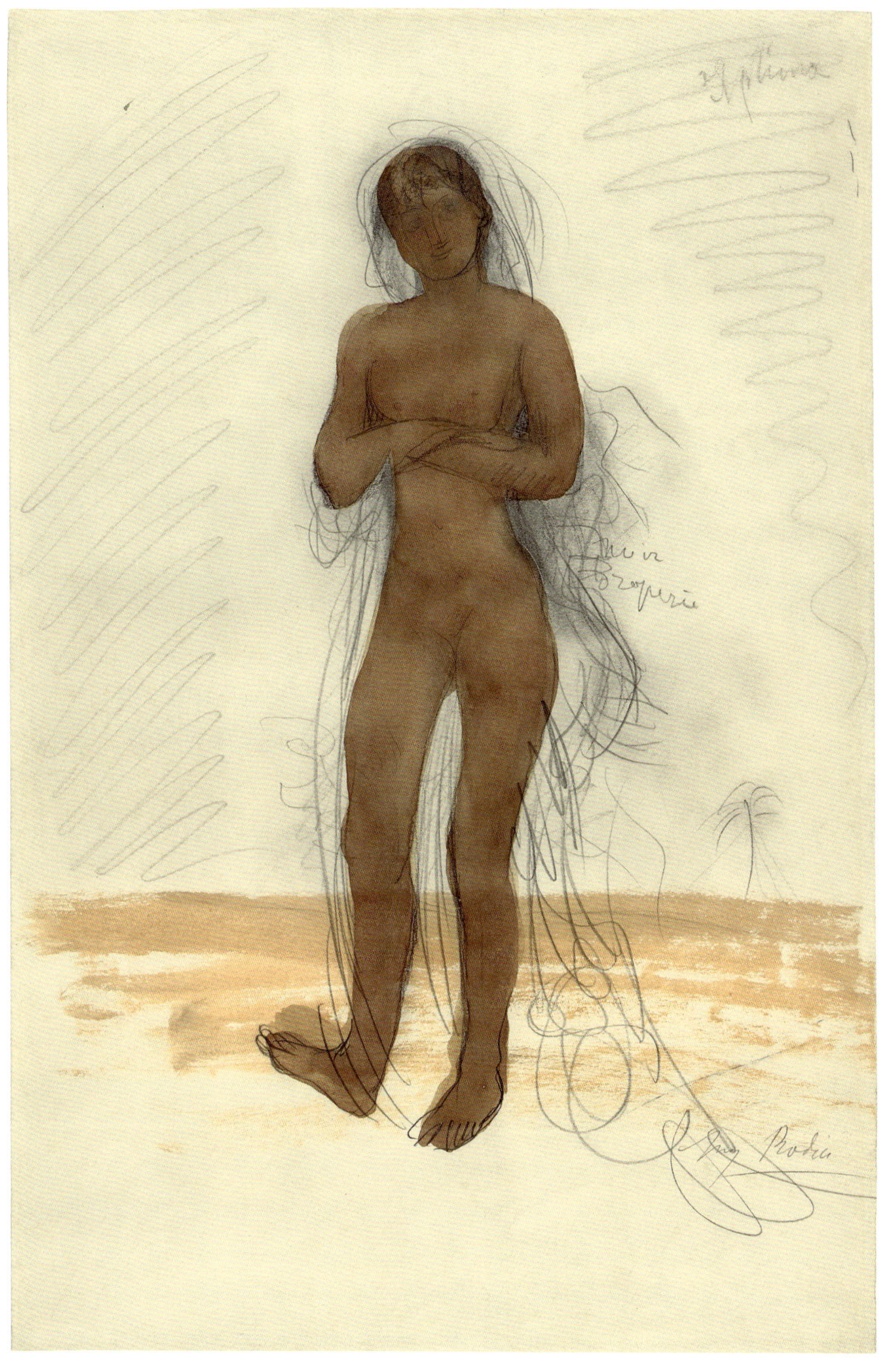

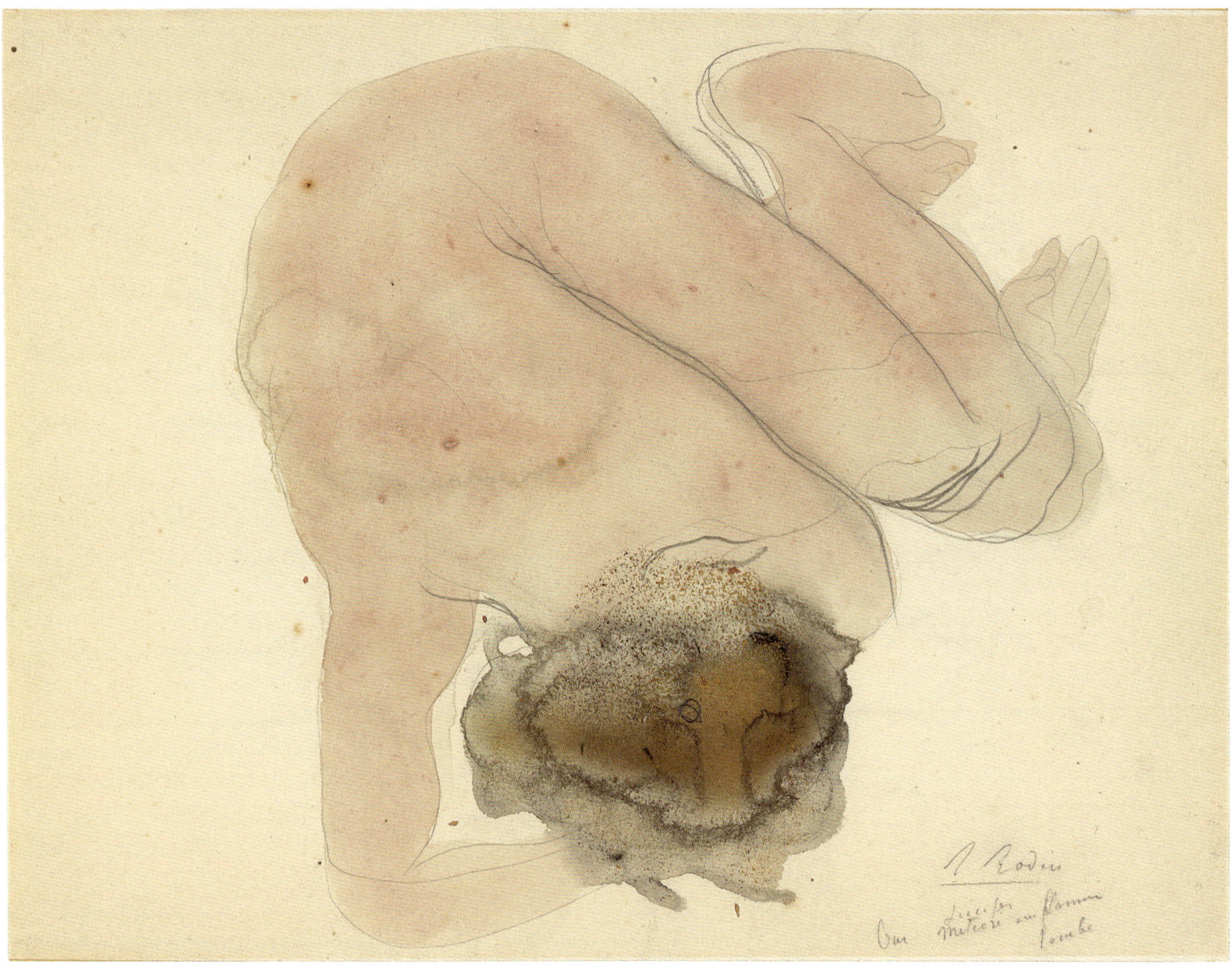

CAT. 99
LUCIFER (FALLING METEOR IN FLAMES)

c. 1898–1900
Graphite and watercolor on wove paper
9⅜ × 12⁷⁄₁₆ in. (23.8 × 31.6 cm)
Signed and inscribed in graphite, lower right:
A. Rodin / bas / Lucifer / Meteore en flamme / tombe
Inscribed in pen and ink lower right on mount:
inv.n°134
Morgan Library & Museum, New York
Gift of Alexandre P. Rosenberg, 1981.10

The provenance of *Lucifer*, known as *Falling Meteor in Flames*, is connected to the tragic events of World War II, when one of the most important dealers in French modern art, Paul Rosenberg, was forced to flee to the United States to escape the Nazis. Stripped of his nationality under the anti-Semitic laws of the Vichy government, he fled Paris when his famous gallery at 21 rue de la Boétie was "Aryanized" (a Nazi term referring to the confiscation [looting] of Jewish property,

beginning in Germany in 1933 and then in all Nazi-controlled countries, including France, between 1941 and 1945). He first went to Bordeaux, after storing paintings by artists including Henri Matisse and Pablo Picasso. Most of them were stolen. With the help of Alfred Barr, who was then director of the Museum of Modern Art, he was able to reach New York, where he opened a new gallery at 79 East Fifty-Seventh Street in 1941. Was *Lucifer* one of the artworks that could be easily transported and that he did not want to leave behind? This drawing must have been important to him, because it stayed in the Rosenberg family, after its purchase in 1917 at the sale of the collection of fashion designer Jacques Doucet at Hôtel Drouot in Paris, until it entered the Pierpont Morgan Library in 1981. The almost abstract appearance of the drawing, made of lines, spots, and watercolor drips, was exactly the thing to catch the eye of a gallerist who was passionate about modern art.

Rodin executed the drawing in two stages. First, he sketched the silhouette of a crouching woman seen from above and foreshortened. Then, he reworked the figure, turning the sheet upside down, which gives the impression of a figure falling into an abstract space. This is the definitive orientation of the work, as indicated by the word *bas* (down) and the location of the signature. The crouching woman assumed the role of Lucifer — the two drips extending from the hair might represent horns — and recalls the Gospel of Luke 10:18, where Jesus tells his disciples, "I saw Satan fall like lightning from Heaven." The splashes of watercolor and the rock-like appearance of the ball of hair may have led Rodin to associate them with a flaming meteor.
CBU

EMERGING FROM THE CLOUDS (NIJINSKY)

1912
Graphite with stumping and watercolor on laid paper
18 ½ × 12 ¼ in. (47 × 31.1 cm)
Inscribed in graphite, top left: *sortant des nuages*
Rappaport Rodin Collection

Rodin attended the premiere performance of *The Afternoon of a Faun* by the Ballets Russes at the Théâtre du Châtelet in Paris on May 29, 1912. Vaslav Nijinsky (1889–1950) was the choreographer and the main dancer in this one-act ballet set to the music of *Prelude to the Afternoon of a Faun* (1894) by Claude Debussy, which was itself inspired by Stéphane Mallarmé's poem of the same title, published in 1876. Nijinsky had created a kind of tableau vivant where the dancers, located on the edge of the stage, imitated figures of ancient bas-reliefs. In addition to a statuette, which was never cast in bronze during the artist's lifetime, Rodin produced three rough sketches of Nijinsky (all Musée Rodin, Paris) in poses that can easily be recognized as part of the choreography (perhaps he asked the dancer to pose or drew him from photographs).

In this more spontaneous drawing, which we also propose identifying as Nijinsky, the muscles of the torso and arms are emphasized, as if the body's energy were concentrated in its upper part (cf. the *Apollo* from the Maryhill Museum of Art, cat. 53). The pelvis and legs are reduced to the very minimum, as in the statuette. They serve as a base for the sculpture, and in the drawing, they are barely visible, with no color. In this drawing, we find the animal nature of the Faun, emphasized by heavy makeup giving the eyes an almond shape. The red watercolor enveloping the figure recalls a scarf. Describing Nijinsky's performance, Rodin noted, "Nothing is more striking than his momentum when, in the conclusion, he stretches out with his face to the ground on the hidden veil that he kisses and holds with the fervor of passionate sensuality."[1] It seems Rodin wished to express the emotion imprinted by such amorous passion in *Emerging from the Clouds*.

Like *The Thinker* (cat. 94), the drawing is now in an important California private collection and will be part of the collector's plans for a public Rodin Gallery displaying over fifty works, including bronzes, plaster casts, and drawings, opening in the near future.
CBU

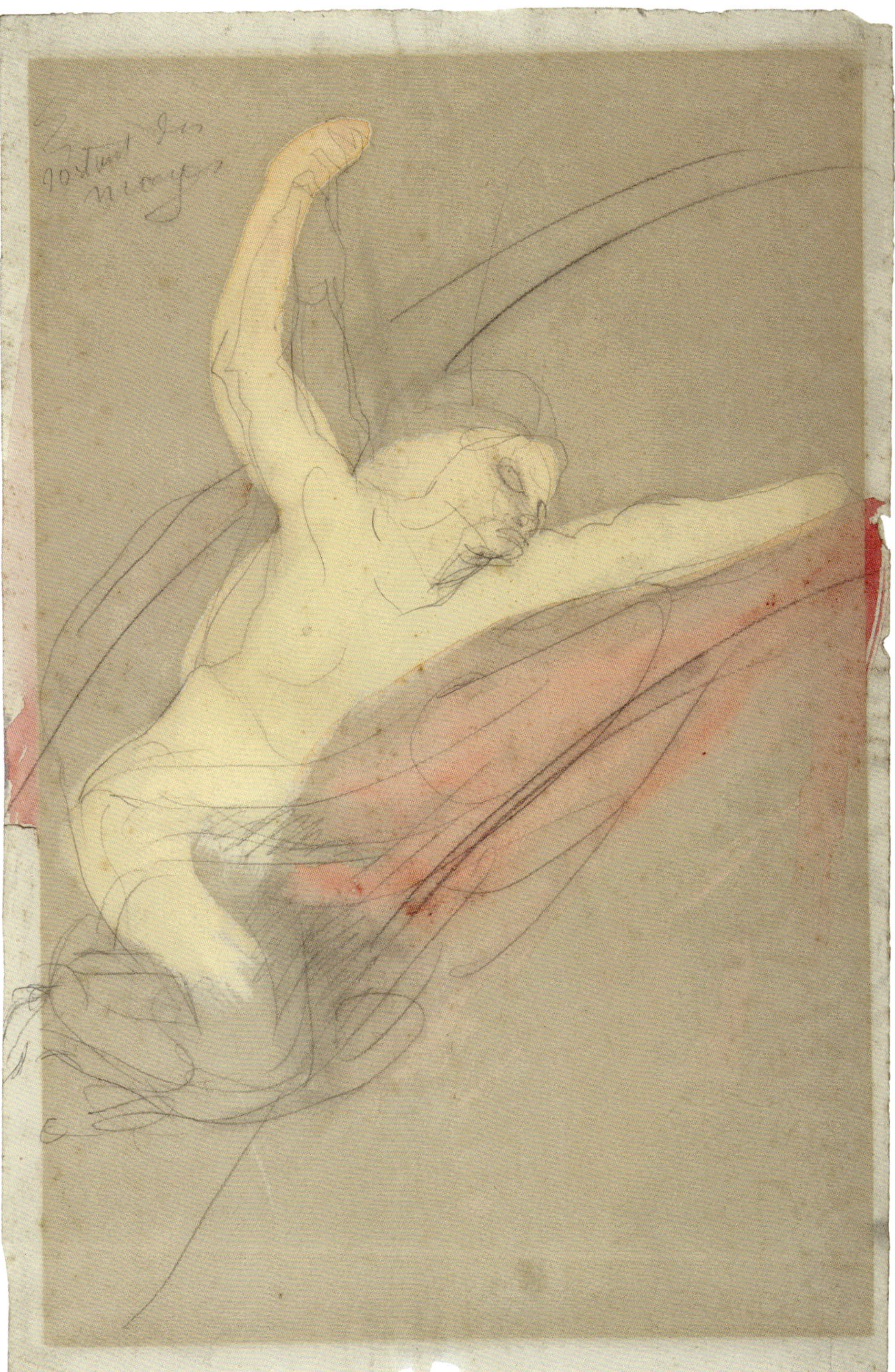

1. Auguste Rodin, "La Rénovation de la danse: Loïe Fuller, Isadora Duncan, Nijinski," *Le Matin*, May 30, 1912.

CHRIST AND MARY MAGDALENE

Original model 1894
Marble, carved by Victor Peter, 1908
43 × 33 ½ × 31 in. (109.2 × 85.1 × 78.7 cm)
Signed on base: *A. Rodin*
J. Paul Getty Museum, Los Angeles, 2014.32

The recent acquisition of this spectacular marble sculpture by an important institution indicates that Rodin has returned to the same level of admiration in the United States that he enjoyed a century earlier. This is the second marble version of this work, which was one of the compositions by Rodin most influenced by the contemporary Symbolist movement. As the title of the work changed, from *Genius and Pity* and *Prometheus and an Oceanid* in previous iterations to *Christ and Mary Magdalene*, a shift occurred, assimilating the suffering of the genius to the suffering of Christ. As Rodin told art critic Paul Gsell, "Sometimes his [the artist's] heart is tortured, but even more strongly than the suffering, he feels the bitter joy of understanding and expressing. In everything that he sees, he seizes clearly the intentions of destiny."[1] Perhaps this sculpture's special connection with its creator explains why this group was never shown during the artist's lifetime, although many photographs and admiring comments from those who saw it indicate that it would have received an enthusiastic reception.

The initial composition is traditionally dated to 1894, a time when Rodin returned again to a small figure of a damned woman that he was introducing at the same time into the *Monument to Victor Hugo*, where she embodies poetry. This very sensual figure is pressed against the body of Christ, depicted in agony with his head thrust so far forward that it seems almost disconnected from his body.

The first marble *Christ and Mary Magdalene* (c. 1905) was acquired by August Thyssen in 1908 (Carmen Thyssen Collection). Loïe Fuller, for lack of bronze casts that were never produced, arranged for plaster casts of it to join the collections of both Alma de Bretteville Spreckels and Samuel Hill. The second marble followed immediately. The same size as the first, it makes a strong impression by the huge mass of rough stone, hewn with the point of the knife, that surrounds the two figures, which are handled with great precision. Rodin plays on contrasts here, between the fluidity of the drapery and the almost methodically carved block of stone, between very different approaches to the sculpting of the stone, and, finally, between shadows and light. Mary Magdalene's left arm stands out from a deep cavity carved into the stone, while the face of Christ appears in full light in the front of the composition.

ALNR

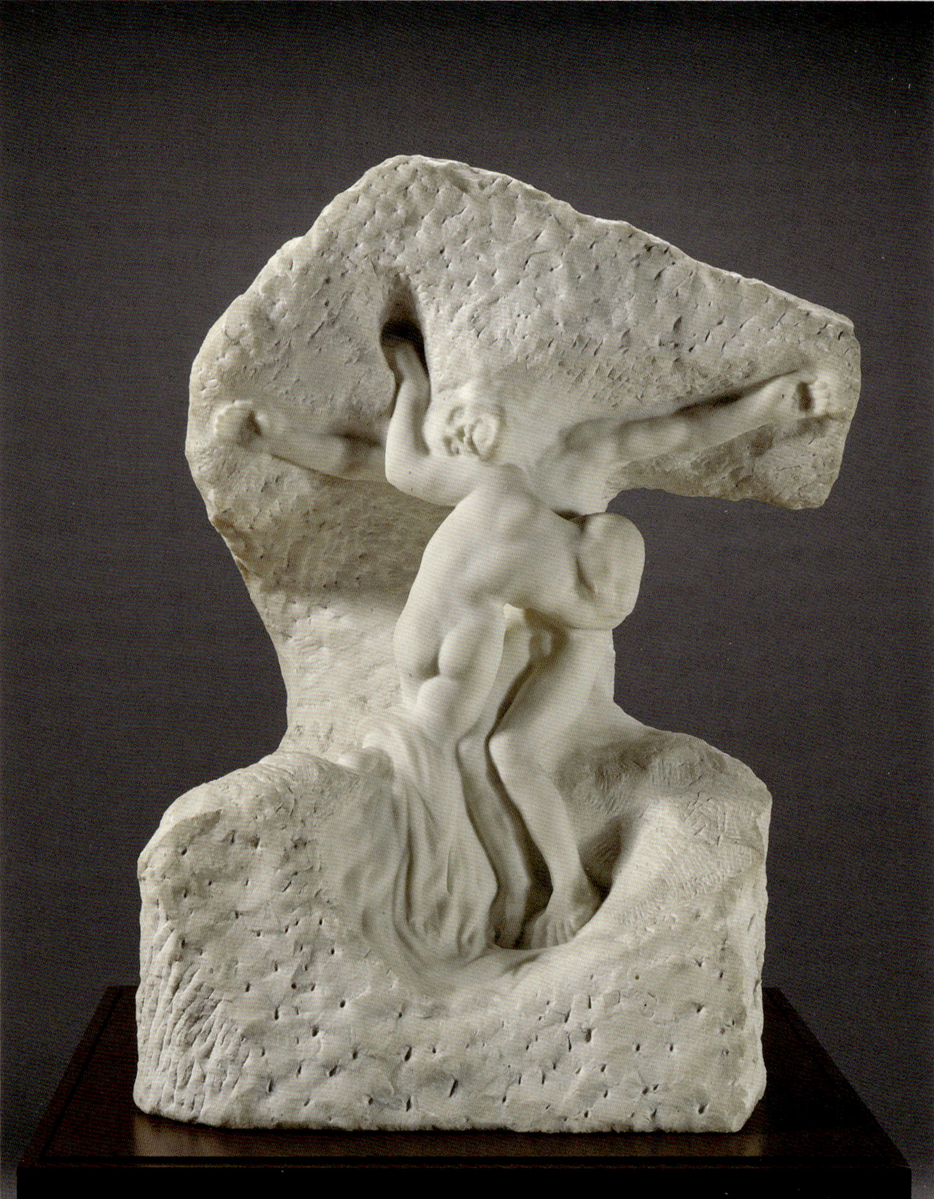

1. Auguste Rodin, *Art: Conversations with Paul Gsell* [1911], trans. Jacques de Caso and Patricia B. Sanders (Berkeley: University of California Press, 1984), 54.

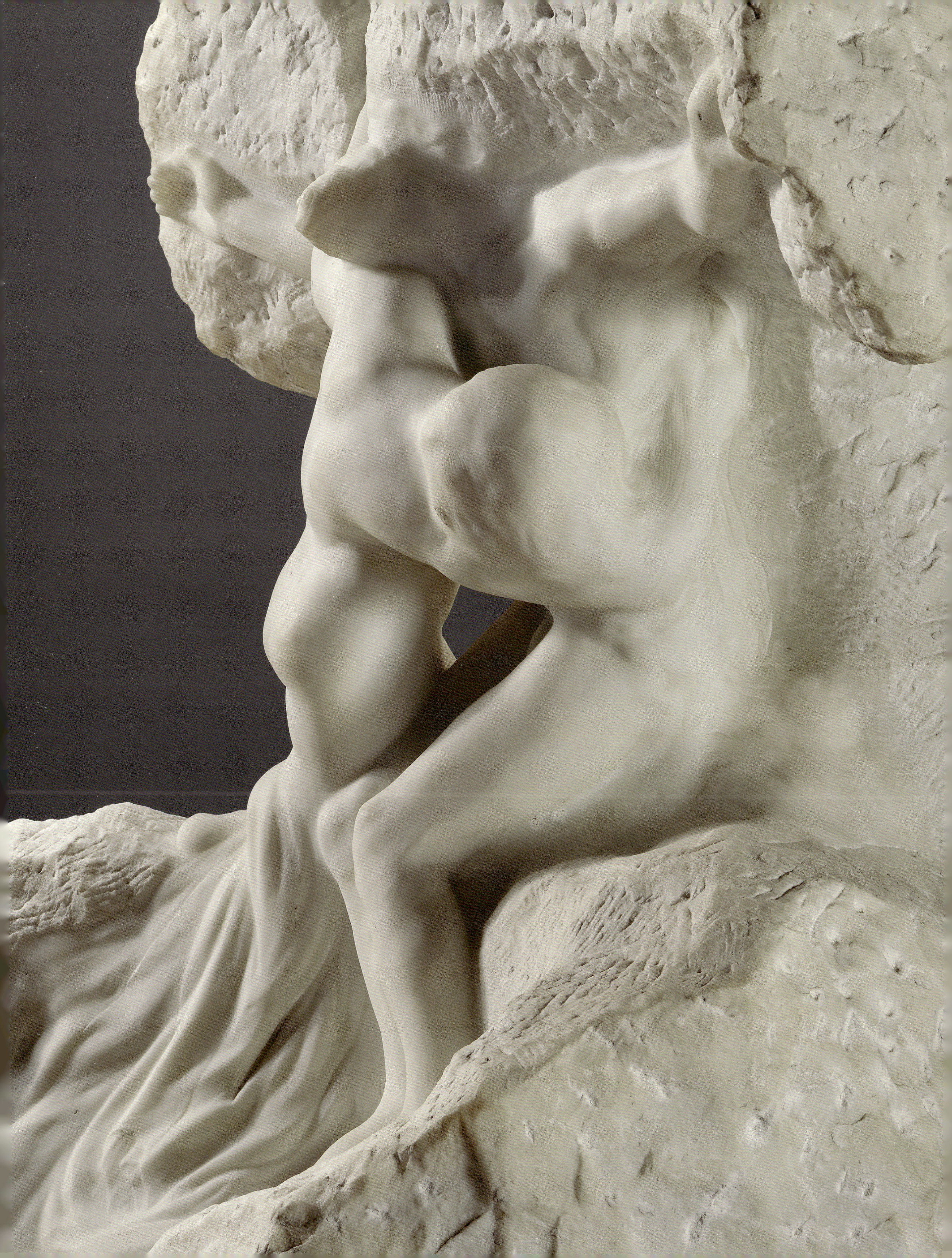

THE GENIUS OF SCULPTURE

c. 1880
Pen and ink on wove paper
10 3/8 × 7 7/16 in. (26.3 × 18.9 cm)
Inscribed in graphite on previous mount: *le génie de la sculpture*
Cleveland Museum of Art
Bequest of Muriel Butkin, 2008.404

The Genius of Sculpture is a rare example of a drawing from the 1880s depicting an artist in the process of creating—a symbolic self-portrait, as Kirk Varnedoe suggests.[1] It can be compared to the bas-relief of the *Creator* for *The Gates of Hell*, which has also been identified as a self-portrait, not of a god-like artist in action but of an artist "cogitating, in the manner of the *Thinker*."[2] As Rosalyn Frankel Jamison pointed out describing this drawing, Rodin does not portray the act of creation itself, however, because the figure's two hands are not sculpting.[3] *The Genius of Sculpture* depicts three phases of creativity at the same time: inspiration (the muse in the form of a weightless woman / airborne genius instead of a traditional winged muse, whispering an idea in the artist's ear), thought (the artist, with his right hand over his forehead), and the artwork (his left arm surrounds his

figurine on the stand). Thanks to a striking second version of the theme with the addition of gouache (the Cleveland *Genius of Sculpture* is probably a preliminary sketch), we can confirm the intention of a self-portrait. In the gouache drawing, only known by a black-and-white reproduction, Rodin's signature appears on the bottom right of the sheet and on the drawn pedestal. The latter supports what seems now to be the depiction of a sculpted group—meaning Rodin is not only the author of the drawing, but he is also doubly and symbolically the author of the sculpture he is representing: a sculptor in the process of creating (comparable to the work *I Am Beautiful*). Around 1889, Rodin would develop the iconography of the creator/poet/thinker with his projects for the *Monument to Victor Hugo*.
CBU

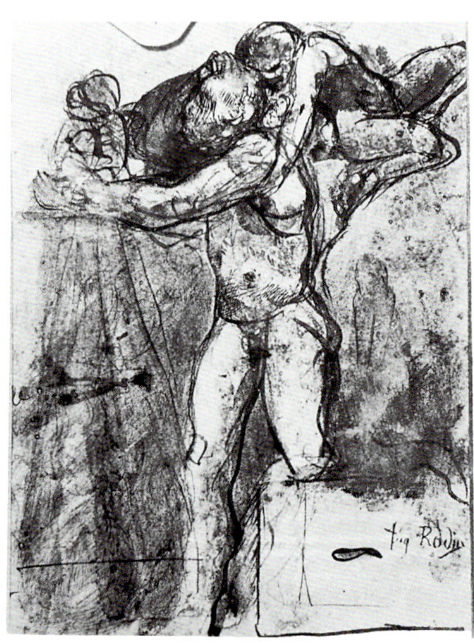

Auguste Rodin, *The Sculptor*, c. 1880. Pen and ink and gouache on paper, dimensions and location unknown.

1. J. Kirk T. Varnedoe, "Rodin's Drawings," in *Rodin Rediscovered*, exh. cat., ed. Albert E. Elsen (Washington, DC: National Gallery of Art, 1981), 169.
2. Albert E. Elsen, *The Gates of Hell by Auguste Rodin* (Palo Alto, CA: Stanford University Press, 1985), 221.
3. Rosalyn Frankel Jamison, "Rodin's Humanization of the Muse," in *Rodin Rediscovered*, exh. cat., ed. Albert E. Elsen (Washington, DC: National Gallery of Art, 1981), 106.

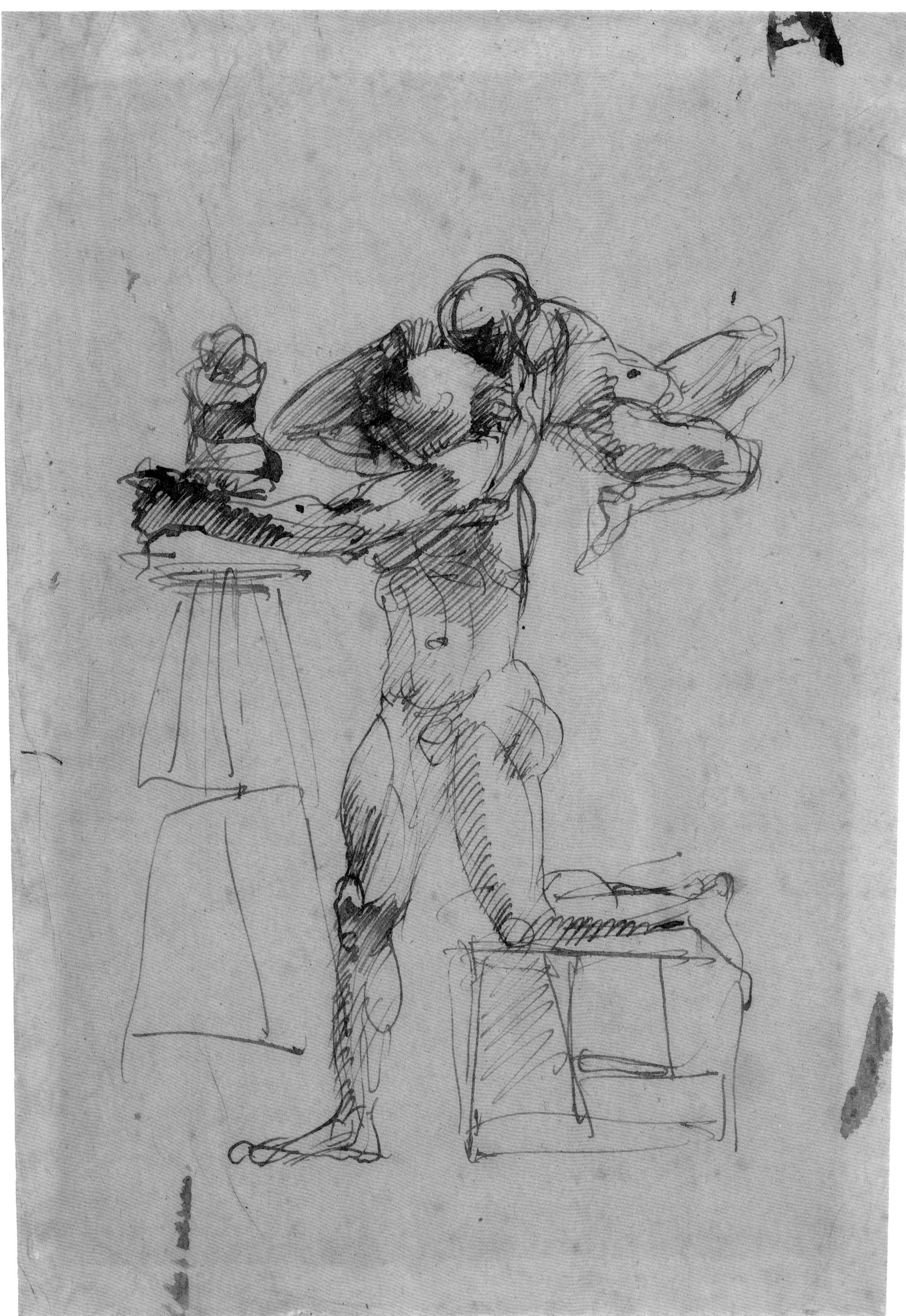

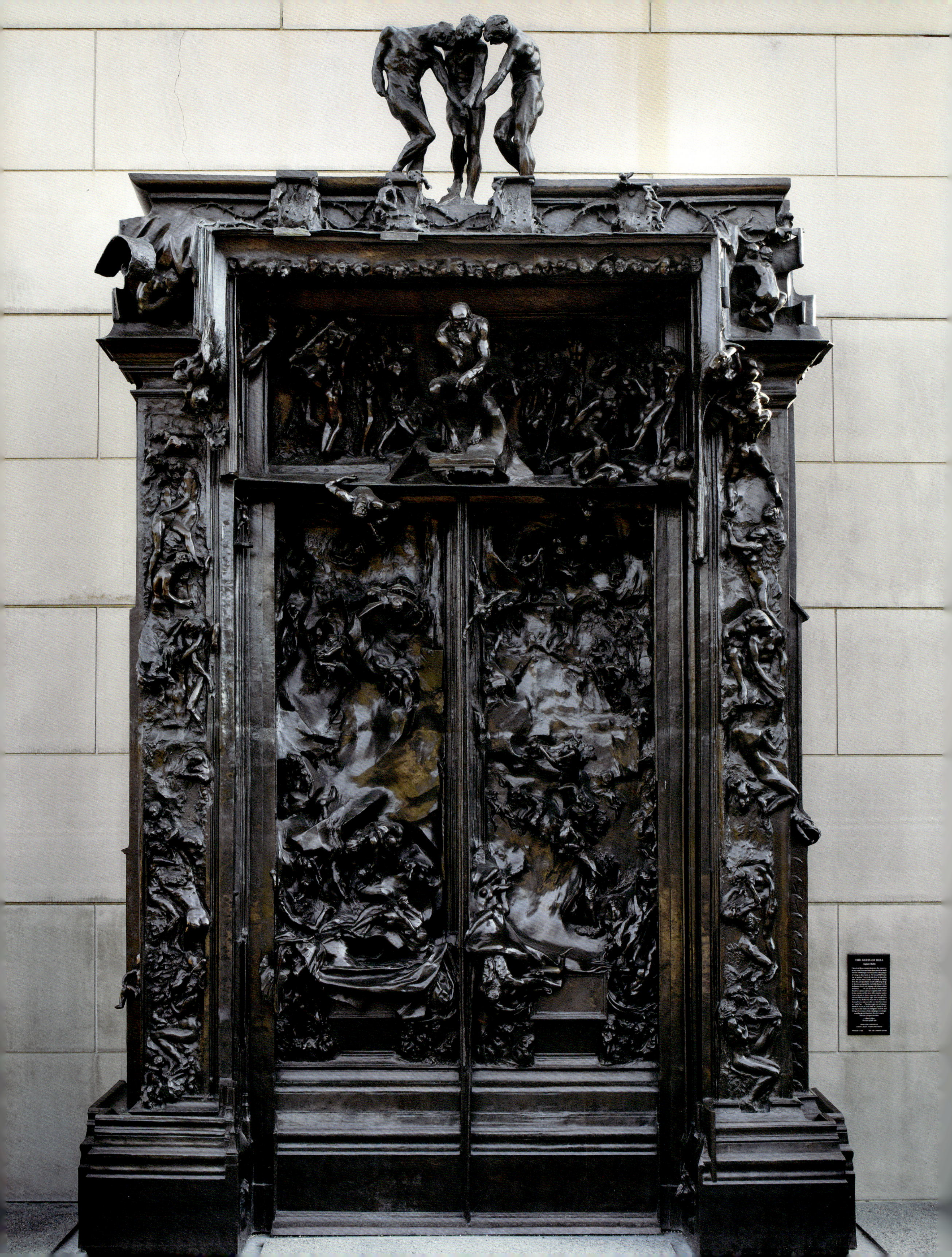

STAGING *THE GATES OF HELL*

PATRICK R. CROWLEY

In 1974, the financier and philanthropist B. Gerald Cantor donated eighty-nine sculptures by Auguste Rodin to what was then the Stanford University Art Museum (now the Iris & B. Gerald Cantor Center for the Arts).[1] It was, at the time, the largest bequest of sculpture to any university museum. With important exceptions (including the Legion of Honor, located nearby in San Francisco, which boasts an outstanding collection of lifetime casts assembled by Alma de Bretteville Spreckels), chances are good that if you are seeing Rodin's bronzes in the United States, you are seeing them through the eyes of both Gerald and Iris Cantor, who shares her late husband's fervent passion for Rodin. But you are also seeing them through the eyes of Albert E. Elsen, a professor of art history at Stanford, who was largely responsible for the rehabilitation of Rodin's reputation in the mid-twentieth century. Elsen worked closely with the Cantors over many years, and it was he who helped to shepherd their major gift to Stanford.

Of the many museum collections across the country that include Rodin's bronzes, Stanford's is the largest, and the third largest in the world after the Musée Rodin in Paris. In contrast to the Spreckels collection, however, Stanford's comprises mostly posthumous casts.[2] While Gerald Cantor, like many collectors, favored lifetime casts, both he and Elsen were strongly committed to the educational value of posthumous casts, believing that a university museum was an appropriate venue for a major center for Rodin research. For Elsen, establishing the value of the posthumous casts—not only for educational purposes, but also as legitimate works in their own right, especially in the United States—would become a kind of passion project. In 1974, in his capacity as president of the College Art Association, Elsen drafted the organization's Statement on Standards for the Production and Reproduction of Sculpture (which remains in place with some modifications today).[3] And in 1979, with John Henry Merryman,

FIG. 8.1

Auguste Rodin (French, 1840–1917), *The Gates of Hell*, 1880–c. 1900, cast in 1981. Bronze, 250 ¾ × 158 × 33 ⅜ in. (636.91 × 401.42 × 84.77 cm). Iris & B. Gerald Cantor Center for Visual Arts at Stanford University. Gift of the B. Gerald Cantor Collection, 1986.85.

a professor at Stanford Law School, Elsen wrote *Law, Ethics, and the Visual Arts* (where Rodin features prominently in several sections), which was the first, and would remain the standard, reference in the emerging field of art law.[4]

Elsen's rather pragmatic approach to the status of posthumous casts would be tested in 1981 when a conflict erupted between him and Rosalind Krauss, a critic and, at the time, professor of modern art at Hunter College, over the new cast of *The Gates of Hell*, commissioned by the French government and financed by Gerald Cantor in 1977 (fig. 8.1). These *Gates*, which have anchored the Rodin Sculpture Garden at Stanford since 1985, were cast between 1978 and 1981 to serve as the centerpiece of *Rodin Rediscovered*, a major exhibition in 1981–82 at the National Gallery of Art in Washington, DC.[5] The acrimonious debate between Elsen and Krauss served as a crucial turning point in the critical reception and understanding of Rodin's legacy in the United States, one that would have a lasting impact more generally in reframing the story of modernism in twentieth-century art criticism.

In the autumn 1981 issue of the journal *October*, Krauss published her seminal essay "The Originality of the Avant-Garde: A Postmodernist Repetition," in which she deployed the unlikely figure of Rodin in her opening gambit.[6] Unlikely because Rodin was about as far from the avant-garde as one could conceivably get—an artist who had achieved such widespread popularity in his own time, and whose name had become so synonymous with mass production that, in Krauss's words, he was "induced to participate in the transformation of his own work into kitsch."[7] The *Gates* offered a perfect test case for Krauss, since Rodin worked on them between 1880 and 1900 but left them incomplete upon his death in 1917. Shortly before he died, Rodin made it clear in a letter to Léonce Bénédite, the first curator of the Musée Rodin, that he wanted the *Gates* to be cast. The first two versions, financed by Jules Mastbaum for his own Rodin Museum in Philadelphia and the Musée Rodin, were cast between 1925 and 1928; a third and fourth, now in Tokyo and Zurich, respectively, were cast by Alexis Rudier for Kojiro Matsukata and Hermann Göring on behalf of Adolf Hitler.[8] The Stanford *Gates*, cast by the Coubertin Foundry, are the fifth version of the *Gates* to be cast, but they have the distinction of being the first to be cast using the lost-wax process, rather than sand-casting. This history of posthumous casts of the *Gates* and their different conditions of patronage, making, and viewing forms the context for Krauss's essay. What does it mean, she wondered, to cast such a work after the literal death of the author? Cast for different patrons, in different foundries, using different methods, in different places?

> The National Gallery's exhibition included, for example, a brand new cast of *The Gates of Hell*, so absolutely recent that visitors to the exhibition were able to sit down in a little theater provided for the occasion to view a just completed movie of the casting and finishing of this new version.
>
> To some—though hardly all—of the people sitting in that theater watching the casting of *The Gates of Hell*, it must have occurred that they were witnessing the making of a fake. After all, Rodin had been dead since 1918 [*sic*], and surely a work of his produced more than sixty years after his death cannot be the genuine article, cannot, that is, be an original. The answer to this is more interesting than one would think; for the answer is neither yes nor no.[9]

There is not now, nor has there ever been, any genuine doubt as to whether *The Gates of Hell* cast by the Coubertin Foundry constitutes a strictly "legitimate" work by Rodin. Krauss well understood the legal stipulations of Rodin's will, who left his estate to France, granting the state the right to cast new

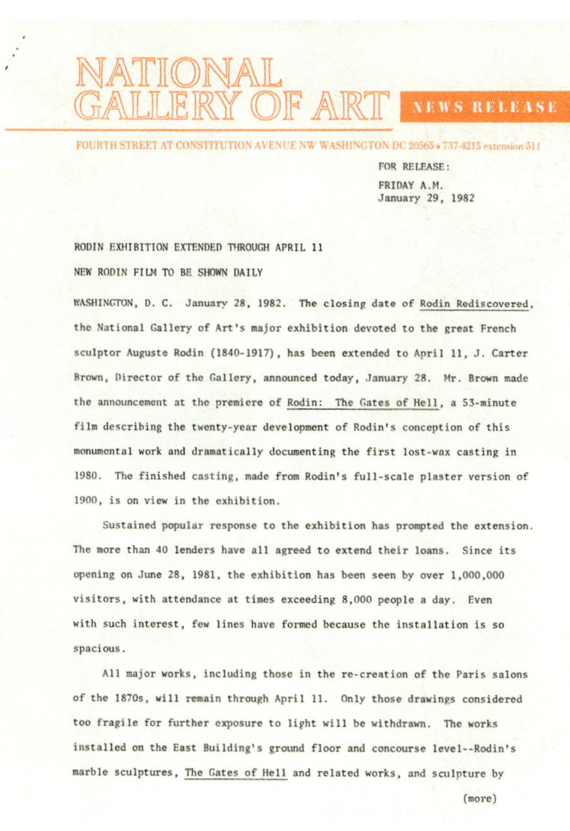

FIG. 8.2

National Gallery of Art Press Release, January 28, 1982, announcing that the exhibition *Rodin Rediscovered* would be extended through April 11, with the new Rodin film to be shown daily.

bronzes (in editions of twelve, as determined by French statute).[10] "But once we leave the lawyer's office and the terms of Rodin's will," she wrote, "we fall immediately into a quagmire. In what sense is the new cast an original?"[11] The point, as Krauss put it, was not legal but structural and aesthetic. "We do not care if the copyright papers are all in order; for what is at stake are the aesthetic rights of style based on a culture of originals. Sitting in the little theater, watching the newest *Gates* being cast, watching this violation, we want to call out, 'Fraud.'"[12]

Elsen was furious. Such destabilizing doubt, he believed, threatened to undermine his entire project of affirming the legal and ethical legitimacy of certain posthumous casts. Despite the fact that Krauss never called the 1978–81 *Gates* a fake and, indeed, pointedly declared it to be legitimate and a "real original," her quite reasonable question about the limits of the role of the lawyer's office or the copyright papers appear to have struck Elsen as an almost personal affront. In a letter to the editors of *October*, Elsen characterized Krauss's essay as a willful massaging of the facts and a malicious smear on his legacy, not to mention the hugely successful exhibition he had organized.[13] To bolster his counterclaims, Elsen supplied plentiful historical documentation about Rodin's own collaboration with enterprising technicians responsible for the reproduction and patination of his bronzes, as well as his clearly stated intentions about the dissemination of his work.[14]

But Elsen saved his most scathing rebuttal for last, accusing Krauss of essentially making up the whole scene of "the little theater" where "visitors to the exhibition were able to sit down" and view a film documenting the casting of the new *Gates*[15]: "As of this writing, January 12, 1982, no film on the casting has been shown to the public in any size theater of the National Gallery. . . . Just what do we call out when a critic invents issues, makes up contradictions, promotes a double standard, and reviews an event that has not yet happened?"[16] In a footnote to her lengthy rejoinder to Elsen's letter (which the editors published in full), Krauss explained that she knew about the film from Elsen's description of it at an informational meeting at the National Gallery in the spring of 1981, in the months preceding the opening of *Rodin Rediscovered*.[17] Although Krauss was aware that the film was not yet ready at the opening of the show (unbeknownst to her because the first pouring of the *Gates* had failed), she retained the bit about the theater because the issue was already going to press and she believed (rightly, as it turned out) that the film would later be incorporated into the exhibition. And so, as she playfully conceded in her reply to Elsen's letter, "The inclusion of the scene of the 'film' in the published essay was, reportorially, journalistically, an error. And yet . . . and yet . . . the 'staging of the film' is part of the staging of *The Gates* as a theoretical entity at the beginning of a general inquiry on originality within the conceptual frame of modernism."[18]

A press release from the National Gallery attests that sixteen days after the writing of Elsen's letter, the film was, in fact, screened in the East Building Auditorium multiple times daily for several months (fig 8.2).[19] That auditorium is hardly a "little theater" of the kind that was initially intended to be installed in one of the galleries (the original idea, according to Krauss's report of Elsen's description, was that the galleries were conceived as a suite of "imaginative spaces," including, most notably in the context of the present essay, the atelier). Indeed, the auditorium, designed by I. M. Pei, is often called the "Large Theater" and seats up to five hundred people. But for Krauss, as she went on to explain

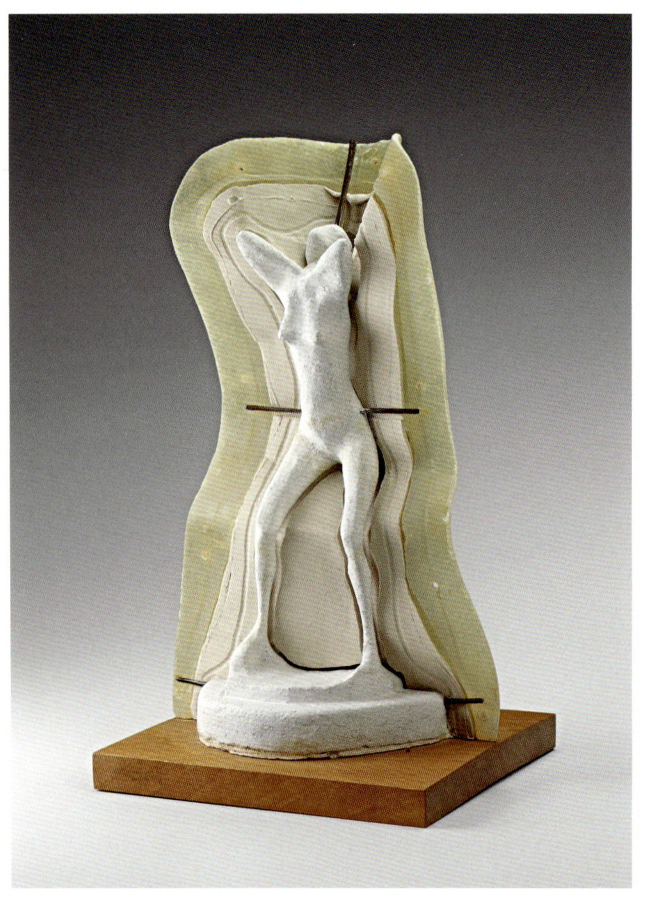

Coubertin Foundry (French, established 1963) after Auguste Rodin, *Small Fauness*, step four in the eleven-step lost-wax casting process, 19th century, cast 1981. Plaster, wax, metal, synthetic material, 9 ½ × 4 × 3 ¼ in. (24.1 × 10.2 × 8.3 cm). Iris & B. Gerald Cantor Center for Visual Arts at Stanford University. Gift of the B. Gerald Cantor Art Foundation, 1992.188.4.

in her reply, the specific conditions of the screening were moot: "This imaginary scene, with its onset of doubt, could be staged anywhere: in the galleries of a Rodin exhibition, in a darkened room where a movie of the casting of *The Gates* is shown, or in a meeting with the education department of a museum where a discussion about how to explain very late posthumous casts to a possibly dubious public takes place."[20]

What has been overlooked in accounts of the critical controversy surrounding the *Gates* is the compelling and historically significant fifty-three-minute film itself—the very film that ignited Krauss and Elsen's quarrel in the first place. *Rodin: The Gates of Hell* (1981), financed by Gerald Cantor, was the brainchild of Iris Cantor, who coproduced it along with David Saxon. The Cantors commissioned this documentary record of the bronze-casting process—one that can understandably seem deeply mysterious, given its highly technical and, indeed, literally invisible operations within the mold and the furnace—in keeping with their strong commitment to the education of the museum public.[21] Four decades later, an excerpt from the film demonstrating lost-wax casting still plays in the Rodin gallery of Stanford's Cantor Arts Center alongside a set of didactic texts and a specially commissioned set of replicas of *The Small Fauness* alternately sliced open in sections, encased in the investment mold, or left with its sprues and gates revealed so that she metamorphoses, Daphne-like, into a tree (fig. 8.3). Yet beyond their museological function as what Elsen called an "illustrative record" of the casting process, these figures present a similar interpretive challenge in the sense that they stand in a kind of ontological limbo: they are neither "authentic" works by Rodin, nor are they fakes or forgeries. Likewise, the film, for all its narrative and technical clarity, raises as many questions as it answers. Despite its painstaking representation of Rodin's preferred lost-wax casting method, the film also draws attention to the decidedly contemporary interventions made by the Coubertin Foundry in the use of fiberglass and other "space-age" materials that were unavailable to Rodin. In this way, the uneasy admixture of both high fidelity and technological enhancement threatens to undermine the very purpose of the film—and the didactic frame that surrounds it in the gallery—to help us understand and come to terms with the posthumous origins of the *Gates*.

The *Gates* film opened to much fanfare at the National Gallery of Art in January 1982; it was on this occasion that the gallery's director, J. Carter Brown, announced that *Rodin Rediscovered*, which had already received one million visitors since its opening, would be extended through Easter. Following close-up shots of various figures on the *Gates* and its installation in the exhibition, the film proceeds to introduce the principal protagonists of the film. Jean Bernard, the master founder at Coubertin, greets the Cantors and Monique Laurent, director of the Musée Rodin, at the Chateau de Coubertin. There, Bernard displays to the group a deluxe volume of engravings by Pierre-Jean Mariette depicting the lost-wax casting process. One of these, showing an equestrian statue of Louis XV, closely resembles that of Louis XIV in Denis Diderot's famous *Encyclopédie* (fig. 8.4). The film then tracks the entire casting endeavor, with all its risks and rewards: the construction of the massive furnace; the making of the molds (fig. 8.5); the drama of the pour before 300 spectators, including the Cantors, a delegation from the Musée Rodin, and throngs of townspeople peering through the windows from outside (fig. 8.6); and the painstaking finishing touches on the resultant cast, once again shown installed in the National Gallery, but now with visitors who marvel over the *Gates*, themselves mirroring the museum visitors in the film's audience.

Usually described as an educational film (indeed, it won an award in that category at the American Film Festival in 1983), it is also a quintessential example of what film historian Salomé Aguilera Skvirsky has recently identified as the "process genre."[22] For Skvirsky, this genre involves a distinctive syntax and expository structure that outlines a recipe-like series of steps with a clear beginning, middle, and end resulting in the achievement of a goal. Although processual representation is not unique to cinema—Skvirsky looks at early modern prints, such as Diderot's, as important precursors—cinema nevertheless offers a unique capacity for depicting motion and fostering absorptive states of attentiveness. It does so, according to Skvirsky, by aestheticizing labor as a form-giving activity that, unlike mere toil, straddles the boundaries between work and leisure. Process films thus make even industrial labor look artisanal and, indeed, almost magical. In Marxian terms, the durational character of cinema reveals how much labor time is congealed in the commodity, thus enhancing the product's value. The film makes this labor painfully clear when revealing that the first attempt at casting the *Gates* in a single pour resulted in failure: the narrator notes that thousands of hours had been spent on this fruitless endeavor (Bernard, in his memoir of the event, provides a very specific number: 5,518).[23] Besides the suspense it builds toward the triumphant denouement, the revelation of this initial failure is itself revealing: Bernard, according to the narrator, has a bad feeling about the result before he even lays eyes on it; his artisanal experience provides him with a kind of supersensory intuition. But perhaps Skvirsky's most useful insight, in terms of the *Gates*, is her recognition of an internal tension in the process film between the generic and the singular: on one hand, the genre exhibits techniques as eminently repeatable; on the other, its interpretive conventions (through the script, editing, and so on) allegorize the singular instance of production. Thus, "even when a process film was intended and functions as a how-to, it remains at the same time a unique, particular instance of doing or making."[24]

What makes the *Gates* film especially compelling is the way its genre *as* a process film aligns so neatly with the role of process in Rodin's sculptural practice. Recalling Leo Steinberg's landmark 1963 essay on the processual aspects of Rodin's sculpture and its relationship to modernism, Krauss, in her 1981 text, observed that "the revelation of process works to expose the means of reproduction; in formalist terms, it bares the device."[25] The film similarly enacts its own processual representation in an astonishing moment when the camera pans to the wooden platform of VIP spectators (fig. 8.7), revealing another camera capturing the event from their vantage point (the townspeople watching from outside play an important role in the social dynamics of spectatorship as well, standing in as they do for the museum public beholding the *Gates* at the end of the film). In this inversion of perspective and subjectivity, the viewer of the film, facing the lens of the second camera, displaces and occupies the position of the maker— and perhaps even the *Gates* themselves—to become the object of their own gaze. The effect evokes Roland Barthes's account of Diderot's *Encyclopédie* and the didactic goals of its illustrations (not coincidentally, the ones devoted to bronze casting): namely, that Diderot's process imagery is "fascinated, at reason's instance, by the *wrong side* of things: it cross-sections, it amputates, it turns inside out, it tries to get *behind* Nature."[26] The *Gates* film, and the cast cross-sections of the *Small Fauness* now flanking it in the Stanford gallery, make this desire explicit.

Forty years later, it is tempting to regard the dispute between Krauss and Elsen as a museum piece in twentieth-century art criticism. But this would be a

FIG. 8.4

Jean Bernard showing an engraving illustrating the lost-wax casting process to B. Gerald and Iris Cantor and the delegation from the Musée Rodin. Still from *Rodin: The Gates of Hell* (1981).

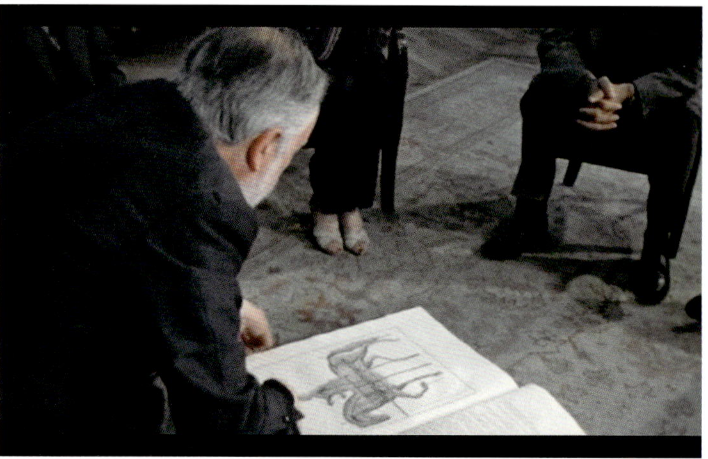

FIG. 8.5

A technician at Coubertin Foundry applies a layer of liquid rubber to a plaster model for the making of a new mold. Still from *Rodin: The Gates of Hell* (1981).

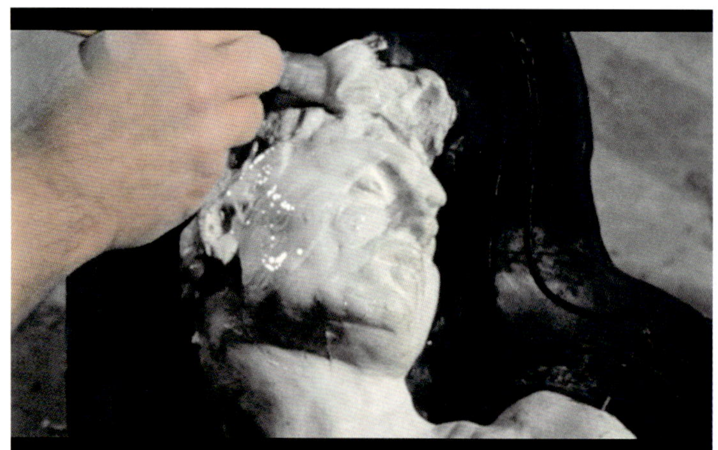

FIG. 8.6

Spectators peer through the windows to catch a suspenseful glimpse of the *grande coulée*, the "big pour." Still from *Rodin: The Gates of Hell* (1981).

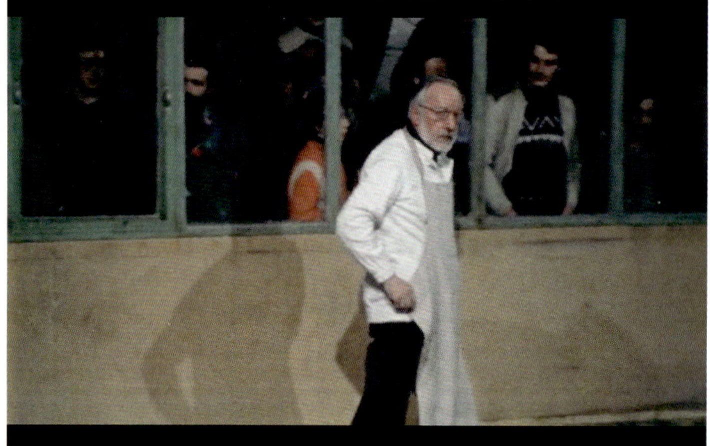

FIG. 8.7

The VIP viewing scaffold at Coubertin Foundry, showing another camera capturing the pouring of Rodin's *Gates of Hell* from a different vantage point. Still from *Rodin: The Gates of Hell* (1981).

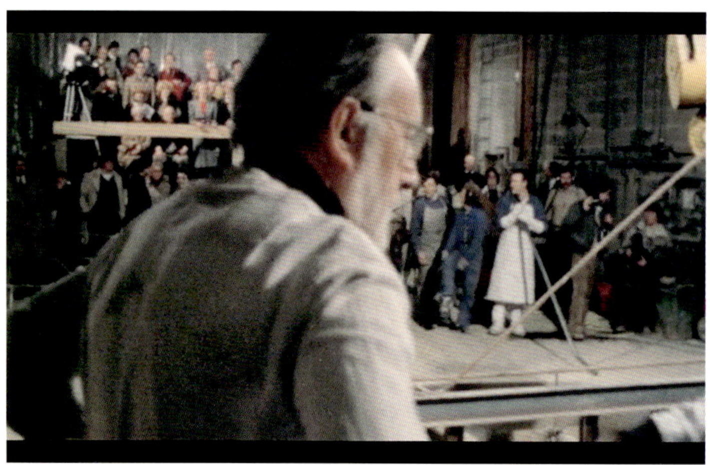

grave mistake, for the stakes of originality, although historically specific there to the emergence of postmodernism in the early 1980s, remain just as compelling today: it is no coincidence that Rodin remains central to contemporary questions about the relationship between law and technology (especially with regard to new techniques of sculptural reproduction, such as 3D printing), which a university museum such as the Cantor is uniquely equipped to explore, drawing from the broad range of expertise across a variety of constituents on campus. Of course, much has changed; another way to look at the historical context of the quarrel would be to see it as an allegory of the rise of theory and the fall of connoisseurship—a shift that has arguably been overturned, or at least greatly attenuated, with the more recent valorization of connoisseurship in conjunction with a material turn and what historians of science have called "artisanal epistemology."[27] Indeed, examining the embodied knowledge of craft production, and the concomitant attention to the role of making, marks one of the most significant interdisciplinary turns in object-driven research in American universities over the past decade. This approach has the potential to interweave the historical connections between Rodin's art and the many skilled technicians who have helped bring his works to light, both before and after his death. The pedagogical mission of the university museum, especially at Stanford with its reputation as a cutting-edge hub of technological innovation, offers an ideal context for the presentation and study of the *Gates* as a technical triumph in this expanded field of makers and viewers: one where the dynamics of teaching and learning are catalyzed by—what else?—repetition.

NOTES

1. For an introduction to the history of the collection at Stanford, see, especially, Albert E. Elsen, "B. Gerald Cantor and the Stanford Rodin Collection," in *Rodin's Art: The Rodin Collection of the Iris & B. Gerald Cantor Center for Visual Arts at Stanford University*, ed. Albert E. Elsen and Bernard Barryte (New York: Oxford University Press, 2003), 5–11.

2. On posthumous casts of Rodin, see, especially, Monique Laurent, "Vie posthume d'un fonds d'atelier: Les éditions de bronzes du musée Rodin," in *La sculpture du XIXe siècle, une mémoire retrouvée: Les fonds de sculpture* (Paris: Rencontres de l'École du Louvre, 1986), 245–53.

3. College Art Association, "Statement on Standards for the Production and Reproduction of Sculpture," adopted February 17, 2013, http://www.collegeart .org/standards-and-guidelines/guidelines/sculpture. Cf. Sylvia Hochfield, "Problems in the Reproduction of Sculpture," *ArtNews* 73 (November 1974): 21–29.

4. John Henry Merryman and Albert E. Elsen, *Law, Ethics, and the Visual Arts*, 2 vols. (New York: Matthew Bender, 1979). See also Albert Elsen and John Merryman, "Art Replicas: A Question of Ethics," *ArtNews* 78 (February 1979): 61.

5. Albert E. Elsen, ed., *Rodin Rediscovered*, exh. cat. (Washington, DC: National Gallery of Art, 1981). For an introduction to *The Gates of Hell* at Stanford, see, especially, Elsen and Barryte, *Rodin's Art*, 155ff.

6. Rosalind Krauss, "The Originality of the Avant-Garde: A Postmodernist Repetition," *October* 18 (1981): 47–66. References to this text are taken from the reissued version of the essay in Rosalind E. Krauss, *The Originality of the Avant-Garde and Other Modernist Myths* (Cambridge, MA: MIT Press, 1985), 151–70.

7. Krauss, *Originality of the Avant-Garde*, 157.

8. Elsen and Barryte, *Rodin's Art*, 34n5.

9. Krauss, *Originality of the Avant-Garde*, 151. The film Krauss refers to is *Rodin: The Gates of Hell* (1981), coproduced by Iris Cantor and David Saxon, http://www.amazon.com/gp/video/detail /B00SQYRI3Y/ref=atv_dp_share_cu_r.

10. For a superb introduction to the legal issues surrounding Rodin's estate, see, especially, Deborah M. Hussey, "The *Sine Qua Non* of Copyright," *Journal of the Copyright Society of the USA*, 51 (2004): 763–95. On the status of copies in copyright law and the role of copies in museum collections, see Hillel Schwartz, *The Culture of the Copy: Striking Likenesses, Unreasonable Facsimiles* (New York: Zone, 1996), 241–57.

11. Krauss, *Originality of the Avant-Garde*, 151.

12. Krauss, *Originality of the Avant-Garde*, 157.

13. Albert E. Elsen, "On the Question of Originality: A Letter," *October* 20 (1982): 107–9.

14. For a discussion of originality and the seeming oxymoronic status of the "original copy," see, especially, Jean Chatelain, "An Original in Sculpture," in Elsen, *Rodin Rediscovered*, 275–82.

15. See Krauss, *Originality of the Avant-Garde*, 151, as quoted above.

16. Elsen, "On the Question of Originality," 109.

17. Rosalind Krauss, "Sincerely Yours: A Reply," *October* 20 (1982): 110–30.

18. Krauss, *Originality of the Avant-Garde*, 181n16.

19. Records of Public Relations and Communication, Press Releases, 1939–present, RG14A, National Gallery of Art, Washington, DC, Gallery Archives, accessed November 18, 2021, http://www.nga.gov /content/dam/ngaweb/research/gallery-archives /PressReleases/1989-1980/1982/14A11_44463 _19820128.pdf.

20. Krauss, *Originality of the Avant-Garde*, 180n16.

21. Elsen and Barryte, *Rodin's Art*, 31–33. Due to spatial constraints, the eleven-step process was reduced to eight in the present installation.

22. Salomé Aguilera Skvirsky, *The Process Genre: Cinema and the Aesthetic of Labor* (Durham, NC: Duke University Press, 2020).

23. Jean Bernard, "Memoire sur la cinquième fonte de la Porte de l'Enfer," *Fonderie de Coubertin* (1976–1981), archival object file for *The Gates of Hell* (1985.86), Cantor Arts Center, Stanford University.

24. Skvirsky, *Process Genre*, 85.

25. Krauss, *Originality of the Avant-Garde*, 186. Cf. Leo Steinberg, "Rodin," in *Other Criteria: Confrontations with Twentieth-Century Art* (New York: Oxford University Press, 1972).

26. Roland Barthes, "The Plates of the *Encyclopedia*," in *New Critical Essays* (Evanston, IL: Northwestern University Press, 2009), 39. Cf. Skvirsky, *Process Genre*, 42.

27. See, especially, Pamela Smith, "Making Things: Techniques and Books in Early Modern Europe," in Paula Findlen, *Early Modern Things: Objects and Their Histories, 1500–1800* (New York: Routledge, 2012), 173–203. Cf. Jennifer L. Roberts, "Things: Material Turn, Transnational Turn," *American Art* 31 (2017): 64–69.

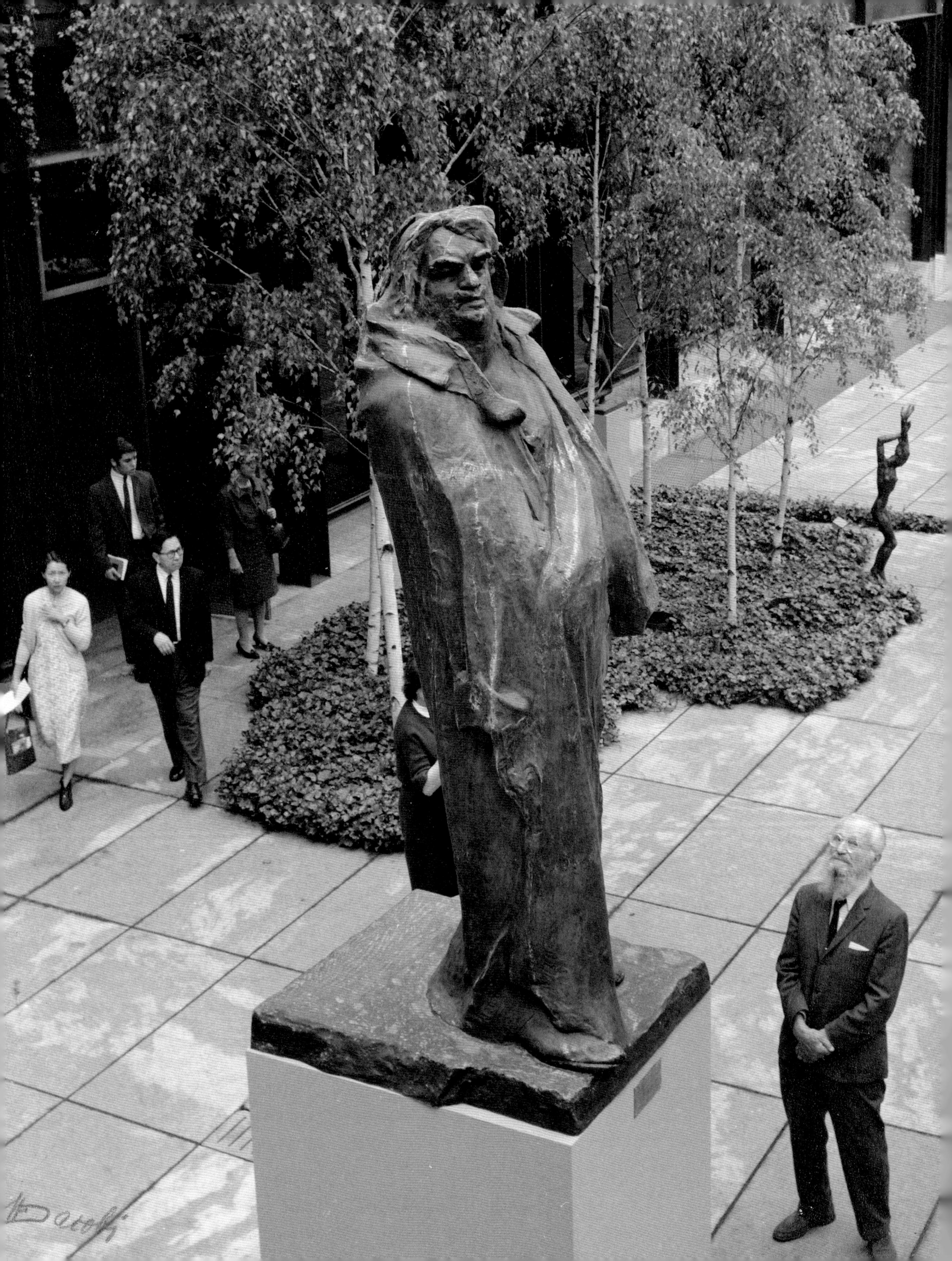

CHRONOLOGY

NORA M. ROSENGARTEN

Auguste Rodin Biographical Dates

The following events from the life of Auguste Rodin trace the evolution of his artistic practice from his birth in 1840 to his death in 1917. While the events here are by no means comprehensive, they mark pivotal shifts in his work across media, as well as his own self-fashioning as an artist. In particular, these dates and descriptions attend to and reach toward the other two timelines, in the hopes of provoking new sets of questions and connections pertaining to this canonical artist.

1840

François-Auguste-René Rodin is born in Paris on November 12 to Jean-Baptiste Rodin (1803–1883), a police clerk, and Marie Cheffer (c. 1806–1871). He will become especially close with his elder sister, Anna-Marie (1837–1862), who goes by Maria.

1847–1854

Rodin first attends École des Frères de la Doctrine Chrétienne and later enrolls in a private boarding school in Beauvais.

Selected World Events

Highlighting a selection of significant world events, with priority given to those relating to the United States and France, this timeline intends to provoke new associations and questions about the relevance of a broader geopolitical context, both to Rodin's oeuvre and to the collecting practices it generated even decades after the artist's death. What, how, and why a collector acquires a piece of art is always political, if indirectly so. The following events are meant to serve as familiar coordinates within the span of nearly two hundred years one must traverse to grasp Rodin's influence in the United States, as well as jumping-off points for future scholarship.

1851

The Great Exhibition takes place in London, becoming the first world's fair.
Louis Napoleon takes power in France by coup.

1852

On March 6, the US Supreme Court hands down the Dred Scott decision.
Frederick Douglass delivers the speech "The Meaning of July Fourth for the Negro" in Rochester, New York.

1853

Matthew C. Perry of the US Navy aggresses the Japanese capital city of Edo with gunships in a bid to initiate trade between the United States and Japan.

Collecting Rodin in the United States

This timeline presents some of the crucial episodes in the history of collecting Rodin's work in the United States. Arranging these events in relationship to both a geopolitical landscape and key events in Rodin's life makes visible the degree to which this history of collecting is shaped by a complex network of events. One collector acquiring a single work of art is a consequence of hundreds of smaller events that, in concert, produced the networks of patronage this catalogue articulates.

Auguste Rodin Biographical Dates

1854
Rodin enters the Paris École Impériale Spéciale de Dessin et de Mathématiques, also known as the Petite École, where he studies under Horace Lecoq de Boisbaudran (1802–1897).

1855
Rodin wins the second-place award for achievement in drawing at the Petite École; the next year, he will win first place.
Rodin discovers sculpture.

1857–1859
Rodin is rejected three times in his repeated bids for admission to the prestigious École Supérieure des Beaux-Arts in Paris.

1861
Maria Rodin enters a convent in Paris.

1862
Maria Rodin dies.
Overcome with grief, Rodin becomes a novice in the order of the Pères du Très-Saint-Sacrement, Paris. Pierre-Julien Eymard, the order's leader, tells Rodin to devote himself to art. Rodin leaves the order. Photographer Charles Aubry produces two photos of the young Rodin, one in which the artist is shown as a craftsman, clad in dirty overalls, and one in which he appears dressed in a top hat—a member of bourgeois society (figs. 9.1, 9.2).

1863
Rodin works on decorative sculpture for the Théâtre des Gobelins.

1864
Rodin enrolls in classes from sculptor Antoine-Louis Barye (1796–1875) at the Musée d'Histoire Naturelle in Paris.
Rodin meets Rose Beuret (1844–1917), who will become his lifelong companion and, at the end of their lives, his wife. She worked as his studio assistant during the early years of his career.
Rodin is first employed by famous French sculptor Albert-Ernest Carrier-Belleuse.

1865
The Man with the Broken Nose—a portrait of a workman with a broken nose, named Bibi, whom Rodin had met in 1863 or 1864—is made into a mask following an accident due to a very cold winter. The mask is refused by the French Salon.

1866
Birth of Auguste Beuret, Rose Beuret and Rodin's only son.

Selected World Events

1853–1856
The Crimean War

1859–1869
The Suez Canal is built under the leadership of French diplomat Ferdinand de Lesseps.

1861–1865
The American Civil War between the Union and the seceding Confederacy.

1861–1867
French invasion of Mexico, resulting the Second Mexican Empire.

1863
On January 1, US President Abraham Lincoln delivers the Emancipation Proclamation.
Cambodia becomes a French protectorate.

1865
On April 9, Robert E. Lee surrenders to Ulysses S. Grant in Virginia.
On April 14, Abraham Lincoln is assassinated while attending a performance at Ford's Theater in Washington, DC.
On December 6, the Thirteenth Amendment to the Constitution of the United States is ratified, prohibiting and abolishing slavery.

1866
The Austro-Prussian War

1867
The United States purchases Alaska from Russia.

1868
The Fourteenth Amendment to the Constitution of the United States is ratified.

Collecting Rodin in the United States

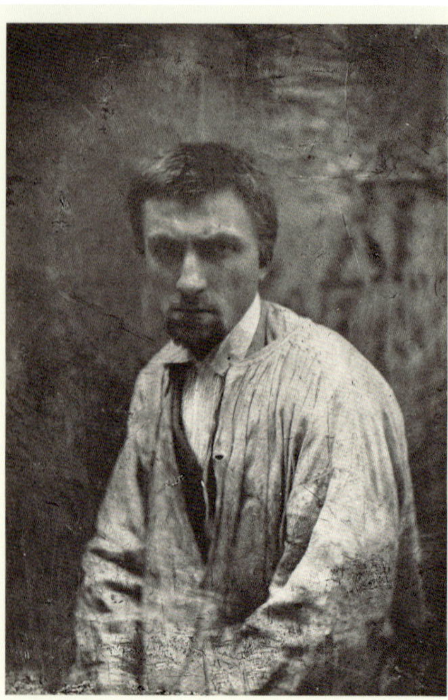

FIG. 9.1
Charles Hippolyte Aubry (French, 1811–1877), *Portrait of Auguste Rodin in Overalls*, c. 1862. Photograph on albumen paper. Musée Rodin, Paris. Ph.00004.

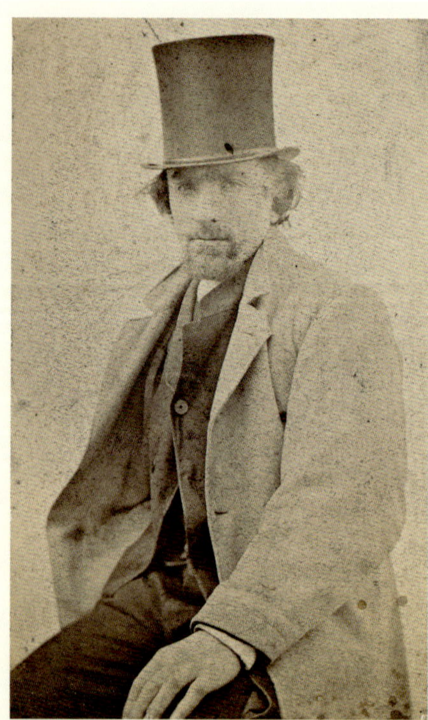

FIG. 9.2
Charles Hippolyte Aubry, *Auguste Rodin in Top Hat*, c. 1862. Photograph on albumen paper. Musée Rodin, Paris. Ph.00003.

1870
The Franco-Prussian War begins. Rodin is conscripted into the 158th Regiment of the Garde Nationale as a corporal.

1871
Rodin is discharged from the National Guard for nearsightedness. He follows Carrier-Belleuse to Belgium and is joined by Beuret shortly thereafter. He will not return to France until 1877.

1875
Living in Brussels, Rodin begins work on a standing nude later known as *The Age of Bronze* (cf. cat. 87).

1876
In spring, Rodin travels in Italy, visiting Turin, Genoa, Rome, Naples, Siena, and Florence. He studies sculpture by Michelangelo (1475–1564), Donatello (c. 1386–1466), and Raphael (1483–1520).

1877
The plaster model of *The Age of Bronze*, the first full-scale figure Rodin exhibits publicly under his own name, is shown at the Cercle Artistique in Brussels.
Rodin returns to Paris.
The Age of Bronze is exhibited at the Paris Salon of the Société des Artistes Français. Due to the work's verisimilitude, Rodin is accused of having cast it from a live model.

1880
Convinced of Rodin's integrity, French Undersecretary of Fine Arts Edmond Turquet commissions a cast of *The Age of Bronze*. On August 16, Turquet also commissions a decorative gate for the Musée des Arts Décoratifs in Paris, intended for construction on the site where the Musée d'Orsay is today. He begins working with enthusiasm; however, *The Gates of Hell* will not be completed in the artist's lifetime.
The beginning of Rodin's so-called black drawings period, where the artist explored drawing with ink and gouache.

1882
Rodin meets a nineteen-year-old sculptor named Camille Rosalie Claudel (1864–1943) (fig. 9.3). Claudel becomes Rodin's student, working in his studio as an assistant and model for the next decade. The two artists also engage in a romantic relationship.

1883
For the first time, Rodin exhibits a small selection of drawings, in Paris.

1868–1878
The Ten Years' War breaks out between Cuba and Spain.

1869
On May 10, the first transcontinental railroad in North America is completed.

1870–1872
The Franco-Prussian War

1871
The Paris Commune briefly controls the French capital city.

1876
The Battle of the Little Bighorn ends in victory for the Lakota, Cheyenne, and Arapaho.

1876
Philadelphia
Rodin exhibits eight decorative busts in the Centennial International Exhibition.

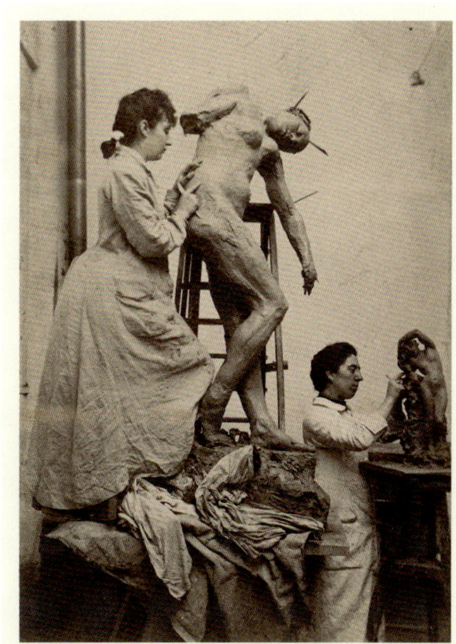

FIG. 9.3
William Elborne (British, c. 1858–1952), *Camille Claudel* [left] *with Fellow Sculptor Jessie Lipscomb in Their Studio*, mid-1880s. Musée Rodin, Paris. Ph.01773.

1884

The Municipal Council of Calais votes to install a commemorative monument. Numerous artists submit designs for consideration.

1885

On January 28, Rodin wins the commission for the monument honoring heroes of Calais.

1887

Paul Gallimard commissions Rodin to produce twenty-seven pen-and-ink drawings directly on Gallimard's personal copy of Charles Baudelaire's *Les fleurs du mal* (1857) (fig. 9.4).

1889

Rodin wins the commission for a monument to the writer Victor Hugo in the Panthéon in Paris (fig. 9.5). In 1881, the French government had decreed the building a mausoleum for "the golden ages and great men of France." Hugo was the first to be entombed there following this declaration.
The exhibition *Claude Monet—A. Rodin* takes place at the Georges Petit Gallery. Needing a large sculpture to occupy the center of this space, Rodin elects to complete *Monument to the Burghers of Calais* (see fig. 1.5) rather than *The Gates of Hell*; he will not return to work on the latter project until 1900.

1891

In July, the Société des Gens de Lettres commissions a monument to Honoré de Balzac for the Palais-Royal in Paris.

1892

The romantic relationship between Rodin and Claudel ends.

1893

Rodin is elected president of the Société Nationale des Beaux-Arts section of sculpture.

1894

Rodin moves to Meudon, which will become his primary residence (fig. 9.6).

1895

Monument to the Burghers of Calais is inaugurated on June 3.

1896

Rodin invents his pure linear style and from this period on draws nearly exclusively with crayon and watercolor.

1887

Cambodia becomes part of the French "Indochina Union," a conglomeration of colonial territories in southeast Asia that would come to include Vietnam, Laos, and Kwangchowan.

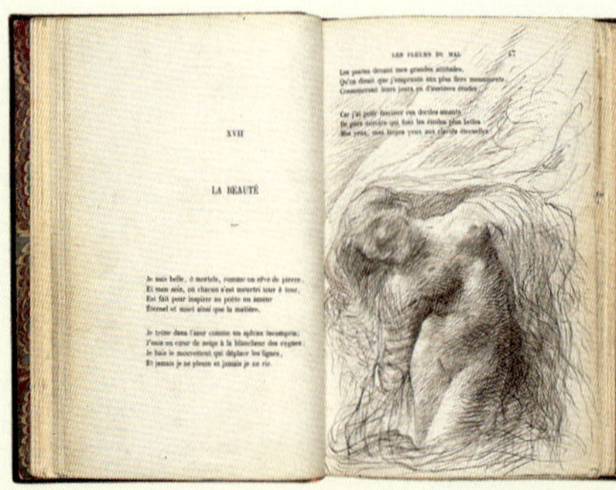

FIG. 9.4

Charles Baudelaire, *Les fleurs du mal, Paris, Poulet-Malassis et de Broise* (*The Flowers of Evil*), 1857, page 47, with drawing by Auguste Rodin. Ink on printed, bound paper. Musée Rodin, Paris. D.7174(E).

1893

The World's Columbian Exposition in Chicago is opened to the public.
United States forces overthrow the Hawaiian government.

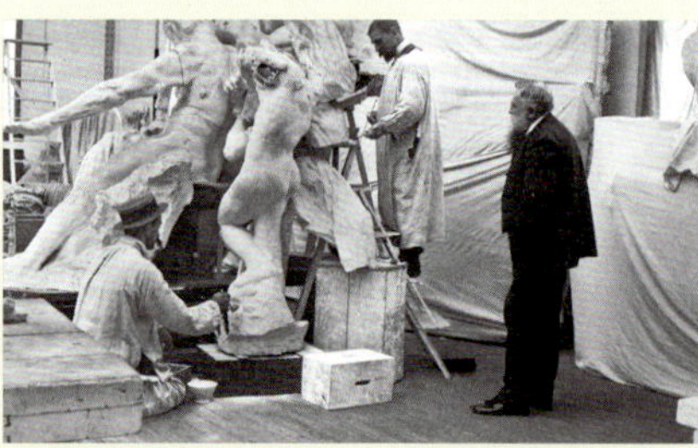

FIG. 9.5

Rodin observes work on the *Monument to Victor Hugo* in the studio of his assistant Henri Lebossé, 1896. Library of Congress.

1896

In Plessy v. Ferguson, the United States Supreme Court rules that states have the right to legally segregate public facilities.

Before 1887
Paris

Samuel Isham acquires the marble *Fallen Caryatid* (cat. 2).

1889

Between January 19 and June 15, Truman H. Bartlett publishes ten articles in the *American Architect and Building News* that constitute the first detailed analysis of Rodin's work in the United States.

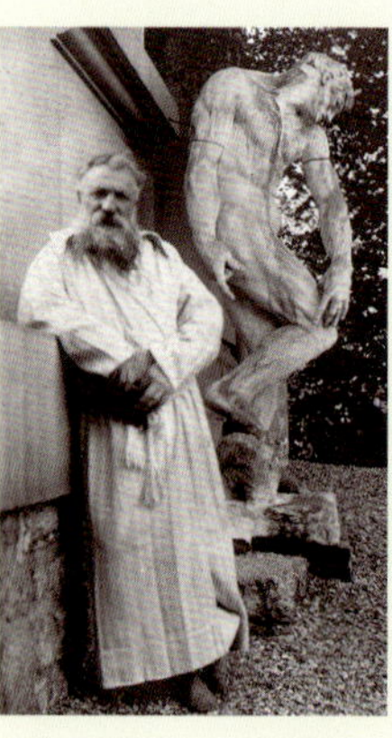

FIG. 9.6

Rodin in the garden of his villa at Meudon, near Paris, c. 1900. Behind him is the original plaster of *Adam*, also called *The Creation of Man*. Edward Gooch Collection / Getty Images.

1893
New York

Philanthropist Samuel P. Avery gifts Rodin's *St. John the Baptist* (cat. 3) to the Metropolitan Museum of Art (the Met) in New York, marking the first acquisition of the artist's work by a US museum.
Chicago
Rodin exhibits five sculptures at the World's Columbian Exposition: two in the French pavilion and three in a special section curated by American Sara Tyson Hallowell, at whose behest Rodin selected works to be shown. Rodin's works attract significant critical attention for their sensuality—what one journalist described as "their rigorous truthfulness."

1894
Chicago

After seeing Rodin's showing at the Columbian Exposition, financier Charles T. Yerkes begins collecting the artist's work.

Auguste Rodin Biographical Dates

1897

Eternal Spring is exhibited at the Paris Salon under the title *Cupid and Psyche*—not to be confused with the 1893 work by the same title (cat. 4).

Rodin completes the maquette for the *Monument to Balzac*.

Maison Goupil reproduces 142 of Rodin's "black drawings," with sponsorship from Maurice Fenaille. The result is the so-called *Album Fenaille*.

1898

Monument to Balzac (original model 1897; cf. cat. 85) and *The Kiss* (original model c. 1881–82; cf. cat. 68) are exhibited at the SNBA Salon. *The Kiss* is favorably received, whereas *Balzac* is rejected by the Société des Gens de Lettres.

1899

Rodin and Claudel cut all remaining personal and professional ties.

Gallerist and publisher Ambroise Vollard commissions a drawing by Rodin for the frontispiece of the *Jardin des Supplices* by Octave Mirbeau (1899). Rodin subsequently gives the drawing, *Salome* (cat. 96), to Claude Monet.

Traveling from Brussels to Rotterdam, Amsterdam, and The Hague, Rodin's first solo exhibition (fig. 9.7) features more than 100 works, including a number of important drawings.

1900

Rodin creates a display in the pavilion at the Pavillon de l'Alma featuring 150 sculptures, as well as 128 drawings and photographs (fig. 9.8). Designed to coincide with the Parisian Exposition Universelle, this showing functioned as a retrospective of the artist's oeuvre up to that point.

1902

Edward Steichen visits Rodin in Paris, producing a series of photographs of the artist and his sculpture (see fig. 4.3).

Vollard publishes a second, deluxe edition of Octave Mirbeau's *Jardin des supplices*, featuring twenty drawings by Rodin reproduced in lithographs by Auguste Clot.

1904

The large version of *The Thinker* (later acquired by the Met, see fig. 9.9) is exhibited at the SNBA Salon, while a plaster copy is on view at the Louisiana Purchase Exposition in St. Louis, Missouri.

Selected World Events

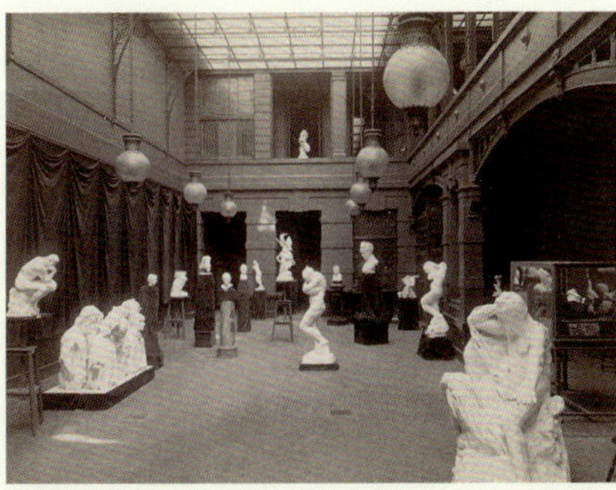

FIG. 9.7

The Rodin exhibition at the Maison d'Art, Brussels. Musée Rodin, Paris. Ph.01798.

1900

Paris hosts the Exposition Universelle.

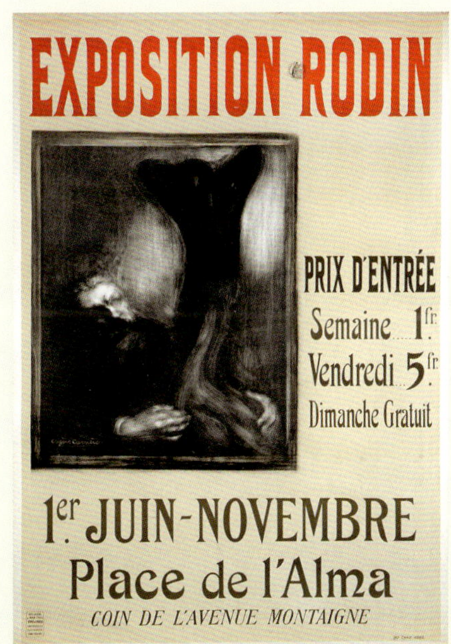

FIG. 9.8

Eugène Carrière (French, 1849–1906), poster for *Exposition Rodin* at the Palais de l'Alma, Paris, 1900. Lithographed poster. Musée Rodin, Paris. Inv. Af. 106-1.

Collecting Rodin in the United States

1898
Philadelphia

The Pennsylvania Academy of the Fine Arts acquires a cast of *The Age of Bronze* (cast 1898; now in the National Gallery of Art, Washington, DC) to serve as a model for young artists.

1902–1903
Paris

The artist creates a portrait in marble of Katherine (Kate) Seney Simpson (cat. 12), who, with her husband John Woodruff Simpson, would become one of the most important Americans collecting Rodin.

1903
New York

Loïe Fuller organizes *Exhibition of Statuary and Paintings Belonging to Miss Loïe Fuller*. She shows a selection of sculptures and drawings, but nothing is sold.

Boston

Rodin sculptures from the collection of Henry Lee Higginson are on view at the Museum of Fine Arts.

Pittsburgh

A couple of Rodin's drawings are exhibited at the Carnegie Institute. This is the first exhibition of his drawings in the United States.

1904
New York

The first Rodin sculptures acquired by Kate and John Simpson arrive in New York. Among these works is *The Thinker* (modeled 1880, cast 1901; now in the National Gallery of Art, Washington, DC; cf. cat. 21).

Auguste Rodin Biographical Dates

1906

Rodin creates approximately 150 drawings of the Cambodian Royal Ballet (cats. 57, 65, 81, 97) following their performances as part of the Colonial Exposition at Marseilles. The festivities were to celebrate a diplomatic trip undertaken by the recently coronated King Sisowath I of Cambodia. Rodin produces a unique series of portraits in watercolor, among them: *Nathalie de Goloubeff* (Musée Rodin, Paris), *Nourye de Rohozinska* (Musée Rodin, Paris), *King Sisowath* (Musée Rodin, Paris; Staatliche Sammlung, Munich; Yale University Art Gallery, New Haven), and *Hanako* (cat. 26).

1907

The Walking Man (original model 1907; cf. cat 86) is exhibited at the Salon of the Société Nationale des Beaux-Arts in Paris.

1909

Monument to Victor Hugo is inaugurated in the gardens at the Palais Royal on September 30.

1911

The Walking Man is given to the French state and installed in the heart of the French Embassy in Rome, at the Palazzo Farnese.

Selected World Events

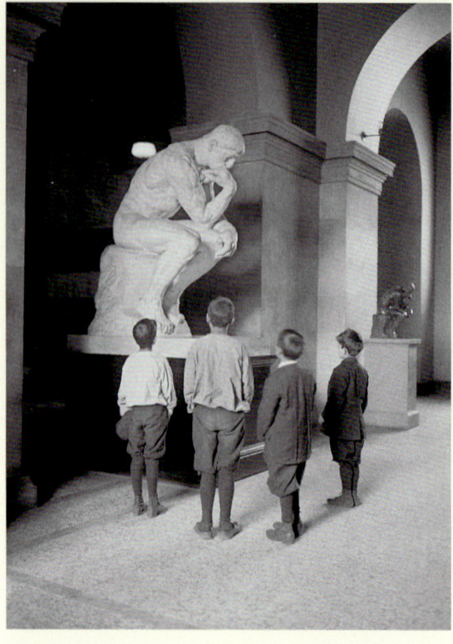

FIG. 9.9

Four boys viewing a monumental plaster cast of Rodin's *The Thinker* (original model probably 1880) at the Metropolitan Museum of Art, New York, in 1913. Visible at rear is the small, original-sized bronze cast of *The Thinker* from the museum's collection, cast c. 1910.

1912

The African National Congress is founded.
The end of the Chinese Empire; the Republic of China is founded.
On April 15, the *RMS Titanic* sinks.

Collecting Rodin in the United States

1905
Boston

The Copley Society hosts an exhibition titled *Loan Collection of Paintings by Claude Monet and Eleven Sculptures by Auguste Rodin*, featuring works from the collections of Kate and John Simpson, Henry Higginson, and Eric Pape.

1907
New York

Kate Seney Simpson gives the Met a bronze copy of *The Age of Bronze* (cast c. 1906).

Paris

Denman Waldo Ross visits the Galerie Bernheim Jeune exhibition and purchases *Standing Nude* (1900–1905), *Anxiété* (1900–1906), and *Cambodian Dancer* (1906) for the Museum of Fine Arts, Boston. These are the first Rodin drawings to enter a US public collection.

1908
New York

With encouragement from Edward Steichen, photographer Alfred Stieglitz's Little Galleries of the Photo-Secession, later known as 291, hosts *Drawings by Auguste Rodin*. This important exhibition is the third showing of the artist's drawings in the United States.

1910
New York

Roger Fry purchases the drawing *The Abandoned (Psyche,* cat. 24*)* for the Met thanks to the Rogers Fund. It is the first Rodin drawing to enter the museum's collection.
Rodin's drawings are featured at Stieglitz's 291 gallery, in two separate exhibitions, and the Metropolitan Museum purchases seven with the John Stewart Kennedy Fund.
Collector Thomas Fortune Ryan gives three Rodin sculptures to the Metropolitan Museum, along with a sum of $25,000 to acquire other works by the artist.

1911
Buffalo

A group exhibition at the Albright Art Gallery presents Rodin drawings as representative of the work of the "Société des Peintres et Sculpteurs." The exhibition travels to Chicago, St. Louis, and Boston in 1912.

1912
New York

On May 2, the Rodin gallery opens at the Met (fig. 9.9, see also figs. 5.7, 5.8). It is the first gallery at the museum dedicated in its entirety to a living artist. The gallery is the result of years of advocacy by Kate Seney Simpson, as well as the ardent support of sculptor Daniel Chester French, then chair of the museum's Committee on Sculpture.

1913

On March 10, 1913, Claudel is forcibly committed to the psychiatric hospital of Ville-Évrard in Neuilly-sur-Marne. Despite her many pleas for release, she will remain there for thirty years, until her death in 1943.

1914

Publication of *Les Cathédrales de France* by Rodin.

1916

Rodin bequeaths his estate to France.

1917

Rodin and Rose Beuret (fig. 9.10) marry on January 29; Beuret dies three weeks later.
Rodin dies on November 17 and is buried in Meudon below a cast of *The Thinker* (see fig. 6.2).

1919

The Musée Rodin in Paris, committed to preserving the art and legacy of Auguste Rodin, opens its doors to the public for the first time, on August 4.

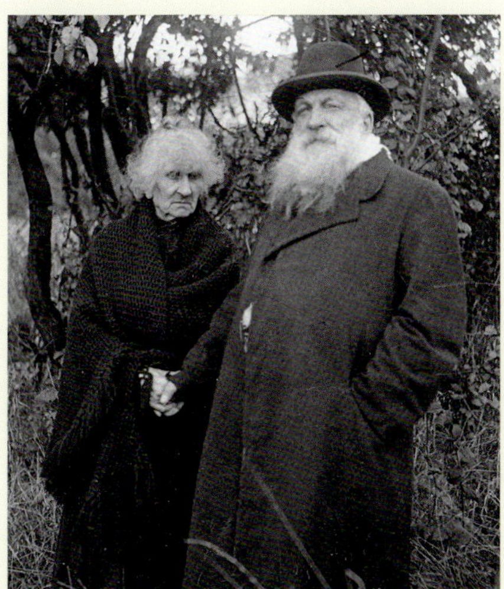

FIG. 9.10

Antoine de Combettes (French), *Rodin with Rose Beuret in the Gardens at the Villa in Meudon*, 1915. Gelatin silver print. Musée Rodin, Paris. Ph.01621.

1914

On June 28, Archduke Franz Ferdinand of Austria is assassinated in Sarajevo, leading to the outbreak of World War I.

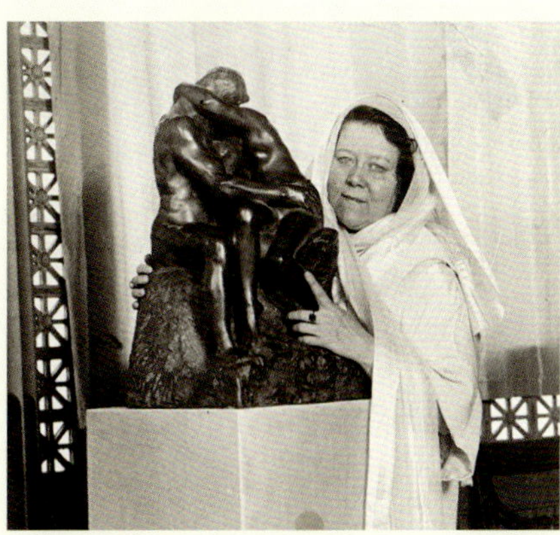

FIG. 9.11

Loie Fuller with Rodin's *The Kiss*, 1916. Jerome Robbins Dance Division, New York Public Library Digital Collections.

1917

On March 8, the Russian Revolution ends the Russian Empire.
On April 6, the United States enters World War I.

1919

The Treaty of Versailles is signed.
The German Revolution ends, resulting in the establishment of the Weimar Republic.

1920

In the United States, prohibition begins.

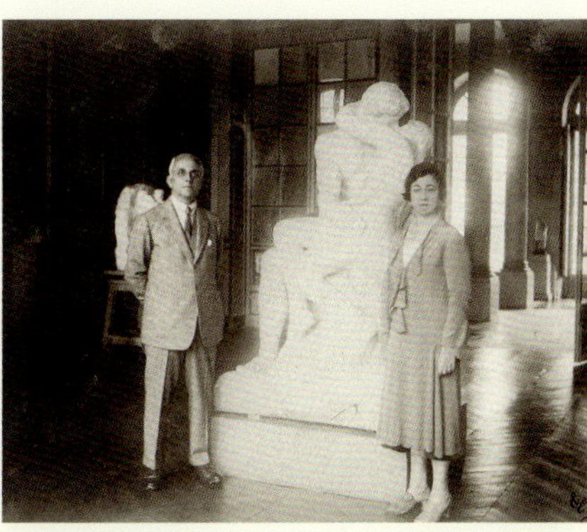

FIG. 9.12

Jules and Etta Wedell Mastbaum with Rodin's *The Kiss* at the Musée Rodin, Paris, in 1925. Photo by Pierre Choumoff. Curatorial files, Department of European Painting and Sculpture, Philadelphia Museum of Art.

1913

New York, Chicago, Boston

The Armory Show takes place. Gertrude Käsebier lends seven Rodin drawings from her collection. A group of Rodin drawings given by Thomas Ryan are on view at the Metropolitan Museum of Art.

1914

Paris

Collector Robert Sterling Clark helps his brother acquire the plaster *Man with Serpent* (cat. 63), which he describes in his diaries as "an unusually fine work."

1915

San Francisco

Alma de Bretteville Spreckels—socialite, philanthropist, and wife of sugar magnate Adolph Spreckels—exhibits her collection of Rodin's work at the Panama-Pacific International Exhibition. Spreckels had begun acquiring pieces by Rodin thanks to efforts by dancer and performer Loïe Fuller (fig. 9.11). Spreckels donates a large version of *The Thinker* (cast c. 1904, Legion of Honor Museum) to the city of San Francisco.

Washington, DC

Rodin dedicates his drawing *Figure Sketch* (cat. 1; now in the National Gallery of Art) to the United States of America. The work is part of a collection of eighty-two pictures given to the United States along with an "album of letters by eminent French statesmen and writers expressing appreciation for the aid rendered by the American people toward relieving the distress occasioned by the European war."

1917

Cleveland

Cleveland Museum of Art trustee Ralph King donates the eighth copy of the large version of *The Thinker* (commissioned from the artist and cast 1916) to the museum.

1921

Providence

Philanthropist Eliza Greene Metcalf Radeke gives one of the first copies of the *Mask of the Man with the Broken Nose* and drawings by Rodin to the Rhode Island School of Design.

1922

New York

The Joseph Brummer Gallery organizes the first important exhibition of Rodin drawings in the United States after the artist's death. The show will travel to the Art Institute of Chicago the following year.

1924

Paris

Philadelphia philanthropist and cinema magnate Jules Ephraim Mastbaum visits the Musée Rodin (fig. 9.12). He purchases one small bronze by the artist; over the next two years, his collection will expand to include more than two hundred sculptures.

San Francisco

Opening of the California Palace of the Legion of Honor, with the Spreckels collection on view.

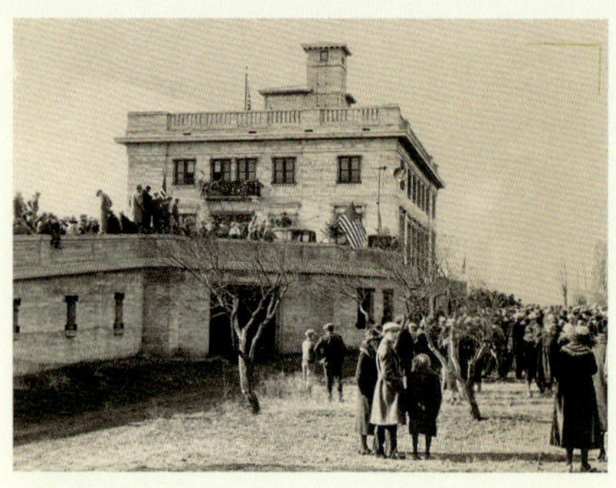

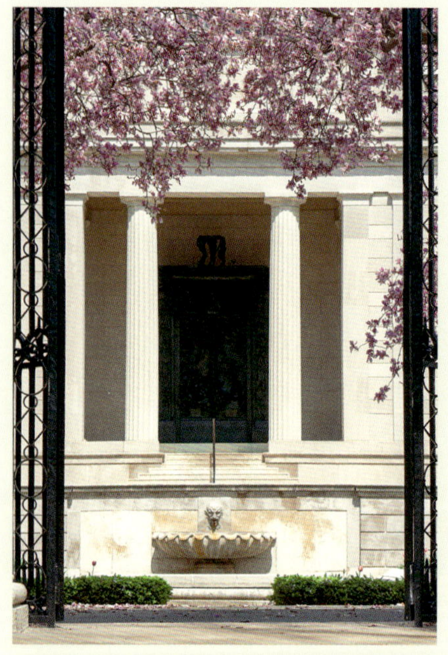

Auguste Rodin Biographical Dates

Selected World Events

1927

Aviator Charles Lindbergh flies nonstop from
New York City to Paris.

1929

On October 24, which comes to be known as Black
Thursday, the New York Stock Exchange collapses.

1933

Adolf Hitler becomes chancellor of Germany. The
first concentration camps open, targeting individuals
of Jewish and Romani heritage, as well as queer
people and members of physically and intellectually
disabled communities.

1939

Nazi invasion of Poland marks the beginning of
World War II.

1941

United States forces are attacked by Japanese military
at Pearl Harbor in Hawai'i. The United States enters
World War II.

1944

D-Day landings occur in Normandy.

1945

End of World War II in Europe.
The Holocaust ends; tens of thousands of people are
liberated from concentration camps.
The Nuremberg trials begin.
United States military planes drop atomic bombs on
the Japanese cities of Hiroshima and Nagasaki.

Collecting Rodin in the United States

1926
Philadelphia

In April, Jules Mastbaum hires architects to build a
Rodin Museum in Philadelphia, at his expense. He
aspires to share his collection with the people of his
city. He campaigns for and obtains official permission
and support from the Musée Rodin in this
undertaking.
Commissioned by Mastbaum, the first two casts of
The Gates of Hell are made. The first cast had initially
been commissioned by the Japanese collector Kojiro
Matsukata for the National Museum of Western Art,
Tokyo, but eventually went to Philadelphia. The
second remained in Paris.
In December, Mastbaum dies suddenly. His widow,
Etta Mastbaum, with their three daughters, oversees
the project's execution.

Goldendale, Washington

With guidance from Loïe Fuller, businessman Samuel
Hill builds a collection that includes more than
eighty works by Rodin. Hill decides to construct a
museum in Goldendale that will house his art
collection. Marie, Queen of Romania, inaugurates the
museum (fig. 9.13). The building, however, remains
unfinished for many years.

1929
Philadelphia

The Rodin Museum opens its doors overlooking the
Benjamin Franklin Parkway (fig. 9.14). The museum's
holdings comprise 150 bronzes, marbles, and plasters,
including a cast of *The Gates of Hell* and a large
collection of drawings.

1930
Philadelphia

Over 390,000 people visit the Rodin Museum in its
first year.

1940
Goldendale, Washington

Nine years after Samuel Hill's untimely death,
the Maryhill Museum of Art opens. Sculptures
and drawings by Rodin are the centerpiece of
the collection.

1942
Washington, DC

Kate Seney Simpson leaves the collection of Rodin
work she and her husband acquired to the National
Gallery of Art.

1943
Cambridge, Massachusetts

Collector Grenville L. Winthrop bequeaths his
sculptures and drawings by Rodin to the Fogg
Museum, Harvard.

1947
New York

Financier B. Gerald Cantor acquires his first Rodin
sculpture, a reduction of *The Hand of God*, inspired
by the marble version in the Met (cat. 22).

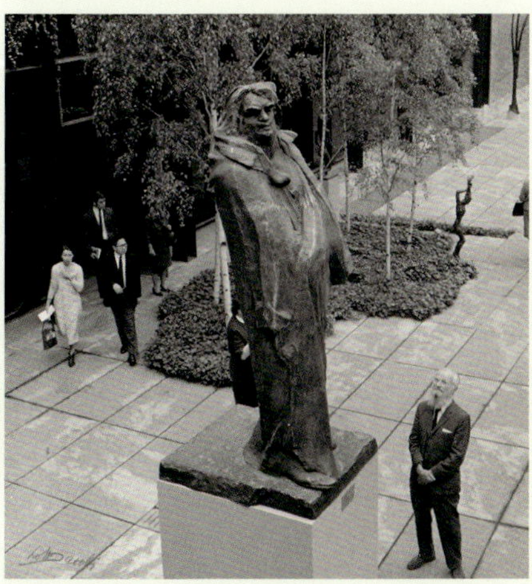

FIG. 9.15
Lotte Jacobi (American, 1896–1990), *Edward Steichen with Rodin's Monument to Balzac in the Courtyard of the Museum of Modern Art, New York*, 1960. Musée Rodin, Paris, Ph.13156.

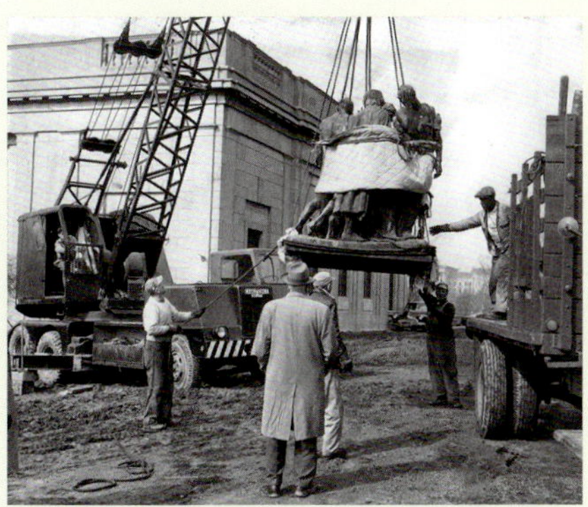

FIG. 9.16
The Burghers of Calais being moved from the Rodin Museum, Philadelphia, on February 17, 1955. Photo by Frank P. Montone. Courtesy of Temple University Libraries, Urban Archives, Philadelphia.

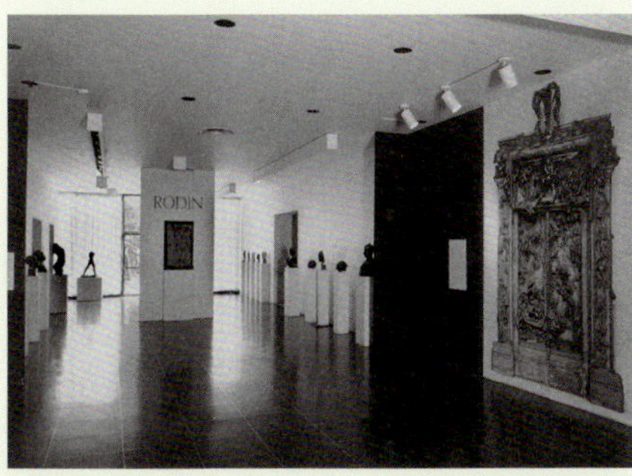

FIG. 9.17
Installation view of the exhibition *Rodin*, Museum of Modern Art, New York, May 1– September 8, 1963. Photo by George Barrows. Photographic Archive, Museum of Modern Art Archives, New York.

1949
Establishment of the People's Republic of China under Mao Zedong.

1950–1953
The Korean War

1953
After French forces fail to regain control following World War II, Cambodia declares independence.

1954
The United States Supreme Court rules segregated schools unconstitutional in Brown v. the Board of Education.

1959
Beginning of the Vietnam War, which will continue until 1975.

1960
Seventeen African nations achieve independence from European colonialism.

1961
Yuri Gagarin of the Soviet Republic becomes the first human in outer space.
Construction of the Berlin Wall begins.

1962
The Cuban Missile Crisis

1963
On November 22, US President John F. Kennedy is assassinated in Dallas, Texas.

1968
Protests break out across the United States, Europe, and Latin America.
On April 4, civil rights leader Martin Luther King Jr. is assassinated in Memphis, Tennessee.

1969
Apollo 11 spaceflight marks the first humans on the moon.

1973
The United States Supreme Court rules in Roe v. Wade.

1949
Chicago
Rodin drawings from the estate of Alfred Stieglitz are given to the Art Institute of Chicago.

1953
Boston
Museum of Fine Arts, Boston, deaccessions *Iris* (cat. 84).

1955
New York
A group of donors give Rodin's *Balzac* (cat. 85) to the Museum of Modern Art in memory of gallerist Curt Valentin. The sculpture has been on view ever since, either in the garden (fig. 9.15) or at the museum's entrance.
Philadelphia
The Burghers of Calais is moved from the Rodin Museum to its new display site, in the Philadelphia Museum of Art (fig. 9.16).

1962
Paris
Rodin inconnu opens at the Louvre. Created under the guidance of curator and art historian Cécile Goldscheider, this exhibition introduces the French public to a more modern Rodin.

1963
New York
Rodin: Sculptures and Drawings opens at the Charles E. Slatkin Galleries. Art historian Leo Steinberg writes an introductory essay for the exhibition catalogue; the essay is republished in 1971 in *Other Criteria: Confrontations with Twentieth-Century Art*.
The exhibition *Rodin* opens at the Museum of Modern Art (fig. 9.17). The catalogue includes essays by Albert E. Elsen and Peter Selz, who writes on Rodin and America.

1965
Princeton, New Jersey
Students of Rodin's former secretary René Chéruy give rare Rodin cut-out drawings to the Princeton University Library.
New York
Dorothy Seiberling publishes the first essay on Rodin's forgers, in *Time* magazine.

1968
Stanford, California
Albert Elsen moves to Stanford University, where he launches a new research initiative focused on Rodin.

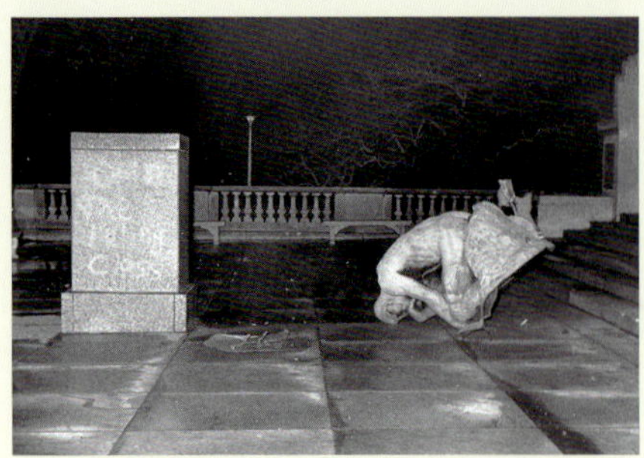

FIG. 9.18

Rodin's *The Thinker* after the bombing of the Cleveland Museum of Art on March 24, 1970. Cleveland Press Collection, Michael Schwartz Library, Cleveland State University.

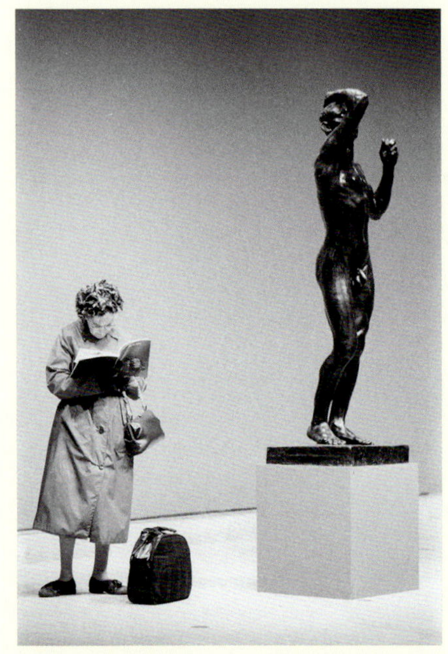

FIG. 9.19

A woman reads a catalogue while standing next to Rodin's *The Age of Bronze* at the exhibition *Rodin: Sculpture and Drawings*, organized by the Arts Council of Great Britain and the Association française d'action artistique at the Hayward Gallery, London, January 27, 1970. Photo by Evening Standard / Hulton Archive / Getty Images.

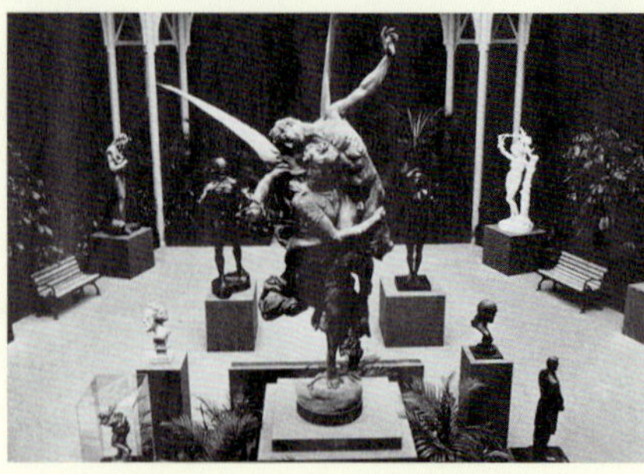

FIG. 9.20

Installation view of *Rodin Rediscovered* at the National Gallery of Art, Washington, DC. Published in *Art Journal* 41, no. 4 (Winter 1981): 371.

1974

Richard Nixon resigns the US presidency in the aftermath of the Watergate scandal.

1975–1979

The Khmer Rouge regime overthrows the Khmer Republic of Cambodia, leading to the Cambodian genocide.

1979

A nuclear accident occurs at Three Mile Island near Harrisburg, Pennsylvania.

1980

Mount Saint Helens erupts in Washington State.

1986

Chernobyl disaster occurs in Ukraine.

1989

On November 9, the Berlin Wall falls.

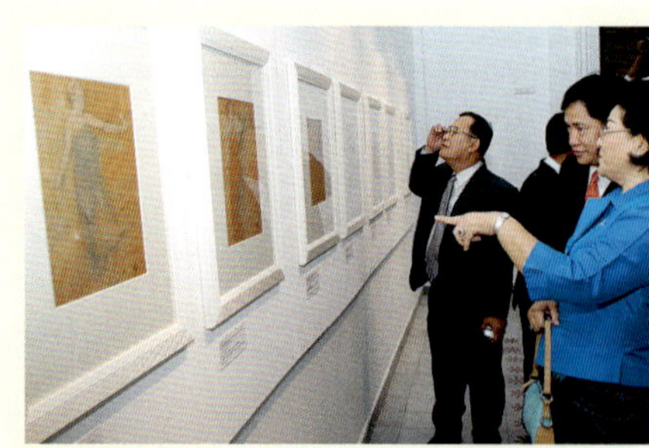

FIG. 9.21

Visitors examine Rodin drawings at the National Museum in Phnom Penh, December 21, 2006. Tang Chhin Sothy / AFP via Getty Images.

1970

Cleveland

At approximately 1:00 a.m. on March 24, the Cleveland Museum of Art's *The Thinker* is bombed in an anonymous act of vandalism. The explosion damages the sculpture's base and the pedestal beneath it; conservators and art historians decide not to repair it (fig. 9.18).

London

The exhibition *Rodin: Sculpture and Drawings*, organized by the Arts Council of Great Britain and the Association Française d'Action Artistique, takes place at the Hayward Gallery (fig. 9.19).

1971

Washington, DC, and New York

Albert Elsen and Kirk Varnedoe organize a groundbreaking exhibition, *Rodin Drawings, True and False*, at the National Gallery of Art and the Solomon R. Guggenheim Museum.

1974

Palo Alto, California

The Iris and B. Gerald Cantor Center for Visual Arts at Stanford University is founded.

1975

San Francisco

Victoria Thorson's *Rodin Drypoints, Illustrations and Related Drawings* opens at the Fine Arts Museums of San Francisco. The exhibition is a groundbreaking investigation into the artist's engravings.

1976

New York

Gertude Käsebier's drawings by Rodin enter the Museum of Modern Art collections.

1977

New York / Saint-Rémy-lès-Chevreuse, France

Gerald Cantor commissions a cast of *The Gates of Hell* from the prestigious Coubertin Foundry (see fig. 8.1).

1981–1982

Washington, DC

Rodin Rediscovered opens at the National Gallery of Art (fig. 9.20). Organized by Ruth Butler, Albert Elsen, and Kirk Varnedoe, the exhibition features more than three hundred objects, including the Cantor cast of *The Gates of Hell*. *Rodin Rediscovered* is so popular that it is extended by three months. By the end of its run, more than one million people have visited the exhibition.

1993

Ruth Butler's biography of the artist, *Rodin: The Shape of Genius*, is published to critical acclaim.

2001

New York

A fragment of a Rodin sculpture is spotted in the rubble at Ground Zero, following the attack on the Twin Towers on September 11 that destroyed hundreds of Rodin works in the Cantor Fitzgerald offices. Photographs of this fragment are shared around the world.

2006

Phnom Penh

Forty of Rodin's drawings depicting dancers from the Cambodian National Ballet are displayed in the National Museum (fig. 9.21).

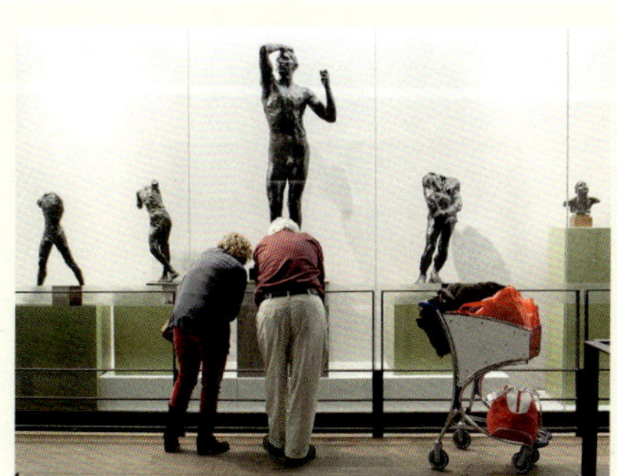

FIG. 9.22

American travelers visit an art gallery installed with works by Rodin at Roissy-Charles de Gaulle Airport, Paris, 2013. Photo by Lauren Fleishman. New York Times / Redux.

2017

Rodin's centenary exhibition is held at the Grand Palais, Paris.

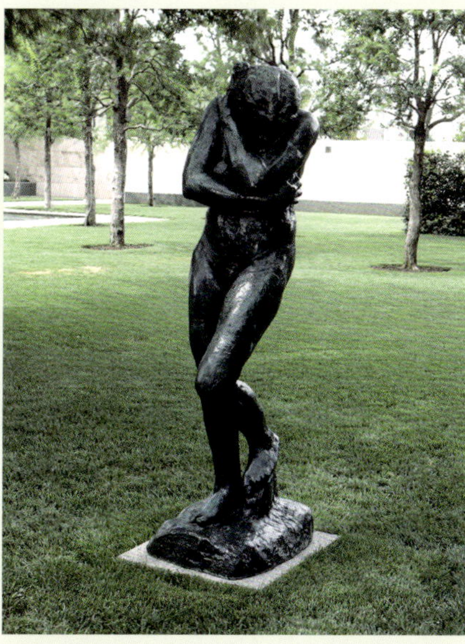

FIG. 9.23

Rodin's *Eve* in situ at the Nasher Sculpture Center, Dallas. Image courtesy of Nasher Sculpture Center. Photo by Tom Jenkins.

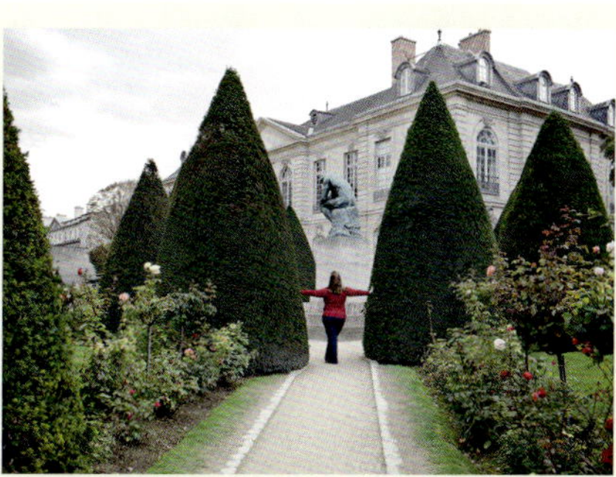

FIG. 9.24

Rodin's *The Thinker* at the Musée Rodin, Paris, as the museum prepared for its grand reopening in 2015. Photo by Guia Besana. New York Times / Redux.

2013
Paris
A small art gallery at Roissy-Charles de Gaulle Airport features several Rodin sculptures for viewers to enjoy as they wander the terminals (fig. 9.22).
Dallas
The Nasher Sculpture Center unveils a new installation of outdoor sculpture to complement Rodin's *Eve* (fig. 9.23).

2014
Los Angeles
The J. Paul Getty Museum purchases Rodin's *Christ and Mary Magdalene* (cat. 101)—an important marble whose acquisition shows the continued enthusiasm for Rodin's work in the United States into the twenty-first century.

2015
Paris
Musée Rodin reopens after a major renovation of the Hôtel Biron building (fig. 9.24).

2017
The centenary of Rodin's death is celebrated worldwide.

2019
Washington, DC
Works by Rodin are on view in the Smithsonian's Hirshhorn Museum and Sculpture Garden.
Philadelphia
The Gates of Hell remains on view at the Rodin Museum, standing in the same spot where the monumental work was installed ninety years prior, in 1929 (fig. 9.25).

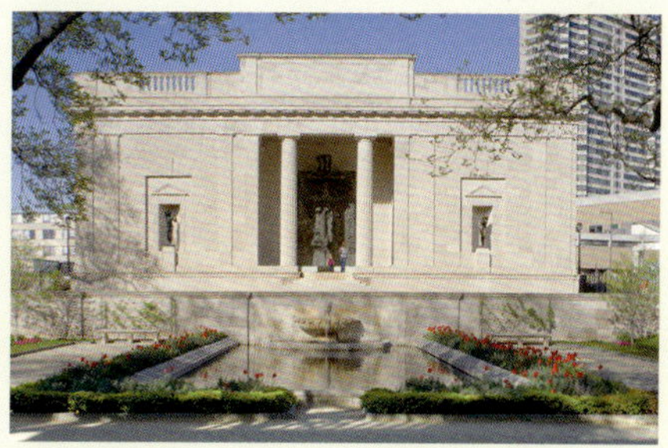

FIG. 9.25

The Rodin Museum in Philadelphia today with *The Gates of Hell* still installed in the portico above the garden. Philadelphia Museum of Art.

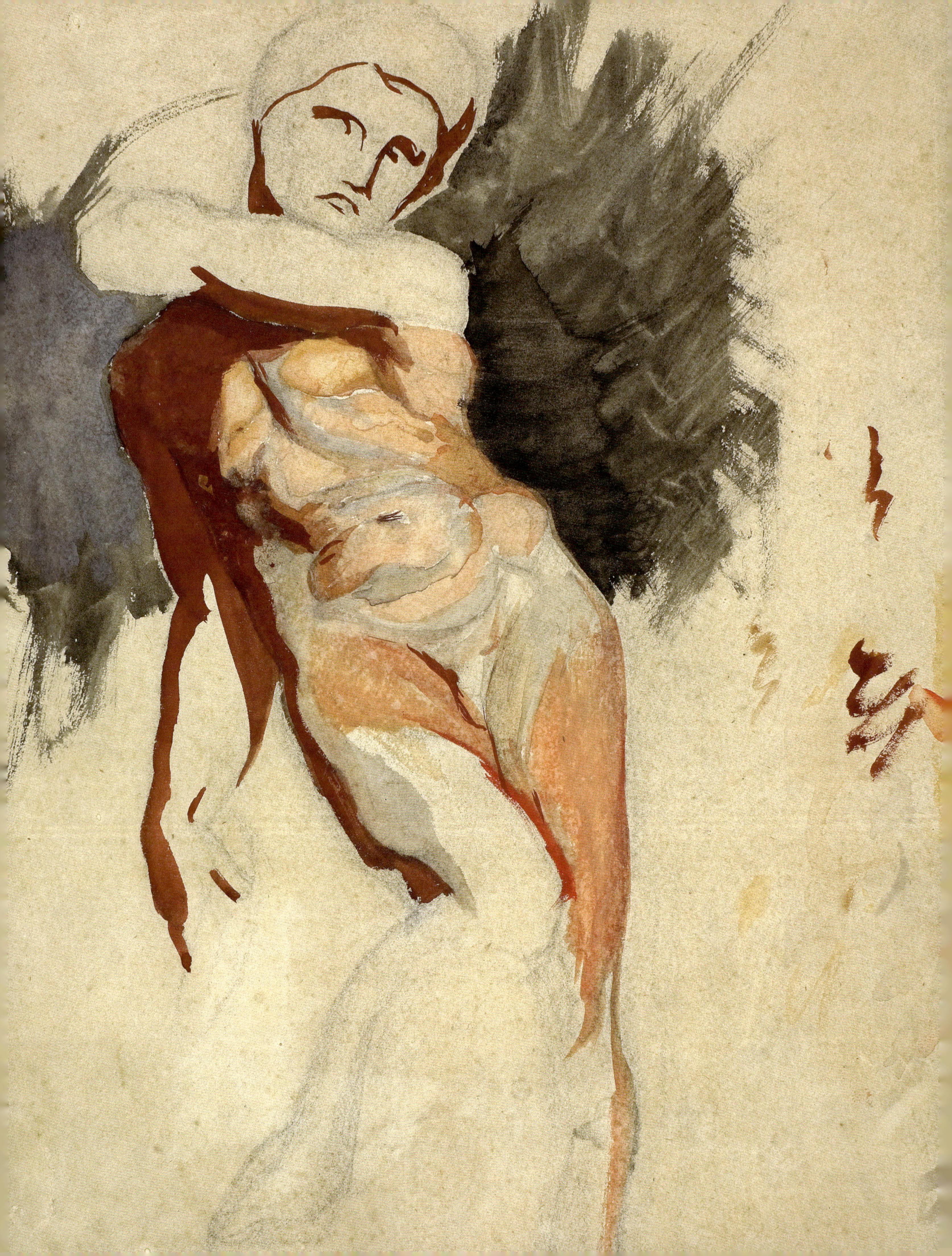

EXHIBITION CHECKLIST

All works are by Auguste Rodin (French, 1840–1917) unless otherwise noted. For further explanations regarding process, title, dating, dimensions, exhibition history, provenance, and references, please see "Notes to the Reader," pp. 10–11. All works appeared at both the Clark Art Institute (Williamstown) and the High Museum of Art (Atlanta) except where noted in brackets.

THE ERA OF COLLECTORS, 1885–1915

Cat. 1

Figure Sketch
c. 1898–1900
Graphite with stumping on wove paper
11 ½ × 7 ¼ in. (29.2 × 18.4 cm)
Dedicated and signed in graphite at lower right:
aux Etats Unis / Auguste Rodin / reconnaissance
Smithsonian American Art Museum, Washington, DC
Gift of the Republic of France, 1915.11.70

Provenance: Republic of France (c. 1915, until given to the US State Department); US State Department (November 6, 1915, transferred to museum); Smithsonian American Art Museum, 1915.

[Williamstown]

Cat. 2

Fallen Caryatid
Original model 1882
Marble, probably carved by Bozzoni, 1882–83
19 ¹¹⁄₁₆ × 12 × 10 ½ in. (50 × 30.48 × 26.67 cm)
Signed on base: *Rodin*
Museum of Fine Arts, Boston
Gift of the Estate of Samuel Isham through Julia Isham (Mrs. Henry Osborn Taylor), 17.3134

Provenance: Possibly Jules Bastien-Lepage (1848–1884), Paris (c. 1883–84); estate of Jules Bastien-Lepage (c. 1884, probably sold to Isham); Samuel Isham (1855–1914), Paris and New York (between 1885 and 1887–1914); estate of Samuel Isham (1914–17, given to museum through Julia Isham); Museum of Fine Arts, Boston, October 4, 1917.

[Williamstown]

Cat. 3

Bust of St. John the Baptist
Original model 1880
Bronze, cast by François Rudier (no marks), 1883
21 ³⁄₈ × 15 ¾ × 11 in. (54.3 × 40 × 27.9 cm)
Signed on base, under left shoulder: *A. Rodin*
Metropolitan Museum of Art, New York
Gift of Samuel P. Avery, 1893, 93.11

Provenance: George A. Lucas (1824–1909), Paris (1888); Samuel Putnam Avery Sr. (1822–1904), New York (until 1893, given to museum); Metropolitan Museum of Art, New York, 1893.

Cat. 4

Cupid and Psyche
Before 1886
Marble
With wooden base, 9 × 27 ½ × 17 ¾ in. (22.9 × 69.9 × 45.1 cm)
Signed on side of base, near figures' feet: *A. Rodin*
Iris Cantor Collection

Provenance: Arcole, Paris, June 20, 1989, no. 175; Cyril Abecassis, Geneva; Sandra Werther and Jamie Szoke, New York; Iris Cantor (b. 1941) and B. Gerald Cantor (1916–1996), New York; Iris Cantor, New York.

[Williamstown]

Cat. 5

Assemblage of a Watchman and a Seated Bather, also known as *The Confidence*
Assembled 1892
Bronze, perhaps cast by Adolphe Gruet, 1892
5 ¹¹⁄₁₆ × 6 ¼ × 3 ³⁄₁₆ in. (14.4 × 15.8 × 9.1 cm)
Dedicated and signed on rock: *épreuve unique / en hommage a Miss Hallowell / Rodin*
Private collection

Provenance: Sara Tyson Hallowell (1846–1924), Chicago, Paris, and Moret-sur-Loing, France (gift from the artist, 1892–1924); Harriet Tyson Hallowell (1873–1943), Moret-sur-Loing, her niece, by descent (until 1943); Galerie Fabius, Paris; private collection.

Cat. 6

Fugit Amor, also known as *The Sphinx*
Assembled before 1887
Bronze, probably cast by Griffoul and Lorge, 1892
14 ¾ × 17 ¹¹⁄₁₆ × 7 ¹¹⁄₁₆ in. (37.4 × 45 × 19.6 cm)
Inscribed and signed on base: *hommage respectueux / a Miss S. Hallowell / A. Rodin*
Private collection

Provenance: Sara Tyson Hallowell (1846–1924), Chicago and Moret-sur-Loing, France (gift from the artist, April 1893–1924); Harriet Tyson Hallowell (1873–1943), Moret-sur-Loing, her niece, by descent (until 1943); probably Galerie Fabius, Paris (c. 1959); private collection.

Cat. 7

Arthur Jerome Eddy
Original model 1898
Bronze, cast by Auguste Griffoul [no mark], 1898
17 ¾ × 19 ½ × 10 ¾ in. (45.1 × 49.5 × 27.3 cm)
Signed and dated, on left side of chest: *A. Rodin 1898*
Art Institute of Chicago
Arthur Jerome Eddy Memorial Collection, 1931.502

Provenance: Arthur Jerome Eddy (1859–1920), Chicago (commissioned from the artist, 1898–1920); Lulu Crapo Orrell Eddy, Chicago, his wife, and Jerome Orrell Eddy (1891–1951), Chicago, his son, by descent (1920–31, given to museum); Art Institute of Chicago, 1931.

Cat. 8

Death of Alcestis
Assembled c. 1899
Bronze, cast 1902
14 ⁹⁄₁₆ × 9 ¼ × 6 ¾ in. (37 × 23.5 × 17.2 cm)

Signed, left of figures, on side of base: *A. Rodin*
Museum of Fine Arts, Boston
Bequest of Major Henry Lee Higginson, 21.2521

Provenance: Henry Lee Higginson (1834–1919), Boston (1903–19, loaned to museum 1903–19, bequest to museum); Museum of Fine Arts, Boston, 1921.

[Williamstown]

Cat. 9
Ceres
1902
Marble
26 × 17 1/2 × 13 3/4 in. (66 × 44.5 × 34.9 cm)
Signed, right side, edge of shoulder: *A. Rodin*
Museum of Fine Arts, Boston
Gift Major Henry Lee Higginson, 06.1910

Provenance: Henry Lee Higginson (1834–1919), Boston (commissioned from the artist 1901; 1902–6, loaned to museum 1902–6, given to museum); Museum of Fine Arts, Boston, 1906.

[Williamstown]

Cat. 10
Thought
Original marble 1895
Marble, carved by Camille Raynaud, 1900–1901
29 1/8 × 17 1/16 × 18 1/8 in. (74 × 43.3 × 46 cm)
Signed, lower-right corner of pedestal: *A. Rodin*
Philadelphia Museum of Art
John G. Johnson Collection, cat. 1148

Provenance: Alexander Harrison (1853–1930) (commissioned for the W. P. Wilstach Collection, Philadelphia, August 1900; instead sold to Johnson); John G. Johnson (1841–1917), Philadelphia (April 1901–17, bequest to city); City of Philadelphia, 1917.

[Williamstown]

Cat. 11
Thought
Original model 1895
Bronze, cast by Alexis Rudier, 1925
17 3/4 × 15 5/8 × 16 1/2 in. (45.1 × 39.7 × 41.9 cm)
Signed on top of base: *A. Rodin*
Rodin Museum, Philadelphia Museum of Art
Bequest of Jules E. Mastbaum, 1929, F1929-7-47

Provenance: Jules E. Mastbaum (1872–1926), Philadelphia (acquired from Musée Rodin, Paris, November 1925–26, bequest to museum); Rodin Museum, Philadelphia, 1929.

[Atlanta]

Cat. 12
Katherine Seney Simpson (Mrs. John W. Simpson)
1903
Marble

21 13/16 × 27 3/16 × 16 5/16 in. (55.4 × 69 × 41.5 cm)
Signed and dated on base: *A. Rodin / 1903*
National Gallery of Art, Washington, DC
Gift of Mrs. John W. Simpson, 1942.5.16

Provenance: Katherine Seney Simpson (1869–1943) and John W. Simpson (1850–1920), New York (commissioned from the artist, 1903–20); Katherine Seney Simpson (1920–42, given to museum); National Gallery of Art, Washington, DC, 1942.

Cat. 13
Mask of Katherine Seney Simpson (Mrs. John W. Simpson)
1902
Plaster
7 × 7 11/16 × 6 in. (17.8 × 19.5 × 15.3 cm)
Inscribed, dated, and signed, left side of chin, in graphite: *Mme K Simpson esquisse pour le portrait / 12 septembre 1909 / A. Rodin*
National Gallery of Art, Washington, DC
Gift of Mrs. John W. Simpson, 1942.5.21

Provenance: Katherine Seney Simpson (1869–1943), New York (1909–42, given to museum); National Gallery of Art, Washington, DC, 1942.

[Williamstown]

Cat. 14
Study for St. John the Baptist, today known as *The Small Walking Man*
Assembled c. 1899
Bronze, cast by Alexis Rudier [no mark], 1903
33 1/2 × 23 9/16 × 10 7/16 in. (85.1 × 59.8 × 26.5 cm)
Signed in incised letters on base between feet: *A. Rodin*; in raised letters on underside of base inside left foot: *A. Rodin*; in raised letters behind right heel, on underside of base: *A. Rodin*
National Gallery of Art, Washington, DC
Gift of Mrs. John W. Simpson, 1942.5.11

Provenance: Katherine Seney Simpson (1869–1943) and John Woodruff Simpson (1850–1920), New York (1903–20); Katherine Seney Simpson (1920–42, given to museum); National Gallery of Art, Washington, DC, 1942.

Cat. 15
A Burgher of Calais (Jean d'Aire)
Original model 1887, reduced 1895
Bronze, probably cast by François Rudier, 1904
18 1/2 × 6 5/16 × 5 1/2 in. (47 × 16 × 14 cm)
Signed on back of base: *A. Rodin*
National Gallery of Art, Washington, DC
Gift of Mrs. John W. Simpson, 1942.5.13

Provenance: Katherine Seney Simpson (1869–1943) and John Woodruff Simpson (1850–1920), New York (before 1905–20); Katherine Seney Simpson (1920–42, given to museum); National Gallery of Art, Washington, DC, 1942.

Cat. 16
Woman and Child (originally titled *First Impression of Love*)
Original model before 1893
Marble, carved 1902
17 × 17 1/2 × 13 1/16 in. (43.2 × 44.4 × 33.1 cm)
Signed, bottom left: *A. Rodin*
National Gallery of Art, Washington, DC
Gift of Mrs. John W. Simpson, 1942.5.19

Provenance: Katherine Seney Simpson (1869–1943) and John Woodruff Simpson (1850–1920), New York (acquired from the artist through agent Samuel Bing, 1902–20); Katherine Seney Simpson (1920–42, given to museum); National Gallery of Art, Washington, DC, 1942.

[Atlanta]

Cat. 17
Nude Woman Carrying Vase on Head (Antique Vase)
c. 1898–1900
Graphite with stumping and watercolor on wove paper
19 13/16 × 12 5/16 in. (50.3 × 31.2 cm)
Dedicated, signed, and dated in graphite on lower right: *à Madame K. Simpson amie / de mon art dès la première heure / Aug. Rodin 1909*
Inscribed upper left, in unknown hand: *1842*
National Gallery of Art, Washington, DC
Gift of Mrs. John W. Simpson, 1942.5.32

Provenance: Katherine Seney Simpson (1869–1943), New York (given by the artist 1909–42, given to museum); National Gallery of Art, Washington, DC.

[Williamstown]

Cat. 18
Figure Facing Forward (Serpentine?)
c. 1906
Graphite with stumping and watercolor on wove paper
12 13/16 × 9 15/16 in. (32.5 × 25.3 cm)
Signed in graphite, lower right: *A. Rodin*
Inscribed in later hand, center-right verso: *Mrs. Nelson Robinson / 23 E. 55*; lower-right verso: *38538*
National Gallery of Art, Washington, DC
Mrs. John W. Simpson, 1942.5.34

Provenance: [Possibly Little Galleries of the Photo-Secession, New York, sold to Robinson, 1908]; Elizabeth "Lillie" Rushmore Seney Robinson (1855–1924), New York (1908–24); Katherine Seney Simpson (1869–1943), New York, her sister, by descent (1924–42, given to museum); National Gallery of Art, Washington, DC, 1942.

[Williamstown]

Cat. 19
Miss Jean Simpson, Seated
1903
Graphite and watercolor on wove paper
12 13/16 × 9 7/8 in. (32.5 × 25.1 cm)
Inscribed and signed in graphite, upper right:
Mademoiselle Jean / 28 Sept. 1903 / A. Rodin
Signed in graphite, lower right: *A. Rodin*
Brooklyn Museum, New York
Gift of the Iris and B. Gerald Cantor Foundation,
87.94.4

Provenance: Jean Walker Simpson (1897–
1980), East Craftsbury, Vermont; estate of Jean
Walker Simpson (1980–82, sale, Sotheby's,
December 10, 1982, no. 113); Iris and B.
Gerald Cantor Foundation (by 1987, given to
museum); Brooklyn Museum, 1987.

[Atlanta]

Cat. 20
Jean Simpson
1903
Graphite on wove paper
12 15/16 × 9 13/16 in. (32.9 × 24.9 cm)
Signed in graphite, lower right: *A. Rodin*
Brooklyn Museum, New York
Gift of the Iris and B. Gerald Cantor Foundation,
87.94.3

Provenance: Jean Walker Simpson (1897–
1980), East Craftsbury, Vermont; estate of Jean
Walker Simpson (1980–82, sale, Sotheby's,
December 10, 1982, no. 119); Iris and B.
Gerald Cantor Foundation (by 1987, given to
museum); Brooklyn Museum, 1987.

[Williamstown]

Cat. 21
The Thinker
Original model 1881–82
Bronze, probably cast by Alexis Rudier [no
marks], 1902 or 1906
20 × 21 1/2 × 20 1/2 in. (50.8 × 54.6 × 52 cm)
Signed on rock and to left of figure: *A. Rodin*
Dedicated, signed, and dated on base near right
foot: *à Loïe Fuller. A. Rodin / 1906*
Yale University Art Gallery, New Haven,
Connecticut
Bequest of Susan Vanderpoel Clark, 1967.82.4

Provenance: Loïe Fuller (1862–1928), Paris
(given by the artist, 1906–); Stephen Clark
(1882–1960), New York and Cooperstown, New
York (date acquired unknown–1960); Susan
Vanderpoel Clark (1889–1967), Cooperstown,
New York, his wife, by descent (1960–67,
bequest to museum); Yale University Art Gallery,
New Haven, Connecticut, 1967.

Cat. 22
The Hand of God
Original model 1895
Marble, carved by Louis Mathet, c. 1907

29 × 23 3/4 × 25 1/4 in. (73.7 × 60.3 × 64.1 cm)
Signed on base: *A. Rodin*
Metropolitan Museum of Art, New York
Gift of Edward D. Adams, 1908, 08.210

Provenance: Edward D. Adams (1846–1931),
New York (commissioned from the artist,
1906–8, given to museum); Metropolitan
Museum of Art, New York, 1908.

Cat. 23
Seated Nude
c. 1900–1908
Graphite with stumping, black crayon, and
eraser on wove paper
12 3/16 × 7 7/8 in. (31 × 20 cm)
Dedicated and signed in graphite, top right:
*à Monsieur Edward / Robinson / directeur
du Musée / Metropolitain / de New York /
en grande sympathie / Auguste Rodin*
Jonathan and Abby Freund, United States

Provenance: Edward D. Robinson (1858–1931),
New York (gift from the artist, 1913–31); Susan
Robinson, New York, by descent (1931–until
given to Lane); Katherine Lane; private collection,
by descent, until sale, Sotheby's New York,
October 7, 2008, no. 1; private collection,
United States.

Cat. 24
The Abandoned (Psyche)
c. 1902
Graphite with stumping on wove paper
7 9/16 × 11 7/8 in. (19.4 × 30.4 cm)
Signed in graphite, lower right: *Aug. Rodin*
Metropolitan Museum of Art, New York
Rogers Fund, 1910, 10.45.20

Provenance: Hôtel Drouot, Paris, May 6, 1909,
no. 119c, sold to Turner; [Percy Moore Turner,
London (1909–10, sold to Roger Fry, agent
of museum)]; Metropolitan Museum of Art,
New York, 1910.

[Williamstown]

Cat. 25
Nero
c. 1900–1910
Graphite with stumping, watercolor, and
gouache on wove paper
12 13/16 × 9 13/16 in. (32.5 × 24.9 cm)
Signed in graphite, lower right: *Aug. Rodin*
Inscribed in graphite, center right: *Néron*
Inscribed in later hand in graphite, lower left: *17*
Metropolitan Museum of Art, New York
John Stewart Kennedy Fund, 1910, 10.66.5

Provenance: [*An Exhibition of Recent and Early
Drawings and Watercolors by Auguste Rodin,*
Little Galleries of the Photo-Secession, New York,
March 31–April 16, 1910, no. 19, purchased
by museum]; Metropolitan Museum of Art,
New York, 1910.

[Williamstown]

Cat. 26
Hanako
July 1906–7
Graphite, pen and ink, crayon, and gouache
on wove paper
11 3/4 × 8 7/16 in. (29.8 × 21.4 cm)
Inscribed and signed in graphite, lower right:
Hanako / Aug. Rodin
Inscribed by later hand in graphite, lower left: *9*
Metropolitan Museum of Art, New York
John Stewart Kennedy Fund, 1910, 10.66.2

Provenance: [*An Exhibition of Recent and Early
Drawings and Watercolors by Auguste Rodin,*
Little Galleries of the Photo-Secession, New York,
March 31–April 16, 1910, no. 12, purchased
by museum]; Metropolitan Museum of Art,
New York, 1910.

[Atlanta]

Cat. 27
Nude Figure on Hands and Knees (Executioner)
c. 1898–1900
Graphite with stumping and watercolor on wove
paper
9 3/4 × 12 13/16 in. (24.8 × 32.5 cm)
Signed in graphite over inscription, lower right:
Aug. Rodin
Inscribed in graphite, lower right: *Bourreau*
Metropolitan Museum of Art, New York
Gift of Thomas F. Ryan, 1913, 13.164.1

Provenance: Metropolitan Museum of Art,
New York, 1913.

[Atlanta]

Cat. 28
Female Nude Reclining
c. 1909–10
Graphite with stumping on wove paper
14 3/16 × 9 1/4 in. (36 × 23.5 cm)
Signed in graphite, lower right: *Aug Rodin*
Metropolitan Museum of Art, New York
Gift of Thomas F. Ryan, 1913, 13.164.4

Provenance: Metropolitan Museum of Art,
New York, 1913.

[Atlanta]

Cat. 29
Honoré de Balzac
1891
Terracotta
With base: 15 × 5 × 5 in. (38.1 × 12.7 ×
12.7 cm)
Signed on back of neck: *A. Rodin*
Metropolitan Museum of Art, New York
Rogers Fund, 1912, 12.11.1

Provenance: Metropolitan Museum of Art,
New York, 1912.

Cat. 30
Young Woman Kneeling
Original model late 19th–early 20th century
Plaster
8 ⅛ × 6 ⁵⁄₁₆ × 4 in. (20.6 × 16.8 × 10.2 cm)
Signed vertically on the figure's back: *Rodin*
Metropolitan Museum of Art, New York
Gift of Auguste Rodin, 1912, 12.12.3

Provenance: Metropolitan Museum of Art,
New York, 1912.

[Williamstown]

Cat. 31
Study of the Left Hand and Arm of "Meditation"
Original model c. 1894
Plaster
4 ⅛ × 9 ⅛ × 6 ⅛ in. (10.5 × 23.2 × 15.6 cm)
Signed around opening of base: *A. Rodin*
Metropolitan Museum of Art, New York
Gift of Auguste Rodin, 1912, 12.12.9

Provenance: Metropolitan Museum of Art,
New York, 1912.

Cat. 32
Study of a Hand
Original model late 19th–early 20th century
Plaster
4 ¾ × 2 × 1 ¼ in. (12.1 × 5.1 × 3.2 cm)
Signed under base: *A. Rodin*
Metropolitan Museum of Art, New York
Gift of Auguste Rodin, 12.12.16

Provenance: Metropolitan Museum of Art,
New York, 1912.

Cat. 33
Study of a Hand
Original model late 19th–early 20th century
Plaster
6 ⅜ × 2 ½ × 3 ¾ in. (16.2 × 6.4 × 9.5 cm)
Signed under base: *A. Rodin*
Metropolitan Museum of Art, New York
Gift of Auguste Rodin, 1912, 12.12.10

Provenance: Metropolitan Museum of Art,
New York, 1912.

Cat. 34
Psyche (Love over the Waters)
c. 1902
Graphite and watercolor on wove paper
9 ¾ × 12 ¾ in. (24.7 × 32.4 cm)
Signed and inscribed in graphite, lower right:
A. Rodin / l'amour porté sur les eaux
Private collection, courtesy of Nicholas Sands &
Company Fine Art, New York

Provenance: Malvina Hoffman (1885–1966),
New York (probably gift from the artist–1966);
Hoffman estate; private collector.

Cat. 35
*Stretching Figure (The Angel Thrown down
to Earth or Trapeze)*
c. 1898–1900
Graphite and watercolor on wove paper
13 × 9 ¾ in. (33.0 × 24.9 cm)
Inscribed and signed in graphite, lower right:
enfer / devant l'effroy / A. Rodin; center right:
rebelle / l'ange précipité / sur la terre / enfer;
upper right: *trapeze*
Museum of Modern Art, New York
Bequest of Mina Turner, 254.1976

Provenance: Gertrude Käsebier (1852–1934),
New York (gift of the artist–1906); Mina Turner,
her granddaughter, by descent (until 1976,
bequest to museum); Museum of Modern Art,
New York, 1976.

[Williamstown]

Cat. 36
Seated Woman (Psyche)
c. 1902
Graphite on wove paper
12 ¼ × 8 in. (31.2 × 20.2 cm)
Museum of Modern Art, New York
Bequest of Mina Turner, 251.1976

Provenance: Gertrude Käsebier (1852–1934),
New York (gift of the artist–1906); Mina Turner,
her granddaughter, by descent (until 1976,
bequest to museum); Museum of Modern Art,
New York, 1976.

[Williamstown]

Cat. 37
Figure of a Woman, "The Sphinx"
Original model before 1888
Marble, carved 1909
23 ¼ × 24 ⁷⁄₁₆ × 22 ¹⁵⁄₁₆ in. (59 × 62.1 × 58.3 cm)
Signed on base, near fingers: *A. Rodin*
National Gallery of Art, Washington, DC
Gift of Eugene and Agnes E. Meyer, 1967,
1967.13.6

Provenance: Agnes Ernst Meyer (1887–1970)
and Eugene Meyer (1875–1959), Mount Kisco,
New York, and Washington, DC (acquired from
the artist, 1910–59); Agnes Ernst Meyer
(1959–67, given to museum); National Gallery
of Art, Washington, DC, 1967.

[Williamstown]

Cat. 38
Horseman (recto); *Horse and Rider* (verso)
c. 1886–89
Graphite, pen and ink, gouache, and traces of
faded ink; graphite (verso) on wove paper,
tipped onto wove paper
8 ⁹⁄₁₆ × 6 ⅞ in. (21.7 × 17.4 cm)
Dated and signed, lower left, on paper support:
1889 / Aug. / Rodin
Art Institute of Chicago
Alfred Stieglitz Collection, 1949.580

Provenance: Edward Steichen (1879–1973)
(possibly gift from the artist–1910, given to
Stieglitz); Alfred Stieglitz (1864–1946),
New York (December 1910–1946); Stieglitz
estate (1946–49, given to museum); Art Institute
of Chicago, 1949.

[Williamstown]

Cat. 39
Lightly Draped Dancing Female Nude
c. 1900
Graphite with stumping on card laid down on
wove paper
12 ¹⁄₁₆ × 7 ¾ in. (30.6 × 19.7 cm)
Dedicated and signed in graphite on lower right:
*hommage / affectueux à madame / C. Steichen
/ Aug. Rodin*
Art Institute of Chicago
Alfred Stieglitz Collection, 1949.898

Provenance: Clara Steichen (d. 1957) (gift of
the artist); Edward Steichen (1879–1973),
her husband, by descent; Alfred Stieglitz
(1864–1946), New York (c. 1908 or 1910–
1946); Stieglitz estate (1946–49, given to
museum); Art Institute of Chicago, 1949.

[Atlanta]

Cat. 40
Reclining Nude
c. 1900
Graphite with stumping on wove paper
12 ⅛ × 8 ¹⁄₁₆ in. (30.8 × 20.4 cm)
Signed in graphite, lower right: *A. Rodin*
Art Institute of Chicago
Alfred Stieglitz Collection, 1949.899

Provenance: Charles H. Caffin (1854–1918),
New York (gift of the artist–1909, given to
Stieglitz); Alfred Stieglitz (1864–1946), New
York (May 1909–46); Stieglitz estate (1946–49,
given to museum); Art Institute of Chicago,
1949.

[Atlanta]

Cat. 41
Witch's Sabbath
c. 1900–1905
Watercolor, gouache, and graphite on
wove paper
12 ¹³⁄₁₆ × 9 ¾ in. (32.6 × 24.8 cm)
Inscribed and signed in graphite, lower right:
sabbat / Aug. Rodin
Metropolitan Museum of Art, New York
Gift of Georgia O'Keeffe, 1965, 65.261.1

Provenance: Alfred Stieglitz (1864–1946);
Georgia O'Keefe (1887–1986), New York and
Santa Fe, New Mexico (by 1965, given to
museum); Metropolitan Museum of Art,
New York, 1965.

[Atlanta]

Cat. 42

The Prodigal Son
Original model before 1887, enlarged 1893
Bronze, cast by Alexis Rudier, 1914
64 × 28 × 34 ½ in. (162.6 × 71.1 × 87.6 cm)
Signed on base, top-right front corner: *A. Rodin*
Stamped inside: *A. Rodin*; stamped rear of base,
right: *Ais. Rudier Fondeur Paris*
Fine Arts Museums of San Francisco, Legion of
Honor
Gift of Alma de Bretteville Spreckels, 1940.137

Provenance: Alma de Bretteville Spreckels
(1881–1968), San Francisco (1915–40, given to
museum); Fine Arts Museums of San Francisco,
1940.

Cat. 43

Female Figure, Half-Length
Original model c. 1910
Bronze, cast by Montagutelli, 1913
29 ¼ × 12 ¼ × 23 ⅝ in. (74.3 × 31.1 × 60 cm)
Signed: *Rodin*
Stamped: *Montagutelli Fres Paris Cire Perdue*
Fine Arts Museums of San Francisco, Legion of
Honor
Gift of Alma de Bretteville Spreckels, 1942.36

Provenance: Alma de Bretteville Spreckels
(1881–1968), San Francisco (1915–42, given to
museum); Fine Arts Museums of San Francisco,
1942.

Cat. 44

The Fallen Angel
Original model c. 1895–1900
Bronze, cast by Alexis Rudier, probably 1915
Signed, top of base, right: *A. Rodin*
Stamped on back: *A. Rudier Fondeur Paris*
20 ⅛ × 21 ½ × 32 in. (51.1 × 54.6 × 81.3 cm)
Fine Arts Museums of San Francisco, Legion of
Honor
Gift of Alma de Bretteville Spreckels, 1940.139

Provenance: Alma de Bretteville Spreckels (1881–
1968), San Francisco (1915–42, given to museum);
Fine Arts Museums of San Francisco, 1942.

Cat. 45

Head of Balzac (last study)
Original model c. 1897
Bronze on tall marble base, cast before 1915
Signed, lower-left side: *A. Rodin*
16 ¾ × 7 ½ × 8 ½ in. (42.6 × 19 × 21.6 cm)
Fine Arts Museums of San Francisco, Legion of
Honor
Gift of Alma de Bretteville Spreckels, 1941.34.5

Provenance: Loïe Fuller (1862–1928), Paris (sold
to Spreckels, 1915); Alma de Bretteville
Spreckels (1881–1968), San Francisco (1915–
41, given to museum); Fine Arts Museums of San
Francisco, 1941.

Cat. 46

*Heroic Head of Pierre de Wissant, One of the
Burghers of Calais*
Original model 1887, enlarged 1908
Bronze, cast by Alexis Rudier, 1916; patinated
by Jean Limet
32 ⅞ × 18 ½ × 21 ¾ in. (83.5 × 47 × 55.2 cm)
Signed on neck, at left: *A. Rodin*
Inscribed, lower back: *Alexis Rudier /
Fondeur-Paris*
Cleveland Museum of Art
The Norweb Collection, 1920.120

Provenance: Emery May Holden Norweb
(1896–1984), Cleveland (1917–20, given to
museum); Cleveland Museum of Art, 1920.

Cat. 47

Model of a Foot (Left Foot)
Original model late 19th–early 20th century
Bronze, cast before 1917
2 ¹³⁄₁₆ × 1 ¾ in. (7.2 × 4.4 cm); length (toe to
heel): 4 ⁵⁄₁₆ in. (11 cm)
Signed over heel: *A. Rodin*
Cleveland Museum of Art
Gift of Loïe Fuller, 1917.372

Provenance: Loïe Fuller (1862–1928), Paris
(until 1917, given to museum); Cleveland
Museum of Art, 1917.

Cat. 48

Eve
1881/82–99
Plaster with graphite guiding marks
67 × 18 ⅛ × 23 ¼ in. (170 × 47 × 59 cm)
Maryhill Museum of Art, Goldendale,
Washington
Bequest of Samuel Hill, 1938.01.0162

Provenance: Possibly Antoine Bourdelle
(1861–1929), Paris (1901–c. 1920); possibly
Loïe Fuller (1862–1928), Paris; Samuel Hill
(1857–1931), Seattle (before 1926–1931);
estate of Samuel Hill (until 1938, bequest to
museum); Maryhill Museum of Art, Goldendale,
Washington, 1938.

[*This work did not travel to the exhibition.]

Cat. 49

Hanako (type A)
1907
Gilded bronze on wood base
6 ½ × 5 × 5 ⅝ in. (16.5 × 12.7 × 14.3 cm)
Dedicated at back on bottom: *A-l'admirable et /
Geniale artiste / Loïe-fuller / A. Rodin*
Fine Arts Museums of San Francisco, Legion of
Honor
Gift of Alma de Bretteville Spreckels, 1941.34.7

Provenance: Loïe Fuller (1862–1928), Paris
(gift from the artist, 1907–19, sold to Spreckels);
Alma de Bretteville Spreckels (1881–1968),
San Francisco (1919–41, given to museum);
Fine Arts Museums of San Francisco, 1941.

Cat. 50

Eve Eating the Apple, known as *Dawn*
Original model c. 1887
Plaster
10 ½ × 6 × 10 ¼ in. (26.7 × 15.2 × 26 cm)
Signed on base: *A. Rodin*
Maryhill Museum of Art, Goldendale,
Washington
Bequest of Samuel Hill, 1938.01.0164

Provenance: Loïe Fuller (1862–1928), Paris;
Samuel Hill (1857–1931), Seattle (before
1926–1931); estate of Samuel Hill (1931–38,
bequest to museum); Maryhill Museum of Art,
Goldendale, Washington, 1938.

Cat. 51

The Hand of God
Original model before 1895
Plaster c. 1900
13 ½ × 11 × 10 ½ in. (34.3 × 27.9 × 26.7
cm)
Dedicated and signed in graphite on base:
A Loïe. Rodin
Maryhill Museum of Art, Goldendale,
Washington
Bequest of Samuel Hill, 1938.01.186

Provenance: Loïe Fuller (1862–1928), Paris
(gift from the artist, before 1917–c. 1926);
Samuel Hill (1857–1931), Seattle (1926–31);
estate of Samuel Hill (until 1938, bequest to
museum); Maryhill Museum of Art,
Goldendale, Washington, 1938.

Cat. 52

The Hand of God
Original model before 1895
Bronze, cast by Alexis Rudier, before 1908
38 × 24 ½ × 17 in. (96.5 × 62.2 × 43.2 cm)
Signed on base: *A. Rodin*
Carnegie Museum of Art, Pittsburgh
Purchase, 20.14.5

Provenance: Musée du Luxembourg, Paris
(1909–19, until transferred to Musée Rodin);
Musée Rodin, Paris (1919–20, until sale,
*Nineteenth Annual International Exhibition of
Paintings*, Pittsburgh, April 29–June 30, 1920,
no. 377, sold to museum); Carnegie Museum
of Art, Pittsburgh, 1920.

Cat. 53

Figure in Pose of Michelangelo's "Apollo"
c. 1876
Charcoal, watercolor, and gouache on wove
paper
13 ¾ × 9 ¼ in. (34.9 × 23.5 cm)
Maryhill Museum of Art, Goldendale,
Washington
Bequest of Samuel Hill, 1938.01.0094

Provenance: Loïe Fuller (1862–1928), Paris
(purchased from the artist, c. 1915 or
1916–21, sold to Hill); Samuel Hill (1857–
1931), Seattle (1921–31); estate of Samuel

Hill (1931–38, bequest to museum); Maryhill
Museum of Art, Goldendale, Washington, 1938.

[Williamstown]

Cat. 54
Before Creation: Chaos
c. 1898–1900
Graphite and watercolor on wove paper
9 ¾ × 12 ¾ in. (24.8 × 32.4 cm)
Inscribed in graphite, center right: *avant /
la creation / Cahos* [*sic*]
Maryhill Museum of Art, Goldendale,
Washington
Bequest of Samuel Hill, 1938.1.116

Provenance: Loïe Fuller (1862–1928), Paris
(purchased from the artist, c. 1915 or 1916–21,
sold to Hill); Samuel Hill (1857–1931), Seattle
(1921–31); estate of Samuel Hill (1931–38,
given to museum); Maryhill Museum of Art,
Goldendale, Washington, 1938.

[Atlanta]

Cat. 55
Psyche
c. 1902
Graphite and watercolor on wove paper
10 ¾ × 12 ½ in. (27.3 × 31.8 cm)
Inscribed in graphite, upper right: *trainée
Psychée* [*sic*] */ attachée par / les cheveux /
à un autel*; center right: *amour / traine par /
les cheveux*; lower right: *gaine priape*; upper
middle: *bas*
Maryhill Museum of Art, Goldendale,
Washington
Bequest of Samuel Hill, 1938.1.107

Provenance: Loïe Fuller (1862–1928), Paris
(purchased from the artist, c. 1915 or 1916–21,
sold to Hill); Samuel Hill (1857–1931), Seattle
(1921–31); estate of Samuel Hill (1931–38,
given to museum); Maryhill Museum of Art,
Goldendale, Washington, 1938.

[Williamstown]

Cat. 56
Psyche
c. 1902
Graphite and watercolor on wove paper
17 × 14 in. (43.2 × 35.6 cm)
Signed in graphite, bottom right: *Aug. Rodin*
Maryhill Museum of Art, Goldendale,
Washington
Bequest of Samuel Hill, 1938.1.104

Provenance: Loïe Fuller (1862–1928), Paris
(purchased from the artist, c. 1915 or 1916–21,
sold to Hill); Samuel Hill (1857–1931), Seattle
(1921–31); estate of Samuel Hill (1931–38,
given to museum); Maryhill Museum of Art,
Goldendale, Washington, 1938.

[Atlanta]

Cat. 57
*Cambodian Dancer in Yellow, at the End of
a Rainbow*
c. 1906–7
Graphite and watercolor on wove paper
12 ¾ × 9 ⅞ in. (32.4 × 25.1 cm)
Signed in graphite, bottom right: *Aug. Rodin*
Maryhill Museum of Art, Goldendale,
Washington
Bequest of Samuel Hill, 1938.01.0099

Provenance: Loïe Fuller (1862–1928), Paris
(purchased from the artist, c. 1915 or 1916–21,
sold to Hill); Samuel Hill (1857–1931), Seattle
(1921–31); estate of Samuel Hill (1931–38,
given to museum); Maryhill Museum of Art,
Goldendale, Washington, 1938.

[Williamstown]

Cat. 58
Female Figure (Assunta Petricca)
1915
Graphite with stumping on wove paper
17 ⁵⁄₁₆ × 23 ¼ in. (44 × 59 cm)
Left page inscribed in graphite in Rodin's hand,
top left: *S Martino / Nathan / O Conner*
Dedicated, signed, and dated, bottom
right: *à Loïe Fuller / la grande artiste créatrice /
Aug Rodin / janvier 1915*
Right page inscribed, signed, and dated in pen
and brown ink in Loïe Fuller's hand: *To Eugène
Rudier from Loïe Fuller. / This beautiful and
incomparable work of the Master was presented
to me as an expression of his love and esteem in
Rome 1915, and in 1927 Presented to Eugene
Rudier, whose life work and that of his father
before him was to put into everlasting Bronze the
works of the master and for which the world
owes its undying gratitude. It is presented as a
rare souvenir of the master we both loved so
profoundly and so well! In 1902 [actually 1903]
I took to America the first collection of the
master's works to show my countrymen in an
exhibition I organized for that purpose in New
York City. Not one person wanted one of his
works, + in one month, all the works were
returned to "him." I tried to present a beautiful
terra cotta of the great Bellone but it was refused
because it was not in bronze or marble. On my
return I promised the master that one day we
would create a French Museum in America as an
education to my new country and we worked
together for that purpose till his death. The news
of the realization of our dream,—of his heart's
desire and our efforts—reached him on his death
bed! It was the Palace of the Legion of Honor at
San Francisco / for which we have to thank Mr.
AB & Alma de Bretteville Spreckels and Mr.
Albert Tirman: and the moral help of an
unknown woman friend of Mrs. Spreckels, Miss
May Slesinger. Paris, July 2nd 1927. Loïe Fuller.*
Fine Arts Museums of San Francisco, Legion of
Honor

Museum purchase, gift of Mrs. John N. Rosekrans
Jr., in memory of her husband, grandson of Alma
de Bretteville Spreckels, 2007.49

Provenance: Loïe Fuller (1862–1928), Paris
(gift from the artist, 1915–27, given to Rudier);
Eugène Rudier (1875–1952), Paris (1927–);
Fine Arts Museums of San Francisco, 2007.

[Atlanta]

Cat. 59
Female Torso
Original model c. 1889–90
Plaster on plaster base
5 ¼ × 3 ¹⁵⁄₁₆ × 3 ¹⁵⁄₁₆ in. (13.3 × 10 × 10 cm)
Fine Arts Museums of San Francisco, Legion of
Honor
Gift of Adolph B. Spreckels Jr., 1933.12.10

Provenance: Eugène Rudier (1878–1952), Le Vésinet,
France (1920s); Adolph B. Spreckels Jr. (1911–1961),
San Francisco(?) (until 1933, given to museum); Fine
Arts Museums of San Francisco, 1933.

Cat. 60
Female Torso with a Slavic Woman's Head
Original models c. 1905
Plaster on marble base
8 × 2 ¾ × 4 in. (20.3 × 7 × 10.2 cm)
Fine Arts Museums of San Francisco, Legion of
Honor
Gift of Adolph B. Spreckels Jr., 1933.12.14

Provenance: Eugène Rudier (1878–1952), Le Vésinet,
France (1920s); Adolph B. Spreckels Jr. (1911–1961),
San Francisco (?) (until 1933, given to museum); Fine
Arts Museums of San Francisco, 1933.

Cat. 61
Two Hands
Assembled c. 1900
Plaster on marble base
4 ⅛ × 3 × 2 ¼ in. (10.5 × 7.6 × 5.7 cm)
Fine Arts Museums of San Francisco, Legion of
Honor
Gift of Adolph B. Spreckels Jr., 1933.12.12

Provenance: Eugène Rudier (1878–1952), Le
Vésinet, France (1920s); Adolph B. Spreckels Jr.
(1911–1961), San Francisco (?) (until 1933, given
to museum); Fine Arts Museums of San Francisco,
1933.

Cat. 62
Camille Claudel
French, 1864–1943
Bust of Auguste Rodin
Original model 1892
Bronze with marble base, probably cast by François
Rudier, c. 1900
16 ¼ × 9 ¾ × 11 ¼ in. (41.3 × 24.8 × 28.6 cm)
Signed on back: *CClaudel*
Fine Arts Museums of San Francisco, Legion of
Honor
Gift of Alma de Bretteville Spreckels, 1968.26.7

Provenance: Loïe Fuller (1862–1928), Paris
(probably acquired from the artist c. 1900–
c. 1915 and 1924, sold to Spreckels); Alma de
Bretteville Spreckels (1881–1968), San Francisco
(c. 1915 and 1924–68, given to museum);
Fine Arts Museums of San Francisco, 1968

Cat. 63
Man with Serpent
1885
Plaster
27 ½ × 22 × 11 ⅞ in. (69.9 × 55.9 × 30.2 cm)
Clark Art Institute, Williamstown, Massachusetts
Acquired by Sterling Clark, 1923, 1955.1023

Provenance: Antony Roux (1833–1913),
Marseille, Monte-Carlo, Paris (1887–1914, his
sale, Paris, May 19–20, 1914, no. 146, sold to
M. Knoedler, agent for Robert Sterling Clark,
who purchased for his brother, Stephen Clark);
Stephen Carleton Clark (1882–1960), New York
and Cooperstown, New York (1914–23,
consigned to Knoedler's); Robert Sterling Clark
(1877–1956), New York (1923–55, given
to museum); Sterling and Francine Clark Art
Institute, Williamstown, 1955.

[Williamstown]

Cat. 64
Mask of the Man with the Broken Nose
Original model 1864–65
Bronze, probably cast by Charles-Adolphe
Gruet, 1881
12 ¼ × 7 ¾ × 6 ½ in. (31.1 × 19.7 × 16.5 cm)
Museum of Art, Rhode Island School of Design,
Providence
Gift of Mrs. Gustav Radeke 1921, 21.341

Provenance: Constantine Ionides (1933–1900),
London (purchased from artist, 1882); [Martin
Birnbaum]; [Scott and Fowles, New York, sold to
Radeke]; Eliza Greene Metcalf Radeke (1854–
1931), Providence (until 1921, given to
museum); Museum of Art, Rhode Island School
of Design, Providence, 1921.

Cat. 65
Cambodian Dancers
c. 1906–7
Graphite, watercolor, and gouache on wove
paper mounted to cardboard
7 ¾ × 11 ⅜ in. (19.7 × 28.9 cm)
Inscribed by René Chéruy (Rodin's secretary) in
graphite, lower right: *Cambodgienne pour servir
de gloire*
Museum of Art, Rhode Island School of Design,
Providence
Gift of Mrs. Gustav Radeke, 21.128

Provenance: Eliza Greene Metcalf Radeke
(1854–1931), Providence (by 1921, given to
museum); Museum of Art, Rhode Island School
of Design, Providence, 1921.

[Atlanta]

Cat. 66
The Mermaid
c. 1898–1900
Graphite and watercolor on wove paper
mounted to cardboard
13 ⅛ × 10 ½ in. (33.3 × 26.7 cm)
Inscribed in graphite, middle right: *bas /
marine* [?]
Museum of Art, Rhode Island School of Design,
Providence
Gift of Mrs. Gustav Radeke, 21.476

Provenance: Eliza Greene Metcalf Radeke
(1854–1931), Providence (by 1921, given to
museum); Rhode Island School of Design
Museum of Art, Providence, 1921.

[Williamstown]

Cat. 67
The Witches' Sabbath (recto); *Sketches of
Centaurs* (verso)
c. 1883–89
Graphite, pen and ink, gouache (recto),
and graphite (verso), on wove paper
5 ¾ × 7 ½ in. (14.6 × 19.1 cm)
Inscribed with pen and brown ink, lower center
(recto): *le sabbat*
Art Institute of Chicago
Gift of Robert Allerton, 1923.943

Provenance: Republic of France (Auguste Rodin's
Donation to the French State, 1916, possibly
sold by the Musée Rodin, Paris, around 1922 to
intermediate purchaser or directly to Allerton),
Robert Allerton (1873–1974), Chicago (by
1923, given to museum); Art Institute of
Chicago, 1923.

[Atlanta]

Cat. 68
The Kiss
Original model c. 1881–82
Bronze, cast by Griffoul and Lorge (no mark),
1888
34 × 19 ½ × 20 ¾ in. (86.4 × 49.5 × 52.7 cm)
Signed on back of base: *Rodin*
Baltimore Museum of Art
Jacob Epstein Collection, 1951.128

Provenance: Alfred Roll (1846–1919), Paris
(by exchange with the artist, until his sale, Paris,
December 7, 1923, no. 35); [Galerie Georges
Petit]; [Hector Brame and Gustave Tempelaere,
sold to Epstein, November 4, 1927]; Jacob
Epstein (1927–45, bequest to city); Mayor and
City Council of Baltimore, 1945; Baltimore
Museum of Art, 1951.

Cat. 69
The Thinker
Original model 1881–82, enlarged 1903
Bronze, cast by Alexis Rudier, 1928
79 × 37 ¾ × 59 in. (200.7 × 95.9 × 149.9 cm)
Inscribed right side, near back: *A. Rodin*; back

left: *Alexis Rudier, Fondeur, Paris*
Baltimore Museum of Art
Jacob Epstein Collection, 1930.25.1

Provenance: Jacob Epstein (1864–1945),
Baltimore (1928–30, given to museum);
Baltimore Museum of Art, 1930.

Cat. 70
The Benedictions
Original model before 1896, version on a round
base probably enlarged 1898
Bronze, cast by Alexis Rudier, by 1926
31 ½ × 23 ¼ × 25 in. (80 × 59.1 × 63.5 cm)
Signed, front of base, at right: *A. Rodin*
Rodin Museum, Philadelphia Museum of Art
Bequest of Jules E. Mastbaum, 1929,
F1929-7-11

Provenance: Jules E. Mastbaum (1872–1926),
Philadelphia (commissioned August 1925–26,
bequest to museum); Rodin Museum,
Philadelphia, 1929.

Cat. 71
Shame (Absolution)
Original model c. 1895–1900
Bronze, cast by Alexis Rudier, 1925–26
25 ¾ × 15 × 12 ½ in. (65.4 × 38.1 × 31.8 cm)
Signed on base: *A. Rodin*
Inscribed beneath left foot of seated figure:
la pudeur; on top of base: *absolution*
Foundry mark, center rear of base: *Alexis Rudier
/ Fondeur Paris*
Rodin Museum, Philadelphia Museum of Art
Bequest of Jules E. Mastbaum, 1929,
F1929-7-16

Provenance: Jules E. Mastbaum (1872–1926),
Philadelphia (commissioned from the Musée
Rodin, Paris, November 1925–26, bequest to
museum); Rodin Museum, Philadelphia, 1929.

Cat. 72
Medea
Original model c. 1880
Plaster
23 ½ × 12 ½ × 9 ½ in. (59.7 × 31.8 × 24.1 cm)
Rodin Museum, Philadelphia Museum of Art
Bequest of Jules E. Mastbaum, 1929,
F1929-7-100

Provenance: Musée Rodin, Paris (until 1927,
given to Mastbaum); Etta Wedell Mastbaum
(1866–1953), Philadelphia (1927–29, given to
museum); Rodin Museum, Philadelphia, 1929.

Cat. 73
Ecclesiastes
Original model before 1899
Plaster
10 × 11 × 10 in. (25.4 × 27.9 × 25.4 cm)
Rodin Museum, Philadelphia Museum of Art
Bequest of Jules E. Mastbaum, 1929,
F1929-7-117

Provenance: Musée Rodin, Paris (until 1927, given to Mastbaum); Etta Wedell Mastbaum (1866–1953), Philadelphia (1927–29, given to museum); Rodin Museum, Philadelphia, 1929.

Cat. 74

Mask of Rose Beuret, Later Mme Rodin
Original model c. 1882
Ground glass refired in a mold (*pâte de verre*), executed by Jean Cros, c. 1911
9 ½ × 6 ¼ × 7 ⅛ in. (24.1 × 15.9 × 18.1 cm)
Rodin Museum, Philadelphia Museum of Art
Bequest of Jules E. Mastbaum, 1929,
F1929-7-43

Provenance: Jules E. Mastbaum (1872–1926), Philadelphia (acquired from the Musée Rodin, Paris, August 1925, bequest to museum); Rodin Museum, Philadelphia, 1929.

Cat. 75

Seated Woman
c. 1900
Graphite and watercolor on wove paper
9 ¹¹⁄₁₆ × 12 ⅞ in. (24.6 × 32.7 cm)
Signed in graphite, lower right: *bas / Auguste Rodin*
Inscribed in graphite, lower left, in the hand of Judith Cladel: *À Monsieur Jules E. Mastbaum / Fondateur du Musée Rodin à Philadelphie / En haute sympathie / Judith Cladel / Cette aquarelle est l'original du dessin / reproduit au trait sur la couverture de / mon livre: "Auguste Rodin. L'œuvre et l'homme." Paris. Juillet 1926*
Rodin Museum, Philadelphia Museum of Art
Bequest of Jules E. Mastbaum, 1929,
1929-7-197

Provenance: Judith Cladel (1873–1958), Paris (until given to Mastbaum, July 1926); Jules E. Mastbaum (1872–1926), Philadelphia (1926, bequest to museum); Rodin Museum, Philadelphia, 1929.

[Williamstown]

Cat. 76

Woman and Two Children
c. 1883
Graphite, pen, ink, and gouache on wove paper
Sheet: 7 ¹⁄₁₆ × 5 ¼ in. (17.9 × 13.3 cm)
Rodin Museum, Philadelphia Museum of Art
Bequest of Jules E. Mastbaum, F1929-7-168

Provenance: Jules E. Mastbaum (1872–1926), Philadelphia (by 1926, bequest to museum); Rodin Museum, Philadelphia, 1929.

[Williamstown]

Cat. 77

Centaur Carrying a Woman (Dawn: Return from the Sabbath)
c. 1883–85
Pen and ink, wash, gouache on cutout and mounted paper

Sheet (irregular): 7 ⅞ × 9 ¹⁵⁄₁₆ in. (20 × 25.2 cm)
Inscribed with pen and brown ink, upper right: *l'aube / retour du sabbat*
Rodin Museum, Philadelphia Museum of Art
Bequest of Jules E. Mastbaum, 1929,
F1929-7-166

Provenance: Jules E. Mastbaum (1872–1926), Philadelphia (until 1926, bequest to museum); Rodin Museum, Philadelphia, 1929.

[Atlanta]

Cat. 78

Dance (Drawing Reconstructed from Memory by Rodin, after a Destroyed Vase)
c. 1887–1907
Pen and ink on wove paper
7 ⅛ × 9 in. (18.1 × 22.9 cm)
Collector's stamp of the Musée Rodin collection(?) on left edge: *AR* (not identified by Lugt)
Collector's stamp of the R.M collection on verso, lower left (not identified by Lugt)
Mr. Hugh Justin Seto and Mrs. Amy T. Seto

Provenance: Jules E. Mastbaum (1872–1926), Philadelphia; [Feingarten Galleries, Los Angeles, 1971, sold to Andersons]; Harry W. and Mary Margaret Anderson; sale 15881, Christie's, New York, December 6–13, 2018, no. 535; Hugh Justin Seto and Amy T. Seto, 2018.

Cat. 79

Group of Figures (Time)
c. 1885–90
Graphite, pen and ink, and gouache on tracing paper mounted to a gray sheet
5 ⅜ × 5 ⅜ in. (13.7 × 13.7 cm)
Collector's stamp of Marcel Louis Guérin on the mount (Lugt 1872b)
Private collection, courtesy of Nicholas Sands & Company Fine Art, New York

Provenance: Marcel Louis Guérin (1873–1948), France; Jules E. Mastbaum (1872–1926), Philadelphia; Mr. and Mrs. Laurence Brunswick Jr., Rydal, Pennsylvania, his daughter, by descent; private collection.

Cat. 80

Standing Female Nude with Drapery
c. 1909–15
Graphite with stumping on wove paper
12 × 7 ⅜ in. (19.7 × 29.8 cm)
Inscribed in graphite, top left: *le/de soleil . . .* [unclear inscription]
Rodin Museum, Philadelphia Museum of Art
Bequest of Jules E. Mastbaum, 1929,
F1929-7-191

Provenance: Jules E. Mastbaum (1872–1926), Philadelphia (by 1926, bequest to museum); Rodin Museum, Philadelphia 1929.

[Atlanta]

Cat. 81

Cambodian Dancer with Swirling Drapery
c. 1906–7
Graphite and watercolor on wove paper
12 ³⁄₁₆ × 8 in. (31 × 20.3 cm)
Inscribed in graphite, lower right, by Rodin's secretary, René Chéruy: *Cambodgienne pour servir de gloire*
Rodin Museum, Philadelphia Museum of Art
Bequest of Jules E. Mastbaum, 1929,
F1929-7-196

Provenance: Jules E. Mastbaum (1872–1926), Philadelphia (by 1926, bequest to museum); Rodin Museum, Philadelphia, 1929.

[Williamstown]

Cat. 82

Kneeling Nude Male
c. 1900–1905
Graphite with stumping and watercolor on wove paper
7 ⅞ × 12 ¼ in. (20 × 31.1 cm)
Signed in graphite, lower left: *Aug. Rodin*
Inscribed in graphite, top right: *haut bas relief*
Rodin Museum, Philadelphia Museum of Art
Bequest of Jules E. Mastbaum, 1929,
F1929-7-185

Provenance: Jules E. Mastbaum (1872–1926), Philadelphia (by 1926, bequest to museum); Rodin Museum, Philadelphia, 1929.

[Atlanta]

Cat. 83

Reclining Nude Woman (Alda Moreno)
c. 1910
Graphite with stumping on laid paper with watermark (Drey . . . K)
9 ⁷⁄₁₆ × 15 ¹⁄₁₆ in. (24 × 38.3 cm)
Collector's stamp of the musée Rodin collection (?) lower right: *Rodin* (Lugt 2142)
Collector's stamp of the R.M collection on verso (not identified by Lugt)
Rodin Museum, Philadelphia Museum of Art
Bequest of Jules E. Mastbaum, 1929,
F1929-7-176

Provenance: Jules E. Mastbaum (1872–1926), Philadelphia (by 1926, bequest to museum); Rodin Museum, Philadelphia, 1929.

[Williamstown]

THE REVIVAL, 1950–2014

Cat. 84

Iris, Messenger of the Gods
Original model 1895
Bronze, cast by Alexis Rudier, probably c. 1950
32 ½ × 34 × 14 ¾ in. (82.5 × 86.3 × 37.5 cm)
Signed under left foot: *A. Rodin*
Hirshhorn Museum and Sculpture Garden, Smithsonian Institution, Washington, DC

Gift of Joseph H. Hirshhorn, 1966, 66.4330
Provenance: [Probably Musée Rodin, Paris; Curt Valentin Gallery, New York (1953–55, sold to Hirshhorn)]; Joseph Hirshhorn (1899–1981), Greenwich, Connecticut (1955–66, given to museum); Hirshhorn Museum and Sculpture Garden, Washington, DC, 1966.

Cat. 85

Monument to Balzac
Original model 1897, enlarged 1898
Bronze, 4th cast, cast by Georges Rudier, 1954
111 × 48 ¼ × 41 in. (282 × 122.5 × 104.2 cm)
Signed behind figure's left foot, top of base: *A. Rodin*
Museum of Modern Art, New York
Presented in memory of Curt Valentin by his friends, 1955, 28.1955

Provenance: Musée Rodin, Paris; Museum of Modern Art, New York, 1954.

Cat. 86

The Walking Man
Original model 1907
Bronze, cast by Georges Rudier, 1965
Numbered 9, but actually the 11th cast
Signature and date incised in base: *A. Rodin © by Musée Rodin. 1965*
Incised on figure's right, in base: · *Georges Rudier · / · Fondeur · Paris*
88 ³⁄₁₆ × 29 ½ × 53 ⅛ in. (224 × 75 × 135 cm)
Smith College Museum of Art, Northampton, Massachusetts
Purchased 1965, SC 1965.30

Provenance: Smith College Museum of Art, Northampton, Massachusetts, 1965.

Cat. 87

The Age of Bronze
Original model 1876
Bronze, cast by Alexis Rudier, c. 1910–20
71 × 20 × 20 in. (180.3 × 50.8 × 50.8 cm)
Signed on base: *A. Rodin*
Inscribed on back: *Alexis Rudier Fondeur Paris*
Stamped in relief, inside: *A. Rodin*
Iris & B. Gerald Cantor Center for Visual Arts, Stanford University, Palo Alto, California
Gift of the B. Gerald Cantor Foundation, 1983.300

Provenance: Reynaud Icare, Paris; [Wildenstein Gallery]; Charles Zadak (1896–1984), New York and Milwaukee; [Bruton Gallery, Somerset, New York]; B. Gerald Cantor (1916–1996), New York and Los Angeles (until 1983, given to museum); Iris & B. Gerald Cantor Center for Visual Arts at Stanford University, 1983.

Cat. 88

Three Female Nude Cutout Figures
c. 1900–1906
Graphite and watercolor on wove paper, cut out and mounted to wove paper
22 ½ × 28 ½ in. (57.2 × 72.4 cm)
Graphic Arts Collection, Princeton University, Princeton, New Jersey
Gift of René Chéury's students, HSV / 71 / GA 2006.01573, 2006.01574, 2006,01575

Provenance: René Chéury (1880–1965), Windsor, Connecticut, and Tucson, Arizona; Princeton University Library, Princeton, New Jersey, 1965.

[Atlanta]

Cat. 89

Female Nude Cutout Figure
c. 1900–1906
Graphite and watercolor on wove paper mounted to a later support
13 × 8 ⅞ in. (33 × 22.5 cm)
Graphic Arts Collection, Princeton University, Princeton, New Jersey
Gift of René Chéury's students, 2006.01560 HSV / 71 / GA

Provenance: René Chéury (1880–1965), Windsor, Connecticut, and Tucson, Arizona; Princeton University Library, Princeton, New Jersey, 1965.

[Williamstown]

Cat. 90

Dance Movement H
c. 1911
Bronze, cast by Georges Rudier, 1965
11 ¼ × 3 × 4 ¼ in. (28.6 × 7.6 × 10.8 cm)
Signed on right arm: *A. Rodin*
Inscribed on right ankle: *Georges Rudier Fondeur Paris*; below: *No. 11 / © by Musée Rodin 1965*
Iris & B. Gerald Cantor Center for Visual Arts, Stanford University, Palo Alto, California
Gift of the Iris & B. Gerald Cantor Foundation, 1975.84

Provenance: Sale, Sotheby's London, July 2, 1970, no. 48, purchased by the Cantors; Iris Cantor (b. 1931) and B. Gerald Cantor (1916–1996), New York and Los Angeles (until 1975, given to museum); Iris and B. Gerald Cantor Center for Visual Arts, Stanford University, Palo Alto, California, 1975.

Cat. 91

Ugolino and His Sons
Original model c. 1881–82
Bronze, cast by Eugène Gonon, 1883
15 ⅞ × 16 ³⁄₁₆ × 25 ⅜ in. (40.3 × 41.1 × 64.5 cm)
Signed on base: *Rodin*
Inscribed on base: *E. GONON FONDEUR*
Private collection, London, on loan to the Clark Art Institute

Provenance: Henry Lerolle (1848–1929), Paris (acquired from the artist 1887); Jacques Lerolle, Paris, by descent; sale, Millon & Associés, Hôtel Drouot, Paris, March 19, 2004, no. 54; sale, Sotheby's New York, May 7, 2013, no. 47; private collection, London.

Cat. 92

Ugolino and His Sons: Fifth Day (recto); *Dante and Virgil: Anatomical Studies* (verso)
1876–80
Graphite and pen and ink on graph paper
6 ⅛ × 3 ¾ in. (15.6 × 9.6 cm)
Inscribed in pen and ink, top left: *5*; top right: *ugolin 5ᵉ jour*
Inscribed by another hand in red pencil, right margin: *9 cent 1/2*; in blue pencil, top left: *1338/68*
Metropolitan Museum of Art, New York
Anonymous Gift, 2012, 2012.222.2 a, b

Provenance: François Thiébault-Sisson (1856–1936), Paris (until 1936); private collector (given to museum, 2012); Metropolitan Museum of Art, New York, 2012.

[Williamstown]

Cat. 93

Study for Ugolino and His Sons (recto); *Sketch of Ugolino and Son* (verso)
c. 1876–80
Graphite and pen and ink on graph paper
5 ⅝ × 3 ¹¹⁄₁₆ in. (14.3 × 9.3 cm)
Inscribed with pen and ink, at bottom right: *Ugolin*; at top left (verso): *planche*
Unauthenticated initials in graphite, lower right: *A.R.*
Iris and B. Gerald Cantor Center for Visual Arts, Stanford University, Palo Alto, California
Gift of the Iris & B. Gerald Cantor Foundation, 1987.39

Provenance: Iris and B. Gerald Cantor Foundation (until 1987, given to museum); Iris & B. Gerald Cantor Center for Visual Arts, Stanford University, Palo Alto, California, 1987.

[Atlanta]

Cat. 94

The Thinker (*The Prophet* or *Ugolino*) (recto); *Study for Ugolino* (verso)
c. 1880
Graphite, ink, and gouache (recto) and graphite (verso) on lined paper
7 ½ × 4 ⁵⁄₁₆ in. (19 × 11 cm)
Inscribed in pen and ink, upper right: *prophète*
Collector's stamp of the Musée Rodin collection(?), recto and verso: *Rodin* (Lugt. 2142)
Rappaport Rodin Collection

Provenance: Private collection, France; sale, Sotheby's Paris, June 1, 2016, no. 34; Rappaport Rodin Collection, 2016.

Cat. 95
Charybdis
c. 1883
Graphite, ink, watercolor, and gouache on wove
paper, cut out, torn, and glued on support
8 ¼ × 3 ⅜ in. (21× 8.6 cm)
Inscribed and signed in ink, upper left: *Charybe
[sic] / A. Rodin*
Private collection, courtesy of Nicholas Sands &
Company Fine Art, New York

Provenance: Leo Lentelli (1879–1961), Rome
and New York (acquired as gift by 1930);
private collection.

Cat. 96
Salome
c. 1895
Graphite, pen and ink, watercolor, and gouache
on laid paper
6⅞ × 4⁷⁄₁₆ in. (17.4 × 11.2 cm)
Private collection

Provenance: Claude Monet (1840–1926),
Giverny, France (gift from the artist, April
1897–1926); Michel Monet (1878–1966),
France, his son, by descent (1926–until given to
Verneiges); Rolande Verneiges (1914–2008),
France, his daughter, by descent (1966–2008);
family of Verneiges, until sale, Christie's, Hong
Kong, November 26, 2017, no. 121; private
collection, 2017.

[Williamstown]

Cat. 97
Cambodian Dancer
1906
Watercolor over graphite pencil on paper
11⁷⁄₁₆ × 7 ¹¹⁄₁₆ in. (29 × 19.6 cm)
Museum of Fine Arts, Boston
Bequest of John T. Spaulding, 48.851

Provenance: John Taylor Spaulding (1870–
1948), Boston (until 1948, bequest to museum);
Museum of Fine Arts, Boston, 1948.

[Williamstown]

Cat. 98
Sphinx
c. 1898–1900
Graphite with stumping and watercolor on wove
paper
19³⁄₁₆ × 12¾ in. (48.7 × 32.4 cm)
Signed, lower right: *Aug. Rodin*
Inscribed in graphite, upper right: *sphinx;*
on right toward middle: *noir draperie*
J. Paul Getty Museum, Los Angeles
2008.60

Provenance: [Galerie Bérès, Paris (until 2008,
sold to museum)]; J. Paul Getty Museum,
Los Angeles, 2008.

[Williamstown]

Cat. 99
Lucifer (Falling Meteor in Flames)
c. 1898–1900
Graphite and watercolor on wove paper
9 ⅜ × 12⁷⁄₁₆ in. (23.8 × 31.6 cm)
Signed and inscribed in graphite, lower
right: *A. Rodin / bas / Lucifer / Meteore en
flamme / tombe*
Inscribed in pen and ink lower right on mount:
inv.n°134
Morgan Library & Museum, New York
Gift of Alexandre P. Rosenberg, 1981.10

Provenance: Jacques Doucet (1853–1929), Paris
(until his sale, Hôtel Drouot, Paris, December
28–29, 1917, no. 294, acquired by Rosenberg);
Paul Rosenberg (1881–1959), Paris and New
York; Alexandre P. Rosenberg (1921–1987),
New York, his son, by descent (until 1981, given
to museum); Morgan Library & Museum,
New York, 1981.

[Atlanta]

Cat. 100
Emerging from the Clouds (Nijinsky)
1912
Graphite with stumping and watercolor on
laid paper
18 ½ × 12 ¼ in. (47 × 31.1 cm)
Inscribed in graphite, top left: *sortant des nuages*
Rappaport Rodin Collection

Provenance: Shoji Kawahara (by 1954), Japan;
private collection (1954–2020, until sale,
Sotheby's New York, October 5, 2020, no. 88);
Rappaport Rodin Collection, 2020.

Cat. 101
Christ and Mary Magdalene
Original model 1894
Marble, carved by Victor Peter, 1908
43 × 33 ½ × 31 in. (109.2 × 85.1 × 78.7 cm)
Signed on base: *A. Rodin*
J. Paul Getty Museum, Los Angeles, 2014.32

Provenance: Karl Wittgenstein (1847–1913),
Vienna (commissioned in 1907, delivered in
1909–13); Paul Wittgenstein (1887–1961),
Vienna, his son, by descent (1913–61); estate of
Paul Wittgenstein (1961–64); Wittgenstein estate
sale, Sotheby's London, April 19, 1964, no. 82,
sold to Pon; Bernardus Marinus Pon (1904–
1968) (1964–68); Cornelia Clasina Pon-Parlevliet
(1904–1980), The Netherlands, his wife, by
descent (1964–80); Mr. Pon, The Netherlands, her
son, by descent; [consigned with Pieter
Hoogendijk, sold to Katz, 2013]; [Daniel Katz
Ltd, London (2013–14, sold to museum)]; J. Paul
Getty Museum, 2014.

Cat. 102
The Genius of Sculpture
c. 1880
Pen and ink on wove paper
10⅜ × 7⁷⁄₁₆ in. (26.3 × 18.9 cm)
Inscribed in graphite on previous mount:
le génie de la sculpture
Cleveland Museum of Art
Bequest of Muriel Butkin, 2008.404

Provenance: Marcel Louis Guérin (1873–1949),
Paris (until his sale, Hôtel Drouot, Paris,
December 9, 1932, no. 70); [Shepherd Gallery,
New York, sold to Butkin]; Muriel Butkin
(1916–2008), Shaker Heights, Ohio (until 2008,
bequest to museum); Cleveland Museum of Art,
2008.

[Williamstown]

CONTRIBUTORS

Christina Buley-Uribe is an independent art historian specializing in Auguste Rodin's graphic work. Her books include *Rodin: Drawings and Watercolours* (2006/2017), *Mes sœurs divines: Rodin et 99 femmes de son entourage* (2013), and *Naissance de la modernité: Mélanges offerts à Jacques Vilain* (2009). She has contributed to numerous exhibition catalogues, most recently *Rodin: La lumière de l'antique*, Musée de l'Arles Antique (2013); *Rodin: L'accident et l'aléatoire*, Musée d'Art et d'Histoire, Geneva (2014); and *Rodin: L'exposition du centenaire,* Grand Palais, Paris (2017). She is writing the catalogue raisonné of Rodin's drawings and preparing a 2023 Rodin exhibition for the Museum of Fine Arts of Mons, Belgium.

Patrick R. Crowley is the associate curator of European art at the Iris & B. Gerald Cantor Center for Visual Arts at Stanford University. From 2013 to 2020, he was assistant professor of art history at the University of Chicago. His research has been supported by the Getty Research Institute, the National Endowment for the Humanities, and the Center for Advanced Study in the Visual Arts, Washington, DC. He is the author of *The Phantom Image: Seeing the Dead in Ancient Rome* (2019).

C. D. Dickerson III serves as curator and head of the department of sculpture and decorative arts at the National Gallery of Art in Washington, DC. Prior to joining the curatorial staff of the gallery in 2015, he spent eight years at the Kimbell Art Museum in Fort Worth as curator of European art. Among the exhibitions he has curated are *From the Private Collections of Texas: European Art, Ancient to Modern* (2009–10), *Bernini: Sculpting in Clay* (2012–13), and *The Brothers Le Nain: Painters of Seventeenth-Century France* (2016–17), at the Kimbell; and *Alonso Berruguete: First Sculptor of Renaissance Spain* (2019–20), at the National Gallery of Art.

Antoinette Le Normand-Romain holds the title of Conservateur Général Honoraire du Patrimoine. She was director of the Institut National d'Histoire de l'Art (INHA), Paris, from 2006 to 2016; curator of sculpture at the Musée Rodin from 1994 to 2006; and curator at the Musée d'Orsay from 1977 to 1994. Her writings examine nineteenth- and early twentieth-century sculpture (*Mémoire de marbre: La sculpture funéraire en France 1804–1914*, 1995), with a focus on Rodin (*Rodin et le bronze: Catalogue des œuvres conservées au musée Rodin*, 2007; *Rodin*, 2013), Camille Claudel, and Maillol. She has curated many exhibitions, including *Rodin: L'exposition du centenaire*, Grand Palais, Paris (2017) and *Maillol: La quête de l'harmonie*, Musée d'Orsay, Paris / Roubaix, Zurich (2022–23).

Laure de Margerie is the director of the French Sculpture Census, a survey of French sculpture (1500–1960) in American public collections and the subject of her forthcoming book *French Sculpture, An American Passion* (2022). She previously worked at the Musée d'Orsay, where she curated exhibitions on Jean-Baptiste Carpeaux and Charles Cordier. Her recent publications include essays on sculpture collections in Chicago, Dallas, New York City (2018), and Saratoga Springs, New York (2019), as well as French Art Deco sculpture in the United States (2021).

Véronique Mattiussi is head of the research center at the Musée Rodin, Paris, and scientific manager of its historical collection. She is coauthor of *Rodin–Bourdelle: Correspondance 1823–1920* (2013) and author of *Auguste Rodin, artiste libre et affranchi* (2017). She was co-curator of *Camille Claudel: 1864–1943*, Fundación Mapfre, Madrid, and Musée Rodin, Paris (2007–8); *Rodin in Meštrović's Zagreb*, Muzeji Ivana Meštrovića, Zagreb (2015); *Rodin: The Centennial Exhibition*, Grand Palais, Paris (2017); *Auguste Rodin–Anselm Kiefer*, Musée Rodin, Paris, and the Barnes Foundation, Philadelphia (2017–18); and *Picasso–Rodin*, Musée Rodin and Musée Picasso, Paris (2021).

Elyse Nelson is assistant curator in the department of European Sculpture and Decorative Arts at the Metropolitan Museum of Art, New York. Before assuming this role in 2019, she took part in the organization of *Rodin at The Met* (2017) and *Like Life: Sculpture, Color, and the Body* (2018). She is the organizing curator of *Fictions of Emancipation: Carpeaux Recast* (2022) and coeditor of its accompanying volume.

Nora M. Rosengarten is a doctoral student in the history of art and architecture at Harvard University, where her research focuses on the history of prints and printmaking. She holds a BA from Georgetown University (2014) and an MA from the Williams College / Clark Art Institute Graduate Program in the History of Art (2019).

Jennifer A. Thompson is the Gloria and Jack Drosdick Curator of European Painting and Sculpture and Curator of the John G. Johnson Collection at the Philadelphia Museum of Art. Since 2008, she has also been curator of the Rodin Museum in Philadelphia. Her publications include *Impressionism and Post-Impressionism: Highlights from the Philadelphia Museum of Art* (2019) and *Rodin Museum, Philadelphia* (2012). She has also contributed to *The John G. Johnson Collection: A History and Selected Works* (2018); *Discovering the Impressionists: Paul Durand-Ruel and the New Painting* (2015); *Van Gogh Up Close* (2012); and *Renoir in the 20th Century* (2010).

SELECTED BIBLIOGRAPHY

Aldaheff, Albert. "Rodin: A Self-Portrait in the Gates of Hell." *Art Bulletin* 48, nos. 3–4 (September–December 1966): 393–95.

Ariot, Chloé, Agnes Cascio, and Guylaine Mary. "In Search of Hanako: Fifty Portraits by Rodin." *Burlington Magazine* 162, no. 1411 (October 2020): 851–59.

Audeh, Aida. "Rodin's *Gates of Hell* and Aubé's *Monument to Dante*: Romantic Tribute to the Image of the Poet in Nineteenth Century France." *Journal of the Iris and B. Gerald Cantor Center for Visual Arts at Stanford University* 1 (1998–99): 33–46.

Barbier, Nicole, ed. *Rodin sculpteur: Œuvres méconnues*. Paris: Musée Rodin, 1992. Exhibition catalogue.

Barbour, Daphné S., and Lisha Deming Glinsman. "Auguste Rodin's Lifetime Bronze Sculptures in the Simpson Collection." In *Facture: Conservation, Science, Art History*, vol. 2, *Art in Context*, edited by Daphné S. Barbour and E. Melanie Gifford, 54–81. Washington, DC: National Gallery of Art, 2015.

Barryte, Bernard, and Roberta K. Tarbell, eds. *Rodin and America: Influence and Adaptation 1876–1936*. Stanford, CA: Iris and B. Gerald Cantor Center for Visual Arts, 2011. Exhibition catalogue.

Bartlett, Truman H. "Auguste Rodin, Sculptor." *American Architect and Building News* 25, nos. 682–703 (January 19–June 15, 1889).

Beausire, Alain. *Quand Rodin exposait*. Paris: Éditions du musée Rodin, 1988.

Biass-Fabiani, Sophie. *Dessiner-découper*. Paris: Musée Rodin, 2018. Exhibition catalogue.

Blanchetière, François, ed. *L'Enfer selon Rodin*. Paris: Musée Rodin, 2016. Exhibition catalogue.

Buley-Uribe, Christina. "L'aliénabilité *de facto* de dessins du musée Rodin?" *Cahiers d'histoire de l'art*, no. 19 (2021): 96–107.

———. *Mes sœurs divines: Rodin et 99 femmes de son entourage*. Paris: Relief, 2013.

Butler, Ruth. *Rodin in Perspective*. New York: Prentice-Hall, 1980.

———. *Rodin: The Shape of Genius*. New Haven, CT: Yale University Press, 1993.

Butler, Ruth, Suzanne Lindsay Glover, and Alison Luchs. *European Sculpture of the Nineteenth Century: The Collections of the National Gallery of Art Systematic Catalogue*. Washington, DC: National Gallery of Art, 2001.

Carr, Carolyn Kinder. *Sara Tyson Hallowell: Pioneer Curator and Art Advisor in the Gilded Age*. Washington, DC: Smithsonian Institution Scholarly Press, 2019.

Caso, Jacques de. "Rodin's Mastbaum Album." *Master Drawings* 10, no. 2 (Summer 1972): 155–61.

Caso, Jacques de, and Patricia B. Sanders. *Rodin's Sculpture: A Critical Study of the Spreckels Collection, California Palace of Legion of Honor*. San Francisco: Fine Arts Museums, 1977.

Chevillot, Catherine, and Antoinette Le Normand-Romain, eds. *Rodin: L'Exposition du centenaire*. Paris: Grand Palais, 2017. Exhibition catalogue.

Cladel, Judith. *Rodin*. Translated by James Whitall. New York: Harcourt, Brace, 1937.

———. *Rodin: The Man and His Art with Leaves from His Notebook*. Translated by S. K. Star. New York: Century, 1917.

Cousseau, Henry-Claude, Christina Buley-Uribe, and Véronique Mattiussi, eds. *Naissance de la modernité: Mélanges offerts à Jacques Vilain*. Paris: Relief, 2009.

Current, Richard Nelson, and Marcia Ewing Current. *Loïe Fuller, Goddess of Light*. Boston: Northeastern University Press, 1997.

Dunn, Ashley. *Not Rodin: Misattributed Drawings in the Met Collection*. The Met blog, November 28, 2017. http://www:metmuseum:org/blogs/now-at-the-met/2017/auguste-rodin-misattributed-drawings.

Elsen, Albert E. *Auguste Rodin: Readings on His Life and Work*. Englewood Cliffs, NJ: Prentice Hall, 1965.

———. *The Gates of Hell by Auguste Rodin*. Stanford, CA: Stanford University Press, 1985.

———. *Origins of Modern Sculpture: Pioneers and Premises*. New York: George Braziller, 1974.

———. *The Partial Figure in Modern Sculpture: From Rodin to 1969*. Baltimore: Baltimore Museum of Art, 1969. Exhibition catalogue.

———. *Rodin*. New York: Museum of Modern Art, 1963.

———. "Rodin's Drawings and the Art of Matisse." *Arts Magazine* 61, no. 7 (March 1987): 32–39.

———. *Rodin's Thinker and the Dilemmas of Modern Public Sculpture*. New Haven, CT: Yale University Press, 1985.

Elsen, Albert E., ed. *Rodin Rediscovered*. Washington, DC: National Gallery of Art, 1981. Exhibition catalogue.

Elsen, Albert E., and Bernard Barryte eds. *Rodin's Art: The Rodin Collection of the Iris and B. Gerald Cantor Center for Visual Arts at Stanford University*. New York: Oxford University Press, 2003.

Elsen, Albert E., and J. Kirk T. Varnedoe, eds. *The Drawings of Rodin*. New York: Praeger, 1971.

Fletcher, Valérie J. *A Garden for Art: Outdoor Sculpture at the Hirshhorn Museum*. Washington, DC: Hirshhorn Museum and Sculpture Garden, 1998.

Fuller, Loïe. *Fifteen Years of a Dancer's Life*. London: H. Jenkins, 1913.

Fusco, Peter, and H. W. Janson. *The Romantics to Rodin: French Nineteenth-Century Sculpture from North American Collections*. Los Angeles: Los Angeles County Museum of Art, 1980. Exhibition catalogue.

Gerstein, Alexandra. *Rodin and Dance: The Essence of Movement*. London: Courtauld Gallery, 2016. Exhibition catalogue.

Greenough, Sarah, ed. *Modern Art and America: Alfred Stieglitz and His New York Galleries*. Washington, DC: National Gallery of Art, 2001. Exhibition catalogue.

Grunfeld, Frederic V. *Rodin: A Biography*. New York: Henry Holt, 1987.

Holtz, Maureen. *Images of America: Robert Allerton, His Parks and Legacies*. Mount Pleasant, SC: Arcadia, 2021.

Judrin, Claudie. *Inventaire des dessins*, 6 vols. Paris: Éditions du musée Rodin, 1987–92.

Kessler, Comte Harry. *Journal: Regards sur l'art et les artistes contemporains (1889–1937)*, 2 vols. Translated by Jean Torrent. Edited by Ursel Berger, Julia Drost, Alexandre Kostka, Antoinette Le Normand-Romain, Dominique Lobstein, and Philippe Thiébaut. Paris: Édition Maisons des sciences de l'homme, 2017. doi: http://doi.org/10.4000/books.editionsmsh.10922.

Lacasse, Yves, and Antoinette Le Normand-Romain, eds. *Camille Claudel and Rodin: Fateful Encounter*. Quebec: Musée national des Beaux-Arts du Québec, 2005. Exhibition catalogue.

Lampert, Catherine. *Rodin: Sculpture and Drawings*. London: Arts Council of Great Britain, 1986. Exhibition catalogue.

Lampert, Catherine, and Antoinette Le Normand-Romain, eds. *Rodin*. London: Royal Academy of Arts, 2006. Exhibition catalogue.

Le Normand-Romain, Antoinette. "The Arc of Creation: Auguste Rodin at the Dallas Museum of Art." In *Impressionism and Post-Impressionism at the Dallas Museum of Art*, the Richard R. Brettell Lecture Series, edited by Heather MacDonald, 109–19. New Haven, CT: Yale University Press, 2013.

———. "Auguste Rodin and the Question of the Original in Sculpture." In *Facture: Conservation: Science, Art History*, vol. 4, *Series, Multiples, Replicas*, edited by Daphné S. Barbour and E. Melanie Gifford, 102–27. Washington, DC: National Gallery of Art, 2019.

———. "Le musée Rodin 1916–1940: Un lieu de référence." *Revue de l'art*, no. 162 (April 2008): 11–19.

———. *Rodin*. New York: Abbeville, 2014.

———. *Rodin et le bronze: Catalogue des œuvres conservées au musée Rodin / The Bronzes of Rodin: Catalogue of Works in the Musée Rodin*, 2 vols. Paris: Éditions du musée Rodin / Réunion des musées nationaux, 2007.

Le Normand-Romain, Antoinette, ed. *1898: Le "Balzac" de Rodin*. Paris: Éditions du musée Rodin, 1998. Exhibition catalogue.

———. *Rodin en 1900: L'Exposition de l'Alma*. Paris: Musée du Luxembourg, 2001. Exhibition catalogue.

Le Normand-Romain, Antoinette, and Christina Buley-Uribe. *Rodin: Drawings and Watercolours*. London: Thames & Hudson, 2006.

Le Normand-Romain, Antoinette, and Laurence Madeline. *Rodin: L'accident et l'aléatoire*. Geneva: Musée d'Art et d'Histoire, 2014. Exhibition catalogue.

Lehni, Nadine. *Rodin, son musée secret*. Paris: Albin Michel, 2017.

Lugt, Frits, and Fondation Custodia. *Les Marques de collections de dessins et d'estampes*. Online journal. Paris: Fondation Custodia, Collections Frits Lugt, [2010]–.

Magnien, Aline, ed. *Rodin: La chair, le marbre*. Paris: Musée Rodin, 2012. Exhibition catalogue.

Marandel, Patrice J. "Rodin's Thinker: Notes on the Early History of the Detroit Cast." *Bulletin of the Detroit Institute of Arts* 62, no. 4 (1987): 33–52.

———. "Rodin's Thinker: Notes on the Early History of the Detroit Cast." *Bulletin of the Detroit Institute of Arts* 63, no. 3/4 (1988): 33–55.

Margerie, Laure de. French Sculpture Census / Répertoire de sculpture française, 2014. http://frenchsculpture.org/.

Margerie, Laure de, with Antoinette Le Normand-Romain. *French Sculpture: An American Passion*. Paris: Institut national d'histoire de l'art, 2022.

McCauley, Elizabeth Anne, "Auguste Rodin, 1908 and 1910: The Eternal Feminine." In *Modern Art and America: Alfred Stieglitz and His New York Galleries*, edited by Sarah Greenough, 71–78. Washington, DC: National Gallery of Art, 2001. Exhibition catalogue.

Michaels, Barbara L. *Gertrude Käsebier: The Photographer and Her Photographs*. New York: Harry N. Abrams, 1992.

Picard, Pascale, ed. *Rodin: La lumière de l'antique*. Arles: Musée de l'Arles Antique, 2013. Exhibition catalogue.

Rodin, Auguste. *Art: Conversations with Paul Gsell* [1911]. Translated by Jacques de Caso and Patricia B. Sanders. Berkeley: University of California Press, 1984.

———. *Correspondance de Rodin, 1860–1917*, vols. I–IV (vol. I, *1860–1899*, 1985; vol. II, *1900–1907*, 1986; vol. III, *1908–1912*, 1987; vol. IV, *1913–1917*, 1992). Edited by Alain Beausire, Hélène Pinet, Florence Cadouot, and Frédérique Vincent. Paris: Musée Rodin, 1985–92.

Scharlach, Bernice. *Big Alma, San Francisco's Alma Spreckels*. San Francisco: Scottwall Associates, 1990.

Seiberling, Dorothy. "The Great Rodin: His Flagrant Faker." *Life*, June 4, 1965, 64–71.

Steinberg, Leo. "Rodin." In *Other Criteria: Confrontations with Twentieth-Century Art*, New York: Oxford University Press, 1972. Originally published in *Rodin: Sculpture and Drawings*. New York: Charles E. Slatkin Gallery, 1963. Exhibition catalogue.

Tancock, John L. *The Sculpture of Auguste Rodin: The Collection of the Rodin Museum of Philadelphia*. Boston: David R. Godine, 1976.

Thorson, Victoria. *Rodin Graphics: A Catalogue Raisonné of Drypoints and Book Illustrations*. San Francisco: Fine Arts Museums of San Francisco, 1975.

———. "Symbolism and Conservatism in Rodin's Late Drawings." In *The Drawings of Rodin*, edited by Albert E. Elsen and J. Kirk T. Varnedoe, 121–39. New York: Praeger, 1971.

Varnedoe, J. Kirk T. "Early Drawings by Auguste Rodin." *Burlington Magazine* 116, no. 853 (April 1974): 197–202.

Viéville, Dominique, Christina Buley-Uribe, and Hélène Pinet, eds. *Rodin: The Figures of Eros: Drawings and Watercolours, 1890–1917*. Paris: Musée Rodin, 2006. Exhibition catalogue.

Vilain, Jacques, ed. *Rodin and the Cambodian Dancers: His Final Passion*. Paris: Musée Rodin, 2006. Exhibition catalogue.

Vincent, Clare. "Rodin at the Metropolitan Museum of Art: A History of the Collection." *Metropolitan Museum of Art Bulletin* 38, no. 4 (Spring 1981): 23–48.

Weisberg, Gabriel P., and Laurinda S. Dixon. *The Documented Image: Visions in Art History*. Syracuse, NY: Syracuse University Press, 1987.

Wiegand, Steve. *The Dancer, the Dreamers and the Queen of Romania: How an Unlikely Quartet Created America's Most Improbable Art Museum*. Baltimore: Bancroft, 2019.

Wolohojian, Stephan, ed., assisted by Anna Tahinci. *A Private Passion: 19th-Century Paintings and Drawings from the Grenville L. Winthrop Collection*. New York: Metropolitan Museum of Art, 2003. Exhibition catalogue.

Zarobell, John. "La modernité de Rodin: Les dessins tardifs et leur accueil aux États-Unis." In *Rodin: La saisie du modèle: 300 dessins: 1890–1917*, edited by Dominique Viéville and Nadine Lehni, 71–85. Paris: Musée Rodin, 2011. Exhibition catalogue.

Published on the occasion of the exhibition
Rodin in the United States: Confronting the Modern
presented at:

Clark Art Institute
Williamstown, Massachusetts
June 18–September 18, 2022

High Museum of Art
Atlanta, Georgia
October 21, 2022–January 15, 2023

Rodin in the United States: Confronting the Modern
is organized by the Clark Art Institute and
guest curated by independent scholar Antoinette Le
Normand-Romain.

This exhibition is made possible by Denise Littlefield
Sobel and Diane and Andreas Halvorsen. Major
funding is provided by the Acquavella Family
Foundation, with additional support from Jeannene
Booher, Robert D. Kraus, the Robert Lehman
Foundation, Carol and Richard Seltzer, and the
Malcolm Hewitt Wiener Foundation. This exhibition
is supported by an indemnity from the Federal
Council on the Arts and the Humanities.

Produced by the Publications Department of the
Clark Art Institute, 225 South Street, Williamstown,
Massachusetts 01267
clarkart.edu

Anne Roecklein, Managing Editor
Kevin Bicknell, Editor
Annie Jun, Assistant Editor
David Murphy, Rights and Image Use Associate

Essays translated by Damion Searls
Additional translations by Kate Deimling as translator
    and David Auerbach as editor, courtesy Eriksen
    Translations Inc.
Copyedited and proofread by Kristin Swan
Designed by Roy Brooks, Fold Four, Inc.
Composed in Apollo MT and Futura LT
Image acquisitions by David Murphy
Color separations by VeronaLibri
Printed on Gardamatt Art and Fedrigoni Nettuno
    by VeronaLibri

Distributed by Yale University Press, New Haven and
London, P.O. Box 209040, New Haven, Connecticut
06520-9040
yalebooks.com/art

Printed and bound in Italy
10 9 8 7 6 5 4 3 2 1

Cataloging-in-Publication Data is available from the
Library of Congress.
978-1-935998-51-8 (Clark Art Institute)
978-0-300-26406-7 (Yale University Press)

Photography Credits